FINANCIAL INSTITUTIONS

MARKETS AND MANAGEMENT

McGraw-Hill Series in Finance

CONSULTING EDITOR

Charles A. D'Ambrosio, *University of Washington*

Brealey and Myers: Principles of Corporate Finance
Campbell: Financial Institutions, Markets, and Economic Activity
Christy and Clendenin: Introduction to Investments
Coates: Investment Strategy
Doherty: Corporate Risk Management: A Financial Exposition
Edmister: Financial Institutions: Markets and Management
Francis: Investments: Analysis and Management
Francis: Management of Investments
Garbade: Securities Markets
Haley and Schall: The Theory of Financial Decisions
Hastings and Mietus: Personal Finance
Henning, Pigott, and Scott: International Financial Management
Jensen and Smith: The Modern Theory of Corporate Finance
Lang and Gillespie: Strategy for Personal Finance
Levi: International Finance: Financial Management and the International Economy
Martin, Petty, and Klock: Personal Financial Management
Robinson and Wrightsman: Financial Markets: The Accumulation and Allocation of Wealth
Schall and Haley: Introduction to Financial Management
Sharpe: Portfolio Theory and Capital Markets
Stevenson: Fundamentals of Finance
Troelstrup and Hall: The Consumer in American Society: Personal and Family Finance

McGraw-Hill Finance Guide Series

CONSULTING EDITOR

Charles A. D'Ambrosio, *University of Washington*

Bowlin, Martin, and Scott: Guide to Financial Analysis
Farrell: Guide to Portfolio Management
Gup: Guide to Strategic Planning
Riley and Montgomery: Guide to Computer-Assisted Investment Analysis
Smith: Guide to Working Capital Management
Weston and Sorge: Guide to International Finance

FINANCIAL INSTITUTIONS

MARKETS AND MANAGEMENT

SECOND EDITION

Robert O. Edmister, Ph.D.

Associate Professor of Finance
University of Maryland

McGRAW-HILL BOOK COMPANY

New York   St. Louis   San Francisco   Auckland   Bogotá
Hamburg   Johannesburg   London   Madrid   Mexico   Montreal   New Delhi
Panama   Paris   São Paulo   Singapore   Sydney   Toyko   Toronto

This book was set in Times Roman by Better Graphics, Inc.
The editor was Paul V. Short;
the cover was designed by Carla Bauer;
the production supervisor was Charles Hess.
Project supervision was done by Caliber Design Planning, Inc.
R. R. Donnelley & Sons Company was printer and binder.

FINANCIAL INSTITUTIONS

Markets and Management

2 3 4 5 6 7 8 9 0   DOCDOC   8 9 8 7

ISBN 0-07-019015-1

Library of Congress Cataloging-in-Publication Data

Edmister, Robert O.
    Financial institutions.

    (McGraw-Hill series in finance)
    Includes bibliographies and index.
    1. Financial institutions.   2. Finance.
I. Title.   II. Series.
HG173.E43   1986   332.1   85-15215
ISBN 0-07-019015-1

For Todd and Tracy

CONTENTS

PREFACE

Managerial, regulatory, and consumer changes which occurred in recent years have outdated the traditional concept of financial institutions as having natural, well-defined missions. Today the financial institution should be viewed generically as a business which intermediates or brokers funds from savers to borrowers and accounts for transactions among economic units. Legal and operating differences among once-distinct institutions are blurring, as institutional managers concentrate on serving economic needs and ignore traditional roles.

This book emphasizes the *economics* of the financial markets and the *business management* of financial institutions. It builds upon previous courses in economics and business finance to provide students with a basic source of information on the operation and management of financial markets and institutions. The first and second parts of the book concentrate on the financial markets, the third part describes the businesses conducted by different financial institutions, the fourth part develops managerial methods applicable to most types of financial institutions, and the fifth part relates public policy concerns to the operations of financial institutions.

SCOPE

Textbooks covering financial institutions have traditionally been macroeconomic descriptions of institutions, markets, and securities. Issues and analyses dealt with in such books usually have related to public policy rather than to institutional management. Although public-policy-oriented books are appropriate for courses taught in economics departments, they lack the microeconomic analysis desired for courses taught in business and management schools. Furthermore, texts oriented toward public policy suggest that regulatory conditions are subject to change, while institutional behavior is a given condition. Business school texts should adopt the opposite concept: institutional behavior is controlled by the manager, subject to the given constraint of public policy. Like texts available for corporate finance and investments courses, a text is needed for business school courses aimed at financial institutions management.

This book is oriented toward students who are interested in managing and dealing with financial institutions and markets. My belief is that preparation for either role, manager or client, requires a basic understanding of the economics, markets, and regulation of financial institutions. Consequently, the primary approach taken in this book progresses from the concept of financial institutions themselves, through financial markets, institutional strategies, and government regulation, to financial planning and analysis. On the other hand, courses which emphasize capital markets, institutional characteristics, or commercial banks would use selected portions of the book. Suggestions for chapter sequences appropriate for alternative approaches are discussed immediately following the description of the primary approach.

PEDAGOGICAL TECHNIQUES

Upper-class and graduate students enter financial markets, financial institutions, and banking courses with a wide range of backgrounds. Those with business majors usually are strong in accounting and financial management, while those with economics majors are educated in micro-, macro-, and monetary economics. A minimal grounding in accounting, finance, and economics is assumed. However, topics generally begin with basic material both as a starting point and a review. Thus, some material is review for one group of students but an initial learning experience for others. The goal throughout has been to give students with minimal business backgrounds the opportunity to understand and master the essential concepts and analytical techniques of the financial markets and institutions.

To develop mastery as well as general understanding, many of the concepts and techniques are taught in four phases:

1 The concept is described generally.
2 The relationship is expressed graphically or algebraically, if applicable.
3 The concept or relationship is repeated with an example in the text.
4 The concept or relationship is further reinforced with an end-of-chapter question or problem.

This four-part sequence moves students from conceptualization to actualization and application. For example, interest rates are presented in the usual present value function to describe the concept of the time value of money. Then, equations relating interest rates for a number of common securities are presented, explained, and illustrated. Following this course, students should be able to compute and compare interest rates on dozens of securities with different terms and tax consequences. Although the student's depth of knowledge would not rival the professional who specializes in security analysis, it would be an excellent foundation for managing or negotiating with financial institutions.

After researching the major journal articles and books published over the years, particularly the last 10 years, I have found that substantially more good research is reported than could be encompassed in one intermediate-level book. Rather than omit reference to studies which explore a particular point in depth but not in general, I have cited a number of articles in footnotes and end-of-chapter reference lists. For efficiency in exposition, most footnoted references are listed at the end of chapters and referred to with standard journal notation, such as Fama (1970), and Benston (1982). The intent of the citation is to direct interested readers toward an author who investigates a specific topic in detail. Thus, the citations provide an "indexed" bibliography for advanced students who are extending their knowledge by studying and writing term essays in the field.

An instructor's manual contains answers to end-of-chapter questions and other teaching support. Most of the questions and test items came from my classes and have been classroom-tested. The questions can be worked with tables (see Appendix A) and a hand held calculator with the y^x function; calculators with the present value functions are recommended but not required.

ACKNOWLEDGMENTS

I want to begin by thanking William Longbrake, Jonathon Fiechter, Susan Krause, and the staff at the Office of the Comptroller of the Currency. As a Visiting Scholar, I was afforded a firsthand view of the rapidly changing commercial bank and financial services industry. At the office of the Comptroller of the Currency, colleagues and students have been a continual source of mostly friendly and helpful criticism, which prodded and directed me toward improving the text, questions, and organization. A particular note of thanks is due to Robert Schietzer at the University of Delaware for his lengthy and insightful reports. Charles D'Ambrosio, who acted as shepherd to the first edition, continued to provide key ideas which were used in this edition as well. A special thank you is due to Elizabeth Shields, who had instructed with the first edition, for revising tables and reviewing the manuscript very carefully. Also, Gina Vacca deserves a special acknowledgment for carefully compiling this version from my often-cryptic writings. Further, as the author of a text, I gratefully acknowledge the researchers in finance who have devoted their time and effort to publishing the vast number of journal articles on which this compilation rests.

Robert O. Edmister

PART ONE

FINANCIAL INSTITUTIONS AND MARKETS

ORIENTATION

In the first three chapters, the basic relationship between savers and borrowers is analyzed and then expanded to encompass the U.S. flow of funds and financial institutions. Borrower and lender needs for financial services, discussed in Chaper 1, are the foundation supporting the financial markets and institutions. The structure and change of the U.S. financial markets are best described by the flow of funds, Chapter 2. Supply and demand for funds are equated by prices in the chapter on interest rate equilibrium (Chapter 3). The basic concepts, definitions, and facts about the financial markets, presented in this part, are an important foundation for more detailed analysis in subsequent sections of the book.

CHAPTER 1

FINANCIAL MARKETS, SERVICES, AND INSTITUTIONS

Changes in the forms and delivery modes of financial services offered by commercial banks and other financial institutions have taken place at an unprecedented pace in the last decade. Pressure from innovative nonbank institutions such as money-market funds spurred the Congress to pass banking legislation in 1980 and 1982 that opened competitive markets for depository institutions. High-technology solutions to the movement of funds, selection of investments, and other operations have geometrically speeded and expanded the flow of financial information and transactions in every dimension. Furthermore, high-technology businesses are part of the loan, leasing, and equity portfolios of financial institutions.

Survival in the rapidly changing financial market is no more assured for existing financial institutions than for existing animal species in a changing environment. Bank closings so far in the 1980s have occurred at five times their previous record levels. Savings and loans have been forced to merge in unprecedented numbers as a result of unprofitable operations during the past decade. But while others failed, new banks, savings and loans, brokerage firms, finance companies, and other financial institutions opened for business. Many new and old institutions not only have survived, but have prospered in high-technology operations and investments.

To understand how financial institutions compete successfully in a rapidly changing environment requires a thorough understanding of the money and capital markets, institutional positions, management techniques, and governmental regulatory structure. Such an understanding transcends time, because the behavior of savers and borrowers is relatively static compared with the ways of delivering financial services. For example, today's bankers who finance oil shipping serve savers and borrowers in fundamentally the same way as twelfth-century Venetian bankers served Rennaissance ship owners and lenders.

In this chapter we discuss fundamental financial services provided by financial institutions. The definitions and concepts presented here are more than a simple introduction, however, they provide the underlying form upon which the details of interest-rate analysis, institutional structure, managerial methods, and government oversight are based. Learning the basics in this chapter affords a strong foundation for understanding the more specific areas discussed later in this book and observed in the financial markets.

ROLE OF FINANCIAL INSTITUTIONS IN MONEY AND CAPITAL MARKETS

Money markets are exchange systems for trading short-term (less than one year), high-quality securities such as U.S. Treasury bills. *Capital markets* are exchange systems designed to transfer ownership of long-term (over one-year) debt and equity securities, such as corporate bonds, U.S. Treasury bonds, and common stock. *Financial institutions,* such as commercial banks and insurance companies, are specialized businesses that efficiently operate most of the money and capital markets. Financial institutions and markets are inseparable in practice, because the markets are often created and operated by financial institutions.

The creation and operation of financial institutions are the responsibilities of financial institution managers. Managers are responsible for the proper functioning of the financial institution, a difficult task in our very competitive and uncertain financial markets. Competition is fierce in virtually every financial market, from the local savings deposit market to the U.S. Treasury bill market and from the domestic commercial loan market to the Eurodollar bond market. To survive and prosper in today's money and capital market, financial institutions must be managed by people who understand the economics of financial institutions, the flow of funds from savers to borrowers, the competitive positions of major financial institutions, financial analysis techniques for a wide range of securities, and the status and trend of government regulations.

Financial institutions play the important role in the money and capital markets of moving funds from savers to borrowers. (See Figure 1-1.) Savers consume less than their income and borrowers consume more than their income, with interest rates acting as the driving force for allocating funds. Imagine how difficult it would be to allocate funds without interest rates and without a competitive market open to all savers and borrowers.

Using interest rates as a means of allocating capital and savings opportunities is an excellent solution to an otherwise complex societal problem. The problems of expulsing free money and capital markets are obvious in many of the noncapitalistic, administered countries in the world. In recent years the

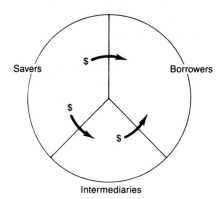

FIGURE 1-1
Financial intermediaries facilitate the flow of funds (depicted by arrows) from savers to borrowers.

Savers

Borrowers

Intermediaries

largely administered economies of China and Hungary have opened selected parts of their economies to the capitalistic approach in an effort to improve efficiency and consumer welfare. A convenient, efficient money and capital market does not exist, however, without a great deal of effort and expertise. A modern, efficient financial market requires experts to transmit and analyze financial information, create new financial contracts, transact money and securities, and maintain a reliable, trusted custodianship. Also, knowledgeable investors are needed to select intelligently among competitive investments, price risk accurately, and respond to change quickly. Who provides the expertise? Who assures that investors receive reliable information? Who is the trusted custodian of our securities?

In the United States, Canada, and other capitalistic economies, financial institutions provide financial expertise and services and governments oversee the financial institutions. Attracted by profits earned by providing financial services, financial institutions deal in the financial markets to satisfy the needs of businesses, households, and governments. The financial institutions view money as a commodity to be brokered, refined, and stored, just as nonfinancial businesses process oil, wheat, or computer chips.

The intangible nature of money and financial assets separates financial businesses from their nonfinancial counterparts. Money is a creation of our mind and exists because of the strength of our faith. That is, securities and deposits are supported *not by a physical resource but by the confidence and desire of investors*. Consequently, financial institutions are supported by intangible assets and are subject to decline or collapse when trust and confidence wane. The supporting forces of government regulation and efficient management are discussed in this book. Furthermore, the book shows how new securities are created to extend the financial frontier.

United States financial institutions are usually private, profit-making businesses. They are run by managers who report to owners, and the owners invest in financial institutions to earn profits. Therefore, the typical managerial objective is to produce the greatest profit possible for a given level of risk. That is, managers operate the financial institution to maximize the wealth of the owners—shareholders and association members.

The decision analyses in this book evaluate the risks and returns expected for alternative strategies in the money and capital markets. Managers are concerned not only with the risk of financial collapse (a remote possibility), but also with the risk of failing to achieve competitive returns. The excitement of managing a financial institution comes with positioning the institution so that it profits from future financial conditions. This book discusses how bank, savings and loan, insurance, and other managers direct their institutions into the most lucrative financial markets. These are the people who decide the most profitable ways to move money from savers to investor. Financial institutions management may be thought of as a billion-dollar game—played with real money.

Desired Securities and Investor Confidence

Financial institutions must be managed so that (1) *desired securities* are created and funds flow optimally to satisfy capital needs, and (2) *trust and confidence* in the institutions exist to a degree sufficient to create the securities. Because financial institutions create their own financial contracts, they are an important part of the contract; that is, banks create and form a part of demand deposits, and stockbrokers are a valuable adjunct to listed stocks. The value of the security, therefore, is enhanced by an institution that stands ready to redeem or market it. Consequently, understanding financial markets requires knowing about both securities and institutions.

Wealth Maximization

The manager's objective is usually to maximize the wealth of the institution's stockholders, where wealth is measured by the market value of common stock.[1] The institutional manager analyzes, selects, and implements strategies for creating and exchanging securities that benefit stockholders. Strategies are developed by:

1 *Recognizing* individuals, governments, and businesses qualified to borrow and invest money
2 *Facilitating* the movement of money provided by savers
3 *Controlling* the timing and terms of repayment

---

[1] Institutional managers are the officers and managerial personnel who direct and commit the institution in the financial marketplace. Some financial intermediaries, such as savings banks, credit unions, and savings and loans, are mutual associations owned by the deposit and borrowing members. Managers of mutual associations are legally responsible to the members. In a general sense, mutual association managers serve to improve the wealth of members, including both those who borrow and those who lend funds.

The institutional manager operates in the money and capital markets to achieve the stockholder's objective and makes decisions on the basis of *expected returns and risk*. Like stockholders, managers value future returns by discounting them at a risk-adjusted rate. Returns usually accrue from strategies involving a combination of an investment portfolio and financial service package that solves important household or business financial problems.

FINANCIAL MARKET STRUCTURE AND FUNCTIONS

Financial markets consist of agents, brokers, institutions, and intermediaries transacting purchases and sales of securities. The many persons and institutions operating in the financial markets are linked by laws, friendships, contracts, and communications networks that form an externally visible *financial market structure*. One view of the current market structure is seen in Figure 1-2.

The financial market is divided between investors and financial institutions. The term *financial institution* is a broad one, referring to organizations that act as agents, brokers, and intermediaries in financial transactions. Financial institutions are easily distinguished from nonfinancial businesses by looking at

FIGURE 1-2
Classification of participants in the financial markets.

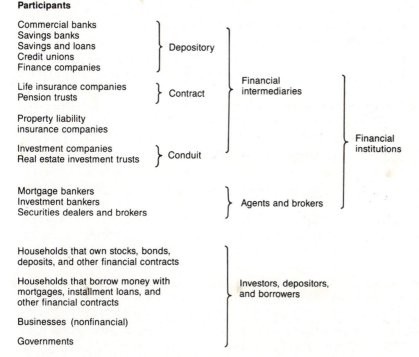

the asset side of the balance sheet. Whereas nonfinancial businesses own real assets (inventory, equipment, real estate, etc.), financial institutions own financial contracts (loans, securities, leases, etc.). *Agents and brokers* contract on behalf of others; intermediaries sell for their own account. *Financial intermediaries* purchase securities for their own account and sell their own liabilities and common stock. For example, stockbrokers and savings and loans are classified differently. The stockbroker is classified as an agent and broker, and the savings and loan is called a financial intermediary. Brokers and savings and loans, like all financial institutions, buy and sell securities, but they are classified separately because the primary activity of brokers is buying and selling as an agent for others rather than buying and holding an investment portfolio of their own. Financial institutions are classified according to their primary activity, although they frequently engage in overlapping activities. Next we see that financial markets provide our specialized, interdependent economy with many financial benefits, including:

1 Time preference
2 Risk separation and distribution

Functions of Financial Markets

Time Preference Time preference refers to the value of money spent now relative to money available for spending in the future. Business executives must judge between outlays that provide a return in the near term and those that pay off many years from now. They must decide upon commitments requiring funds now and those requiring funds later. They must allocate not only funds that they expect to receive currently, but also those that they expect to receive in the future. Planning the best uses for the investment of current surpluses, arranging to borrow to cover deficits, and forecasting future flows are the essence of financial planning. In a capitalistic economy, the money and capital markets price funds so that businesses and governments can make rational economic allocations of capital. The price of capital is set in a competitive marketplace by supply and demand forces (discussed in Chapter 3). The market price of capital is compared by businesses with the expected returns in proposed capital expenditures. Businesses allocate their capital to real investments whose return is at or above the cost of capital. Long-term investments are compared with short-term investments using the financial-market-determined cost of capital. Consequently, the allocation of capital between short-and long-term investments depends on the free play of supply and demand in an open market.

Also, consumers may decide upon a time pattern for expenditures that does not necessarily coincide with their current or expected income flows. Financial markets allow consumers to implement time adjustments in the payment for goods. Without them, there would be no opportunity to earn interest on savings, and expenditures would be limited to current receipts and cash. Saving allows many consumers to postpone consumption and to receive returns from investments. On the other hand, borrowing to purchase an automobile, for example, provides physical and psychic returns, as does a vacation to the Florida beaches. (Fisher's time preference model is discussed in Chapter 3. His eloquent model is a classic representation of our utility for present and future expenditures.)

Risk Separation and Distribution   In addition to allocating money capital, the financial markets distribute economic risks. Employment and investment risks are separated by the creation and distribution of financial securities. The person who builds and operates a new restaurant may not want to risk his or her capital, while another person may be in a position to chance receiving a low return or a loss on a restaurant investment. On a larger scale, the money and capital markets transfer the massive risks of steel plants, electronics research, and oil exploration from people actually performing the work (employment risks) to savers who accept the risk of an uncertain return. The chance of failure for a $100 million plastics manufacturer may be divided among thousands of investors living and working all over the world. If the plastics business fails, each investor loses only part of his or her wealth and may continue to receive income from other investments and employment.

In addition to permitting individuals to separate employment and investment risks, the financial markets allow individuals to diversify among investments. Diversification means combining securities with different attributes into a portfolio. Ordinarily, a diversified portfolio of financial claims is less risky than a portfolio consisting of one or at most a handful of similar securities. Total risk is reduced because losses in some investments are offset by gains in others. The benefits of diversification are possible due to the existence of large, diversified financial markets where investors may buy and sell securities with minimum impediments (transactions costs, regulatory interference, and so forth).

Functions of Financial Intermediaries

We have seen that financial markets facilitate the movement of funds from those who save money to those who invest money in capital assets. Savings are distributed among investments and expenditures through securities traded in the financial markets. Now we go on to show how financial institutions facilitate and improve the distribution of funds, money, and capital in several respects:

1 Payments mechanism
2 Security trading
3 Transmutation
4 Risk diversification
5 Portfolio management
6 Income taxes

All of these functions are important to an efficient financial system, and managers are improving execution capability through improved electronic communication, information processing, and institutional design. Financial intermediaries are special types of agents that collect information about economic entities, evaluate financial information, and package financial claims.[2] The following sections discuss these six functions of financial intermediaries.

Payments Mechanism   Financial intermediaries facilitate payments by enabling businesses, governments, and consumers to complete transactions without cash. Checks and credit cards are used for the bulk of purchases, as measured by the dollar amount of transactions. Check payments going through banks in standard metropolitan areas of the United States now exceed $10 trillion annually. Check clearings exceed fourteen times our net national income. Checking account balances of $250 billion are twice as great as currency in circulation. Employees are paid for their labor by check and stockholders receive dividends by check. In turn, consumers pay for housing, electricity, gas, water, clothing, and most of their own bills by check or credit card. Most businesses and consumers make all their payments by check because it is *economical* (computers can write checks more easily than they can count bills and coins), *safe*, and *preferred by the recipient*. Although banks have traditionally operated most of the payment systems, savings and loans and other institutions are entering the transactions services market. Computer technology advances are making *point-of-sale automated teller machines* and home computers competitive alternatives to bank lobbies, and are opening the way for securities brokers and investment companies to provide payments services to consumers. By linking payments services to securities portfolios, consumers can invest or spend their wealth more quickly and conveniently than when money and securities are separated by legal and operational barriers. Thus, advances in the payments mechanism not only improve the convenience of the point of sale, but also increase the liquidity of capital investments.

Security Trading   The most straightforward security trading system is the network of investment dealers and the related communications facilities. For example, brokerage houses, securities dealers, banks, savings and loans, and the New York and American Stock Exchanges are part of a national system that trades equities, corporate bonds, municipal bonds, and federal government debt issues. In the investment banking chapter we take a closer look at investment brokers and bankers. These agents trade thousands of primary securities every day. *Primary securities*, defined as securities issued by the unit making the real capital investment, are marketed throughout the country to lenders and borrowers, who are continually informed about capital market transactions by sophisticated communications networks. Transactions are reduced to a routine, and costs of trading are minimized by the national scope of the market.

---

[2] The agency theory of financial intermediation is discussed in Draper and Hoag (1978).

The intense effort of the dealers produces a broad array of security offerings. Massive issues, even amounts over $100 million, are assimilated quickly and at a cost of only a few percent of the amount sold.

Even the best trading system cannot overcome, however, the difficulties associated with savers directly purchasing primary securities. The terms desired by savers may not suit the borrowers, or vice versa. Consumers, who provide the bulk of savings funds, generally prefer short-term over long-term investments. On the other hand, business borrowers prefer long-term securities that match their expected return from capital investment and decrease the frequency with which they must enter the capital market. Consequently the disadvantages of the longer-term securities are reflected in a premium rate. To overcome this, financial intermediaries issue securities with terms suitable to consumers on the one hand and buy securities desired by businesses on the other hand. We define and discuss the process of changing the package of terms, called *transmutation*, in the next section. Changing the terms of money flowing from savers to investors is an important function of financial intermediaries and a significant reason why financial intermediaries exist and earn profits.

Transmutation The financial intermediary, by purchasing primary securities and issuing secondary securities, *adds* choices to borrowers and lenders. Issues of financial intermediaries are termed *secondary securities*. The secondary security choices are designed more nearly to reflect the lender's preferences, and therefore the lender is willing to provide funds at a lower rate of interest. For example, time deposits at commercial banks are preferred by small savers over corporate bonds because the saver can withdraw his or her "money" at any time with only a small loss of principal and cost. Funds from time deposits are invested in corporate loans and other primary securities that are well suited to the borrowers' needs. We also observe pension funds and life insurance companies arranging the terms of debt directly with corporate borrowers so as more nearly to satisfy the borrowers' preferences. Banks are issuing certificates of deposit in the exact amount and with the exact maturity date needed by firms desiring to invest temporarily idle funds. The process of changing the terms of money bought and sold by financial intermediaries is termed *transmutation*. For example, savings and loan associations obtain money with short-term, small-balance savings deposits to make 20- to 30-year mortgage loans in amounts usually exceeding $10,000. Timing and amount are usually changed through transmutation, with alterations limited only by the creativity of the financial institution and the acceptance of its customers.

Risk Diversification Because of their immense size, financial institutions are able to purchase a large number of investments and reduce the negative effect of one investment returning a much lower than expected rate. The potential negative effect of one asset in a small portfolio, which many investors have, is mitigated by the holdings of hundreds of assets. Individuals cannot as easily achieve a well-diversified portfolio as a large financial institution. The services and transactions are provided at a relatively low cost, as institutions usually achieve substantial economies of scale. Therefore, large institutions can efficiently invest in a number of securities, such as hundreds of stocks and bonds, thousands of mortgage loans, or tens of thousands of consumer loans. Although some investments do not produce the expected return, others return more profits than expected. The average return will approximate the expected return more closely if many securities are owned than if only a few securities are held. The concept of spreading investment to reduce risk is called diversification.

Portfolio Management   Financial institutions also act as portfolio managers and advisers over most of the primary securities owned in the United States. The private financial sector manages most of the home mortgages, commercial mortgages, consumer loans, state and local government securities and business loans. In addition, nearly one-fourth of outstanding common stocks are managed by investment companies, and a large portion of the remaining shares of stock are invested with the advice of trust institutions.

The most important reasons for obtaining institutional management are:

1 Convenience
2 Protection against fraud
3 Quality of investment selection
4 Low transaction cost

Financial intermediaries provide a convenient place where savers can safely invest excess money and consumers can easily borrow funds. Investments are protected against unscrupulous borrowers by loan officers and a bevy of collectors and attorneys. Well-trained investment analysts and loan officers seek good investment opportunities and screen prospective securities so as to obtain the best yield available for the risk level that suits the investors' preferences.

Income Taxes   Income-tax differentials among individuals and businesses are mitigated by intermediaries, which transfer tax deductions from one time period to another and from low- to high-income taxpayers. For example, income invested in and earned by pension funds is not taxed until retirement, when rates are generally lower than before retirement. Leasing intermediaries, a type of finance company, pass depreciation tax shields from equipment users in low-tax brackets to equipment owners in high-tax brackets. The depreciation and other expenses reduce income taxes more for high- than for low-tax-bracket investors.

Also, income taxes are not applied to some services provided by financial institutions. When services are provided in lieu of interest payments, customers are said to receive *implied interest.* For example, depositors often receive checking accounts, traveler's checks, and low-rate loans in return for the use of their money. These benefits are a form of implicit interest and usually are exempt from income taxes, whereas explicit interest payments are generally subject to income taxes.

SPECIALIZATION BY MAJOR FINANCIAL INSTITUTIONS

Each type of financial institution approaches the financial markets from a different angle. We characterize kinds of institutional specialization as *strategies*, because institutional managers develop strategies for making profits in the financial markets. Strategies are developed by:

1 Recognizing individuals, governments, and businesses who want to buy and sell primary and secondary securities

2 Selecting security transactions that are profitable to the institution

3 Efficiently utilizing labor and capital to execute transactions

Although we characterize certain institutions as having roles to play, the managers of those institutions are bound to such roles but are persistently specializing in given securities. For example, insurance companies specialize in marketing, policy underwriting, and organizing people to meet financial needs caused by unexpected deaths. Of the numerous types of life insurance that a company may sell, it will choose the most profitable ones. If a life insurance policy line becomes unprofitable, then it may be eliminated from the company's offerings.

We note that most financial institutions specialize in one or a few securities, such as life insurance, savings deposits, or consumer loans. Financial institutions specialize to increase the efficiency of labor and capital in executing transactions. Life insurance companies, for example, develop a well-trained sales staff, smoothly functioning operations personnel, and knowledgeable management by utilizing all their resources in one line—life insurance. Furthermore, the efficiency advantage of specialization tends to create larger financial institutions. Large financial institutions are able to use specialized personnel and equipment to buy, process, and sell securities. Cost reductions achieved by size are called *economies of scale* and are very significant for some financial institutions. Through specialization in the selection of security lines and productive resources, financial institutions are able to trade securities more cheaply than can individuals and institutions that do not specialize. Consequently most financial institutions are specialists in selected securities and markets.[3]

In Chapters 8 to 14, we discuss the strategies, securities, and operations of major financial institutions. Here it is necessary only to survey the major institutions as preparation for Chapter 2. We are concerned primarily with the following institutions (chapters covering each institution are given in parentheses):

---

[3] Benston and Smith (1976) identify three sources of comparative advantage.

Commercial banks (Chapters 8 and 15)
Savings banks (Chapter 9)
Savings and loans (Chapter 9)
Credit unions (Chapter 9)
Finance companies (Chapter 10)
Life insurance companies (Chapter 11)
Property and liability insurance companies (Chapter 11)
Pension trusts (Chapter 12)
Mortgage bankers (Chapter 13)
Investment brokers and bankers (Chapter 13)
Investment companies (mutual funds) (Chapter 14)
Real estate investment trusts (Chapter 14)

The relative sizes of many of these institutions are shown in Table 1-1, and each is described briefly as follows:

1 *Commercial banks* are the most numerous of all U.S. financial institutions; they are an intermediary that attracts funds with deposits and invests money in consumer and business loans, state and local government bonds, and U.S. government bonds in domestic and international markets.

2 *Savings banks* raise funds with deposits and invest primarily in long-term securities, bonds, residential mortgages, consumer loans, and commercial loans.

3 *Savings and loans* sell deposits and invest in mortgage, consumer, and commercial loans.

4 *Credit unions* are a consumer savings and lending intermediary that pools savings to make mostly installment-type loans to its members.

TABLE 1-1
TOTAL FINANCIAL ASSETS OF MAJOR
FINANCIAL INSTITUTIONS,
DECEMBER 31, 1984
(AMOUNTS IN BILLIONS)

Commercial banks	$2,012.9
Savings banks	206.4
Savings and loans	989.9
Credit unions	115.8
Finance companies	294.1
Life insurance companies	692.4
Private pension funds	623.3
Investment bankers	60.5
Investment companies	161.9
Real estate investment trusts	4.7
Money market funds	209.7

5 *Finance companies* grant installment loans to consumers and many types of loans to businesses.

6 *Life insurance companies* and *pension trusts* accumulate savings by individuals and insure people against the financial misfortune of untimely death.

7 *Property and casualty insurance companies* collect premiums from those subject to a small chance of a large loss and pay benefits to the unfortunate few who suffer losses.

8 *Mortgage bankers* and *investment bankers and brokers* facilitate the creation and exchange of virtually all publically traded securities.

9 *Investment companies* exist in several forms but are best known as *mutual funds*. Mutual funds provide diversification by investing our money in many marketable stocks and bonds selected by professional money managers.

10 *Real estate investment trusts* are the real estate counterparts to investment companies. Only two decades old, real estate investment trusts are emerging, with growing pains, as a dynamic and demanded type of financial intermediary.

We list many financial institutions here, but we hasten to add that others exist and more are coming to the financial markets. Although we concentrate on the biggest institutions, we do not slight any profit-oriented financial business that serves a legitimate economic role. We point out that the basic management concepts developed in this book extend beyond these eleven to virtually all financial institutions.

Further, the practical ability to manage financial institutions serving many markets simultaneously has been increasing, as institutions merge. Once entirely separate, banks, brokers, and insurers are now often owned and managed by a single corporation. The trend is toward financial conglomerates, sometimes called *financial supermarkets*, which combine many of the services of the eleven separate institutions.

Importance of Information Economics in Financial Institutions

Financial institutions are substantial users and producers of information. Any information relevant to financial decisions is likely to be produced, including such things as stock and bond prices, financial reports, production records, governmental actions, legal actions and decisions, agricultural weather conditions, and international political events. They use information to analyze and judge investments in securities, loans, leases, and other financial opportunities. They develop and sell information to potential investors regarding deposit interest rates, stock dividends, bond rates, and insurance policy earnings and benefits. They produce information by researching corporate finances, tax laws, securities contracts, and borrower backgrounds. Information production and acquisition are costly, requiring people to conduct research, equipment to store their findings, and distribution networks to transfer reports to users. The users pay for information, either in the form of fees or reduced investment yields, which they find of greater value than its cost. Therefore, financial institutional managers attempt to produce or acquire information whose value exceeds its cost.

Some of the investment information acquired by financial intermediaries is confidential. Internal financial statements and operating plans of businesses are confidential, because this information could be helpful to competitors. Financial statements, legal proceedings, and plans of individuals are regarded as confidential for personal or professional reasons. Businesses and individuals who prefer to maintain the confidentiality of their affairs do not want to distribute their information to the public financial markets. Rather, they open the books, records, and plans for a confidential inspection by a banker, investment officer, loan officer, or other officer who can authorize a loan or investment directly. Thus, a business or individual can borrow without publicly revealing trade secrets, finances, or personal facts to the world at large. Only financial intermediaries combine the ability to lend and collect confidential information, a unique combination that may explain the existence of financial intermediaries.[4] At the very least, successful intermediary management requires shrewdly deciding what information should be obtained, efficiently acquiring that information, and discreetly using confidential information in judging investment opportunities.

PUBLIC POLICY

To accumulate sufficient amounts of capital requires a safe, sound, and controlled money and capital market. Because of the continuing opportunity for fraud, gross mismanagement, lack of concern for external effects, and other deficiencies of a purely laissez-faire financial market, governments establish a public policy with respect to financial institutions. *Public policy* is a set of laws, regulations, and popular attitudes that motivate financial institutions to perform in a publicly acceptable manner.

Actions taken by the U.S. government to achieve public policy goals may be grouped into three categories:

1 Active supervision of financial institutions
2 Disclosure of investment information
3 Control of the money supply

These topics are discussed briefly here and more thoroughly in Part Five.

Active Supervision of Financial Institutions

A major public policy goal is the assurance of a safe and sound financial system. Safety and soundness are important because people and businesses are

---

[4] See Campbell and Kracaw (1980), Thakor and Callaway (1983), and Chan (1983) for theoretical treatments of information economics in bank credit markets.

severely disrupted by the collapse of the financial system. In the liquidity crises of 1973, 1884, 1893, and 1907, and the depression of the 1930s, financial disaster caused widespread real economic hardship—unemployment, hunger, and despair. The severe *external consequences* of financial failure have focused public concern on safety.

The Federal Reserve Act of 1913 and the Banking Act of 1933 established two important governmental agencies, the Federal Reserve and the Federal Deposit Insurance Corporation, to deal with two significant public banking problems, illiquidity and insolvency. Both agencies subsequently developed large staffs to actively supervise commercial banks.

Under active supervision government-imposed penalties are the primary approach to regulation, because examiners use directives and legal action to prohibit or correct undesired institutional practices. Regulatory directives are usually delivered to management and boards of directors, who respond either by implementing or challenging the examiners' recommendations. Legal actions may be instituted to require compliance with directives or to reconcile differences of opinion regarding management or disclosure practices, but legal proceedings are relatively rare.

Disclosure of Investment Information

Investment information *disclosure* is the public dissemination of facts and opinions that are material to forming investment decisions. Disclosure is necessary for effective *market discipline*, an important means of regulating financial institutions and securities. Market discipline operates through private investors, including depositors, who allocate their funds among the institutions and securities that are most acceptable. If a financial institution fails to meet the public's expectations, then it is "disciplined" by investors who withdraw their funds. Forming accurate investment opinions requires good investment information; hence, disclosure of investment information by all financial institutions and on securities issues is essential for good market discipline.

Currently financial disclosure is required primarily by the Securities and Exchange Act (1940) and its amendments. Also, financial disclosure is required by some Federal Reserve regulations covering deposit and loan terms offered to consumers. State and federal agencies regulating corporations, banks, insurance companies, brokerage firms, and other financial institutions routinely collect and make publicly available a wide range of financial statements and management reports.

Control of the Money Supply

Many governments, including that of the United States, influence the quantity of funds and interest rates in the money markets by controlling the money supply. For example, the Federal Reserve controls the total amount of money in the United States and other U.S. dollar economies by regulating commercial bank reserve levels and requirements. Reserve levels are varied regularly to achieve public policy goals, such as stimulating economic growth, moderating price inflation, and stabilizing the dollar relative to foreign currencies.

SUMMARY

The financial markets consist of financial institutions, lenders, and borrowers. Financial institutions are agents and owners that market securities to lenders, borrowers, and one another. The flow of funds from lenders to borrowers is facilitated by financial institutions, which trade existing securities and create new securities. Institutions provide an important payments mechanism, operate markets for trading securities, transmute funds by creating securities with new terms, manage portfolios, and reduce risk through diversification. Financial intermediaries, by demanding and selling securities in desired quantities and at minimum transaction costs, make profits in the process of allocating funds among users of capital.

Through specialization in selected strategies, financial institutions develop competitive advantages in segments of the financial markets. They obtain labor and capital economies of scale not achievable by individual lenders and borrowers and nonspecialized institutions. Over time the specialized strategy matures into a commonly recognized role in the financial markets. Specialized institutions playing important roles in today's financial markets are commercial banks, savings banks, savings and loans, credit unions, finance companies, life insurance companies, pension trusts, mortgage bankers, investment brokers and bankers, investment companies, and real estate investment trusts.

Although often specialization provides cost benefits, it constrains the types of financial services offered. In recent years financial institutions have attempted to maintain the cost advantages of specialization while eliminating the limited service constraints by merging different types of financial institutions. The resulting institution is a horizontally integrated financial supermarket offering a large array of services. The conglomerate strategy is too new to evaluate on the basis of experience, but it does offer the potential of greater consumer convenience for payment transactions, securities transactions, risk diversification, and portfolio management.

TERMS

financial markets	transmutation
financial institutions	portfolio management
savers	payments mechanism
borrowers	primary securities
financial contracts	secondary securities
financial intermediaries	economies of scale
agents and brokers	public policy
time preference	market discipline
risk diversification	investment information disclosure

QUESTIONS

1 List five services (functions) of financial intermediaries.

2 What is the objective of the financial institution manager and how does he or she accomplish this objective? Why might it be in the public interest to allow a financial intermediary to go out of business?

3 What is the difference between primary securities and secondary securities?

4 How is saving (real) transferred to investment (real) through financial intermediaries?

5 What is meant by transmutation?

6 What are the two major classes of financial institutions? How do their functions differ?

7 Name three reasons why businesses and consumers prefer to make payments by check.

8 How are strategies and profits of financial institutions developed?

9 What are the three types of actions taken by the U.S. government to achieve public policy goals?

SELECTED REFERENCES

Benston, G. J., and C. W. Smith, Jr.: "A Transactions Cost Approach to the Theory of Financial Intermediation," *Journal of Finance*, May 1976, pp. 215–231.

Campbell, Tim S., and William A. Kracaw: "Information Production, Market Signaling, and the Theory of Financial Intermediation," *The Journal of Finance*, September 1980, pp. 863–882.

Chan, Yuk-Shee: "On the Positive Role of Financial Intermediation in Allocation of Venture Capital in a Market with Imperfect Information," *Journal of Finance*, December 1983, pp. 1543–1568.

Demsetz, Harold: "The Cost of Transacting," *Journal of Quantitative Economics*, February 1968, pp. 33–53.

Dobrovolsky, Sergei P.: *The Economics of Corporation Finance*, McGraw-Hill, New York, 1971, chap. 12.

Dougall, Herbert E.: *Capital Markets and Institutions*, Prentice-Hall, Inc., Englewood Cliffs, N.J., 1970.

Draper, Dennis W., and James W. Hoag: "Financial Intermediation and the Theory of Agency," *Journal of Financial and Quantitative Analysis*, November 1978, pp. 595–711.

Smith, Gary, and William Brainard: "A Disequilibrium Model of Savings and Loan Associations," *The Journal of Finance*, December 1982, pp. 1277–1293.

Spellman, Lewis J.: *The Depository Firm and Industry*, Academic Press, New York, 1982.

Thakor, Anjan, V., and Richard Callaway: "Costly Information Production Equilibria in the Bank Credit Market with Applications to Credit Rationing," *Journal of Financial and Quantitative Analysis*, June 1983, pp. 229–256.

CHAPTER 2

FLOW OF FUNDS THROUGH UNITED STATES FINANCIAL MARKETS AND INSTITUTIONS

The last chapter discussed the concept of funds flowing from savers to borrowers. (See Figure 1-1.) This chapter presents the amounts of funds actually flowing through the U.S. financial system. It sets the stage for later chapters, which analyze banks, savings and loans, other institutions, loans, bonds, and other securities. Here financial institutions and trillions of dollars comprise the financial markets of the United States. We call this area *macrofinance*, because we study the entire ("macro") financial system. As participants in the financial markets, financial institutions managers need a working knowledge of all financial markets to understand fully the position of their particular institution. We see here that financial institutions do not exist independently of one another but interact daily to move money and negotiate interest rates.

This chapter begins by surveying the ownership of securities—the stock of financial wealth—in the United States. Next we look at the flow of funds and trace the movement of funds from household savers to business and government investors. The intersection of supply and demand schedules determines the equilibrium level of interest rates, as will be seen in the next chapter. Interest rates are the prices bid, asked, and charged for funds in the financial markets.[1] This chapter concentrates on describing the flow and ownership of money capital in the United States (a subsequent chapter describes interna-

---

[1] *Interest rate* is a term with two meanings, and the usage determines the appropriate meaning. When describing a specific security, interest rates are fixed rates of return and refer only to fixed return securities such as bonds and mortgages. On the other hand, when describing the flow of funds and the stock of money capital in general, the term "interest rate" refers to the price of all money capital, regardless of the types of securities which represent investment transactions.

tional investment) and the following chapter analyzes supply and demand equilibrium quantities and interest rates.

FINANCIAL ASSETS AND LIABILITIES

The present stock of financial assets is now the unimaginable figure of $16 trillion dollars ($16,000,000,000) in the United States, and many times that amount for the entire world. Although $16 trillion overestimates the wealth of the United States in real assets, it is a good estimate of the size of the U.S. *financial market*. The financial asset and liability matrix (Table 2-1) reports the financial positions of households, businesses, governments, and financial institutions. A great deal of information is contained in Table 2-1, but we can deal only with a few sectors and securities because this is just an overview.

Households own about $7 trillion (44 percent) of the financial assets in the U.S. economy. They own nearly $1.5 trillion worth of the corporate shares, although we see later that households are reducing their direct ownership of stock in favor of indirect ownership through pension plans. Households invest the other 57.8 percent of their money primarily in financial institutions, a tribute to the ability of institutional managers to sell (supply) securities to households. Financial sector investment is almost entirely primary securities. Of the financial sector's $6.6 trillion of assets (line 1, under "financial sector"), $2.3 trillion is placed in corporate shares and other credit market instruments (total of lines 20 and 21). Credit-market instruments (line 21, Table 2-1) are primary securities such as bonds, home mortgages, consumer loans, and bank loans. The financial sector owns $5.4 trillion of the $7.1 trillion of the credit-market debt (line 21) securities and about one-half of government debt (lines 22–24). Thus, *a pattern in the financial markets is shown by the statement of financial assets and liabilities: households invest their savings in financial intermediaries, and, in turn financial intermediaries buy (demand) securities directly from businesses and governments.*

Descriptions of the flow of funds through the U.S. financial markets are based largely on the *flow-of-funds* statements prepared by the Board of Governors of the Federal Reserve. At this point in our discussion, we are concerned only with tracing funds through the financial markets. In the next section, we look at the concept of tracing funds from savers to investors.

Tracing Funds from Savings to Investment

Tracing the savings through the financial markets cannot be accomplished by following a particular dollar, because that dollar passes through numerous financial transactions before it returns to the GNP flow. Rather the flows are characterized by *paths* that usually leave the main trail, branch out, and eventually return to the main trail. The path begins with savings flows; when our consumption expenditures (C) are less than income (Y), then saving (S) is created.

TABLE 2-1

FINANCIAL ASSETS AND LIABILITIES, DECEMBER 31, 1984 (AMOUNTS OUTSTANDING IN

	Private		Domestic		Nonfinancial		Sectors		Foreign Sector		U.S. Government	
	Households		Business		State & Local Governments		Total					
	A	L	A	L	A	L	A	L	A	L	A	L
1 Total financial assets	6608.5		1400.3		344.2		8353.0		670.6		303.7	
2 Total liabilities		2223.8		2698.5		425.9		5348.0		599.5		1557.5
3 Gold									38.2		—	
4 S.D.R.'S									21.0		5.6	
5 I.M.F. position										11.5	11.6	
6 Official foreign exchange										6.7	3.1	
7 Treasury currency												17.5
8 Checkable deposits & currency	386.5		87.7		.4		474.6		19.6			21.9
9 Private domestic	386.5		87.7		.4		474.6					
10 Foreign									19.6			
11 U.S. government												21.9
12 Small time & savings deposits	1688.6				7.7		1696.3				1.1	
13 Money market fund shares	209.7						209.7					
14 Large time deposits	179.6		81.4		64.3		325.3		39.4			
15 Fed. funds & security RP's			40.3		19.6		60.0					
16 Deposits abroad			13.4				13.4			34.6		
17 Life insurance reserves	248.8						248.8					9.9
18 Pension fund reserves	1433.0						1433.0					130.0
19 Interbank claims									−26.6			
20 Corporate equities	1492.5						1492.5		94.5			
21 Credit market instruments	844.9	2133.8	166.2	2056.3	231.8	404.0	1242.9	4594.1	298.3	247.5	229.6	1376.8
22 U.S. treasury securities	317.3		28.3		114.2		459.7		193.1			1373.4
23 Federal agency securities	89.2		1.7		50.2		141.1				—	3.2
24 State & local govt. secur.	205.3	51.3	4.1	102.4	10.0	385.5	219.3	539.2				
25 Corporate & foreign bonds	40.2			453.5			40.2	453.5	63.4	66.4		
26 Mortgages	184.9	1373.6		648.3	57.5		242.4	2021.9			51.3	.1
27 Consumer credit		593.6	76.1				76.1	593.6				
28 Bank loans N.E.C.		36.0		543.6				579.6		28.1		
29 Open-market paper	8.0		56.1	79.6			64.1	79.4	41.8	82.3		
30 Other loans		79.3		229.1		18.5		326.9			70.6	178.2
31 Security credit	24.9	47.5					24.9	47.5	-	-		
32 Trade credit		25.8	587.1	479.2		21.9	587.1	526.9	26.3	13.9	31.9	23.4
33 Taxes payable				10.5	20.4		20.4	10.5			−16.2	
34 Miscellaneous	99.9	16.7	424.2	152.3			524.1	169.0	159.7	285.4	15.1	0

Note: "A" refers to assets and "L" to liabilities. Asterisk indicate negligible amounts.
Source: Board of Governors of the Federal Reserve System.

BILLIONS OF DOLLARS)

				Financial		Sectors							
Total		Spons. Ag. & Mtg. Pools		Monetary Authority		Commercial Banking		Pvt. Nonbank Finance		All Sectors		Floats And Discr.	
A	L	A	L	A	L	A	L	A	L	A	L	A	
6775.9		587.1		218.4		2012.9		3957.6		16103.0		−29.7	1
	6470.3		579.5		218.4		1867.9		3804.4		13975.3		2
11.1				11.1						49.3			3
										26.7			4
−.1				−.1						11.5	11.5		5
3.6				3.6						6.7	6.7		6
21.0				21.0						21.0	17.5	−3.5	7
63.5	623.1	1.3			171.4	10.5	409.3	51.7	42.4	579.7	623.1	43.3	8
63.5	582.2	1.3			165.1	10.5	374.7	51.7	42.4	538.2	582.2	44.1	9
	19.6				.4		19.2			19.6	19.6		10
	21.2				5.8		15.4			21.9	21.2	−.7	11
10.0	1707.4						812.9	10.0	894.5	1707.4	1707.4		12
	209.7								209.7	209.7	209.7		13
67.0	431.7						282.9	67.0	148.8	431.7	431.7		14
92.3	191.6	22.5					146.2	69.8	45.5	152.2	191.6	39.4	15
21.2								21.2		34.6	34.6		16
	239.0								239.0	248.8	248.8		17
	1303.0								1303.0	1433.0	1433.0		18
44.9	29.7			4.4	40.5	40.5	−10.7			18.3	29.7	11.4	19
596.9	161.9					.1		596.8	161.9	2183.8	161.9		20
5350.3	902.8	552.9	530.5	169.6		1740.0	81.1	2887.8	291.1	7121.0	7121.0		21
720.5		2.5		160.9		183.0		374.2		1373.4	1373.4		22
387.7	525.5	.7	525.5	8.8		78.5		299.6		528.7	528.7		23
319.9						172.0		143.8		539.2	539.2		24
535.9	119.6					17.6	37.0	518.3	82.6	639.5	639.5		25
1730.4	2.1	437.5				374.2		918.8	2.1	2024.1	2024.1		26
517.5						259.6		257.9		593.6	593.6		27
638.1	30.4			—		638.1			30.4	638.1	638.1		28
201.3	145.6	.8		—		17.0	44.1	183.5	101.4	307.2	307.2		29
298.9	79.6	111.4	5.0					187.5	74.6	477.1	477.1		30
77.0	54.3					35.0		42.0	54.3	101.9	101.9		31
24.3								24.3		669.5	564.2	−105.3	32
	1.9					−.3		1.6		4.2	12.3	8.2	33
393.0	614.2	10.4	49.0	8.8	6.6	186.9	146.0	187.0	412.6	1091.6	1053.6	−23.3	34

$$\text{Saving } (S) = \text{Income } (Y) - \text{Consumption } (C) \qquad (2\text{-}1)$$

We normally think of saving in terms of a positive amount of money. [Negative saving (Y less than C) is called dissaving, such as college students borrowing money to finance their educations; we are going to discuss only saving here.] Surplus units are savers and deficit units are borrowers of funds. The flow of savings from surplus to deficit units must take one or a combination of the following paths:

1 Real investment: the purchase of a house, machine, tool, etc.
2 Financial investment: the purchase of bonds, stocks, etc.
3 Repayment of indebtedness: payments on maturing bonds, installment loan repayments, etc.
4 Hoarding cash: increases in currency

FIGURE 2-1
Alternative paths for savings dollars.

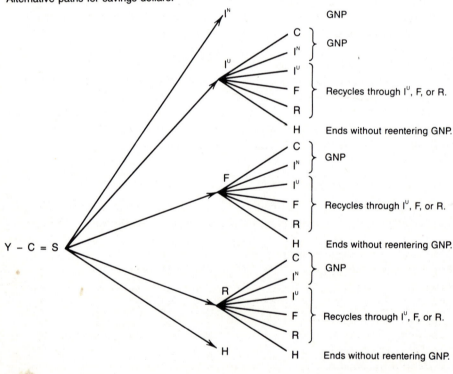

Legend

Y is income	I^N is real asset purchase—new	R is repayment of indebtedness
S is saving	I^U is real asset purchase—used	H is hoarding
C is consumption	F is financial investment	GNP is gross national product

Figure 2-1 illustrates some of the paths that saving may take.

Saving flows that are spent for new equipment (real investment expenditures) leave the savings paths and reenter the gross national product (GNP) as income. The purchase of capital equipment by one company is simultaneously a sale by an equipment manufacturer. Money leaves the savings paths whenever it is invested in new real assets. Similarly, saving lent to someone who spends it for consumption leaves the savings paths and flows into GNP. On the other hand, money that is hoarded leaves the saving paths but does not flow into GNP. Hoarding is a transaction that fails to return money to the income stream. For example, money is hoarded by burying currency in the garden or hiding it under the mattress. Hoarding reduces investment and GNP by failing to recycle money for consumption and investment. Note that branch H, Figure 2-1, does not return funds to the financial system nor add to gross national product.

Purchases of used equipment, financial investments, and debt repayment with savings do not move money back into the GNP but transfer funds to the next person in line. Persons (businesses) who sell used assets, issue new securities, and receive debt payments may choose any of three paths for their money. Used equipment sales, debt repayments, and security issues are transactions that move money to a new decision point. In many cases, that decision point is in the financial market where many alternative investment opportunities are available. Thus the financial investment and debt repayment paths are taken, because they offer more profitable opportunities than a direct real investment by the saver. Financial institutions open financial investment trails for savers; the benefits of improved savings allocation are split between the institution (for operating expenses and profits) and the saver.

Flow of Funds Accounting

The *flow-of-funds* report is the financial accounting counterpart of the National Income Accounts of the Department of Commerce.[2] Descriptions of the financial markets in this text are based largely upon the flow of funds, and a full understanding of the numbers presented requires a basic understanding of their birth. Flow-of-funds reports are used by institutional managers as they prepare interest rate forecasts and plan for future markets and operations. After working through the accounts, basic money flows will be traced through the financial system using the 1984 *flow-of-funds*.

The flow-of-funds accounting system divides the economy into a number of sectors for which sources and uses of funds statements are constructed. *Sectors* are subdivisions of the economy (such as household or business) which make common decisions and are relatively homogeneous in other respects.

---

[2] This section is based on the discussion by Ritter (1963), which summarizes the Federal Reserve's flow-of-funds accounting. The Federal Reserve first published such statistics in 1955 and made major revisions in 1959.

Financial institutions are separated from other business firms in the flow of funds so as to differentiate those making primarily real expenditure decisions from those making financial investments. A sources and uses of funds statement reports the flow of funds by type of *security*. The statement form is a matrix with sector headings and security captions. Flow-of-funds statements are prepared quarterly and annually.

The sectoral statement is a hybrid of balance sheet and income statement information reported to the Federal Reserve by a multitude of business and government entities. The construction of the flow of funds begins with a balance sheet, such as the following generalized version:

Assets	Liabilities and net worth
Financial assets	Liabilities
1 Primary securities	1 Short-term
2 Secondary securities	2 Long-term
Real assets	Net worth
Total assets	Total liabilities and net worth

Each sector would, of course, have characteristic accounts in its balance sheet. For example, business firms would substitute cash and accounts receivable for "financial assets" and plant and equipment for "real assets." Households would show home mortgage loans or automobile loans as long-term liabilities.

The distinction between primary and secondary securities is related to the difference between nonfinancial and financial businesses. *Nonfinancial businesses* are distinguished from financial businesses by the large proportion of real assets owned; *financial business* (institution) assets are principally securities representing claims against others. *Primary securities* are those issued by nonfinancial businesses, while *secondary securities* are claims generated by financial businesses. Note that every financial asset appears on two balance sheets, that of the person owing the funds and that of the owner of the claim. Unlike real assets such as furniture, grain, or lumber, financial assets are claims against someone else or another business. The net worth of any one sector is equal to total assets, real and financial, less liabilities.

However, the net worth, or *wealth*, of the whole economy can equal only the value of all real assets. Financial assets and liabilities serve to divide wealth among economic units or sectors and do not change the real wealth of the economy. Increasing the national debt owed to the country's citizens, for example, does not make a country poorer. Although a liability of the government, government bonds are financial assets belonging to someone. As long as the national debt is held within the country, increases in it increase individuals' financial assets as much as the government debt. A country becomes more or less wealthy only when its real assets or international assets and liabilities change.

Funds Flows from Stock Statements

Balance sheet statements are limited to assets and liabilities at a moment in time. They are like a road map that depicts where a driver has been but not how fast the driver is traveling. The question is whether to look at stocks or flows in an economic analysis. Financial flows depict the "action" in the money game, while stocks represent players' stakes. We compute the amount of flows by looking at the changes in balance sheets from one time period to the next. How *much more or less* does a unit have now than it had last year? How much money is the consumer sector supplying and who is using it? What securities have the state and local government been issuing over the last year? These questions are answered by converting stock information into flow data.

Sector statements of *flows of financial claims* are created by computing the changes in balance sheet accounts, as shown in the following general form:

Financial uses	Financial sources
Financial assets (lending)	Liabilities (borrowing)
1 Δ Primary securities	1 Δ short-term debts
2 Δ Secondary securities	2 Δ long-term debts
	Δ Equity securities

Note that repaying a debt or repurchasing securities is a use of funds, while selling some of our financial assets is a source of funds. Making monthly car payments or mortgage payments takes money—it is a use of our funds. Alternatively, one can purchase a new car or repay old debts by drawing money out of a savings account or selling shares of stock.

The financial flows would be complete now, but the statements would not balance because changes in real assets and net worth are ignored. The "nonfinancial" sources and uses of funds, arising from the sale or purchase of real assets, accrue from transactions on *capital accounts* or *current accounts*.[3] Purchases of real assets with an expected useful life of one year or longer are referred to as *capital expenditures*. Business firms make capital expenditures for plant and equipment, while households make capital outlays for houses, washing machines, boats, and similar goods.

Knowing the changes in financial and real assets, the sector's *net worth* is computed as the difference between total assets and liabilities. Increases in net worth, therefore, are the net result of increases in assets over liabilities. Saving is defined as increase in net worth and is derived from the current transactions accounts. The excess of a sector's current receipts over its current expenditures is also a measure of saving. The funds saved may be used to increase financial or real assets, but the total stock of assets must increase by the amount saved. For example, a household receiving income of $10,000 during a

---

[3] Reported in the National Income and Product Distribution Accounts. See issues of the *Federal Reserve Bulletin*, Board of Governors of the Federal Reserve, Washington, D.C.

TABLE 2-2
EXAMPLE OF SAVINGS BY A SECTOR

Source of funds

Income $10,000
   Less: Consumption 9,000
Saving .... $ 1,000

Use of funds

Increase in primary securities .... $ 200
Increase in secondary securities........... 800
Increase in financial assets .... $ 1,000

year may spend $9000 on consumption (including depreciation and taxes) and save $1000, which it may hold in cash, invest in bonds, spend on capital goods, or apply to debts. For example, Table 2-2 shows a sector saving $1000, of which $200 is invested in primary securities and $800 issued to purchase securities. Whatever the decision, total assets must rise or liabilities fall in an amount equaling the household's savings over the year, i.e., $1000. Net worth of the household must increase by $1000. Saving and the change in net worth are identical, a relationship crucial to the construction of the United States flow-of-funds accounts, which are compiled from only partially complete balance sheet and income statement data.

General Form of Sector Statement

A complete sources and uses of funds statement consists of current nonfinancial sources and uses, financial transactions, and capital nonfinancial transactions. The general form of the sources and uses of funds statement, a simplification of the actual statements, is shown in the following table:

General Form of the Sector Sources and Uses of Funds Statement

Uses		Sources
		Gross savings less capital consumption
		Net saving
Investmemt (increase in real assets)		Saving (increase in net worth)
Lending (increase in financial assets)		Selling securities (decrease in financial assets)
Debt repayment (decrease in liabilities)		Borrowing (increase in liabilities)
Hoarding (increase in money)		Dishoarding (decrease in money)
Total	Equal	Total sources

Deficit sectors are those which invest more than they save, while surplus sectors save more than they invest in real assets. Conversely, we can say that deficit sectors spend more on current and capital goods than they receive in current income. The consumption and investment spending of surplus sectors, on the other hand, are less than their current income. The gap between income and expenditure (i.e., saving) may be greater than or less than investment; the difference is made up through sector lending or borrowing. For instance, the billions of dollars of excess money earned but not spent by the household sector is lent to business and government sectors whose real expenditures exceed their saving. For example, highway and school building programs of the state governments are largely financed by borrowing in the financial markets.

Flow-of-Funds Matrix

A two-sector example will serve to show how the separate sector statements are assembled into the flow-of-funds matrix. The flow of funds is an interlocking, complete system that depicts the balanced sources and uses of funds for each sector, the interrelationships among sectors, and the saving, investment, borrowing, lending, and money flow totals for a 3-month or 1-year period. Again, a simple, generalized version is presented to highlight the major elements:

Generalized Form of the Flow-of-Funds Matrix

	Sector 1		Sector II		All sectors	
	Uses	Sources	Uses	Sources	Uses	Sources
Net saving (net worth)	$\cdots$	S_1	$\cdots$	S_2	$\cdots$	$S_1 + S_2$
Real assets (investment)	I_1	$\cdots$	I_2	$\cdots$	$I_1 + I_2$	$\cdots$
Money (hoarding)	H_1	$\cdots$	H_2	$\cdots$	$H_1 + H_2$	$\cdots$
Financial assets (lending)	L_1	$\cdots$	L_2	$\cdots$	$L_1 + L_2$	$\cdots$
Liabilities (borrowing)	$\cdots$	B_1	$\cdots$	B_2	$\cdots$	$B_1 + B_2$

The actual flow-of-funds matrix for 1984, shown in Table 2-3, is merely a more elaborate and detailed version of the generalized form. We see this by taking a closer look at some of the columns. For example, the generalization contained only two sectors, but the actual matrix consists of eight sectors classified into four groups: private domestic nonfinancial, United States government, financial, and rest of the world. The private domestic nonfinancial sectors are household, business, and state and local government. The financial sectors are broadly defined as monetary authority (an immodest self-reference to the Federal Reserve and the U.S. Treasury), commercial banks, and nonbank finance (savings and loan associations, credit unions, etc.). The discrepancy column is a handy basket to place errors in when sector uses or sources fail to balance, as frequently happens. Deficiencies and inconsistencies in the data arise from errors in data collection, omission, differences in classification or coverage, and various other statistical problems. The recognition of a discrepancy is preferable to burying the error arbitrarily.

TABLE 2-3

SUMMARY OF FLOW-OF-FUNDS ACCOUNTS FOR THE YEAR 1984 (BILLIONS OF DOLLARS)

Private Domestic Nonfinancial Sectors (Households, Business, State & Local Governments, Total); Foreign Sector; U.S. Government. "U" = uses, "S" = sources.

	Households U	Households S	Business U	Business S	State & Local Govts U	State & Local Govts S	Total U	Total S	Foreign Sector U	Foreign Sector S	U.S. Government U	U.S. Government S
Gross saving		606.4		429.5		13.5		1049.4		90.9		-193.4
Capital consumption		300.6		321.2				621.8				
Net saving (1-2)		305.8		108.3		13.5		427.6		90.9		-193.4
Gross Investment (5+11)	654.2		391.8		12.5		1058.5		68.5		-204.5	
Pvt. capital expenditures	464.2		477.8				942.0				-7.9	
Consumer durables	318.5						318.5					
Residential construction	131.7		22.0				153.7					
Plant and equipment	13.9		390.1				404.0					
Inventory change			57.9				57.9					
Mineral rights			7.9				7.9				-7.9	
Net financial investment	189.9		-86.0		12.5		116.5		68.5		-196.6	
Financial uses	433.4		85.8		46.5		565.7		87.4		28.3	
Financial sources		243.5		171.8		33.9		449.2		19.0		224.9
Gold & off. fgn. exchange									-1.0	1.4	2.5	
Treasury currency												.6
Checkable deposits & curr.	30.9		-4.1		.5		27.3		2.0		5.5	
U.S. government											5.5	
Foreign									2.0			
Private domestic	30.9		-4.1		.5		27.3					
Small time & savings dep.	150.6				-2.6		148.0			.4		
Money market fund shares	47.2						47.2					
Large time deposits	58.0		4.7		7.2		69.8		4.0			
Fed. funds & security RP's			2.5		2		2.4					
Foreign deposits			-3.4				-3.4			-4.1		
Life insurance reserves	8.0						8.0					.2
Pension fund reserves	124.1						124.1					18.0
Interbank claims									14.7			
Corporate equities	-46.5			-72.1			-46.5	-72.1	-2.7	1.1		
Credit mkt. instruments	103.8	241.6	18.1	241.9	37.1	33.0	159.0	516.5	45.7	1.7	16.7	198.8
U.S. treasury securities	49.7		2.9		27.0		79.7		26.8			199.0
Federal agency securities	30.0		-.1		4.4		34.4		—			-.1
State & local govt. secur.	31.5	10.7	-.1	18.5	.4	25.4	31.8	54.6				
Corporate & foreign bonds	-6.2			32.2			-6.2	32.2	17.5	2.7		
Mortgages	1.0	130.9		70.7	5.2		6.2	201.5			.4	-.1
Consumer credit		100.6	12.2				12.2	100.6				
Bank loans N.E.C.		-3.3		74.8				71.5		-6.2		
Open-market paper	-2.2		3.2	23.8			1.0	23.8	1.4	.4		
Other loans		2.8		21.9		7.6		32.3		4.8	16.3	
Security credit	5.5	-.5					5.5	-.5	—	—		
Trade credit		1.8	43.7	38.0		1.0	43.7	40.8	3.6	.2	5.7	2.6
Taxes payable				.7	4.4		4.4	.7		-4.0		
Equity in noncorp. bus.	-55.6			-55.6			-55.6	-55.6				
Miscellaneous	7.4	.6	24.3	18.8			31.7	19.4	21.0	18.7	1.6	4.9

Note: "U" refers to uses and "S" to sources of funds. Asterisks indicate negligible amounts.
Source: Board of Governors of the Federal Reserve System.

The "national saving and investment" column reports domestic saving and investment. It is computed by adding saving and investment data from the "all sectors" column to "discrepancies" and subtracting the "rest of the world"

	Total		Spons. Ag. & Mtg. Pools		Monetary Authority		Commercial Banking		Pvt. Nonbank Finance		All Sectors		Discr.	Natl. Svg. & Inv.	
	U	S	U	S	U	S	U	S	U	S	U	S	U		
		16.8		1.2		1.1		12.8		1.6		963.7		872.8	1
		15.0						11.7		3.3		636.8		636.8	2
		1.8		1.2		1.1		1.2		-1.7		326.0		326.0	3
	27.8		.6		1.1		19.2		6.8		950.2		13.5	887.0	4
	21.4							14.7		6.7		955.5	8.2	955.5	5
												318.5		318.5	6
	.1									.1		153.8		153.8	7
	21.3							14.7		6.6		425.3		425.3	8
												57.9		57.9	9
															10
	6.4		.6		1.1		4.5		.2		-5.3		5.3	-68.5	11
	744.1		85.3		14.6		193.8		450.5		1425.5		5.3	19.0	12
		737.7		84.7		13.4		189.3		450.3		1430.8		87.4	13
	-.1				-.1						1.4	1.4			14
		.7				.7					.7	.6	-.1		15
	8.6	46.8		.6		15.8	2.7	23.6	5.4	7.5	43.5	46.8	3.3		16
		5.5				1.7		3.8			5.5	5.5	.1		17
		2.0				*		2.1			2.0	2.0			18
	8.6	39.2		.6		14.2	2.7	17.7	5.4	7.3	36.0	39.2	3.2		19
	.3	148.8						70.7	.3	78.1	148.8	148.8			20
										47.2	47.2	47.2			21
	2.3	76.1						27.5	2.3	48.6	76.1	76.1			22
	26.9	30.7	9.9					9.2	17.0	21.4	29.4	30.7	1.3		23
	-.7									-.7	-4.1	-4.1			24
		7.9								7.9	8.0	8.0			25
		106.2								106.2	124.1	124.1			26
	*	27.2			2.0	-2.0	-2.0	29.1			14.7	27.2	12.5		27
	19.4	41.1					*	.8	19.4	40.3	-29.8	-29.8			28
	622.1	126.5	71.8	74.2	8.4		176.1	12.7	365.8	39.6	843.5	843.5			29
	92.5			-.1	8.9		3.9		79.8		199.0	199.0			30
	39.8	74.2	.2	74.2	-.1		-.5		40.1		74.1	74.1			31
	22.8						9.4		13.4		54.6	54.6			32
	38.1		14.5				4.5	6.5	33.6	8.0	49.4	49.4			33
	195.0		*		55.6		46.3		93.1	*	201.5	201.5			34
	88.4						46.0		42.4		100.6	100.6			35
	66.2		.9		—		66.2			.9	66.2	66.2			36
	42.9	21.2	*			-.4	.3	6.1	43.0	15.0	45.3	45.3			37
	36.5		15.7		16.0		—		20.5	15.7	52.8	52.8			38
	5.8		11.9				6.3		-.5	11.9	11.4	11.4			39
	2.0									2.0	55.0	43.5	-11.4		40
				-.2				*		-.2	.3	.5	.2		41
											-55.6	-55.6			42
	56.8	67.6	3.0	10.5	3.7	—	10.7	15.6	39.4	42.0	111.0	110.6	-.4		43

sector. Claims on foreigners are included here, even though the foreign claims are financial in nature.

Turning now from columns to lines, we find that the third line, "net saving" is what we generally refer to as *saving*. The "gross saving" on the first line is current income less current expenditures; net saving is gross saving less depreciation (capital consumption). The "private capital expenditures" (line 5) corresponds to *investment*, which is further broken down as consumer durable, residential construction, plant and equipment, and inventory. The "financial uses" (line 12) refers to *lending*, while "financial sources" (line 13) corresponds to *borrowing*. The rest of Table 2-3 breaks down lending and borrowing by the security involved, such as bank loans, time and savings accounts, security credit, or trade credit.

TRACING THE 1984 FLOW OF FUNDS

The flow-of-funds matrix for 1984 will be used to illustrate how the effects of substantial money flows can be traced through the system (Figure 2-2). Although the analysis admittedly is rough, it will serve as an overview of the actual saving-to-investment pipeline. The matrix is entered at the top left, "gross saving" of households and business (see Table 2-4). Households and businesses had gross savings of $606.4 billion and $429.5 billion (line 1), respectively. Households added $243.5 billion (line 13) of funds to their savings by borrowing. Spending $464.2 billion (line 5) on capital goods, households had $433.4 billion (line 12) remaining for financial investment.

Household financial investment consisted primarily of the purchase of secondary securities from financial institutions. The five major investments by households were (Table 2-3 line numbers are given in parentheses):

1 Checkable deposits and currency (line 16)
2 Small time and savings deposits (line 20)
3 Life insurance reserves (line 25)
4 Pension fund reserves (line 26)
5 U.S. government securities (line 30)

The predominance of financial intermediation of household funds is dramatized by a pie diagram (Figure 2-3) which shows 1984 investment selections.

FIGURE 2-2
Household funds, 1984, in billions. (*Source*: Table 2-3.)

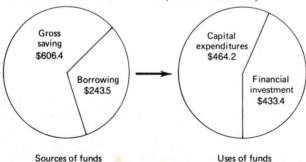

Sources of funds   Uses of funds

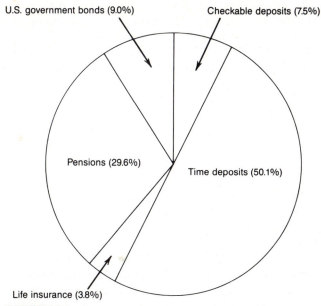

FIGURE 2-3
Household financial investment, (amounts in billions). (*Source*:
Table 2-3.)

Although a use of funds to the household sector, demand and time deposits, life insurance reserves, and pension fund reserves are also a source of funds to the financial sector. With the bulk of household financial investment being made in secondary securities, it is relatively easy to trace them *across* the matrix to the commercial banking and private nonbank finance sectors. If we then move *down* to lines 28 through 36 in Table 2-3, we find that the financial intermediaries were using the funds to purchase primary securities:

1 Corporate shares (line 28)
2 U.S. government obligations (line 30)
3 State and local obligations (line 32)
4 Corporate and foreign bonds (line 33)
5 Home mortgages (line 34)
6 Other loans (line 36)
7 Consumer credit (line 35)
8 Bank loans N.E.C. (line 36)

Part of the household financial investment returned to the household sector, but a large portion went to business, state and local government, and U.S. government sectors. The business sector was a $86.0 billion net user of funds, borrowing $171.8 billion from the money and capital markets. The funds made available to businesses were used primarily for real investment of $477.8 billion. United States government debt issues to fund fiscal deficits are shown on line 30 as $199.0 billion; the U.S. government was a net user of fund in the amount of $196.6 billion in 1984. From a macromarkets perspective, we observe that the U.S. government debt funding came primarily from the private household sector and secondarily from the foreign sector, while the domestic business sector was a relatively small user of funds.

Characteristics of Household Savers

Households are clearly the major source of funds for the financial markets. They are the major source of funds for commercial banks, savings and loans, mutual savings banks, credit unions, life insurance companies, investment companies, and other financial institutions. But it would be naive to believe that all households save and invest equally. Which households save a little? Which save a great deal? What are the characteristics that distinguish the amount of savings by different households?

These important questions about household saving characteristics prompt the Federal Reserve to conduct surveys of household financial assets. Excerpts from the survey are reported in Table 2-4. Total financial assets are reported here; generally the conclusions drawn apply equally well to liquid assets— checking accounts, certificates of deposit, savings accounts, money-market accounts, and savings bonds. Five characteristics are important:

1 Income
2 Age
3 Life cycle
4 Education
5 Occupation

Income You might guess that income determines household financial assets, and you would be partially correct. However, notice that income is a significant factor *only in the upper brackets*. For households with annual incomes of less than $25,000, financial assets are about the same regardless of the income level.

Age and Life-Cycle Stages The most consistently significant determinant of household financial assets is *age*, as is evident in Figure 2-4. People needs, interests, abilities, and opportunities change as they age. Read through the life-cycle stages in Table 2-5 from both a personal and a professional perspective. (Stages I to IV are under 45; stages V to IX are 45 and over.) Most people can easily point to their current stage and relate to past stages but protest vigorously at the suggestion that they will go through later stages! Note that in the 45-and-over stages the need for and ability to save is substantially greater than in the under-45 stages. Whereas younger persons are concerned about children's needs and the struggling to develop a career, older persons are con-

TABLE 2-4
MEDIAN TOTAL FINANCIAL ASSETS OF
FAMILIES HOLDING SUCH ASSETS, 1983

Family Income (dollars)	
Less than 5,000	$ 513
5,000–7,499	$ 1,000
7,500–9,999	$ 848
10,000–14,999	$ 2,205
15,000–19,999	$ 1,780
20,000–24,999	$ 2,385
25,000–29,999	$ 3,349
30,000–39,999	$ 5,950
40,000–49,999	$10,631
50,000–and over	$31,658
Age of family head	
Under 25	$ 746
25–34	$ 1,514
35–44	$ 3,750
45–54	$ 4,131
55–64	$ 9,338
65–74	$11,400
75–and over	$10,350
Life-cycle stage of family head	
Under 45 years	
Unmarried, no children	$ 1,700
Married, no children	$ 2,894
Married, with children	$ 1,842
45 years and over	
Head in labor force	$ 8,199
Head retired	$ 8,747
Education of family head	
0–8 grades	$ 1,502
9–11 grades	$ 1,800
High school diploma	$ 2,550
Some college	$ 3,785
College degree	$10,977
Occupation of family head	
Operative, labor, or service worker	$ 1,316
Miscellaneous	$ 1,372
Craftsperson or supervisor	$ 2,775
Clerical or sales	$ 4,225
Professional, technical	$ 7,727
Farmer or farm manager	$10,203
Manager	$10,650
Self-employed manager	$15,150

Source: Federal Reserve Bulletin, Board of Governors of the Federal Reserve System, Washington, D.C., September 1984: 696.

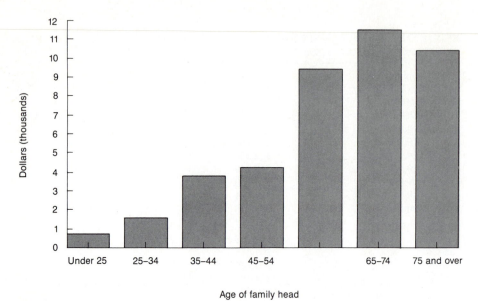

FIGURE 2-4
Total financial assets by age of the head of the household. (*Source*: *Federal Reserve Bulletin*, Board of Governors of the Federal Reserve System, Washington, D.C., September 1984, p. 696.)

cerned about retirement and medical needs and reaping the rewards of their (often dual) careers. With both desire and ability to save, persons 45 and over tend to build portfolios of financial assets.

Education and Occupation Clearly persons with college degrees tend to own more financial assets than those of lesser education. These same persons are likely to be in occupations that tend to require college degrees: professionals, farmers, managers, and self-employed managers. The median amount of financial assets of managers is several times larger than that of operators, laborers, service workers, craftspeople, supervisors, and the like. Thus, a college student who graduates and becomes a manager is likely to be in the upper brackets of financial assets!

Future Capital Flows

During the past couple of decades, there has been growing concern about a possible "capital shortage" in the United States.[4] The question is whether or not future savings will be great enough to meet projected investment needs. The basis for projecting a capital shortage lies in the slow rate of U.S. capital accumulation since World War II. The United States has accumulated capital

---

[4] This section is based primarily on the comprehensive review and analysis by Andersen (1976).

TABLE 2-5
SUMMARY OF FINANCIAL STATUS AND NEEDS OF INDIVIDUALS OVER THEIR LIFE CYCLE

Stage   I   Bachelor stage; young single people not living at home
1 Few financial burdens
2 Fashion-opinion leaders
3 Recreation oriented
4 Buy: basic kitchen equipment, basic furniture, cars, equipment for mating game, vacations

Stage   II   Newly married couples; young, no children
1 Better off financially than they will be in the near future
2 Highest purchase rate and highest average purchase of durables
3 Buy: cars, refrigerators, stoves, sensible and durable furniture, vacations

Stage   III   Full nest 1; youngest child under 6
1 Home purchasing at peak
2 Liquid assets low
3 Dissatisfied with financial position and amount of money saved
4 Interested in new products
5 Like advertised products
6 Buy: washers, dryers, TV, baby food, chest rubs and cough medicine, vitamins, dolls, wagons, sleds, skates

Stage   IV   Full nest 2; youngest child 6 or over
1 Financial position better
2 Some wives work
3 Less influenced by advertising
4 Buy larger-sized package, multiple-unit deals
5 Buy: many foods, cleaning materials, bicycles, music lessons, pianos

Stage   V   Full nest 3; older married couples with dependent children
1 Financial position still better
2 More wives work
3 Some children get jobs
4 Hard to influence with advertising
5 High average purchase of durables
6 Buy: new, more tasteful furniture, auto travel, unnecessary appliances, boats, dental services, magazines

Stage   VI   Empty nest 1; older married couples, no children living with them, head in labor force
1 Home ownership at peak
2 Most satisfied with financial position and money saved
3 Interested in travel, recreation, self-education
4 Make gifts and contributions
5 Not interested in new products
6 Buy: vacations, luxuries, home improvements

Stage   VII   Empty nest 2; older married couples, no children living at home, head retired
1 Drastic cut in income
2 Keep home
3 Buy: medical appliances, medical care, products that aid health, sleep, and digestion

Stage   VIII   Solitary survivor, in labor force
1 Income still good, but likely to sell home

Stage   IX   Solitary survivor, retired
1 Same medical and product needs as other retired group; drastic cut in income
2 Special need for attention, affection, and security

at a slower pace than other major industrialized countries, and the United States has produced no increase in real capital investment. ("Real" means that the expenditures are adjusted for price-level changes.) The threat posed by a capital "gap" is that output per worker-hour will not rise at as rapid a rate as previously. The impact of capital on labor productivity may have been confirmed by the 1970s when real investment was about zero and increase in labor output per worker-hour lagged. The steel, auto, and other basic industries in the United States have not raised capital for modern equipment, thus causing them to be less competitive in the market for their products.

On the other hand, the empirical studies and projections of capital gaps have been based on assumptions inconsistent with the theory of capital accumulation. They naively extrapolate past trends, with few modifications for economic influences. A common shortcoming of them all is that "they tended to ignore the market process by which the interaction of these economic influences jointly determines the actual amount of capital accumulation and its allocation."[5] Supply and demand interact to determine the market rate of interest (interest rate equilibrium is discussed in the next chapter), and the amount of capital accumulated. According to price theory, the equilibrium interest rate and capital accumulation quantity respond to changes in individual consumption demands and the productivity of capital investments. In short, sufficient capital is provided by savers through foregone consumption to meet worthwhile investment opportunities, because the equilibrium level of interest moves to the point where desired supply and demand are equal. A capital shortage will not exist, because the investment opportunities will offer the individual a sufficiently high return to induce him to save rather than consume his income.

Thus, the debate regarding capital shortages poses empirical studies against price theory. The empirical studies extrapolate past trends to present a gloomy future, while price theory argues that the free market will induce all changes necessary to balance savings and investment. In the remainder of the book, the reader will see that both arguments are supportable. In the next chapter, it will be seen that interest rates are determined in a relatively free financial market but that institutional constraints prevent the attainment of a perfect market. Later chapters describe the major institutions and governmental bodies, organizations which not only improve the efficiency of the financial markets but also form a rigid structure tending to retard the development of new, more efficient markets. However, the pressures of investors and savers for an efficient market are strong, and substantial profits can be earned by institutions which promote the flow of capital. Through planning and management, such as that discussed in Parts Four to Seven, financial institutions can earn profits by facilitating capital flows, and the U.S. economy can generate sufficient quantities of capital. Thus, the debate depends in part on the efficiency of the United

---

[5] Andersen (1976), p. 259.

States capital markets and the institutions which serve them.[6] Interest-rate equilibrium and market efficiency are major topics discussed in the next chapter.

SUMMARY

We have seen that financial intermediaries are the primary vehicle for moving funds saved by individuals (and trust and nonprofit organizations) to the businesses, individuals, and governmental units needing funds. The Federal Reserve's *flow-of-funds* report provided empirical data with which to trace savings through the financial sector to nonfinancial sectors. The concept of investing savings in real investment, financial investment, repayment of indebtedness, and hoarding was applied to the flow-of-funds matrix for the United States economy. This chapter presented a broad view of how funds move in the entire economy and the effects of changes in such flows on various kinds institutions.

The chapter also presented the characteristics of savers. The important characteristics are income, age, life cycle, education, and occupation. Owing to both life needs and career abilities, persons with large financial asset balances are likely to earn more than $25,000 per year (1983 dollars), be age 55 or older, hold a college degree, and be employed in a professional, managerial, or farm, position, or be self-employed.

TERMS

macrofinance	capital shortage
financial market	capital gap
supply of funds	household sector
demand for funds	business sector
surplus units	state and local government sector
deficit units	private domestic nonfinancial sectors
flow of funds	financial sectors
real investment	hoarding cash
financial investment	life cycle

QUESTIONS

1 List four purposes for which money is saved.
2 Name six major financial investments made by households.

---

[6] The debate also depends on the willingness of individuals to forgo current consumption in return for greater future consumption. Free market adherents argue that a sufficiently high interest rate will also clear the market. On the other hand, opponents contend that interest rate insensitivity on the part of savers in the short run could produce insufficient quantities of capital to sustain labor productivity increases and cause economic decline.

3 What are the eight major primary securities purchased by financial intermediaries?

4 What is macrofinance? What does it attempt to study?

5 Distinguish between financial assets and real assets. How does this distinction explain the discrepancy between the stock of financial assets in the United States and the concept of United States wealth?

6 What sector of the U.S. economy owns the greatest proportion of financial assets? What is that proportion? What two securities are preferred by that sector?

7 In flow-of-funds accounting, what is a sector? What is a sector statement?

8 What is the difference between financial business and nonfinancial business? Primary and secondary securities?

9 How are sectoral balance sheet statements coverted to funds flows?

10 Can deficit sectors be saving?

11 Why are some people concerned that the United States may suffer from a capital shortage in future years? Why do the free-market theorists believe that sufficient capital will be available in the future? What is your opinion?

SELECTED REFERENCES

Andersen, Leonall C.: "Is There a Capital Shortage: Theory and Recent Empirical Evidence," *Journal of Finance*, May 1976, pp. 257–268.

Ando, Albert, and Franco Modigliani: "The 'Life Cycle' Hypothesis of Savings; Aggregate Implications and Tests," *American Economic Review*, March 1963, pp. 55–84.

Federal Reserve Bulletin, Board of Governors of the Federal Reserve, Washington, D.C., see June and November issues.

The Flow of Funds Approach to Social Accounting, National Bureau of Economic Research, Washington, D.C., 1962.

Ritter, Lawrence S.: "The Flow-of-Funds Accounts: A New Approach to Financial Market Analysis," *Journal of Finance*, May 1963, pp. 219–230.

CHAPTER 3

MONEY AND CAPITAL MARKET EQUILIBRIUM

The flow of funds, studied in the last chapter, is important not only because it describes the U.S. capital markets, but also because it shows the supply and demand forces determining interest rates. The supply and demand for funds determines the equilibrium level of interest rates, and in turn, interest rates allocate the supply of capital among individual, business, and government borrowers. Factors influencing the capital supply and demand, and thereby interest rates, are discussed in this chapter. Impediments to the achievement of an equilibrium interest rate, such as the existence of transactions costs and a lack of information, are studied in the context of ideal financial market criteria.

The U.S. financial markets are found to be close to the ideal in some cases and less well developed in other cases. The existence of financial markets of varying degrees of perfection suggests important implications for financial institutions management, and two of these implications are discussed as a foundation for the chapters which follow in the next part. Also, the recent history of interest rates is discussed in the context of supply and demand equilibrium. The historical review serves as an application of interest rate concepts to the real world and as background information for later chapters describing financial institutions and market phenomena. Thus the chapter brings together the flow of funds and interest rates, first from a theoretical viewpoint of market equilibrium, and second from a practical viewpoint of actual rates negotiated under recent economic conditions.

SUPPLY AND DEMAND EQUILIBRIUM

Supply and demand interact to price funds flowing through the financial market. For the entire market, economists refer to "the interest rate" to represent many different rates existing in the market. The concept of one interest rate is convenient for analysis of the aggregate market but should be recognized as an oversimplification. Many interest rates exist at any time because of differences in credit standing, maturity, call provisions, and other factors. In later chapters we expand our discussion to include securities with different risks, maturities, and other characteristics.[1] However, before we are ready to consider the complex structure of interest rates in the real world, we need to build a theoretical foundation.

The equilibrium interest rate is determined by simultaneously equating supply and demand in the security market. Like markets for guns, shoes, and butter, supply and demand forces are assumed to set the price. The flow of funds, described in the last chapter, is increasingly used in financial models to explain changes in interest rates.[2] Flow-of-funds models provide for analyzing security supplies and preferred habitats of different economic sectors. On the flow-of-funds supply side, investment by business and borrowing by governments are analyzed.[3]

Supply of Funds

Aggregate saving is the difference between income and consumption. As in the flow-of-funds, saving is divided between personal and business saving. Personal saving is disposable personal income of households after taxes less current consumption. Business saving is net income less dividends, that is, retained earnings. Substantially all saving in the United States is retained by households and businesses from income (salaries, wages, and so forth) and net profit.

Classical and neoclassical economists regarded the amount of saving desired as positive function of interest rates. Higher interest rates were believed to induce saving, while lower rates would depress saving. The underlying assumption was that present consumption is preferred to future consumption, but people would forgo current expenditures if properly rewarded by higher interest. There would be no saving at a zero interest rate, and greater and greater saving would occur as the interest rate increased without limit.

Although the classical and neoclassical economists considered a direct correlation between saving and interest rates irrefutable, modern scholars have taken issue with certain assumptions. The absolute adherence to the time preference assumption (Appendix 3-1) ignores other reasons for saving, such as smoothing expenditures from year to year when income varies or accumulating funds for retirement. Furthermore, the time preference assumption does not

---

[1] The computation, analysis, and managerial implications of interest rates are major topics discussed extensively in chapters 4, 5, and 6.

[2] Hendershott and Orlando (1976) review financial models and state: "Flow-of-funds models represent a major conceptual advance in financial model building."

[3] Seven sectors are incorporated in the flow-of-funds model developed by Hendershott and Orlando (1976).

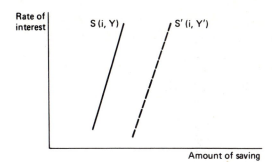

FIGURE 3-1
Supply of saving (S) as a function of
the rate of interest (i) and income (Y).

imply that society as a whole abstains from current consumption for future
consumption. The classical saving function is postulated for a given full employment level of income. At lower levels of income, the ability to save
diminishes and the amount saved falls. Accustomed to a high level of consumption, people tend to reduce their saving drastically to maintain their life-style
when income temporarily declines. Studies of low-income countries show that
capital formation is very low despite high interest rates.

While not dismissing interest rates as unrelated to saving, economists are
inclined to give them second place behind income. Contemporary economists
of the Keynesian school of thought believe that income is the primary determinant of saving and the supply funds. For given levels of income, interest
rates may act to slightly increase or decrease desired saving, but people
probably would save some amount even if offered a small rate of return. The
saving schedule drawn in Figure 3-1 shows the saving curve ($S(i, Y)$). The slope
is slightly positive, reflecting the positive relationship between interest rates (i)
and saving. An increase in interest rate encourages and increases the amount
saved, and vice versa. Also, the saving curve shifts to the right when income
(Y) increases. [The shift is shown as a change from $S(Y)$ to $S'(i, Y')$.] For any
level of interest rate, more money is saved at higher than at lower income
levels. Thus, we represent interest-rate-induced changes in saving as movements along the saving line, and show income-generated changes in savings as
shifts in the saving schedule ($S(i, Y)$).

Demands for Funds

We can divide the demand for funds into subsector components—business
investment and government borrowing. Business firms require funds for investment purposes (I), such as new machines, building, or inventories, in amounts
far exceeding their depreciation flows. The investment demand curve by businesses is downward sloping with respect to interest rates; it also shifts with
changes in income expectations as firms plan expansion in anticipation of
market changes.

Investment Demand for Funds   The investment demand curve is a reflection of business "investment opportunity schedule" (see Figure 3-2). The downward slope shows that firms do not have unlimited investment opportunities. As illustrated in Figure 3-2, the firm has $120 million of investments that are expected to return 15 percent or more, but only $100 million that have an

FIGURE 3-2
The investment opportunity schedule.

Frame a.

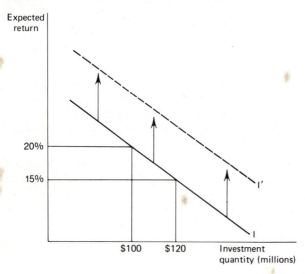

Frame b.

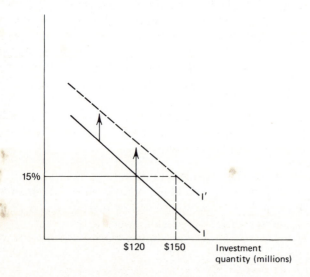

expected return of 20 percent or more for investment curve I. Also, we may interpret the investment opportunity schedule as the amount of investment that will be undertaken at different opportunity rates. If similar investment opportunities yield 20 percent, then the firm will invest $100 million. On the other hand, if alternative investments yield only 15 percent, then the firm will undertake $120 million. The investment opportunity schedule shows the amount of investment undertaken at various rates of return.[4] The demand for investment funds is derived by adding the investment opportunity schedules of individuals and businesses.

Next we see that the investment demand curve changes over time in response to changing expectations. For example, sales expectation rises when the demand for goods and services increases.[5] Higher sales expectations usually imply a greater cash flow for new investments. For instance, an increasing demand for new cars means higher revenues can be anticipated for investments in machinery, plant, and equipment used to produce cars. Greater revenues mean higher rates of return on new investments—a machine that was expected to yield 15 percent may now yield 20 percent. A general rise in demand and revenue expectations causes the entire investment demand curve to shift up, as shown in Figure 3-2, from I (solid line) to I' (broken line).

An upward shift in the investment demand curve means not only a higher expected return for a given quantity of new investment but also a greater quantity of investment for a given rate of return. The effect of I shifting to I' is shown in frame b of Figure 3-2. By extending the horizontal (15 percent) return line to the new investment schedule (I') and projecting downward to the quantity axis, the greater investment quantity, $150 million, is found. Thus we see that investment demand can change as a result of a shift in the investment demand (opportunity) schedule.

Government Demand for Funds   Also, the federal, state, and local governments require funds to meet expenditures not supported from tax revenues. Governmental borrowing (G), largely related to fiscal deficits and long building programs, is generally unrelated to the current market interest rate. Therefore, the government demand curve is drawn vertically, as shown in Figure 3-3, frame a. In frame b, the investment demand curve is shown again, but the vertical axis is labeled "interest rate" instead of "expected return." The terms are interchanged by assuming that investment is undertaken up to the point where expected return from investment equals the interest rate paid for investment funds. The assumption moves the analysis from the investor to the capital

---

[4] Major firms increasingly utilize rate of return evaluation tools for capital expenditures and develop investment schedules. However, small outlays and investments by small firms are evaluated with simpler methods which recognize interest rates only to a limited extent. See Gitman and Forrester (1977) for a survey of capital expenditure techniques used by business.

[5] Changing expectations about inflation affect capital budgeting decisions, as well as expectations regarding future sales. Higher inflation rates increase business taxes and reduce investment rates of return. See Nelson (1976).

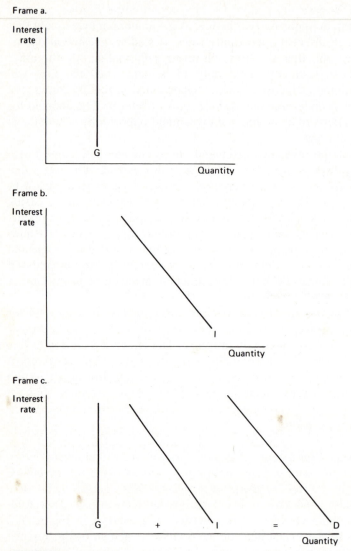

FIGURE 3-3
Demand for funds schedule.

market. Now, the government demand curve (G) can be added to the investment demand curve (I) to derive a total demand curve (D) shown in frame c.[6] The total demand curve for funds (D), therefore, is the sum of investment and governmental demand schedules:

$$D = I + G \qquad (3\text{-}1)$$

[6] Interaction between tax cuts and investment expenditures are considered by Hendershott (1976).

Dynamics of Interest Rates

The total demand and supply schedules for 2 years are depicted in Figure 3-4. The supply schedule is drawn nearly vertically, while the demand function is negatively sloped. Supply and demand functions both shift from the first to the second year, as is usually the case. The supply curve usually shifts to the right due to annual increases in income, and demand curve frequently (but not always) shifts to the right due to the growing market opportunities and technological developments. Interest rates may rise or fall in the second year depending on the shifts in supply and demand *relative* to their first-year positions. As shown in Figure 3-4, a shift in the demand schedule (D_1 to D_2) greater than a shift in the supply schedule (S_1 to S_2) causes an excess demand for funds during the second year, *if current interest rates prevail*. Equilibrium is restored when interest rates rise to i_2 (security prices fall) whereby the quantity of funds demanded falls and the quantity of funds supplied rises to LF_2. Similarly, a large shift in the supply curve would lead to a fall in interest rates until sufficient investment projects are undertaken.

Effect of Inflation on Interest Rates

Definition of Inflation   Inflation means that the prices of goods and services are increasing generally. During an inflationary period, the prices of food, housing, cars, dry cleaning, and most, but not all, other things increase. Of course, not all prices change at the same rate—some may fall while others rise. For example, rapidly developing technology in the electronics industry resulted in falling prices for hand-held calculators during a period when the average price of consumer goods rose by about 6 percent per year. By dividing the index of prices at one point in time (CPI_{t+1}) by the index of prices at an earlier point in time (CPI_t) and then subtracting 1, we find rate of change in prices. The percentage is designated as the inflation rate (ΔCPI):

$$\Delta CPI = \frac{CPI_{t+1}}{CPI_t} - 1 \tag{3-2}$$

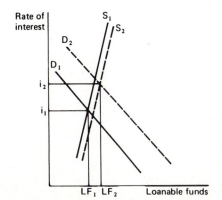

FIGURE 3-4
Supply of and demand for funds schedules and equilibrium.

For example, suppose we borrowed $500 in 19X1 and repaid it 1 year later in 19X2. The CPI in 19X1 and 19X2 was 161.2 and 169.2 respectively. The loss in value to inflation is calculated as:

$$\Delta CPI = \frac{CPI_{t+1}}{CPI_t} - 1 = \frac{169.2}{161.1} - 1$$
$$= 0.0496 = 4.96\%$$

The $500 borrowed in 19X1 is repaid with 19X2 dollars, which are worth 4.96 percent or $24.80 less than the 19X1 dollars borrowed.

Past Experience with Inflation and Deflation For 85 years, prices have been trending up in the United States, but the changes have been neither smooth nor constant. Prices rose rapidly during every major war: War of 1812, Civil War, World War I, World War II, and the Vietnam war. After each of the first three wars, prices dropped and we experienced deflation for decades.[7] In more recent times, prices have not dropped but have risen steadily during peacetime (Figure 3-5). In the cold war "peace" between the Korean and Vietnam wars, prices rose an average 1.4 percent per year. In the years from 1973 through 1984 inflation vacillated at annual rates from 5 to 15 percent.

[7] Deflation is not necessarily desirable; employment and economic growth rates were low during the three postwar periods.

FIGURE 3-5
Percentage changes in consumer price index from previous year, 1950 to 1984. (*Source*: Board of Governors of the Federal Reserve System.)

Effect of Unanticipated Inflation   Past experience provides investors with valid reasons for attempting to anticipate inflation. For example, prices rose a trillionfold during the hyperinflationary period in Germany from 1920 to 1923 and in Hungary after World War II. Consequently the purchasing power of money dropped so fast that owners of fixed-income securities lost their wealth within a few years. German university endowments and life insurance assets were destroyed. On a smaller scale, U.S. Treasury bill holders have steadily lost ground to inflation over the last two decades. The annual return after inflation for Treasury bills has ranged from -3.1 to 2.3 percent. The facts are startling: In 4 out of 20 years, investors actually lost real wealth by investing in the "safest asset."[8] After 20 years of foregoing consumption, the U.S. Treasury bill investor would have increased his or her initial real wealth of $100 by only $12. This is before income taxes; the investor might not have earned anything after taxes!

On the other hand, owners of real property earn large profits from unforeseen inflation. The value of real property, inventories, tools, and business enterprises rises as their owners increase the selling prices of their goods and services. If real property is financed with long-term debt, then it is possible to earn even higher returns. While the dollar value of the property rises with inflation, the dollar obligation to repay debt remains constant. The equity owner realizes a profit while making interest and principal payments with dollars having less real worth.

Fisherian Effect   Hardened by past experience with inflation, investors learn to adjust for inflation and to include expected inflation in interest rates. After a period of rising inflation rates, investors adjust their expectations and demand a higher rate of interest on fixed income securities. Thus, over the long run, the market rate of interest includes expected inflation. *The market rate is termed the "nominal" rate* ($i_{nominal}$) *and consists of the real interest rate* (i_{real}) *plus the expected inflation rate* (ΔCPI). The concept of nominal and real interest rates is named for its author, Irving Fisher, and inflation influences are called "Fisherian effects."[9] Fisher's classic relationship between nominal and real interest rate follows:

$$i_{nominal} = i_{real} + \Delta CPI \qquad (3\text{-}3)$$

Individuals attempt to earn the same real rate of return over time, although the price level changes.[10] Estimates of expected price level changes are made by

[8] Ibbotson and Sinquefield (1976). Common stocks are not necessarily a better hedge against inflation. See Ibbotson and Sinquefield (1976), Bodie (1976), and Jaffe (1976).

[9] See Bomberger and Makinen (1977) for a recent review of Fisherian interest-rate dynamics. The original works are Fisher (1911) and Fisher (1930). Fisher did not use the CPI as an inflation measure; we introduce it as the most commonly accepted measure.

[10] The theory of capital structure and capital budgeting under inflation is present in a model by Hagerman and Kim (1976).

comparing past inflation and interest rates in a lagged regression model.[11] Apparently investors adjust their expectations slowly over a period of several years, and respond more to longer periods of price movements than to those lasting only a few months.

Example of Nominal and Real Rates   An investor expecting 4.96 percent inflation adds 4.96 percent to a desired real interest rate. If this real rate is 4 percent, then the nominal rate is computed as Eq. (3-3):

$$
\begin{aligned}
i_{\text{nominal}} &= i_{\text{real}} + \Delta\text{CPI} \\
&= 4.00\% + 4.96\% \\
&= 8.96\%
\end{aligned}
$$

Investors demand 8.96 percent and cause the market rate to adjust. Adjustments for expected inflation are observed in Brazil, Chile, and other countries with a long history of chronic inflation. United States investors are adjusting to inflation, too, and tend to include anticipated inflation in interest rates.

Because nominal interest rates include inflation, changes in anticipated inflation cause adjustments in nominal interest rates. If inflation increases and investors expect it to be 6 percent next year, then interest rates increase from 8.96 to 10 percent (6 percent inflation plus 4 percent real interest). Changing expectations about inflation can and do push nominal interest rates up and down, even though the demand and supply for real capital remains constant.[12]

OTHER SUPPLY AND DEMAND DETERMINANTS

The supply and demand equilibrium level of interest rates is one that is always approached but rarely achieved. If there were enough time and markets were sufficiently perfect, then we could assume that the interest rates we observe are the same as the theoretical equilibrium level of interest rates. However, there are real world conditions that may prevent savers and borrowers from actually supplying or demanding funds that are theoretically "correct" from a capital viewpoint. There are at least four market conditions that impede fund flows:

1 The stock of securities already outstanding may influence the quantity of new securities supplied or demanded.

2 Unlike our initial assumption of one interest rate and market, there are many interest rates for the many markets that exist.

[11] Sargent (1969), Hendershott and Van Horne (1973), and Choate and Archer (1975). Estimation and definition problems of empirical work are discussed by Amihudy and Barnea (1977).

[12] Changes in nominal interest rates are believed to cause changes in real saving and the allocation of real capital. Fisher's theory of the business cycle hinges on changes in real loanable funds caused by price level changes (see Bomberger and Makinen, 1977). Inflation-induced changes in interest rates impact on the housing industry (Jackson, 1976) and real investment expenditures by business (Nelson, 1976), for example. Consistent with the scope of this book, the effect of inflation on real economic conditions is not discussed.

3 Information does not travel instantaneously and transactions are not executed immediately.

4 Transactions, buying and selling, are costly. It may not be profitable to trade securities even when the investor knows that the interest rate is intrinsically wrong.

Next, we discuss each of the four conditions in order to understand better the acutal working of the capital market.

Stocks versus Flows

At any instant in time, only stocks of securities exist. Security stocks are the inventories of existing loans, bonds, common stocks, and other financial assets. In the context of supply and demand analysis, security stocks mean all types of financial instruments which exist, not just common stock issues. Therefore, we might argue that interest rates are set so as to equate the supply and demand for the existing stock of financial assets. Over time, however, newly issued securities come into market for sale to persons or businesses generating funds. The impact of newly created securities on existing securities depends upon the substitutability of the new for the old and the relative size of each. The existing stock is usually large in comparison with the new offerings and traded in an active secondary market. Some economists consider security stocks and the secondary market to be the dominant force in determining the interest rate.[13] Metzler contends that the new securities arising from saving and investment affect market rates only *indirectly*. On the other hand, many contend, as does this text, that market rates of interest are primarily determined by the *flow of funds*. The stock and flow supply and demand equations interact. Separation of their independent or relative effects is difficult, but reason suggests that flows are the relevant measure. The financial markets are analogous to a fruit market: prices are haggled and agreed upon by the vendors and shoppers according to the volume of fruit coming to the market and the consumption demand of the shoppers; oranges still hanging on the trees or stored at home are only indirect factors in setting the price.

Multiple Markets

The equilibrium level of interest clears the market for funds in each market. Supply and demand forces reflect the *behavior* of investors, businesses, and others issuing securities. Supply and demand equilibrium is dependent upon consistent behavior by market participants. Disequilibrium may be caused by:

1 Altered portfolio preferences by market participants
2 Altered preferences of those creating securities
3 Private wealth formation and government saving or dissaving

[13] Metzler (1951).

For example, suppose that the New York Port Authority issues a large volume of bonds, causing the municipal bond demand curve to shift to the right. As was shown in Figure 3-4, the shift in demand from D_1 to D_2 caused the equilibrium interest rate to run from i_1 to i_2. That is, the municipal bond rate increases in response to a sudden demand for funds by the New York Port Authority. Municipal bonds, whether issued by New York Port Authority or others, are now more attractive to some investors than other investments such as corporate or Treasury bonds. Some investors will adjust their portfolios to substitute municipals for other securities. As investors sell corporate and Treasury bonds and purchase municipal bonds, the supply of funds to the municipal market drives up their price and reduces their interest rate. Conversely, the sale of corporate treasury bonds tends to lower their price and raise their interest rate. This process continues toward equilibrium until all the financial markets are in equilibrium or until another disequilibrating force is exerted and the cycle resumes.

The financial markets are international in scope, and consequently interest-rate equilibrium depends on financial conditions in all countries. For example, interest-rate increases in the Eurobond market attract funds from investors in the United States. An increase in the Eurobond market interest rate attracts funds from U.S. investors, causing interest rates to rise in the U.S. bond market. Of course, the process works equally well in reverse. Suppose that federal government deficits cause the U.S. Treasury to borrow funds. The demand for funds in the U.S. bond market pushes up interest rates in the United States. Foreign investors, attracted by relatively higher yields in the United States, supply increased quantities of funds to the U.S. capital market and thereby bid interest rates down in the United States and up elsewhere. Thus, funds tend to move to and from countries, particularly large industrialized countries, in response to interest-rate conditions. The fund movements among countries continues until interest rates in any one country are somewhat comparable to rates in any other country. Frictions such as laws, customs, communications lags, and political expediency prevent full adjustment, such as that occurring among states within the United States, but interest rates (adjusted for currency value differences) tend to be very similar across international markets, at least in the free world.[14]

Adjustment Period

The adjustment period before equilibrium is not instantaneous. Different factors cause longer or shorter time periods before equilibrium is restored. During the *reaction period*, information is disseminated and recognized. High-speed stock quotation systems, such as those of the New York Stock Exchange, report stock prices within minutes after each transaction, while news service

---

[14] See Solnik and Grall (1975).

Teletypes distribute financial, business, and governmental news for an eager audience. The rapid transmittal of information and quick recognition by investors effect speedy price adjustments. On the other hand, the speed and efficiency of a secondary market are diminished considerably if the potential buyers and sellers must seek each other on their own. Changing conditions are less well known due to the longer information lag and the smaller number of ready buyers and sellers. The result is a slower adjustment time and a larger transaction cost.

Transaction Costs

From a comprehensive perspective, transaction costs consist of three items:

1 Commissions paid by investors to brokers and dealers for buying and selling securities, plus
2 Dealer spread—the difference between the dealer bid and asked prices, plus
3 Adverse price changes caused by buying and selling securities.

Commission costs are explicit charges levied for trading securities and providing security information. The commission rate varies from less than one-half of 1 percent for large common stock trades of institutional investors to 6 percent for transactions involving small amounts of relatively unknown securities. In addition to commissions, transactions sometimes involve a securities dealer who quotes a higher price to buyers (*asked price*) than the price quoted to sellers (*bid price*). The difference between the bid and asked price is called the *spread* and compensates the dealer for offering to buy and sell immediately. The spread may be as large as several percent, but it is usually a fraction of 1 percent.

Although the U.S. financial markets are large and relatively well able to assimilate substantial buy and sell orders, the supply or demand for a large amount of any particular security causes its price to change. As in the New York Port Authority example, security returns and prices are changed by variations in supply and demand. When an investor decides that a particular stock is no longer desirable, then the investor begins selling it. If the investor is a large financial institution, then the sale is a large one—often millions of dollars worth of stocks and bonds. The sale from an institutional portfolio is analogous to a new issue by a corporation—the supply of securities offered in the market increases substantially. Consequently, price decreases until a new equilibrium is struck between supply and demand. The institution that sells the security causes the price to decline and, consequently, receives a price below the market level that would have existed in the absence of its decision to sell. Buying and selling large quantities during a short time period usually cause adverse price effects, ranging rom 1 to 5 percent. (Estimating adverse price effects is subject to error; it is always difficult to estimate what the security price would have been without a large buy or sell order.) Thus, a security purchase or sale involves transaction costs in the form of (1) commissions, (2) dealer spreads, and (3) adverse price effects.[15]

The costs of good information and trading securities are sometimes large. Not everyone knows about current rates all of the time, and small changes in rates do not inspire people to adjust their portfolios. They may desire to hold a different portfolio of claims than they do, but find the cost of changing too great. These market imperfections make the concept of equilibrium no less valid, but suggest that the market is more often striving for than achieving equilibrium.

EFFICIENCY OF FINANCIAL MARKETS

Price Analysis in Well-Developed Markets

Investors, both private and institutional, constantly gather and analyze information about securities traded in the financial markets. Supply and demand for funds are forecasted, shifts in the types and quantities of securities brought to the market are considered, international monetary conditions are evaluated and inflation rates are predicted. The credit quality and dividend prospects of the issuer are analyzed extensively by expert analysts equipped with computers, interview reports, and financial statements. After careful study, investors assess the present values of securities traded in the financial markets.

Alert analysts look for market disparities between the estimated present value (intrinsic value), obtained by analyzing the security, and the market price. When the market price is below the intrinsic value, then the security is purchased and demand forces the price up. On the other hand, if the market price is greater than the present value, then the security is sold, and the increased supply depresses the price. In a free and well-developed market, investors actively analyze, buy, and sell securities that are temporarily inefficiently priced. If the market is particularly active and trading costs are small, then the price disparities are short-lived and the prevailing price reflects the composite belief of investors.

Definition of Efficient Markets

When a security's price is a good estimate of its investment value, then the market is termed "efficient." Financial markets are defined as efficient when security prices fully reflect all available information.[16] The market must be perfect to achieve efficiency. Although perfect markets do not exist, it is important to know what conditions must prevail to achieve an efficient market. Perfect capital markets are characterized by the following attributes:

---

[15] Definitions of transaction costs are discussed in Demsetz (1968), pp. 35–40.

[16] The theory of efficient capital markets is discussed concisely in Fama and Miller (1972), pp. 335–340.

1 Information is equally available without cost to all traders.

2 Security prices are independent of individual buyers, sellers, and issuers.

3 Transactions costs are zero—there are no brokerage fees, transfer taxes, or other transactions costs incurred when securities are exchanged.[17]

Information must be readily available if investors are to be able to evaluate fairly the present value of securities. (Imposing a cost for information would reduce its availability.) After analyzing information and deciding to buy or sell, traders must be able to execute a transaction without a significant price change. Also, impediments to trading, including transactions costs, must be nonexistent to allow all investors to adjust their portfolios to exactly the desired composition.

Under conditions for perfect markets, financial institutions would not exist.[18] Information purveyors expect to be paid for their services just as other business persons are compensated. For example, security analysts are real people who deserve to be compensated for their time and effort. Consequently, market efficiency cannot be tested against a strict ideal standard but against modified forms of the perfect market assumptions.

Efficient Market Hypotheses

Three forms representing varying degrees of market efficiency are generally recognized by researchers and analysts; the three levels of efficiency are referred to as:

1 Weakly efficient market hypothesis
2 Semistrongly efficient market hypothesis
3 Strongly efficient market hypothesis

The three forms of efficient market hypotheses are differentiated by the type of data believed to be available to investors.[19] The weakly efficient market hypothesis implies that all historical price and volume data for securities are reflected in the price; that is, past price and trade volume information do not contain information useful for predicting future prices. For example, a three-day increase in the price of RCA common stock does not mean that the price will increase or decrease tomorrow, according to the weak-form hypothesis.[20]

The *semistrongly efficient market hypothesis* states that prices reflect all publicly available information. For example, information published in *The Wall Street Journal, Moody's,* and *Valueline* is available to the general investing

---

[17] Implicitly, income taxes are assumed to be nonexistent or equal for all types of securities and security returns. That is, ordinary and capital gains income are taxed equally. Fama and Miller (1972), p. 21.

[18] Financial institutions reduce security market imperfections, but they can not eliminate imperfections without disappearing themselves!

[19] The three hypotheses are suggested first in Fama (1965) and summarized in Fama (1970).

[20] Studying past prices and sales volume to predict future price changes is called *technical analysis.*

public. Note that the scope of the information published is much greater than simply historical price and volume data. Publicly available information includes earnings reports, new product developments, marketing plans, acquisitions, Federal Reserve monetary actions, and thousands of other facts, figures, and opinions.

The *strongly efficient market hypothesis* states that all information, public and private, is reflected in present security prices. Private information encompasses everything from financial statements prior to public release to secret inventions and business relationships. Managers and executives, so called "insiders," are privy to a great deal of information that is not normally disclosed for competitive, legal, personal, and other reasons. The strong-form hypothesis assumes that insiders are not able to profit from their special knowledge, because prices currently reflect all relevant information.

Studies of Market Efficiency

Tests of the efficient market hypotheses solidly affirm the weak form, partially affirm the semistrong form, and refute the strong form.[21] Empirical tests of the weakly efficient market hypothesis consist of statistical tests of relationships between current prices and previous prices and volumes. The relationships can be stated as filter rules, serial correlations, runs tests, and other functional forms. A filter rule states, for example, that an investor should buy a security when the price rises or falls by at least x percent from a base level. That is, "buy General Motors stock when it breaks through a level 10 percent above its two-year low." Extensive testing of many different filter rules (an infinite number exists) fails to produce a viable strategy.[22] Scientific investigations of other technical analyses show that price strategies do not consistently yield returns greater than a buy-and-hold approach. Thus, the evidence supporting the weakly efficient market hypothesis is uniformly affirmative, and the hypothesis is generally accepted as true.

The semistrong form is more difficult to test than the weak form, because the range of information is essentially infinite. Over the past decade, a number of studies have covered the major public sources of information. Possible information that would affect security prices and be subject to scientific study include earnings announcements, Federal Reserve discount rate announcements,[23] the prices of leading and lagging stocks and bonds, various U.S. government bonds, the Department of Commerce Index of Leading Indicators, and stock splits and dividends.[24] In general, news published in the financial

---

[21] Empirical tests are reviewed by Fama (1970) and Francis (1976), chap. 21.

[22] See Alexander (1961) and Fama and Blume (1966).

[23] The "discount rate" is the interest rate charged to banks who borrow from the Federal Reserve. See Chapter 19.

[24] See Waud (1970), Francis (1975), Fama, Fisher, Jensen, and Roll (1969), Garbade and Hunt (1978), and Brick and Thompson (1978).

press and filed with the Securities and Exchange Commission is widely available to investors, and investors correctly interpret this news quickly and accurately. Immediately following the announcements and filings, investors begin trading, and prices adjust toward the new intrinsic values. Research shows, also, that prices begin to adjust prior to announcements, as investors *anticipate* information releases. The validity of the hypothesis is frequently affirmed and rarely challenged by empirical studies.[25]

The strongly efficient market hypothesis is the most easily disproved: evidence showing that insiders profit from their information refutes this hypothesis. One group of traders who possess "insider" information is composed of the stock exchange specialists. Stock exchange specialists are designated members of organized securities exchanges (discussed in Chapter 14) who "make a market" in securities. The specialist buys or sells securities when no one else is immediately available to meet an incoming buy or sell order. Also, the specialist records buy and sell bids and asked prices offered by investors. Thus, the specialist knows the prices and quantities investors are bidding for securities. Only the specialist knows the stocks' supply and demand schedules; and, under the rules of the exchanges, is not permitted to share supply and demand information with others. Can specialists earn excess profits from their insider information? Apparently, they do earn speculative trading profits.[26]

Another group of insiders who might earn better than average profits from monopolistic information are corporate officials who trade their company's stock. The Securities and Exchange Commission maintains a file of trading by insiders, recording the stock traded, the date of the transaction, number of shares traded, end-of-month holding of the insider, buy and sell codes, and daily closing prices. Analysis of this data for the years 1969 through 1972 showed that "it is apparent that in the short-run insiders are able to identify profitable as well as unprofitable situations in their own companies."[27] The strongly efficient form can be refuted, but refutation by specific examples does not imply that all insider information is valuable or that all persons close to insider information are able to earn trading profits. For example, mutual fund managers and analysts deal in the securities markets everyday, study security values intensively, and maintain many contacts who supply information quickly. It is a reasonable expectation that "Wall Stret analysts" possess and utilize insider information. However, the mutual fund managers are "apparently unable to forecast returns accurately enough to recover their research and transactions cost. . ."[28] In summary, the evidence indicates that some insiders with monopolistic information do earn speculative trading profits but that most professional analysts, with or without insider information, are unable to consistently earn a premium. The market prices of securities are the intrinsic (pre-

[25] A rare exception is the Box-Jenkins transfer function model developed in Umstead (1977).
[26] Jaffe (1974).
[27] Finnerty (1976), p. 1146.
[28] Jensen (1969), p. 170.

sent) values; that is, relevant information appears to be reflected in the market price. Consequently, we conclude that the securities markets are very efficient.[29]

RECENT HISTORY OF INTEREST RATES

The theory of interest-rate pricing was discussed in the last section as a function of supply and demand. Here some of the major shifts in supply and demand for funds are related to fluctuations in interest rates over the past few decades as seen in Figures 3-6 and 3-7. Note that there are long secular changes in interest rates as well as short-term fluctuations; and, unfortunately, many of the shifts would have been impossible to predict prior to their occurrence.

1940–1959

The low and stable rates existing during World War II reflect an agreement between the Federal Reserve System and the U.S. Treasury to stabilize rates at

[29] The conclusion is limited to organized securities markets and listed securities, because studies of other unlisted securities (such as bank time deposits, mortgages, and insurance reserves) are not available.

FIGURE 3-6
Long and short-term interest rates. (*Source*: Board of Governors of the Federal Reserve System.)

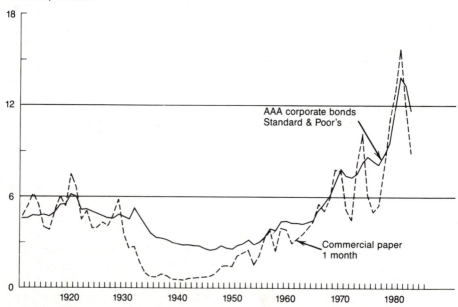

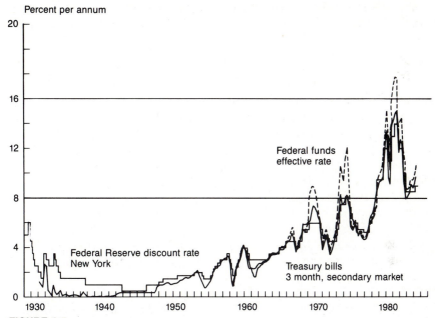

FIGURE 3-7
Short-term interest rates. Money market: discount rate, effective date of change; all others, quarterly averages. (*Source*: Board of Governors of the Federal Reserve System.)

a low level for the duration of the war. A growing demand for short-term capital to finance business expansion occurred after the Second World War and led to climbing commercial paper rates until 1953. Short- and long-term rates fell precipitously during the recession of 1953–1954 and then recovered their secular upswing until 1956. The 1957–1958 business recession brought a sluggish demand for funds, allowing Treasury bill rates to fall below 1 percent. (Treasury bills have been as high as 9 percent in recent years.) Business activity picked up in the late 1950s and rates began a steady rise that did not culminate until a decade later.

1960–1969

A long, sustained upward drive in the economy drew heavily upon capital, and interest rates rose steadily from 1961 to 1966. An extraordinary burst in rates occurred in late 1966 when the Federal Reserve first tightened credit sharply, then fearing a recession or depression, flooded funds into bank reserves in the fall of 1966. Inflationary conditions in early 1967 then suggested another more moderate reversal of policy toward tight credit and higher interest rates. The combination of strong credit demand and credit restraint squeezed interest rates up to peaks in 1969 and early 1970. Such periods are called "tight credit" conditions, during which borrowers must compete vigorously for funds and not infrequently obtain less than they would under more normal circumstances.

1970–1979

With the advent of a mild recession in 1970–1971, short-term rates fell precipitously and long-term rates waned from historic highs. Money-market rates moved higher during 1972, but credit-market conditions were more settled and interest rates were less volatile than during the previous few years. The economy expanded at a strong pace in 1972, but the supply of funds shifted as well so that interest rates ended the year at about the same level as they started. The expansion begun in 1972 continued through 1973, although the pace in 1973 was slower than in 1972, as uncertainties about fuel shortages increased. The continued business expansion again shifted the demand curve in 1973, as firms undertook increasing amounts of capital expansion, and the supply of funds continued strong as households saved funds as a precaution against job layoffs. Interest rates, therefore, moved through the year 1973 at relatively high levels but without major incident.

In 1974 and 1975, a combination of severe inflation and slackened economic activity beset the industrialized countries, including the United States. The effects of strong demand dating from the mid-1960s and unprecedented inflation stimulated by rising oil prices generated an inflation rate unprecedented for a peacetime period. As industrial production faltered and the unemployment rate rose, the demand schedule for funds shifted down. Short-term interest rates began falling in mid-1974 and continued to decline through 1975 and 1976. A somewhat faltering recovery began in late 1975 and continued through 1978 for the industrialized world. The U.S. economic recovery was similar to previous post-World War II growth periods—in the first year real gross national product increased at a rate of 7.3 percent. Demand for funds began increasing, but the supply of funds rose, as well. Saving grew with the recovery in employment and corporate profits. Consequently, short-term interest rates continued to decline (see Figure 3-6), as the demand for funds was satiated by a strong stream of savings and a reservoir of liquid assets built up during the 1973–1974 recession. In late 1977 and through 1979, interest rates began to rebound and increased two percentage points (not shown in Figure 3-6). The expansion began in 1975 and heavy federal government borrowing outpaced the savings flows of 1977–1979, so that the demand curve intersected the supply of funds curve at substantially higher rates. The 1975 economic recovery and money market were typical, because:

1 In the early years of expansion, the demand for funds is easily met with a supply of funds accumulated during recession.

2 In the later part of economic expansion, increases in the demand for funds outruns increases in the supply; then, interest rates begin rising in response to increasing competition for money capital.

1980–1985

United States inflation rates increased *unexpectedly* from single-to double-digit levels in the late 1970s, causing massive losses for fixed-income security holders. As would be predicted by Fisher's equation (3-3), nominal interest rates rose as investors adjusted their inflation expectations upward. The prime rate at major banks peaked at 22.00 percent, and the 3-month Treasury bill secondary market rate exceeded 15.00 percent in 1981. Further, (nominal) interest rates remained high although economic activity was sluggish. The strange and unwanted combination of recession and historically high interest rates cast an aura of gloom over the economic future of the U.S. financial markets. However, interest rates tumbled in 1982, because of slack funds demand for investment and falling inflation rates. Apparently, a commitment by the Federal Reserve to tighten the money supply increased the value of the dollar, thereby decreasing inflationary expectations. Decreased inflationary expectations alone would have caused interest rates to fall, but the drop in interest rates was further stimulated by a recessionary economy. In particular, real estate construction reached a two-decade low, as housing inflation rates fell below mortgage interest rates. That is, the inflationary force that had spurred real investment in earlier years now favored financial investment. The combination of the real rate of interest at a historically high rate of 6 percent on low-risk securities and renewed confidence in the value of the dollar moved nominal interest rates toward their 1970 levels in 1983, 1984, and 1985. Thus, the 1980s demonstrated the validity of Fisher's inflation expectations formulation, first as inflation rates rose, and later when they fell.

SUMMARY

Interest rates were introduced in this chapter as the equilibrium rent for capital. Supply and demand for funds are equated in the financial markets by the interest rate negotiated by savers and (real) investors. The supply of funds orginates from saving, primarily saving by the household sector and the demand for funds accrues from business, governments, and household sector real investment. Shifts in the supply and demand schedules for funds tend to cause changes in interest rates, although other factors exert pressures on interest rates, as well. Expected inflation is a significant factor, because bond and other fixed-income securities must return a nominal yield sufficient to compensate for both the use of money and the change in the value of money. Research of past interest and inflation rates has shown that changes in expected inflation cause changes in nominal interest rates, as modeled by Fisher.

The adjustments to inflation and other factors are rapid in the organized United States financial markets. Although changes in interest rates are modified by the influences of existing stocks of securities, multiple markets, and transactions costs, the markets are generally found to be "efficient." That is, interest rates quickly reflect all information available. According to the availability of information, the efficient market concept is divided into three hypotheses: weakly efficient, semistrongly efficient, and strongly efficient market hypotheses. Empirical evidence clearly affirms the weakly efficient market hypothesis and supports the semistrongly efficient market hypothesis. However, the strongly efficient market hypothesis has been refuted by studies of insiders who use monopolistic information to earn abnormal profits.

Market efficiency depends on the maintenance of perfect markets—markets where information is available to all investors, traders are too small to affect prices, and transactions costs are zero. Relatively efficient markets are created largely by financial institutions that provide information to large numbers of investors, develop large exchanges where individual trades exert minimum influence on prices, and reduce transactions costs with operating economies of scale. By pursuing perfect market ideals, financial institutions managers create the relatively efficient financial system of specialized but interrelated institutions that exists today and will serve consumers and businesses in the future.

APPENDIX 3-1: Fisher's Time Preference Theory

The time preference for present and future income is given formal representation by economists in the *theory of interest*. The discussion here is a theoretical representation of the desired timing of expenditures and the determination of interest rates. Obviously, risk affects substitution of expenditures among time periods, but substantially more complex models than this one are required to account for risk. The investor's preference curves are risk specific. Each set of opportunities presented here are the certainty equivalents for uncertain income flows; that is, appropriate adjustments are made for risk in the definition of income. The investor's preference curve is affected by risk as well, but meaningful adjustments cannot be made in the context of the simple model presented.[30]

The geometric representation is drawn with opportunity, preference, and interest-rate curves. The Fisherian *opportunity* curve is a production function for capital, showing the amount of future income that would be produced given current income. As greater amounts of current income are forgone, more future income results, but at a declining rate. Hence, the opportunity curve is drawn concave to the origin. (*VV* in Figure 3-8). A steeper slope indicates a greater productivity of capital than a more horizontal opportunity curve.

The *time preference* curves (*PP* in Figure 3-8) depict indifference points of an individual between present and future income.[31] The individual receives diminishing marginal utility from incremental income; therefore, the curves show time preference for a set of satisfaction levels. Curves farther from the origin (higher numbers) are more desired than those closer to the origin.

---

[30] The discussion here is largely based on Fisher (1939). For a discussion of risk in the determination of interest rates, see Hirshleifer (1961, 1965).

[31] Fisher (1930) called these "willingness" curves.

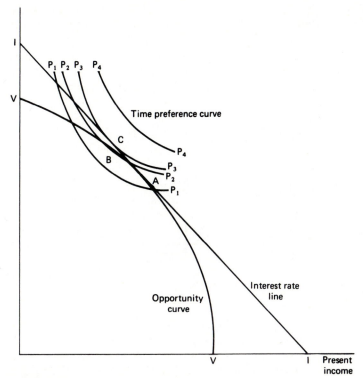

FIGURE 3-8
Fisherian interest-rate curves. (Note: A = point of tangency between
interest-rate line and opportunity curve; B = point of tangency
between opportunity curve and time-preference curve; C = point of
tangency between time-preference curve and interest-rate line.)

The interest-rate line (II in Figure 3-8) represents the cost of external financing that
will permit transfer of income from the future to the present or reward the forbearance
of present income for greater future income. The interest-rate line is tangent to the
opportunity curve at point A and to the time preference curve P_3P_3 at point C, and the
opportunity curve is tangent to the time preference curve P_2P_2 at point B.

Consider now a set of preference curves of which one is tangent to the opportunity
curve at a point *below* A. These curves and points are shown in Figure 3-9. The
individual may now *borrow* to increase present income from $0Q$ to $0R$, if one is willing to
reduce one's future income from $0Q'$ to $0R'$. The cost of increasing present income at
the expense of future income is given by the investment function line II. The borrower
increases personal satisfaction by moving from preference curve P_2P_2 to P_3P_3, when he
or she borrows for current income the amount QR and promises to pay $R'Q'$ in the
future. The borrower cannot move to P_4P_4 because external financing opportunities are
unavailable for that set of indifference points.

The optimal point of trade-off between present and future income lies on the highest
preference curve the individual can attain. Suppose that one starts at point S on

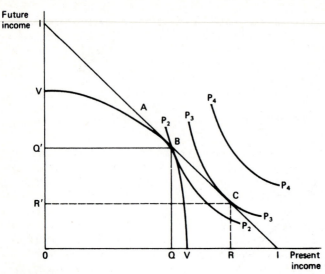

FIGURE 3-9
Borrower's optional position.

FIGURE 3-10
Moving to the optimal position in the absence of external financing.

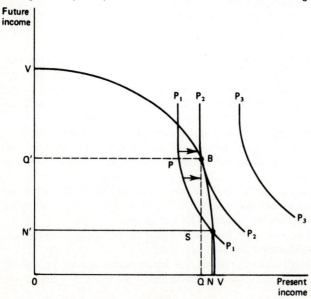

preference curve P_1P_1 as shown in Figure 3–10. Then present income is $0N$ and future income is $0N'$, giving the satisfaction commensurate with curve P_1P_1. However, better preference curves intersect the opportunity curve, and the individual will move to higher curves until reaching point B on P_2P_2. Present income is reduced from $0N$ to $0Q$ in order to increase future income from $0N'$ to $0Q'$. The higher curve indicates that the new income levels are preferable to the previous ones and the individual's satisfaction is greater than before. One cannot move to curve P_3P_3, although one would like to, because production opportunities (curve VV) do not exist for those income levels, without external financing.

With external financing available (represented with line II on Figure 3-11), individuals may move to a higher preference curve. Consider an individual whose preference curve is tangent to the opportunity curve *above* point A; that person will be a *lender*. The best preference curve for a potential lender in the absence of external financing is P_2P_2. However, external financing permits the individual to reduce present income from $0Q$ to $0R$ by lending the amount RQ, with the expectation that future income will increase from $0Q'$ to $0R'$ when the debt is repaid. The new income levels are preferable to the previous ones, and the investor moves to point C on the higher curve P_3P_3.

For the entire financial system, the amount borrowed must equal the amount lent; that is, borrowers and lenders are on preference curves that are tangent to the investment curve, which results in an equilibrium supply and demand position. Suppose that the original II curve implies a rate of interest at which more funds would be lent than borrowed (see Figure 3-12). The individual who is currently on preference curve $P_3^BP_3^B$ can borrow to increase present income. The decline in interest rates that induces borrowing is represented by the shift in the investment curve from II to $I'I'$. At the lower interest rate, lenders move to lower preference curves and increase their present income by lending less. Also, individuals with preference curves tangent above point A but

FIGURE 3-11
Lender's optimal position.

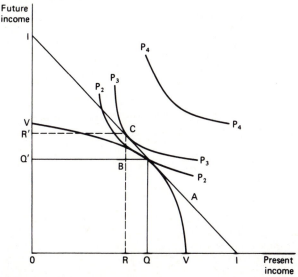

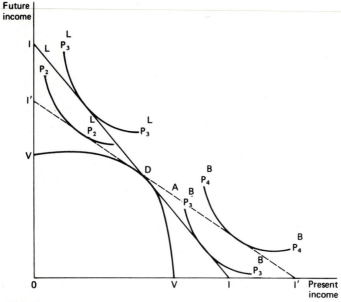

FIGURE 3-12
Achieving an equilibrium interest rate with Fisher's model.

below point *D* change from lending to borrowing. Shifts in the investment function will continue until the supply and demand for funds is in equilibrium.

TERMS

yield	nominal interest rate
interest-rate equilibrium	real interest rate
stock of securities	real investment
multiple markets	efficiency of financial markets
adjustment period	perfect market
transaction costs	weakly efficient market hypothesis
spread	semistrongly efficient market hypothesis
investment opportunity schedule	strongly efficient market hypothesis
CPI	

LIST OF EQUATIONS

Demand for funds

$$D = I + G$$

Nominal and real interest rates

$$i_{nominal} = i_{real} + \Delta CPI$$

QUESTIONS AND PROBLEMS

1 What are the two major determinants of interest-rate equilibrium in the flow of funds?
2 What two sectors constitute the major demand for funds?
3 Using a graph similar to Figure 3-4, illustrate and explain how interest-rate equilibrium is reestablished when the supply of funds schedule and demand for funds schedule both drop, with demand dropping twice as fast as supply.
4 What four factors other than supply and demand affect interest-rate equilibrium?
5 What is the spread in a securities transaction?
6 What do we mean by the term *"inflation"*?
7 What are two measures of price stability that are published by the federal government?
8 Based on the chart in Figure 3-5:
  a What was the longest period of stable prices in the United States?
  b In what year was the highest level of inflation experienced?
  c When was the most precipitous deflation experienced?
  d What economic condition explains most inflationary peaks?
9 What was the real rate of return over 1 year for a 1-year bond yielding 10 percent when the inflation rate was 6 percent?
10 What is the expected nominal rate of interest if the expected inflation rate is 9.00 percent, assuming a normal real rate of interest?
11 Advanced question. Cite periods in history when the *ex ante* and *ex post* real rates of interest were unequal. What accounted for the differences?
12 Using Fisher's interest-rate curves, demonstrate how individuals can achieve higher levels of satisfaction with external financing than they can without it.
13 Show that there is only one optimal interest rate. (*Hint*: Graphically determine the equilibrium supply and demand for funds.)
14 Will most individuals in an economic system achieve a higher level of satisfaction with financing than without it? What persons will benefit by the introduction of borrowing and lending?

SELECTED REFERENCES

Alexander, S.: "Price Movements in Speculative Markets: Trends or Random Walks," *Industrial Management Review*, May 1961, pp. 7–26.
Alhadeff, D. A.: "Bank Management and Inflation," *California Management Review*, Spring 1976, pp. 14–20.
Amihudy, Y., and A. Barnea: "A Note on Fisher Hypothesis and Price Level Uncertainty," *Journal of Financial and Quantitative Analysis*, September 1977, pp. 525–529.
Bodie, Z.: "Common Stocks as a Hedge against Inflation," *Journal of Finance*, May 1976, pp. 459–470.

Bomberger, W. A., and G. E. Makinen: "The Fisher Effect: Graphical Treatment and Some Econometric Implications," *Journal of Finance*, June 1977, p. 719.

Brick, J. R., and H. E. Thompson: "Time Series Analysis of Interest Rates: Some Additional Evidence," *Journal of Finance*, March 1978, pp. 93–103.

Choate, G. M., and S. H. Archer: "Irving Fisher, Inflation, and the Nominal Rate of Interest," *Journal of Financial and Quantitative Analysis*, November 1975, pp. 675–685.

Demetz, Harold: "The Cost of Transacting," *Journal of Quantitative Economics*, February 1968, pp. 33–53.

Fama, Eugene F.: "The Behavior of Stock Market Prices," *Journal of Business*, January 1965, pp. 34–105.

Fama, Eugene F.: "Efficient Capital Markets: A Review of Theory and Empirical Work," *Journal of Finance*, May 1970, pp. 383–417.

Fama, Eugene F., and Marshall E. Blume: "Filter Rules and Stock Market Trading," *Journal of Business*, January 1966, pp. 226–241.

Fama, Eugene F., and Morton H. Miller: *The Theory of Finance*, Dryden Press, Hinsdale, Ill., 1972.

Fama, Eugene, L. Fisher, Michael Jensen, and Richard Roll: "The Adjustment of Stock Prices to New Information," *International Economic Review*, February 1969, pp. 1–21.

Finnerty, Joseph E.: "Insiders and Market Efficiency," *Journal of Finance*, September 1976, pp. 1141–1148.

Fisher, Irving: *The Purchasing Power of Money*, Macmillan, New York, 1911.

Fisher, Irving: *The Theory of Interest*, Macmillan, New York, 1930.

Francis, J. C.: "Intertemporal Differences in Systematic Stock Price Movements," *Journal of Financial and Quantitative Analysis*, June 1975, pp. 205–220.

Francis, Jack Clark: *Investments: Analysis and Managment*, 3d ed., McGraw-Hill, New York, 1980.

Friedman, Benjamin M.: "Effects of Shifting Saving Patterns on Interest Rates and Economic Activity," *Journal of Finance*, March 1982, pp. 37–62.

Garbade, K. D., and J. F. Hunt: "Risk Premiums on Federal Agency Debt," *Journal of Finance*, March 1978, pp. 105–116.

Gitman, L. S., and J. R. Forrester, Jr.: "A Survey of Capital Budgeting Techniques Used by Major U.S. Firms," *Financial Management*, Fall 1977, pp. 66–71.

Hagerman, R. L., and E. H. Kim: "Capital Asset Pricing with Price Level Changes," *Journal of Financial and Quantitative Analysis*, September 1976, pp. 381–391.

Hendershott, P. H.: "A Tax Cut in a Multiple Security Model: Crowding Out, Pulling In and the Term Structure of Interest Rates," *Journal of Finance*, September 1976, pp. 1185–1199.

Hendershott, P. H., and F. S. Orlando: "The Interest Rate Behavior of Flow-of-Funds and Bank-Reserves Financial Models," *Journal of Money, Credit and Banking*, November 1976, pp. 497–512.

Hendershott, Patric, and J. Van Horne: "Expected Inflation Implied by Capital Market Rates." *Journal of Finance*, May 1973, pp. 301–314.

Hirshsleifer, J.: "Risk, the Discount Rate, and Investment Decisions," *American Economic Review*, May 1961, pp. 112–120.

Hirshsleifer, J.: "Investment Decision under Uncertainty Choice-Theoretic Approaches," *Quarterly Journal of Economics*, November 1965, pp. 509–536.

Ibbotson, Roger G., and Rex A. Siquefield: "Stocks, Bonds, Bills, and Inflation: Year-by-Year Historical Returns (1926–1974)," *Journal of Business*, January 1976, pp. 11–47.

Jackson, P. C.: "Statements to Congress," *Federal Reserve Bulletin*, February 1976, pp. 100–103.

Jaffe, Jeffrey F.: "Special Information and Insider Trading, *Journal of Business*, July 1974, pp. 410–428.

Jaffe, J. F., and G. Mandelker: "Investigation," *Journal of Finance*, May 1976, pp. 447–458.

Jensen, Michael, "The Risk, the Pricing of Capital Assets, and the Evaluation of Investment Portfolios," *Journal of Business*, April 1969, pp. 167–247.

Jensen, Michael C.: "Capital Markets: Theory and Evidence," *Bell Journal of Economics and Management Science*, Autumn, 1972, 357–398.

Metzler, L. A., "Wealth, Saving, and the Rate of Interest," *Journal of Political Economy*, April 1951, pp. 93–116.

Mundel, Robert, "Inflation and Real Interest," *Journal of Political Economy*, June 1963, pp. 380–383.

Nelson, C. R.: "Inflation and Capital Budgeting," *Journal of Finance*, June 1976, pp. 923–931.

Sargent, Thomas J.: "Commodity Price Expectations and the Interest Rate," *Quarterly Journal of Economics*, February 1969, pp. 127–140.

Solnik, B. H., and J. Grass: "Eurobonds: Determinants of the Demand for Capital and the International Interest Rate Structure," *Journal of Bank Research*, Winter 1975, pp. 218–230.

Umstead, David A.: "Forecasting Stock Market Prices," *Journal of Finance*, May 1977, pp. 427–441.

Waud, R. N.: "Public Interpretation of Discount Rate Changes: Evidence on the 'Announcement Effect,'" *Econometrica*, March 1970, pp. 231–250.

PART TWO

INTEREST-RATE ANALYSIS

ORIENTATION

The last part described interest *rates* from a macroeconomic perspective as if only *one* rate existed for the entire economy. Obviously many interest rates exist, because we see them quoted daily. The next chapters develop your ability to reconcile or explain differences in interest rates. The capability to evaluate interest rates is an important ability in the financial markets, because the rule of caveat emptor applies to everyone except consumers.

The mathematics of interest rates (Chapter 4) lays down the basic definitions and relationships. (Those with good financial management backgrounds may find this simply a review chapter.) Interest rates in the real world (Chapter 5) is an application of interest-rate mathematics to financial contracts often used by financial institutions. Interest-rate structure (Chapter 6) explains why term to maturity and other factors cause multiple yields to exist in the financial markets. Term-structure management (Chapter 7) follows with institutional management uses for term-structure concepts.

Prepare yourself to deal with *past, present,* and *expected future* interest rates for all types of financial contracts in this part. The time dimensions for interest rates include future periods beginning at future dates; contracts include principal and interest payment terms that are stated in nonconventional ways. The consistent framework presented in this part provides a means for analyzing timing and other terms into a meaningful number for decision-making purposes.

CHAPTER 4

MATHEMATICS OF INTEREST RATES

Financial institution managers are keenly interested in the rate of return received on their investments and the rates paid on borrowed money. Rate of return is the relationship between investment returns (interest, dividends, and price appreciation) and the amount of money invested. It is the single most important result of any investment and weighs heavily in every investment decision. Managers find that even small decreases in the rate of return on investment can mean substantial changes in profits when millions of dollars are invested. Interest rate changes of small proportions are so important to professional money managers that they quote rates in *basis points*. Each basis point is equal to one-hundredth of 1 percent. Unlike most consumers, financial intermediary managers are very concerned about interest differences of even a few basis points.

We need to sharpen our ability to compute interest rates, so that we can tell the difference between two securities that seem to promise the same return but actually yield significantly different returns. Although interest is a simple idea, the various ways of paying interest, defining investment, and computing interest payments are institutional peculiarities camouflaging true rates of return on investment.

MANAGEMENT RESPONSIBILITY FOR INTEREST-RATE ANALYSIS

Legal Reasons APR

The possibility of misleading consumer borrowers is well recognized and is the reason for the Truth in Lending Consumer Leasing Act at the federal level and the Uniform Commercial Code and Uniform Consumer Credit Code on the state level. Credit has been an important subject of the present consumer movement, and credit disclosure is a legal responsibility of financial institutions dealing with consumers. Title I of the Consumer Credit Protection Act deals with credit transaction and credit advertising. This title is explained by the Commerce Clearing House[1]:

> Its [Consumer Credit Protection Act] purpose is to provide for a complete and conspicuous disclosure of credit charges in dollars and cents and as an annual percentage rate. The annual percentage rate will become the uniform standard of measurement in credit cost comparison. To make the rate meaningful, the Act contains a comprehensive definition of a finance charge so that there will be no doubt as to the component items that must be disclosed and reflected in the rate calculation.

The Consumer Credit Protection Act means that lenders must tell consumers all the terms of credit and the annual cost and the annual percentage rate (APR) being charged. Commerce Clearing House goes on with its interpretation[2]:

> The basic philosophy behind the advertising mandates of Trust-in-Lending is all-of-it or none-of-it. You cannot tell part of the story of your credit terms without telling all.

Financial institutions managers are responsible for providing consumer borrowers with information on the total amount of interest to be charged and the annual percentage rate of interest. The intermediary may use loan terms of its choosing, but the intermediary manager must compute and provide the individual borrower with the APR accurate to within ⅛ of 1 percent. The manager must know a great deal about interest rate-of-return computations to avoid inadvertent violations of law.

Business Reasons

On the other hand, there are no laws to protect the financial institutions manager who misunderstands the terms of a security. He or she must rely upon his or her own knowledge and wits. Pricing in the money markets is largely caveat emptor. The burden of understanding and fairly interpreting money-market interest-rate statements is placed primarily on the manager of the financial institution.

The purpose of this chapter is to show how to evaluate interest-bearing securities. We introduce a basic yield equation, which is used throughout this and later chapters to compute yields for many common lending arrangements. We use a common solution equation and notation to emphasize the similarity of different loans and investments. The ability to compute yields for investment problems successfully is useful in many more situations than the select few described here. A summary of equations is provided at the end of the chapter,

---

[1] Cissell and Cissell (1969), p. 6.
[2] Cissell and Cissell (1969), p. 45.

and several interest-rate tables are located in the appendixes at the end of the book to facilitate computation.

STATED RATE VERSUS YIELD

Before proceeding to the numerical analysis, three important interest-rate terms need to be defined precisely. The important terms are *stated rate, annual percentage rate,* and *yield*. The definitions are listed separated so that they may be compared:

1 Stated rate refers to a period rate that is multiplied times the principal amount of the loan to compute interest charge.
2 Annual percentage rate is an annualized interest rate that adjusts the stated rate for the number of periods per year and the amount of principal actually borrowed.
3 Yield is the rate that is equivalent to a financial contract meeting three conditions:
   a the full amount is actually borrowed (lent)
   b at the beginning of the year
   c and then repaid at the end of the year with interest.

The first definition, stated rate, bases interest rates on the *contract terms*. The second definition, annual percentage rate, adjusts selected contract terms to compute an interest-rate equivalent. The third definition, yield, undertakes all adjustments necessary to compute a rate equivalent to a clearly defined standard. The standard for comparison is the simple-interest rate, discussed in the following section. Thus, yield is a computed value that transforms stated or annual percentage rates into their simple-interest equivalents. Consequently, yield analysis begins with a discussion of simple-interest rates.

Simple-Interest Rate

Simple interest refers to interest charged for the use of money for exactly 1 year and paid at the end of the year. Interest on single-payment notes maturing in exactly 1 year is simple interest. The yield on a simple-interest note is the same as the stated interest rate, because it fully meets the definition presented previously.

The interest-rate equation for simple interest is a good starting point for understanding interest-rate relationships. We designate the interest rate with an i, the amount paid at the end of each period as C, the amount of money borrowed (principal) as P. The letter C is chosen because interest payments on bonds are called *coupons*; these are sometimes attached to bonds and periodically clipped from the bond and presented for payment. We can now express the definition for simple interest algebraically as:

$$i = C/P \equiv R \tag{4-1}$$

where the simple rate is equal to the interest coupon divided by the principal sum borrowed. In this case only, the interest rate i is equal to the yield R. After our example we define yields for many situations that differ from this simple case and where i and R are unequal.

Example of Interest Rate

Simple interest is notoriously easy to compute. What is the interest rate on a 1-year note of $1000 principal with an $80 interest charge?

$$i = C/P = 80/1000$$
$$= 0.0800 = 8.00\%$$

The interest rate is 8.00 percent, rounded to the nearest basis point. Recall that 1 basis point equals one-hundredth of 1 percent.

One-Year-Bond Yield

The price of a bond is not always equal to the par value but may be less than or greater than the amount received at maturity. When the current price is above the maturity (par) value, the investment declines in value at maturity. Our yield is less than the coupon rate for bonds selling at a premium price and greater than the coupon rate in the case of bonds selling at a discount.

The simple-interest-rate equation, Eq. (4-1), provides an inexact figure for the yield. Money-market traders call the interest to current price relationship the *current yield*. By referring to the current price as P_0 we can compute yield (*CR*) as:

$$CR = C/P_0 \tag{4-2}$$

Current yield is the annual interest coupon divided by the current price.

The *yield* for a 1-year bond is computed on the basis of current price (P_0) and the maturity (par) value (P_1). We subscript P to indicate time as current (0) or one period from now (1). Yield (R) is the rate at which we discount the interest coupon and the future price. The 1-year-yield equation is:

$$P_0 = \frac{C}{(1 + R)} + \frac{P_1}{(1 + R)} \tag{4-3}$$

The yield (R) in Eq. (4-3) is the yield for a 1-year bond with current price P_0, coupon C, and ending price P_1. *Note that as current prices fall, yields rise, and as prices rise, yields decline.*

Example of One-Year-Bond Yield

Yield and stated interest rates are the same when P_0 and P_1 are the same. From our previous example, P_0 equals $1000 and P_1 equals $1000; we calculate C as $80. What is the yield, R?

$$1000 = \frac{80}{(1 + R)} + \frac{1000}{1 + R)}$$

Solving this equation, we find that R equals 8.00 percent.

Now consider the same bond that is selling at a discount for a price (P_0) of 95 (quoted as 95 in newspapers and meaning 95 percent of 1000 par value). What is the yield?

$$950 = \frac{80}{(1 + R)} + \frac{1000}{(1 + R)}$$
$$R = 13.68\%$$

We find that the rate increases to 13.68 percent, as the price decreases to 95.

Holding Period Yield

Holding period yield, commonly used in investment analysis, is a useful variation on the 1-year-bond equation (4-3). After rewriting the one-period yield equation, we see the holding period yield form familiar to investment analysts:

$$R = ((P_1 + C/M) / P_0)^M - 1 \qquad (4\text{-}4)$$

In words, Eq. (4-4) says that "yield equals the sum of interest (or dividends) plus sales price less purchase price all divided by the purchase price." M is the number of periods per year; it adjusts the annual coupon rate and compounding frequency for monthly, quarterly, and semiannual periods.

The holding period yield relationship is one of the most important tools in financial management, because it is both simple and precise. Holding period yields can often be analyzed for bonds, stocks, and other financial contracts. An example of its use is presented in the following; also note that Ibbotson and Sinquefield used holding period yield to compare returns of U.S. Treasury bills, long-term bonds, and common stocks (Table 4-1).

Example of Holding Period Yield

Again using our bond, which currently sells at 95 and pays 8 percent interest annually, and matures for 100 percent of face value after 1 year, we can compute the yield—this time with Eq. (4-4):

TABLE 4-1
ONE-YEAR HOLDING PERIOD RETURNS (1926–1974) FOR BILLS, BONDS, AND STOCKS

Year	Risk-free asset U.S. Treasury bills due within 90 days	Long-term bonds U.S. Treasury bonds (coupon and price change)	Common stocks S & P 500 (dividends and price change)
1926	2.54%	7.79%	11.61%
1927	2.52	8.92	37.45
1928	3.68	0.09	43.60
1929	4.96	3.42	−8.41
1930	2.40	4.65	−24.90
1931	1.20	5.85	−43.35
1932	1.19	16.84	−8.20
1933	0.31	−0.07	53.97
1934	0.18	10.02	−1.43
1935	0.13	5.01	47.66
1936	0.18	7.51	33.92
1937	0.29	0.24	−35.02
1938	0.00	5.52	31.14
1939	0.00	5.95	−0.42
1940	−.03	6.08	−9.78
1941	0.03	0.93	−11.58
1942	0.27	3.25	20.33
1943	0.36	2.10	25.91
1944	0.35	2.84	19.73
1945	0.33	10.71	36.41
1946	0.36	−0.09	−8.07
1947	0.51	−2.62	5.77
1948	0.81	3.39	5.51
1949	0.74	6.47	18.76
1950	1.22	0.04	31.74
1951	1.46	−3.96	24.01
1952	1.63	1.17	18.35
1953	1.73	3.61	−0.99
1954	0.84	7.18	52.62
1955	1.60	−1.11	31.54
1956	2.38	−5.77	6.55
1957	2.86	7.46	−10.79
1958	1.50	−6.08	43.37
1959	2.80	−2.26	11.98
1960	2.47	13.77	0.46
1961	2.05	0.97	26.89
1962	2.67	6.85	−8.73
1963	2.94	1.20	22.77
1964	3.30	3.53	16.51
1965	3.71	0.70	12.45
1966	4.32	1.26	−10.05
1967	3.74	−9.18	23.99
1968	4.78	−0.29	11.08
1969	5.96	−5.03	−8.43
1970	5.99	12.06	3.95
1971	4.03	13.21	14.32

TABLE 4-1 (*continued*)

Year	Risk-free asset U.S. Treasury bills due within 90 days	Long-term bonds U.S. Treasury bonds (coupon and price change)	Common stocks S & P 500 (dividends and price change)
1972	3.53	5.71	18.97
1973	6.72	5.52	−14.67
1974	8.04	4.40	−26.45
1975	5.80	9.19	37.20
1976	5.08	16.75	23.84
1977	5.12	−0.67	−7.18
1978	7.18	−1.16	6.56
1979	10.38	−1.22	18.44
1980	11.24	−3.95	32.42
1981	14.71	1.85	−4.91
1982	10.54	40.35	21.41
1983	8.80	0.68	22.51
1984	9.85	15.43	6.27

Source: Roger G. Ibbotson and Rex A. Sinquefield. "Stocks, Bonds, Bills, and Inflation. Simulations of the Future (1976–2000)," Table A1, *The Journal of Business*, April 1976, pp. 313–338.

$$R = ((100 + 8/1) / 95)^1 - 1$$
$$= 13.68\%$$

Note that *all* of the values substituted in this equation are dollar amounts. The same result would have been obtained if *all* values were fractional equivalents of percentages. In solving these problems, the values substituted must be either percentages or dollar amounts, as mixing the two is likely to lead to the wrong answer.

Next, consider a more complicated example. What is the yield for a loan of $3 million with a stated interest rate of 12 percent per year paid semiannually, if it is sold after 6 months in the secondary market for $2,900,000? The annual interest coupon is $360,000 (12 percent of $3,000,000). By substituting into Eq. (4-4), we find:

$$R = ((2,900,000 + 360,000/2) / 3,000,000)^2 - 1$$
$$= 5.40\%$$

The result, 5.40 percent, is the yield—a return equivalent to that earned by investing in a 1-year loan at the beginning of the year and receiving principal and interest at the end of the year. Because yields in both examples are adjusted to the same standard, they are comparable. Thus, the yield was greater for the bond than for the loan, although the stated rate was higher on the loan than the bond. This example illustrates one of the many situations in which the stated rate is substantially different from the yield.

Multiperiod-Bond Yield

Bonds usually pay interest over 20 to 30 years, rather than only once as depicted previously. Yield is computed as the sum of the present values of all future interest coupons plus the present value of the principal repaid at maturity. The price (P_0) of an N-period bond is computed as follows:

$$P_0 = \frac{C}{(1 + R)} + \frac{C}{(1 + R)^2} + \cdots + \frac{C}{(1 + R)^N} + \frac{P_N}{(1 + R)^N} \qquad (4\text{-}5)$$

Equation (4-5) is an expansion of the simple-interest equation, Eq. (4-3). The principal borrowed is not repaid at the end of a year, as in Eq. (4-3), but used for N years, and the interest is paid each year. Consequently, Eq. (4-5) discounts coupon terms and the principal for N years.

Multiperiod Example

Suppose that a bond is offered to us with an $80 coupon (payable annually) and a maturity of 3 years. If we can purchase a similar bond in the market and earn 6 percent, then we will discount the coupon payments of the proposed bond at the 6 percent rate to find its price. That is, we want to value the $80 coupon bond when the going market yield is 6 percent. An illustration of this procedure is shown in Figure 4-1, and the computations for Eq. (4-5) are as follows:

$$P_0 = \frac{80}{(1 + 0.06)} + \frac{80}{(1 + 0.06)^2} + \frac{80}{(1 + 0.06)^3} + \frac{1000}{(1 + 0.06)^3}$$

FIGURE 4-1
Present value illustration.

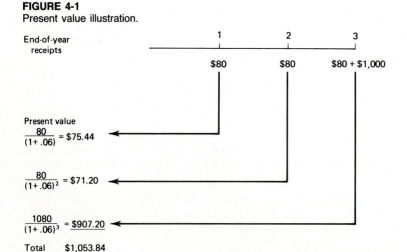

End-of-year receipts	1	2	3
	$80	$80	$80 + $1,000

Present value

$\dfrac{80}{(1+.06)} = \$75.44$

$\dfrac{80}{(1+.06)^2} = \$71.20$

$\dfrac{1080}{(1+.06)^3} = \$907.20$

Total $1,053.84

The present value of a future amount (PV) such as $1/(1 + 0.06)$ or $1/(1 + 0.06)$ is common to many financial decisions. The factors are evaluated in Appendix B [e.g., $1/(1 + 0.06) = 0.943$]; the foregoing equation is solved by substituting the PV values from the 6 percent page of the table in Appendix B. (Alternatively, many calculators can be used to compute present values.)

$$P = 80\,(0.9434) + 80\,(0.8900) + 80\,(0.8396) + 1000\,(0.8396) = \$1,053.44$$

We note that the \$80 coupon is an annuity. When the same coupon is paid at a regular interval, the payment is called an annuity. (Also, many calculators compute annuity values.)

Annuity Present Value

The equation for annuity present value (APV) may be rewritten as follows:

$$P_0 = C \sum_{t=1}^{N} \frac{1}{(1 + R)^t} + \frac{P_N}{(1 + R)^N} \tag{4-6}$$

The summation expression is the annuity factor and is evaluated in Appendix B, a table of present values for \$1-per-period annuities of different lengths of time. By substituting from Appendix B into the above illustration, we have the price we would pay:

$$
\begin{aligned}
P_0 &= 80 \sum_{t=1}^{3} \frac{1}{(1 + 0.06)^t} + \frac{1000}{(1 + 0.06)^3} \\
&= 80\,(2.673) + 1000\,(0.8396) \\
&= 1053.44
\end{aligned}
$$

Bond interest is usually paid semiannually or quarterly. Equation (4-5) is modified when interest payments occur more than once per year. If M is the number of times per year that the coupon is paid or interest is compounded, then the current price is calculated as follows:

$$P_0 = \sum_{t=1}^{n} \frac{C/M}{(1 + i/M)^t} + \frac{P_n}{(1 + i/M)^n} \tag{4-7}$$

where $n = (N)(M)$.

If we consider the 8 percent coupon bond that matures in 1 year as one paying interest semiannually rather than annually, we find that the price is as follows:

$$
\begin{aligned}
P_0 &= \sum_{t=1}^{6} \frac{80/2}{(1 + 0.06/2)^t} + \frac{1000}{(1 + 0.06/2)^6} \\
&= \$1054.19
\end{aligned}
$$

The value of the bond increases from $1053.84 to $1054.19 when the interest compounding increases from an annual to a semiannual frequency. Hence the effective yield increases and the bond value increases by $0.35, as a result of semiannual compounding. *More frequent compounding, such as quarterly or monthly interest payments, would increase the value further.*

Example of Annuity Method Yield Computation

Assume that we invest $900 in a bond that pays a $90 coupon annually for 10 years plus the principal at the end of 10 years. We receive $90 each year on our investment of $900 for a current yield of 10.0 percent. What is the effective yield to maturity? We know the maturity value (P_N), the coupon (C), the term to maturity (N), and the price (P_0). Noting that the current price is below par value, we begin with a yield above the coupon rate. Using a trial discount rate of 12 percent, we compute a price:

$$P_0 = \sum_{t=1}^{10} \frac{90}{(1 + 0.12)^t} + 1000 \frac{1}{(1 + 0.12)^{10}}$$
$$= \$830.52$$

The computed price ($830.52) is less than the market price ($900.00); therefore, the trial yield is too high. We then select a lower yield, 10 percent for example, and compute the price again using Appendix B:

$$P_0 = \sum_{t=1}^{10} \frac{90}{(1 + 0.10)^t} + 1000 \frac{1}{(1 + 0.10)^{10}}$$
$$= \$938.51$$

These calculations tell us what purchase prices and yields are close to the price and yield of our bond. Because the price lies between $830.52 and $938.51, the yield must fall between 10 and 12 percent. We can closely approximate the actual yield by interpolation. Some calculators perform the interpolation between 10 and 12 percent automatically, but other calculators do not. If your calculator does not interpolate annuity and lump sum payments to find the internal rate of return, then you must interpolate manually. To interpolate manually, first record upper, interpolated, and lower rates and present values, as follows:

	Interest rate, percent	Present value, dollars
Upper	12	830.52
Interpolated	R	900.00
Lower	10	938.51

Then make the rate change proportionate to the present value change:

$$\frac{\text{Upper rate} - \text{Interpolated rate}}{\text{Upper rate} - \text{Lower rate}} = \frac{\text{Upper value} - \text{Interpolated value}}{\text{Upper value} - \text{Lower value}}$$

$$\frac{12 - R}{12 - 10} = \frac{830.52 - 900.00}{830.52 - 938.51}$$

Then solve for R,

$$R = 10.70\%$$

EQUAL MONTHLY PAYMENTS

Monthly Payment Amount

Monthly payments are equal for mortgage and installment loans, hence more of the monthly payment is paid for interest than principal during the early years of the loan. If we repay a portion of the principal each month, then the ending principal balance will be zero. That is, fully amortized loans are set so that P_n equals zero. Each payment contains some interest (C_n) and some principal (P_n):

$$PAY = C_n + P_n \qquad (4\text{-}8)$$

where $n = (N)(M)$

Payments (PAY) for a \$1 loan are calculated as:

$$PAY = \frac{i}{1 - (1 + i)^{-n}} \qquad (4\text{-}9)$$

To compute payments for loans of initial amount P_0, multiply P_0 by PAY. The value of PAY is found in Appendix B or computed by some calculators.

Example of Equal Monthly Payments

What are the monthly payments for a 20-year mortgage at 9 percent annually (¾ percent monthly) when \$50,000 is borrowed? The terms of the loan are substituted into Eq. (4-9) and the payment factor from Appendix B is substituted to find:

$$\begin{aligned} \text{Payment} &= 50,000 \, (0.00900) \\ &= \$450.00 \end{aligned}$$

We find that 240 equal monthly payments of \$450.00 exactly amortizes a \$50,000 loan with a 9.00 percent interest rate.

COMPOUND INTEREST

Compound interest is earned on interest previously received during the year. Investors can reinvest interest, which then begins bearing interest itself. Compounding increases the yield in proportion to the frequency that interest is paid. For example, our savings passbook account yield is greater if we receive interest each quarter than if we receive interest at the end of the year. The quarterly interest payment can be redeposited and bear interest in following quarters, whereas an annual interest payment cannot produce an additional return until the following year.

We can compare compound interest with our simple-interest benchmark. We can find a simple-interest equivalent to the compound interest accumulated during the year. The yield (R) for a simple-interest bond is equated to the compound value produced by bonds paying interest more frequently than once per year. If the interest rate is quoted as i and compounded M times per year, then the relationship is expressed as:

$$(1 + R) = (1 + i/M)^M \qquad (4\text{-}10)$$

Equation (4-10) says that the year-end total principal and interest from a simple-interest security (left side) is equivalent to the ending value for a compound-interest security (right side). We can simplify the algebra by subtracting 1 from both sides and find the yield for a compound-interest rate:

$$R = (1 + i/M)^M - 1 \qquad (4\text{-}11)$$

Example of Compound-Interest Payments

How much more is paid on a savings account when interest is paid quarterly rather than annually? Suppose that the interest rate is 8 percent. The two types of accounts are compared in the following statements:

	Balance at end of quarter	
	Quarterly interest	Annual interest
Beginning balance	$1000.00	$1000.00
Balance after first quarterly interest payment ($1000.00) (0.08/4) and (0)	$1020.00	$1000.00
Balance after second quarterly interest payment ($1020.00) (0.08/4) and (0)	$1040.40	$1000.00
Balance after third quarterly interest payment ($1040.00) (0.08/4) and (0)	$1061.21	$1000.00
Balance after fourth quarterly interest payment ($1061.21) (0.08/4) and ($1000) (0.05)	$1082.43	$1080.00

The quarterly account builds interest faster than the annual account, resulting in greater interest payments. The intermediary is paying not 8 percent but 8.24 percent, an additional 24 basis points due soley to compounding effects.

Example of Compounding Equation

We can compute the effect of compounding easily by using Eq. (4-11). Substituting 0.08 for i and 4 for M, we can compute the yield for an 8 percent account compounded quarterly:

$$
\begin{aligned}
R &= (1 + i/M)^M - 1 \\
&= (1 + 0.08/4)^4 - 1 \\
&= (1.02)^4 - 1 \\
&= 0.0824 = 8.24\%
\end{aligned}
$$

Thus, the yield is increased by 24 basis points. (*Note:* When using a calculator with a y^x function, enter $1 + i/M$ for y and M for x.)

Example of Compounding Using Table of Compound-Interest Equivalents

In Appendix A a table is presented that provides the interest equivalents for varying rates of interest and compounding frequencies. This table provides the solutions to Eq. (4-11) for all the values of i presented in the column on the left and the values of M designated across the top row.

If we wished to determine the effective yield of an 8 percent savings account where interest is paid monthly, the solution to Eq. (4-11) (substituting 0.08 for i and 12 for M) can be found directly from the table or calculated with a calculator.

$$
\begin{aligned}
R &= (1 + i/M)^M - 1 \\
R &= 8.30\%
\end{aligned}
$$

SUMMARY

This chapter covered interest-rate concepts. These are applied in the following chapter to compare yields for alternative loans and investments. They are used by practitioners to compare hundreds of different types of securities bought and sold daily. The equations from this chapter are summarized in the list of equations.

We began with the familiar simple-interest equation and gradually progressed to multiperiod bond and mortgage equations. The 1-year-bond equation was an extension of the simple-interest equation and provided a means of computing yield for 1-year bonds selling at discounts or premiums. The multiperiod equation extended the bond equation to time periods beyond 1 year, and the compound bond equation was designed for quarterly and semiannual interest payments. Then equal payment contracts (mortgages and installment loans) were evaluated. Finally we saw that compounding interest daily, monthly, quarterly, or semiannually increased the effective yield, as interest is earned on interest received during the year.

APPENDIX 4-1: Call Options

A *call option* written into a bond indenture (agreement) allows issuers to retain the right to repay the debt and retire the bond before maturity. *Deferred-call bonds* provide that the option may not be exercised for a given number of years. In effect the bond issuer has the right to buy a particular bond (its own) at a *stated price* during a *limited period of time*.

The call option is a clause in nearly all corporate and state government bonds, and frequently a part of loans from financial intermediaries. Although disguised by other terminology, the call option is a common part of loan agreements. Mortgage loans may usually be repaid if the mortgaged property is sold, and an automobile installment loan may be prepaid anytime for a small, fixed penalty: Note that a noncallable bond is a special case in which the call deferment equals the maturity term.

The option is exercised when less costly bonds may be issued to replace outstanding, callable bonds or borrowers find their own bonds the most attractive investment alternative.

The value of the option is illustrated by the following scenario.

January, 1985 *Bonds issued at current market rates*	$1 million of 20-year bonds are issued. The bonds are sold at par, pay 9 percent interest, and are *callable at 102* any time.
March, 1990 *Bond yields decline*	Yield to maturity on 15-year bonds (a 20-year bond 5 years later) is 7 percent; the bond is now selling at *118.22*.
Issuer reduces interest expense by refunding	Exercising its call option, the issuer repurchases the bonds for $1,020,000; funds are raised by selling a 15-year bond at 7 percent. Interest expense is reduced by $20,000 per year for 15 years with a one-time outlay of $20,000. this process is termed *refunding*.
Investors loss	Investors owning the security when the call option is exercised sustain a $162,200 loss. The loss equals market value less call value.

Of course, neither the issuer nor investors know with certainty that refunding will be worthwhile. The probability that bonds will be called depends upon the deferment period, call-price distribution of future interest rates, and cost of refunding. The present value of a call right is a function of call likelihood and value when exercised. Callable issues command a premium up to 1 percent in yield over immediately noncallable bonds, when yields are historically high.

TERMS

rate of return	simple interest
basis points	present value
yield	semiannual payment
holding period yield	semiannual compounding
Consumer Credit Protection Act	current yield
annual percentage rate (APR)	term to maturity
interest rate	interpolation
coupon	equal monthly payment

LIST OF EQUATIONS

$$i = C/P$$

$$P_0 = \frac{C}{(1 + R)} + \frac{P_1}{(1 + R)}$$

$$R = ((P_1 + C/M)/P_0)^M - 1$$

$$P_0 = \frac{C}{(1 + R)} + \frac{C}{(1 + R)^2} + \cdots + \frac{C}{(1 + R)^N} + \frac{P_N}{(1 + R)^N}$$

$$P_0 = \sum_{t=1}^{n} \frac{C/M}{(1 + i/M)^t} + \frac{P_n}{(1 + i/M)^n}$$

$$\text{Payment} = P_0 \frac{R}{1 - (1 + R)^{-n}}$$

$$R = (1 + i/M)^M - 1$$

QUESTIONS AND PROBLEMS

1 This morning's newspaper reported that U.S. Treasury bills now yield 12 basis points more than last week. How much has the yield increased in percent?

2 How much more would you earn in a year if your investment of $2 million increased from a 7.10 to a 7.30 percent yield? What dollar return would you receive by investing idle cash of $2 million over the weekend at 7.30 percent?

3 How much would you receive each year from a $5000 par value bond with an interest rate of 9 percent? If interest is paid each quarter, what is the quarterly coupon?

4 What is the current yield for a $1000 par value bond paying an 8 percent coupon and selling at a price of 89?

5 Calculate the holding period yield on the following security transactions: 1000 shares of Thor Corporation purchased at $1.00 per share on September 1, 19X0, and sold at $2.00 per share on March 1, 19X1; a dividend of $0.10 per share was paid on December 1, 19X0.

6 What is the yield to maturity for a $1000 par value bond paying an 8 percent coupon, selling at a price of 89, and maturing in 7 years?

7 How many basis points would the yield to maturity decrease for the bond in Question 6, if the selling price increased to 94?

8 How much would you pay for a bond maturing in 15 years which has a 6 percent coupon, when the yield to maturity on similar bonds is 8 percent? (Use present-value tables in the Appendixes.)

9 The Security Bank is currently offering 9.50 percent certificates of deposit maturing in 1 year with interest payable upon maturity. Several competing banks sell certificates with the same stated rate (9.50 percent) but First National pays interest quarterly and Second State advertises "daily compounding." Security management is divided about what difference, if any, interest payment timing has on the cost of funds. Prepare an analysis of the three CD offerings discussed.

10 What would the true yield be for a certificate of deposit advertised as follows: 4-year maturity, 7.5 percent interest rate, and interest compounded quarterly?

11 Compute the yield to maturity for a 20-year bond with a coupon of 6 percent, when the current price is 108.

12 Which 2-year certificate of deposit has a greater yield? (Use tables found in Appendix A.)
  a 6¾ percent interest rate compounded daily
  b 7¼ percent interest rate compounded annually

13 What monthly payment amount would be required on a $75,000, 30-year mortgage at 8 percent? At 12 percent?

SELECTED REFERENCES

Cissell, Robert, and Helen Cissell: *Mathematics of Finance*, Houghton Mifflin, Boston, 1956.

Cissell, Robert and Helen Cissell: *Truth in Lending*, Commerce Clearing House, Chicago, 1969.

Cole, Robert H.: *Consumer and Commercial Credit Management*, Richard D. Irwin, Homewood, Ill., 1972.

Johnson, Robert W.: *Financial Management*, 4th ed., Allyn and Bacon, Boston, 1971.

Van Horne, James C.: *Function and Analysis of Capital Market Rates,"* Prentice-Hall, Englewood Cliffs, N.J., 1970.

CHAPTER 5

INTEREST RATES IN THE REAL WORLD

Loans, bonds, and other financial contracts frequently yield substantially more or less than the quoted or stated interest rate. Discounted notes, compensating balances, installment payments, tax exemptions, and transactions costs may all change the yield. To compare yields on competing securities and to set rates on loans and investments, financial managers need to know how to compute yield to maturity for nonstandard investment arrangements. This chapter contains a few examples of institutional securities that have a true yield different from the nominal interest rate. In practice nearly every security merits the type of scrutiny applied to the selected investments seen here.

In the case of loans and securities that pay interest more frequently than once per year, the rate is compounded to find the yield. Two steps are used to find yields for compound interest situations:

1 Adjust for specific terms such as discounting, points, and compensating balances to compute the annual percentage rate (APR).
2 Adjust for compound-interest effects to compute yield (R).

Step 1 is sufficient only for 1-year bonds and loans, and step 2 must be added for securities paying daily, monthly, quarterly, or semiannual interest installments. The rates computed in step 1 are designed as i', and the yields calculated by step 2 are denoted by R. Computations in this chapter require a four-function calculator with a y function. Beyond such a basic calculator, one with present-value functions is recommended because it is more efficient than searching through tables and interpolating between table values. Explanation of tables has been retained to assist those with a basic calculator and may be ignored by those with a present-value calculator. See your calculator's manual for a description of its capability and operation.

DISCOUNTED NOTE

Discounted notes are sold at a price below the par value; a discounted bank loan is one in which the interest is subtracted from the amount of the loan, when the loan is granted. The discount is the difference between the cost (or price) of a security and its maturity value. After the initial issue, the discount is the difference between selling price and par value. When we issue a discounted note or receive a discounted loan, we are agreeing to pay back more at maturity than we borrowed at inception. Part of the so-called principal payment is interest, and discounts are generally amortized over the life of the bond by accounting practice.

The amount loaned (P_0) is the loan principal (P_1) less the amount of interest charged for the first period. The borrower receives P_0 and repays the amount P_1, which includes interest. The relationship is expressed as:

$$P_0 = P_1 - (i/M)(P_1) \qquad (5\text{-}1)$$

P_0 is equal to the amount of note less interest for the period (M periods per year).

Example of Discount Computation

Suppose that our bank deducts interest in advance on a $1000, 8 percent note. The note is to be outstanding for 90 days. How much will the borrower receive? We apply Eq. (5-1) to the problem by substituting $1000 for P_1, 0.08 for i and 4 for M (365/90 days; $n = 4$ periods per year):

$$\begin{aligned} P_0 &= 1000 - (0.08/4)\,(1000) \\ &= 980 \end{aligned}$$

The borrower receives $1000 less interest of $20.

Yield on Discounted Note

The yield on a discounted note is greater than the stated rate for two reasons:

  1 Interest is computed on the stated amount of the loan, which is greater than the amount actually borrowed.
  2 Interest paid during the year is reinvested, and the rate is compounded.

The effective yield is found in two steps:

1 Compute the rate (i') to reflect the discounting effect.
2 Compound the discounted note rate (i') to its annual equivalent yield (R).

In the first step, the rate i is adjusted for discounting with the following equation[1]:

$$i' = \frac{i}{1 - i/M} \tag{5-2}$$

The effective rate (i') is the nominal rate (i) divided by 1 minus the interest discount. The higher the interest rate, the greater is the (positive) effect on yield.

The second step is to compound the effective rate (i') when interest is collected and reinvested during the year. Interest is earned on interest charges every time the note is paid or refinanced. The computation is made by substituting i' for i in Eq. (4-11):

$$R = (1 + i'/M)^M - 1$$

Here we are compounding the effects of discounting to find the true yield.

Example of Discounted Note Yield

What is the yield for our 8 percent, 90-day, $1000 note? The effect of discounting is computed with Eq. (5-2):

$$i' = \frac{0.08}{1 - 0.08/4}$$
$$= 0.0816 = 8.16\%$$

Discounting increases the yield by 16 basis points to 8.16 percent. Quarterly compounding further increases the yield. With Eq. (5-2) we find R:

$$R = (1 + i'/M)^M - 1$$
$$= (1 + 0.0816/4)^4 - 1$$
$$= 0.0841 = 8.41\%$$

The yield is really 8.41 percent and not 8.00 percent on a 90-day discounted note. The lender increases interest income by $4100 annually on every million dollars by using 90-day discounted notes rather than annual simple-interest notes. Discounting can, and often does, make a significant contribution to interest revenues and profits.

---

[1] Equation (5-2) is derived from Eq. (4-7) by recognizing that the value of C is zero (because interest is not paid until maturity), by setting $N = 1$ and $n = 1$, and by rearranging terms.

MORTGAGE POINTS

In mortgage lending *points* are frequently added to the initial cost of a loan. Each point is equal to 1 percent of the amount of the loan, and points are paid when the loan is granted. Charging points is customary for commercial mortgages and mortgages guaranteed by the VA, FHA, and other government insurance agencies. Yield is increased by points in the same way as yield is increased by interest discounting. The points are retained by the lender (or paid to the lender as a finder's fee), rather than disbursed to the borrower.[2] Thus the borrower receives a cash amount less than the loan amount.

To compute the amount the borrower receives, both the amount of the mortgage and the number of points must be considered. The following equation (5-3) provides a general framework for this analysis:

$$P_0' = P_0 (1 - POINTS/100) \tag{5-3}$$

where P_0' equals the amount of funds received by the mortgagee; P_0 equals the stated amount of the mortgage loan at origination; and *POINTS* equals the number of points charged to the borrower.

Points are paid at the time the loan is made and are not returned to the borrower, although the loan may be paid before maturity. Three points on a $50,000 mortgage, for example, amount to $1500, which is paid to the lending institution. If the borrower repays the loan after a couple of years, then the lender receives the full balance owing on the original $50,000 loan. The points are paid, in such cases, for the use of money over 2 rather than 30 years. Clearly, the lender receives a higher yield from prepaid than from full-term loans. He or she has lent $48,500 and must wait only 2 years to be repaid the full $50,000, when the borrower voluntarily prepays the loan in 2 rather than 30 years.

Prepayment is very common in residential mortgage lending, because homeowners frequently repay their loans when moving to a new house or area. Households in the United States move on an average of once every 7 years, often selling one house and buying another when they relocate. Although prepayment depends on the type of mortgage contract and interest-rate conditions, it is customary for investors in fixed-rate, long-term mortgages to compute yields on the basis of a 12-year maturity rather than the stated 25- or 30-year maturity. Federal National Mortgage Association mortgage yields are computed on the basis of a 12-year maturity, as are most other mortgage market instruments. The computation is made using the basic yield equation by specifying N equal to 12 and P_0 equal to the stated amount of the loan.

---

[2] Charging points is illegal under some state laws and limited under Veterans Administration legislation. Although these laws restrict the practice of having borrowers pay points, they do not prohibit real estate developers or home sellers from paying points. Consequently developers and sellers may include in the price of real estate points paid to mortgage lenders. Although the seller technically pays the points, in effect the real estate buyer incurs the cost of points.

Example of Mortgage Points

Consider now the insurance company loan officer who is about to make a $40,000 mortgage loan to finance a new house. The loan officer charges a 12 percent interest rate plus 2 points for a 20-year mortgage. It is the responsibility of the manager to tell the borrower how much money will be loaned and what the yield is equal to after deducting the 2 points. How much is disbursed to the borrower and what is the effective yield to the lender? What are the monthly payments? These are basic questions important in any mortgage loan proceeding.

The amount of money given to the borrower is computed with Eq. (5-3), solving for P_0. The amount of the loan to be repaid during the next 20 years is symbolized by P_N. *POINTS* equals 2, the number of points charged to the borrower. With Eq. (5-3) we find the amount of money lent after points are deducted.

$$
\begin{aligned}
P_0 &= P_N \, (1 - POINTS/100) \\
&= \$40,000 \, (1 - 2/100) \\
&= \$39,200.00
\end{aligned}
$$

The $40,000 of principal to be repaid is used here to compute the 240 (12 months times 20 years) equal monthly payments, using Eq. (4-9) from the previous chapter.

$$
\begin{aligned}
PAY &= P_N \, [(0.12/12)/(1 + (1 - 0.12/12)^{-240})] \\
&= 40,000(0.01100) \\
&= 440.00
\end{aligned}
$$

The monthly payment factor (PAY) per dollar of loan amount is taken from Appendix B or computed with an x^y function on a calculator.

In effect the mortgage payment table evaluates the equation for common situations. Now, we recall that only $39,200.00 is actually lent. What effective rate (i') is earned on a $39,200.00 loan with 240 equal monthly payments of $440.00? Because the note is discounted and paid monthly, the yield is greater than the stated rate of 12 percent. To find the exact yield, we work through the following steps:

1 Compute the payment factor for the proposed loan. Example of payment factor computation:

$$
\begin{aligned}
PAY/P_0 &= 440.00/39,200 \\
&= 0.0112
\end{aligned}
$$

2 Look up the payment factor in Appendix B. Example: For a 240-month mortgage, the computed payment factor is between 0.0110 and 0.0132.

3 Interpolate between the payment factors to find the approximate yield.

Example: We know that the yield is between 1.00 and 1.25 percent. Therefore, the yield *R* is computed as follows:

Interest rate	Payment factor
1.00	0.0110
APR/12	0.0112
1.25	0.0132

The unknown APR is found by setting up the following proportion.

$$\frac{1.00 - APR/12}{1.00 - 1.25} = \frac{0.0110 - 0.0112}{0.0110 - 0.0132}$$

and solving for APR,

$$APR = 12.27\%$$

4 Compute the simple-interest equivalent of a monthly payment with the compound-interest equation or Appendix A.

Example of compound-interest equation:

$$
\begin{aligned}
R &= (1 + i/M)^M - 1 \\
&= (1 + 0.1227/12)^{12} - 1 \\
&= 12.98\%
\end{aligned}
$$

Thus, a 12 percent, 20-year mortgage with 2 points yields 13.12 percent to maturity. Furthermore, the yield will be much greater if the loan is repaid in the first few years.

COMPENSATING BALANCES

Compensating balances have been a requirement since interest on demand deposits was outlawed in the early 1930s. Despite articles and speeches decrying the practice as unprofitable, compensating balances are an entrenched part of bank relationships. Compensating balances are demand deposits (non-interest-bearing) maintained at the lending bank in excess of balances needed for transactions or other needs. In effect the customer is keeping some of his or her loan on deposit at the bank. As Nadler quips, "In no other industry is the customer sold something and then told he must leave in the store 15% or 20% of what he bought in order to augment the seller's remaining inventory."[3]

---

[3] Nadler (1972), p. 113.

Customers who have to borrow from the bank to meet their compensating balance requirement would be as well off with a $100,000 loan at 12 percent with no requirement as they would be with a $125,000 loan at 10 percent with a $25,000 compensating balance. Either way the customer pays annual interest of $12,000 ($100,000 times 12 percent or $125,000 times 10 percent).

In general the interest coupon is equal to the interest times the amount borrowed and applied to both the borrower's needs and compensating balances. Note that compensating balances change the interest cost only when borrowers increase their intended loans to obtain required deposits. If a borrower normally maintains deposit balances satisfactory to the lending bank, then balances will not be increased after the loan is made.[4] Consequently interest cost and rate are based solely on the amount of funds needed by the borrower, when the borrower maintains balances adequate for the amount borrowed.

The effect compensating balances have on yield can be seen by modifying the 1-year-bond equation. Interest cost is computed as:

$$C = i(P_0 + CB) \tag{5-4}$$

where CB refers to the compensating balance (amount) and P_0 is the amount needed by the borrower—who borrows and repays $P_0 + CB$. By substitution we find the yield on a single-payment, 1-year loan to be:

$$R = i\frac{P_0 + CB}{P_0} \tag{5-5}$$

Example of Compensating Balances

Consider the example in which the bank offers a $100,000 1-year loan at 11 percent without a compensating balance, or a $125,000 loan at 10 percent with a $25,000 compensating balance. The yield on the $100,000 loan is equal to the simple-interest rate of 11 percent. What is the yield on the compensating balance alternative? We substitute values for i, P_0, and CB into Eq. (5-5). The interest rate (i) is 10 percent (0.10), the principal amount borrowed and used (P_0) is $100,000, and the compensating balance (CB) is $25,000. By substitution we can find the yield (R):

$$R = 0.10\left(\frac{100,000 + 25,000}{100,000}\right)$$
$$= 0.125 = 12.50\% \text{ (rounded to nearest basis point)}$$

---

[4] Careful cash managers maintain their demand deposit accounts at the minimum possible level at which the business can be operated efficiently. Whether or not normal cash balances are considered adequate by the lending bank depends upon the individual bank's costs and policies.

INSTALLMENT LOANS

Financial institutions determine interest charges on installment loans in a number of different ways. The method of computing interest charges makes a substantial difference in the yield. Consequently, understanding installment loan interest computations is very important.

Interest on Unpaid Balance

Interest charges may be calculated on the balance owed and unpaid. For example, we may charge credit card holders 18 percent on unpaid balances. If a customer owes \$300 for 30 days, then we charge him or her \$4.44 (i.e., 0.18 times $\frac{30}{365}$ times \$300). We are charging simple-interest rates and collecting the interest monthly on the actual amount lent. Therefore, the yield ($R = 19.56$ percent) is the compound equivalent of the interest rate i (18.00 percent).

Interest on Original Balance

The total amount of interest charged may be based on the original balance, although the loan balance is reduced by regular payments. This is termed "add-on interest." For instance, if we borrow \$1000 for 1 year at 7.5 percent and agree to make equal monthly payments of interest and principal, then the interest charge will be \$75 and the monthly payment will be \$89.58. (The monthly payment is equal to \$1075.00/12.)

In general the monthly payments (PAY) are computed as follows:

$$PAY = \frac{P_N + P_N(i)(N)}{n} \tag{5-6}$$

where

$$i = \text{add-on rate} \tag{5-7}$$
$$n = (N)(M)$$

The monthly payment reduces the principal balance each month, because only a portion of the \$89.58 is needed to pay interest.

Figure 5-1 illustrates the differences between the actual balance owed and the assumed balance for interest computation. The loan begins with a balance of \$1000 at P_0. At the end of the sixth period, about one-half of the loan has been repaid and the principal balance stands at P_6. However, interest is computed on the basis of the original loan principal of \$1000. In effect interest is charged for principal the borrower has repaid. Principal continues to decline over the life of the installment loan, although the interest charge is constant and calculated on the basis of the starting loan balance.

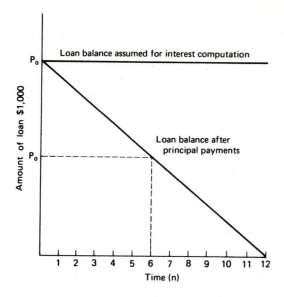

FIGURE 5-1
Illustration of loan balances used in computing yield on installment loans.

The nominal annual percentage rate of an installment loan can be computed using the monthly payment information. The nominal annual rate is equivalent to a simple-interest rate, except for compounding effects. The monthly payment on an installment loan is mathematically equivalent to a monthly payment on a mortgage loan. Therefore, we can apply the monthly loan equation equally well for consumer installment as for mortgage loan computations. Equation (4-9) from Chapter 4 is:

$$\text{Payment} = P_0 \frac{i'}{1 - (1 + i')^{-n}}$$

where i' is the annual percentage rate.

We rearrange terms to solve the payment factor, which is payment divided by the beginning principal. Then we find the yield by consulting Appendix B for an n-period loan. By interpolation we can find the yield associated with the factor PAY/P_0 for an n-period loan, as was done for a mortgage loan with points. Alternatively, some calculators and computers perform this computation.

Example of Installment Loan

How is yield represented and computed for our example? We substitute the example values for P_0, n, M, and i into the equation to obtain the following:

$$\text{Payment}/P_0 = 89.58/1000$$
$$= 0.0896$$

What rate would produce a *PAY* factor of 0.0896 for a 12-month loan? In Appendix B we find the following:

Interest rate (percent)	Payment factor (A/P)
1.00	0.0888
i'/M	0.0896
1.25	0.0903

By interpolation, as in the mortgage loan example, we find the adjusted rate *i'* equal to 13.56 percent. (*Note*: Some calculators make the previous calculations directly.) This completes step 1, and we are ready for step 2.

To find the effective yield from a 13.56 percent adjusted rate (from monthly payment example), compound the nominal rate 12 times. Equation (4-11) is used:[5]

$$R = (1 + i'/M)^M - 1$$
$$R = (1 + .1356/12)^{12} - 1$$
$$= 0.1444 = 14.44\%$$

Thus the yield for a 7.5 percent, 1-year, add-on installment loan is 14.44 percent.

Installment Yields: Rules of Thumb

A common rule of thumb for estimating installment loan annual rates is to multiply the stated rate by 2 and subtract 1. This handy rule is reasonably accurate, as may be illustrated with our example. The rule-of-thumb rate is 14 percent [(7.5 × 2) − 1], only 0.44 percent different from the exact yield computed previously.

PRETAX EQUIVALENT YIELDS

State and local government securities are often exempt from federal taxation, and sometimes exempt from state and local taxes as well. The differential tax treatment afforded tax-exempt securities is of great importance to institutions and individuals in high income-tax brackets. Life insurance companies, which pay only a limited amount of tax, are able to take only partial advantage of tax-exempt securities. Commercial banks, however, which are subject to income taxes in excess of 50 percent, may gain a great advantage with the judicious use of tax-exempts.

---

[5] Alternatively we could find the compound yield equivalent in Appendix A by interpolating between 13 and 14 percent.

Yields on taxable and tax-exempt securities cannot be compared directly but should be compared on a *pretax* basis. Taxable security yields are quoted on a pretax basis, because we will pay taxes on the interest yielded on the security. However, tax-exempt securities are quoted on an after-tax basis, as income from tax-exempt securities is not included in taxable income. The tax equivalent yield on tax-exempt securities is designated i' and is given by the following equation:

$$i' = \frac{i}{1 - tax} \tag{5-8}$$

where i is the annual rate quoted on tax-exempt securities and *tax* is our marginal income tax rate. That is, the tax equivalent rate is equal to the tax-exempt rate divided by 1 minus the marginal income tax rate.

Example of Pretax Equivalent Yields

What would the tax equivalent yield be for a 6 percent municipal bond which is not subject to income taxes, when our marginal income tax rate is 40 percent? We can find the annual percentage rate (i') by substituting 40 percent for the tax rate (tax) and 6 percent for the interest rate (i):

$$i' = \frac{0.06}{1 - 0.40} = 10.00\%$$

This example points up the substantial advantage that tax-exempt municipal securities often enjoy over taxable securities for investors in high income-tax brackets.

TRANSACTION COSTS

Transaction costs are the expenses associated with buying and selling securities and investments. Moving our money into investments, receiving money from customers, repaying our debts, and making other transactions are all very costly. Institutional managers recognize that the net return earned on an investment depends on both the gross pretax yield and the cost of buying and holding that investment. Often the important yield to compute for decision-making purposes is not the gross yield but the net yield after transaction cost. Bankers are faced with deciding between a U.S. Treasury bill yielding 10.00 percent and a prime commercial loan yielding 12.00 percent. Insurance company money managers are comparing U.S. Treasury bills with a shopping center investment expected to yield 11.00 percent. The transaction costs for U.S. Treasury bills is very low, while the transaction cost for direct loans is relatively high. Which investment produces the greatest yield net of transaction cost?

Example of Transaction Costs

Consider a savings and loan that receives a 12 percent gross yield on a mortgage to a home buyer. The marginal cost of bookkeeping, managing, and collecting payments is about 1.4 percent of the principal amount. The government taxes the savings and loan association about 0.6 percent of the principal amount. The rest of the revenue represents the net return on the mortgage investment. The computation is made as follows[6]:

Gross yield on mortgage		12%
Less:		
Loan administration expense	1.4%	
Income taxes	0.6%	2%
Net yield on mortgage		10%

The savings and loan would compare the mortgage net yield (10 percent) with alternative investment net yields, as part of its security evaluation and decision process.

SUMMARY

The chapter covered the major lending instruments and provided the methodology for finding yields on many instruments now in existence and others yet to be created. The basic-yield equation gave us a formula for finding the simple-interest equivalent for discounted notes, mortgage loans with points, installment loans with add-on interest, and commercial bank loans requiring compensating balances. In addition, the effect of exemption from income taxes and transaction costs was shown to be very significant to some institutions. Many other types of securities could have been analyzed in the same way, although space prohibited the inclusion of more examples.

TERMS

discounted bond or note   add-on interest
mortgage points   installment loan
prepaid loans   pretax equivalent yield
compensating balances   transaction cost

---

[6] Figures are based on the expenses of an individual savings and loan and may not be representative for other savings and loan institutions.

LIST OF SELECTED EQUATIONS

Discounted note:

$$P_0 = P_1 - (i/M)(P_1)$$

$$i' = \frac{i}{1 - i/M}$$

$$R = (1 + i'/M)^M - 1$$

Mortgage points:

$$P_0 = P_N (1 - POINTS/100)$$

Compensating balances:

$$C = i(P_0 + CB)$$

$$R = i\frac{(P_0 + CB)}{P_0}$$

Monthly payments on installment loans:

$$PAY = \frac{P_0 + P_0(i)(N)}{n}$$

$$\text{Payment} = P_0 \frac{R}{1 - (1 + R)^{-n}}$$

Tax-exempt securities equivalent yield:

$$i' = \frac{i}{1 - tax}$$

QUESTIONS

1 Suppose that you wish to borrow $47,500 for 6 months and it is the bank's policy to deduct interest in advance at a rate of 10 percent. What must the face value of the note be to yield proceeds of $47,500?

2 What is the effective yield in Question 1?

3 A mortgage is granted which calls for repayment of $80,000 at 7 percent in monthly installments over 30 years. The mortgage institution retains three "points" on new mortgages issued. What is the yield on this mortgage, assuming it is held to maturity?

4 To obtain $100,000 of needed financing, a borrower is required by the bank to maintain a minimum $25,000 in a demand deposit with the bank. To satisfy this requirement, the borrower obtains a $125,000 loan at 8 percent. Calculate the yield on the loan and briefly explain why compensating balance requirements increase yield rates.

5 The Second National Bank finances the purchase of a $6000 automobile over 3 years, with add-on interest of 7 percent. Compute the monthly payment and the effective yield on the auto loan.

6 Using the "rule-of-thumb" method, compute the yield on the installment loan described in Question 5.

7 You have alternative investment opportunities involving a choice between a municipal bond yielding 5.8 percent and a bank certificate yielding 7 percent. Assuming you

are in a 40 percent marginal tax bracket, which of the securities offers the highest tax equivalent yield?

8 An insurance company is considering investment in an industrial mortgage with a 9 percent gross yield. The administrative expense of managing the investment is estimated to be 15 percent of gross yield, and income tax on earnings averages 8 percent of gross yield. What is the net yield that may be expected on the mortgage?

SELECTED REFERENCES

Makliel, Burton G.: *The Structure of Interest Rates: Theory, Empirical Evidence, and Applications*, McCaleb-Sieler Publishing Company, New York, 1970.

Nadler, Paul S.: "Compensating Balances and the Prime at Twilight," *Harvard Business Review*, January–February 1972, pp. 112–120.

Van Horne, James C.: *Function and Analysis of Capital Market Rates*, Prentice-Hall, Englewood Cliffs, N.J., 1970.

Weil, Roman L.: "Realized Interest Rates and Bondholders' Returns," *American Economic Review*, June 1970, pp. 502–511.

CHAPTER 6

INTEREST-RATE STRUCTURE

Interest-rate structure refers to differences in yields that arise as a result of different characteristics of loans and securities. Characteristics discussed here are (1) term, (2) default, and (3) taxation.

TERM STRUCTURE

Term structure is the relationship between the yield to maturity and the time to maturity of bonds, loans, and other debt securities. Term is the number of periods, such as days, weeks, and years, until the security matures and the borrower repays all the principal and interest owed. In this chapter the concepts and theories of term structure are discussed. The theoretical foundation laid here is essential for understanding profit and risk management techniques developed in later chapters.

The ideas and equations presented in this chapter are a basis for interest-rate, profit, and risk-control policies of many types of financial intermediaries. The uses of term-structure concepts vary greatly, depending on the needs of the investors and institutions, but we may generalize by saying that nearly everyone participating in the money or capital markets encounters term-structure decisions in managing money.

Overview of Term-Structure Problem

The underlying problem of the term-structure decision is, "Should we buy a long-term bond and receive a known return for a long period of time, or should we buy a short-term bond now and receive an unknown return on future short-term investments?'' ''Is the 7 percent 5-year loan better than the 8 percent 10-year loan?'' Also, decisions must be made when borrowing money: ''Which is a lower cost source of $5 million: certificates of deposit for 1-year at 5 percent or for 3 years at 6 percent?''

We know what rates are quoted today, but we are uncertain what rates will exist when we reinvest or refinance. Thus, we are unsure whether we should use short-term securities now and go back to the market later or simply commit to long-term investments now. Depending on future interest-rate conditions, either alternative may produce the greater profit. As is shown later, the profit or loss from right and wrong decisions is substantial; the profit from trading gains and losses may easily exceed the profits from normal operations.

YIELD-CURVE CONSTRUCTION

The yield curve is a chart depicting the relationship between bond yield and time to maturity. The horizontal axis is the length of time to maturity, and the vertical scale depicts yields. Bonds of similar characteristics are plotted on the graph point by point according to maturity and yield. Then a smooth curve is fitted statistically or by hand so as to highlight the general shape of the term structure.

Example of Yield-Curve Construction

Using yields based on U.S. Treasury bonds quoted in *The Wall Street Journal*, we may illustrate the construction of a yield curve. *The Wall Street Journal* prints dealer quotations daily, and by plotting these quotations, a graph, such as that shown in Figure 6-1, can be constructed. The curve shown in Figure 6-1 is a freehand fit to the points and presents the general term structure of rates as of the date for Treasury bonds. Issues with different tax, default, or other features present a somewhat different yield curve.[1]

Yield-Curve History

Yield curves usually approximate one of four shapes; ascending, descending, flat, or humped. The four characteristic yield-curve shapes are depicted in Figure 6-2. Also, periods during which the characteristic yield curve were observed are noted next to each curve in Figure 6-2. We note that short-term yields are far more volatile than long-term yields. Restrictive credit conditions usually cause short-term rates to rise considerably more than long-term rates, with short-term yields falling more precipitously in subsequent easy credit

---

[1] The additional bonds fill in maturity gaps and provide a better basis for drawing the ''term structure curve.'' Care was taken to avoid plotting issues with very high coupons or very low coupons because the difference between capital gains and regular income tax rates might affect their yields. For example, ''flower bonds'' issued to the U.S. Treasury have a low yield because they can be used at par value (now below market value) to pay federal estate taxes.

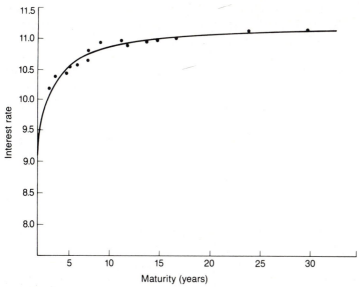

FIGURE 6-1
Yield curve.

times. That is to say, short-term interest rates are more volatile than long-term interest rates.

Example of Yield-Curve History

The yield curve drawn in Figure 6-1 displays a smooth form and may fit one of the four descriptions of yield curves. Is the curve in Figure 6-1 ascending, descending, flat, or humped? Obviously the curve is ascending, as rates increase continually. Other term structures can be identified similarly by drawing yield curves at different times. Again, note that yield curves depict interest rates at one point in time, not over time. The following sections, which analyze yield curves, explain why yields vary with respect to maturity at a given point in time.

TERM-STRUCTURE THEORIES

We have seen that yield curves have taken on various forms during the past half-century. What is the relationship between short- and long-term yields? What is the relationship between present yields, expected future yields, and actual future yields? Theorists have postulated and tested many concepts of term-structure relationships to answer these questions. In this section we consider the major theories which have been advanced to explain the term structure of interest rates.

Panel a.

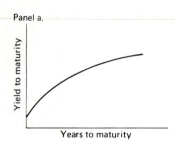

Ascending Curve:
  Interest rates are lowest for short
    term issues and increase monotonically
    at a diminishing rate as the maturity
    increases.
  Observed from 1930 until about 1965
    and again in the early 1970s and 1980s.
  Characteristic curve during periods of
    relatively easy credit and low short-term
    interest rates.

Panel b.

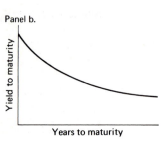

Descending Curve:
  Yields are highest for short-term
    issues and decrease monotonically
    at a diminishing rate with increases
    in maturity.
  Observed for high-grade corporate
    bonds from 1906 to 1929, but not
    again until the late 1960s and 1970s.
  Characteristic curve during periods of
    relatively high short-term interest
    rates and tight credit.

Panel c.

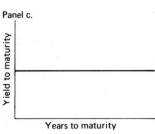

Flat Curve:
  Short- and long-term yields are
    approximately equal.
  Observed for short periods of time
    since 1901.
  Curve found during transition from
    low interest rates to high rates,
    or vice versa.

Panel d.

Humped Curve:
  Yields rise to a peak during the
    first few years to maturity, then
    decline thereafter.
  Observed for U.S. Treasury securities
    in 1957, 1959, 1960, 1966–1970 for
    short periods of time.
  Most frequently occurs when interest
    rates are high and credit is becoming
    increasingly tight.

FIGURE 6-2
Characteristic yield curves.

Economists hypothesize three causes for differing term structures. The *expectations theory* argues that investors select short-term or long-term bonds so as to maximize expected returns over a given investment horizon, on the basis of their predictions for future short-term bond interest rates. The *liquidity-preference theory* asserts that short-term bonds are less risky and, therefore, modifies the expectation theory by adding a premium to long-term issues.

The *segmented-markets theory* segments the market by maturity and argues that yields for each maturity are determined by relatively independent supply and demand forces.

Expectations Theory

The yield-curve shape, according to the expectations theory, is a function of investor predictions of future yields. Consider the simple case of having three bonds with maturities of 1, 2, and 3 years and yields of 5, 6, and 7 percent, respectively. If an investor plans to own bonds for 3 years, which one will result in the greatest return? A 1-year bond offers the lowest rate but affords the opportunity of reinvesting the higher yielding 1- or 2-year bonds at the end of the first year. The 2-year bond offers a higher yield, but the possibility of reinvesting in possibly higher yielding 1-year bonds is deferred for 2 years. Which bond is the better choice? The answer depends upon the *expected yields* of 1-year bonds next year and the year after. The validity of the expectations theory depends on investors who think and act on the basis of expected future interest rates.

A survey of major institutional investors in the United States revealed that professional security analysts do hold interest rate expectations.[2] At the time of the 1966 survey, investors believed that bond yields were unusually high (yields were at historic highs) and that future rates were likely to be lower. Further support for believing that professional investors have expectations is implied by bond price and yield behavior, explained in the next section.

The actual 2-year-bond yield, in the example, is compared with the present 1-year yield and the expected 1-year yield next year:

$$(1 + {}_tR_2)(1 + {}_tR_2) \lesseqgtr (1 + {}_tR_1)(1 + {}_{t+1}r_1) \qquad (6\text{-}1)$$

The left-hand terms are identical and may be rewritten as a square:

$$(1 + {}_tR_2)^2 \lesseqgtr (1 + {}_tR_1)(1 + {}_{t+1}r_1) \qquad (6\text{-}2)$$

where R denotes *actual* (market) yields to maturity, and r stands for future yields *expected* by investors. The postsubscript is the bond's maturity. The presubscript is the time (date) of the yield (t is always the present time). The ${}_tR_2$ refers to the actual yield (R) at the present time (t) for a 2-year maturity (postscript 2) bond. Reference to an investor's expectation for 1-year maturity (1) bond yields 1 year from now ($t + 1$) is given as ${}_{t+1}r_1$.

Other information presented for this example can be denoted as ${}_tR_1 = 5$ percent, ${}_tR_2 = 6$ percent, ${}_tR_3 = 7$ percent, ${}_{t+1}r_1 = 7$ percent, ${}_{t+2}r_1 = 9$ percent. Check your understanding of the notation by identifying the algebraic relationships presented in this paragraph with the earlier description of the problem.

---

[2] Kane and Malkiel (1967).

Using the figures from the example, $(1 + 0.06)^2 = (1 + 0.05)(1 + 0.07)$, so that the investor expects a terminal wealth 112.4 percent under either investment strategy. The investor would be indifferent with regard to long-term and short-term bond alternatives in this example. Other situations exist where the investor will clearly prefer short-term or long-term bonds.

In general actual long-term yields can be expressed as a series of shorter term yields. An N-year bond is equated with 1-year bonds as:

$$(1 + {}_tR_N)^N \lessgtr (1 + {}_tR_1)(1 + {}_{t+1}) \cdots (1 + {}_{t+N-1}r_1) \qquad (6\text{-}3)$$

Clearly any yield-curve shape can be explained by the expectations hypothesis. A descending curve stems from the belief that future short-term rates will be less than current short-term rates. An ascending curve results from investor forecasts of higher short-term rates. Even the humped yield curve can be explained: rates are expected to rise in the near term before they decline in the distant future.

Liquidity-Preference Theory

A variant of the expectations theory, the liquidity-preference theory argues that long-term bonds should yield more than shorter term bonds. Investors desire liquidity, quick convertibility into cash with only a small loss of principal. Therefore, investors demand a premium yield for longer term securities. Security issuers are willing to pay a premium to avoid frequent refundings, which are costly and risky. Refunding requires the replacement of an old debt issue through the sale of a new issue. By issuing long-term securities, borrowers avoid the transactions costs each time a short-term security matures and is refinanced.

Thus, the actual yield curve is composed of expected future short-term rates and liquidity premiums for longer term commitments. Liquidity premiums are algebraically expressed by adding the term L to expected short-term yields (r) in the basic expectations equation. The liquidity-preference equation is as follows:

$$(1 + {}_tR_N)^N = (1 + {}_tR_1)(1 + {}_{t+1}r_1 + L_2) \cdots (1 + {}_{t+N-1}r_1 + L_n) \quad (6\text{-}4)$$

Liquidity-Premium Example

For example, if $L_2 = 2$ percent and $L_3 = 4$ percent, then the expected short-term rates (${}_{t+1}r_1$ and ${}_{t+2}r_1$) must be less than previously stated for actual short- and long-term rates to be in equilibrium. With a liquidity premium, the 3-year bond example becomes:

$$(1 + 0.07)^3 = (1 + 0.05)(1 + 0.05 + 0.02)(1 + 0.05 + 0.04)$$

Short-term rates are expected to remain constant and the yield curve is flat, except for the liquidity premium.

Segmented-Markets Theory (Institutionalists)

The strongest criticism of the expectations and liquidity-preference theories comes from institutional investors contending that short-, intermediate-, and long-term bond markets are segmented. The institutionalists assert that independent supply and demand forces operate along the maturity axis, with the yield at each maturity clearing the specialized market of institutions and individuals preferring securities of that maturity. Commercial banks, according to segmentation advocates, seek highly liquid investments for temporary deposit inflows, while life insurance companies demand long-term bonds to meet annuity and life insurance reserve commitments. Life insurance companies make long-term yield commitments, which they hedge with the purchase of long-term bonds. Moreover, there are pension plans and individual savers who find price fluctuations an inconsequential risk compared with the possibility of lower than anticipated yields. Many more significant money-market participants could be named, each having strong maturity preferences that induce them to purchase bonds in a narrow maturity band. Institutionalists contend that substitutability among maturities is severely impeded by the preferred habitats of participants, and yields along the maturity spectrum are set independently of future expected rates and bond yields at other maturity points.

YIELD-CURVE ANALYSIS

Arbitrage

Arbitrage is buying and selling a security simulatneously to earn a profit from the difference between the bid and asked price. One benefit the yield curve may be to investors is to identify particular issues that carry a higher or lower than usual yield. Those particular issues which are off the yield curve become visible once the yields are plotted and a curve fitted. Issues below the curve are overpriced and should be sold short. If the bond is plotted well above the curve, it may be regarded as underpriced and a good purchase candidate. A small security segment may be underpriced when a large new issue is being marketed, for example, and close attention to the yield curve could be useful in detecting such temporary anomalies.[3]

Speculation

Whereas arbitrage transactions embody little risk because purchases are covered by sales, and vice versa, speculation may be highly risky. Speculation in the bond market requires the investor to take a position, either a short position or a net long position.[4] Successful speculation occurs when we forecast future

---

[3] Arbitrage opportunities, although often present, are difficult to recognize in practice and require great agility to exploit. Bond-house traders monitor market prices closely and, of course, seek to make short-run profits through arbitrage trading.

[4] A short position occurs when the trader has sold borrowed securities which the trader promises to return on or before some future date. A long position is simply buying and holding bonds.

actual yields more accurately than the market in general. The nature of term-structure speculation and risk is discussed in terms of forward positions, forward rates, and expected rates.

Market Expectations

Expected future yields are implied by and can be calculated from existing market interest-rate structures. We assume here the market yields referred to so far are all "spot" yields or actual yields for a specific period of time *ex post facto*. On the other hand, expected yields are security returns predicted for future points in time.

In general, the market's expected 1-year yield is computed for a future period $(t + N - 1)$ using *ex post* rate quotations in the following equation:

$$_{t+N-1}F_1 = \frac{(1 + {}_tR_N)^N}{(1 + {}_tR_{N-1})^{N-1}} - L_N - 1 \qquad (6-5)$$

Roughly translated into words, Eq. (6-5) says that the market expected future yield is equal to the ratio of yields for period N and period $N - 1$ less the liquidity premium; the value "1" may be thought of as principal first invested (included in the yield ratio) and then repaid (subtracted at the end of the equation). If we know the spot yields for bonds maturing at the beginning and end of a future period and the liquidity premium, then this formulation allows us to compute the market expected yields for 1-year bonds for the future period.

Forward-Yields Example

Take the example of a 1-year maturity bond bearing an interest rate $({}_tR_1)$ of 6 percent and a 2-year maturity bond that yields $({}_tR_2)$ 6½ percent. Assume the liquidity premium is 1 percent (1 percent $\equiv 0.01$). The market expected $({}_{t+1}F_1)$ yield is:

$$_{t+1}F_1 = \frac{(1 + {}_tR_2)^2}{(1 + {}_tR_1)} - L_N - 1$$

$$= \frac{(1.065)^2}{1.06} - 1.01$$

$$= 6.00\%$$

Thus, the market expects 1-year bonds to yield about 6 percent again next year.

Forward Positions

To profit from our expectations (correct, of course!) about future interest rates, we must take forward positions in securities. The term "position" refers to an ownership or other contractual commitment in a security. Purchasing a security creates a *long* position. When we buy a $1000 bond, we establish a long position. If the bond has a term to maturity of 10 years, then we have a 10-year long position. We may also reverse our field and establish a *short* position.

A short sale of securities occurs when the seller borrows the securities that he or she sells; he or she later repurchases the borrowed securities and returns them to the original owner. For example, we can "short" $1 million of U.S. Treasury bonds by borrowing them (through a broker) and selling them: we will later repay our loan by repurchasing an equal number of bonds at whatever price may prevail in the market. We profit when prices fall and suffer losses when prices rise.

We need forward positions to profit from expectations about future interest rates. How can we establish *long or short positions* in the future? One way to establish a forward position is simultaneously to buy and sell bonds of different maturities.

Example of Forward Positions

For example, we may purchase a 2-year bond and simultaneously sell a 1-year bond short to obtain a long position in a 1-year maturity bond 1 year hence. To the extent that securities of different maturities are available in the market, financial institutions may establish long and short positions for any future period. Of course, we want to establish positions that we believe to be profitable. We combine our ideas about forward yields and positions to decide when and how to speculate.

Forward Yields and Positions

Consider now comparing the market expected yield ($_{t+N-1}F_1$) and *our* expectations for the same future period ($_{t+N-1}r_1$). If the forward and expected yield are the same, then we agree with the market rate. However, we may believe that the market expected yield is too low and that rates will increase to the level we expect. When the rates do increase, the security price will decline.

Profit from falling security prices is made by establishing a forward short position. In a *short sale*, we sell the bond now and buy it back later at a lower price, because the price will fall as yields rise. On the other hand, we might believe that the market expected yields are too high. We believe that in the future yields will be much lower than expected by the market. In this third case, we would want to be the proud owner of bonds, because bond prices rise as bond yields decline. When we believe that market expected yields are too high, we establish a forward long position to own the bond as it rises in price and declines in yield to maturity. A summary of the three cases is given in Table 6-1.

Futures Contracts

Futures contracts are transacted on the Chicago Board of Trade (CBT), and prices are quoted in financial papers (see Table 6-2). Government National

TABLE 6-1
SUMMARY OF THREE POSSIBLE FORWARD-RATE COMPARISONS
AND FORWARD POSITIONS

Case 1

$$_{t+N-1}F_1 = {}_{t+N-1}r_1$$

We are indifferent between a one-period loan now and a forward loan,
Action: None

Case 2

$$_{t+N-1}F_1 < {}_{t+N-1}r_1$$

We should issue *N*-period loans, because the market expects the future yield to be less than that expected by us. Security prices will fall, if our expectations are confirmed, and we will be able to redeem our loan at a lower price.
Action: Sell *N* maturity bond short and purchase *N* − 1 maturity bond.

Case 3

$$_{t+N-1}F_1 > {}_{t+N-1}r_1$$

Market expected rate is greater than our expectations. We should make one-period-forward loans.
Action: Sell *N* − 1 bonds short and buy N period bonds.

Mortgage Association (GNMA) certificates, representing marketable shares in pools of Federal Housing Administration and Veterans Administration mortgage loans, are traded in units of $100,000 principal. Each unit of $100,000 is traded on the basis of an 8 percent interest rate and a 12-year maturity. On the floor of the CBT, traders buy and sell units of the GNMA futures contracts,

TABLE 6-2
GNMA FUTURES PRICES AND YIELDS,
DECEMBER 1, 19X1

	Price	Yield
December 19X1	66–17	13.951
March	66–02	14.065
June	65–20	14.172
September	65–09	14.257
December 19X2	65–00	14.326
March	64–24	14.389
June	64–17	14.444
September	64–11	14.491
December 19X3	64–06	14.531
March	64–02	14.563
June	63–31	14.587

Note: GNMA 8 percent (CBT) − $100,000
principal; points are thirty-seconds of 100 percent.

bidding and offering to buy or sell units with various expiration dates up to 12 years in the future. Traders are guaranteed contract payment and delivery by the CBT, because all contracts are made directly with the CBT. Of course, few actual deliveries are expected. Most buyers "close" by selling an identical contract, and most sellers "close" by buying the same contract prior to the expiration date. Each transaction carries with it a commission charge, but transactions costs are small relative to the amount of the contract.

Rate-of-Return Example

The return from GNMA certificates held from December to June can be computed from information in our previous example. Assume that instead of selling short we are purchasing an 8 percent certificate on December 1, 19X1, and agree to sell it the following June. The December purchase price is $66^{17}/_{32}$, and the June sales price (guaranteed by the futures contract) is $65^{20}/_{32}$. (See Table 6-2.) During the 6-month period, we receive interest of 4.00 percent. The return earned is computed by substituting into Eq. (4-4), as shown here:

$$R = \left(\frac{C + P_1}{P_0}\right)^M - 1$$

$$= \left(\frac{4.00 + 65.63}{66.53}\right)^2 - 1$$

$$= 9.54\%$$

The return (R) is equal to the interest coupon earned (C) plus the selling price (P_1) less the purchase price (P_0), all divided by the purchase price; then the holding period return is compounded M times per year. The (annual) yield is equal to 9.54 percent, based on the receipt of interest of 4 percent semiannually and on a loss of 1.35 percent in price during each 6-month period. Note that the 6-month rate is compounded twice to compute the annual yield.

Three Forward-Yield Cases

What forward position should we take when 1-year bonds are yielding 9.00 percent and 2-year bonds are yielding 10.50 percent? We see that the yield curve is ascending and conclude that the market expects short-term yields to rise. We agree with the market's implication that "rates will be higher next year," and forecast 1-year rates to be about 13 percent at this time next year. Is there an opportunity to profit from our analysis?

To decide what the best forward position would be, we compare our expectation of a 13 percent 1-year yield with the 1-year forward yield $(_{t+1}F_1)$ using Eq. (6-5), recognizing that R_1 equals 9.00 percent and $_rR_2$ equals 10.50 percent.

$$_{t+2-1}F = \frac{(1 + _rR_2)^2}{1 + _rR_1} - L_N - 1$$

$$= \frac{(1 + 0.1050)^2}{1 + 0.09} - 0.01 - 1$$

$$= \frac{1.2210}{1.0900} - 1.01$$

$$= 11.02\%$$

The forward yield for 1-year bonds for a time 1 year from now ($_{t+1}F_1$) is 11.02 percent. Next, we compare our expectations about next year's 1-year rates with the forward yield.

Our forward-yield computation shows that the market believes that 1-year yield will be higher next year, just as we believe that 1-year yield will rise. However, we cannot stop here and conclude that we are indifferent between 1- and 2-year bonds. The extent of the expected increase may be viewed differently by the market and ourselves. Suppose that we believe that 1-year rates will increase to 13.00 percent next year, a larger increase than that expected by the market. We can express the relationship as case 2, Table 6-1:

$$_{t+1}F_1 = 11.02 < {_1}r_1 = 13.00$$

What position should we take now to profit from our expectation that interest rates will increase more than that implied by the market? The higher yield will mean that 1-year bonds will sell for lower than expected prices. We can profit by buying 1-year bonds next year, if we sell the equivalent bond now. We want to sell the bond that will be a 1-year bond next year. What bond will be a 1-year bond, after 1 year? Obviously, a 2-year bond will become a 1-year bond next year. Therefore, we sell a 2-year bond, which we borrow from someone else. In market parlance, we take a short position in 2-year bonds. The proceeds from the short sale are used to purchase a bond maturing 1 year hence, thus neutralizing our position during the first year. The proceeds from the maturing 1-year bond are used to repurchase a bond to cover the short position.

On the other hand, suppose that we expect rates to fall dramatically to 8.00 percent. Prices of 1-year bonds will be much higher than expected, in our opinion. This is a case 3 situation. Prices on 1-year bonds are going to go up next year, when the market recognizes what we foresee now. Profits can be earned by buying the 2-year security now, so that we will own a 1-year bond next year. In the meantime, we sell a 1-year bond short, neutralizing our position during the first year. (We have a long position in 2- and a short position in 1-year bonds, so that the positions cancel each other during the first year.) At the end of a year, we sell the 2-year bond at a price higher than the market anticipated. After covering the short position, we take our profit.

What would happen if we forecasted future rates incorrectly and established the wrong position? Obviously, we would suffer losses equal to the profits of those who undertook the correct position. We profit from a case 2 position only when the actual rate is greater than the forward rate and from case 3 only when the actual rate falls below the forward rate. We never know with certainty that we have taken the correct position, until *expected rates* become *actual rates*. Only after the fact can we say with assurance what the best course of action would have been. Therefore, we must regard forward positions as risky investments, except when used as a hedge to reduce risk of an opposite position.

INSTITUTIONAL AND DEFAULT RISK CAUSES OF YIELD DIFFERENCES

Interest rates vary with respect to institutional as well as term characteristics. Important institutional characteristics are:

1 Transactions costs
2 Taxes
3 Default risk
4 Marketability

Because institutional differences remain relatively constant from time to time, interest-rate differentials among debt instruments is a constant part of the yield structure.

For example, consider the yields on four instruments of similar maturity: U.S. government bonds, state and local government bonds, utility bonds, and conventional mortgages. On the same date, the yields were 12.94, 11.39, 14.25, and 15.65 percent for the three bonds, respectively, shown in Table 6-3. The U.S. government bonds are used as a basis for comparing other instruments. The yield differential for state and local government bonds of − 1.55 percent is caused primarily by the income-tax structure; interest received on such bonds is largely exempt from state and federal income taxes. The positive differential on the utility bonds is caused by the relatively greater cost of transacting, the greater risk of default (yes, utilities occasionally fail to make scheduled interest and principal payments), and the smaller market available for individual utility bonds than for the billions of dollars of U.S. government bonds. Finally, the conventional mortgage has all of the disadvantages of the utility bonds plus increased default risk (individual homeowner versus a public utility company)

TABLE 6-3
YIELD DIFFERENTIALS FOR INSTRUMENTS OF SIMILAR
MATURITIES (PERCENTAGE YIELDS TO MATURITY)

Instrument	Yield	Differential
U.S. government bonds	12.94	—
State and local government bonds	11.39	− 1.55
AAA utility bonds (new issue)	14.25	2.86
Conventional mortgages	15.65	4.26

Source: Federal Reserve Bulletin, 69 (September 1983), Board of Governors of the Federal Reserve: A3.

and reduced marketability (one mortgage on a specific property versus a publicly traded security administered by a trustee); therefore, the largest yield differential (4.26 percent) would be expected for conventional mortgages. Although yield differentials vary over time as institutional characteristics change, the overall structure tends to remain the same and explains much of the difference in yields among securities.[5]

SUMMARY

This chapter has concentrated on the term-to-maturity aspect of securities. We have built yield curves and identified four common yield-curve shapes. We have reviewed the theories that have been advanced to explain the shape and level of present yields for differing maturities. Then we proceeded to develop trading rules, based on our expectations of future interest rates. We saw how to compute the forward-market rates implied by today's rates. Then we discovered ways of buying and selling that allow us to establish forward security positions. Combining our analysis of rates and positions provided the means and decision criteria for speculating on interest rates.

Financial institutions may speculate on future spot rates, as traders do, by purchasing securities to acquire a long position and selling their own securities to place themselves in a short position. They do speculate on forward rates, although speculation is usually not a major objective, and sometimes not even a desired action of the institution. However, whenever the marketing strategy of the institution calls for the institution to purchase a security of one maturity and sell a similar security of differing maturity, then the institution is speculating on forward rates. In the next chapter, we investigate ways in which a manager can control the term structure of his or her financial institution.

APPENDIX 6-1: Empirical Evidence on Term Structures of Interest Rates

Expectations Theory

Statistical tests of the expectations theory began with the comparison of actual and the expected rates. Did investors correctly anticipate future interest rates?

Macaulay (1938) and Culbertson (1957) concluded that no relationship existed between expected future rates and actual future rates. Fama (1976) shows in tests of the more recent 1959-to-1974 period that the prediction errors of the naïve model (future yields are forecasted to be equal to current yields) are less than the errors of forward rates. He concludes that the naïve model is a better predictor of future spot rates than the forward rates, although the naïve model simply predicts that interest rates will

---

[5] See Feder and Ross (1982), Ferri and Gaines (1980), and Skelton (May 1983).

remain unchanged. Such studies showed investors to be pathetic rather than prophetic predictors but did not disprove the expectations hypothesis. Only in a world of perfect certainty would *anticipated* and *actual* yields be equal.

Meiselman (1962) developed and tested an *error-learning* model of interest rate expectations. Investors are hypothesized to revise their expectations systematically as they experience forecasting errors; the revised expectations are manifest in term structure changes. By observing forecast errors and consequent shifts in interest rates, the hypothesis is tested empirically. Meiselman formally stated that the expected short-term rates would vary as a function of forecasting error in the last period. His equation was:

$$_{t+n}r_{1,t} - {}_{t+n}r_{1,t-1} = F(_{t}R_1 - {}_{t}r_{1,t-1}) \tag{6-6}$$

where $n = 1, \ldots, N$.

Equation (6-6) can be rewritten as:

$$\Delta_{t+N}r_{1,t} = g(E_t) \tag{6-7}$$

where E_t was the forecasting error defined on the right-hand side of Eq. (6-6). Estimating a linear form of the above equation, Meiselman found that the expected 1-year rates were highly correlated with the forecast error, although the correlation declines rapidly with term to maturity. Short-term forecasts are revised more than long-term forecasts, as near-term rates are more earnestly regarded than those in the remote future. Meiselman is regarded as having lent great support to the expectations theory, and others have followed with similar empirical studies. In general the error-learning concept has been supported in subsequent studies, although some researchers have been unable to replicate the Meiselman work satisfactorily.

Fama (1976) also provides support for the expectations theory by providing evidence that forward rates are consistent with the efficient markets proposition. The efficient markets theory would require that forward rates reflect the information provided by past spot rates. Fama finds that forward rates, adjusted for variations in risk premiums, predict future spot rates about as well as forecasts based on the past spot rates. Furthermore, the market reacts appropriately in setting bill prices and rates to monthly changes in the spot rate.

Although direct evidence supporting it does not exist, implicit support and logical reasoning combined provide strong support for the expectations theory. Variations between forward rates and actual future spot rates seem to be caused more by changes in expectations fostered by new information than by a lack of expectations at the outset. Thus, we can reasonably explain apparent discrepancies and uncover consistent and significant evidence in support of the expectations hypothesis.

Liquidity-Preference Theory

Since the Civil War, the slope of the yield curve has usually been ascending, and short rates have averaged less than long rates. Kessel (1965) reported that short-term government bonds yields averaged less than long-term yields during nine business cycles spanning 40 years. Cagan (1969) obtained similar results from an analysis of short-term U.S. government bonds for the period from 1951 to 1965. These studies indicate that investors have received a liquidity premium on average over long time periods.

Segmented-Markets Theory

Malkiel examined portfolios of institutions, particularly U.S. government holdings, to test the segmentation tenet that certain institutions strictly purchase securities of a given maturity. He concluded that "aggregate statistics on institutional holdings of governments during the decade from 1955 to 1965 revealed no evidence of complete portfolio specialization in narrow maturity ranges."[6] Institutions, such as commercial banks and insurance companies, do substitute among similar maturities. Substitution on the basis of rates is common policy in most institutions, and portfolio managers regard maturity policy as flexible and subject to managerial control. Consequently, the segmented markets theory has not been empirically confirmed and appears to be, at most, a weak force in term-structure determination.

APPENDIX 6-2: Duration

Duration is a time-domain concept that serves as an alternative to the single-term-to-maturity concept. However, duration is considered to be conceptually superior to term to maturity because it reflects the amount and timing of all cash flows rather than simply the maturity cash flow. Whereas term to maturity ignores semiannual interest payments, for example, duration includes and weights them relative to their timing.

Definition of Duration

Duration is an average term measured by the ratio of the sum of the time-weighted present values to the bond's present value itself. The numerator is the sum of the present value of the coupon payments and face value weighted by the respective time elements; the denominator is the sum of the present value of coupon payments and face value. Thus duration is expressed as the following ratio:

$$\text{Duration} = \frac{\text{time weighted present value}}{\text{present value}} \tag{6-6}$$

Present values are computed by discounting future cash flows to the present. Time-weighted present values are present values multiplied by number of time periods from the present to cash receipt period.

Examples of Duration Computation

To illustrate the calculation of duration, consider a 3-year bond with a 10 percent coupon and a $1000 face value. If the market rate of interest is 10 percent, then D is calculated as shown in Table 6-4. The computation follows the following steps:

1 Transform future cash payments (coupons and principal) from bond to their present value equivalents (column 1 times column 3 equals column 4). The purpose of this adjustment is to remove the time value of money (interest) effects, leaving values with a common (present) time period. Unlike cash flows in different time periods, the present values may be added together.

[6] Malkiel (1970), p. 21.

TABLE 6-4
DURATION COMPUTATION FOR BOND EXAMPLE

Item	(1) Cash payment	(2) Time period	(3) Discount factor 10 percent Rate	(4) Present value (1) × (3)	Time-weighted present value (2) × (4)
Coupon	$ 100	1	0.9091	90.91	90.91
Coupon	$ 100	2	0.8264	82.64	165.28
Principal and coupon	$1100	3	0.7513	826.43	2479.29
Total				999.98	2735.48
Duration =	2.74 years				

2 Time weight present values by multiplying each present value by its time period. The purpose of time weighting is to relate the importance of each cash flow, as measured by the present value for that time period, to time. Time-weighted present values may be compared to show the relative importance of each time period on duration. Note that period 3 is relatively more important on a time-weighted basis than on a present-value basis (Table 6-4). This results from the largest cash flow (principal repayment) occurring in the largest time period (3). This result is typical for bonds, because bonds usually repay principal as a lump sum at maturity. Mortgages and other installment-type financial contracts would have much different time-weighted present values.

3 Average the time-weighted present values by dividing total time-weighted present values (column 5) by total present value (column 4). [See Eq. (6-6).] The purpose of averaging is to compute a single time measure of duration for all cash flows. In this example, the duration of 2.74 years is the ratio of the time-weighted present values (2,735.48) and the present values (999.98).

Duration is equally applicable to the evaluation of other financial contracts. For example, consider an insurance contract that collects a single premium at inception and pays benefits over a period of years. Benefit payments are expected to be $330, $484, and $399 in years 1, 2, and 3, respectively. What is the expected duration of this insurance contract?

TABLE 6-5
DURATION COMPUTATION FOR INSURANCE EXAMPLE

Item	(1) Cash payment	(2) Time period	(3) Discount factor 10 percent Rate	(4) Present value (1) × (3)	Time-weighted present value (2) × (4)
Benefit payments	$ 330	1	0.9091	300.00	300.00
Benefit payments	$ 484	2	0.8264	400.00	800.00
Benefit payments	$ 399	3	0.7513	300.00	900.00
Total				1000.00	2000.00
Duration =	2.00 years				

Duration is computed for the insurance example with the same three steps as applied in the bond example. In step 1 insurance benefits are transformed to present values. As shown in Table 6-5 the present values are more nearly equal across all years. In step 2 time weights are introduced, resulting in time-weighted distributions. In step 3 duration is calculated as 2.00 years (2000.00/1000.00).

Next compare the duration in the bond and insurance examples. Both examples are designed with the same maturity and total present values, but the bond duration is longer than the insurance duration. Why is the bond duration longer than the insurance duration? The answer is that the present values from bond flows occur mainly in period 3, whereas present values for insurance benefits are substantial in the early periods (1 and 2) as well as in period 3. Thus the bond and insurance examples illustrate the general statement made earlier that "duration is considered to be conceptually superior to term to maturity because it reflects the amount and timing of all cash flows rather than simply the maturity cash flow."

Bond Price Volatility

Bond price volatility is the change in bond prices caused by a change in market interest rates. (Note that the word "bond" is used in its generic sense; as illustrated in the previous example, bond duration is equally applicable to all financial contracts.) Previously we noted that long-term bonds are more volatile than short-term bonds, given the same change in market interest rates. Similarly, bonds with longer durations have greater price elasticities than those with shorter durations, because the time value of money becomes increasingly important as the time interval until payment increases.

Definition of Volatility   Bond price volatility is a function of duration and interest rates, as shown here:

$$\text{Price change } \% = -D\frac{(_1R_D - {}_0R_D)100}{100 + {}_0R_D} \qquad (6\text{-}7)$$

where:

$$
\begin{aligned}
D &= \text{duration of the bond in years} \\
{}_0R_D &= \text{interest rate now (0) for a } D\text{-year bond} \\
{}_1R_D &= \text{interest rate 1 year from now for a } D\text{-year bond}
\end{aligned}
$$

Thus the change in price is inversely related (minus sign) to duration (D) times the change in interest rates [$(_1R_D - {}_0R_D)$ 100] divided by the interest-rate adjustment ($100 + {}_0R_D$).

Example of Volatility   For example, what is the price volatility of a bond with a 2.74-year duration? Applying Eq. (6-7), we find the price change caused by an increase in interest rates from 10 percent to 11 percent as follows:

$$\text{Price change } \% = -2.74\frac{11.00 - 10.00}{100 + 10}$$

$$= -2.48\%$$

Thus, an increase in market interest rates of 1.00 percent would effect a decrease of 2.48 percent in the price of the bond. For each $1 million in the bond portfolio, a loss of $24,800 (2.48 percent times $1,000,000) occurs when market interest rates increase by 1.00 percent.

For the insurance example in which duration is equal to 2 years, the price volatility is computed as -1.82 percent for a 1.00 percent change in market interest rates. Therefore, an insurance liability present value of $1 million would decrease by $18,200 as market interest rates rise from 10.00 to 11.00 percent. Note that the change in duration to 2.74 from 2.00 years causes price volatility to decrease from $24,800 to $18,200 per $1 million of value. This illustrates the general statement that "bonds with longer durations have greater price elasticities than those with shorter durations."

TERMS

interest-rate structure
term structure of interest rates
yield curve
ascending yield curve
flat yield curve
humped yield curve
expectations theory
liquidity theory
institutional theory
spot rate

forward rate
expected future rate
liquidity premium
segmented-markets theory
arbitrage
speculation
short position
long position
duration (Appendix 6-2)
bond price volatility (Appendix 6-2)

EQUATIONS

$$(1 + {}_tR_N)^N = (1 + {}_tR_1)(1 + {}_{t+1}r_1) \cdots (1 + {}_{t+N-1}r_1)$$
$$(1 + {}_tR_N)^N = (1 + {}_tR_1)(1 + {}_{t+1}r_1 + L_2) \cdots (1 + {}_{t+N-1}r_1 + L_n)$$
$${}_{t+N-1}F_1 = \frac{(1 + {}_tR_N)^N}{(1 + {}_tR_{N-1})^{N-1}} - 1 - L_N$$

QUESTIONS AND PROBLEMS

1 What relationship is expressed by a yield curve?
2 Using a recent issue of *The Wall Street Journal*, construct a yield curve for U.S. Treasury bonds.
3 What type of yield curve would you see if interest rates were expected to be higher during the next 3 years but then decline after that?
4 In what manner does the expectations theory relate short- and long-term rates of interest? Do yield curves relate present and future term structures?
5 Can the relationship between current long-term rates and current short- and expected future short-term rates be expressed algebraically? Write the equation.
6 What is the difference between the expectations theory and the liquidity-preference theory?

7 Why would investors consistently accept a lower return from short-term than from long-term bonds?

8 What market segments are associated with long-term bonds? Short-term bonds?

9 If short-term and long-term bonds are highly substitutable for each other, what is the effect on the segmented-markets theory? What empirical evidence can you cite about substitutability of short- and long-term bonds? (See Appendix 6-1.)

10 In a theoretical sense, does an arbitrager undertake any risk? What practical problems might change your answer to that question?

11 What is the basic difference between arbitrage and speculation?

12 How can we establish a short position in a bond now for period 2 without simultaneously establishing a (short or long) position during period 1? Describe required transactions and illustrate.

13 How are forward rates implied by current spot rates? What is the algebraic relationship?

14 The World has four securities outstanding from the All Powerful Being (who is also riskless). The securities have 1-, 2-, 3-, and 4-year maturities that have a yield of 4 percent, 5 percent, 5 percent, and 4 percent respectively. You estimate that rates will remain at 5 percent after the first year on 1-year maturity securities. You wish to obtain the best yield possible from trading in these securities. What are the optimal short and long positions that should be taken?

15 The U.S. Treasury has decided to issue notes to enhance President Reagan's economic recovery plan. The notes have 1-year, 2-year, 3-year, and 4-year maturities with an annual rate of 9 percent, 10¼ percent, 10 percent, and 10¾ percent, respectively. Interest on these notes is paid semiannually and they have annual yields of 9.56 percent, 10.44 percent, 10.17 percent and 11.02 percent, respectively. As a smart investor trading in these securities, you would like to receive the best yields possible. On the other hand, you have estimated that rates will be 10 percent after the first year on 1-year maturities and 10.50 percent for the following 2 years on 1-year maturities.

Describe the optimal position that you would take on these securities and tell why.

16 For the instruments listed in the following table, construct a yield-differential table, and describe the causes of yield differentials among the instruments.

Instrument	Yield
U.S. government bonds	12.94
State and local government bonds	11.39
AAA utility bonds (new issue)	14.25
Conventional mortgages	15.65

17 Using a recent issue of the *Federal Reserve Bulletin* or other source, list yields for different instruments with similar maturities, construct a yield-differential table, and describe the causes of yield differentials among the securities you list.

18 (Based on Appendix B) Compute the duration for a 3-year bond with a 12 percent coupon and a $1000 face value when the market rate of interest is 9 percent.

19 (Based on Appendix B) What is the price elasticity for a 3-year installment loan with payments of $400 per year when market interest rates are 9 percent?

20 For the instruments listed in the following table, construct a yield-differential table, and describe the causes of yield differentials among the instruments.

Instrument	Yield
U.S. government bonds	12.94
State and local government bonds	11.39
AAA utility bonds (new issue)	14.25
Conventional mortgages	15.65

SELECTED REFERENCES

Buse, A.: "Interest Rates, the Meiselman Model and Random Numbers," *Journal of Political Economy*, February 1967, pp. 49–62.

Cagan, Phillip: "A Study of Liquidity Premiums on Federal and Municipal Government Securities," In Jack M. Guttentag and Phillip Cagan (eds.), *Essays on Interest Rates*, Columbia University Press for the National Bureau of Economic Research, New York, 1969.

Cargill, T. F.: "The Term Structure of Interest Rates: A Test of the Expectations Hypothesis," *Journal of Finance*, June 1975, pp. 761–772.

Carleton, W. T., and I. A. Cooper: "Estimation and Uses of the Term Structure of Interest Rates," *Journal of Finance*, September 1976, pp. 1067–1083.

Cox, John C., Jonathon E. Ingersoll, Jr., and Stephen A. Ross: "A Reexamination of Traditional Hypotheses About the Term Structure of Interest Rates," *The Journal of Finance*, September 1981, pp. 769–799.

Culbertson, John M.: "The Term Structure of Interest Rates," *Quarterly Journal of Economics*, November 1957, pp. 485–517.

Dobson, S. W.: "Estimating Term Structure Equations With Individual Bond Data," *Journal of Finance*, March 1968, pp. 75–92.

Durand, David: *Basic Yields of Corporate Bonds, 1900–1942*, Technical Paper 3, National Bureau of Economic Research, 1942.

Echols, M. E. and J. W. Elliott: "Measuring the Shoulder of the Yield Curve," *Journal of Bank Research*, Winter 1975, pp. 264–268.

Elliott, J. W., and M. E. Echols: "Market Segmentation, Speculative Behavior and the Term Structure of Interest Rates," *Review of Economics and Statistics*, February 1976, pp. 40–49.

Fama, Eugene F.: "Forward Rates as Predictors of Future Spot Rates," *Journal of Financial Economics*, June 1976, pp. 361–377.

Feder, Gershon, and Knud Ross: "Risk Assessments and Risk Premiums in the Eurodollar Market," *Journal of Finance*, June 1982, pp. 679–691.

Ferri, Michael C., and James P. Gaines: "A Study of Yield Spreads in the Money Market: 1971 to 1978," *Financial Management*, Autumn 1980, pp. 52–59.

Fisher, Irving: *The Theory of Interest*, Augustus M. Kelly, New York, 1970.

Fisher, Lawrence: "Determinants of Risk Premiums on Corporate Bonds," *Journal of Political Economy*, June 1959, pp. 217–237.

Grant, J. A. G.: "Meiselman on the Structure of Interest Rates: A British Test," *Economica*, February 1964, pp. 51–71.

Haugen, Robert A., and Dean W. Wichern: "The Term of a Risk-Free Security," *Journal of Financial and Quantitative Analysis*, March 1980, pp. 41–52.

Hawawini, Gabriel A., and Ashok Vora: "Yield Approximations: A Historical Perspective," *Journal of Finance*, March 1982, pp. 145–156.

Hessel, Christopher A., and Lucy Huffman: "The Effect of Taxation on Immunization Rules and Duration Estimation," *Journal of Finance*, December 1981, pp. 1127–1142.

Kane, Edward J.: "The Term Structure of Interest Rates: An Attempt to Reconcile Teaching with Practice," *Journal of Finance*, May 1970, pp. 361–374.

Kane, Edward J., and Burton G. Malkiel: "The Term Structure of Interest Rates: An Analysis of a Survey of Interest-Rate Expectation," *Review of Economics and Statistics*, August 1967, pp. 343–355.

Kessel, Reuben A.: *The Cyclical Behavior of the Term Structure of Interest Rates*, Occasional Paper 91. National Bureau of Economic Research. 1965.

Lee, Wayne Y., Terry Maness, and Donald L. Tuttle: "Nonspeculative Behavior and the Term Structure," *Journal of Financial and Quantitative Analysis*, March 1980, pp. 53–84.

Livingston, Miles, and Suresh Jain: "Flattening of Bond Yield Curves for Long Maturities," *Journal of Finance*, March 1982, pp. 157–167.

Macaulay, Frederick R.: *The Movements of Interest Rates, Bond Yields, and Stock Prices in the United States Since 1856*, National Bureau of Economic Research, 1938.

Malkiel, Burton G.: *The Structure of Interest Rates: Theory, Empirical Evidence, and Applications*, McCaleb-Seiler Publishing Company, New York, 1970.

McCulloch, J. H.: "The Tax-Adjusted Yield Curve," *Journal of Finance*, June 1975, pp. 811–830.

Meiselman, David: *The Term Structure of Interest Rates*, Prentice-Hall, Englewood Cliffs, N.J., 1962.

Metzer, L.A.: "Wealth, Savings, and the Rates of Interest," *Journal of Political Economy*, April 1951.

Modigliani, Franco, and Richard Sutch: "Innovations in Interest Rate Policy," *American Economic Review: Papers and Proceedings*, May 1966, pp. 178–197.

Modigliani, Franco, and Richard Sutch: "Debt Management and the Term Structure of Interest Rates: An Empirical Analysis," *Journal of Political Economy*, August 1967 Supplement, pp. 569–589.

Modigliani, Franco, and Richard Sutch: "The Term Structure of Interest Rates: A Reexamination of the Evidence," *Journal of Money, Credit and Banking*, February 1969, pp. 112–120.

Pesando, J. E.: "Determinants of Term Premiums in the Market for United States Treasury Bills," *Journal of Finance*, December 1975, pp. 1317–1327.

Roll, Richard: *The Behavior of Interest Rates*, Basic Books, New York, 1970.

Ross, Myron H.: "'Operation Twist': A Mistaken Policy?" *Journal of Political Economy*, April 1966, pp. 195–199.

Santomero, A. M.: "The Error-Learning Hypothesis and the Term Structure of Interest Rates in Eurodollars," *Journal of Finance*, June 1975, pp. 773–784.

Skelton, Jeffrey L.: "Relative Risk in Municipal and Corporate Debt," *Journal of Finance*, May 1983, pp. 625–634.

Van Horne, James C.: "Interest Rate Risk and the Term Structure of Interest Rates," *Journal of Political Economy*, August 1965, pp. 344–351.

Van Horne, James C.: *Financial Market Rates and Flows*, Prentice-Hall, Englewood Cliffs, N.J., 1978.

Wood, John H.: "Expectations, Errors, and the Term Structure of Interest Rates," *Journal of Political Economy*, April 1963, pp. 160–171.

Wood, John H.: "Expectations and the Demand for Bonds." *American Economic Review*, September 1969, pp. 522–530. See also Richard Roll, "Expectations and the Demand for Bonds: Comment," *American Economic Review*, September 1969, pp. 225–228.

CHAPTER 7

TERM-STRUCTURE MANAGEMENT

Term-structure management is planning and controlling the maturity structure of assets and liabilities. It is important to manage the term structure so that the financial intermediary can survive and profit under both present and future economic conditions. Monetary conditions change rapidly in the United States economy, which is tied to the cyclical swings of domestic and international trade. Managers cannot commit themselves to short-term or long-term positions and be confident that adverse interest rates and flows of funds will not occur unexpectedly. Recent experience shows that banks that borrow substantial amounts of short-term funds to finance long-term commitments may find themselves paying far more for deposits than they receive from loans and investments. Savings and loans can suffer major decreases in the market value of their mortgage portfolios during periods of high interest rates, while the cost of deposits soars. On the other hand, interest-rate changes are extremely beneficial and profitable to those in the right position. Although some intermediaries attempt to take advantage of increasing short-term rates by financing with long-term liabilities, most banks and many savings and loans match the term structure of assets and liabilities, immunizing themselves from the risk of rising and falling interest rates.

Term structure is a fundamental policy decision of all financial intermediaries, and a policy which is made in concert with marketing, credit, liquidity, capital, and other policies. Life insurance companies market a long-term liability and cannot shorten the term structure of liabilities without simultaneously destroying their major product, whole life insurance. Long-term mortgages are not well matched with short-term deposits of the savings and loan association, but both mortgages and deposits are difficult to alter without upsetting the marketing mix. Likewise, credit, liquidity, capital, and other policies and programs influence the term structure and explain why banks, savings and loan associations, credit unions, insurance companies, investment bankers, mortgage bankers, and savings bankers make different term-structure decisions. Thus, term structures are suited to the (1) regulatory structure, (2) market demand, and (3) stockholder preference of each intermediary.

This chapter does not prescribe a term structure for any type of individual intermediary but analyzes alternative term-structure strategies in terms of profitability and risk. The first section shows methods of managing the term structure to profit from the interest-rate cycle. Risks of insolvency and illiquidity may result from incorrect forecasts of the business cycle. Favorable and unfavorable term-structure positions are analyzed in the second section. Here we consider means of controlling or eliminating risk. Portfolio turnover policies, asset and liability maturity adjustments, and hedging can substantially reduce the susceptibility of a financial intermediary to adverse market conditions. This chapter assesses the impact of future interest rates on alternative term structures as a means of evaluating term-structure policy. The proper term structure balances expected future results under the range of future interest-rate conditions with other policy decision areas of the individual financial institution.

INTEREST-CYCLE MANAGEMENT

Interest-cycle management is a concept for varying the maturity of assets and liabilities in anticipation of changes in interest rates. For example, a manager might believe that the economy is at an extremely high level of activity and interest rates are very high—say 20 percent. Funds are scarce, as credit is tight. In applying business-cycle management, some managers attempt to increase future profits of their financial intermediary by changing their investment strategies from short-term to long-term loans and assets. Thus they fix the rate of return on the asset portfolio at a high level for a long period of time. In the following periods, they continue to earn a high rate of interest, despite declines in the short-term interest rate. Managers who recognized the 1969, 1973, and 1982 peaks and prepared for subsequent lower interest rates earned high rates of return for their institutions in later years.

The example for the 1978–1982 period can be generalized into an interest-rate-cycle management concept. The cycle periods are shown in Figure 7-1, and the typical business conditions for those periods are described in Table 7-1; we can ignore risk considerations until later. We can think of the peak conditions of 1982 as being represented by phase 1. Interest rates were at their highest level and credit demand was very great. The correct position for the financial structure in phase 1 is for liquidity to be fully depleted, investments to be at their longest terms, and liabilities to be at their shortest term. This position serves two purposes: (1) investments are locked into high rates for some years to come, and (2) liabilities are shortened so that the cost of funds

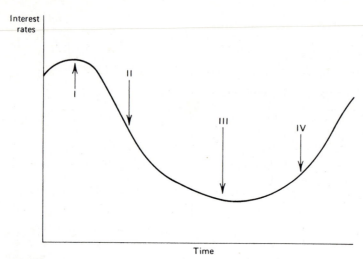

FIGURE 7-1
Business cycle periods.

declines quickly with falling rates. In phase 2 interest rates are declining and the demand for loans is dropping sharply. Phase 2 is a good opportunity to rebuild liquidity while long-term investments provide a high level of interest income. Liability structure, which was shortened in the last period, can now be lengthened at more favorable rates. Interest rates continue to drop along with loan demand in phase 3. The bottom of the business cycle is represented by phase 3, during which interest rates and credit demand are at their lowest levels of the entire cycle. The recommended position for phase 3 is to rebuild liquidity to its maximum level, shorten investment maturities, and extend the liability term structure as far forward into the future as possible.

TABLE 7-1
SUMMARY OF BUSINESS CONDITIONS AND RECOMMENDED FINANCIAL STRUCTURES

Business conditions	Cycle phase			
	1	**2**	**3**	**4**
Interest rates	High	Declining	Low	Rising
Credit demand	Great	Dropping	Small	Increasing
Recommended position				
Liquidity	Depleted	Increasing	Maximum	Reduced
Investment maturity structure	Longest	Long	Short	Long
Liabilities maturity structure	Short	Long	Longest	Long

Short-Run versus Long-Run Profits

It is important to note that interest-cycle management usually maximizes long-run rather than short-run profits. *Long-run* profits are used here to mean the present value of profits earned over many years, while short-run profits refer to profits earned during the current quarter or year. Current-year profits are often sacrificed for long-run profits, as the manager positions the institution for the next phase of the interest-rate cycle. Interest-income management, on the other hand, is a policy of purchasing assets with the highest yield and raising funds with liabilities having the lowest cost now, regardless of maturity. If the yield on commercial loans is higher than that on 30-year bonds, then we invest in loans under an interest-income policy. When passbook-deposit accounts can supply funds more cheaply than longer-term certificates of deposit, then we acquire funds with passbook accounts. Under an interest-income policy, the manager decides which securities to buy and sell strictly on the basis of current income and without regard to future capital gains and losses.

The differences in when and how much profit is earned with interest-cycle and interest-income management approaches are striking. A comparison of ordinary income and capital gain and loss income for the four phases of the interest-rate cycle is shown in Table 7-2. During phase 1, interest-cycle management is producing moderate profits without capital losses, while interest-income management results in high current interest income but large capital losses. In order to invest in high-yielding, short-term assets, the interest income managers must sell their long-term, lower yielding bonds at depressed prices and pay high rates for short-term liabilities. In phase 2 both approaches result in capital gains, but the interest-cycle manager can take greater capital gains, because the manager invested in long-term assets at the peak of the

TABLE 7-2
COMPARISON OF PROFITS FOR INTEREST-CYCLE MANAGEMENT AND
INTEREST-INCOME MANAGEMENT OVER THE INTEREST-RATE CYCLE

Cycle phase	Type of profit/loss	Interest-cycle management	Interest-income management
Phase 1: Peak	Ordinary income	Moderate	High
	Capital gain/loss	None*	Large losses
Phase 2: Decline	Ordinary income	High	Moderate
	Capital gain/loss	Large gains	Small gains
Phase 3: Trough	Ordinary income	Low	Moderate
	Capital gain/loss	Moderate gains	Small gains
Phase 4: Recovery	Ordinary income	Moderate	Moderate
	Capital gain/loss	None†	Moderate losses

* Assumes ascending yield curve during phase 3 and descending yield curve during phase 1 of the interest-rate cycle.
† No asset capital gains but low-rate long-term liabilities reduce the cost of funds to the institution using interest-cycle management.

cycle. During phase 3, interest-cycle management is most costly; funds are invested in low-yielding short-term assets and purchased with high-cost long-term liabilities in anticipation of the coming recovery. Interest-income managers invest in higher yielding long-term assets and fund their institution with the readily available short-term sources of funds, producing moderately high current profits. Both approaches continue to produce some capital gains, although the interest-cycle policy produces more capital gains. During the recovery of phase 4, both approaches produce moderate ordinary income, although the interest-income manager begins taking capital losses as switches are made from long- to short-term assets at unfavorable prices.

Clearly, neither the interest-cycle nor the interest-income approach consistently dominates. The better strategy for financial planning (Chapter 19) depends on both ordinary income and capital gains and losses. Furthermore, the benefits of each depend on how long the phases last. If the trough endures for a long period of time, then the interest-income management policy is better than the interest-cycle management. While the interest-cycle manager is suffering through a period of poor ordinary income and taking the last of any capital gains, the interest-income manager is harvesting good operating profits. A prolonged trough leaves the interest-cycle managers looking foolish, like prophets whose miracles never materialize. On the other hand, the interest-income manager may be a current success but a long-run disaster. When the economy moves through the interest-rate cycle rapidly, the current-income-conscious manager is frequently "absorbing" securities losses like the unfortunate grasshopper who learns that it is best to prepare for the days of necessity.[1] Most financial institutions realize the risk of adopting either policy in whole and seek a balance that produces moderate income throughout the interest-rate cycle.

The 1975–1976 Recovery: An Exception

Interest-rate-cycle management is dependent on business cycles repeating themselves. However, business cycles rise and fall with different intensity and duration. Sometimes parts of the economy lag behind other parts, while a typically slow sector spurts ahead unexpectedly. The conditions being experienced by businesses and governments do not change in a perfectly predictable and uniform pattern. Consequently, the financial markets do not move through the business cycle in a perfectly predictable and uniform pattern.

A good example of an unexpected condition during a business recovery was the failure of bank loans to increase during the 1975–1976 recovery. Unlike four previous recoveries (1954–1956, 1958–1959, 1961–1963, and 1970–1973), the 1975–1976 recovery failed to bring an increase in business loans of commercial banks. With a lackluster demand from businesses, commercial loans declined by 5 percent during the first 16 months of the 1975–1976 recovery. Figure 7-2

[1] Aesop, "The Ant and the Grasshopper."

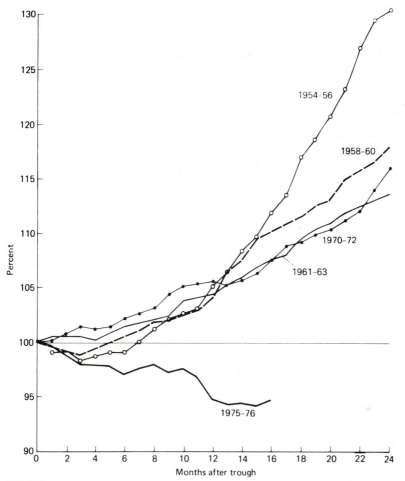

FIGURE 7-2
Business loans in the first 24 months of recoveries. For all commercial banks, seasonally
adjusted trough equals 100. (*Source*: Board of Governors of the Federal Reserve System.)

shows the remarkable contrast between business loans in the 1975–1976 recovery and all other post-World War II recoveries. In the 1975–1976 recovery,
inventories increased slowly, profits generated ample internal cash flow, and
capital market financing provided large amounts of external capital. After years
of declining liquidity and increasing reliance on short-term sources of funds,
corporations decided to rebuild their liquid reserves. Furthermore, they made
relatively small capital expenditures for plant and equipment. In summary,
businesses borrowed less than ever before at this stage of the business cycle
and, further, turned from banks to the securities markets.

The exceptional conditions of the 1975–1976 recovery were not difficult to
explain after they had occurred. Predicting that the business cycle would not

repeat itself for the fifth time was not likely, however, in 1974. The unexpected has happened, and will happen again. This is but one example of many that could be cited to prove that business-cycle theory is a good concept but risky to implement. In the following sections of this chapter, we consider the effects of wrongly forecasting future interest rates and ways of reducing the need to forecast interest rates.

Term-Structure Risk Example

Consider the case of a simple, hypothetical financial institution borrowing and lending funds with securities of three maturities. The assumption that transactions costs are zero is made without affecting the validity of the results. Assets consist of $30 million short-term (1-month), $50 million intermediate-term (1-year), and $20 million long-term (10-year) securities, while liability issues are $50 million short-, $28 million intermediate-, and $11 million long-term securities. Equity is set at $11 million. The beginning balance sheet appears as follows:

Example Balance Sheet

Short-term	$ 30,000,000	Short-term	$ 50,000,000
Intermediate-term	50,000,000	Intermediate-term	28,000,000
Long-term	20,000,000	Long-term	11,000,000
Total assets	$100,000,000	Total liabilities	$ 89,000,000
		Equity	11,000,000
		Total liabilities and equity	$100,000,000

Rates earned and paid are 5, 5, and 5 percent, respectively, for the short, intermediate, and long securities at the beginning of the period. (The yield curve is the solid line in Figure 7-3.)

However, during the period, interest rates rise to 8 percent for the intermediate securities. That is, the yield curve shifts from flat to humped. The institu-

FIGURE 7-3
Yields to maturity at beginning (solid line) and end (dashed line) of period.

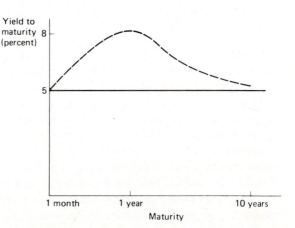

tion's securities, which had been selling at par (assuming a 5 percent coupon), now decline 2.9 percent in price. Prices are taken from financial market quotations or estimated with present-value analysis. (See Chapters 4 and 5.)

The price decline is reflected in both intermediate asset *and* liability values but has *greater impact on assets than liabilities* due to the unequal maturity weighting. The ending balance sheet appears as follows:

Example Balance Sheet
End of Period

Short-term	$30,000,000	Short-term	$50,000,000
Intermediate-term . . .	48,550,000	Intermediate-term	27,188,000
Long-term	20,000,000	Long-term	11,000,000
Total assets	$98,550,000	Total liabilities	$88,188,000
		Equity	10,362,000
		Total liabilities and equity	$98,550,000

The institution lost $638,000 (5.8 percent of equity) when the interest rate on intermediate-term securities increased. Such losses are real, immediate, and not uncommon. *When an institution has an unequal asset-and-liability term structure, it is open to security losses that adversely affect the market value of the equity.*

TERM-STRUCTURE RISK CONTROL

Although a financial intermediary may profit from anticipating the interest-rate cycle, it may suffer losses. An incorrect forecast of future rates might lead to exactly the opposite position from the correct one. Capital losses are sustained as market yields rise and prices fall on its long-term loans and securities. The intermediary may be committed to borrowing short-term sources of funds, as the short-term rate soars above historical highs. Playing the interest-rate cycle necessarily implies assuming term-structure position and risk. We take a long-term or short-term position, leaving the financial intermediary exposed to money-market forces that may blow favorably or unfavorably.

Many financial intermediaries want to control term-structure risk. They control their risk exposure at the expense of lowering their rate of return. The stockholders may object to lengthening the maturities of assets or liabilities on the basis of an uncertain money market forecast. If earnings are greatly depressed by unfavorable interest-rate conditions or large securities losses, then dividends may be cut and the stock price may decline. *Careful management of a financial intermediary requires that we assess the degree of term-structure risk, and limit the extent of risk to a prudent level.* Even when we decide to assume term-structure risk, we should adopt an investment strategy that gives us the highest return for the risk taken. To control risk and select investment strategies, we need to analyze alternatives using past data.

In this section we look at portfolio strategies and risk as they relate to term structure. We see that *term-structure* risk is a controllable, not an uncontrollable, factor for financial intermediaries.

Maturity Management

In deciding what maturity and what portfolio strategy to select, we need to consider what level of portfolio variability is acceptable. That is, how much interest-rate risk is acceptable and consistent with the liquidity, capital, and other policies of the intermediary. This is one important point where capital adequacy is related to the asset and liability portfolios. By constraining the variability (standard deviation) of returns, the risk to be absorbed with capital is limited. Earnings are smoothed and the retained earnings account is protected from large losses, when specific limits are placed on the variability of portfolio returns. Variability is directly related to maturity; consequently, we can control variability by constraining the term to maturity.

The Cramer and Seifert results, depicted in Figure 7-4, show the trade-off between variability (measured by the standard deviation) and rate of return (annual return). If we can accept a portfolio with a standard deviation equal to 2 percent of the portfolio, then we may expect to earn more than if we constrain the standard deviation to 1 percent. A more aggressive, well-capitalized intermediary would adopt the higher risk and return portfolio, whereas the more conservative management would accept the lower risk and return option. Each intermediary would then select a maturity consistent with its risk capital position.

FIGURE 7-4
Standard deviation—return frontier composite with CDs for Strategy 1. (*Source*: Cramer and Seifert, 1976.)

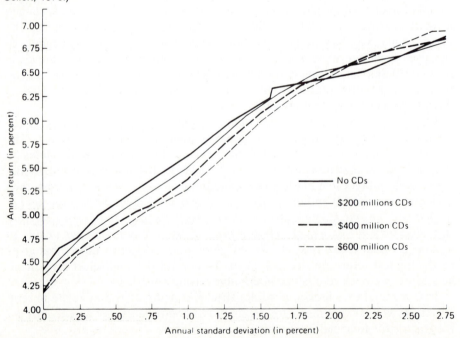

Asset/Liability Covariability

Maturity management, however, closes the door to long-term investments and loans for many institutions. How can a bank make 20-year mortgages with only a 5 percent capital-to-asset ratio? What institution can make 20-year fixed-rate loans? One solution to this problem is to apply the principle that *the rate of return on securities of similar maturity tend to vary in unison*. Consequently an intermediary finds that increased returns on its assets are accompanied by increased costs for sources of funds (liabilities), when the assets and liabilities are about the same maturity. The tendency of interest rates to vary in unison is termed *covariance*.

Financial intermediaries can use the covariance among securities to manage their term-structure risk. Risk is reduced if either long term loans are matched with long-term liabilities, or long-term liabilities are matched with long-term bonds. For example, savings and loans are successfully selling long-term certificates of deposit rather than short-term savings accounts to better match asset and liability returns. Insurance companies reduce the long-term liability risk from long-term life insurance and pension commitments by purchasing mortgages having substantial prepayment penalties and equity "kickers" that extend the effective maturities of assets. Commercial banks are issuing long-term bonds as a source of capital that increases the average maturity of liabilities and counteracts the long position of the loan portfolio. Because bond returns are generally positively correlated with one another, the best way to neutralize an asset position is with a similar liability position, and vice versa.

A risk-reduction technique closely related to term-structure matching is *variable-rate pricing* for long-term loans. Variable-rate loans are long-term commitments (longer than 1-year) to extend credit (loan funds) with a rate change provision. Rate changes are computed using an index that is independent of the lending institution.

Adjustable-Rate Mortgage (ARMs)

The most popular current alternative to the fixed-rate mortgage is the adjustable-rate mortgage (ARM).[2] The initial interest rate is increased or decreased to reflect current money market conditions under an adjustable-rate mortgage. In contrast the interest rate remains the same until maturity in the case of a fixed-rate mortgage. A common method for varying the interest rate is to tie the interest rate to a short-term index. California savings and loan associations use a cost-of-funds index published by the Federal Home Loan Bank of San Francisco. With an established index, the computation of the change in the mortgage rate is simple. The mortgage rate is computed by adding the initial

---

[2] We point out that other solutions have been suggested for the thrift institution problem, including diversification of assets and flexible-rate mortgages. Both of these suggestions would, of course, remove interest-rate risk. However, these suggestions are inconsistent with our national objective of encouraging residential construction, since asset diversification would tend to supply funds to non-mortgage-type securities and variable rates would increase the homeowner's risk.

mortgage to the change in the index. The mortgage rate changes from one time period to the next, as the index increases and decreases.

The adjustable mortgage rate is represented with the subscripted symbol i_t. Time is shown with the subscript t for the mortgage rate i. We can call the value INDEX$_t$ for the value of the cost-of-funds index. The relationship between the current mortgage rate and the index is the following equation:

$$i_t = i_0 + (\text{INDEX}_t - \text{INDEX}_0) \tag{7-1}$$

The initial mortgage rate and index value indicated as i_0 and INDEX$_0$ respectively. Thus the current mortgage rate (i_t) is equal to the initial loan rate plus the current index value less the initial index value.

Although the variable-rate mortgage may reduce risk for the financial intermediary, it may increase the credit risk of the borrower. Consider the case of rising short-term interest rates, which in turn cause the mortgage index and the mortgage rate to rise. Some adjustable-rate mortgages pass increased interest rates through to the borrower as higher monthly payments, while other adjustable-rate mortgages account for increased interest rates by adding to the amount owed. These adjustments raise the question of whether or not the mortgagee can repay more than originally agreed upon. If monthly payments rise, is there sufficient cash flow to meet higher monthly payments? If the mortgage debt amount increases, will the value of the property rise also? Because the borrower's ability to repay higher interest rates may be limited by his or her specific circumstances, default risk is increased by the adjustable-rate feature. Thus, a disadvantage of the adjustable-rate mortgage is the potentially greater default risk than that for a fixed-rate mortgage.[3]

Example of Adjustable-Rate Mortgages

Suppose the mortgage borrower agrees to an adjustable-rate contract with an initial rate of 12.00 percent. At the time that the mortgage is signed, the cost-of-funds index stands at 11.50 percent. During the first month, the borrower pays interest at the 12.00 percent rate. At the first adjustment date, the rate is adjusted for changes in the index. If the index stands at 11.25 percent at the end of the first time period ($t = 1$), then the interest rate decreases. The new rate is computed with Eq. (7-1):

$$
\begin{aligned}
i_1 &= i_0 + (\text{INDEX}_t - \text{INDEX}_0) \\
&= 12.00 + (11.25 - 11.50) \\
&= 11.75\%
\end{aligned}
$$

---

[3] The combined interest-rate and credit risk of variable-rate loans is described theoretically by Santomero (1983).

The mortgage rate for the second month is 11.75 percent. If the index changes at the end of the second month, then the mortgage rate is adjusted again.[4] For an index value of 11.60 percent, the mortgage rate would be computed as:

$$i_2 = 12.00 + (11.60 - 11.50)$$
$$= 12.10\%$$

The index of 11.60 percent is above the initial value (11.50 percent) and the mortgage rate rises above the initial 12.00 percent to 12.10 percent. In each computation the initial rate and index remain the same, while the current index value changes to adjust the current loan rate to the current cost of funds. Consequently the risk of increasing cost of funds is passed through the institution to the borrower. The borrower bears the risk of changing short-term rates, as the loan rate rises with the cost of funds index. On the other hand, ARM borrowers also get the benefit of falling short-term rates. As the index declines, the loan rate falls and borrowers pay less interest.

Hedging with Future Contracts

Hedging is a means of guaranteeing a rate of return in the face of potentially unfavorable changes in market prices with respect to a position already taken.

The financial intermediary manager can hedge against rising and falling rates with bond futures contracts. Futures contracts are agreements to buy or sell a security for a specific price at a future date. Short and long hedges are possible. A short hedge uses a futures contract to *deliver* a financial contract and protects the intermediary against a net long position during rising interest rates or a net short position during falling interest rates. The intermediary might also use futures contracts as a long hedge to protect itself against a net short position. A long hedge uses a futures contract to *buy* a financial contract at a future date. In this section we discuss how futures contracts are traded and how financial intermediaries can hedge short and long positions to reduce term-structure risk.

Short hedges are used by banks, savings and loan associations, savings banks, credit unions, and other thrift intermediaries with long-term assets and short-term liabilities. Interest-rate hedging transactions are summarized in Table 7-3. The commitment to sell a long-term asset of comparable maturity to assets actually owned is effectively the same thing as committing to sell mortgages and other long-term loans of the intermediary's customers. How-

---

[4] Many adjustable rate mortgages permit changes in rates only quarterly or annually. Some ARMs limit the size of changes and the frequency of changes during any year. We choose to use the most straightforward case of monthly adjustments for our example, but point out that many variations on the ARM idea exist.

TABLE 7-3
SUMMARY OF INTEREST-RATE HEDGE

Transactions on March 1	*Position after transaction*
Mortgages are granted and placed in the loan portfolio	Long in mortgages
Futures contracts in GNMA certificates are sold	Short in GNMA certificates
Transaction on September 30	
Purchase GNMA certificates in spot market and deliver on September 30 contract or repurchase the maturing September 30 contract from CBT	Long in mortgages

ever, the intermediary need not and will not sell loans made to its customers, because the personal relationship with its customers is an important part of its business. Rather than sell its own loans when the commitment due date arrives, it will reverse the original transaction by buying contracts in the spot market, or, more commonly, by closing the futures contract directly in the futures market. During the period between the original short-sale date and the closing date, the intermediary has hedged losses on the long-term mortgages with the futures contract, and, for the same reasons, hedged profits on the long-term mortgages. Thus, hedging eliminates the opportunity for profit as it eliminates risk of loss.

Bacon and Williams (1976) show how GNMA futures contracts can be used to hedge against rising and falling rates. For example, a hedge can protect an intermediary against an increase in the future level of interest rates on long-term loans. Consider the situation of a savings and loan that owns $20 million of mortgages with an average expected maturity of 12 years. It fears that long-term interest rates may increase and the value of its mortgages decline.

The risk is largely eliminated by the sale of $20 million in futures contracts now. Suppose that the current price on GNMA future contracts is $66 17/32 for contracts with a 6-month delivery date. (We are using Table 6-2 prices in our discussion.) This price provides a 13.951 percent yield on a 30-year certificate with a stated interest rate of 8 percent.[5] At today's quote for future delivery, 305 ($20,000,000/$100,000 x 65.53 percent) contracts are sold to hedge the $20 million loan portfolio. If interest rates for both GNMA certificates and the loan portfolios rise by 0.54 percent over the next 6 months, then the spot market price of contracts declines to 64 11/32. The intermediary covers the short position with the purchase of 305 contracts in the spot market (or closes the futures contract). To see how the profit from the futures contracts offsets the loss in the loan portfolio, make the following comparison:

---

[5] Compounding effects are ignored here, because exposition is greatly simplified without loss of generalization.

	Loan portfolio (long position)	GNMA Futures contract (short position)
December	Value: $20 million	Price: Sell: 305 contracts
June	Value: $19.50 million	Price: 64 11/32 Purchase: 305 contracts Value: $19,625,000
March-to-September change in value	$392,000	– $392,000
Gain or loss to intermediary	$392,000	$392,000

In this example the market value remains constant because the S & L has a long position in the loan portfolio and an offsetting short position in the futures contracts. The declining mortgage value is a loss in the loan portfolio because this is a long position; the corresponding decline in GNMA certificates is a gain because the S & L sold (short position) GNMAs in December.

The market value of the savings and loan portfolio falls during periods of rising interest rates. However, an equal gain is made from the futures market transactions, because contracts are purchased for $19.47 million on September 30 to cover the March 1 commitment to sell certificates at $20 million. During the 6-month period from March 1 to September 30, the savings and loan received interest income equal to 8 percent of the $20 million loan portfolio, as expected, and fully protected itself from the adverse change in interest rates. At September 30 the savings and loan may sell GNMA futures again to continue to hedge against further unfavorable changes in interest rates.

SUMMARY

This was the last in a four-chapter sequence dealing with interest rates. Here we applied the term-structure concepts to the difficult but persistent problem of structuring the maturities of assets and liabilities. The greatest opportunity to earn profits was seen to be from managing the portfolio to anticipate the interest-rate cycle. Interest rates were found to increase and decrease cyclically over time, giving financial intermediaries an opportunity to adjust their maturity structure so as to profit from conditions expected during the next phase. At the peak of the *cycle* (phase 1), the intermediary invests in long-term assets and reduces the liabilities maturity to the shortest term possible. After a period in which interest rates decline, economic conditions and rates decline to the trough (phase 3), and the intermediary prepares for the next business boom. Assets are kept at minimum maturities, liabilities are extended to the longest possible term, and liquidity is rebuilt. The interest-rate strategy was seen to produce large profits during the phase after conditions are correctly forecasted to change, although short-run profits are sacrificed. Also, we noted that interest-cycle management depends on correct forecasts of interest rates and leads to short-run losses when the cycle fails to repeat itself as soon as expected. The risk of incorrect forecasts and temporary losses was shown to be an undesirable but necessary part of managing the balance sheet in anticipation of future interest-rate conditions.

To avoid the risks inherent in taking a short or long position in assets or liabilities, we next considered limiting the maturity of assets and liabilities. We were looking for methods of controlling term-structure risk of commercial banks, savings and loan associations, life insurance companies, pension funds, and other intermediaries. By first measuring the risk, maturity, and return relationships over time, we found a means of relating acceptable risk levels determined by considering capital and liquidity policies to maturity. Increases in asset maturity were seen to lead to increases in the variability of returns. By analyzing the acceptable variability to optional maturity-strategy alternatives, and comparing expected returns of portfolio options, we found a portfolio with the highest expected return for a given level of risk. We also used the covariability between assets and liabilities having similar maturities to offset asset or liability term-structure risks.

However, some intermediaries may not be able to control interest risks entirely with the securities available for sale or purchase. Additional risk reduction was achieved by hedging with bond futures contracts. As an example, GNMA futures contracts to buy or sell GNMA certificates were shown to be an effective technique for shifting the interest-rate risk to CBT investors. Long-term asset positions are hedged with short sales, and long-term liability positions are hedged with purchases of GNMA futures contracts.

Thus, we saw that intermediaries may assume the interest-rate risk in hope of earning capital gains and unusually large profits by anticipating the interest-rate cycle. If they want to limit interest-rate risk exposure, they may control the maturity of assets and liabilities. If they want to eliminate substantially the term-structure risk, intermediaries may hedge. Thus, term-structure risk arises from many of the common transactions of financial intermediaries but may be managed. The decision to accept or eliminate term-structure risks is an important decision variable in the operation of financial intermediaries. Fortunately large banks, as a group, have successfully immunized themselves from market-rate fluctuations in recent years.

APPENDIX 7-1: Immunization

In Appendix 6-2 of Chapter 6, we discussed bond duration and recognized that bonds with different durations have different price volatilities. Then in this chapter, we noted that financial institutions make asset and liability commitments that have different terms to maturity. Now consider the case in which maturity is measured with duration, and a financial institution owns assets with a duration different from the duration of its liabilities. What is the effect of changing market interest rates on the equity value of the financial institution?

The equity value of the financial institution is equal to the asset value less the liability value, and consequently the change in equity value is equal to the change in asset value less the change in liability value. Thus the effect of market interest rate changes on equity depend on the price volatilities assets and liabilities, which in turn depend on duration. (See Appendix 6-2, Chapter 6, for the price elasticity explanation.) Equity value may change in one of three ways:

1 If asset duration exceeds liability duration, then equity value falls as market interest rates rise.
2 If asset duration is less than liability duration, then equity value rises as market interest rates rise.
3 If asset duration equals liability duration, then equity value remains constant as market interest rates rise.

Note that the controlling variable affecting equity value is the relative duration of assets and liabilities at the time that market interest rates change. The risk of equity loss due to mismatched durations may be avoided by *immunization*, which means *creating asset and liability portfolios with equal durations*. When both asset and liability durations are equal, interest-rate changes will cause approximately offsetting changes in value (and future returns) for both assets and liabilities. Consequently, the net effect on equity is nearly zero.

For the bond portfolio/insurance benefit example presented previously, if the asset duration is decreased to the insurance liability duration of 2.00 years, then any interest-rate change will cause equal and offsetting value changes in both assets and liabilities. If interest rates rise by 1 percent, then the bond portfolio decline of $18,200 per $1 million would be offset by the decline of the present value of insurance benefits of $18,200 per $1 million. Consequently, the net position—equity—is constant regardless of fluctuating market interest rates.

TERMS

term-structure management
maturity structure of assets
maturity structure of liabilities
short-term position
long-term position
interest-rate cycle
interest-cycle management

GNMA certificates
GNMA futures contracts
hedging
adjustable-rate mortgage
covariance of asset and liability returns
immunization (Appendix)

LIST OF EQUATIONS

$$i_t = i_0 + (INDEX_t - INDEX_0)$$

QUESTIONS AND PROBLEMS

1 Explain why each of the following institutions continues to assume term-structure risk:
a life insurance companies
b mortgage bankers

2 Compare the maturity structure of assets and liabilities of a financial institution with the following balance sheet to answer the questions below:

(Amounts in Millions)

Assets		Liabilities	
Cash	$ 10	Demand deposits	$ 300
Short-term investments	200	Short-term savings deposits......	600
Mortgage loans (fixed-rate)......	800	Capital	$ 160
Land and building.............	50	Total	$1,060
Total	$1,060		

a Are the asset and liability maturity structures the same? How do they differ?
b Is the term-structure position short or long on balance?
3 What are the four phases of the interest-rate cycle?
4 How does an institution profit by purchasing long-term assets during phase 1 of the interest-rate cycle?
5 If the institution attempts to profit from interest-cycle management, what liquidity and term-structure position does it take in phase 1? In phase 3?
6 Why is the 1975–1976 economic recovery an exception to the interest-rate cycle?
7 What risk is suggested by the exceptional 1975–1976 economic recovery?
8 Does interest-cycle management maximize current profits? Explain.
9 (Advanced problem) Using the following information, explain the portfolio positions that would be taken to maximize the yield from interest and capital gains. Calculate the annual yields that would be obtained for each possible position.

	Short-term			Long-term		
Date	Int. rate	Yield to maturity	Price	Int. rate	Yield to maturity	Price
Jan. 1, 19x0	8.00%	8.00%	100	8.00%	8.00%	100
Jan. 1, 19x1	9.00%	9.00%	100	8.00%	8.25%	95
Jan. 1, 19x2	10.00%	10.00%	100	8.00%	8.45%	92
June 30, 19x2	9.00%	9.00%	100	8.00%	8.35%	94
June 30, 19x3	7.00%	7.00	100	8.00%	7.94%	102
Jan. 1, 19x4	8.00%	8.00%	100	8.00%	8.00%	102

The following format may be used to construct a table to summarize the annualized yields for each position:

	Short-term securities				Long-term securities			
Time Period	C	P_0	P_1	R	C	P_0	P_1	R
	—	—	—	—	—	—	—	—

Using information from the table, do you feel that the profits potential of the maximum-profit approach would have been worth the risk of earning the lowest return?

10 Why is it often inappropriate for a savings and loan association to set current deposit and loan rates on the basis of a constant rate spread?

11 Using the futures prices (Exhibit 6-2), show that a 1-year deposit rate of 6.00 percent is unprofitable for savings and loan associations which invests in 8.248 percent mortgages in March 1977. Assume that marginal operating expenses are equal to zero and the percentage is fully hedged.

12 Describe the transactions involved in hedging a GNMA certificate for 1 year beginning in December and ending in December.

13 What rate of return is earned on a fully hedged GNMA certificate for 1 year beginning in December and ending the following December? (Use Table 6-2.)

14 Compute the capital gain or loss the market expects from holding a GNMA certificates without hedging for the same period as above.

15 A variable-rate mortgage is signed on January 30, 1977, which specifies a rate of 8½ percent adjusted for any change in the cost-of-funds index. If the cost-of-funds index was 6.14 percent on January 30, what will the mortgage rate be on November 30 when the index stands at 6.38 percent?

16 (Advanced problem) A good customer of your financial institution has asked that you lend her funds for 1 year to purchase 20-year U.S. government bonds on a 90 percent basis. While the customer is a good account and you have no reservations

FIGURE 7-5
Yield curves for U.S. government securities. (*Source: Monthly Review,* Federal Reserve Bank of New York, New York, April 1973, p. 86.)

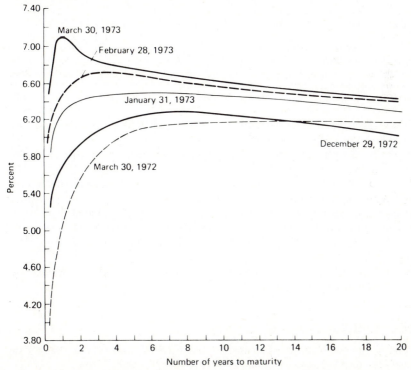

about the value of the relationship, you do desire explicitly to describe the risk associated with this transaction in a memo "for the file" and in a letter to the customer. Accordingly, on April 1, 1973, you obtain from the *Monthly Review* a graph of "yields on United States Government Securities" (Figure 7-5). With mathematical rigor and intuitive logic, prepare a brief statement discussing the speculative nature of the proposed transaction. Suggest an alternative method of speculating on the 20-year bonds that does not require the customer to sign a note.

17 Suppose the safe S & L goes out into the market and purchases a GNMA certificate in March 19X1. To limit your risk from price fluctuations, you decide fully to hedge your GNMA certificate for 1 year ending in March 19X2. What rate of return would you earn on this fully hedged GNMA certificate? Use the following data:

	Price	Yield
March 19X1	61–10	15.287
June	61–05	15.330
September	61–02	15.355
December	60–31	15.381
March 19X2	60–29	15.398
June	60–27	15.415
September	60–25	15.433
December	60–23	15.450
March 19X3	60–21	15.467
June	60–20	15.476
September	60–19	15.484
December	60–18	15.493
March 19X4	60–17	15.502
June	60–16	15.510

Note: GNMA 8 percent (CBT) — $100,000 principal; points are thirty-seconds of 100 percent.

18 (Based on Appendix A) In Questions 17 and 18 of Chapter 6, you evaluated duration for the following two financial contracts:
1 A 3-year bond with a 12 percent coupon and a $1000 face value when the maket rate of interest is 9 percent.
2 A 3-year installment loan with payments of $400 per year when the market interest rate is 9 percent.
   a If a financial institution borrows funds with 3-year bonds and lends with 3-year installment loans, is it immunized against fluctuations in market interest rates?
   b If it is not immunized, then what will be the percentage change in equity value for a 1 percent change in market interest rates?
   c What are two alternatives for immunizing this financial institution against fluctuations in market interest rates?.

SELECTED REFERENCES

Bacon, Peter W., and Richard E. Williams: "Interest Rate Futures: New Tool for the Financial Manager," *Financial Management*, Spring 1976, pp. 32–38.

Baesel, Jerome B., and W. B. Brueggeman: "The Mechanics of Variable Rate Mortgages and Implications for Home Ownership as an Inflation Hedge," *Appraisal Journal*, American Institute of Real Estate Appraisers, April 1976, pp. 236–246.

Bradley, S. P., and D. B. Crane: "Simulation of Bond Portfolio Strategies: Laddered vs. Barbell Maturity Structure," *Journal of Bank Research*, Summer 1975, p. 122.

Cramer, R. H., and S. L. Hawk: "The Consideration of Coupon Levels, Taxes, Reinvestment Rates and Maturity in the Investment Management of Financial Institutions," *Journal of Financial and Quantitative Analysis*, March 1975, pp. 67–84.

Cramer, Robert H., and James A. Seifert, "Measuring the Impact of Maturity on Expected Return and Risk," *Journal of Bank Research*, Autumn 1976, pp. 229–235.

Deshmukh, Sudhakar D., Stuart I. Greenbaum, and George Kanatas: "Bank Forward Lending in Alternative Funds Environments," *Journal of Finance*, September 1982, pp. 925–939.

Epley, D.: "A Re-examination of Federal Mortgage Rate Insurance," *Journal of Risk and Insurance*, March 1977, pp. 151–154.

Fama, E. F.: "Forward Rates as Predictors of Future Spot Rates," *Journal of Financial Economics*, October 1976, pp. 361–377.

Findlay, M. C., and D. R. Lapuzza: "The Variable Rate Mortgage and Risk in the Mortgage Market," *Journal of Money, Credit and Banking*, May 1977, pp. 356–364.

Flannery, Mark J., "Market Interest Rates and Commercial Bank Profitability: An Empirical Investigation," *Journal of Finance*, December 1981, pp. 1085–1101.

Fogler, H. R., W. A. Groves, and J. G. Richardson: "Managing Bonds: Are 'Dumbbells' Smart?," *Journal of Portfolio Management*, Winter 1976, pp. 54–60.

Fogler, H. R., W. A. Groves, and J. G. Richardson: "Bond Portfolio Strategies, Returns, and Skewness: A Note," *Journal of Financial and Quantitative Analysis*, March 1977, pp. 127–140.

Hempel, George H., and Stephen R. Kretschman: "Comparative Performance of Portfolio Maturity Policies of Commercial Banks," *Mississippi Valley Journal of Business and Economics*, Fall 1973, pp. 55–75.

"Interest Rate Behavior in the Current Economic Recovery," *Quarterly Review*, Federal Reserve Bank of New York, Winter 1976, pp. 33–39.

James, Christopher: "Analysis of Bank Loan Rate Indexation," *Journal of Finance*, June 1982, pp. 809–825.

Kaufman, George G., "The Thrift Institution Problem Reconsidered," *Journal of Bank Research*, Spring 1972, pp. 26–32.

Leibowitz, M. L.: "Horizon Analysis for Managed Bond Portfolios," *Journal of Portfolio Management*, Spring 1975, pp. 23–34.

Santomero, Anthony M.: "Fixed Versus Variable Rate Loans," *Journal of Finance*, December 1983, pp. 1363–1380.

Stansell, S. R., and J. A. Millar: "An Empirical Study of Mortgage Payment to Income Ratios in a Variable Rate Mortgage Program," *Journal of Finance*, May 1976, pp. 415–425.

Tucker, D. P.: "Financial Innovation and the Mortgage Market: The Possibilities for Liability Management by Thrifts," *Journal of Finance*, May 1978, pp. 427–437.

Worley, R. B., and S. Diller: "Interpreting the Yield Curve," *Financial Analysts Journal*, November/December 1976, pp. 37–45.

PART THREE

MAJOR FINANCIAL INSTITUTIONS

ORIENTATION

Until recently financial service offerings and institutions were easily recognizable as counterparts or, more strongly, as stereotypes. Commercial banks granted commercial loans, mortgage bankers bought mortgage loans for resale, and so forth. We might even have reversed it with some degree of accuracy: commercial loans were granted by commercial banks, mortgage loans were brokered by mortgage bankers, and so forth. Today, however, every type of financial institution is stretching to offer profitable financial services, regardless of its traditional market position. Commercial banks are granting mortgage loans, and savings and loan associations are granting commercial loans, for example.

Now financial institutions are creating holding companies to form horizontally integrated conglomerates, broad-line providers of financial services sometimes called "financial supermarkets." The conglomerate may run a bank, a securities trading firm, and an insurance company that sell financial services under a common name to consumers and businesses. Further marketing economies are sought by nonbank firms such as national retail chains that combine financial service offerings with their other product and service offerings. The result is a national or international supermarket of financial services often operated by a firm like Sears, Roebuck and Company, better known for its nonfinancial than for its financial services.

In a world increasingly characterized by financial supermarkets, one may ask, "Why is studying individual institutions important?" The reason is simply that these institutions are the basic elements of the financial conglomerate, because legal restrictions and managerial expertise tend to require or favor separating financial service operations by the type of service. Also, close inspection of a financial supermarket reveals a group of commonly owned but independently managed financial institutions, each offering a different set of services. If each of those institutions is well understood, then the conglomerate is understandable as a combination of them.

Although the correspondence between financial service offerings and institutional types is fading with deregulation of the financial industry, it remains strong enough to describe securities and services within the context of individual institutions. For example, commercial loans are discussed under commercial banking (Chapter 8) and consumer time deposits are covered in the discussions of savings and loans (Chapter 9). Such classifications indicate historical importance rather than current conditions. As deregulation proceeds, chances are good that institutional distinctions will become insignificant. When a financial institution is no longer identifiable by its balance sheet, then the type of institution is probably no longer a meaningful classification. As you read the balance sheets in this section, see if you can guess the type of institution by analyzing its financial statement.

CHAPTER 8

COMMERCIAL BANKS

CONCEPT OF BANKING

The primary business of banking is one of collecting funds from the community and extending credit (making loans) to people for useful purposes. Banking organizations are also involved in nonbanking financial services, described in subsequent chapters of this part.

The origin of banking is traceable to the ancient Assyrians, Babylonians, and Athenians, but the forerunners of modern banks are considered to be the Bank of Venice (1171), the Bank of Genoa (1320), and the Bank of Amsterdam (1609). The Martins Bank in London has been operating on its original site since Sir Thomas Gresham, a goldsmith, established it in 1563 "at the Sign of Grasshopper." Banking in America is strongly influenced by its heritage, although banks have evolved into professionally managed and electronically connected money brokers.

Today banks are the most important and most complex institution in the U.S. financial system. We deposit our money in banks in return for checking, savings, and time deposit instruments to the tune of $2500 billion. As consumers, business managers, and governmental officials, we borrow those billions of dollars to create a better economic world. The banker is the custodian whom we trust to invest our funds wisely.

Furthermore, the bank is responsible to its stockholders. Banking is a profit-seeking business, not a community charity, which attempts to maximize the wealth of shareholders.

Banks and other financial institutions are best described by two financial reports: (1) statement of condition, and (2) income statement. We are going to

TABLE 8-1
FINANCIAL ASSETS AND LIABILITIES OF THE COMMERCIAL BANKING SYSTEM, DECEMBER 31, 1972–1984 (BILLIONS OF DOLLARS)

		1972	1973	1974	1975	1976	1977	1978	1979	1980	1981	1982	1983	1984
Total financial assets	1	640.7	728.8	800.1	834.6	906.0	1003.5	1147.7	1277.4	1390.5	1525.0	1608.1	1756.5	2012.9
Demand deposits and currency	2	.7	1.0	0.8	0.9	0.7	1.3	1.5	2.2	2.9	3.9	5.6	7.8	10.5
Total bank credit	3	587.0	668.3	733.1	764.6	831.1	921.1	1047.0	1167.1	1268.8	1377.7	1457.8	1596.0	1775.0
U.S. government securities	4	90.0	88.8	89.5	119.5	139.6	138.5	139.0	146.5	172.1	183.9	211.8	263.8	261.5
Treasury issues	5	68.1	59.2	56.3	84.9	103.6	101.7	95.2	95.3	111.2	113.1	133.6	183.2	183.0
Agency issues	6	22.0	29.6	33.2	34.6	36.0	36.8	43.8	51.2	60.9	70.7	78.2	80.6	78.5
State & local obligations	7	90.0	95.7	101.1	102.9	106.0	115.2	126.2	135.6	149.2	154.2	158.7	159.6	172.0
Corporate & foreign bonds	8	5.2	5.6	6.6	8.4	7.8	7.7	7.4	7.1	7.7	7.7	9.2	13.0	17.6
Total loans	9	401.6	478.1	535.7	533.6	577.5	659.5	774.3	877.8	939.7	1031.8	1078.0	1159.6	1323.9
Mortgages	10	99.3	119.1	132.1	136.2	151.3	179.0	214.0	245.2	263.0	284.5	301.7	329.7	374.2
Consumer credit	11	87.0	99.6	103.0	106.1	118.0	140.3	166.5	186.4	180.2	184.2	190.5	218.9	259.6
Bank loans n.e.c.	12	188.5	237.3	278.4	266.1	272.5	302.1	359.7	410.9	458.6	519.2	541.5	565.1	638.1
Open-market paper	13	8.3	7.0	9.2	10.3	14.0	14.3	13.0	15.2	16.9	17.7	18.1	16.7	17.0
Security credit	14	18.6	15.2	13.0	15.0	21.7	23.9	21.0	20.2	20.9	26.2	26.2	29.1	35.0
Corporate equities	15	0.1	0.2	0.2	0.2	0.2	1 0.2	1 0.1	1 0.1	1 0.1	1 0.1	1 0.1	1 0.1	.1
Vault cash	16	8.6	10.7	11.6	12.3	12.1	13.9	15.5	18.5	19.8	18.6	19.5	20.7	18.7
Member bank reserves	17	25.6	27.1	25.8	26.1	25.2	26.9	31.2	29.8	27.5	25.2	26.5	21.4	21.8
Miscellaneous assets	18	18.8	21.8	28.8	30.8	36.9	40.4	52.4	59.7	71.6	99.6	98.7	110.5	186.9

Total liabilities	19	604.2	688.1	756.0	787.7	853.0	945.3	1082.8	1205.0	1310.4	1438.2	1516.1	1656.9	1867.9
Checkable deposits	20	222.6	235.4	235.2	242.8	256.1	280.6	305.9	332.4	341.9	350.5	369.7	385.5	409.3
U.S. government	21	10.9	9.9	4.8	3.1	3.0	7.3	14.1	14.5	11.9	10.8	16.9	10.9	15.4
Foreign	22	7.9	10.9	13.5	13.2	16.2	18.7	18.3	22.7	22.9	19.0	15.6	17.0	19.2
Private domestic	23	203.8	214.6	216.9	226.5	236.9	254.6	273.5	295.3	307.0	320.7	337.3	357.6	374.7
Small time & savings deposits	24	232.4	245.1	263.3	303.2	357.8	386.0	399.3	428.7	473.7	514.0	612.4	742.9	812.9
Large time deposits	25	84.5	122.5	161.9	152.0	136.7	162.7	211.2	225.0	272.2	323.8	307.8	253.7	282.9
Fed funds & security RPs	26	9.2	25.4	23.5	26.9	40.6	49.5	69.5	85.6	103.9	118.3	130.4	142.7	146.2
Net interbank claims	27	10.3	6.7	7.1	-4.8	-12.7	-17.3	-7.3	12.3	-16.1	-28.5	-65.4	-49.1	-10.7
To monetary authority	28	6.0	4.4	2.3	3.9	2.6	4.1	7.7	8.2	6.3	3.4	3.5	2.5	4.4
To domestic banks[2]	29	-2.4	-1.8	0.7	-3.1	-4.0	-9.4	-8.6	-10.1	-13.5	-15.9	*	1.7	11.4
To foreign banks	30	6.8	4.1	4.1	-5.7	-11.5	-12.0	-6.3	14.3	-8.9	-15.9	-68.8	-53.3	-26.6
Credit market debt	31	10.9	14.1	18.7	19.5	25.5	28.1	35.4	42.1	49.2	57.4	60.0	68.6	81.1
Corporate bonds	32	8.3	9.2	10.4	10.8	17.7	18.9	19.6	21.7	23.2	24.4	25.5	30.6	37.0
Open-market paper	33	2.6	4.9	8.3	8.7	7.9	9.1	15.8	20.4	25.9	33.0	34.6	38.0	44.1
Profit taxes payable	34	0.7	0.8	0.9	0.6	0.6	0.8	0.9	1.4	0.8	0.5	0.4	0.3	.3
Miscellaneous liabilities	35	33.4	38.1	45.5	47.5	48.3	54.9	67.8	77.5	84.8	102.2	100.8	112.3	146.0
Memo: Credit market funds advanced	36	568.3	652.9	720.0	749.4	809.2	897.0	1025.9	1146.8	1247.8	1351.4	1431.5	1566.8	1740.0

[1] Consists of U.S.-chartered commercial banks, their domestic affiliates, Edge Act corporations, agencies and branches of foreign banks, and banks in U.S. possessions. Edge Act corporations and offices of foreign banks appear together in these tables as "foreign banking offices."

[2] Floats and discrepancies in interbank deposits and loans.

use these two terms as a framework for discussing banks in this chapter and nonbank financial institutions in later chapters. The *statement of condition* reveals the important securities bought and sold, and the *income statement* shows the primary sources of income and expense. How do banks obtain money to lend? The bank statement of condition reports that deposits are their primary source of funds. Now let us take a closer look at the business of banking and the financial contracts used by bankers.

SOURCES OF COMMERCIAL BANK FUNDS

What do bankers provide that is so popular among consumers and businesspeople? Bankers are not popular for their personalities alone! We like banks because they help us spend our money more efficiently or invest our savings more wisely. In Fisherian terms, banks link those desiring to defer their consumption and those preferring to borrow at an interest rate that satisfies both groups at the margin. The links are financial contracts developed primarily by the bank. Now let us look at three financial contracts that banks use to account for our money: (1) demand (checking) deposits, (2) savings deposits, and (3) time deposits. These are the keystone sources of funds for most banks and well worth further description here.

Look at the banking sector's financial assets and liabilities shown in Table 8-1. Money is obtained by issuing (selling) securities listed under "liabilities." The most important liabilities are:

1 Checkable deposits ($385.5 billion, 22 percent of liabilities)
2 Time deposits ($996.9 billion, 57 percent of liabilities)
3 Federal funds and security repurchase agreements ($142.7 billion, 8 percent of liabilities)

Exactly what are these securities and who buys them? In this section we take a closer look at these three major securities sold by commercial banks.

Checkable Deposits

Checkable deposits are checking account balances maintained at commercial banks. We write checks ordering the bank to pay a third party from our demand deposit. Commercial banks and the depository institutions are permitted by law to issue demand deposit accounts. There are important advantages to using checks, and most payments are made by check. They eliminate the need for us to carry a large amount of cash. Payment is easily mailed rather than hand-carried to pay telephone, electric, and other bills. Our canceled check serves as a receipt for proof of payment. The benefits of check payment are many but not new; see Exhibit 8-1 for the interesting history of bank checks.

Banks compete vigorously for demand deposits, and consumers can choose among many banks. The reputation and location of the bank are very important

EXHIBIT 8-1
Origin of bank checks.

In England, the modern bank check had its start with the British goldsmiths. In the early 1600s there were no banks of deposit in England. The practice of merchants in those days was to store their surplus gold in the Tower of London. In 1640, Charles I found he was short of money and forcibly borrowed large sums from the merchants' stocks. This impelled the merchants to find a safer place for their funds. They chose the shops of goldsmiths, and the custom of depositing surplus funds with them began. Until that time, the chief business of goldsmiths had been that of manufacturing gold and silver plate and jewelry and purchasing and selling jewels.

In time, goldsmiths began to serve individuals as well as businessmen. The unsettled conditions of the Civil War (1642–49) caused the nobility to have their gold and silver plate melted down. The metal was deposited with the goldsmiths for safekeeping.

As this business grew, many goldsmiths became bankers. The receipts they issued to depositors ("goldsmith notes") were the forerunner of the latter-day bank note. Goldsmiths also began to lend their depositors' money to businessmen.

Soon merchants began to call on goldsmiths for assistance in transacting business with third parties. In the earliest days of English banking, the depositor and the payee appeared together at the goldsmith's place of business to arrange the transfer of the deposit. Then, businessmen began drawing bills of exchange or drafts on the goldsmiths. This practice apparently started about 1650.

It was not until the latter part of the 18th century that the word "check" came into use to describe these instruments.

Source: Quoted from *The Story of American Banking,* The American Bankers Association, Washington, D.C., 1963.

to the majority of depositors. Individuals are concerned with the quality and availability of services, as well as with the fees charged for services and interest rates paid on deposits. As in any business, the product, place, price, and promotion are all part of a bank service package.

The following figures are for typical banks that average $181,233,735 in demand deposits, of which $134,984,383 is available for investment in the portfolio. Banks are required by law to hold a fraction of their deposits in cash and demand deposits at the Federal Reserve or qualifying commercial banks. The background and details of reserve requirements are discussed later (Chapter 22), and it is necessary only to recognize that non-interest-bearing reserves and other requirements reduce the amount of investible funds to less than deposit balances. Therefore, when analyzing costs and revenue, the total package is considered.

Although a substantial amount, service charges cover only a small proportion of the processing costs. That is, banks provide far more service than is paid for explicitly with fees and charges. Economists refer to the provision of such services in return for the use of money as *implicit interest.* Unlike *explicit interest,* which is paid in cash, implicit interest is provided in the form of goods (calculators, balloons, and other gifts) and services (check clearing, financial advice, and 24-hour teller machines, for example). In a perfect market depositors would prefer explicit over implicit interest payments, but because of legal restrictions and tax differentials, implicit interest is sometimes an advantage.

For example, income taxes are not assessed on bank services provided in return for the use of a minimum deposit checking account.

Income:	
Service charge	$2,070,784
Other income	396,255
Total income	2,467,039
Interest expenses	1,798,442
Processing expenses	9,220,868
Net loss	($8,552,270)

From the bank's viewpoint, the operating loss on demand deposits is a fair trade for the use of the deposit balances. In exchange for a loss of $8,552,270, the bank receives the use of $134,984,735. We can consider the operating loss as a type of interest payment. The interest rate (i_D) is calculated by dividing the net loss by the amount of deposits less reserves. Net losses are equal to service charges and fees minus interest and operating expenses. That is,

$$i_D = \frac{\text{net loss}}{\text{investible funds}}$$
$$= \frac{8,552,270}{134,984,735} \tag{8-1}$$
$$= 6.34\%$$

The effective "interest rate" (i_D) for demand deposits is estimated as 6.34 percent.

The trend in recent years has been toward higher service fees by banks and smaller deposit levels by customers. In an attempt to better relate service value and price, banks have been raising service fees. However, the total implicit and explicit cost of consumer funds has continued to rise toward money-market rates in recent years. (The rate i_D increased from 3.73 to 6.34 percent from 1978 to 1982 for the medium-size bank example presented here.) At the same time, customers are learning to use their checking accounts more actively, thus keeping a smaller balance per dollar of income. Commercial customers have been controlling demand balances particularly well under "cash management" programs. Consequently the net loss has been increasing faster than the increase in deposits less reserves and the effective interest rate (i_D) for demand deposits has been trending upward.

Time Savings Deposits

Time and savings deposits are interest-bearing liabilities payable at some future date or after notice. Although the names may differ from bank to bank and region to region, there are three types of consumer deposits, savings and time deposits.

Type of Account	Characteristics
1 Savings deposits (regular) also called *passbook savings*.	Convenience and liability are provided while interest rates are low and regulated. As part of the "full service" concept of banking, passbook savings fulfill the short-term savings needs for demand deposit customers. Banks generally permit the holder to withdraw funds on demand, waiving the legal right to require 30 days' notice.
2 Time deposits, also called *nonnegotiable certificates of deposit (CDs)*	Consumer certificates of deposit mature at fixed dates after 30 days and are usually denominated in amounts of $1000 or more.
	Interest-conscious savers are attracted to the higher yields (permitted by regulation) on CDs. A wide variety of forms are offered to suit customers' needs, including interest payments by check, automatic renewal, and premature redemption (with a penalty).
3 Money-market deposit and Super NOW accounts	MMDAs and SNOWs are savings accounts exempt from rate ceilings as long as a $1,000 minimum or average balance is maintained; also, there is no minimum term and preauthorized or draft transfers are permitted. (Authorized by the Garn-St. Germain Depository Institutions Act of 1982.)

In addition to consumer time and savings deposits, money-center banks sell negotiable certificates of deposit (CDs). Only the few money-center banks sell large CDs, because they have the substantial credibility demanded by money-market investors. Negotiable means that the CDs can be sold to someone else. Unlike nonnegotiable CDs, which are redeemable only at the bank, negotiable CDs are traded in a secondary market. *Large negotiable CDs* are money-market instruments that represent bank deposit accounts transferable from one party to another. They are issued in amounts of $100,000 or more and mature within 30 to 180 days. Specific maturities are tailored to corporate cash needs such as dividend dispersals and tax payments, and CDs in units of $1 million or

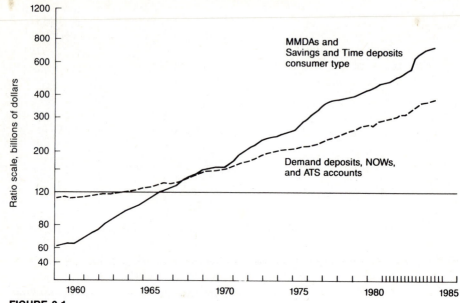

FIGURE 8-1
Demand and time deposits in commercial banks, 1960–1983. (*Source*: Board of Governors of the Federal Reserve System.)

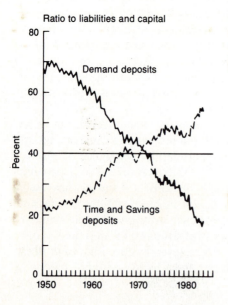

FIGURE 8-2
Demand deposits and time deposits of all commercial banks as percents of liabilities plus capital. (*Source*: Board of Governors of the Federal Reserve System.)

more may be sold in an active secondary market operated by security dealers. As discussed earlier, although interest payments are substantially higher for certificates of deposit, the total cost to the bank is not much greater than the cost of passbook savings. In computing the cost of deposits, banks add operating costs to interest costs and exclude deposits held as nonearning reserves.

We see in Figure 8-1 that since the early 1940s savings deposit balances at banks have been growing faster than demand deposit balances. The Banking Act of 1980 relaxed regulation Q, which opened the way to higher interest payments on time accounts. To raise funds banks have aggressively sought and successfully obtained time deposits, both passbook savings and certificates of deposit. Consequently the mix of demand and time deposits has changed dramatically during the past 20 years. As shown in Figure 8-2, demand deposits have declined from about 60 percent to about 30 percent of liabilities and capital, while time deposits have increased from 30 percent to 50 percent of total liabilities and capital. The composition of deposit liabilities at commercial banks has changed from largely demand to largely interest-bearing time deposits. The trend is toward an even greater proportion of interest-bearing deposits but future interest-bearing deposits will be in both demand and time accounts. See commercial bank flow of funds in Table 8-2 for this and other banking trends.

Federal Funds

Commercial banks lend one another funds through the Federal Reserve or through a correspondent bank which is a member of the Federal Reserve. The lending bank notifies the Federal Reserve of the transaction, and the Federal Reserve simultaneously debits the lending bank's account and credits the borrowing bank's account. The transaction is usually a 1-day loan, involves any amount specified, and costs very little to execute. Federal funds loans are an excellent way for a bank with excess funds to lend to a bank with insufficient funds for very short periods of time.

For example, the National Bank money desk may believe that it has excess balances with the Federal Reserve of $1 million today at 11:00 a.m. The money may be needed tomorrow or the next day, and National Bank is unwilling to commit the funds for more than one day. After contacting several banks for bids, National Bank decides to sell its funds. The transaction is executed by wiring the regional Federal Reserve bank, which reduces National Bank's account by $1 million and increases the account of the borrowing bank by a like amount. National Bank is said to have "sold" federal funds, and the borrowing bank refers to the loan as *Federal funds bought*. On the following day, the Federal Reserve credits National Bank's account for principal plus interest. These are frequently referred to as *overnight funds*.

Regional banks purchase Federal funds from small local banks for their needs or for resale to large money center banks. Local banks are generally sellers in the Federal funds market and develop relationships with the regional

TABLE 8-2
COMMERCIAL BANKING FLOW OF FUNDS, 1972–1984 (BILLIONS OF DOLLARS)

	1972	1973	1974	1975	1976	1977	1978	1979	1980	1981	1982	1983	1984
Current surplus	4.25	4.5	4.6	4.3	4.5	5.3	6.7	7.9	7.6	7.5	9.3	12.7	12.8
Plant and equipment	4.3	5.7	5.4	2.3	4.1	6.7	9.3	10.7	9.8	10.7	12.4	14.8	14.7
Net acq. of financial assets	73.7	80.1	70.9	34.5	71.3	97.6	144.1	134.6	108.7	134.4	120.0	148.4	193.8
Demand deposits and currency	N/A	N/A	-0.2	0.1	-0.2	0.5	.3	0.7	0.6	1.0	1.7	2.2	2.7
Total bank credit	73.7	75.6	64.8	31.5	66.5	90.0	126.2	122.2	101.8	108.8	108.5	138.2	182.4
U.S. government securities	3.1	-1.4	0.7	30.0	20.2	-1.1	.5	7.9	25.6	11.7	27.7	51.9	3.4
Treasury issues	2.1	-8.7	-2.9	28.6	18.7	-1.9	-6.5	0.4	15.9	1.9	20.4	49.6	3.9
Agency issues	3.8	7.4	3.6	1.4	1.5	0.8	7.0	7.6	9.7	9.8	7.3	2.4	-.5
State & local obligations	7.1	5.6	5.4	1.8	3.0	9.2	9.6	9.5	13.6	5.0	4.7	0.9	9.4
Corporate bonds	1.7	0.4	1.0	1.8	-0.6	*	-.3	-0.1	0.6	*	1.9	3.8	4.5
Total loans	59.3	71.0	57.7	-2.1	43.8	82.0	116.4	104.8	62.0	92.2	74.2	81.6	165.1
Mortgages	16.8	19.6	12.8	3.8	15.1	27.4	35.1	30.6	17.8	21.5	16.1	29.5	46.3
Consumer credit	12.6	12.6	3.4	3.1	12.0	22.3	26.2	19.9	-6.2	4.0	6.3	28.4	46.0
Bank loans n.e.c.	25.5	43.1	41.5	-12.1	6.4	29.9	59.3	53.0	47.8	60.6	51.4	22.1	66.2
Open market paper	-0.3	-1.5	2.2	1.1	3.7	0.3	-1.3	2.0	1.8	0.8	0.3	-1.4	0.3
Security credit	4.6	-2.8	-2.2	2.1	6.6	2.2	-2.9	-0.9	0.8	5.3	*	2.9	6.3
Corporate equities	1.1	1.2	*	*	*	*	*	*	*	-0.1	*	*	*

Vault cash & mem. bank res.	-1.0	3.4	-0.3	0.8	-1.0	3.5	5.9	1.6	-1.0	-3.4	2.2	-3.9	-2.0
Miscellaneous assets	1.0	1.0	6.5	2.0	6.1	3.5	11.8	10.1	7.3	28.0	7.5	11.9	10.7
Net increase in liabilities	71.8	77.2	68.5	32.6	69.6	92.9	138.7	128.0	101.2	128.2	115.4	141.6	189.3
Checkable deposits	24.2	12.5	-0.2	7.6	13.4	24.5	25.3	26.5	4.9	8.7	19.2	15.8	23.6
U.S. government	0.7	-1.0	-5.1	-1.7	-0.1	4.3	6.8	0.4	-2.6	-1.1	6.1	-6.0	3.8
Foreign	1.5	2.2	2.6	.3	3.0	2.4	-.3	4.1	0.3	-3.9	-3.4	1.6	2.1
Private domestic	34.4	11.2	2.3	9.6	10.4	17.8	18.8	22.0	7.2	13.7	16.5	20.2	17.7
Small time & savings deposits	25.7	12.7	17.4	39.9	54.6	28.2	13.3	29.3	45.0	40.3	97.0	130.6	70.7
Large time & deposits	17.0	37.1	39.3	-9.9	-15.3	26.0	48.6	13.8	47.2	51.5	-8.8	-54.1	27.5
Fed. funds & security RP's	1.6	16.1	-1.9	3.5	13.6	9.0	20.0	15.6	18.3	14.4	12.0	12.3	9.2
Net interbank claims	-5.3	-5.8	0.4	-11.9	-7.8	-4.6	10.1	21.1	-28.5	-12.4	-14.3	16.3	29.1
To Federal Reserve	-0.3	-0.7	-2.1	1.6	-1.3	1.4	3.6	0.5	-1.9	-2.9	0.1	-1.0	2.0
To domestic banks	-6.1	-3.3	2.5	-3.8	-0.9	-5.4	.8	-1.7	-3.4	-2.4	15.7	1.7	12.5
To foreign banks	-0.7	-0.8	*	-9.8	-5.7	-0.7	5.7	22.3	-23.2	-7.0	-30.1	15.6	14.7
Corporate equity issues	1.1	1.2	1.0	1.0	1.6	0.6	1.1	1.3	0.4	0.5	0.6	0.7	0.8
Credit market debt	4.0	15.1	4.6	0.8	6.1	2.5	7.3	6.7	7.1	8.2	2.5	8.5	12.7
Corporate bonds	1.1		1.1	0.5	6.9	1.3	.6	2.1	1.5	1.2	1.1	5.1	6.5
Open market paper	0.7	2.2	3.5	0.3	-0.8	1.3	6.7	4.5	5.6	7.0	1.4	3.5	6.1
Profit taxes payable	-0.2	0.1	0.1	-0.3	—	0.2	.1	0.5	-0.5	-0.4	-0.1	-0.1	*
Miscellaneous liabilities	7.3	12.7	7.7	2.1	3.4	6.7	12.9	13.2	7.4	17.4	7.3	11.5	15.6
Discrepancy	-2.0	-4.1	-3.2	0.1	-1.4	-6.1	-8.0	-9.4	-9.7	-9.3	-7.7	-9.0	-6.4
Memo: Credit market funds advanced	69.0	78.4	67.0	29.5	59.8	87.8	129.0	123.1	101.1	103.6	108.5	135.3	176.1

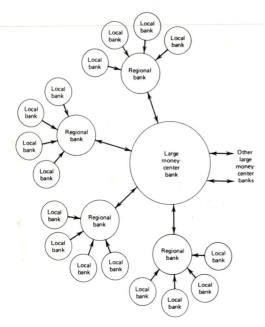

FIGURE 8-3
Federal funds market structure.

banks in which the regional bank purchases all excess funds at the going market price, less a small transactions fee. In turn, the regional bank often sells the funds to large money-center banks, which are generally net purchasers of funds. The market structure is illustrated for a few banks in Figure 8-3. Money traders within the larger banks regularly monitor rates at regional and money-center banks and execute arbitrage trades when even small rate disparities surface. Consequently, Federal funds rates tend to be uniform throughout the United States for local, regional, and large money-center banks. Rates are very responsive to changes in supply and demand, varying from zero (when it is too late in the day to reinvest 1-day funds) to over 20 percent per annum. Hourly fluctuations of several percentage points are not uncommon, particularly during periods when loan demand is strong and the Federal Reserve is rationing credit.

The Federal funds market provides an extremely efficient facility for balancing short-term liquidity surpluses and deficits. Cash flows of banks are very large and volatile, so that daily surpluses and deficits are commonplace. Amounts as small as $100,000 can be profitably invested overnight, and sums in the millions can be placed with a phone call. However, Federal funds are not a dependable source of liquidity during tight credit conditions, because the price soars and supplies are short. Regional banks, which are usually sellers, retain the funds they purchase to meet loan demands of their customers, rather than wholesaling funds to the large money-center banks. The large banks vie for a dwindling supply to meet loan commitments and primary reserve requirements.

Eurodollar Market

Large banks with foreign branches turned to the Eurodollar market for funds during the liquidity pressures of 1966 and 1969. Regulation Q rate ceilings prevented banks from selling new CDs to refund maturing obligations, while loan demand and rates set record highs. As shown by Mastrapasqua (1973), foreign branches of U.S. banks received substantial increases in dollar deposits from 1964 to 1969. London branches of U.S. banks increased their dollar deposits by 610 percent from 1964 to 1969, while the liabilities of American banks to their branches abroad increased 675 percent. Not subject to Regulation Q but under the control of U.S. banks, the foreign branches met competitive interest rates and remitted funds to domestic affiliates. The precipitous drop in Eurodollar borrowings beginning in 1970 was caused by the imposition of substantial reserve requirements on liabilities coupled with a reduction in liquidity needs. Foreign-branch borrowings remain a viable but expensive source of short-term funds, although the monetary authorities impose reserve requirements and monitor foreign-branch transactions more closely now than during the 1960s.

INVESTMENTS BY COMMERCIAL BANKS

Commercial banks put their deposit money to work by making loans and buying bonds. Loans are made to businesses and individuals for thousands of reasons and uses. Bonds are purchased from state, local, and national governments that are financing capital assets and fiscal deficits. In this chapter we look at three important investments: (1) loans, (2) state and local government bonds, and (3) money-market securities. In later chapters we consider consumer credit and mortgage loans, which are important not only to banks but to other institutions as well.

Loans

Loans are an essential aspect of commercial banking. First, income from loans contributes 80 percent of all revenues of the average bank. Second, lending money to people in a confidential manner is a valuable service, as discussed in Chapter 1. Attracted by lending services, many people and businesses deposit their funds in the local bank. The synergistic lending and deposit relationship reduces banking costs over those of financial institutions offering only loan or deposit services. Third, lending money spurs business development and supports a growing economy. Whether loans are made to businesses for inventory and equipment investment or to consumers for purchases of durable goods, business activity increases.

Loans are negotiated directly between the bank (lender) and the customer (borrower). The loan agreement is an understanding between two parties—the

bank (or group of banks) and the borrower. Because the agreement is negotiated and involves only a small number of parties, the terms are tailor-made to
suit both the bank and the customer. For example, a businessperson may
request a 90-day loan for the purchase of inventory. After the banker listens to
the request and asks about the finances of the borrower, he or she may respond
that the loan agreement must include a pledge of collateral and a limit on
additional borrowing. In response, the customer may argue for a high limit on
later borrowings, perhaps a limit based on sales and profits. The negotiation
continues until both the bank and the borrower agree to the amount, maturity,
interest rate, and covenants (restrictions) of the loan.

Although keeping flexibility in mind, we characterize bank loans as three
types:

1 Commercial (business and farm)
2 Consumer
3 Mortgage (real estate)

We consider commercial loans in the next section and consumer and mortgage
loans in following chapters. Banks make all three types of loans, but it is more
interesting to discuss consumer and mortgage lending in the context of institutions that specialize in these types of instruments.

Commercial Loans

The traditional mainstay of bank lending is the commercial loan. These loans
meet many diverse credit needs of business enterprises. A common grouping of
commercial loans by purpose is:

1 Seasonal loans
2 Permanent working capital loans
3 Term loans

Seasonal Loans   Seasonal loans are granted for periods of less than 1 year,
usually 90 to 180 days. Borrowers use seasonal loans to buy inventory and
finance accounts receivable during their peak sales season. The loan is repaid
as inventory and receivables are converted into cash when the rate of sales
declines. We call seasonal loans *self-liquidating,* because repayment follows
from the normal liquidation of inventory and receivables. Under seasonal
lending arrangements, the bank is repaid in a few months; and the bank
partially depends upon repayments to meet the needs of other borrowers or to
repay depositors. As one borrower passes a peak period and begins repaying
the loan, another is often entering a seasonal period when additional funds are
needed.

For example, a farmer needs money in the spring to purchase seed, fertilizer, fuel, and equipment. The bank makes a seasonal loan to the farmer, who
will receive cash from the sale of the crop later in the summer or fall. When the

crop is sold, the bank is repaid. However, a local grain elevator may purchase the grain from the farmer and need money to finance its inventory. Again, the bank is called upon to make a seasonal loan. As soon as the grain elevator sells its inventory, it repays the bank, which may relend the money to someone else. Clearly, banks perform an important and profitable service by moving money from one seasonal borrower to the next.

Permanent Working Capital Loans   When our inventory and accounts receivable needs continue throughout the year, then we need a permanent working capital loan. Many businesses carry a big stock of merchandise on their shelves all of the time, and they do not plan to reduce that stock so long as they continue in business. If we sell on credit as well, then we are carrying accounts receivable from past sales. We need a loan to finance our inventory and receivables, although we will not be able to repay the loan from a reduction in assets.

How do we repay a permanent working capital loan? Usually we will repay from future profits and depreciation or from the sale of bonds or common stock. Banks generally find profits and refinancing less secure sources of repayment than the seasonal liquidation of working assets. To assure better repayment, banks often require borrowers to pledge good-quality collateral and limit dividend payments from profits. Collateral, however, "only makes a good loan a better one, never makes a poor loan a good loan."

Term Loans   Term loans are credits extending from 1 to 10 years in the future. If our business buys a new machine, we will usually need many years of operation to earn sufficient profits to repay the loan. If we need a large loan to buy the machine but can afford only small periodic payments, we negotiate a term loan with the bank to spread the principal repayment over several years. Typically term loans mature in 3 to 10 years and are repaid in monthly or quarterly installments. Banks are careful in analyzing term-loan applications, because they will be exposed to default risk for a long time. Banks look at the capacity of the business to generate good cash flows from profits and depreciation under different economic conditions, as well as the current prospects for sales and operations. The additional hazards of term loans do not deter banks from granting long-term credits but do require them to investigate each situation more fully and define credit terms more carefully.

Growth and Variability of Business Loans

We see in Figure 8-4 that commercial loans have been growing since the end of World War II. Now commercial loans account for about one-third of total loans outstanding at banks; the remaining loans are real estate and consumer types. You may note in Figure 8-4 that commercial loans vary widely over time. We can examine the changes in commercial loans more fully by graphing the year-to-year increases and decreases. Changes in business loans of banks are

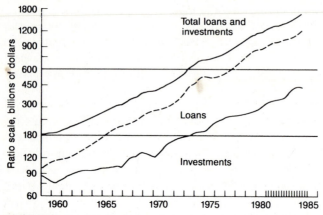

FIGURE 8-4
Loans and investments of banks, 1960–1983. (*Source*: Board of
Governors of the Federal Reserve System.)

graphed in Figure 8-5 on an exploded scale. Although business loans usually
increase each year, the amount of additional loans varies widely and somewhat
unpredictably. We see swings from zero growth in 1961 to nearly a $38 billion
growth in 1973 to a $10 billion decline in 1975. Alternatively, the manager is
deluged with loan requests during business booms and loan repayments during
recessions. Keep in mind that the bank manager must face those swings and
satisfy the credit needs of the community. We will face the management
problem more directly in Chapter 20, where we plan institutional investment
strategy.

STATE AND LOCAL GOVERNMENT BONDS

Also called municipal bonds, state and local government (SLG) bonds are
issued by state and city governments. The SLG bonds are studied next,
because they are the second highest yielding asset in the average bank. The
federal government exempts SLG bonds from income taxes, because the

FIGURE 8-5
Changes in bank loans to businesses and open-market paper
issues of nonfinancial businesses. (*Source*: Board of Governors of
the Federal Reserve System.)

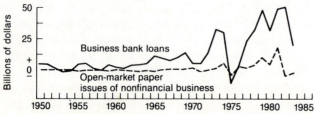

United States Constitution prohibits the federal government from levying taxes on the states and their political subdivisions. It is important to recognize that only interest payment is exempt from federal income taxes and that price appreciation is taxed as usual. Furthermore, the interest payments and value of state and local bonds may or may not be subject to state taxes. However, state taxes are far less than federal taxes, and the tax-exempt status of SLG bonds is a' major reason for banks to buy them. All the interest income flows from revenue to net income without deductions for federal income taxes. Anyone can buy tax-exempt SLG bonds, but commercial banks benefit more than most of us. Banks are often in high-tax brackets, paying over 46 percent of their earnings as income taxes. A dollar of tax-exempt income produces a full dollar of net income, whereas a dollar of taxable interest results in only 54 cents of net income.

The tax implications of state and local government bonds are easily understood with an example using Eq. (5-8) from Chapter 5. Consider a bank with two investment alternatives: (1) quality loans at 12.00 percent and (2) quality tax-exempt notes at 8.00 percent. Assume that the investments are equivalent in all respects but the quoted yields. Which is the better alternative? Before comparing the yields, we recognize that the loan yield is *pretax* but the tax-exempt yield is *posttax*. Therefore, the tax-exempt yield must be converted to its *pretax equivalent yield*. The marginal tax rate (tax) is applied, because the investment decision affects incremental income and taxes. Using Eq. (5-8), we find:

$$R = \frac{i}{1 - tax}$$
$$= \frac{8.00}{1 - 0.46}$$
$$= 14.81\%$$

Thus, the tax-exempt note yield of 14.81 percent is found to be far greater than the 12.00 percent yield on loans. Such pretax equivalent yield advantages often occur and make tax-exempt securities desirable investments for banks. However, the extent to which tax-exempt securities are useful in banks is limited by the amount of taxable income expected, the demand deposits associated with direct lending, and the yield differential between taxable and tax-exempt alternatives. The limiting factors change over time and differ across banks; consequently, we observe that banks vary their tax-exempt security investments as economic conditions change. They determine their needs for these and other securities using planning techniques, such as those described in Chapter 20.

MONEY-MARKET SECURITIES

Money-market securities are sources of liquidity, in that they can be sold at nearly full value quickly—usually within a business day. Also, trading profits are earned by regularly dealing in such securities. Banks commonly deal in the following money-market instruments:

1 U.S. Treasury and agency bills and notes
2 Federal funds sold to other banks (discussed in prior section)
3 Repurchase agreements
4 Bankers' acceptances
5 Commercial paper
6 Prime-quality demand and call loans and loan participations that may be liquidated at a small cost

U.S. Treasury Bills

U.S. Treasury bills are short-term obligations of the U.S. government that are sold in enormous quantities. Maturities range from 30 days to 1 year, and denominations typically range from thousands to millions of dollars. Because they are a direct obligation of the government, default risk is extremely low. Because they can be purchased and sold on short notice in a large, well-organized market, they are an ideal liquidity instrument.

Treasury bills are purchased either from the Treasury (through the Federal Reserve) or from bond dealers. The Treasury offers bills for sale on competitive bids on Mondays except for holidays. Invitations are sent to persons interested in bidding, and bidders return the invitation, stating the price and the amount they are willing to purchase. Also, bidders may submit a noncompetitive offer for less than $200,000 worth of bonds. Bills purchased on a noncompetitive bid basis are priced at the average of the competitive bids. On Tuesday the Treasury announces the amounts and price range of the accepted bids and notifies bidders whether or not their bids were accepted. Payment is made on Thursday in maturing Treasury bills or immediately *available funds*. Deposits at the Federal Reserve are available because they can be spent immediately by the Treasury. On the other hand, a personal check delivered on Thursday would not be immediately available because a delay of 1 or more days is required in processing the check. Ownership is accounted for by the Federal Reserve's automated bookkeeping system. Purchases and sales are recorded for Treasury bills in a manner similar to that for deposits and withdrawals to any deposit account.

Banks have not increased their investments in U.S. Treasury securities, although they have been and continue to be the major holder of such securities (see Figure 8-6). Since World War II banks have owned virtually the same dollar amount of U.S. Treasury bills, notes, and bonds. As bank assets in total have increased, the proportion of U.S. Treasury securities has declined. Why have banks reduced their proportionate holdings of this low-risk security? The answer is probably the relative tax consequences of U.S. Treasury and SLG securities. As we saw earlier, SLG securities produce more net income after taxes so long as banks pay the 48 percent corporate income tax rate. Although

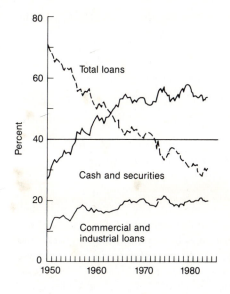

FIGURE 8-6
Cash and securities, commercial and industrial loans, and total loans of all commercial banks as percents of total assets. (*Source*: Board of Governors of the Federal Reserve System.)

SLG bond yields are lower than U.S. Treasury note yields, the after-tax yield is greater for SLGs than for U.S. Treasury notes. Furthermore, as shown in Figure 8-6, banks have reduced cash and security holdings as a percent of total assets. They have invested proportionately more in loans than in cash and securities. This trend may not continue in the future because legal and liquidity requirements may constrain the extent to which banks can make further reductions in cash and securities.

Repurchase Agreements

Repurchase agreements (RPs) are contracts in which an owner sells Treasury bills to another and pledges to repurchase them within a short time at a stated price. The seller "borrows" the value of the Treasury bills under an RP and "repays" the funds a few days or weeks later by repurchasing the bills. The buyer is protected against default risk, because he or she owns the high-quality Treasury bill. Also, buyers are protected against interest-rate risk because the RP is short-term and states the repurchase price. Thus, the institution can invest funds under an RP with safety and security.

The market for RPs is very large and well developed. The raw material, U.S. Treasury debt, is abundant and the daily trading volume enormous. Communications equipment—telephones, telexes, and computers—forms a vast network linking securities dealers, institutions, nonfinancial corporations, and speculators. Information travels nearly instantaneously and professional money managers act quickly to negotiate RPs, which are priced at favorable rates. Payment is made in Federal funds through the commercial bank, and funds are available the same day as the transaction. Transactions costs are very small, and reasonable returns can be earned by investing as little as $100,000 over the weekend.

Bankers' Acceptances

Bankers' acceptances are time drafts issued by a business firm (bills of exchange) on the face of which a bank has written the word *Accepted* over its signature. The bank assumes the liability when it accepts the draft, although the business firm remains liable as well. The bank's credit is added to that of the business, thereby making the draft less risky and more marketable. Bankers' acceptances of major banks are widely traded throughout the world. Interest rates on bankers' acceptances are higher than those for Treasury bills and reflect the slightly greater risk involved in lending to a United States bank rather than the Treasury. The spread between Treasury bills and bankers' acceptances ranges from about 30 to 50 basis points, depending on maturity and money market conditions. Generally the bankers' acceptance rate is very close to the bank prime rate.

Commercial Paper

Commercial paper refers to short-term notes of leading industrial corporations sold through brokers in the open market and directly to lenders in large denominations. This is one of the highest quality investment instruments available from the private sector. Only corporations with national reputations and good to excellent credit ratings are accepted by the commercial paper market. The major industrial firm's paper is referred to as *industrial paper,* and finance company notes are called *finance paper.* Industrial paper is usually placed through dealers, while finance paper is typically sold directly by the finance companies.

Industrial paper is purchased as a liquid asset by banks during periods of slack loan demand. The paper is bought and sold strictly on the basis of price and does not involve a personal relationship. Consequently a bank may sell or fail to renew the paper at maturity, if the funds are needed.

Federal and some state savings and loan associations are not permitted to purchase commercial paper by law. Insurance companies and other financial institutions buy commercial paper to invest idle funds temporarily, if the interest rate is attractive.

Commercial paper yields are slightly higher than Treasury bills of the same maturity, reflecting the marginally higher default risk of a private sector firm. Occasionally a private corporation that issues commercial paper falls into bankruptcy. An example is the Penn Central Railroad. The greater default risk is the reason that commercial paper yields more than Treasury bills yield. The yield spread between commercial paper and Treasury bills varies from about 25 to 50 basis points, depending on the maturity of the note and money market conditions. Finance paper usually yields 10 to 30 basis points less than industrial paper.

COMMERCIAL BANK INCOME AND EXPENSE

The bank income statement reports exactly how each bank or a group of banks earns profits by borrowing funds at one interest rate and selling funds at a higher interest rate. For example, consider the income statement of all banks as a percent of total assets presented in Table 8-3. The interest expense of 6.36 percent is the cost of funds relative to total assets, and the total interest revenue of 9.50 percent is the return on those funds. The difference between interest revenue and interest expense is *net interest revenue,* also called *net interest margin.* From the financial market's perspective, net interest margin is the value added to funds by the bank's credit services. From the bank management perspective, net interest margin is the primary source of income for paying operating expenses and compensating stockholders. Noninterest income of 1.12 percent is an important and growing source of income. Loan loss provisions were increasing during this period as a result of unexpected commercial loan defaults. After paying operating expenses and providing for losses, the bank computes its net income by subtracting income taxes and security gains or losses. Income taxes average less than 46 percent, because banks invest in tax-exempt securities and tax-sheltered leases. The net income is divided between cash dividends and retained earnings, as stockholders receive part of the net income immediately in cash while some net income is invested with the expectation of greater dividends in the future.

Commercial bank operating revenues have been rising rapidly in recent years due to increasing interest rates and loan portfolios. Operating revenues are graphed in Figure 8-7 (frame a) on a ratio scale. (A straight line would indicate a constant percentage increase, and the upward curve shows an increasing rate of increase.) Increasing operating revenues have been matched by increasing operating expenses, however. The major expense item, interest

TABLE 8-3
INCOME AND EXPENSES OF ALL INSURED BANKS AS A PERCENT OF AVERAGE CONSOLIDATED ASSETS, 1980–1983

	1980	1981	1982	1983
Gross interest income	9.87	11.81	11.19	9.50
Gross interest expense	6.78	8.75	8.02	6.36
Net interest margin	3.09	3.07	3.17	3.15
Noninterest income	0.89	0.99	1.05	1.12
Loan-loss provision	0.25	0.26	0.39	0.47
Other noninterest expense	2.63	2.76	2.91	2.95
Profits before tax	1.10	1.04	0.91	0.84
Taxes	0.28	0.24	0.17	0.18
Other	−0.03	−0.04	−0.03	−0.01
Net income	0.79	0.76	0.71	0.67
Dividends	0.29	0.30	0.31	0.33
Retained income	0.50	0.46	0.40	0.34

Source: Deborah J. Danker and Mary M. McLaughlin, "Profitability of Insured Commercial Banks in 1983," *Federal Reserve Bulletin,* vol. 70, no. 11 (November 1984): 814.

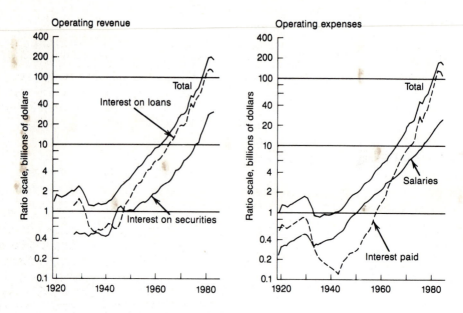

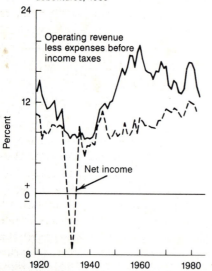

FIGURE 8-7
Revenue, operating expenses, and net income of member commercial banks. Frame a.
Operating revenues have increased at a faster rate since 1969 than before 1960. Frame b.
Total operating expenses rise rapidly as a result of increasing interest payments. Frame c. Net
income as a percent of capital, 1919–1968 (equity capital plus subordinated rates and
debentures). (*Source*: Board of Governors of the Federal Reserve System).

paid, has risen rapidly since the 1950s. Banks have successfully balanced increasing operating revenues and costs, and average net income as a percent of capital has remained at approximately 11 percent for the last 30 years (see frame c, Figure 8-7). Maintaining profitability during the past 20 years of rising interest and salary expenses has been difficult, and the likelihood of further expense increases and uncertainties poses a real challenge for bankers in the future.

UNITED STATES BANKING STRUCTURE

The concept of bank structure encompasses the conglomeration of banking institutions *and* the laws and customs surrounding them. One aspect of banking structure is the type of bank organization:

1 Correspondent banking
2 Group banking
3 Branch banking

All these structures are similar in that many banks or offices of a bank operate under a well-defined agreement, the relationship becoming increasingly closer as it moves from a correspondent to a holding company to a branch structure.[1]

Correspondent Relationships

The correspondent banking system consists of a network of informal relationships among small, medium, and large banks. The smaller banks maintain demand deposits at larger banks in return for services provided by the larger banks. The more important of the correspondent services are summarized here.[2]

1 Loan participation—Large banks participate in credits exceeding the smaller bank's lending authority and directly support the smaller bank during the peak demand for agricultural loans.

2 Check collection—Small banks in towns and villages forward items for collection to their correspondent in larger towns, where they are collected directly or sent into the Federal Reserve clearing system.

3 Accounting—Bank accounting, including the maintenance of the bank's own books, as well as customers' records, requires a substantial outlay for computers and related peripheral equipment. Many large banks provide complete accounting services for their correspondent banks, particularly in states limiting banks to a single office (unit banking).

4 Investment advice and transaction—The staffs at larger banks provide counsel regarding the merits of particular securities, forecast yields, and make

---

[1] Banking structure refers also to the number and size of banking institutions.
[2] Ranked in order of importance by American Banker's Association survey. See Summers (1978).

recommendations for the smaller bank's liquidity position. Larger banks also invest excess funds from small banks through the Federal funds market and bid for U.S. Treasury securities for resale to the smaller bank.

The economic rationale for correspondent banks stems from (1) their role as the money center intermediary between smaller, country banks and the New York money market, and (2) the attainment of economies of scale in bank operations through the investment in large efficient capital equipment to process records and the employment of specialized personnel to give advice on technical financial and operational problems.

Group Banking

Group banking is conducted by a corporation or syndicate that controls two or more legally independent banks. A corporation owning more than one bank is a *bank holding company,* and a syndicate or other small group of individuals with common interests owning more than two banks is referred to as *chain banking.* Bank holding companies are subject to the Bank Holding Company Act (1956) and regulated by the Federal Reserve. Group banking arose to circumvent state laws prohibiting branch offices, and the groups attempt to operate banks within their control as if they were part of one entity.

Chain banks are controlled through a common ownership, common board of directors, and a recognized organizational hierarchy beyond that of the individual banks. A principal "key" bank frequently coordinates the management of the entire group and also serves as the depository for required reserves of state chartered holding company banks. Furthermore, excess funds from one bank are channeled to deficit banks via the principal bank or at its direction. Bank holding companies attempt to invest the combined resources of the group banks as if they managed one portfolio of assets. Of course, the principal bank performs the usual correspondent services for the smaller affiliates, such as accounting, marketing analysis, personnel training, and legal counseling.

Branch Banking

Obviously, branch banking is the most highly integrated bank structure possible, as all offices are owned and operated by the same legal entity. Although most banks conduct their business from a single office (unit banks), a large number operate branch facilities. Indeed the branch offices far surpass the unit bank offices. Branch banking is expanding more through mergers than through establishment of new facilities by existing banks. We see the growth of branch banks in Figure 8-8. Branches may be opened with minimal legal and regulatory approval, compared with the chartering of new banks. Banks demonstrating the managerial capacity to operate new branches are generally permitted to open new facilities, so that the major consideration in branch establishment is profitability.

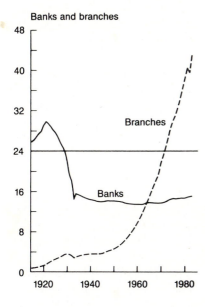

FIGURE 8-8
Number of banks and branches in the United States.
(*Source*: Board of Governors of the Federal Reserve
System.)

Significance of a Few Large Banks

Although the U.S. banking industry consists of 14,500 banking corporations, a few very large banks account for a large share of bank assets and deposits. The largest 100 banks in the United States attract about one-half of all bank deposits (demand and time) and make about one-half of all bank loans.

The large banks are important sources of capital for large corporations, because they can grant substantial loans and hire specialized lending officers. Also, large banks operate in widely disparate geographical markets within and outside of the United States. However, the large banks encounter fierce competition from smaller banks that coexist successfully with the major banks.

REGULATION OF COMMERCIAL BANKS

Banks are subject to a more complex system of supervision than any other type of institution. Responsibility for supervision is divided among many state and federal agencies. Three federal agencies share supervisory functions:

1 Office of the Comptroller of the Currency
2 Board of Governors of the Federal Reserve System
3 Federal Deposit Insurance Corporation

Each state performs audits on state chartered banks. The complexity of the system is shown in Figure 8-9.

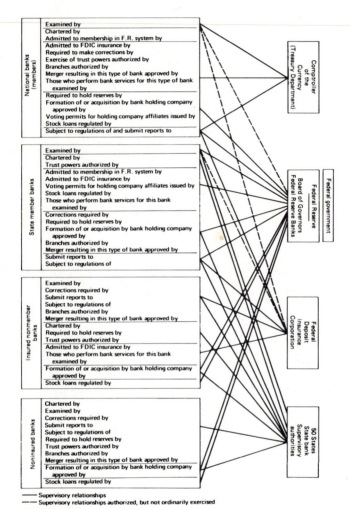

—— Supervisory relationships
--- Supervisory relationships authorized, but not ordinarily exercised

FIGURE 8-9
Supervision of the commercial banking system; principal relationships. (*Source*: Board of Governors of the Federal Reserve System.)

Federal Deposit Insurance Corporation

Virtually all commercial banks participate in federal deposit insurance. Under the Federal Deposit Insurance Act, each depositor is protected for deposits up to $100,000 in each insured bank. Time and savings deposits of governmental units of the bank's own state are insured up to $100,000 for each depositor. An annual fee of one-twelfth of 1 percent of deposits is usually assessed to fund this insurance. The FDIC protects deposits by restructuring failing institutions in one of three ways: (1) merging the failing institution into a strong bank, (2) replacing nonperforming loans with cash and changing management, or

(3) paying insured depositors in failed banks and liquidating the assets. The FDIC attempts to arrange a merger through the purchase of assets and assumption of liabilities as often as is possible. Also, it may directly assist the purchasing bank financially by buying some assets of the failing bank or indemnifying the purchasing bank against losses. After assuring that insured deposit liabilities are safeguarded, the FDIC selects a course of action which reduces the risk or loss to federal deposit reserves.

Federal Reserve

The Federal Reserve provides special services to member and nonmember banks (national and voluntary state banks). Important services are borrowing privileges, check clearing operations, deposit insurance, and statistical reporting.[3] Member banks, which are temporarily short of funds, may borrow directly from their Federal Reserve Bank. Borrowing from the Federal Reserve is an alternative to selling some of the bank's securities, borrowing from other banks, refusing to make new loans, or borrowing with certificates of deposit in the money market. Enabled by the Federal Reserve Act of 1913, the so-called "discount window" is a safety valve for the banking system and individual banks. Banks that are temporarily unable to meet their reserve requirements can obtain funds quickly from the Federal Reserve and later adjust their loan and investment portfolio. Credit is ruled by Regulation A, which states, in part:

> Federal Reserve credit is generally extended on a short-term basis to a member bank in order to enable it to adjust its asset position when necessary because of developments such as a sudden withdrawal of deposits or seasonal requirements for credit beyond those which can reasonably be met by use of the bank's own resources. . . .
>
> In considering a request for credit accommodation, each Federal Reserve Bank gives due regard to the purpose of the credit and to its probable effects upon the maintenance of sound credit conditions. . . . It keeps informed of and takes into account the general character and amount of the loans and investments of member banks. It considers whether the bank is borrowing for the purpose of obtaining a tax advantage or profiting from interest differentials and whether the bank is extending an undue amount of credit for the speculative carrying of or trading in securities, real estate, or commodities. . . .

That is, banks are not supposed to borrow continuously from the Federal Reserve. Repeated, frequent borrowing implies that a bank is unable to repay its debts by adjusting the asset portfolio, and suggests that further examination of the bank is warranted. Needless to say, most bankers avoid added Federal Reserve scrutiny by limiting their use of the discount window.

Check Collection Check collection is a second important service of the Federal Reserve. Measured in hours worked, this is the largest job of

---

[3] Indirectly, many of these services are available to nonmember banks. By dealing through a member bank, a nonmember can route its checks through the Federal Reserve clearing facilities.

the Federal Reserve. Over $4 trillion worth of checks per year are cleared by the Federal Reserve without charge. Basically the clearing operation transfers checks from the recipient's bank to the depositor's bank.

Example of Check Clearing Joan banks with State Bank and merchant Mike deals with National Bank. Joan buys $100 worth of tools from Mike. Both Joan and Mike use their bank accounts to transfer money. How does the Federal Reserve help the banks move Joan's money to Mike's account? Mike takes Joan's check to his bank, National Bank, which credits his account for $100. Then National Bank takes Joan's check (and many others) to the Federal Reserve clearinghouse. A check clearinghouse is a place where messengers from member banks meet to exchange bundles of checks drawn on other banks. National Bank deposits Joan's $100 check at the Federal Reserve, and the Federal Reserve credits the National Bank account for $100. Then the Federal Reserve sends the check to State Bank for collection and reduces the State Bank account. The books are changed as shown in the following T account:

1 Mike's deposit is sent to Fed.

2 Fed changes deposits of member banks.

National Bank	
Federal Reserve +100	Deposits: Mike +100

Federal Reserve	
	Deposits: National Bank +100 State Bank −100

3 Check reduces Joan's account.

State Bank	
Federal Reserve −100	Deposits: Joan −100

The clearing process is complete. Joan's checking account is reduced by $100 to increase Mike's account in payment for the tools.

Statistical Reporting Statistical reporting services of the Federal Reserve are numerous. Information is distributed in monthly written and computer-readable forms. Two reports illustrate the micro- and macrostatistics developed by the Federal Reserve. An example of microstatistics is the functional cost analysis (FCA) discussed earlier in this chapter. Macrostatistics are published in reports such as the *Federal Reserve Bulletin*. In over 100 tables per monthly issue, the *Bulletin* provides financial statistics on monetary aggregates and interest rates, U.S. government finances, securities market trading, real estate, finance, consumer credit, business activity, and international trade and money markets. The cost of producing information services is borne by the Federal Reserve and often provided to the financial community at nominal cost.

SUMMARY

Commercial banks are the most important and most complex financial institution in the United States. The statement of condition and the income statement of a bank provide valuable information concerning its resources and operations. The statement of condition shows that the principal financial contracts issued by banks are demand deposits, savings deposits, and time deposits. Commercial banks compete vigorously for customers' deposits with demand, time, and NOW accounts. Although banks experience a net loss on demand deposit account services, the bank obtains the use of customers' money. Although customers are not paid interest on their demand deposits balances, they do receive benefits in the form of checking account services.

Time and savings account deposits appear in two basic forms: passbook savings and certificates of deposit. The certificates may be nonnegotiable or negotiable. In the latter case, the certificates may represent a transferable bank deposit account, which is a money market instrument. Another principal source of bank funds is purchase of federal funds and borrowing. These are day or weekend loans from other banks and are transacted through the Federal Reserve.

The funds banks obtain from deposits and the Federal Reserve are invested in individual and business loans and securities. The securities are generally limited to state, local, and federal government bonds. Loans made by banks benefit the bank in the form of interest revenue and benefit the community by satisfying commercial, consumer, and mortgage needs. In turn commercial loans, subdivided into three basic types—seasonal, permanent working capital, and term —have increased and decreased sporadically since World War II.

Banks invest heavily in state and local government bonds because the interest from these investments is exempt from federal income tax. Since banks are generally in high-income-tax brackets, the tax-exempt feature can boost net yields by as much as 60 percent.

Bank investments in federal government securities include investments ranging from short-term Treasury bills to long-term bonds. These investments carry a comparatively low yield, but banks are the major holders of these securities.

The difference between investment income received by banks and interest paid on deposits is the interest margin from which banks pay operating expenses. Earnings remaining after expenses are divided among tax payments, dividends to stockholders, and retained earnings.

Three basic bank structures function in the United States: correspondent banking, group banking, and branch banking. The corespondent banking system consists of a network of informal relationships in which small banks forward and maintain deposit balances in large money-center banks in exchange for which the small bank is provided with check clearing, accounting, banking, advisory, and other services.

Group banking is typically carried on through a bank holding company. A bank holding company is a corporation created to hold the stock of one or more banks whose affiliation is limited due to bank laws that prohibit branch offices.

Branch banking, which represents the greatest number of bank locations, consists of a number of different bank offices owned and operated by a single legal entity. Expansion of bank branches increases profitability and benefits the consumer public in a variety of ways, including lower loan rates and more liberal credit.

TERMS

financial contracts	self-liquidating loans
demand deposits	municipal bonds
savings deposits	tax-exempt notes and bonds
time deposits	net interest revenue
certificates of deposit (CDs)	correspondent banking
Federal funds	group banking
"full service" banking	bank holding company
money market	branch banking
seasonal loans	chain banking
term loans	functional cost analysis

QUESTIONS

1 What are the principal types of accounts offered by banks?
2 Which two financial statements best describe banks and other financial institutions?
3 What financial institutions are permitted to hold demand deposits?
4 List three advantages that checking accounts offer over currency.
5 Calculate the effective interest rate on demand deposits given the following information:

Average collected demand deposit balances	$15,000,000
Annual service fee income	67,500
Annual processing expenses	750,000
Reserves (percent of demand deposits)	12 percent

6 Compare passbook savings account with nonnegotiable certificates of deposit with respect to maturity dates, minimum denominations, and interest rates.
7 Why are negotiable CDs considered money-market instruments?
8 Country National Bank has a surplus money supply, while Central City National Bank is currently short of funds. Both banks are in touch with Mid City National Bank, a correspondent bank of both. Explain and illustrate the procedures that

would be followed in a federal funds transaction between Country Bank and Central City Bank.

9 a What are the three types of commercial loan needs served by banks?
b Which of these types is considered self-liquidating?
10 What feature of state and local government bonds make them most attractive to banks? What effect does this feature have on the yield of these bonds?
11 Compute net interest revenue for Peoples National Bank, which has income and expenses as follows:

Income from U.S. Treasury bonds	$10,000
Income from municipal bonds	7,000
Income from loans	24,000
Income from other services	4,000
Interest expense	19,000
Operating expenses	12,000
Taxes	2,000

12 What five important services are provided by correspondent banks?
13 What legal restriction do bank holding companies attempt to circumvent? How does group banking accomplish this? What is chain banking?
14 How does branch banking differ from group banking?
15 What six benefits are derived from branch banking?

SELECTED REFERENCES

Ali, M. M., and S. I. Greenbaum: "A Spatial Model of the Banking Industry," *Journal of Finance,* September 1977, pp. 1283–1303.

Benston, George J.: "The Optimal Banking Structure: Theory and Evidence," *Journal of Bank Research,* Winter 1973, p. 220.

Boltz, P. W.: "Survey of Terms of Bank Lending," *Federal Reserve Bulletin,* May 1977, pp. 442–445.

Bozcar, G. E.: "Market Characteristics and Multibank Holding Company Acquisitions," *Journal of Finance,* March 1977, pp. 131–146.

Brewer, V. L., and W. P. Dukes: "Empirical Evidence on the Risk-Return Relationships between Banks and Related Bank Holding Companies," *Review of Business and Economic Research,* Spring 1976, pp. 56–65.

Burns, A. F.: "Statements to Congress," *Federal Reserve Bulletin,* July 1977, pp. 636–643.

Campbell, T. S.: "A Model of the Market for Lines of Credit," *Journal of Finance,* March 1978, pp. 231–244.

Chase, S., and J. Morgo: "The Regulation of Bank Holding Companies," *Journal of Finance,* May 1975, pp. 282–292.

Coldwell, P. E.: "Statements to Congress," *Federal Reserve Bulletin,* February 1976, pp. 113–119.

Eisemann, P. C.: "Diversification and Congeneric Bank Holding Company," *Journal of Bank Research,* Spring 1976, pp. 68–77.

Eisenbeis, R. A.: "Differences in Federal Regulatory Agencies' Bank Merger Policies," *Journal of Money, Credit and Banking,* February 1975, pp. 93–104.

Gardner, S. S.: "Statements to Congress," *Federal Reserve Bulletin,* November 1976, pp. 912–915.

Gilbert, G. G.: "An Analysis of Federal Regulatory Decisions on Market Extension Banks Mergers," *Journal of Money, Credit and Banking,* February 1975, pp. 81–92.

Gilbert, G. G., and M. O. Peterson: "The Impact of Changes in Federal Reserve Membership on Commercial Bank Performance," *Journal of Finance,* June 1975, pp. 713–720.

Greenbaum, S. I., M. M. Ali, and R. C. Morris: "Monetary Policy and Banking Profits," *Journal of Finance,* March 1976, pp. 89–101.

Hall, William: "How the American System of Bank Regulations Developed," *The Banker,* September 1974, pp. 1101–1107.

Haslem, John A., and William A. Longbrake, "The Productive Efficiency of North Carolina Commercial Banks," Research Paper 21, Graduate School of Business Administration, University of North Carolina, Chapel Hill, February 1975.

Heggestad, A. A., and J. J. Mingo: "The Competitive Condition of D. C. Banking Markets and the Impact of Structural Form," *Journal of Finance,* June 1977, pp. 649–662.

Horvitz, Paul M., "Failures of Large Banks: Implications for Banking Supervision and Deposit Insurance," *Journal of Financial and Quantitative Analysis,* November 1975, pp. 589–601.

James, J. A.: "Banking Market Structure, Risk, and the Pattern of Local Interest Rates in the United States, 1893–1911," *Review of Economics and Statistics,* November 1976, pp. 453–462.

Kohers, T.: "Commercial Banks and Bank Holding Companies: A Financial Performance Comparison," *University of Michigan Business Review,* July 1977, p. 6–10.

Mayne, L. S.: "Management Policies of Bank Holding Companies and Bank Performance," *Journal of Bank Research,* Spring 1976, pp. 37–48.

Mayne, L. S.: "A Comparative Study of Bank Holding Company Affiliates and Independent Banks, 1969–1972," *Journal of Finance,* March 1977, pp. 147–158.

Murphy, Neil B.: "The Relationship between Organizational Size and the Administrative Component of Banks: A Comment," *Journal of Business,* January 1976, pp. 62–65.

Peterson, R. L.: "Factors Affecting the Growth of Bank Credit Card and Check Credit," *Journal of Finance,* May 1977, p. 553.

Rhoades, S. A.: "Sharing Arrangements in an Electronic Funds Transfer System," *Journal of Bank Research,* Spring 1977, pp. 8–15.

Spellman, G. S.: "Competitive for Savings Deposits in the U.S.: 1936–1966," *Journal of Financial and Quantitative Analysis,* November 1975, pp. 567–576.

Summers, "Correspondent Services, Federal Reserve Services, and Bank Cash Management Policy," *Economic Review,* November–December 1978, pp. 29–38.

CHAPTER 9

SAVINGS AND LOAN ASSOCIATIONS, SAVINGS BANKS, AND CREDIT UNIONS

Savings and loan associations, savings banks, and credit unions specialize in consumer deposits and loans but, as permitted by expanded depository and lending powers granted in the recent years, offer services to businesses as well. Savings and loans and savings banks, once highly specialized institutions concentrating on the local consumer savings market niche, are rapidly converging with their diversified brother—the commercial bank. On the other hand, credit unions continue to specialize in the consumer savings and loan market and operate under a preferential but restricted legal status. Why are these instutions different from banks? Why do they continue to specialize in particular financial markets? These questions are answered largely by their histories, from their inceptions as limited-purpose institutions meeting the needs of a small group of savings and borrowers through turbulent periods of fluctuating interest rates in the money and capital markets.

SAVINGS AND LOAN ASSOCIATIONS

Starting as small, informal cooperatives pooling and accumulating funds so that a few members could purchase homes, savings and loan associations (S & Ls) have matured into an established intermediary serving masses of savers and home buyers. The basic strategy of savings and loan associations has been to purchase funds directly from middle-income savers and lend funds to real estate buyers. Innovative lending and savings policies, such as early entry into government lending programs, heavy promotional efforts, and attractive facilities, have appealed to the general public. The S & Ls continue to appeal to savers by making the thrift concept meaningful and practical. To create the image of a progressive and friendly savings institution paying a high rate of return with safety, the S & L industry has spent more on promotion and advertising than any other type of financial institution.

Savings Trends at Savings and Loan Associations

During the 20-year period following World War II and prior to 1964, savings balances at savings and loan associations doubled about every 5 years. Furthermore, the growth was stable from year to year, and associations could predict with confidence that savings would increase each year. Substantial changes in the money and capital markets in recent years have ushered in a new environment characterized by uncertainty and unsettling shifts in the savings growth rates. (Savings-share amounts are shown in Table 9-1, and changes in savings shares are shown in Table 9-2.)

Wide fluctuations in interest rates and historically high rates produced substantial shifts in the flow of funds. The historically high interest rates in 1969, 1974, and 1980 caused periods of disintermediation. Household deposits flowed out of savings and loans and into primary securities such as Treasury bills, because savings interest rates did not increase as fast as primary security rates. Savings institution rates were restricted by government regulation, while primary security rates were unregulated and negotiated freely in the open market. (The reasons for regulation of interest rates are many, as discussed in Chapter 21.)

The impact of restricted interest rate payments on deposits was substantial. Net savings (deposits less withdrawals) at associations dipped below zero during periods of high short-term interest rate. (See Figure 3-7 for interest rates.) In response to the shift in interest rates and funds flows, associations began issuing a wide assortment of savings accounts in the 1970s and 1980s. The accounts were distinguished by the interest rate paid and the maturity of the account. Consequently the proportions of passbook savings and certificate and special accounts have changed significantly. In one decade certificates of deposit have grown from only about 5 percent to over 75 percent of total savings. S & L management responded quickly to the loss of funds in traditional savings accounts by developing and promoting the higher yielding certificates.

Loans and Investments

Savings flows provide the major source of growth for associations, and most of the funds are invested in mortgages (Table 9-2). Conventional mortgage investments are made in one- to four-family dwellings directly to owners who provide a 20 percent down payment. During the 1960s about 95 percent of the mortgages were conventional loans rather than mortgage loans insured by the Veterans Administration (VA) or the Home Loan Bank (FHA). In the 1970s, however, associations began purchasing mortgages insured by the VA and

TABLE 9-1

SAVINGS AND LOAN STATEMENTS OF FINANCIAL ASSETS AND LIABILITIES, 1972–1984 (BILLIONS OF DOLLARS)

		1972	1973	1974	1975	1976	1977	1978	1979	1980	1981	1982	1983	1984
Total financial assets	1	236.9	267.2	292.3	333.1	385.1	449.3	512.8	569.4	621.9	657.8	706.0	821.7	989.9
Mortgages	2	199.0	227.1	246.1	273.5	316.2	371.3	422.1	466.1	494.4	512.2	482.2	526.3	606.3
Consumer credit	3	3.5	6.5	7.4	8.2	9.3	10.8	11.0	14.8	17.4	17.2	20.2	26.6	43.3
Other assets	4	34.4	33.6	38.9	51.4	59.6	67.3	79.7	88.5	110.2	128.4	203.6	268.8	340.3
Demand deposits & currency	5	1.2	1.0	1.0	1.3	1.6	1.5	1.6	2.1	2.6	3.6	5.5	9.1	10.3
Time deposits	6	3.4	2.9	3.6	8.1	6.7	6.8	7.2	5.0	7.5	6.8	14.0	15.2	16.0
Federal funds & security RPs	7	0.9	2.2	4.8	3.8	5.0	7.3	9.0	11.5	10.8	15.0	15.4	21.1	22.5
U.S. government securities	8	15.0	15.4	14.9	19.6	25.2	29.1	33.6	34.6	48.4	51.4	88.0	130.2	170.7
Treasury issues	9	5.4	3.4	1.8	2.4	7.3	6.3	6.3	3.4	9.0	5.5	13.6	27.9	49.0
Agency issues	10	9.6	11.9	13.1	17.2	17.9	22.8	27.4	31.2	39.3	45.9	74.4	102.3	121.7
State & local obligations	11	0.2	0.2	0.5	1.5	1.2	1.2	1.3	1.2	1.2	1.3	0.8	0.9	0.9
Open-market paper	12	3.3	2.0	1.8	2.7	2.6	2.3	2.7	3.4	4.9	6.1	8.8	12.5	8.7
Miscellaneous assets	13	10.4	10.0	12.3	14.4	17.3	19.2	24.3	30.8	34.8	44.2	71.1	79.9	110.8
Total liabilities	14	221.7	250.1	273.9	313.3	363.1	424.1	483.8	536.8	588.6	629.4	679.9	794.7	966.3
Deposits	15	206.8	227.0	243.0	285.7	335.9	386.8	431.0	470.0	511.8	531.8	580.8	678.0	796.1
Fed. funds & security RPs	16	0.3	0.3	1.8	1.9	1.8	3.8	5.9	6.4	8.5	11.3	15.1	25.2	45.5
Credit market instruments	17	9.5	17.1	23.3	19.1	17.4	24.3	37.8	50.3	57.8	73.4	70.4	71.6	93.9
Corporate bonds	18	—	—	—	0.1	0.1	1.3	2.0	3.4	3.7	3.2	3.2	3.5	3.5
Bank loans n.e.c.	19	1.5	1.9	1.5	1.2	1.4	2.8	3.1	5.1	5.1	5.0	1.2	9.2	15.7
Fed. Home Loan Bank loans	20	8.0	15.1	21.8	17.8	15.9	20.2	32.7	41.8	49.0	65.2	66.0	59.0	74.6
Profit taxes payable	21	0.2	0.2	0.3	0.4	0.6	0.8	1.0	0.8	0.5	0.1	0.1	0.1	*
Miscellaneous liabilities	22	4.9	5.6	5.5	6.2	7.3	8.5	8.2	9.2	10.1	12.7	13.5	19.8	30.9
Memo: Total cr. mkt. assets	23	221.1	251.2	270.6	305.5	354.5	414.6	470.8	520.0	566.2	588.2	600.2	696.4	830.0

* Negligible amount.

TABLE 9-2
SAVINGS AND LOANS FLOW OF FUNDS, 1972–1984 (BILLIONS OF DOLLARS)

	1972	1973	1974	1975	1976	1977	1978	1979	1980	1981	1982	1983	1984
Current surplus	1.6	2.0	1.5	1.4	2.0	2.7	3.6	3.3	1.4	-3.7	-2.9	1.0	-0.8
Net acq. of financial assets	35.9	30.3	25.1	40.8	52.0	64.3	63.5	56.6	52.6	35.8	55.3	115.6	159.6
Mortgages	30.5	28.0	19.0	27.7	42.7	55.1	51.4	44.2	28.7	18.3	-23.5	44.1	77.0
Consumer credit	-0.1	1.2	0.9	0.8	1.1	1.5	0.3	3.7	2.6	-0.2	3.3	6.3	13.7
Other assets	5.5	0.9	5.2	12.3	8.2	7.7	11.8	8.6	21.3	17.7	75.4	65.2	69.0
Demand deposits & currency	0.2	-0.2	—	0.3	0.3	-0.2	0.1	0.5	0.5	1.0	1.9	3.6	1.8
Time deposits	1.0	*	0.7	4.5	-1.4	0.1	0.4	-2.2	2.5	-0.7	7.2	1.2	0.8
Fed Funds & Security RPs	0.3	1.3	2.6	-1.0	1.2	2.3	1.7	2.5	-0.7	4.2	0.4	5.7	1.2
U.S. Treasury securities	0.1	-2.0	-1.6	0.6	4.9	-1.0	*	-2.9	5.7	-3.5	7.5	14.3	19.7
U.S. government agency securities	2.4	2.3	1.2	4.1	0.7	4.9	4.6	3.9	8.1	6.6	29.8	27.8	17.5
State & local obligations	*	*	0.3	1.0	-0.3	*	0.1	-0.1	*	0.1	-0.5	*	*
Open-market paper	0.5	-1.3	-0.2	0.9	-0.1	-0.3	0.4	0.7	1.5	1.2	2.7	3.6	-3.8
Miscellaneous	1.7	1.3	2.3	1.9	2.9	1.8	4.6	6.3	3.7	8.8	26.4	8.8	31.8
Net increase in liabilities	34.2	28.4	23.7	39.5	49.7	61.1	59.6	53.0	51.9	40.8	59.6	114.8	160.9
Deposits	32.5	20.1	16.0	42.8	50.2	50.9	44.2	39.1	41.8	20.0	45.5	97.2	112.3
Security RPs	0.3	*	1.5	0.1	-0.1	1.9	2.1	0.5	2.1	3.0	3.8	16.5	21.4
Credit market instruments	0.4	7.5	6.2	-4.2	-1.7	6.9	13.5	12.6	7.4	15.5	-3.0	-5.2	20.1
Corporate bonds	—	—	—	0.1	-0.1	1.2	0.7	1.4	0.4	-0.5	*	*	-0.1
Bank loans n.e.c.	0.4	0.4	-0.4	-0.3	0.2	1.4	0.3	2.0	-0.1	-0.2	-3.8	1.8	4.5
Fed. Home Loan Bank loans	*	7.1	6.7	-4.0	-2.0	4.3	12.5	9.2	7.1	16.2	0.8	-7.0	15.7
Profit taxes payable	*	*	0.1	0.1	0.2	0.2	0.2	-0.2	-0.3	-0.3	*	*	-0.1
Misc. liabilities	0.9	0.6	-0.1	0.7	1.1	1.2	-0.3	1.1	0.9	2.6	13.3	6.3	7.2
Discrepancy	*	0.1	0.1	*	-0.2	-0.5	-0.2	-0.3	0.7	1.2	1.4	0.1	0.5
Memo: Acq. of credit mkt.	32.5	28.3	19.5	35.1	49.0	60.1	56.7	49.4	46.6	22.6	19.4	96.2	124.0

* Negligible amount.

FHA, to take advantge of regional interest-rate disparities. The Federal Home Loan Bank Board (FHLBB), an S & L regulatory agency, now permits S & Ls to lend up to 95 percent of the property value, if the principal balance in excess of 90 percent is insured by a private mortgage insurer or a specific S & L reserve. Conventional mortgages remain the mainstay of S & L lending, however, because of a rate differential favoring conventional mortgages over insured mortgages.

Operating Income and Expense

Mortgage interest income accounts for most of the S & Ls' gross income, and interest paid to savers is the major expense item. The mortgage loan portfolio also generates mortgage loan fees, commissions, and premiums. Of course, the major expense item is interest paid to savers. Operating expenses are largely for personnel compensation, office space, and advertising.

Profitability Trends

Profitability, as measured by net additions to reserves divided by total reserves at the begining of the year, ranged between 13 and 17 percent from 1950 through 1962. Dropping in 1963, the rate reached a low of 5 percent in 1966, fluctuated in the 7 to 9 percent range in the late 1960s and 1970s, and fell to a 15 percent loss in 1981 and 1982. Three of every four savings and loans reported a net operating loss in 1981 and 1982; in the more favorable interest-rate environment of 1983, one out of four savings and loans reported a net loss. The fluctuations in profitability are largely a function of short-term interest rate fluctuations, which affect interest expense and savings flows. When short-term rates increase in the money markets, the savings and loans must increase their rates to remain competitive. However, gross income changes very little because interest income from mortgages remains constant for the life of the mortgage—up to 30 years. Net operating income declined, therefore, during tight credit and high-interest-rate periods—such as occurred during the high-inflation-rate era of the early 1980s.

Government Regulation

Most savings and loan associations are regulated by the Federal Home Loan Bank Board (FHLBB), although some S & Ls are regulated only by the laws of their states. The FHLBB supervises the operating as well as financial affairs in great detail. During unannounced audits the FHLBB examiners verify accounts, review management decisions, and evaluate the efficiency of operations. The FHLBB promulgates rules to interpret congressional legislation that applies to S & Ls and studies problems facing the industry and its public.

The Federal Home Loan Bank Board provides many of the same lending and statistical services to S & Ls as the Federal Reserve gives the commercial

banks. S & Ls may borrow from FHLBB for a broader range of needs, however. They may borrow to meet a decline in deposits or an increase in mortgage
demand. The need may be seasonal and the loan repaid within a few months, or
the demand for funds may continue for an extended period. When home
building proceeds at a brisk pace, new mortgage money is needed. By supporting the S & Ls with loans up to 17½ percent of savings deposits, a vast amount
of money is made available to S & Ls. Because of the investment restrictions
imposed on S & Ls, the advances tend to be invested in home mortgages. Most
of the FHLBB advances are invested ultimately in home mortgages and thus
support the housing industry. Congress supports housing finance as a matter of
good public policy. In the process S & L managers gain an important source of
emergency and expansion funding.

Just as the FDIC provides deposit insurance for commercial banks, the
Federal Saving and Loan Insurance Corporation provides deposit insurance for
savings and loan associations. Again, the insurance amounts to $100,000 per
account and the insurance fee is one-tenth of 1 percent of deposits annually.

Savings and loan standards are set by the FHLBB. In addition to initial
capital, S & Ls must retain some of their income each year. The retained
income is transferred to a capital account until the capital-to-deposit ratio
reaches 5 percent. The average capital-to-assets ratio for savings and loans is
about 3.7 percent.

The Federal Home Loan Bank Administration (FHLBA), like other regulatory agencies, requires periodic reporting of financial and other information
by its member institutions. Much of this information forms the basis for
statistical data reported in the FHLBA's monthly publication, *The Journal*. In
addition to statistics, *The Journal* provides articles of current interest and
industry developments. *The Journal* is also the vehicle used for publishing the
FHLBA's annual report. The FHLBA's Office of Economic Research publishes a monthly newsletter, *Economic Briefs,* which is a digest of newsworthy
information affecting the savings and loan industry.

MUTUAL SAVINGS BANKS

Mutual savings banks (MSBs) channel deposits primarily into long-term investments and liquid assets. Mortgage loans represent about two-thirds of all
assets, while U.S. government and corporate securities account for most of the
remainder. Like savings and loan associations, savings banks attract funds
from small investors. Mutual savings banks do not make extensive use of
money-market borrowings for liquidity and have no capital stock. In general
savings banks adhere closely to the concept of channeling depositor's savings
into low-risk investments, as prescribed by law and conservative management
policies.

The Middle Atlantic and New England states host 90 percent of the MSBs.
The geographical concentration in the northeastern United States is a historical
phenomenon, unique to the savings bank industry. All are state-chartered
organizations subject to legal restrictions that prevent geographic extension.

The greatest number of associations are located in Massachusetts, followed by New York, Connecticut, Maine, and New Hampshire, but the greatest concentration of savings bank assets is in New York.

Deposit Trends at Savings Banks

Savings bank deposits have increased astride with other thrift instutitions. Since World War II, deposits have increased every year, although the rate of growth has varied widely from year to year. In recent years the most rapid growth rate was in 1983 and the slowest growth rate was during 1974. (Mutual savings bank assets, liabilities, and flow of funds are shown in Tables 9-3 and 9-4.)

Growth at savings banks was related to (1) yields on competitive money-market instruments, and (2) development of new depository accounts by savings banks and their competitors. The fluctuations in net deposit gains corresponded very closely with the yield spread between interest rates on savings bank deposits and average yields on 3- to 5-year U.S. government securities. Like other thrift institutions, savings banks are subject to disintermediation when money-market rates increase sharply.

Loans and Investments

Mortgages comprise a larger portion of investments at savings banks than at commercial banks but are proportionally less than at savings and loan associations. Most of the asset growth from 1950 to 1978 has been in mortgage securities, which increased from 36 to 68 percent of total assets (see Table 9-4). Delinquency rates on mortgages have been relatively low. Savings banks experienced delinquency rates of about 0.6 to 0.7 percent on FHA- and VA-insured mortgages and 0.5 percent on conventional mortgages. Foreclosure rates were about 0.09 percent for FHA, 0.05 percent for VA, and 0.02 percent for conventional mortgages.

Funds used to increase the mortgage portfolio at mutual savings banks were derived from net deposit inflows and decreases in U.S. government securities. Note in Table 9-5 the net outflow in U.S. government bonds for nearly every year from 1948 to 1974. Yields for U.S. government bonds were less than mortgage yields throughout the post-World War II period, drawing thrift institution funds out of U.S. Treasury bills, notes, and bonds. Furthermore, savings banks have been investing heavily in corporate bonds during the past decade and in Federal funds, open-market paper, and short-term marketable securities in recent years.

Capital Resources

The amount of reserves at savings banks increased, but not as rapidly as deposits, from 1951 to 1980. Furthermore, operating losses sustained in

TABLE 9-3
MUTUAL SAVINGS BANKS STATEMENT OF FINANCIAL ASSETS AND LIABILITIES DECEMBER 31, 1972-1984 (BILLIONS OF DOLLARS)

		1972	1973	1974	1975	1976	1977	1978	1979	1980	1981	1982	1983	1984
Total financial assets	1	101.5	106.8	109.1	121.1	134.8	147.3	158.2	163.3	171.5	175.3	174.3	191.5	206.4
Demand deposits and currency	2	1.0	1.1	1.1	1.2	1.3	2.1	3.0	2.8	3.9	5.1	5.2	4.3	4.6
Time deposits	3	0.6	0.8	1.0	1.1	1.1	0.3	0.7	0.4	0.4	0.3	1.8	1.1	.4
Fed. funds & security RPs	4	0.8	1.5	1.2	1.1	1.5	2.1	2.1	3.1	3.7	5.2	5.3	6.2	6.6
Corporate equities	5	4.5	4.2	3.7	4.4	4.4	4.8	4.8	4.7	4.2	3.2	3.3	4.2	4.3
Credit market instruments	6	92.4	96.8	99.4	110.1	122.9	134.1	143.4	148.0	154.3	155.8	151.0	166.6	178.9
U.S. government securities	7	7.7	7.2	7.0	10.9	14.9	17.6	18.3	19.5	22.8	23.7	23.8	33.0	34.3
Treasury issues	8	3.5	3.0	2.6	4.7	5.8	5.9	5.0	4.8	5.6	5.4	6.0	9.8	9.9
Agency issues	9	4.2	4.2	4.4	6.1	9.1	11.7	13.4	14.7	17.2	18.4	17.8	23.2	24.4
State & local obligations	10	0.9	0.9	0.9	1.5	2.4	2.8	3.3	2.9	2.4	2.3	2.5	2.2	2.1
Corporate & foreign bonds	11	14.2	13.1	14.0	17.5	20.3	21.5	21.6	20.5	21.2	20.3	19.0	21.7	21.0
Mortgages	12	67.6	73.2	74.9	77.2	81.6	88.1	95.2	98.9	99.9	100.0	94.1	96.0	103.3
Consumer credit	13	1.6	1.9	2.1	2.3	2.6	3.1	3.9	3.9	4.3	4.2	4.9	6.0	11.3
Commercial paper	14	0.6	0.5	0.5	0.6	1.0	1.0	1.2	2.2	3.7	5.3	6.8	7.8	7.0
Miscellaneous assets	15	2.1	2.4	2.6	3.2	3.6	3.9	4.1	4.4	5.0	5.6	7.9	9.1	11.6
Total liabilities	16	93.6	99.0	101.6	112.6	125.8	137.3	147.3	151.9	160.2	165.7	165.0	180.4	195.0
Deposits	17	91.6	96.3	98.7	109.9	122.9	134.0	142.6	146.0	153.5	156.5	157.0	172.3	181.6
Miscellaneous liabilities	18	2.0	2.6	2.9	2.8	2.9	3.3	4.7	5.9	6.7	9.2	7.9	8.1	13.4

TABLE 9-4
MUTUAL SAVINGS BANKS FLOW OF FUNDS, 1972–1984

	1972	1973	1974	1975	1976	1977	1978	1979	1980	1981	1982	1983	1984
Current Surplus	0.4	0.5	0.5	0.4	0.4	0.7	0.9	0.7	-0.4	-1.2	-0.9	*	0.8
Net acq. of financial assets	11.0	6.0	3.8	11.5	13.8	12.5	10.9	5.2	8.2	4.2	4.4	16.6	12.0
Demand deposits & currency	*	0.1	*	0.1	*	*	1.0	-0.3	1.1	1.2	0.1	-0.8	0.1
Time deposits	0.1	0.1	0.2	0.1	—	*	0.3	-0.3	*	-0.1	1.4	-0.7	-1.4
Fed. funds & security RPs	0.1	0.7	-0.3	-0.1	0.4	0.6	*	0.9	0.6	1.5	*	0.9	1.9
Corporate equities	0.6	0.3	0.2	0.2	0.1	0.4	0.1	-0.1	-0.5	-0.6	-0.5	0.3	*
Credit market investments	9.5	4.3	3.1	10.7	12.8	11.1	8.8	4.4	5.9	0.9	0.6	15.7	10.9
U.S. Treasury securities	0.2	-0.4	-0.4	2.2	1.1	0.1	-0.9	-0.2	0.8	-0.2	0.7	3.8	*
U.S. government agency securities	1.1	*	0.2	1.7	2.9	2.6	1.7	1.3	2.5	1.2	1.2	5.4	0.7
State and local obligations	0.5	*	*	0.6	0.9	0.4	0.5	-0.4	-0.5	-0.1	0.2	-0.3	-0.1
Corporate bonds	2.1	1.1	0.9	3.5	2.8	1.2	0.1	-1.1	0.7	-1.0	-1.1	2.7	-1.0
Mortgages	5.4	5.7	2.2	2.3	4.4	6.5	6.5	3.6	0.6	-0.4	-2.6	2.0	7.4
Consumer credit	0.1	0.3	0.2	0.2	0.3	0.5	0.7	0.1	0.4	*	0.6	1.1	2.8
Commercial paper	0.1	0.1	0.1	0.1	0.4	*	0.2	1.1	1.5	1.5	1.6	1.0	1.0
Misc. assets	0.5	0.2	0.5	0.6	0.4	0.3	0.7	0.5	1.0	1.2	2.7	1.1	0.5
Net increase in liabilities	10.3	5.3	3.4	11.0	13.1	11.5	10.0	4.6	8.3	5.5	5.0	15.4	11.9
Deposits	10.1	4.7	3.1	11.2	13.0	11.1	8.6	3.4	7.5	3.0	5.3	15.3	8.8
Misc. liabilities	0.2	0.6	0.3	-0.1	0.1	0.4	1.4	1.2	0.8	2.6	-0.3	0.1	3.1
Discrepancy	-0.2	-0.1	0.1	-0.1	-0.2	-0.3	-0.1	*	-0.2	0.2	-0.2	-1.2	0.7

TABLE 9-5
CREDIT UNIONS STATEMENTS OF FINANCIAL ASSETS AND LIABILITIES, 1972–1984 (BILLIONS OF DOLLARS)

		1972	1973	1974	1975	1976	1977	1978	1979	1980	1981	1982	1983	1984
Total financial assets	1	24.6	27.8	31.1	36.9	43.3	51.5	58.4	63.1	71.6	75.1	86.8	103.1	115.8
Demand deposits and currency	2	0.9	0.9	1.0	0.9	0.8	0.8	0.9	1.1	1.3	1.4	1.4	1.5	1.6
Time deposits	3	0.1	0.3	0.5	0.1	0.8	0.9	0.9	0.8	2.9	2.2	2.2	2.2	2.4
Savings and loan deposits	4	3.6	2.9	3.3	3.3	3.3	4.2	3.6	5.4	9.3	9.7	10.8	10.2	10.0
Credit market instruments	5	20.1	23.7	26.4	31.7	38.4	45.6	52.9	55.8	58.2	61.8	72.4	89.1	101.9
U.S. government securities	6	2.1	2.6	3.0	4.1	4.7	5.2	5.3	5.3	9.6	10.8	19.6	29.6	27.5
Home mortgages	7	1.0	1.4	1.5	2.0	2.5	2.8	3.4	4.0	4.5	5.0	5.5	6.0	6.5
Consumer credit	8	17.0	19.6	21.9	25.7	31.2	37.6	44.3	46.5	44.0	46.0	47.3	53.5	67.9
Credit union shares	9	21.6	24.5	27.5	33.0	39.0	46.7	53.0	57.5	65.7	68.9	80.1	95.9	108.0

1980–1982 reduced reserves. Reserves at savings banks have declined to a position similar to that of other deposit intermediaries, with capital and reserves equal to about 5.8 percent of assets (capital is discussed again in Chapter 17).

Income and Expense

The shift to higher yielding assets and generally higher interest rates in the post-World War II period has been reflected in higher asset yields. Operating income has advanced steadily with higher yields and larger portfolios. Savings bank asset yields have been less than savings and loans, but the gap has narrowed as savings banks have increased the proportion of their portfolio invested in mortgages.

Increases in current operating income have been paralleled by increases in interest and operating expenses. Earnings increased during the 1971–1972 period. Earnings dropped in 1973–1974 as short-term interest rates rose. From 1974 to 1976, net realized losses on mortgages rose and credit-market rates increased, forcing some savings banks to liquidate long-term investments with capital losses. Then in the 1980–1982 period, losses from operations resulted from interest expenses rising faster than interest revenues, as was the case for savings and loans.

Government Regulation

Mutual savings banks are unique among banking institutions in that there is no separate federal regulatory agency having jurisdiction over MSBs. They are, like savings and loans, able to join the FHLB and take advantage of credit available through the FHLB. In addition, New York MSBs and Massachusetts MSBs can borrow through the Savings Banks Trust Company in New York and the Mutual Savings Central Fund in Massachusetts, respectively. All MSBs are insured either by the FDIC or, in Massachusetts only, by the Mutual Savings Central Fund, Inc. While some elements of MSB statistics are included in government publications that deal with financial institutions generally, the primary source of MSB statistical information is industry publications.

Mutual savings banks must meet capital requirements set by the chartering state or the FDIC. Of the two requirements, the FDIC is the more stringent. Although a specific capital ratio is not mandated by Congress, the FDIC is empowered to set capital levels. Under the FDIC formula, new savings banks are required to begin with capital equal to 8 percent of assets projected at the end of 3 years of operation. States require mutual, nonstock MSBs to augment capital reserves with retained earnings. In New York, for example, 10 percent of net income (after interest payments on deposits) must be retained when capital is less than 10 percent of deposit liabilities.

CREDIT UNIONS

Credit unions are deposit intermediaries that borrow and lend money to a group of consumers with a common association. Three ingredients are needed to form a credit union: (1) a group of people with a common bond, (2) a pool of savings from members, and (3) a portfolio of loans to members. Credit union members share a common bond, such as a labor union, church, fraternal order, employer, or neighborhood. Members buy "shares" in the credit union with their savings and are extended the privilege of borrowing from the credit union after becoming a savings member.

The 17,000 credit unions are all mutual associations that may begin without capital or reserves. (Depositors technically are shareholders who would participate in losses if there were any.) These are cooperative, self-help societies chartered to serve their members. Although individual members may deposit or borrow money for profit motives, the credit union is not a free-enterprise, profit-oriented institution. Ordinarily the treasurer is the only salaried officer, and other officials serve on a voluntary, part-time basis. Thus credit unions tend to be relatively small institutions; 85 percent of them have total assets of less than $5 million.

Savings Shares

The major part of credit union funds (about 85 percent) comes from member savings in the form of shares and deposits. The small saver is the traditional bulwark of the credit union. Accounts average only $890 and members may "join" the credit union with as little as $5. Members are encouraged to be thrifty, and sponsoring organizations often cooperate by making payroll deductions at the request of the member. Savings share amounts, shown in Tables 9-5 and 9-6, are growing at a very substantial rate.

Loans and Investments

The major source of revenue for the credit union is interest paid on loans. The loans are nearly always consumer loans to members, but some states allow the credit unions to make real estate mortgage loans as well. State laws set maximum loan maturities, amounts, and rates. Federal credit unions are subject to federal laws and certain state laws. For federal credit unions, loans to any borrower may not exceed 15 percent of unimpaired capital and surplus.[1]

In addition to loans to its members, a credit union is permitted to invest in loans to other credit unions and to federally insured mutual savings banks and savings and loans associations, and to purchase U.S. government securities. Some state credit unions are also permitted to purchase high-quality municipal bonds, corporate bonds, and mortgage loans.

[1] For further details, see the *1976 Annual Report* of the National Credit Union Administration, pp. 5–9.

TABLE 9-6
CREDIT UNIONS FLOW OF FUNDS, 1972-1984 (BILLIONS OF DOLLARS)

	1972	1973	1974	1975	1976	1977	1978	1979	1980	1981	1982	1983	1984
Current surplus	0.2	0.3	0.3	0.3	0.4	0.5	0.6	0.3	0.2	0.4	0.5	0.4	0.4
Net acq. of financial assets	3.5	3.1	3.3	5.8	6.4	8.2	6.9	4.8	8.5	3.5	11.7	16.3	13.3
Demand deposits & currency	*	*	*	-0.1	-0.1	0.1	0.1	0.2	0.1	0.1	0.1	0.1	0.1
Time deposits	*	0.2	0.2	0.5	-0.2	0.1	*	*	2.1	-0.7	—	*	0.1
Savings and loan deposits	0.6	-0.6	0.4	*	0.1	0.8	-0.5	1.8	3.9	0.4	1.1	-0.5	0.3
Credit market instruments	2.9	3.5	2.7	5.4	6.6	7.2	7.3	2.8	2.4	3.7	10.6	16.7	12.8
U.S. government securities	0.5	0.5	0.4	1.1	0.6	0.5	0.1	*	4.3	1.2	8.8	10.0	-2.1
House mortgages	2.1	2.6	0.1	0.5	0.5	0.3	0.6	0.6	0.5	0.5	0.5	0.5	0.5
Consumer credit	3.2	2.6	2.3	3.8	5.5	6.4	6.7	2.2	-2.5	1.9	1.3	6.2	14.4
Credit unions shares	3.2	2.9	3.0	5.5	6.0	7.7	6.4	4.4	8.3	3.1	11.2	15.8	12.9

TABLE 9-7
SELECTED SIGNIFICANT RATIOS OF FEDERALLY INSURED SAVINGS INSTITUTIONS

Year	FSLIC-insured savings institutions				FDIC-insured savings banks			
	Asset utiliza-tion[1]	Profit margin[2]	Return on equity[3]	Return on average assets[4]	Asset utiliza-tion[1]	Profit margin[2]	Return on equity[3]	Return on average assets[4]
1960	5.55%	15.55%	12.35%	0.86%	4.25%	11.50%	5.76%	0.49%
1965	5.72	11.63	9.83	0.67	4.93	9.33	5.83	0.46
1970	6.60	8.56	8.02	0.57	5.87	4.31	3.37	0.25
1971	6.93	10.24	10.51	0.71	6.15	7.59	6.56	0.47
1972	7.02	11.01	12.14	0.77	6.38	9.05	8.41	0.58
1973	7.34	10.31	12.15	0.76	6.68	7.88	7.64	0.53
1974	7.63	7.03	8.63	0.54	6.87	4.89	4.76	0.34
1975	7.73	6.06	7.82	0.47	7.06	5.08	4.79	0.36
1976	8.01	7.87	11.10	0.63	7.29	6.09	6.18	0.44
1977	8.23	9.32	13.94	0.77	7.43	7.23	8.13	0.54
1978	8.50	9.57	14.84	0.81	7.75	7.58	8.76	0.59
1979	9.08	7.37	12.06	0.67	8.23	5.42	6.53	0.45
1980	9.60	1.38	2.44	0.13	8.67	1.58	− 2.47	− 0.17
1981	10.48	− 6.96	− 15.44	− 0.73	9.41	− 9.89	− 15.56	− 0.93
1982	11.27	− 5.64	− 16.13	− 0.64	9.69	− 8.12	− 14.76	− 0.79
1983*	11.49	2.37	7.05	0.27	9.51	2.35	4.27	0.22

Note: Beginning in 1982, average assets exclude certain contra-asset balances which had been reported as liabilities.
* Preliminary.
[1] Total income divided by average assets (net of loans in process or contra-assets).
[2] Net after-tax income divided by total income.
[3] Net after-tax income divided by average net worth.
[4] Net after-tax income divided by average assets (net of loans in process or contra-assets).
Sources: Federal Deposit Insurance Corporation; Federal Home Loan Bank Board; United States League of Savings Institutions.

Credit unions realize good investment revenues from consumer loans and experience low expenses because of the close affiliation of members who are all owners as well as customers of the credit union. During 1982 they grossed 13.6 percent on loans, and 12.3 percent on other investments. Many state and federal credit unions make interest refunds to borrowing members; refunds are usually equal to about 10 percent of interest paid. The return of interest paid to borrowers is unique in the money and capital markets and points up the cooperative spirit of the credit union form of organization.

Government Regulation

Credit unions are regulated by state or federal agencies and laws; the federally chartered credit unions are regulated by the National Credit Union Administration (NCUA). As in the regulation of savings and loans, credit union regulation covers supervision, deposit insurance, and financial condition.

Federally chartered credit unions are insured by NCUA. Coverage—up to $100,000 per share account—is funded by an annual fee paid by each member credit union of one-twelfth of 1 percent of share deposits as of each December 31. Federal credit union insurance is also available to state-chartered credit unions. As of 1982, nine states required that their state-chartered credit unions be covered by federal insurance and 34 other states had optional state insurance programs that could be elected.

Federal regulations (enforced by the NCUA) require national credit unions to transfer funds from undivided earnings to a reserve for bad loans. Similarly, states require state-chartered credit unions to transfer a percentage of net income to a reserve fund. The percentage ranges from 5 to 20 percent, and transfers are not required once the reserve equals from 5 to 20 percent of shares or assets.

Credit unions, like savings and loans, can borrow from government agencies. The Federal Intermediate Credit Bank discounts eligible customer loans to provide funds when needed. Federal and state credit unions are usually permitted to borrow from commercial banks, although regulations vary from state to state.

The NCUA collects statistical and other data, which are published in the *Annual Report of the National Credit Union Administration* and the *NCUA Quarterly*. In addition, the NCUA publishes several topical newsletters that contain trade-oriented current and technical developments.

SUMMARY

Three financial institutions specialize in consumer savings instruments: savings and loan associations, mutual savings banks, and credit unions. Savings and loan associations (S & Ls) obtain funds in the form of savings from middle-income savers and lend these funds to purchasers of real estate. Following World War II, S & Ls experienced a strong, stable 20-year growth period.

Beginning in the mid-1960s, financial market instability necessitated a more aggressive policy toward attracting savings, including introduction of new savings vehicles such as certificates of deposit.

Until the 1980s S&Ls invested primarily in "conventional" home mortgages. In the past decade, however, S & Ls have selectively entered the VA- and FHA-insured mortgage market to take advantage of the large mortgage loan volume available in these markets. Mortgage interest is the principal source of income of S & Ls and, correspondingly, interest paid on savings is the major disposition of this income. More recently, S & Ls have entered the commercial loan market as part of a trend toward greater asset diversification. Ownership is reflected by reserve accounts. Following a period of steady, high profits in the 1950s, S & Ls have faced volatile profitability since 1963. While returns on mortgage investments are fixed at the begining of the long-term mortgage period, short-term interest rates have fluctuated, forcing the institutions to pay competitive (higher) rates on savings accounts.

Mutual savings banks (MSBs) are a regional phenomenon existing in the northeastern United States. Functioning in much the same manner as S & Ls, MSBs are state chartered, although they may be federally insured. As is true about S & Ls, unsteady short-term interest rates have created volatile deposit gains. An innovative deposit medium adopted by MSBs was the negotiable order-of-withdrawal account (NOW account), an interest-bearing checking account. In addition to real estate mortgages, investments of MSBs include corporate bonds, Federal funds, open-market paper, and short-term marketable securities.

Credit unions are savings institutions that are formed around a common association, such as membership in a church, residence in a neighborhood, or employment by a common employer. The source of funds is savings by members, which are represented by shares. Funds are invested in loans to members, generally consumer loans, although real estate loans may be made. Credit unions are restricted in the amounts that may be lent on secured and unsecured loans as well as the term of loans and the interest rates that may be charged.

TERMS

thrift institutions

savings and loans (S & Ls)

mutual savings banks (MSBs)

Federal Deposit Insurance Corporation (FDIC)

Federal Home Loan Bank Board (FHLBB)

general reserve account

reserves

credit unions

interest rebate

conventional mortgage

insured mortgage

QUESTIONS

1 What are the seven major reasons for which households maintain savings deposits?
2 Why do commercial and savings banks, savings and loan associations, and credit unions attract a large share of household savings?
3 What five services do financial intermediaries provide to savers?

4 What was the response of S & Ls to rising short-term interest rates in the 1970s?

5 What is the largest category of investment made by savings and loans? What percentage of assets is accounted for by this type of investment?

6 What is the difference between conventional and insured mortgages?

7 What is the major source of revenue to S & Ls?

8 What are S & L "reserves"? How are reserves increased? decreased?

9 How would you characterize the trend in profitability of S & Ls over the past decade?

10 What assets and liabilities of MSBs and S & Ls are similar?

11 Where are most MSBs located? Which state has the greatest number of MSBs? Which state has the largest concentration of MSB assets?

12 What two features influence savings flows into MSBs?

13 What has been the trend in reserves of MSBs? Are annual earnings growing as fast as deposits and reserves? What has been the trend of the earnings-to-reserves ratio? In general, has MSB profitability been increasing or decreasing over the past 10 years?

14 What are the three characteristics that distinguish credit unions from other financial institutions?

15 What investments are credit unions permitted to make by law? What is the major investment? Describe the typical credit union loan.

16 What advantage do credit unions have as compared with savings and loans and mutual savings banks in minimizing operating expenses?

17 What is the maximum dividend rate permitted for credit unions? What rates have they usually paid? How much do borrowers share in the earnings of credit unions?

SELECTED REFERENCES

Benston, George J.: "Savings Banking and the Public Interest," *Journal of Money, Credit, and Banking,* February 1972, pp. 133–226.

Fortune, P.: "The Effectiveness of Recent Policies to Maintain Thrift-Deposit Flows" *Journal of Money, Credit, and Banking,* August 1975, pp. 297–315.

Goldsmith, Raymond W.: *A Study of Savings in the United States,* 3 vols., Princeton University Press, Princeton, N.J., 1955–1956.

Harless, Doris E.: *Nonbank Financial Institutions,* Federal Reserve Bank of Richmond, October 1975.

Kaveman, H. M.: "An Analysis of the Behavior of Federal Mortgage Market Agencies," *Journal of Money, Credit, and Banking,* May 1977, pp. 349–355.

National Fact Book of Mutual Savings Banking, National Association of Mutual Savings Banks, New York, annual publication.

Annual Report of the National Credit Union Administration, Washington, D.C., annual publication.

O'Brien, James M.: "The Household as a Saver," *Business Review,* Federal Reserve Bank of Philadelphia, June 1971, pp. 14–23.

Savings and Loan Fact Book, United States Savings and Loan Association, Chicago, annual publication.

Schaaf, A. H.: "Reforming the Residential Mortgage Market," *California Management Review,* Spring 1976, pp. 76–85.

Yearbook, Credit Union National Association, Inc., Madison, Wis., annual publication.

Yearbook: Financial Intermediaries in the American Economy since 1900, Princeton University Press, Princeton, N.J., 1958.

CHAPTER 10

FINANCE COMPANIES

Finance companies specialize in *lending money to consumers and businesses,* and therefore the discussion in this chapter is divided into two parts: consumer credit and commercial credit. Some firms specialize in consumer or commercial credit, others specialize in one type of financial contract, whereas still others offer a broad range of contracts to many different types of borrowers. It would be a mistake to stereotype finance companies with respect to either people or financial contracts. Perhaps because this type of institution is the least regulated of the financial institutions, it has evolved into the most forms. Finance company operations vary from $100 signature loans through the mail to multimillion dollar leases for tankers and airplanes. However, the common element that generally separates finance companies from other financial institutions is that *they borrow funds from investors and bankers in large denominations and lend directly to consumers and businesses.*

CONSUMER CREDIT

Consumer credit has been an accepted fact of life in the United States since colonial days. Consumer credit is defined by the Federal Reserve as "short- and intermediate-term credit that is extended through regular channels to finance the purchase of commodities and services for personal consumption, or to refinance debts incurred for such purposes." Although the legend of pioneer days depicts colonists as sturdy, self-reliant cash-and-carry patrons of the general store and saloon, actually pioneers depended upon credit to carry them from crop to crop and to meet unexpected financial problems. The general store usually did not levy an explicit finance charge, but the merchandise markup included an amount sufficient to defray the cost of credit. As it is today, furniture was purchased on an installment basis. Sewing machines, books, and pianos were purchased on the installment plan as early as 1850. Monthly payments for automobiles began around 1910, and the rapid growth in the credit sale of automobiles thereafter contributed to the development of the mass market for cars and a tremendous expansion of consumer credit. Today, finance companies are a major lender to consumers and businesses needing money to buy cars, television sets, boats, industrial equipment, retail inventories, home repairs, or hospital services.

"It's all mine . . . and the bank's."

A major shift to asset ownership from asset "rental" is continuing to occur. As automobile travel substitutes for public transportation, automobile loans replace municipal borrowings. Likewise, the consumer seeks financing for home washing machines and dryers rather than drop quarters in the laundromat machines and for a television set in place of admission tickets to movie theaters. Consumers build equity in their autos and appliances, as they usually repay their installment loans before the end of the asset's life. The returns from ownership are often significant, as was shown in one study prepared for the Commission on Consumer Credit. The annual rate of return on a consumer-owned washer and dryer ranged from 6.7 to 29.0 percent for three and seven loads per week, respectively.[1]

Not only have consumers increased their ownership of autos and appliances but homes, too. Home ownership has increased from 55 percent of housing units in 1950 to 64 percent in 1970. The increase in ownership occurred in connection with the exodus from city to suburb and brought with it the desire for ownership of refrigerators, washing machines, lawn mowers, swimming pools, and a second car. As women were freed from daily chores by labor-saving appliances and gained mobility with the purchase of the second family car, they began moving into the labor force. We might also argue that the movement of women into the labor force spurred the demand for home appliances. Whether we argue that increasing desire for employment or recreation caused the demand for labor-saving home appliances or vice versa, we clearly see that the demand for homes and consumer durables has been strong and that substantial consumer financing has been an important ingredient in satisfying that demand. The demand for consumer loans for durable goods depends on the current spending habits, tastes, and confidence of consumers. Consequently, institutions watch consumer purchasers to spot profitable loan opportunities in the consumer credit market.

Generally, we distinguish between two types of consumer finance lending— personal finance and sales finance. As will be described more fully in the following sections, personal finance operations deal directly with the borrower

[1] Dunkleberg and Stevenson (1972), table 5.

whereas sales finance operations arrange loans through the sellers of goods and services.

Personal Finance Companies

The unique aspects of personal finance companies are that they deal directly with consumers and grant cash loans. People who need a small amount of money—the average loan is about $1000—apply directly to finance companies at their offices or through the mail. The total amount of personal cash loans outstanding from finance companies is about $19 billion and represents about 11 percent of total installment credit granted by all financial institutions. The purposes for which these loans are granted include purchases of automobiles, appliances, and recreation vehicles, and for vacations, education, and consolidation of debts. Personal loans are categorized according to whether they are durable goods or cash loans.

Durable Goods Loans   Consumer finance companies are granting about 52 percent of their loans for the purchase of durable goods. Not surprisingly, automobiles are the major durable goods financed—33 percent of total loans granted by consumer finance companies are used to buy cars. The rate of interest on automobile loans averages 13.21 percent for new cars and 17.82 percent for used cars. The rates on auto loans are less than the rates on other durable goods, for which the average charge is 19.60 percent.

Personal Cash Loans   Frequently referred to as *signature loans,* personal cash loans are generally not secured by collateral. Unlike durable goods loans for which the borrower pledges a car or sofa as collateral, personal cash loans are based largely on the ability of the borrower to earn money in the future. Interest rates vary from as low as 12 percent on large, high-quality loans to 36 percent on small signature loans; the average rate is about 21.23 percent. The variability in rates charged reflects two characteristics of this type of loan: (1) the relatively high cost of collecting payments on small loans and (2) the relatively high default risk level. The cost of processing loan applications, credit reports, and investigations for loans becomes proportionately smaller as loans become larger. (In Chapter 16, we analyze the trade-off between loan size and interest rates in detail.) Default risk on consumer loans is relatively high and is increasing over time with the rise in personal bankruptcies. Cash loans are used to consolidate existing bills 31 percent of the time. Individuals who are indebted to many institutions and people are more likely to declare bankruptcy than those borrowers who owe on only one or two loans secured by durable goods. Consequently we find that cash loans carry a higher interest rate than durable goods loans. It does not follow, however, that greater profits are earned on cash than durable goods loans, because cash loans are more expensive to administer and default more often than durable goods loans.

Sales Finance Companies

Sales finance companies develop the profit potential of consumer lending by fostering a close relationship with durable goods retailers. The retailer writes the loan at the point of sale, but the finance company specifies the maturity, down payment, charges, and other terms. Then the retailer sells the loan to the finance company. Loans are purchased on three bases:

1 Full recourse
2 Nonrecourse
3 Repurchase

In the event of default, the dealer must repay a contract purchased on a full-recourse basis. On the other hand, the finance company assumes all risk and collection costs on nonrecourse loan purchases. Under a repurchase arrangement, the dealer reposesses the merchandise and resells it for the unpaid balance.

Example of Sales Finance Arrangements   For example, Charlie's Appliance Store sells a $300 washing maching to Larry Grant. Larry deposits $50 and signs an installment loan contract for $250 plus interest. Charlie's Appliance Store (Charlie) then sells the contract to XYZ Sales Finance Company at the market price for installment loan contracts, $275. If Grant fails to make his payments, then Charlie is obligated as follows:

Sale Arrangement	*Obligation*
Full recourse	XYZ Finance Company returns the installment contract to Charlie for a full reimbursement of the balance owed XYZ.
Nonrecourse	Charlie is not obligated; XYZ attempts to collect from Grant.
Repurchase	Charlie repossesses and sells the washer; proceeds from sale are used to pay balance owed on installment contract.

The arrangement agreed upon by Charlie and XYZ depends primarily on the quality of the installment contracts and the reliability and reputation of Charlie. Sales finance companies continually monitor the quality of installment contracts bought from each retailer and make purchase decisions on the basis of past and expected payment experience of the store's customers.

Captive Sales Finance Companies   Clearly the relationship between a retailer and sales finance company grows close through frequent dealing. In many cases the finance companies are organizationally related as well. When a dealer or manufacturer owns the finance company, the financing subsidiary is called a *captive finance company*. For example, General Motors Acceptance Corporation (GMAC) is a captive finance company of General Motors (GM). Auto and truck dealers place huge quantities of their "paper" (loans) with GMAC, which is profitable in its own right and benefits GM by facilitating the sale of GM cars, trucks, and other products.

Most of the large finance companies are owned by manufacturing and retailing firms. Financing goods and services is part of the total "product" sold by many firms, and financing is provided by a subsidiary finance company called a *captive*. As mentioned above, GMAC is a captive finance company owned by GM. When a customer buys a new Oldsmobile, he or she can finance it from GMAC through the car dealer. By owning GMAC, GM can assure dealers a service of financing and provide consumers a simple means of borrowing money.

Floor-Plan Loans   Sales finance companies (and banks) support retailers with *floor-plan* loans. Dealers need financing to support their inventories, particularly when the inventory includes cars, boats, and other "big ticket" goods. We can take the case of an automobile dealership that buys cars from the manufacturer. The financing is done in sequence:

1 After receiving assurance that the cars will be financed, the manufacturer ships the cars to the dealer with a *sight draft* drawn on the finance company and sends the *bill of lading* to the finance company.

2 A sight draft is like a check which the finance company signs to pay for the cars. The finance company pays for the cars in return for a loan signed by the dealer.

3 A bill of lading is a transportation receipt, which the dealer uses to take possession of the cars. The dealer is given the bill of lading after signing the finance company loan. Now, the manufacturer is paid, the finance company has a floor-plan loan as an asset, and the dealer is borrowing to finance the cars standing on the showroom floor.

4 The cars are held by the dealer in trust to the finance company, which holds a *trust receipt* issued by the dealer. As cars are sold, the dealer redeems the trust receipts and repays the floor-plan loan. Frequently, the dealer pays the finance company by assigning consumer loan contracts on the cars themselves.

Thus, only a small amount of money may change hands, as cars and other merchandise move from dealer showrooms to consumer homes. Payment is deferred first by floor-plan loans to dealers and second by installment loans to consumers.

COMMERCIAL CREDIT

Commercial credit includes loans to businesses to finance accounts receivable, inventory, fixed assets, research and development, and other assets. Important approaches to meeting business needs are leasing, secured lending, and factoring.

Leasing

Leasing is an arrangement in which the finance company holds title to equipment while the lessee uses it. Unlike an installment purchase, the finance company retains title to the equipment after the termination of the lease. Most leases finance a greater percentage of the equipment cost and extend for a longer period than term loans. Therefore, leasing often improves the lessee's cash flow during the early years of the lease. Further, tax consequences are sometimes more beneficial to the finance company than to the lessee; through negotiation with the lessee, some of the finance company's tax benefits are obtained by the lessee.

Lease terms vary widely but tend to fall into the following categories:

True lease: finance company holds title, takes investment tax credits and depreciation expense, and sells or releases property upon termination.

Leverage lease: trustee holds title, finance company borrows 60 to 80 percent of the equipment cost by pledging the equipment as security, either the finance company or lessee receives tax benefits.

Conditional sale: finance company holds title, receives tax benefits, sells equipment to lessee at bargain price upon termination.

Full payout: finance company holds title, receives lease payments sufficient to cover all capital and interest, and passes title to lessee for nominal amount at termination.

Secured Lending

Secured loans are backed by pledges of accounts receivable, inventory, and fixed assets. This form of credit is sometimes termed *asset-based lending*. With adequate safeguards against the loss of the collateral and expertise in marketing repossessed collateral, finance companies can structure an acceptable loan from a situation that otherwise would be excessively risky. For example, accounts receivable from high-quality customers may be sufficiently secure to warrant lending to a high-risk technological venture that otherwise would be rejected for debt financing at going interest rates. In general, the advantage of secured financing is that low-risk assets are financed with low-interest-rate loans, when such assets are segregated from high-risk assets. The segregation and management of loan collateral are complicated by legal, physical, and marketing requirements. Therefore, a specialized group of personnel, supported by legal and operating functions, is required. Finance companies and departments of commercial banks are the most common institutions specializing in secured lending.

Factoring

Finance companies sometimes purchase accounts receivable from businesses. The finance company views the accounts receivable as an investment, and the business considers the sale of accounts receivable a source of cash flow. The sale of accounts receivable is termed *factoring*. The business receives full or nearly full payment immediately, and the finance company receives funds when customers remit payments. For example, a textile mill may sell yard goods to a dressmaker. Rather than wait until the dressmaker remits payment, the textile mill may sell the account receivable to a factor. By receiving funds when the textiles are shipped, the mill accelerates its cash flow and reduces the need for other financing. Like secured financing, factoring is a complicated credit arrangement requiring well-qualified and -supported lending personnel.

Trends in Loans

Over the past 30 years, finance companies have expanded consumer credit (all types of loans to consumers), but in the last 20 years business loans have been growing faster than other types of loans. As shown in Figure 10-1, business loan volume has grown to a level equal to consumer credit. Banks, credit unions, savings and loans, and other financial institutions have competed vigorously and successfully against finance companies for loan volume. On the other hand, finance companies have continued to develop a strong position in the business loan market.

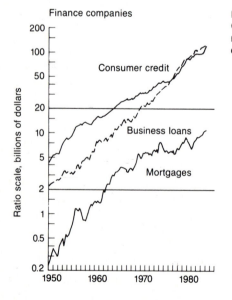

FIGURE 10-1
Growth in consumer and business loans by finance companies. (*Source*: Board of Governors of the Federal Reserve System.)

Sources of Funds

How do finance companies raise money to make loans? What financing instruments do they use and what financial markets are tapped for money?

The major sources of funds are obtained with loans from commercial banks, commercial paper in the money market, and long-term bonds in the capital market. Finance companies tap all three sources to raise the $294.1 billion shown in Table 10-1. Finance companies have grown from $79.2 to $294.1 billion from 1972 to 1984, about a 12 percent annual compound rate of growth. In recent years the growth has been financed with increases in long-term debt (corporate bonds, line 9, Table 10-2) and commercial paper (open-market paper, line 11, Table 10-2), while bank loans (line 10) have decreased. The changes in the sources of funds clearly show that finance companies are changing their financing strategy from bank to direct money and to capital market sales of their securities. Finance companies are taking advantage of the lower rates that usually prevail for commercial paper than for bank loans.

Commercial banks make loans to finance companies under preapproved *lines of credit*. A line of credit is an agreement between a bank and a customer whereby the bank agrees to lend up to a given amount to the customer. The customer may borrow as much of the line as required, although finance companies are required by the bank to pay off their loans to the individual bank for a few months each year. The finance company supplies current financial information and must remain in a sound condition or its line may be canceled by the bank. To pay off individual bank loans periodically, finance companies increase their loans elsewhere. Thus, National Bank is paid from funds borrowed from Super Bank. In turn, Super Bank is paid out in 6 to 9 months by a loan from National Bank (or other borrowings). The finance companies satisfy commercial bank requirements for *seasonal loans* by rotating from one bank to another. This process continues as long as the banks are satisfied with the finance company's condition but ends abruptly when a major bank cancels the line of credit. The chain is broken when the finance company cannot find funds to pay off bank loans that are due for their periodic rest, and the finance company may be declared bankrupt. Because of the importance of maintaining lines of credit, finance companies keep in close contact with the banks, and money market analysts watch the relationship closely.

Finance companies borrow huge amounts of money with *commercial paper*. Commercial paper refers to notes issued in large denominations, due in 30 to 270 days, and negotiable in the money market. In most cases commercial paper issues are supported by lines of credit from banks. For example, the banks agree to lend the finance company $100 million. The finance company then borrows $20 million from the banks and $40 milion by selling commercial paper. If the finance company cannot repay maturing commercial paper by selling new notes, then it can borrow from its banks under the line of credit agreement. Finance companies usually compensate the banks for unused lines of credit by keeping demand deposits equal to about 10 percent of the approved

TABLE 10-1

FINANCE COMPANIES' STATEMENTS OF FINANCIAL ASSETS AND LIABILITIES, 1972–1984 (BILLIONS OF DOLLARS)

	1972	1973	1974	1975	1976	1977	1978	1979	1980	1981	1982	1983	1984
Total financial assets	79.2	90.8	96.0	98.8	110.7	133.4	157.5	184.8	198.7	224.9	229.6	252.7	294.1
Demand deposits and currency	3.2	3.5	3.7	3.9	4.1	4.3	4.4	4.6	4.7	4.8	4.9	5.0	5.1
Credit market instruments	76.0	87.4	92.3	94.9	106.6	129.1	153.1	180.2	194.0	220.0	224.7	247.7	289.0
Mortgages	10.6	12.5	10.6	9.3	9.0	10.2	11.1	11.9	12.4	15.4	16.5	17.8	20.5
Consumer credit	38.0	42.6	44.6	44.7	48.2	55.9	67.5	83.7	93.5	107.2	112.1	116.9	135.5
Other loans (to business)	27.4	32.3	37.2	40.9	49.5	63.0	74.5	84.6	88.1	97.5	96.1	113.0	133.0
Total liabilities	79.2	92.5	98.6	103.7	146.6	140.0	163.7	190.2	204.1	229.5	239.9	256.2	297.1
Credit market instruments	61.1	70.7	76.2	76.7	81.2	97.9	116.2	132.7	138.9	152.9	161.1	172.0	190.5
Corporate bonds	23.3	26.2	28.0	30.7	33.8	41.6	48.0	52.3	57.7	57.0	58.2	70.3	78.4
Bank loans n.e.c.	16.0	20.6	20.8	18.0	16.1	16.7	20.8	19.7	21.0	21.8	28.8	17.7	11.0
Open-market paper	21.9	23.8	27.4	28.0	31.3	39.6	47.4	60.7	60.1	74.1	74.1	84.0	101.1
Profit taxes payable	0.3	0.3	0.3	0.3	0.3	0.4	0.5	0.4	0.2	0.1	*	*	*
Funds from parent companies	3.0	4.3	5.0	8.4	14.7	14.2	16.9	22.4	26.8	34.7	35.7	40.2	52.2
Other miscellaneous liab.	14.9	17.2	17.1	18.2	20.3	27.4	30.1	34.7	38.2	41.9	43.1	43.9	54.4

TABLE 10-2
FINANCE COMPANIES' FLOW OF FUNDS 1969–1978 (BILLIONS OF DOLLARS)

	1972	1973	1974	1975	1976	1977	1978	1979	1980	1981	1982	1983	1984
Net acq. of financial assets	9.7	11.6	5.1	2.9	11.9	22.7	24.1	27.3	13.9	26.2	4.7	23.1	32.6
Demand deposits & currency	0.3	0.2	0.2	0.2	0.2	0.2	0.2	0.2	0.1	0.1	0.1	0.1	0.1
Credit market instruments	9.4	11.4	4.9	2.6	11.7	22.5	24.0	27.1	13.8	26.1	4.6	23.0	32.6
Mortgages	1.7	1.8	−1.9	−1.3	−0.4	1.2	0.9	0.8	0.6	2.9	1.1	1.4	1.0
Consumer credit	3.5	4.6	1.9	0.2	3.4	7.8	11.6	16.2	9.8	13.7	4.9	4.8	11.6
Other loans (to business)	4.2	5.0	4.8	3.7	8.6	13.5	11.5	10.1	3.4	9.5	−1.4	16.9	20.0
Net increase in liabilities	11.3	13.2	6.6	5.1	12.7	23.6	23.5	26.6	14.0	25.5	7.1	22.6	29.7
Credit market instruments	6.6	9.6	6.0	0.5	4.3	16.9	18.1	16.6	6.3	14.1	4.9	17.2	19.5
Corporate bonds	3.6	3.0	1.8	2.7	3.1	7.8	6.4	4.3	5.4	−0.8	1.2	12.1	8.1
Bank loans n.e.c.	4.2	4.6	0.7	−2.8	−2.1	0.7	3.9	−1.0	1.4	1.0	6.9	−4.8	−3.7
Open-market paper	−1.3	2.1	3.6	0.6	3.3	8.4	7.8	13.3	−0.5	13.9	−3.3	9.8	15.1
Profit taxes payable	*	*	—	—	0.1	0.1	0.1	−0.1	−0.2	−0.2	*	*	*
Inv. by parent companies	2.4	1.4	0.7	3.4	6.4	−0.5	2.7	5.5	4.4	7.9	1.0	4.5	5.2
Other misc. liabilities	2.4	2.3	−0.1	1.2	2.1	7.1	2.6	4.6	3.5	3.6	1.2	0.9	5.0

line. Thus, the line of credit plays a dual role in finance company borrowing: it is essential for continuous, rotating bank loans and to warrant the high quality of its commercial paper issues. Buyers of commercial paper—large corporations and institutions with excess cash to invest for a short time—must be assured that they will be repaid when the notes come due in a few days, weeks, or months. In turn, the finance companies borrow large amounts at low rates in the commercial paper market.

Generally, commercial paper is highly marketable, because it is frequently issued by secure businesses and traded by major brokerage firms. The market is made by corporate treasurers, finance company treasurers, and brokers. Each day these people call one another to offer and bid for commercial paper. They negotiate the rates and maturities of commercial paper issues, which are later reported in the financial press.

Bonds issued by finance companies are primarily long-term subordinated debentures. The bonds are subordinated to bank loans and commercial paper and, consequently, constitute debt capital. Should the finance company fail, the subordinated (below bank loans, senior debt, and other debt not subordinated) debenture holders would receive their money after senior claims are satisfied. With less assurance of being repaid in full, investors demand a higher return for subordinated debentures than they do for senior debt instruments. The investors are the "capital market" individuals and institutions who can undertake the risk in exchange for an interest premium. Such investors are located by investment banking syndicates who market finance company bonds. We will study investment banking further in Chapter 13.

SUMMARY

Finance companies are a significant factor in the consumer and commercial credit financial market. Finance companies serve as financial intermediaries by purchasing wholesale quantities of money and then reselling it to individual consumers and businesses in retail quantities at retail prices. The growth of these financial institutions can be directly tied to changes in life-styles, preference for private homeownership, and the related demand for consumer durables.

Three principal types of finance companies are sales finance companies, personal finance companies, and business finance companies. Sales finance companies cater to the loan needs of retailers and their customers by maintaining a close relationship with the dealer. Sales finance companies may make loans to the dealer's customers on one of three bases: full recourse, non-recourse, or repurchase, depending upon whether the dealer or the finance company assumes the risk in case of default. Finance companies that are subsidiaries of dealers or manufacturers are called captive finance companies. In addition to providing financing to customers of the dealer, sales finance companies sometimes provide financing of the dealer's inventory or floor stock.

Personal finance companies provide consumers with small, short-term, direct loans which may be secured by collateral or unsecured. These loans are repaid from consumer's discretionary income. Business finance companies serve commercial loan needs by providing secured loans on inventory, receivables, and fixed assets or by factoring accounts receivable. Financing is also provided in the form of long-term lease agreements on fixed assets.

Finance companies raise funds from bank loans, sales of commercial paper, and issuances of long-term debt. The bank loans are typically lines of credit a finance company maintains with several banks simultaneously. These loans are rotated and paid off periodically at each bank to provide a "rest period" from borrowing at any one individual bank. Commercial paper, which refers to short-term notes issued in large amounts, provides a huge source of funds to finance companies through the money market. Long-term subordinated debentures provide a more permanent source of funds to the finance companies in the form of debt captial. Because these bonds are subordinated to the claims of other creditors and therefore are riskier, they command a higher rate of return than commercial paper and other senior debts.

TERMS

consumer credit	floor-plan financing
full recourse	commercial paper
nonrecourse	subordinated debentures
repurchase	factoring
money market	sight draft
capital market	bill of lading
sales finance company	trust receipt
personal finance company	signature loan
business finance company	discretionary income
captive finance company	line of credit
commercial credit leasing	

QUESTIONS

1 Indicate the two types of financing provided by a sales finance company which benefit an affiliated dealer.
2 Explain the distinction between the money market and the capital market. What securites does a finance company sell in each market to raise funds?
3 List and describe the four steps followed in a floor-plan financing; define the terms sight draft, bill of lading, and trust receipt.
4 What is a signature loan? What kind of finance company grants signature loans?
5 Using the yellow pages of a metropolitan area phone book or other available source, locate examples of two captive finance companies and describe the relationship you would expect these companies to have with dealers.
6 On what three bases can a sales finance company purchase accounts receivable from a retailer? Which of these results in the retailer continuing to bear the risk of default? Which results in the finance company bearing the risk of default?

7 What are three types of financing services provided by business finance companies?

8 What is factoring of accounts receivable? How does this differ from a loan secured by accounts receivable?

9 Who are the participants in the money markets who negotiate rates and maturities on commercial paper?

10 What is a bank line of credit? In what way is the bank usually compensated for unused lines of credit? What dual role does the line of credit play?

SELECTED REFERENCES

Consumer Credit in the United States, Report of the National Commission on Consumer Finance, Washington, D.C., December 1972.

Dunkleberg, William C., and James Stevenson: *Durable Goods Ownership and the Rate of Return*, prepared for National Commission on Consumer Finance, Washington, D.C., 1972.

Durkin, T. A.: "Consumer Loan Costs and the Regulatory Basis of Loan Sharking," *Journal of Bank Research*, Summer 1977, pp. 108–117.

Finance Facts Yearbook, National Consumer Finance Association, Washington, D.C., annual publication.

Greer, D. F.: "Rate Ceilings and Loan Turndowns," *Journal of Finance*, December 1975, pp. 1376–1383.

Harless, Doris E.: *Nonbank Financial Institutions*, Federal Reserve Bank of Richmond, Va., October 1975.

Holmes, D. N., Jr.: "Excess Demand, Undercapitalization, and the True Interest Rate for Credit Union Loans in Unorganized Money Markets," *Journal of Finance*, September 1974, pp. 1063–1076.

Hurley, E. M.: "The Commercial Paper Market," *Federal Reserve Bulletin*, June 1977, pp. 525–536.

Katona, George, Lewis Mandell, and Joy Schiedeskamp: *1970 Survey of Consumer Finances*, University of Michigan Press, Ann Arbor, 1971.

Ostas, J. R.: "Effects of Usury Ceilings in the Mortgage Market," *Journal of Finance*, June 1976, pp. 821–834.

CHAPTER 11

INSURANCE COMPANIES

LIFE INSURANCE COMPANIES

Life insurance companies apply Benjamin Franklin's 185-year-old adage that ". . . in this world nothing is certain but death and taxes." Life insurance companies predict the time of death, a feat that we cannot do as individuals. Of course, life insurance companies cannot predict when an individual will die, but they can and do predict how many will die out of a large group of people at a certain age. Using the law of large numbers, we can estimate with accuracy what percent of our age group will die next year, the year after, and so forth. Percentages of persons dying each year are referred to as *mortality statistics*. An example of mortality statistics is shown in Table 11-1; take a look at your age group to find the chances of your dying next year and your life expectancy, if you can stand to know the facts! Mortality statistics are an important aspect of portfolio management because the timing and frequency of death affect the timing and amount of liquid assets that life companies need. To see how the business of life insurance influences portfolio asset selection of life companies, we next describe the principles of life insurance.

Insurance Function of Life Companies

Life insurance companies (or *life insurers*) collect *premiums* from each of us, invest the receipts until needed, and pay *death benefits* to heirs of those who die. (The amount of the death benefit is commonly called the *face value*.) Premiums are charges by the insurance company each year (or quarter or month) for the insurance policy. By paying the premium, we are assured in the

TABLE 11-1
COMMISSIONER'S 1958 STANDARD ORDINARY MORTALITY TABLE (1950–1954)

Age	Deaths per 1000	Expectation of life (years)	Age	Deaths per 1000	Expectation of life (years)
0	7.08	68.30	48	6.95	25.27
1	1.76	67.78	49	7.60	24.45
2	1.52	66.90	50	8.32	23.63
3	1.46	66.00	51	9.11	22.82
4	1.40	65.10	52	9.96	22.03
5	1.35	64.19	53	10.89	21.25
6	1.30	63.27	54	11.90	20.47
7	1.26	62.35	55	13.00	19.71
8	1.23	61.43	56	14.21	18.97
9	1.21	60.51	57	15.54	18.23
10	1.21	59.58	58	17.00	17.51
11	1.23	58.65	59	18.59	16.81
12	1.26	57.72	60	20.34	16.12
13	1.32	56.80	61	22.24	15.44
14	1.39	55.87	62	24.31	14.78
15	1.46	54.95	63	26.57	14.14
16	1.54	54.03	64	29.04	13.51
17	1.62	53.11	65	31.75	12.90
18	1.69	52.19	66	34.74	12.31
19	1.74	51.28	67	38.04	11.73
20	1.79	50.37	68	41.68	11.17
21	1.83	49.46	69	45.61	10.64
22	1.86	48.55	70	49.79	10.12
23	1.89	47.64	71	54.15	9.63
24	1.91	46.73	72	58.65	9.15
25	1.93	45.82	73	63.25	8.69
26	1.96	44.90	74	68.12	8.24

policy agreement that an amount (the death benefits) will be paid to our estate or beneficiary in the event of our death. Therefore, we are sure that our spouse and children will have some money, the funeral director will bury us according to our wishes, or a business partner can buy our shares of the firm. We pay the premium to provide financial security to those who live after our death.

Note that the death rate increases with age. This not surprising natural fact is shown in the mortality statistics of Table 11-1. Each year the insurance company pays greater death benefits for insured persons our age, because we grow older and are more likely to die. With greater death benefits paid, the insurance company would need to raise premiums each year. To prevent premiums from increasing with age, life insurers sell a *level premium* type of policy. In the early years of our lives, we pay a premium in excess of death benefits and administrative costs so as to build a reserve for later years. The reserve funds are invested by the life insurance company and earn interest. In later years large

TABLE 11-1 (*continued*)
COMMISSIONER'S 1958 STANDARD ORDINARY MORTALITY TABLE (1950–1954)

Age	Deaths per 1000	Expectation of life (years)	Age	Deaths per 1000	Expectation of life (years)
27	1.99	43.99	75	73.37	7.81
28	2.03	43.08	76	79.18	7.39
29	2.08	42.16	77	85.70	6.98
30	2.13	41.25	78	93.06	6.59
31	2.19	40.34	79	101.19	6.21
32	2.25	39.43	80	109.98	5.85
33	2.32	38.51	81	119.35	5.51
34	2.40	37.60	82	129.17	5.19
35	2.51	36.69	83	139.38	4.89
36	2.64	35.78	84	150.01	4.60
37	2.80	34.88	85	161.14	4.32
38	3.01	33.97	86	172.82	4.06
39	3.25	33.07	87	185.13	3.80
40	3.53	32.18	88	198.25	3.55
41	3.84	31.29	89	212.46	3.31
42	4.17	30.41	90	228.14	3.06
43	4.53	29.54	91	245.77	2.82
44	4.92	28.67	92	265.93	2.58
45	5.35	27.81	93	289.30	2.33
46	5.83	26.95	94	316.66	2.07
47	6.36	26.11	95	351.24	1.80
96	400.56	1.51	98	668.15	0.83
97	488.42	1.18	99	1000.00	0.50

Note: Mortality rates contained in the commissioner's standard ordinary tables were obtained from experience of the years indicated, but contain an added element designed to generate life insurance reserves of a conservative nature in keeping with the long-term guarantees inherent in life insurance contracts. Premiums for life insurance policies, on the other hand, are based on assumptions that include expected mortality experience. Everyone is assumed to die by age 100; those who live to age 100 receive the face value of the policy.
Source: Life Insurance Fact Book '77, American Council of Life Insurance, New York, pp. 108–109.

death benefits are paid from the accumulated investments, as well as from current premiums. The reserves are a form of savings, collected as a life insurance premium and repaid as a death benefit to our heirs. The life insurer's reserves represent our investment in the life policy and are a liability of the insurance company.

Financial Intermediary Function of Life Companies

Life insurance companies are enormous financial intermediaries, because they collect and invest vast amounts of premiums on level-payment policies. Young policyholders are paying premiums which include deposits to their reserve accounts. The insurance company collects millions of small payments and invests them in multimillion-dollar loans. Life insurance companies today invest over $239 billion of policy reserves in bonds, stocks, mortgages, and policyholder loans. The portfolio of loans and investments is managed by the insurance company for the benefit of the life policyholders. When the policyholder decides to cancel his or her policy or dies, the insurance company liquidates some of its loan portfolio and pays off the policy.

Sources of Funds

Life insurance companies accumulate vast sums of money by selling life policies. To understand better the character of insurers' sources of funds, we must look at the two major types of policies:

1 Term life
2 Whole life

The difference between term and whole life insurance is the subject of the next section, and the marketing channels for life policies (ordinary life insurance, group life insurance, and credit life insurance) are discussed in a following section. Sales of term and whole life insurance through the above three channels produce funds for investment. In the final section, we look at the growth in life insurance reserves over the past two decades.

Term and Whole Life Types of Policies

Term Life   Term insurance of all types accounts for about 31 percent of total life insurance in force. Term life policies insure us for a specific period of time, such as 1, 5, or 10 years. The premiums are paid in advance each year or quarter and are based on mortality tables like Table 11-1. A regular term policy requires larger premium payments each year, as the mortality rates increase. If we do not want to commit to increasing premiums, we can buy a decreasing term policy. Under decreasing term life, the amount of insurance declines each year. Thus, the decreased amount of insurance compensates for the increased mortality rate.

Whole Life   The oldest and most widely used form of life insurance protection is whole life. It accounts for about one-half of all life insurance in force in the United States. Premiums are payable for a specified number of years (limited-payment life) or for a lifetime (straight or ordinary life). Whole life insurance provides a constant amount of insurance for the same premium over a lifetime.

The premium charged in earlier years is higher than the actual cost of insurance, as represented by the shaded area below the horizontal line in Figure 11-1. The excess premium is paid until age 47 (in this illustration), and the insurance company holds the excess premium as a *reserve* to be used in later years to meet costs of death benefits and operations which are substan-

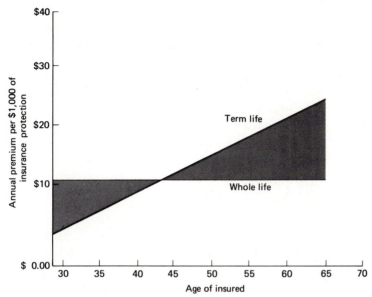

FIGURE 11-1
Illustration of whole life and term life insurance premiums for ages 30 to 70.

tially greater than the premiums collected from older persons. The deficiency after age 47 is represented by the shaded area above the horizontal line in Figure 11-1. It is an important feature of whole life policies that excess premiums are placed into reserves, because these reserves provide investable funds to the life insurance company.

The reserve is a liability of the insurance company and is recognized in the insurance policy as *cash surrender value*. Under the terms of contract, the cash surrender value is the amount available in cash upon voluntary termination of a policy by its owner before it becomes payable by death or maturity. (If you live to age 100, the policy matures and the insured collects your life insurance before you die!) A policyholder is entitled to the cash value if he or she cancels the policy. Also, the policyholder may borrow from the insurance company against the cash value of the policy.[1] Thus, policy reserves may be viewed equally as a legal liability of the insurance company and as an investment of the policyholder. Additions are made to the cash surrender value by policyholders in the form of life insurance premiums in excess of those needed immediately, and the insurance company recognizes the excess premiums as increases to policy reserves.

---

[1] Such borrowings are termed "policy loans" and are discussed later in this chapter.

Group Life Insurance

After tripling in only 10 years, group life now accounts for 43 percent of all life insurance in force in the United States. As implied by the name, group policies insure many people under a single agreement. Each insured person receives a certificate showing that he or she is covered. Premiums are paid by the individual or the group—employer, union, or professional organization. A recent development is the provision for monthly benefits to survivors rather than a lump-sum payment. The surviving spouse, children, or other beneficiary may receive continuing monthly payments related to the insured's income. Total group life in force now totals more than $1 trillion.

Credit Life Insurance

Credit life insurance is used to repay a debt in the event that the borrower dies. Credit life is a form of decreasing term insurance. As the loan is repaid, the insurance decreases with the balance owed. The lender and the borrower's family are protected against unpaid debt left by the deceased borrower. Policies are issued through banks, finance companies, credit unions, and retailers who grant credit to consumers. Often credit life is a part of consumer credit contracts and is purchased at the time the loan is signed. Mortgage loans are sometimes covered for the first 10 years and the premiums collected as part of the monthly mortgage payment. Credit life is a convenient method for many people to protect themselves against specific debts. It is growing rapidly, and now about $124 billion of credit life insurance is in force in the United States.

The popularity of credit life is apparently due to the ease with which it is purchased and paid for by consumers. Loan application forms often include a box for "checking off" credit life and adding the premium to the regular monthly payment. This practice has generated criticism from some consumer rights groups. Critics claim that consumers are intimidated by the lender who encourages them to sign up for credit life. Fearful that their loan will be denied if they refuse credit life, consumers are forced to buy life insurance which they do not want or necessarily need. Critics claim that lenders oversell credit life because lenders receive a fee for each sale. The controversy over this potential conflict of interest continues to rage. Although disclosure of fees and consumer rights is now required by law for most types of lending, additional legislation is likely.

Life Insurance Policy Reserves

Policy reserves of U.S. life insurance companies are accumulated in tremendous amounts, particularly for whole life policies. Each company is required by state law to maintain reserves sufficient to meet future obligations. Actuaries (statisticians specializing in insurance statistics) compute the amount of reserves needed now, given expected future interest earnings, operating expenses, and mortality rates. Reserves are growing rapidly, as shown in Table

TABLE 11-2
LIFE INSURANCE COMPANIES' STATEMENTS OF FINANCIAL ASSETS AND LIABILITIES, 1972–1984 (BILLIONS OF DOLLARS)

	1972	1973	1974	1975	1976	1977	1978	1979	1980	1981	1982	1983	1984
Total financial assets	232.4	244.8	255.0	279.7	311.1	339.8	378.3	419.6	464.2	507.5	567.5	636.5	692.4
Demand deposits and currency	2.0	2.1	2.0	1.9	2.0	2.1	2.4	2.7	3.2	4.3	4.6	4.6	3.5
Corporate equities	26.8	25.9	21.9	28.1	34.3	32.9	35.7	39.8	47.4	47.7	55.7	65.1	63.8
Credit market instruments	192.5	204.8	217.7	234.6	258.3	285.8	318.9	352.3	385.1	419.8	463.2	514.6	568.7
U.S. government securities	4.6	4.3	4.4	6.2	7.7	9.3	11.4	14.3	17.0	22.5	35.2	49.0	74.7
Treasury issues	3.8	3.4	3.4	4.7	5.4	5.3	4.8	4.9	5.8	8.2	16.5	25.0	41.5
Agency issues	0.7	0.9	1.1	1.4	2.3	4.0	6.5	9.4	11.1	14.3	18.6	24.0	33.2
State & local obligations	3.4	3.4	3.7	4.5	5.6	6.1	6.4	6.4	6.7	7.2	9.0	10.7	9.4
Corporate & foreign bonds	86.6	92.5	96.4	105.5	122.4	141.2	158.5	170.1	178.8	186.1	202.3	221.0	240.7
Mortgages	76.9	81.4	86.2	89.2	91.6	96.8	106.2	118.8	131.1	137.7	141.9	150.2	157.3
Open-market paper	3.0	3.0	4.1	4.8	5.1	4.9	6.3	8.0	10.1	17.6	21.7	29.3	32.0
Policy loans	18.0	20.2	22.9	24.5	25.8	27.6	30.1	34.8	41.4	48.7	53.0	54.5	54.6
Miscellaneous assets	11.1	12.0	13.4	15.0	16.5	19.0	21.4	24.9	28.5	35.8	44.0	52.1	56.5
Total liabilities	216.3	230.1	243.9	267.0	296.1	324.8	359.2	396.9	438.4	482.9	540.0	604.4	656.1
Life insurance reserves	136.1	143.5	150.1	158.6	166.8	178.1	189.9	202.0	213.5	223.4	237.3	253.0	239.0
Pension fund reserves	52.3	56.1	60.8	72.2	89.0	101.5	119.1	139.2	165.8	192.7	228.9	270.6	324.8
Profit taxes payable	0.8	0.8	0.8	0.7	0.9	1.3	1.6	1.6	1.2	0.7	0.7	0.6	0.4
Miscellaneous liabilities	27.1	29.6	32.2	35.5	39.4	44.0	48.8	54.1	57.9	66.1	73.1	80.2	91.8

TABLE 11-3
LIFE INSURANCE COMPANIES FLOW OF FUNDS 1972–1984 (BILLIONS OF DOLLARS)

	1972	1973	1974	1975	1976	1977	1978	1979	1980	1981	1982	1983	1984
Current surplus	1.2	2.2	3.1	2.5	2.8	3.6	4.3	4.9	6.3	7.7	6.9	8.0	7.5
Physical investment	1.1	1.2	1.6	2.3	2.0	1.9	2.2	3.0	3.9	5.3	4.6	4.2	6.4
Net acq. of financial assets	14.4	16.8	16.6	20.4	28.2	31.2	35.7	37.8	37.4	45.9	55.3	64.3	60.2
Decreased deposits & currency	0.2	0.1	-0.1	-0.1	0.1	0.1	0.2	0.3	0.5	1.1	0.3	*	-0.5
Corporate equities	3.5	3.5	2.3	1.9	3.0	1.2	-0.1	0.6	0.5	2.9	3.4	4.7	*
Credit market instruments	9.7	12.2	12.9	16.9	23.7	27.5	33.1	33.4	32.8	34.7	43.4	51.5	54.3
U.S. government securities	0.1	-0.1	0.1	1.7	1.5	1.6	2.0	2.9	2.7	5.5	12.7	13.8	20.2
Treasury issues	*	-0.4	-0.1	1.4	0.6	-0.1	-0.5	0.1	1.0	2.3	8.4	8.5	12.9
Agency issues	0.1	0.1	0.2	0.4	0.9	1.7	2.5	2.8	1.8	3.1	4.3	5.4	7.3
State & local oblig.	*	*	0.3	0.8	1.1	0.5	0.4	*	0.3	0.5	1.9	1.7	-0.6
Corporate bonds	7.0	5.8	4.0	9.1	16.9	18.8	17.3	11.6	8.7	7.3	16.2	18.7	21.6
Mortgages	1.4	4.4	4.9	2.9	2.4	5.2	9.4	12.6	12.3	6.7	4.2	8.3	5.7
Open-market paper	0.2	*	1.1	0.7	0.4	-0.3	1.5	1.6	2.2	7.4	4.2	7.5	6.8
Policy loans	0.9	2.2	2.7	1.6	1.4	1.7	2.6	4.7	6.6	7.3	4.3	1.5	0.5
Misc. assets	1.0	0.9	1.4	1.7	1.5	2.5	2.4	3.5	3.6	7.3	8.1	8.2	6.4
Net increase in liabilities	13.8	15.4	15.6	19.8	27.6	31.1	35.1	35.1	35.5	46.1	53.7	60.6	57.9
Life insurance reserves	6.7	7.4	6.6	8.5	8.2	11.3	11.7	12.3	11.4	9.9	13.9	15.7	7.9
Pension fund reserves	4.4	5.4	6.4	8.1	15.3	14.9	18.3	17.5	20.6	28.6	32.7	37.9	40.8
Profit taxes payable	*	*	*	-0.1	0.1	0.4	0.3	*	-0.4	-0.5	*	-0.1	-0.2
Misc. liabilities	2.6	2.5	2.6	3.3	3.9	4.6	4.8	5.3	3.8	8.2	7.0	7.1	9.4
Discrepancy	*	-0.4	0.5	-0.4	0.2	1.5	1.6	-0.7	0.5	2.6	0.7	0.1	-1.2

11-2 (line 15) and Table 11-3 (line 17). The influx of new money, about $60 billion per year, raises the question: "How do life insurance companies invest the policyholders' reserves?" That question brings us to the subject of the next section.

Uses of Life Insurance Funds

Life insurance companies invest life and pension reserves in primary securities. (Pension funds are managed by life companies, too. We'll discuss pensions later.) The major investments of life companies are shown in Table 11-2 and graphed in Figure 11-2.

As portfolio managers, life insurance companies purchase and maintain a portfolio of securities to meet the financial needs of individuals in the distant future. Safety of principal is paramount, because the solvency of the insurance company and the financial security of the policyholder depend upon the future value of the portfolio being at least equal to the life insurance contract obligation. The penalty for a substantial portfolio loss is much more important than the benefits from an unexpectedly large portfolio gain. Thus, insurance company managers invest in securities with a low risk of loss. Important assets are corporate bonds and stocks, mortgages, and policy loans.

Insurance companies try to earn the highest rate possible on investments, consistent with risk objectives, because policy premiums are related to invest-

FIGURE 11-2
Principal earning assets of life insurance companies. (*Source*: Board of Governors of the Federal Reserve System.)

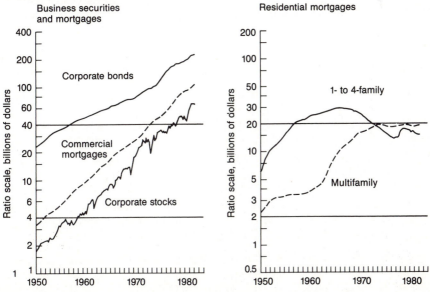

ment performance. As the rate of return on investments increases, the company can lower the premiums it charges on new policies. Higher rates of return provide higher earnings on reserves (cash values) and lessen the need for premium revenues. Because premium rates are a competitive factor, high investment returns are crucial in maintaining and improving a life company's sales position. Strong investment performance supports growth in policy sales and future portfolio expansion.

Forward Commitments and Direct Placements

Life insurance companies compete for new investment with two attractive features: (1) forward commitments and (2) direct placements. *Forward commitments* are firm contracts to buy mortgages of large projects, such as factories, utility plants, office buildings, condominiums, and apartment complexes. These projects are planned well in advance and a great deal of money is at risk during the development stage. Developers are willing to pay a premium for the assurance that permanent financing will be available after construction is completed. *Direct placements* are issues of bonds which are negotiated directly between the borrower and the lender. The borrower (seller of the bond) negotiates directly with the insurance company for the terms and amount he or she needs. Small borrowers gain considerable advantage by directly placing rather than publicly offering their bonds. Legal and marketing costs are reduced substantially, because only a few parties are involved and government filing requirements are minimal. Also, the insurance company allows greater flexibility in the terms and covenants of the bond agreement than would an investment banker who needs to market a standard instrument. In turn the insurance company receives a rate of return of ½ to 1 percent more on directly placed than on publicly marketed bonds. Consequently, insurance companies acquire a majority of their bonds through private placements rather than public issues.

Policy Loans

Life insurance companies make loans against the cash value of whole life insurance policies. The policyholder has the right to borrow from the insurance company any amount up to the cash value at a specified rate of interest. For example, if our life insurance policy has a cash value of $3000, then we can borrow $3000 at the rate stated in our policy.[2] Currently, life companies are lending about $26 billion (8 percent of total assets) to policyholders against cash values.

Tight money conditions combined with low interest rates on policy loans have caused policy loans to increase rapidly during periods of high interest

---

[2] Some policies may limit borrowing to 95 percent of cash value; the remaining cash value is collateral against interest payment defaults.

rates. In the tight-money conditions of 1973–1974, policyholders discovered that the loan rates were below the prevailing credit market rates. Consequently they borrowed against their cash values to invest in certificates of deposit, Treasury bills, and other money-market instruments. The insurance companies were bound by the insurance policy to grant loans at low interest rates. Higher policy-loan rates were needed by insurance companies to provide sufficient investment return to meet policy commitments and prevent unexpected massive outflows of funds to policyholders during periods of high credit. There was no way to change the terms of existing policies, but states have begun to allow insurance companies to state higher rates in new policies. By 1976 two-thirds of the states had passed legislation allowing insurance companies to charge market interest rates on new policies.

Investment Performance

Investment performance is important to life insurance company growth in two ways: (1) investment returns add to the asset base, and (2) high investment returns aid in selling additional policies. The basic criterion for measuring investment performance of a life insurance company is the rate of return on assets. Annual returns of the portfolio represent a weighted average of past investments made at different times and under different conditions.

How well have life insurance companies performed? The overall rate of return on assets is increasing but is still below current market rates. It generally lags behind current market returns, because the portfolio contains many long-term securities purchased in past years. This situation results from a long-term structure for assets, as discussed in Part II. Most insurance companies are immunized against interest-rate fluctuation, because their policy contracts are a long-term fixed-rate commitment. For example, a policy written in 1970 would provide for a lower rates of return than one written in 1980, when market interest rates were higher. The insurance company can hold the lower returning 1970 assets until maturity, because they satisfy the 1970 policy agreements.

Income and Expenses of Life Companies

Premiums for life and health policies account for 78 percent of total income, while earnings from the asset portfolio represent 22 percent of income. The proportions of premium income and investment earnings depend on the type of life insurance company. For mutual companies the proportion of income from premiums is about 74 percent and investment earnings account for about 26 percent. On the other hand, premiums account for about 83 percent and investment earnings about 17 percent of income for stock companies. The differences in income sources are due to differing proportions of group life and group health insurance. Group policies create smaller reserves than ordinary life insurance and produce lower levels of investment earnings relative to the amount of premium income. Stock company business emphasizes group policies, and thus their income sources reflect the lower level of investment earnings typical for group insurance. Also, proportions of premiums income and investment earnings differ by size of company; large companies generally receive a greater share of their income from investments than do smaller companies.[3]

Current and future benefit payments are accounted for as current-year payments (49 percent) and additions to policy reserves (28 percent). Thus 77 percent of total income is paid as benefits or reserved for future benefit payments. The remaining 23 percent is divided among commissions to agents (7 percent), home and field office expenses (9 percent), income taxes (4 percent), additions to reserves (2 percent), and stockholder dividends (1 percent). Of course, outflows vary by major line of business, and individual companies vary from the average. For the life insurance type of business, about 50 percent of income is paid in benefits and 20 percent is added to reserves. In the case of health insurance, about 75 percent is paid in current benefits and policy dividends.[4]

Home and field office expenses have been rising for life insurance companies in recent decades. Insurance companies, like other financial institutions, have attempted to counteract rising personnel and occupancy costs with the following operating changes: (1) increased electronic data processing, (2) improved office management, and (3) increased usage of group policies. Computers achieve favorable economies of scale for large insurance companies, although they increase fixed costs. (Equipment depreciation and specialized computer staff expenses tend to be more fixed than are clerical and occupancy expenses.) Increasing attention is being given to managerial efficiency in an effort to reduce processing and legal costs. Also, greater emphasis on group insurance reduces costs by cutting selling expenses, the number of policies written, and mortality rates. Insurance company managers are seeking new ways to control rising expenses and meet growing competition among the 1750 companies in the insurance business.

PROPERTY AND LIABILITY INSURANCE

Life insurance is reserved exclusively for life insurance companies by law. In the United States, companies that write property and liability insurance are separate from those that write life insurance (annuities and title insurance are also separated by law); this ''compartmentalization'' of insurance underwriters is unique in the world and is known as the *American system*. Although a British insurer may be authorized to write any type of insurance throughout the world, United States companies are restricted to specific types of insurance.[5]

---

[3] For further analysis see a recent *Life Insurance Fact Book*.

[4] Policy dividends are premium rebates resulting from unexpectedly favorable investment income.

[5] For an extensive discussion of the history, advantages, and problems of alternative insurance systems, see Michelbacher (1970), pp. 1–10.

The two major forms of nonlife insurance are *property* and *liability* insurance. Property insurance is a general term covering the following specific types of insurance:

1 Fire
2 Ocean and inland marine
3 Theft
4 Fidelity and surety bonds
5 Water damage, boiler and machinery, glass breakage, data processing, domestic credit, foreign credit, title, and crop insurance

Similarly, liability insurance is a broad term referring to insurance against obligations arising from negligence lawsuits.

A third form is the combination property and liability insurance, which includes the following:

1 Automobile
2 Aviation

In general, property and liability insurance provide financial protection against losses and damage to property and losses accruing from legal liability.

Property Insurance

Fire insurance indemnifies (repays) the insured person or business for losses and damage to buildings and personal property caused by fire, lightning, windstorm, hail, explosion, and a number of other perils. Coverage may extend beyond the destruction of the actual asset to include loss of income and extra expense resulting from the loss of use of the destroyed asset. For example, fire insurance may indemnify a homeowner against the loss of a house due to fire and the resulting hotel bills incurred until he or she purchases another house.

Marine insurance is broader than the name implies—it covers loss and damage during transportation. There are two types of marine insurance: ocean and inland. Ocean marine insurance covers perils at sea to ships and their cargos. Inland marine insurance protects domestic shipments not only by ships and barges on inland waterways, but also by railroads, trucks, airplanes, mail, parcel post, express, armored car, messenger, and other forms of transportation. Furthermore, inland marine insurance includes personal property *floater risks* or property that is mobile, such as jewelry, furs, clothes, construction equipment, and animals.

Theft insurance provides protection against the criminal acts of others.[6] Burglary, robbery, and theft by persons other than employees of the insured are covered and generally referred to as nonemployee crime coverages. Crimi-

---

[6] Theft insurance is a type of *casualty insurance*. The term casualty is gradually being abandoned, because it vaguely refers to everything but fire insurance. Theft, fidelity bonds, automobile, health and accident, and aviation insurance are all classified under the general heading of casualty insurance.

nal acts by employees are protected separately under fidelity bonds. *Fidelity bonds* protect a business against dishonest employees. When bonded employees embezzle funds or steal money, the bonding company pays for the loss. (Most financial institutions are required by law to bond their employees, because it reduces the risk of failure due to internal embezzlement and fraud.) *Surety bonds* are different from fidelity bonds, because they insure that a specific obligation of one party to another party will be met, rather than indemnifying against criminal acts. The insurance company (the *surety*) agrees to pay a third party (the *obligee*) if the individual or business (the *principal*) defaults on a debt or obligation. For example, when a court requires that bail is a condition for release from jail, the surety posts bail to the court (obligee) for the release of the prisoner (principal). If the principal fails to appear in court as ordered, then the surety pays (forfeits) the bail. Another common example of surety bonding is in the construction industry. Contractors are principals bonded to insure performance on construction contracts. If the contractor fails to perform because of a lack of technical or financial capability, then the insurance company underwrites the resulting losses to the building owner.

Liability Insurance

Individuals and businesses are subject to the risk of legal actions requiring substantial payments for negligence. Negligence is defined primarily by common law, although some statutes provide legal definition. Under common law doctrine, people are obligated to act as a reasonable and prudent individual would. Failure to behave in such a manner constitutes negligence, and a legal liability may be imposed if loss or damage actually results from the negligent action. Liability insurance contracts underwrite obligations created by legal actions against negligent parties. Up to the maximum limit of the policy, the insurance company agrees to pay legal liabilities of the insured to injured third parties. Also, most liability policies provide for legal defense of the insured in any lawsuit related to acts covered in the insurance agreement.

Combination Insurance and Aviation Insurance

Automobile aviation insurance protects against both property and liability perils. Equipment theft and accident damage are covered like other types of property insurance. (Note that personal property stolen from inside the automobile is a criminal act covered by theft rather than automobile insurance.) Legal liabilities arising from the ownership and use of automobiles and airplanes are covered as well. For example, lawsuits arising from accidents are settled or paid by insurers under such policies. Also, special types of health and accidental injury insurance are included in automobile and aviation packages.

Financial Structure

The financial statements of property and liability (P & L) insurance companies show the liabilities created in the process of writing insurance policies, the assets and investments they have selected, and the income, expense, and profits generated from insuring property and liability risks. This section analyzes the balance sheets and income and expense statements of P & L insurers. The key items to analyze on the balance sheet are (1) policy payables and (2) bonds and stocks on the asset side (see Table 11-4). Policy payables provide about 60 percent of the total liabilities and capital, and bonds and stocks constitute about 85 percent of total assets. It is important to understand how policy payables are created, because they are the major source of funds to P & L insurance companies.

Policy Payables

In general, policy payable accounts are items on the liability side of the balance sheet (or an offsetting item on the asset side) which recognize an existing, an expected future, or a contingent obligation. State laws require insurance companies to establish *statutory reserves* (policy payables) for existing, expected, and contingent obligations incident to the P & L insurance business. Statutory reserves are mandated for the following:

1 Unearned premiums
2 Unpaid claims
3 Reinsurance obligations, rate credits for policyholders, contingent commissions, taxes, pension obligations, and dividends declared but not paid.

The major items are unearned premiums and unpaid claims, which are explained next.

Unearned-Premium Reserves The unearned-premium reserve is the pro rata portion of premium payments that is not yet earned. Policyholders frequently pay the full premium in *advance* for a policy term of from 1 to 3 years. On the other hand, insurance protection is provided over the entire 3-year period, not only at the time when the premium payment is received. Proper accounting requires that premium payments for future periods of protection be regarded as a reserve (liability) and invested in quality securities (assets). Then in future periods, the reserve and investment account are reduced to provide funds for the cost of insurance protection promised in those periods.

The unearned-premium reserve account has been growing over time, because the amount of P & L insurance in force has been growing. New insurance policies and renewal of old policies generate an inflow of payments which add to the reserve account, while expiring policies reduce the reserve account. The growing volume of insurance underwriting has produced a net increase in insurance outstanding and a net addition to the unearned-income reserve account. The increase in unearned-premium reserves has contributed substantially to the growth in policy payables, as shown in Table 11-4. Increases in policy payables have been an important source of funds, as shown in the statement in Table 11-5. Additions to the unearned premium reserve accounts (not shown in Table 11-5) have been providing new funds to P & L insurance

TABLE 11-4
NONLIFE INSURANCE COMPANIES' STATEMENTS OF FINANCIAL ASSETS AND LIABILITIES, 1972–1984 (BILLIONS OF DOLLARS)

	1972	1973	1974	1975	1976	1977	1978	1979	1980	1981	1982	1983	1984
Total financial assets	67.5	69.5	67.8	77.3	93.9	113.2	133.9	154.9	174.3	185.5	204.5	228.1	240.5
Demand deposits and currency	1.5	1.5	1.6	1.7	1.9	2.2	2.6	2.9	2.9	3.0	6.9	8.6	2.6
Security rps[a]													18.0
Corporate equities	21.8	19.7	12.8	14.2	16.9	17.1	19.4	24.8	32.3	32.4	38.5	48.1	50.0
Credit market instruments	38.3	41.8	46.4	53.7	66.2	83.7	100.2	113.7	123.5	132.0	138.9	149.2	145.6
U.S. government securities	5.2	5.1	5.5	8.0	11.2	14.1	15.3	16.6	18.4	20.5	24.5	33.4	33.9
Treasury issues	2.9	2.8	2.9	4.7	7.3	9.8	10.5	10.7	12.2	13.5	15.0	21.0	20.9
Agency issues	2.3	2.3	2.7	3.3	3.9	4.4	4.9	6.0	6.2	7.0	9.5	12.4	13.0
State & local obligations	24.8	28.5	30.7	33.3	38.7	49.4	62.9	72.8	80.5	83.9	87.0	88.2	87.2
Corporate & foreign bonds	8.1	8.0	10.0	12.2	16.1	19.8	21.6	23.6	23.6	26.3	25.8	25.7	21.8
Commercial mortgages	0.2	0.2	0.2	0.2	0.3	0.4	0.4	0.7	1.0	1.3	1.6	1.9	2.6
Trade credit	5.8	6.5	7.0	7.7	8.9	10.2	11.7	13.6	15.6	18.1	20.2	22.2	24.3
Total liabilities	42.9	47.7	52.6	58.8	69.2	81.9	96.1	110.8	123.0	133.7	144.2	155.2	168.2
Profit taxes payable	0.3	0.3	0.3	0.3	0.4	0.5	0.6	0.6	0.4	0.3	0.3	0.2	0.2
Policy payables	42.6	47.4	52.3	58.5	68.8	81.4	95.4	110.2	122.6	133.4	144.0	155.0	168.0

[a] Reporting begins in 1984; some rps included in other categories in prior years.

TABLE 11-5
NONLIFE INSURANCE COMPANIES' FLOW OF FUNDS, 1972–1984 (BILLIONS OF DOLLARS)

	1972	1973	1974	1975	1976	1977	1978	1979	1980	1981	1982	1983	1984
Current surplus	1.9	1.2	*	-0.7	0.9	4.6	4.6	4.3	5.8	4.1	2.8	3.1	1.4
Net acq. of financial assets	7.8	6.4	4.7	7.3	14.9	20.2	20.4	18.8	15.0	14.1	15.6	16.9	15.2
Demand deposits & currency	*	*	0.1	0.1	0.2	0.3	0.4	0.3	0.1	0.1	3.9	1.6	*
Security rps[a]													4.3
Corporate equities	2.9	2.3	-0.5	-0.7	0.9	1.2	2.0	3.2	3.1	2.0	2.7	2.9	2.0
Credit market instruments	3.6	3.4	4.6	7.3	12.5	17.5	16.5	13.4	9.9	9.4	6.9	10.3	6.9
U.S. government securities	0.1	*	0.4	2.5	3.1	3.0	1.2	1.3	1.8	2.2	4.0	8.9	5.9
Treasury issues	-0.2	*	*	1.9	2.6	2.5	0.7	0.2	1.6	1.4	1.5	6.0	3.5
Agency issues	0.3	*	0.4	0.6	0.6	0.5	0.5	1.1	0.2	0.8	2.5	2.8	2.3
State & local obligations	4.3	3.6	2.2	2.6	5.4	10.7	13.5	9.9	7.7	4.0	3.0	1.3	0.5
Corporate bonds	-0.7	-0.1	2.0	2.2	3.9	3.7	1.8	2.0	*	2.8	-0.5	-0.1	0.2
Commercial mortgages	*	*	*	0.1	0.1	0.1	*	0.3	0.3	0.4	0.3	0.3	0.3
Trade credit	1.1	0.6	0.5	0.6	1.2	1.3	1.5	1.9	2.0	2.6	2.1	2.0	2.0
Net increase in liabilities	5.4	5.3	5.8	7.2	11.3	14.1	15.0	15.6	13.4	11.8	13.4	14.1	13.6
Corporate equity issues	0.4	0.5	0.9	1.0	0.9	1.4	0.8	0.9	1.2	1.1	2.8	3.1	1.6
Profit taxes payable	0.1	*	*	*	0.1	0.1	0.1	*	-0.2	-0.2	*	*	*
Policy payables	4.8	4.8	4.9	6.2	10.3	12.6	14.1	14.7	12.4	10.8	10.6	11.0	12.0

[a] Reporting begins in 1984; some rps included in other categories in prior years.

companies. Collecting premiums *in advance* for as many years' protection as can be reasonably sold is a good decision on the part of insurance company management, because this action builds large reserves,which are invested in earning assets.

Loss Reserves Reserves for unpaid claims, arising from insurance contracts, are called loss reserves. The claims may be for events that have happened or for possible future events. That is, the loss reserve is the estimated liability incurred for:

1 *Reported occurrences*—those accidents and other damages that have been reported to the insurer

2 *Unreported occurrences*—losses that happened but are not known to the insurer

Claims for reported occurrences can only be estimated until fully litigated or paid. For example, medical compensation to persons injured in an automobile accident cannot be determined until after the person is treated and responsibility for the accident determined. Treatment and court actions may continue for years before a final determination is rendered and the claim paid by the insurer. In the meantime, the insurer establishes a loss reserve liability to provide for the possibility of future payments. Similarly, the insurer creates a loss reserve for unreported occurrences that will produce claims in the future. In both reported and unreported occurrences, the insurer *estimates* the amount of reserves needed on the basis of past experience and reports estimated reserves as a liability on the balance sheet.

Loss reserves of P & L insurance companies have been the major source of funds and the largest single liability for over 20 years. In recent years the loss reserves have been accounting for two-thirds of the total funds flow. Note that the flow of funds into both the loss and unearned-premium reserve accounts has been relatively constant and increasing over time. This implies that the funds may be invested in portfolios of long-term assets, except for a portion of liquid assets held as a precaution against an unexpectedly large need.

Investment Portfolio

The major investments of P & L insurance companies are state and local government (SLG) securities, common stocks, and corporate bonds. Unlike life insurance companies, which select corporate bonds for a large portion of their portfolio (36 percent), P & L insurance companies buy corporate bonds for only 10 percent of their investments. SLG bonds (37 percent) and common stocks (22 percent) constitute a substantial 59 percent of P & L insurance portfolios. The vastly different investment portfolios are due largely to differences in the income tax laws and in the insurance regulations restricting permissible types of investments.

Income and Expenses

Property-casualty insurance companies derive nearly all their income from premiums. About 86 percent of total revenue is derived from premiums for all types of property-casualty insurers—stock, mutual, reciprocal, and Lloyds. Underwriting losses take 67 percent, commission expenses require 12 percent, and office expenses absorb 12 percent of revenues. The operating profit of 9 percent of revenue is largely tax exempt, because the portfolio includes substantial holding of preferred stocks and tax-exempt state and local government bonds.

GOVERNMENT REGULATION AND TAXATION

Life insurance companies are subject only to state supervision, according to the federal statute known as the McCarron Act (1945). State statutes governing life insurance companies are numerous and detailed. Provisions of state laws cover organization procedures, minimum capital requirements, annual financial reports, examination by the state agency, investment characteristics, asset valuation, policy reserve computations, annual licensing of sales agents, standard policy provisions, unfair sales practices, prohibited policy provisions, prior approval for policy changes, and remedies for insolvent institutions. Insurance company compliance is further complicated by the requirement that a company must be *licensed in all states* in which it sells insurance. If you are located in New York but sell in Ohio, then you must comply with both New York and Ohio laws. Reports are filed with New York and Ohio, although you are probably subject to only one joint examination once every 3 years. Managers of insurance companies are not subject to federal scrutiny but are not released from the problem of satisfying more than one master.

Federal income taxes are computed according to the Internal Revenue Code, which classifies insurance companies into three groups: life insurance companies, nonlife mutual insurance companies, and insurance companies other than life and mutual.[7] Generally, the same corporate *tax rate* is assessed all insurance companies as is applied to other businesses. However, the definition of expenses, and therefore *taxable income,* is different for some types of insurance companies. Income taxes are a function of both taxable income and tax rate, and, consequently, the definiton of taxable income is as important as the tax rate.

Under the Life Insurance Company Tax Act of 1959, life companies are taxed on only 50 percent of underwriting profit in the year in which it is earned. The other 50 percent is deferred until it is paid out to stockholders. Underwriting profits are separated into two accounts: (1) policyholders' surplus and (2)

---

[7] This section briefly summarizes the Internal Revenue Code sections 801–802 (life), 821–826 (mutual), and 831–832 (other).

shareholders' surplus. The income that goes into the policyholders' surplus account is not taxed, while the income that is placed into the shareholders' surplus account is taxed at the corporate rate. Taxes must be paid on amounts transferred to the shareholders' surplus account, and dividends can be paid only from the shareholders' account. The advantage of the policyholders' surplus account is that taxes on this portion of income are deferred until transferred to the shareholders' account and paid as dividends. Because taxes are deferred, the life insurance companies effectively pay a lower tax rate than they would if they paid taxes on all income during the year earned.

On the other hand, the usual corporate income tax rate is applied to all underwriting profit and investment income of most property and liability companies. Under the Revenue Acts of 1962 and 1964, mutual insurers pay taxes on net income after expenses and allocations to a special *protection against loss* account. A portion of taxable income may be set aside in the special account for 5 years, after which the income is returned to a taxable status if the income is not needed to absorb losses. The net effect is deferment of some income for 5 years in the exceptional case of mutual insurers, which comprise about one-third of the P & L insurance industry by number.[8] Corporate P & L insurers pay corporate tax rates on income in the year earned. Thus, tax advantages of investments are more important to P & L insurance companies than to other insurers, because P & L companies generally pay higher effective rates.

Two types of securites offer tax advantages to P & L companies: (1) SLG securities and (2) stocks. SLG securities are exempt from federal income taxes and some state income taxes. As is shown in Chapter 16, tax-exempt securities generally produce higher after-tax returns than taxable securities to taxpayers in high-tax brackets such as P & L insurance companies and commercial banks.[9] Like banks, the P & L insurance companies buy SLG securities to obtain tax-exempt income.[10] Of the total $385.5 billion in SLG securities outstanding at the end of 1984, commercial banks owned $172.0 billion and P & L insurance companies held $87.2 billion. On the other hand, P & L insurance companies own a large amount of stock, but commercial banks own virtually none. Unlike commercial banks, which are prohibited from purchasing common and preferred stocks, P & L insurance companies may buy quality stocks.[11] Furthermore, P & L companies exercise this privilege, because dividends received are 85 percent exempt from income taxes. (Dividends received from one corporation and paid from another are subject to this general tax provision.) Thus, income tax laws and insurance regulations play an impor-

---

[8] Mutuals with gross income under certain limits are partially or wholly exempted from income taxes.

[9] This is possible only to the point where fully taxable income is replaced with tax-exempt income.

[10] For updated figures, see the *flow-of-funds* reports referenced at the end of Chapter 2.

[11] Except stocks, bonds, and other securities issued by a corporation which invests 20 percent or more in insurance stocks.

tant part in the selection of securities for the P & L company portfolio, and combine to distinguish its portfolio from that of other financial institutions.[12]

Insurance policies written for losses and damage to property are termed *property insurance,* and insurance protection for negligence lawsuits is called *liability insurance*. Combination policies cover both types of risk for commonly insured assets such as automobiles, airplanes, and ships. Insurance premiums, all collected in advance, are accounted for as *unearned premiums* and obligations to pay for damages are booked as *unpaid claims*. Unearned premiums, unpaid claims, and other obligations arise from premium payments and risk underwriting by the insurance companies. Until required for payment, such funds are invested in state and local government securities, common stocks, and corporate bonds. Investment income is small relative to total revenues; however, because the investment portfolio is small relative to premiums, investment funds are working balances for policies usually written for 1 year or less or claims in process for payment. Therefore, property and liability insurance companies conduct a large volume of business with a relatively low funds balance.

SUMMARY

Life insurance companies function as financial intermediaries collecting premiums from insured persons and investing the funds until needed for death benefits. Premiums are the charges made by insurance companies for guaranteeing that benefits are paid to the insured's family, business associates, or other persons in the event of his or her death. On whole life policies, the premium exceeds death benefits in early years so that reserves are accumulated for later years when the death rate increases. On the other hand, term life insurance provides protection for a year or less and becomes more costly as the individual grows older. Life insurance companies accumulate enormous amounts of reserves under whole life policies but very little with term life policies.

Life insurance policies are also classified according to how they are sold. Ordinary life insurance is sold through agents to individuals. Group life insurance is made available through a professional, work, or other association, and participants must be members of that group. Credit life is purchased by borrowers to guarantee that their debt is repaid in the event of their death.

Reserves of life insurers are increasing rapidly, because a large proportion of insurance policies are of the whole life type. Insurance companies invest the reserves in high-quality loans and debt securities, including corporate bonds, mortgages, and policy loans. The corporate bonds are often negotiated directly

---

[12] Many other income tax and regulatory considerations that are not discussed here are important, also. Students are referred to the Internal Revenue Codes cited earlier and the state insurance laws, particularly those of New York State.

with the borrowing business to provide greater flexibility to the borrower and a greater return to the insurance company. Policy loans are secured by the cash values of life insurance policies and made to policyholders under the terms of their contract.

TERMS

mortality statistics	reserves
premiums	group life insurance
death benefit	credit life insurance
level premium policy	forward commitments
ordinary life insurance	direct placements
cash value	policy payables
term life	unearned-premium reserves
whole life	loss reserves

QUESTIONS

1 How do insurance companies determine the percentage of people age 35 who will die next year?
2 Name the three major types of insurance policies, according to the method by which they are sold.
3 What advantage does a whole life policy have over a term life policy? How does cash value relate to this advantage?
4 How can an individual maintain level premium payments under a term life policy?
5 Jane Brown, age 27, is married, the mother of two young children, and is borrowing $40,000 for a new house. She is concerned about the possibility that her family would be forced to sell the house in the event of her death. She is not in a financial position to commit herself to the substantial payments charged for a whole life policy and desires not to be locked into escalating premiums charged for a term life policy. As her insurance agent, what would you advise her to purchase?
6 What is the recent development in group life insurance in which the survivors of the insured do not receive a lump sum death benefit?
7 Name three factors influencing the computation of required life insurance reserves.
8 Rank in order of magnitude the five major classes of life insurance assets.
9 How do investment returns relate to premiums charged on life insurance policies? How does this affect policy sales? Portfolio growth?
10 How does the rate of investment income of insurance companies compare with current market returns?
11 What is meant by the "investment lag" experienced by most insurance companies?
12 What is the American system of insurance company regulation?

SELECTED REFERENCES

Anderson, D. R., and M. L. Fetters: "An Empirical Analysis of State Examiners' Relations to Loss Reserving Patterns," *Journal of Risk and Insurance,* June 1975, pp. 243–262.

Biger, N., and Kahane, Y.: "Purchasing Power, Risk and the Performance of Non-Life Insurance Companies," *Journal of Risk and Insurance,* June 1976, pp. 243–256.

Biger, N., and Kahane, Y.: "Risk Considerations in Insurance Ratemaking," *Journal of Risk and Insurance,* March 1978, pp. 121–132.

Brady, R. P.: "United States Internal Revenue Cases Section 79 Group Ordinary," *Conference of Actuaries in Public Practice, Proceedings,* 1974–1975, pp. 190–196.

Caswell, J. W., and S. C. Goodfellow: "Effect of Including Investment Income in Rate-making Upon Profitability of Non-Life Insurers," *Journal of Risk and Insurance,* June 1976, pp. 305–318.

Cummins, J. D.: "Economies of Scale in Independent Insurance Agencies," *Journal of Risk and Insurance,* December 1977, pp. 539–553.

Day, A. E., and P. H. Hendershott: "Household Demand for Policy Loans," *Journal of Risk and Insurance,* September 1977, pp. 411–423.

Farley, J.: "Disability Income," *Conference of Actuaries in Public Practice, Proceedings,* 1975–1976, pp. 143–146.

Forbes, S. W.: "Capital Gains, Losses, and Financial Results in the Non-Life Insurance Industry," *Journal of Risk and Insurance,* December 1975, pp. 625–638.

Geehan, R.: "Returns to Scale in the Life Insurance Industry," *Bell Journal of Economics,* Autumn 1977, pp. 497–514.

Goshay, R. C.: "Net Income as a Base for Life Insurance Company Taxation in California: Implications," *Journal of Risk and Insurance,* March 1976, pp. 17–41.

Greene, M. R.: "The Government as an Insurer," *Journal of Risk and Insurance,* September 1976, pp. 393–407.

Greene, M. R., J. Neter, and L. I. Tenney: "Annuity Rents and Rate—Guaranteed vs. Current," *Journal of Risk and Insurance,* September 1977, pp. 383–401.

Gustafson, D. R.: "Nonforfeiture, Valuation, and Cash Flow in Variation to Life, Health, and Annuities," *Conference of Actuaries in Public Practice, Proceedings,* 1975–1976, pp. 86–89.

Hadley, G. D.: "Aversion to Loss in Sale of Bonds in the Life Insurance Industry," *Journal of Risk and Insurance,* December 1977, pp. 661–668.

Harmelink, P. S.: "An Empirical Examination of Tax Predictive Ability of Alternate Sets of Insurance Company Accounting Data," *Journal of Accounting Research,* Spring 1973, pp. 146–158.

Humphrys, R.: "Government Supervision and Examination of Life Companies," *Conference of Actuaries in Public Practice, Proceedings,* 1974–1975, pp. 130–141.

Kahane, Y.: "Generation of Investable Funds and the Portfolio Behavior of the Non-Life Insurers," *Journal of Risk and Insurance,* March 1978, pp. 65–77.

Lamont, T.: "Corporate Financing—Private Placements: The Borrowers' Picnic," *Institutional Investor,* January 1977, p. 141.

Life Insurance Fact Book, American Council of Life Insurance, New York, annual publication.

Martin, G. D.: "Lender Discrimination in Pension Plans," *Journal of Risk and Insurance,* June 1976, pp. 203–214.

Michelbacher, G. F.: *Multiple Line Insurers: Their Nature and Operation,* 2d ed., McGraw-Hill Book Company, New York, 1970.

Montgomery, J. O.: "Regulatory Tests in the Life and Health Insurance Industry," *Journal of Risk and Insurance,"* September 1976, pp. 411–430.

Pritchett, S. T., and J. E. Logan: "Economies of Size for Worker's Compensation Business," *Journal of Risk and Insurance,* September 1976, pp. 533–540.

Robertson, R. S.: "Nonforfeiture, Valuation, and Cash Flow in Relation to Life, Health, and Annuities," *Conference of Actuaries in Public Practice, Proceedings,* 1975–1976, pp. 79–83.

CHAPTER 12

PENSION FUNDS

In the last chapter we discussed life insurance policies that protect against the risk of our untimely death. Another kind of risk in life is living long after our income-producing years. After we stop working, how can we provide for food, clothing, and shelter needs? Will the amount we save during our working years provide enough money for our retirement years? Pension plans are a solution to the retirement income problem, and in the process, they are becoming a major force in the financial markets.[1] Here we learn about the concept of pension plans and look at the management of pension reserves.

CONCEPT AND ORGANIZATION OF PENSION PLANS

A pension plan is a fund established and maintained by an employer, union, or individual to provide for the payment of definitely determinable benefits to people during retirement. Several aspects of the definition are important for pension fund management. First, there is a written plan that specifies who participates, benefits, and administers the pension fund. Second, benefits (payments) are contingent on retirement from active employment. Third, the benefits are *definitely determinable* now. Future benefits are determined by a firm contract and are not subject to the whims or fortunes of the employer or union. Contributions are invested in a portfolio of income-producing assets during the employee's working years. The portfolio of investments usually but not always

---

[1] Peter Drucker, a noted economist and management consultant, argues that pension fund "socialism" now influences national economic policy, inflation, retirement, and other crucial national issues. For a discussion of one viewpoint on pension funds and social welfare, see Drucker (1976).

increases in value, and the rate of return may vary widely. The performance of the investment portfolio depends upon the returns produced by securities selected for the portfolio. Whether the employee, employer, or an insurance company benefits from unexpectedly large returns or suffers losses from unexpectedly small returns depends upon the type of pension plan, a subject discussed later.

Investment selection and maintenance is performed by the fund manager, either an insurance company or a trustee. The pension fund is a financial intermediary—in the form of either an insurance company or a trust. Trusts are legally independent entities that hold the assets for the benefit of someone else, employees in this case. The trustee is legally obligated to invest funds paid into the pension fund. Commercial bank trust departments, particularly those of large banks in major cities, aggressively solicit pension funds. Furthermore, a number of commercial bank trust departments not only function as record keepers but also provide investment selection and actuarial planning services. Numerous financial institutions provide services in the pension industry, including all the institutions studied so far. As described in this chapter, numerous pension plan alternatives are available, and there are opportunities for many different financial institutions to provide pension plan services from bookkeeping to investment selection.

The enactment of the Employee Retirement Income Security Act of 1974, following 7 years of debate in the U.S. Congress, is a historical milestone for pension plans.[2] Throughout this chapter the influence of this far-reaching legislation is seen. The act, referred to by the acronym ERISA (pronounced *er-is'-a*), set minimum standards for pension plan contracts, defined investment responsibility, and established a new government-operated insurance program. These and other important features of ERISA are summarized later in the chapter.

Pension plans that qualify under ERISA receive favorable tax treatment, which is a significant reason for complying with ERISA and an important factor in investment selection. Contributions by employers and employees are generally not subject to income taxes until after retirement. That is, the portion of an employee's earnings (or self-employed person's profits) which are contributed to a qualifying retirement plan are excluded from current taxable income, although the employer deducts such contributions as a current business expense like salaries and wages. Participants (persons who are beneficiaries of pension plans) gain two tax advantages: (1) income taxes on contributions are deferred until retirement—often for many years—and (2) income tax rates are often lower after retirement than they are during the working years. Deferment of taxes allows participants to invest money which would normally be paid in taxes; earnings on deferred tax investments accrue to the participants. Then the income tax rate frequently drops after retirement when salary and wage

---

[2] Public Law 93-406, 93d Congress, H.R. 2, September 2, 1974, Employee Retirement Income Security Act of 1974.

income is sharply reduced. Consequently, participants may pay less total tax and always gain the use of deferred income taxes under a qualifying pension plan.[3]

Types of Pension Plans

Insured and Noninsured Plans   In the private sector, pension plans are usually either *insured* or *noninsured*. An insured pension plan uses the premium contributions to purchase an *annuity* from an insurance company. The annuity is a contract that provides income for a number of years or for the lifetime of the retiree. Annuity payments are usually paid monthly but can be paid quarterly, semiannually, or annually. Lifetime annuities provide us with income, regardless of how long we live, and protect us from outliving our income. We remove the risk of retirement poverty by pooling our money now and distributing it to the living later. Payments into the common fund are called contributions or premiums. Actuaries, persons trained in the technical and mathematical aspects of annuities, compute the amount of contributions required for the size of annuity promised in our retirement plan.

Noninsured pension plans invest contributions in a separate, independent trust fund. Future benefits are paid from trust funds assets and are not guaranteed by an insurance company. (We note later that a government agency provides limited insurance protection.) The fund is used to pay benefits under one of the following types of contracts:

1 Defined benefit
2 Defined contribution

In a defined benefit plan, the retirement payments and contributions are estimated by an actuary. For example, the plan may call for annual benefits equal to 60 percent of the employee's last year's salary. The actuary estimates how many people will be retiring and their salaries in future years. In this case the benefit is not a fixed dollar amount, and the actuary makes assumptions about future wage and salary rates. On the other hand, the plan may call for specific contributions, such as 8 percent of wages, and promises retirees a share of the resulting portfolio. As each contribution is added to the pension fund, the employee receives *units* that entitle him or her to a share at retirement age. The share value depends on the performance of the portfolio and is not guaranteed by anyone. Defined contribution plans pass investment returns through to the participants. Thus, in the case of defined contribution plans, the retirement benefits depend in part on future market conditions.

---

[3] For details on pension plan contracts and tax implications, see a guide for establishing plans, such as Bernhard R. Snyder, *Guide to Pension and Profit Sharing Plans under the Employee Retirement Income Security Act of 1974*, rev. ed., Farnsworth, Rockville Centre, N.Y., 1975; Joseph J. Melone and Everett T. Allen, *Pension Planning: Profit Sharing and Other Deferred Compensation Plans*, 3d rev. ed., Dow Jones-Irwin, Homewood, Ill. 1976; *Handbook on Pension Reform Law, Employee Retirement Income Security Act of 1974*, Prentice-Hall, Englewood Cliffs, N.J., 1974.

Self-Employed and IRA Plans   Individuals may make tax-deferrable contributions for retirement plans. Individuals may now contribute up to $15,000 or 15 percent of earned income, whichever is less, to a qualified retirement plan. Also, workers not covered by a retirement plan where they are employed are allowed to make tax-deferrable contributions of $15,000 or 15 percent of earned income, after contributions for retirement, whichever is less, to an individual retirement account (IRA) plan, which may be invested in banks, insurance companies, mutual funds, and certain special government securities. Limitations and penalties exist for transferring and withdrawing funds, prior to retirement. Financial institutions are finding it good business to assist individuals in setting up retirement plans by helping them file the necessary forms, understand the legal aspects, and so forth. In addition to receiving some fees for retirement plan services, the financial institutions are obtaining substantial amounts of long-term money for investment. The next section describes the important role of pension funds as financial intermediaries.

Plans as Financial Intermediaries

In the process of providing for retirement income, pension plans function as intermediaries in the financial markets. The plans receive from individuals small regular amounts that are aggregated and invested in large amounts in corporate securities and other long-term investments. The investment is made with the hope that income and capital growth will, when taken together with the individual contributions, be adequate to meet the pension obligations. As pension obligations come due, the investments should provide the means to furnish the contracted benefits.

Noninsured private plans, which provide pension benefits without insurance company intermediation, may be fully funded, partially funded, or unfunded. A funded plan is one under which funds are segregated in advance in order that the means to provide expected benefits are available. As the terms suggest, a fully funded plan is one in which 100 percent of the needed funds are set aside in advance as compared with a partially funded plan where a lesser percentage of funds is set aside.[4] Obviously an unfunded plan is one in which no funds are set aside for the future benefits.

Pension Fund Growth

Pension funds are growing rapidly from substantial new contributions and the reinvestment of investment income. This section looks at the growth of pension funds in general and for specific institutions. We divide the pension plans into three groups: private plans, government-administered plans, and old-age survivors and disability insurance. Private plans consist of the insured and noninsured types of contracts discussed previously. Government-administered plans

---

[4] The rate and conditions under which funds can be accumulated to assure the success of pension plans is discussed in Bronson (1957).

are the state and federal employee retirement plans, while old-age survivors and disability insurance (OASDI) is commonly referred to as *social security* and provides welfare transfers to a large segment of the population.

Private Plans Private pension plan assets are large and growing rapidly, as shown in Figure 12-1 and Tables 12-1 and 12-2. Private pension plans in 1950 covered 10.3 million persons, which accounted for more than 30 percent of all persons employed in the United States. At that time the private plans had accumulated $12 billion and employers were paying about 85 percent of the total cost. By 1984 the total assets of private pension plans had increased to $623.3 billion.[5]

Common stock, the major assets of private noninsured pension funds, exceeds $100 billion and is growing rapidly. Pension plans are a major owner of listed stocks, and their net purchases exceed those of any other group by a sizable margin. Why have common stocks been chosen as the major type of investment by noninsured private pension funds? Over long periods of time, several decades or more, returns from common stocks have been superior to those obtainable from corporate and government bonds.[6] Although returns from common stocks during the 1970s did not keep pace with historical trends, common stocks have continued to be the major investment. Apparently investment advisers have continued to expect that common stocks are better than

---

[5] For a description of the historical development and growth of private pension plans since 1910, see *Pension Facts 1976*, pp. 7–11.

[6] See Ibbotson and Sinquefield (1976) for a comparison of annual holding period returns (1926–1974) for common stocks, long-term government bonds, long-term corporate bonds, and U.S. Treasury bills.

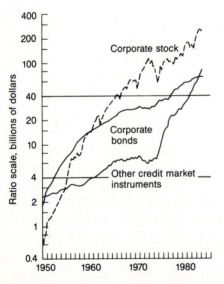

FIGURE 12-1
Growth of investments of private pension funds. (*Source*: Board of Governors of the Federal Reserve System.)

TABLE 12-1
PENSION FUNDS' STATEMENTS OF FINANCIAL ASSETS AND LIABILITIES, 1972–1984 (BILLIONS OF DOLLARS)

		1972	1973	1974	1975	1976	1977	1978	1979	1980	1981	1982	1983	1984
		State and local government employee retirement funds												
Total financial assets	1	80.6	84.7	88.0	104.8	120.4	132.5	153.9	169.7	198.1	224.2	264.2	313.7	354.9
Demand deposits and currency	2	1.0	1.3	1.8	1.4	1.4	1.7	2.7	4.0	4.3	4.4	5.5	6.0	14.0
Corporate equities	3	22.2	20.2	16.4	24.3	30.1	30.0	33.3	37.1	44.3	47.8	60.2	88.1	98.1
Credit market instruments	4	57.4	63.1	69.8	79.1	88.9	100.8	117.8	128.6	149.5	172.0	198.5	219.6	242.8
U.S. government securities	5	5.7	5.8	6.2	7.8	10.9	16.3	23.4	30.1	40.0	50.7	69.0	85.5	113.0
Treasury issues	6	3.6	2.5	1.6	2.5	4.1	6.8	9.5	14.7	20.9	27.6	35.0	45.5	70.0
Agency issues	7	2.1	3.3	4.6	5.3	6.8	9.6	14.0	15.4	19.1	23.1	34.1	40.0	43.0
State & local obligations	8	2.0	1.7	1.0	1.9	3.4	3.5	4.0	3.9	4.1	3.9	3.4	3.0	1.5
Corporate & foreign bonds	9	43.2	48.4	54.9	61.8	66.9	72.9	81.9	85.0	94.5	104.7	112.1	116.6	113.3
Mortgages	10	6.5	7.1	7.7	7.5	7.7	8.0	8.6	9.6	10.9	12.7	14.0	14.5	15.1
		Private pension funds												
Total financial assets	1	156.1	134.3	115.5	146.8	171.9	178.3	198.3	220.0	286.8	293.1	341.6	409.3	623.3
Demand deposits and currency	2	1.6	1.4	1.3	1.5	1.6	1.7	1.8	1.9	1.9	2.0	2.1	2.2	4.2
Time deposits	3	0.3	1.1	3.7	2.4	2.3	4.8	10.3	8.9	10.3	12.0	9.3	7.0	24.6
Corporate equities	4	115.2	90.5	63.3	88.6	109.7	101.9	107.9	123.7	175.8	167.1	200.4	250.7	294.1
Credit market instruments	5	34.0	36.3	41.9	48.9	52.5	64.7	73.0	81.8	92.6	105.4	122.8	142.0	300.5
U.S. government securities	6	3.7	4.4	5.5	10.8	14.7	20.1	22.2	25.0	30.9	40.0	51.5	68.6	171.0
Treasury issues	7	3.0	3.1	3.0	7.4	11.1	15.9	17.5	19.4	24.1	30.6	38.9	49.1	113.1
Agency issues	8	0.7	1.3	2.6	3.3	3.6	114.2	4.7	5.6	6.7	9.3	14.7	19.5	57.9
Corporate & foreign bonds	9	27.6	29.5	34.0	35.8	35.5	42.1	48.0	53.7	58.1	61.7	65.1	68.2	94.5
Mortgages	10	2.7	2.4	2.4	2.4	2.4	2.5	2.8	3.1	3.7	3.7	4.1	5.2	4.6
Miscellaneous assets	11	5.0	5.1	5.3	5.5	5.7	5.2	5.4	5.8	6.2	6.6	7.0	7.4	30.4

TABLE 12-2
PENSION FUNDS' FLOW OF FUNDS, 1972–1984 (BILLIONS OF DOLLARS)

	1972	1973	1974	1975	1976	1977	1978	1979	1980	1981	1982	1983	1984
Private pension funds													
Net acq. of financial assets	6.6	8.3	10.7	11.8	11.2	18.7	15.9	14.0	22.3	22.4	26.6	32.8	26.1
Demand deposits & currency	0.2	-0.2	*	0.1	0.1	0.1	0.1	0.1	0.1	0.1	0.1	0.1	0.7
Time deposits	*	0.8	2.7	-1.3	-0.1	2.5	5.5	-1.4	1.4	1.8	-2.8	-2.3	3.0
Corporate equities	7.3	5.3	2.3	5.8	7.3	4.5	1.9	6.1	9.6	7.3	11.5	15.4	-2.5
Credit market instruments	-0.6	0.2	5.6	7.0	3.6	12.2	8.3	8.8	10.8	12.8	17.4	19.2	24.9
U.S. government securities	1.0	0.7	1.1	5.2	3.9	5.4	2.1	2.8	5.8	9.1	13.6	15.1	18.6
Treasury issues	0.8	0.1	-0.2	4.5	3.7	4.8	1.6	1.9	4.7	6.5	8.2	10.3	12.0
Agency issues	0.1	0.6	1.3	0.7	0.3	0.6	0.5	0.8	1.2	2.6	5.3	4.8	6.7
Corporate bonds	-1.0	1.9	4.5	1.8	-0.3	6.6	5.9	5.7	4.4	3.6	3.5	3.0	2.2
Mortgages	-0.9	-0.3	*	*	*	0.1	0.3	0.3	0.6	0.1	0.4	1.1	0.4
Misc. assets	0.1	0.1	0.1	0.2	0.2	-0.5	0.1	0.4	0.4	0.4	0.4	0.4	3.7
State and local government employee retirement funds													
Net acq. of financial assets	8.5	9.5	9.7	11.3	12.9	15.9	20.7	16.2	26.5	31.0	35.2	39.0	39.3
Demand deposits & currency	0.3	0.4	0.5	-0.4	*	0.3	1.0	1.3	0.3	0.2	1.0	0.5	3.8
Corporate equities	3.6	3.4	2.6	2.4	3.1	3.7	2.6	4.1	5.3	8.3	7.7	17.4	8.4
Credit market instruments	4.5	5.7	6.7	9.3	9.8	11.9	17.0	10.8	20.9	22.5	26.5	21.1	27.1
U.S. government securities	0.3	0.1	0.3	1.6	3.1	5.5	7.1	6.6	9.9	10.7	18.3	16.5	24.8
Treasury issues	-0.3	-1.1	-0.9	1.0	1.5	2.7	2.7	5.3	6.2	6.6	7.4	10.5	19.5
Agency issues	0.5	1.2	1.2	0.7	1.6	2.7	4.4	1.4	3.7	4.1	11.0	5.9	5.3
State & local obligations	-0.1	-0.3	-0.7	1.0	1.4	0.2	0.4	*	0.1	-0.2	-0.5	-0.4	-0.5
Corporate bonds	3.7	5.2	6.5	6.8	5.1	6.0	9.0	3.2	9.5	10.2	7.4	4.5	2.4
Mortgages	0.1	0.7	0.6	-0.2	0.2	0.3	0.5	1.0	1.3	1.8	1.3	0.5	0.4

bonds as a pension fund investment. Corporate bond ownership by private pension plans has increased, also, but not as fast as common stock investment. See Table 12-1 for a listing of major assets.

Federal Government Plans   Government-administered pension plans are public sector funds covering primarily government employees. There are separate plans for federal, state, and local government employees. There are a dozen or more retirement plans for federal employees in different branches of the government. The largest plan is the United States Civil Service Retirement System, which covers 2.7 million active workers. Civil service and other retirement plans hold assets of about $35 billion, an amount substantially less than that needed to pay contractual benefits. The deficiency is called an *unfunded liability* and is estimated at $70 billion. Like other government retirement programs, the federal plans are considered financially troubled. The unfunded liabilities are growing, and either the program will be reduced or funding will be increased in future years to balance promises with contributions.

State and Local Government Plans   State and local government plans cover teachers, police officers, fire fighters, and other employees of states, counties, and cities. Assets total about $355 billion and contributions are $26 billion annually. Recent economic problems are forcing plan administrators to recognize the unfunded liability of such plans. New York City and State pension problems are a public embarrassment and are representative of some other government funds.[7] Economists in general recommend that all local pension systems should be funded fully, thereby preventing irresponsibly legislated increases. The problem of funding past general pension arrangements, sometimes negotiated in exchange for lower salaries and wages, is surfacing. The Employee Retirement Income Security Act of 1974, to be discussed later in the chapter, recognizes this problem area and mandates investigation of possible solutions.

Social Security (OASDI)   Social security is a federal plan for providing payments to retirees and to families of deceased or permanently disabled persons. Taxes are collected from employees and their employers to cover the cost of benefits. We see that the current funding system is inadequate, because benefits have been increased beyond the level supported by past and current taxes. More persons are becoming eligible for benefits than those who are entering the work force. For example, consider the following statistics:

1 In 1900 (35 years before social security existed) there were ten persons over 65 not working for every 100 persons in the working population.

2 In 1975 there were thirty people receiving social security benefits for each 100 workers.

[7] For further discussion and analysis of state and local government pension plans, see Brooks (1975).

3 Within 75 years it is estimated that there will be forty-five recipients of social security for every 100 workers.

That is, projections indicate that one recipient will be supported by only two workers. The system is now too immense and complex even to contemplate complete funding. Extending the retirement age and excluding retirees with other pension benefit sources are actions that have been enacted by Congress. However, social security is in need of more substantive revisions, and Congress is expected to pass more legislation on these issues during the current decade.[8]

SOURCES OF FUNDS

Having established the fact that pension plans are a significant and growing participant in the financial markets, we turn to an analysis of the sources of this growth. Generally the growth is from two factors: (1) contributions by employers and employees and (2) income and capital growth of assets.

Employer-Employee Contributions

In general pension contributions by employers for the benefit of employees is tax deductible by employers in computing taxable income of the employer for the year in which the contribution is made. Until the enactment of recent pension and tax reforms, the availability of tax deductions for pension provisions by individual employees was virtually nonexistent. As a result, employers who offered plans made the major portion of contributions and employees made only a small contribution. Contributions are growing at a compound rate in excess of 15 percent per year due to the growth of employer contributions.

Investment Income, Gains, and Losses

Private noninsured plans receive investment income and asset appreciation, or depreciation on existing investments. In addition to income gains and losses realized by plans, there are usually unrealized gains and losses. The difference between costs of investments owned by plans and the market value of those investments is called unrealized appreciation or depreciation. As the general level of stock market prices fluctuates, unrealized gains and losses are created. Unrealized appreciation generally exists because the stock market trends are up. Whether realized or unrealized, all gains and losses are recognized in computing benefits to plan beneficiaries and in measuring portfolio performance.[9]

---

[8] For an examination of how social security relates to private plans under ERISA, see Greenough and King (1976). Also, see Myers (1975) for a thorough factual description of the various social insurance and allied programs in the United States written by the chief actuary of the Social Security Administration from 1947 to 1970.

[9] SEC Statistical Series presents pension plans statistics annually.

USES OF FUNDS

We have established that the assets of pension funds are substantial and growing. This leads us to the next logical question—how do pension plans use these assets? As previously mentioned, our concern is primarily with private noninsured plans since it is these plans that retain and manage their own contributions. Table 12-1, shown earlier in the chapter, indicates that funds are invested principally in U.S. government and corporate stocks and bonds. Other assets consist principally of mortgages and local and state government obligations.

Investment in Corporate Securities

Traditionally, pension plans have followed conservative investment policies, preferring fixed income obligations such as corporate bonds and U.S. government securities to equity investments. In 1966, U.S. government securities and corporate bonds were 31.8 percent of total assets of private noninsured pension plans, and common stock was 57.2 percent. In 1984 these percentages were 48.2 percent for U.S. government securities and corporate bonds and 47.2 percent for common equity investments. On the other hand, state and local government plans have increased corporate equity investments from 9.2 percent in 1967 to 27.6 percent of assets in 1978. Has the proportion of equity investments been important for performance?

Investment Return and Performance

Experience with noninsured pension plans was studied by Dietz (1966) in early research emphasizing portfolio quality and return on investment rather than actuarial factors.[10] Recent studies have shown that equity investments have not guaranteed the superior performance which pension managers had anticipated.[11] Beebower and Bergstrom (1977) compared total portfolio performance (risk adjusted) against the S & P 500 and found that the relative portfolio performance was largely determined by the portfolio's proportion of equity investment. When stocks outperformed bonds during the period from 1966 to 1970, those portfolios with high-equity commitments outperformed those with low-equity commitments. Then in the period 1971 to 1975, portfolios with large bond commitments outperformed those with a high proportion of stocks, because bonds generally outperformed stocks in the U.S. financial markets. Furthermore, their analysis did not indicate that managers adjusted the debt-

---

[10] Also, see the major study by Lorie et al. (1968). Pension fund performance measurement is still partly art as well as science. Private research houses and some trust advisors provide statistical measures of risk and return, however, for use in evaluating historical performance and estimating future rates of return.

[11] See Beebower and Bergstrom (1977) for estimates and discussion of pension portfolio performance.

stock mix in anticipation of changes in performance.[12] These studies conclude that security analysis and investment by pension plans are subject to the same risks experienced by other investors and, therefore, require varying emphasis depending upon the movements of the financial markets.

EMPLOYEE RETIREMENT INCOME SECURITY ACT (ERISA)

The major law controlling pension funds, pension contracts, and securities management is the Employee Retirement Income Security Act of 1974 (ERISA). ERISA is a massive, comprehensive, and extremely technical legislative compromise to financial and ethical problems in the private pension fund field. New private plans must conform and virtually all pre-1974 plans are being rewritten and portfolios revised to meet the provisions of ERISA. The law sets standards and protects covered employees, but it does not require an employer to set up or retain a pension plan. If an employer has a pension plan that qualifies for federal income tax exemption, then it must conform to the provisions of ERISA.

Major Provisions of ERISA

The provisions cover everything from who is eligible to participate to who is responsible for investment management. Here is a brief rundown on the major provisions.

1 Participation: The plan must include employees age 25 and older, except some part-time workers.

2 Vesting: The right to benefits accrues through service, and some portion of contributions and income is owned by the employee. At a minimum, participants are entitled to 25 percent of accrued pension benefits after 5 years and increasing to 100 percent after 10 years on the job.[13]

3 Spouse option: The plans must allow the option of continuing benefits to a spouse after the retiree dies.

4 Funding standards: Contributions to new plans must be actuarilly sound. That is, current and past benefit promises must be funded by current contributions, except for a time lag to bring unfunded liabilities into line.

5 Portability: Workers are to be able to transfer pension rights when they change jobs.

---

[12] Investment selection and equity portfolio management are discussed in "investments" texts, such as Jerome B. Cohen, Edward D. Zinbarg, and Arthur Zeikel, *Investment Analysis and Portfolio Management*, Irwin, Homewood, Ill.; Charles A. D'Ambrosio, *Principles of Modern Investments*, Science Research Associates, Inc., Chicago, Jack Clark Francis, *Investments: Analysis and Management*, McGraw-Hill, New York.

[13] Vesting makes the fund somewhat portable, because an employee does not lose all pension benefits accrued during past years of employment.

6 Plan termination insurance: Under a federal agency, Pension Benefit Guaranty Corporation ("Penny Benny"), participants are guaranteed that they will receive their vested benefit subject to certain limitations; the guarantee does not cover defined-contribution-type plans.

7 Fiduciary standards: A fiduciary of a pension plan is any trustee, investment adviser, or any other person who has discretionary authority or responsibility in the management of the plan or its assets. Keypoints of the law require the fiduciary to act as a "prudent" person and to perform his or her duties strictly in the interest of the plan participants.

8 Other provisions: The Department of Labor and the Internal Revenue Service share jurisdiction. Extensive reporting and disclosure of information is required to be sent to these two agencies and Penny Benny. Self-employed people can set up their own plan and deduct contributions from income, like employees of the large plans.

ERISA standardizes pension plan management, and in the process, creates a well-defined financial institution, the pension fund. Employers can no longer tie pension funds to their success or failure, because the pension fund and its management are legally independent. Now, we have a separate and viable fund collecting and disbursing payments on actuarilly sound principles. Also, Penny Benny guarantees those funds, as other federal government agencies guarantee bank, savings and loan, and credit union deposits. ERISA imposes greater complexity and cost on pension managers, but it also provides a legal definition for a fast growing financial institution, the private pension fund.

Government Regulation

Prior to the enactment of ERISA, pension plans were virtually unregulated arrangements between employers and employees. ERISA made pension plans subject to regulatory oversight by the Treasury Department, the Labor Department, and a newly created corporation within the Labor Department, the Pension Benefit Guarantee Corporation (Penny Benny). Although no borrowing privileges are available through any of these agencies, Penny Benny specifically operates to administer an insurance plan that pays benefits up to a maximum of $750 per month under plans that are terminated. The insurance is funded through a fee imposed on each pension plan equal to $1 per year for each employee in a single-employer plan and $450 per employee in a multi-employer plan (e.g., union-sponsored collectively bargained plan).

ERISA imposed reporting and disclosure requirements that replaced prior requirements. The information contained in reports made to the Labor Department, Treasury Department (through the Internal Revenue Service), and Penny Benny is made available to the Department of Health, Education, and Welfare, which publishes various statistics in its monthly *Social Security Bulletin*. In addition, the Securities and Exchange Commission publishes pension plan data in its quarterly *Statistical Bulletin*.

SUMMARY

In this chapter we have looked at pension plans as providers of income security to retirees and as financial intermediaries. We have seen that plans may be public employer plans or private employer plans; they may be insured or noninsured; they may be defined benefit plans or defined contribution plans.

Plans that involve a financial intermediary function are those that collect contributions, invest funds, and promise future benefits. This is done through an insurance company for insured plans or directly by the plan itself for noninsured plans. Categorization of plans as unfunded, partially funded, or fully funded depends upon the extent to which assets support expected future benefits. Pension plans in both the private and public sector have grown phenomenally throughout the past three decades.

Because obligations under government-sponsored plans have grown more rapidly than contributions to plans, a tremendous unfunded liability problem has evolved. This problem is a critical and embarrassing industry development, which is being studied now. The most widespread pension system is the social security system administered by the federal government. At the present time this system, which is not fully funded, is obligated to make current payments in excess of current receipts. All projections indicate an imbalance in the social security system which will become acute within the next 50 years.

All pension plans have the same principal source of funds—contributions from employees. Private noninsured funds also generate substantial additional funds from investment income and gains or invested contributions. The investments that generate the investment income and gains are principally common stocks, corporate bonds, and U.S government securities. As state and local government pension plans have come under mounting pressure to improve investment returns, they have shown a tendency to invest proportionately less in fixed obligations (bonds) and more in equity securities (stocks).

The enactment of the Employee Retirement Income Security Act (ERISA) extended federal regulation of pension funds to areas including participation, vesting, funding, portability, and fiduciary standards. Although ERISA contained controversial mandates, it clearly established pension funds as an officially recognized and regulated financial institution.

TERMS

noninsured plan	ERISA
insured plan	social security
annuity	portability
defined benefit	vesting
defined contribution	participation
funded plans	spouse option
unfunded liability	plan termination
private plans	fiduciary standards
public sector plans	

QUESTIONS

1 Cite and describe the eight major provisions of ERISA.

2 What federal agency guarantees pension fund benefits?

3 What is the distinguishing feature between insured and noninsured pension plans?

4 Describe a defined benefit plan. Distinguish this from a defined contribution plan.

5 Distinguish between private pension plans and public sector pension plans.

6 What circumstance has caused pension fund managers to shift pension investments from corporate bonds to corporate equity investments? Has this shift accomplished its purpose?

7 What is an unfunded liability? How does this compare with the concept of a fully funded pension plan?

8 What social and economic conditions are causing social security obligations to exceed contributions?

SELECTED REFERENCES

"Actuary's Responsibilities and Liabilities," *Conference of Actuaries in Public Practice, Proceedings,* 1975–76, pp. 369–375.

Beebower, G. L., and G. L. Bergstrom: "A Performance Analysis of Pension and Profit Sharing Portfolios: 1966–1975," *Financial Analysts Journal,* May/June 1977, pp. 31–41.

Bernstein, P. L.: "Hate: The New Force in America's Stock Market," *Institutional Investor, International Edition,* November 1977, pp. 81–85.

Brooks, John: *Conficts of Interest: Corporate Pension Funds Asset Management,* Twentieth Century Fund, New York, 1975.

Brown, M. V.: "Prudence under ERISA—What the Regulators Say," *Financial Analysts Journal,* January/February 1977, pp. 33–39.

Calderwood, S.: "The Truth about Index Funds," *Financial Analysts Journal,* July/August 1977, p. 36.

Cardon, John A.: "Plan Design for Fiduciary Protection," *Financial Executive,* July 1975, pp. 34–38.

Caswell, J. W.: "Economic Efficiency in Pension Plan Administration: A Study of the Construction Industry," *Journal of Risk and Insurance,* June 1976, pp. 257–270.

Cirino, R. J.: "Controlling AT&T's Pension Explosion," *Institutional Investor,* January 1978, pp. 126–136.

Cottle, S.: "The Future of Pension Fund Management," *Financial Analysts Journal,* May/June 1977, pp. 23–25.

Dietz, Peter O.: *Pension Funds: Measuring Investment Performance,* Free Press, New York, 1966.

Drucker, Peter E.: *The Unseen Revolution,* Harper & Row, New York, 1976.

"Farmland: The Next Pension Fund Investment," *Institutional Investor,* February 1975, pp. 11–12.

Fiske, H.: "Performance Fees: Should a Manager Get a Piece of the Action," *Institutional Investor,* March 1977, pp. 90–91.

"Funding Problems," *Conference of Actuaries in Public Practice, Proceedings,* 1975–1976, pp. 233–237.

Gray, W. S.: "The Major Shortfalls of ERISA," *Financial Analysts Journal,* January/February 1977, pp. 18–20.

Greenough, William C., and Francis P. King: *Pension Plans and Public Policy,* Columbia University Press, New York, 1976.

Haslem, J. A.: "A Note on the Profitability of Commercial Bank Trust Departments," *Journal of Bank Research,* Winter 1975, pp. 260–263.

"How Many Managers Does a Pension Fund Really Need?," *Institutional Investor,* November 1977, pp. 65–66.

"How Pension Funds Monitor the Performance of Their Outside Managers," *Institutional Investor,* May 1976, pp. 65–68.

Ibbotson, Roger G., and Rex A. Sinquefield: "Stocks, Bonds, Bills, and Inflation: Year-by-Year Historical Returns (1926–1974)," *Journal of Business,* January 1976, pp. 11–47.

Jansson, S.: "Regional Banks Close the Gap," *Institutional Investor,* November 1977, pp. 85–92.

Johnson, P. J.: "Cutting the Ticker Tape Umbilical Cord," *Journal of Portfolio Management,* Winter 1976, pp. 61–64.

Kahn, L.: "Lemmings Always Lose," *Financial Analysts Journal,* May/June 1977, pp. 27–29.

Kahn, L. M.: "Plan Amendments—ERISA," *Conference of Actuaries in Public Practice, Proceedings,* 1975–1976, pp. 171–173.

Kaplan, M.: "The U.S. Government's Nonlife Insurance and Guarantee Programs," *Conference on Actuaries in Public Proceedings,* 1974–1975, pp. 143–176.

Klesch, A. G.: "Interpreting the Prudent Man Risk of ERISA," *Financial Analysts Journal,* January/February 1977, pp. 26–32.

Lorie, James H., et al., *Measuring the Investment Performance of Pension Funds for the Purpose of Inter-Fund Comparison,* Bank Administration Institute, Park Ridge, Ill., 1968.

McGill, Dan M.: *Fundamentals of Private Pensions,* 3d ed., Irwin, Homewood, Ill., 1977.

Myers, Robert J.: *Social Security,* Irwin, Homewood, Ill., 1975.

"The 1978 Pensions Directory," *Institutional Investor,* January 1978, pp. 47–130.

Pension Facts, American Council of Life Insurance, New York, annual publication.

Regan, P. J.: "The 1976 BEA Pension Survey," *Financial Management,* Spring 1977, pp. 48–67.

"Should Pension Funds Buy Raw Land," *Institutional Investor,* December 1974, p. 13.

Srodes, J. L.: "The Railroad Retirement Fund: Bumpy Track Ahead," *Institutional Investor,* September 1977, p. 65.

Tepper, I.: "Risk vs. Return in Pension Fund Investment," *Harvard Business Review,* March/April 1977, pp. 100–107.

Voorheis, F. L.: "Do Banks Manage Pension Funds Well," *Financial Analysts Journal,* September/October 1976, pp. 35–40.

Wilson, P. N., and R. I. Cummin: "Pension Officers, Are You Wasting Management and Transaction Costs?" *Financial Analysts Journal,* March/April 1977, pp. 58–62.

CHAPTER 13

INVESTMENT BANKING, SECURITY TRADING, AND MORTGAGE BANKING

This chapter describes intermediaries that own relatively few assets but transact a tremendous volume of securities. *Investment bankers* market new stock and bond offerings to individual and institutional investors around the world. *Security dealers* trade existing securities among millions of investors, both individual and institutional. *Mortgage bankers* grant billions of dollars worth of mortgages for quick resale to institutional investors but act primarily as marketers and retain few securities permanently. These intermediaries contribute their expertise and facilities toward helping individuals, business, and governments bring new security issues to the money and capital markets and to exchange existing securities.

As with other intermediaries described previously, these intermediaries are frequently owned by holding companies that own other types of financial intermediaries. Further, many of the functions described in this chapter are actually performed by institutions other than those designated as investment bankers, security dealers, and mortgage bankers. For example, some commercial banks are taking orders for security transactions from their customers and some savings and loans perform all of the functions attributed to mortgage bankers. Product-line distinctions, once an easy means of classifying institutions, are blurring in today's rush to open financial supermarkets. To avoid the seeming confusion in financial institution structure, we focus not on corporate structures but on the basic financial services that satisfy society's needs for financial intermediation. In this chapter we concentrate on the needs of individuals and businesses to issue financial contracts (securities and mortgages) that can be traded in public capital markets.

INVESTMENT BANKING AND SECURITIES TRADING

Investment banking is defined generally as follows:

> . . . the intermediary activities carried on by securities firms and commercial banks in the sale of new securities. New issues except where otherwise indicated are defined to exclude U.S. government securities and mutual fund shares that do not go through the usual investment banking channels, and to include those secondaries which do.[1]

This part of the chapter discusses investment banking and the related activity of securities trading. The basic difference between investment banking and securities trading is that investment banking is concerned primarily with new issues, whereas securities trading relates to existing securities. For example, Merrill Lynch is acting as an investment banker when it sells a new issue of American Telephone and Telegraph (AT&T) common stock, but it is a securities trader when it participates in the exchange of existing AT&T common stock. Some investment firms, such as Merrill Lynch, Salomon Brothers, and Dean Witter Reynolds, perform both investment banking and securities trading functions, while other, smaller firms specialize in one function.

Investment bankers perform several important fucntions to bring new securities to the investing public. The three major functions of investment bankers are (1) origination, (2) underwriting, and (3) distribution. New securities are created during origination, bought by investment bankers during underwriting, and sold to investors during the distribution phase.[2]

Origination

Security flotations are complex matters, and security issuers look to the investment banker for specialized assistance during origination. Origination is the important function of providing issuers investment advice, information, and assistance. The investment banker commonly:

1 Advises the issuer on the type of security and specific terms that are most acceptable during current financial market conditions.

2 Prepares and assists in filing a prospectus with the Securities and Exchange Commission.

3 Arranges for the efficient distribution of the new issue.

4 Arranges for a number of operational requirements such as trustees, security indentures (contracts), and safekeeping.

Issues frequently depend heavily upon investment bankers who are financial market specialists to create securities that meet most of the issuer's needs and,

---

[1] Friend et al. (1967), p. 2. Parts of this section are based on Friend (1967), chap. 1, and interested readers are referred to this classic study of the investment banking industry.

[2] Institutional and regulatory details are not discussed extensively here but are available in specialized works. See Carosso (1970).

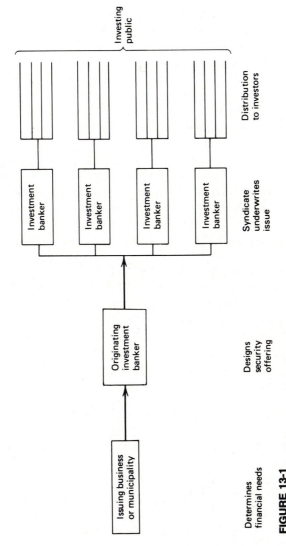

FIGURE 13-1
Organization of new issue distribution syndicate.

Issuing business or municipality

Determines financial needs

Originating investment banker

Designs security offering

Investment banker
Investment banker
Investment banker
Investment banker

Syndicate underwrites issue

Investing public

Distribution to investors

simultaneously, are acceptable for sale to investors.[3] See Figure 13-1 for a depiction of the process.

On the other hand, the investment banker may agree to either (1) a standby agreement or (2) a best-efforts agreement. Standby agreements are commonly used in the case of rights offerings and commit the investment banker to purchase all securities not bought by current stockholders; under the terms of rights offerings, present stockholders are given the privilege of purchasing new stock in proportion to their current ownership before it is offered to other investors. When new stock is sold without rights, then the investment banker may attempt to sell the issue on a best-efforts basis. Investment bankers act as agents and utilizes their best efforts to sell the securities, but the firm or syndicate is not committed to sell the issue. Securities not sold under a best-efforts basis remain unissued. Investment bankers guarantee the sale of securities only under firm underwriting and standby agreements.

Underwriting

Investment banking firms often purchase a new issue or guarantee its sale at a specified price. The investment banking firm *underwrites* the new issue when it assumes the marketing risk. If the security is not sold to investors at the offering price, then the underwriter incurs the loss. For example, XYZ corporation may agree to sell its new stock offering to Big Apple Investment Bankers, Inc., at $20 per share for 1 million shares. Big Apple assumes the risk of selling the stock at $20 or more per share.[4] If XYZ's stock value falls to $19 per share, then Big Apple suffers a loss of $1 per share or $1 million. Underwriting is important to the issuer because it guarantees the amount of money that will be raised by the security issue.

Distribution

The investment bankers distribute the issue to many investors. To sell the issue quickly, a syndicate of many firms is formed for each issue, and the securities are distributed through a large network reaching many potential investors, as illustrated in Figure 13-2. Firms in the syndicate sell the new issue as an alternative to existing securities that they buy and sell. For example, Big Apple offers its customers XYZ stock, as well as General Motors stock. To sweeten the offer, the new issue is priced slightly below its going market price. The new issue discount is an important incentive to customers and allows investment bankers to distribute a new issue quickly. The investment bankers want to sell their inventory of underwritten securities so that they can arrange more new

---

[3] The investment banker is not always compensated for providing origination services because compensation is often tied to underwriting.

[4] Frequently, issues are underwritten by a group of investment bankers, called a *syndicate,* which shares the underwriting risk.

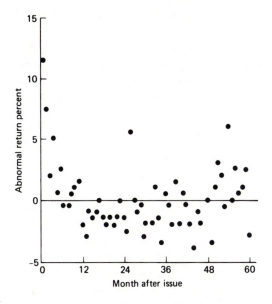

FIGURE 13-2
Abnormal returns for new stock issues, 1960-1969. (*Source*: Roger G. Ibbotson, "Price Performance of Common Stock New Issues," *Journal of Financial Economics*, September 1975, p. 252.)

issues. A high volume of new issues is the key to investment banking success, because fees are based on the volume of securities sold. Ideally, the investment banker can sell a new issue within a few days after it is underwritten.

Compensation

Investment banking revenues are derived from fees for services and price spreads from underwriting securities issues. Fees are charged for origination services when the investment banker is unlikely to handle the underwriting phase. For example, some issuers utilize competitive bidding during the underwriting phase to select the investment banker or syndicate that offers the best overall terms for underwriting and distribution. The investment banker who provided origination services is then compensated with a fee and may be excluded from bidding for distribution. On the other hand, the investment banker may provide origination services without charge when the relationship includes underwriting and distribution. Compensation for underwriting and distribution is typically in the form of price spreads.

Price spread is the difference between the price received by the issuing firm or government and the price paid by the investor. The underwriter commits to pay the issuer a firm price and expects to sell the securities to investors at a higher price. The prices and spread are included in the prospectus filed with the SEC. For example, in one issue of 2 million shares priced to the public at $40, the spread was $1.60 per share (4 percent of the price). The spread was split among the participants of the underwriting. Investment bankers received 32 cents per share for risking their capital, and distributing investment bankers earned 96 cents for each share.[5]

In all underwritings there is both an explicit and implicit spread. The explicit spread is the difference stated in the prospectus, as described previously. The implicit spread is the difference between the offering price and the market price. The implicit spread is important to investment banking management, because it impacts on the effort and risk of selling the issue. If the issue is overpriced (that is, the offering price is above the market price), then it will not sell quickly and the investment banking syndicate may need to stabilize the market.[6] However, an offering price below the market price increases the implicit spread and assures that the securities are sold quickly. The investment banker reaps the benefits of large implicit spreads through reduced risk and distribution expenses. The advantages of large implicit spreads are great, and some observers assert that investment bankers set offering prices below market prices in too many cases.

Recent research indicates that new issues are underpriced.[7] One-month holding period returns in excess of normal returns for a group of new issues underwritten from 1960 to 1969 are shown in Figure 13-2. The holding period is computed for each month after issue for a 5-year period. An abnormal return is one which is greater or less than the normal (risk-adjusted) return. Note that large positive abnormal returns (11.4 percent) are earned by investors who purchase the security on the issue date and then sell it from 1 to 4 months later. The high positive abnormal return implies that the offering price is low relative to the market, because the price tends to rise immediately after the issue date. The abnormal returns beyond the first few months are nearly zero, indicating that investors could not profit by systematically trading in and out of new issues after the first few months. The small positive abnormal returns were not sufficiently large to cover transaction costs of buying and selling. Only by buying at the offering could investors consistently earn abnormal profits from trading in new issues.[8]

Securities Trading

After securities are distributed to the investing public, they are traded in the *secondary* market. Organized securities exchanges, independent brokers and

---

[5] Connelly (1976).

[6] Investment bankers "stabilize" the market for a security by standing ready to purchase the security when the price falls below the offering price. Stabilizing purchases may continue for up to 10 days after the offering date; the amount then is limited by the syndication agreement.

[7] This discussion is based on the work of Ibbotson (1975), and readers are referred to his article for further discussion.

[8] The returns discussed here are *average* returns for 112 new common stock issues. The abnormal return at the end of the offering month for an individual issue is frequently much higher or lower than the average. Therefore, an investor cannot be at all certain that a particular new issue will yield an abnormal return. See Ibbotson (1975) for estimates of return variability on new issues.

dealers, and informal exchange arrangements are all part of the vast and complex secondary market. In the jargon of the industry, there are four markets:

1 *Organized national and regional exchanges,* such as the New York and American Stock Exchanges and the Pacific Coast Stock Exchange

2 *Over-the-counter market,* which is composed of securities dealers and coordinated by the National Association of Securities Dealers (NASD)

3 *Third market,* where securities listed primarily on the New York Stock Exchange (NYSE) are traded by dealers without going through the Exchange

4 *Fourth market,* where large investors buy and sell *directly* among themselves.

Organized Exchanges   The organized stock exchanges are places where a select group of stocks and bonds is traded. As individual investors or managers of financial institutions, we use organized securities exchanges to buy and sell stocks and bonds. Our relationship with organized exchanges is indirect; we deal through a broker who is an exchange member. If we want to buy 100 shares of XYZ Corporation, we call our local broker at Big Apple. We usually place either a *market* order (for which the broker negotiates the best price) or a *limit* order (in which we specify the maximum price that we are willing to pay). Our broker relays the order to one of the exchanges that lists XYZ's stock among those eligible for trading. The order is received by an agent who is on the floor of the exchange and who knows who is willing to sell XYZ. The floor trader buys the stock on our behalf and notifies the exchange of the transaction. The exchange relays, via computerized communications, the transaction amount and price to the thousands of brokerage offices in the United States and around the world.

Commissions   Brokers are paid a commission for selling securities and arranging for the official transfer of ownership. The commission is negotiated between the broker and the investor for each transaction. Large institutional traders are able to negotiate lower commissions than individual traders, because institutional traders need proportionately less advice and personal service than do individual investors. In general institutional traders pay 40 to 50 percent less than individual investors for comparable transactions. The characteristics of the transaction are important determinants of the amount of the commission. The number and price of shares traded account for most of the difference in commissions charged for institutional transaction commissions. However, the commission charges do not increase proportionately with increases in the number of shares or price of shares traded.

For example, look at the change in the commission charge with respect to a change in the size of the stock transaction. Suppose that we compare two transactions, as outlined on the next page:

Transaction	Number of shares	Price per share	Dollar amount
A	100	$40	$4,000
B	100	$80	$8,000

Transaction B is 100 percent larger than transaction A, with respect to the amount of money involved. The following table presents the change in the amount of money involved and the commission charges for typical institutional trade:

Transaction	Dollar amount	Percent change	Commission charges	Percent change
A	$4,000	—	$24	—
B	$8,000	100%	$33	38%

The commission increases only 38 percent when the price increases by 100 percent. A very substantial discount is given for larger dollar volume transactions when the increase is due to higher prices. If we compute commission changes for increases in the number of shares traded, we find that commissions increase by 95 percent when share volume increases by 100 percent. Overall, commissions depend primarily on the number rather than the price of shares traded.[9]

Portfolios of Investment Bankers and Brokers

Most investment bankers are also secondary-market brokers and dealers. They are traders who maintain small inventories of securities, which they plan to sell in the near future. Corporate equity and credit market instrument holdings of security brokers and dealers are shown in Table 13-1, and flows of funds are shown in Table 13-2. Note that the total assets of $61 billion of security brokers are only a small fraction of the total assets of any of the thrift-type institutions. Sources of financing are principally commercial bank loans and customer credit balances. Commercial banks extend *broker loans,* which are very short-term (less than 30 days or on call) credits collateralized by marketable securities. Customer credit balances are amounts due to brokerage customers. Many customers prefer to leave credit balances at brokerage firms to pay for future security transactions, and brokerage firms accept the funds as a short-term source of financing.

---

[9] For individual investor commission rates, see Blum and Lewellen; for institutional investor commission rates, see Edmister (1977, 1978).

TABLE 13-1
SECURITY BROKERS AND DEALERS' STATEMENTS OF FINANCIAL ASSETS AND LIABILITIES, 1972–1984 (BILLIONS OF DOLLARS)

	1972	1973	1974	1975	1976	1977	1978	1979	1980	1981	1982	1983	1984
Total financial assets	21.9	18.3	15.2	18.5	26.8	27.7	27.9	29.1	36.1	39.0	43.3	49.4	60.5
Demand deposits and currency	1.1	0.9	0.8	0.7	0.9	0.9	1.2	2.1	2.6	2.6	4.3	4.1	4.7
Corporate equities	2.4	2.8	2.2	3.4	3.8	4.0	3.7	2.2	2.9	5.7	4.0	4.1	6.5
Credit market instruments	5.0	5.5	4.8	5.8	8.9	8.6	7.2	7.9	7.2	9.6	10.7	-1.3	7.2
U.S. government securities	2.0	2.0	2.3	2.2	4.6	3.8	3.1	5.0	3.6	3.0	4.8	-7.7	-6.6
State & local obligations	0.9	1.1	0.7	0.6	0.9	1.1	0.9	1.0	1.1	1.2	1.0	1.4	2.0
Corporate & foreign bonds	2.0	2.4	1.8	3.0	3.4	3.7	3.3	1.8	2.5	5.3	4.9	5.0	11.9
Security credit	13.5	9.1	7.6	8.6	13.2	14.2	15.8	16.9	23.5	21.1	24.3	42.5	42.0
Total liabilities	19.7	16.2	13.2	16.1	24.1	25.0	25.0	26.2	32.4	34.9	38.3	44.1	55.2
Security credit	19.5	16.1	13.2	16.0	23.9	24.9	24.9	26.0	32.0	34.5	37.7	43.1	54.3
From U.S. chartered banks	13.0	10.3	8.4	10.8	16.8	18.2	15.7	15.0	16.2	20.1	20.5	22.4	27.3
From foreign banking offices	1.2	0.6	0.5	0.4	0.9	1.3	1.4	1.4	1.0	1.6	1.2	1.4	2.2
Customer credit balances	5.4	5.2	4.2	4.8	6.3	5.3	7.8	9.6	14.8	12.7	16.0	19.3	24.9
Profit taxes payable	0.2	0.2	*	0.1	0.2	0.1	0.1	0.2	0.4	0.4	0.6	0.9	0.9

TABLE 13-2
SECURITY BROKERS AND DEALERS' FLOW OF FUNDS, 1972–1984

	1972	1973	1974	1975	1976	1977	1978	1979	1980	1981	1982	1983	1984
Net acq. of financial assets	4.2	-3.6	-3.0	3.2	8.4	0.9	0.2	1.2	7.0	2.9	4.3	6.1	12.9
Demand deposits & currency	*	-0.2	-0.1	*	0.2	*	0.2	0.9	0.5	*	1.6	-0.2	-0.1
Corporate equities	1.0	0.3	-0.6	1.2	0.5	0.2	-0.4	-1.5	0.7	2.8	-0.4	0.1	5.9
Credit market inst.	0.8	0.5	-0.8	1.0	3.1	-0.3	-1.3	0.6	-0.7	2.4	-0.1	-12.0	7.6
U.S. government sec.	0.2	-0.1	0.2	-0.1	2.4	-0.7	-0.8	1.9	-1.4	-0.6	0.4	-12.4	1.0
State & local obl.	-0.1	0.2	-0.4	-0.1	0.3	0.2	-0.2	0.2	*	0.2	-0.2	0.4	0.6
Corporate bonds	0.2	0.3	-0.6	1.2	0.5	0.2	-0.4	-1.5	0.7	2.8	-0.4	0.1	5.9
Security credit	3.7	-4.3	-1.6	1.0	4.6	1.0	1.6	1.1	6.5	-2.3	3.2	18.2	-0.5
Net increase in liab.	4.1	-3.4	-3.0	2.9	8.0	0.8	*	1.2	6.2	2.5	3.4	5.7	12.0
Security credit	4.1	-3.4	-2.9	2.9	7.9	0.9	*	1.1	6.0	2.5	3.2	5.4	11.9
From banks	3.9	-3.2	-1.9	2.2	6.5	1.9	-2.4	-0.8	0.8	4.6	-0.1	2.1	6.4
Customer credit bal.	0.2	-0.2	-1.0	0.6	1.5	-1.0	2.5	1.8	5.2	-2.1	3.3	3.3	5.5
Profit taxes payable	*	*	-0.1	*	0.1	-0.1	*	0.1	0.2	*	0.2	0.4	0.1

Profits of Investment Bankers and Brokers

Revenues of investment bankers and brokers depend heavily on the volume of securities handled. Most firms in this business are both investment bankers and brokers. These institutions are paid for financial transactions, not financial holdings, and they are paid a percentage commission based on the size of the transaction. For example, NYSE member firms' revenues rise with increased trading activity on the exchange. However, the expenses of operating do not change in direct proportion to the change in volume. Expenses tend to remain fixed for many of the productive factors used by investment bankers and brokers. Such expenses as electronic information and data processing systems, administrative salaries, and building costs and rents are fixed expenses. After subtracting expenses from revenues, we find earnings. Because revenues vary more widely than expenses with volume, earnings rise and fall. Revenues, expenses, and earnings of NYSE member firms for the years 1972 through 1976 are given in Figure 13-3. We see losses for the low-volume quarters in 1973 and 1974. Also, we see relatively large earnings for the peak-volume quarters in 1975 and 1976.

THE MONEY MARKET

Although the term *money market* implies the existence of one market, the term refers to a group of financial markets. The money market means a group of markets for short-term credit instruments of high quality, such as Treasury bills, commercial paper, bankers' acceptances, negotiable certificates of deposit, loans to or repurchase agreements with securities dealers, and Federal funds. These instruments involve a small risk due to loss, because they are issued by obligors of the highest credit rating and they mature within 1 year.

FIGURE 13-3
Revenues and expenses of most NYSE firms. (*Source*: Securities and Exchange Commission, "The Effect of the Absence of Fixed Rates of Commissions," Fifth Report to Congress, Washington, D.C., May 26, 1977, p. 22.)

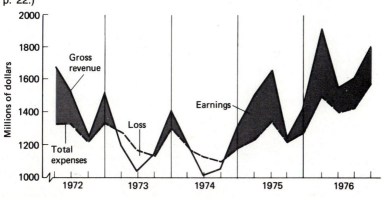

The market features highly efficient transactions machinery for executing trades. Centered in New York, a world financial capital, dealers in these securities are accessible to all parts of the United States and foreign financial centers by telephone. Information is given and trades are made by telephone among the numerous market participants. Major money-market traders are the large New York banks and large banks in other money-center cities, about thirty-four primary government securities dealers, approximately ten commercial paper dealers, a few banker's acceptance dealers, and a number of money brokers who place short-term funds (such as Federal funds) in the money market.

United States Treasury issues are the major security traded in the money market. The daily volume for U.S. Treasury bills averages about $7.5 billion; the daily volume for Federal funds averages about $25.7 billion. Volume is large because the securities mature within a short period, usually 90 days or less, and are "rolled over." That is, maturing securities are repaid with a new issue by the same borrower. Furthermore, investors use the money market to earn interest on funds available for very short periods of time, such as 1 day or over the weekend. Investors may buy a security one day for resale the next. The large volume of transactions is executed at relatively low cost because of the large denomination of the trades ($1 million or more) and the relative ease of finding buyers for high-quality securities.[10]

INVESTMENT BANKING SUMMARY

Investment bankers function as intermediaries between providers and users of capital by their activity in the market for new security issues as well as intermediating between investors in the remarketing of existing securities in the secondary markets.

In the new issues market, the functions of the investment bankers include the negotiations and activities to make new securities acceptable in the market place (origination), the actual purchase of the new security from the issuer at a guaranteed price (underwriting), and the sale of the new security to the investing public through an underwriting syndicate (distribution).

The investment banker also functions as an investment broker-dealer in the secondary securities market. The secondary market comprises organized exchanges and the over-the-counter market as well as the informal third and fourth markets where transactions are not brought to the organized markets.

The broker-dealers are compensated for their intermediation activities in the secondary markets by the receipt of commission charges that are negotiated between brokers and their customers. Empirical study has shown that the commission charges are subject to economies for larger share volume and

---

[10] For further discussion of the money market and its securities, see Cook (1977), which contains a collection of articles originally published in the *Monthly Review* of the Federal Reserve Bank of Richmond.

higher price stock transactions. Since income is based upon transactions volume and expenses involve large amounts of fixed costs for office and electronic equipment, brokerage firms experience great variation in earnings from year to year.

MORTGAGE BANKING

Sometimes known as mortgage companies or mortgage dealers, mortgage bankers are dealers in residential, commercial, apartment, condominium, mobile home, and special-purpose property mortgages. In general they are intermediaries among real estate purchasers using debt financing and investors desiring mortgages or mortgage-backed securities. Mortgage bankers act primarily as a conduit between real estate borrowers and long-term lenders.

The need for mortgage intermediaries is fundamental, and mortgage bankers trace their domestic heritage to the farm mortgage companies that moved capital into the fertile western farms in the 1850s and that fueled the speculative land boom in the 1920s. A dramatic transformation in residential real estate financing followed the financial market collapse in 1929. As the 1929 stock market collapse spread to mortgage institutions, the frequency of mortgage foreclosures increased and the public demand for foreclosure relief grew more insistent. Mortgage moratoriums were in effect in five states by March 1933. After closing banks temporarily for a ''bank holiday,'' state legislatures across the country rushed to pass mortgage relief acts. On the national level, the federal government sought to induce flagging construction with the National Housing Act of 1934, establishing the Federal Housing Administration insurance program.

Housing demand remained soft in the 1930s, in spite of governmental programs, and did not revive until after World War II. After a decade of modest building and the initiation of mortgage guarantee programs by the Veteran's Administration (VA) and the Federal Housing Administration (FHA), the foundation was laid for a burgeoning national mortgage market. With the federal insurance programs, more borrowers qualified for high loan to value mortgages than would qualify for conventional mortgages.[11] The VA and FHA offered mortgage lenders a standardized security, insured by an agency of the federal government, and issued by approved borrowers. Funds could flow easily across state borders and into capital deficit localities. The real estate mortgage was released from being a strictly local arrangement to become a nationally traded security. Although the mortgage market continues to be confined to the local market area of the lending institution, creation of standardized mortgage loan instruments, mortgage loan insurance, and national mortgage loan markets have expanded the geographical scope of mortgage intermediation in the

---

[11] Conventional mortgages are noninsured mortgage loans and are typically held to maturity by the originating institution.

United States financial markets.[12] The mortgage banking industry currently lends approximately $8 billion to the housing industry at any one time, and it transacts an annual volume many times this amount.

Mortgage Banking Functions

In lending funds to real estate buyers and accepting notes secured by real estate mortgages, the mortgage banker *originates* mortgage loans.[13] The loans are *warehoused,* while carried as inventory, until their eventual sale to an institutional investor. When a sufficiently large volume of loans is accumulated in the warehouse, they are packaged for *placement* with an institutional investor. The principal institutions purchasing mortgages for their portfolios are insurance companies, pension funds, mutual savings banks, savings and loans associations, and the Federal National Mortgage Association. Investment institutions retain mortgage bankers as correspondents because (1) mortgage bankers are less costly than direct mortgage lending offices or (2) the investment institution is legally proscribed from mortgage banking activities. Following placement and throughout the life of the mortgage, the mortgage banker represents the institutional investor in *servicing* the loans. That is, the mortgage banker collects payments, inspects the property, accounts for payments and receipts, and initiates proceedings on delinquent loans. The mortgage banking functions

[12] Because of regulatory and operating cost restrictions, the local market is generally concentrated within a radius of 50 to 100 miles from the office(s) of the lending institution or confined to the same state.

[13] The mortgage banking functions described in this section may be performed by financial institutions other than those defined strictly as mortgage bankers. Among the other institutions that act as mortgage bankers, savings and loans are the largest and most active. In areas of the United States which supply more mortgages than local investors demand, savings and loans grant mortgages for resale in the national market.

FIGURE 13-4
Mortgage banking functions.

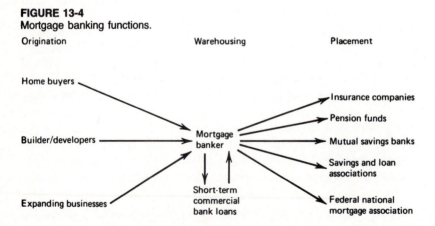

Flow of mortgages and mortgage payments (servicing)

of origination, warehousing, placement, and servicing provide for the flow of mortgages and payment from borrowers to investors. The relationships are depicted in Figure 13-4.

Origination

Solicitation Mortgage bankers cannot rely upon customers calling at their office to apply for mortgage loans. "Walk-in" customers are generally shopping a poor loan around, seeking a loan greater than that generally considered prudent, or requesting a rate below the prevailing rate. Mortgage banking offices are not highly visible to the public, nor are mortgage bankers commonly known by residential real estate purchasers. To develop a growing business and obtain quality mortgages, field agents from the mortgage banker call on real estate brokers and builders. Brokers are responsible for most transfers of real estate and are in an excellent position to know persons needing loans. By providing brokers with information and, occasionally, granting loans to less credit-worthy clients, field agents win the goodwill of real estate brokers. Field agents also solicit builders to obtain mortgages on newly constructed properties. They inspect properties as well as discuss mortgage terms and arrangements. The application is written with the assistance of the mortgage banker early in the origination process. An important part of the mortgage banker's function is to provide current information on institutional investor preferences on mortgage terms.

An essential ingredient in the success of mortgage banking is the development and retention of quality solicitors. Therefore, the method of compensating solicitors is of significant importance.[14] Some solicitors are paid a straight salary, while others (particularly part-time employees) are paid only a commission. Various bonus and incentive payment plans are common. Bonuses are related to the current volume produced and are paid monthly. Mortgage bankers also acquire applications from persons who act as "finders" and who are not regularly employed by the mortgage bank. Finders' fees are paid to real estate brokers, builders, and others responsible for transmitting the applications. Fees are paid usually in one of two ways: (1) cash fee to the agent or (2) absorption of loan fees and legal expenses. Finders' fees of ½ to 2 percent of the principal amount are common and produce healthy profits for finders of million-dollar loans.

Appraisal and Commitment Although "flash" appraisals and informal commitments are sometimes granted by field agents, the normal procedure is to:

---

[14] Salaries and bonuses to field agents are often substantial in mortgage companies but not in commercial bank mortgage departments. Recently bank holding companies have acquired mortgage banking companies. When placed under traditional commercial bank salary schedules, top-producing solicitors move elsewhere and the mortgage banking subsidiary languishes.

1 Review a completed application
2 Appraise the property carefully
3 Investigate the credit history of the applicant

For qualifying borrowers, loan commitments are granted, contingent upon a valid title being produced by the seller upon disbursement of funds. Large loans requiring firm commitments are forwarded to the ultimate lender for approval, and insured loans are forwarded to the insuring agency for authorization prior to granting a commitment.

Role in Financing Large Projects   Financing mass housing projects is a source of volume business for many large mortgage bankers. Consider a builder who desires to construct 300 new houses, each requiring a $30,000 mortgage loan. In all, mortgages of $9 million are required to sell the properties, and the builder wants an assurance that these mortgages will be available to buyers upon completion of construction. The mortgage banker arranges a *take-out letter* committing an investing institution to purchase the mortgage upon completion and occupancy of the properties. With the take-out letter as evidence of a firm commitment for long-term financing, the mortgage banker advances construction financing to the builder. In turn the mortgage banker borrows on a short-term basis from a commercial bank, promising to repay the loan when construction is completed, the houses sold, and mortgage funds obtained from the institutional investor. The take-out commitment not only assures financing for the ultimate home buyer, but supports interim financing arrangements as well.

Warehousing

Mortgages are originated daily, as solicitors and office personnel provide funds for real estate closings, but placements are made from time to time in fulfillment of commitments or in block sales to institutional investors. Unsold mortgages are stored in the "warehouse" for future delivery and pledged as collateral for short-term commercial bank loans. Interest and principal payments on the mortgage accrue to the mortgage banker, and the bank receives interest on the short-term loan to the mortgage banker. When short-term interest rates are higher than long-term interest rates, the mortgage banker receives less interest on mortgages in the warehouse than is being paid to carry them. The mortgage banker expects to recoup warehousing losses during periods when short-term exceed long-term interest rates by charging higher origination fees and commissions.

Like many intermediaries, mortgage bankers turn their capital rapidly and supplement their small equity capital base with bank credit lines. Even large mortgage bankers with bonds and debentures as part of their capital rely heavily upon short-term bank lines to carry their mortgage inventory. On the average, 60 to 90 days are required to disburse a residential single-family mortgage loan and for an investor to remit funds due. If the commercial bank extends loans equal to 90 percent of the mortgage value, then $300,000 of net worth can support a $12 million volume of mortgage originations per year. The relationship between net worth and annual volume is shown below:

$$\text{Volume} = \frac{365}{\text{days}} \times \frac{\text{net worth}}{1 - \text{loan basis}} \qquad (13\text{-}1)$$

where

$\qquad$ days = days mortgages are warehoused

net worth = amount of net worth

$\qquad$ volume = annual volume of originations

loan basis = ratio of bank loan to mortgage value

In applying the formula to the figures given above, we get

$$\text{Volume} = \frac{365}{90} \times \frac{\$300,000}{1 - 0.9}$$
$$= 4\ (\$3,000,000)$$
$$= \$12,000,000$$

Construction financing requires a much greater amount of net worth for the same volume of origination, as construction loans are outstanding for 6 to 18 months. Credit restrictions by commercial banks in the form of smaller loan-to-value ratios likewise necessitate more net worth or reduce the permissible volume by reducing turnover.

Placement

Mortgage placement, the resale of the mortgages in inventory to an institutional investor, is usually arranged in one of three ways:

1 Investor commitment: The mortgage banker and the investor agree to a price before the mortgages are originated, and mortgages originated during the commitment period are transferred at a specified price.

2 Uncommitted origination: The mortgage banker originates loans without an investor commitment. When a portfolio of sufficient quantity is acquired, the loans are sold to the institutional investor at the prevailing price. Strategies number 1 and 2 involve some risk, although the source of risk depends upon whether the loans are originated for a committed investor or for inventory and resale "off the shelf."

3 Commitment option: The mortgage banker purchases an option from the investor to sell a specified quantity of mortgages at a future date and price.

All strategies involve some risk, and mortgage bankers must decide what strategy produces the most acceptable risk. Some of the important advantages and disadvantages of placement commitments are discussed next.

Mortgage bankers occasionally develop a relationship with an investment institution which is so satisfactory that they always know where they can sell their inventory, and the investment institution knows where it can purchase a supply of new mortgages. Informal understandings crystallize into exclusive contracts in which the mortgage banker agrees to sell to only a limited number of investors, and the investors agree to buy only from the mortgage banker mortgages originated in that geographical market.

Although giving both parties a measure of security, the exclusive contract may prove burdensome. Investors feel obligated to purchase from the mortgage banker even when they would prefer to invest funds elsewhere. The mortgage banker, on the other hand, may not be as flexible in shopping for special loans. Generally, mortgage bankers give investors some degree of exclusivity, placing FHA- and VA-guaranteed loans with one investor, conventional loans with another, and so forth. Without an exclusive contract, any party is free to change but recognizes that change breaks long-standing relationships which are generally favorable.

An investor commitment protects the mortgage banker against decreases in market price (as yields rise) from origination to placement. Increases in market yield that decrease market value are not a risk undertaken by the mortgage originator but by the investor. For example, consider a yield increase from 8.09 percent to 8.67 percent on an 8.125 percent, 30-year mortgage. Without a forward commitment to deliver at an agreed upon interest rate, the mortgage banker would lose 5.00 percent of the amount of the mortgage.[15] Such losses are devastating in a business where the origination fee is 1 percent and the annual servicing fee is three-eighths of 1 percent.

However, during a period of declining yields, the commitment to deliver mortgages may prove a burden and result in a lower profit than an uncommitted origination (strategy number 2). Consider the following important sequence of events:

1 Mortgage banker commits to deliver 30-year mortgages yielding 8.09 percent to an investor.

2 Mortgage interest rates decline from 8.09 to 7.98 percent for 30-year mortgages.

3 Mortgage banker originates mortgages at the highest competitive interest rate—7.98 percent.

4 Mortgage banker delivers 7.98 percent mortgages to investor at yield of 8.09 percent by discounting them 1 percent below face value.

---

[15] The change in value is computed using mortgages tables or present value analysis. See Chapter 5.

Thus, the mortgage banker is forced to discount mortgages in step 4 to meet the origination commitment made in step 1. The 1 percent is absorbed as a loss by the mortgage banker. Consequently, we concluded that the placement commitment fails to immunize the mortgage banker from interest rate risk, because the commitment to deliver and the origination of mortgages occur at different times. Clearly, the mortgage banker accepts considerable market risk with either a committed or uncommitted strategy.

Servicing

The mortgage banker's role usually continues after mortgages are placed with an institutional investor. A loan *servicing* function is needed; it typically includes collection of payments, disbursement of taxes and insurance premiums, verification of fire and hazard insurance coverage, and enforcement of contract provisions. In general, the mortgage banker acts for the institutional investor as a local agent. Borrowers make payments at the banker's office, clerks keep track of payments and disbursements, and legal counsel takes action under the mortgage banker's direction. The cost of servicing mortgages is usually less than the typical ⅜ percent fee paid by the investor. Revenues earned from service fees often compensate for losses incurred during origination and warehousing. Although servicing may appear insignificant and mundane, it is the most profitable part of mortgage banking.[16]

MORTGAGE BANKING SUMMARY

Mortgage bankers specialize in creating and placing mortgage loans. They originate, warehouse, and place $6 to $7 billion dollars worth of mortgage loans each year. Then they service the loans for final investors—life insurance companies, savings and loans, pensions funds, and private investors.

TERMS

Investment Banking

investment banker	organized securities markets
origination	over-the-counter market
underwriting	market order
new issues market	limit order
secondary market	security dealer
syndicate	

---

[16] Research by John McConnell shows that origination costs exceed origination revenue and that origination net losses are recouped with net profits from servicing over the life of the mortgage. See McConnell (1974) for an excellent analysis.

Mortgage Banking

mortgage banker

conventional mortgages

Federal Housing Administration

mortgage origination

mortgage warehousing

mortgage placement

mortgage servicing

take-out commitment

QUESTIONS

1 What four functions do mortgage bankers perform to provide for flows of funds between mortgage borrowers and investors?
2 Why must mortgage bankers rely upon solicitation to generate customers? Why cannot they depend upon walk-in customers?
3 What are finders' fees? How are they paid?
4 What four steps are taken in appraising a mortgage loan application?
5 What is a take-out commitment? What two financing arrangements does it facilitate?
6 What are conventional as compared with FHA-insured loans?
7 How does the mortgage banker recoup losses incurred from warehousing loans during periods when short-term interest rates exceed long-term interest rates?
8 If a mortgage banker can obtain 75 percent of needed mortgage funds from a commercial bank and the mortgage bank has capital of $1 million and carries mortgage loans an average of 60 days before remitting funds, what volume of loan originations can it support each year?
9 What is an exclusive outlet? What are the disadvantages of an exclusive outlet in mortgage banking?
10 What activities does the servicing function encompass?
11 What are the three major functions of investment bankers?
12 Identify three kinds of security terms which are designed during the origination phase?
13 What is meant by the observation that the investment banker assumes the marketing risk on a new issue?
14 By what means does an underwriter distribute new securities to the investing public?
15 How is volume of new issues related to investment banking success?
16 What is the secondary securities market?
17 Distinguish between a market order and a limit order.
18 In negotiating brokerage commission rates charged to institutional investors, what factors determine the rate? What factor is most important in accounting for volume discounts?

SELECTED REFERENCES

Blum, Gerald A., and Wilbur G. Lewellen: "Negotiated Brokerage Commissions and the Individual Investor," *Journal of Financial and Quantitative Analysis*, September 1983, pp. 331–343.

Carosso, Vincent P.: *Investment Banking in America*, Harvard University Press, Cambridge, Mass., 1970.

Cohen, Kalman J., and Stephen F. Mairer, Robert A. Schwartz, and David K. Whitcomb: "Market Makers and the Market Spread: A Review of Recent Literature," *Journal of Financial and Quantitative Analysis,* November 1979, pp. 813–836.

Connelly, J.: "Investment Banking: The Rise of Co-Managerships," *Institutional Investor,* June 1975, pp. 23–25.

Connelly, J.: "Is the Syndicate Bid on the Way Out," *Institutional Investor,* May 1976, pp. 61–64.

Cook, Timothy Q. (ed.): *Instruments of the Money Market,* 4th ed., Federal Reserve Bank of Richmond, Richmond, Va., 1977.

Edmister, Robert O.: Management of Commission Costs in Institutional Equity Portfolios," *Journal of Contemporary Business,* Summer 1977, pp. 45–57.

Edmister, Robert O., "Commission Cost Structure: Shifts and Scale Economies," *Journal of Finance,* May 1978, pp. 477–486.

Friend, Irwin, et al.: *Investment Banking and the New Issues Market,* World Publishing, Cleveland, Ohio, 1967.

Friend, Irwin: "Economic Foundations of Stock Market Regulation," *Journal of Contemporary Business,* Summer 1976, pp. 1–27.

Friend, Irwin, and Marshall E. Blume: "Competitive Commissions on the New York Stock Exchange," *Journal of Finance,* September 1973, pp. 795–819.

Government National Mortgage Association Annual Report, Department of Housing and Urban Development, Washington, D.C., annual publication.

Haney, R. L.: "An Empirical Investigation of the Relative Attractiveness of the GNMA Pass-Through Security," *Quarterly Review of Economics and Business,* Winter 1976, pp. 79–89.

Harless, Doris E.: *Nonbank Financial Institutions,* Federal Reserve Bank of Richmond, Richmond, Va., October 1975.

Higgins, W. W., and B. J. Moore: "Market Structure versus Information Costs as Determinants of Underwriters' Spreads on Municipal Bonds," *Journal of Financial and Quantitative Analysis,* March 1980, pp. 85–98.

Ibbotson, Roger G.: "Price Performance of Common Stock New Issues," *Journal of Financial Economics,* September 1975.

Lindvall, J. R.: "New Issue Corporate Bonds, Seasoned Market Efficiency and Yield Spreads," *Journal of Finance,* September 1977, pp. 1057–1067.

McConnell, John Joseph: "Mortgage Companies: A Financial Model and Evaluation of Their Residential Lending Activities," unpublished Ph.D. thesis, Purdue University, 1974.

McConnell, J. J.: "Valuation of a Mortgage Company's Servicing Portfolio," *Journal of Financial and Quantitative Analysis,* September 1976, pp. 433–453.

McConnell, J. J.: "Mortgage Company Bids on the GNMA Auction," *Journal of Bank Research,* Winter 1977, pp. 294–302.

Mandelker, G., and A. Raviv: "Investment Banking: An Economic Analysis of Optimal Underwriting Contracts," *Journal of Finance,* June 1977, p. 683.

Marcus, Bruce W.: *Competing for Capital,* New York, 1975.

MBA Annual Financial Statements and Operating Ratio Reports, Mortgage Bankers Association, Washington, D.C., annual publication.

Osborne, Alfred E., Jr.: "Rule 144 Volume Limitations and the Sale of Restricted Stock in the Over-The-Counter Market," *Financial Analyst's Journal,* May 1982, pp. 505–517.

Report of Special Study of Securities Markets of the Securities and Exchange Commission, U.S. Government Printing Office, Washington, D.C., 1963.

Rhoades, S.: "The Effect of Bank-Holding-Company Acquisitions of Mortgage Bankers on Mortgage Lending Activity," *Journal of Business,* July 1975, pp. 344–348.

Welles, C.: "The War between the Big Board and the Regionals," *Institutional Investor,* March 1977, pp. 131–133.

CHAPTER 14

INVESTMENT COMPANIES AND REAL ESTATE INVESTMENT TRUSTS

The investment company started in Europe 140 years ago when William I established the "Societé Generale des Pays-Bas pour favoriser l'industrie nationale" in Belgium. In 1868 the concept was applied on a large scale in London as the Foreign and Colonial Government Trust. The purpose of the trust was to provide "the investor of moderate means the same advantages as large capitalists, in diminishing the risk of investing in Foreign and Colonial Government Stocks, by spreading the investment over a number of different stocks." Investment companies and real estate investment trusts (REITs, pronounced "reets"), are devices for pooling and investing money in a wide variety and number of securities to obtain portfolio diversification and management efficiency. Investment companies generally invest in marketable bonds, preferred stocks, and common stocks; REITs select from among mortgages, construction financing notes, and real estate equity ownership. Both of these institutions attract large amounts of money from the numerous small investors who seek professional investment management.[1] Now there are over 700 investment companies with more than $371 billion in assets. REITs are fewer and smaller than investment companies; they number about 200 and own assets totaling about $13 billion.

We turn now to an in-depth study of these two interesting financial intermediaries. Investment companies are discussed in the first half, and REITs are surveyed in the second half of the chapter.

---

[1] Also, mutual funds attract substantial amounts from fiduciary, business, and institutional investors. An advantage of mutual funds for pension funds is that they are not subject to fiduciary responsibilities under ERISA.

INVESTMENT COMPANIES

Legal Forms of Organization

We recognize here that mutual funds are one type of investment company.[2] Mutual funds are termed *open-ended investment companies*, because investors may cash in their shares or buy more shares anytime. Share price, called *net asset value,* is determined daily by dividing the market value of all securities plus other assets less liabilities by the number of outstanding shares. Each shareholder may receive his or her portion of the market value of the fund upon surrender of his or her shares. Share prices rise and fall directly and mathematically with changes in the value of portfolio assets. Share values are quoted daily for many mutual funds in *The Wall Street Journal.*

Another form of organization is the *closed-ended investment company.* Unlike open-ended investment companies, shares of closed-ended investment companies are sold only at the initial offering and are not redeemable at net asset value. After the initial sale, shares are traded in the secondary market (stock exchanges) at the market price. Investors buy and sell closed-ended funds at the price determined by supply and demand, rather than the value of the portfolio per se. In fact, closed-ended type shares often trade at prices substantially different from net asset value per share. In a majority of cases the market prices closed-ended investment company shares at a discount from net asset share value.

Both closed- and open-ended investment companies that comply with certain Internal Revenue Code provisions, referred to as Subchapter M of the code, are taxed under the *conduit theory.* An extra layer of taxation is avoided by the conduit theory, which recognizes that shareholders of investment companies are in substantially the same position as individual investors who own primary securities. To qualify under Subchapter M of the Internal Revenue Code, investment companies must distribute at least 90 percent of dividends, interest, and short-term capital gains to shareholders. Of course, the shareholder must report the receipt of these payments on his or her tax return. In effect, the investment company acts as a conduit through which security gains, dividends, and interest are passed to investors. Although the investment company avoids paying taxes, the investor pays taxes as if he or she owned the securities directly. There is no substantial income tax advantage or disadvantage for investing in an investment company as compared with making a direct investment in securities.

---

[2] Trust funds of the type commonly known as *Massachusetts business trusts* are similar to investment companies in most respects. The principal difference is that a shareholder of trusts may, under certain circumstances, be held personally liable as a partner for the obligations of the trust. Mutual funds which are organized as trusts typically protect shareholders from liability by trust agreement exemptions, insurance against lawsuits, and the general conduct of the trust. In practice, there is little distinction between trusts and corporations as investment vehicles, and the distinction is not made in this text for expository convenience.

Objectives of Investment Companies

Investment companies pursue different investment objectives to satisfy varying investor needs.[3] Investment objectives range from long-term growth of capital to current income. The objectives of the investment company determine in large part the types of securities purchased and the investment selection approach. A good means of describing investment companies is to characterize the types of securities in their portfolio. Five common types of investment companies are described next.

Common-stock funds concentrate most of their investments in common stocks. "Blue chip" funds purchase the large, well-known corporations which are industry leaders and offer stable earnings and dividend growth. Other funds emphasize "growth" stocks which are expected to appreciate rapidly in price. Although dividends are small for growth stocks, they offer opportunities for increased income and profits in the future. *Balanced funds* invest in a mixture of bonds and common stocks. Most balanced funds seek more conservative investment goals than do typical common-stock funds. As a result, balanced funds tend to show a smaller gain during rising markets and a smaller loss during falling markets than common-stock funds. *Bondfunds* seek to generate current income by investing in low-, medium-, and high-grade corporate and municipal bonds. Some funds specialize in one grade, and others invest in a balanced portfolio. *Municipal bond funds* invest only in tax-exempt bonds issued by states, cities, and other local governments. Interest income, which is not subject to federal and some state income taxes, is passed through to investors in high-income-tax brackets. *Money-market funds* are portfolios of short-term, prime-grade securities, such as Treasury bills, bank certificates of deposit, bankers' acceptances, and commercial paper.[4] Price movements of money-market securities are relatively minor compared with long-term bonds. Therefore, money-market funds provide current income and safety of principal in a highly liquid form.

Role of Investment Manager

Investment companies usually are associated with an investment manager, which sponsors the fund initially and performs portfolio services on a continu-

---

[3] Investment companies are required to state the purpose of the fund in the offering Prospectus, under the U.S. Securities Act of 1940. Examples of statements of objectives are given in the footnote which follows.

[4] For example, the *Merrill Lynch Ready Assets Trust Prospectus* states:
    The Trust is a no-load money market trust seeking preservation of capital, liquidity and the highest possible current income consistent with the foregoing objectives available from the short-term money market securities in which the Trust invests. Portfolio securities principally consist of short-term United States Government securities, Government agency securities, bank money instruments, corporate debt instruments including commercial paper and variable account master demand notes, and repurchase and reverse repurchase agreements (*Prospectus,* Merrill Lynch Ready Assets Trust, April 28, 1978, p. 1).

FIGURE 14-1
Relationship between the investment company and investment advisor.

ing basis. Under contractual arrangements, the management company receives a fee of from .25 to 2.00 percent of the market value of assets. The manager administers the fund, recommends security transactions, and prepares reports for stockholders and government agencies. We see the relationship between the investment manager and the investment company depicted in Figure 14-1. Although laws require that outsiders sit on the fund's board of directors, the management company and its sponsored investment company employ interlocking staffs and directors. Management contracts are renewed annually and usually with the same management company. Profits are earned by the investment manager, which creates the fund and controls the cost of advisory, clerical, and other services. Fees usually rise directly with asset growth, but operating costs increase by only a fraction of increasing size. Thus, the investment manager's goal is to attract investors and sell shares in the investment company.

Underwriting and Retailing

Closed-ended funds are underwritten like any other large block of securities. A syndicate of investment bankers is formed to buy and distribute the stock offering. The offering price is above the net asset value; the difference or spread represents the charge levied by the syndicate. Investors are willing to pay an underwriting fee in return for the management and other advantages of the fund. Usually, the investment manager is a highly regarded security analyst who has demonstrated outstanding performance. Thus, investors are buying the funds as a mean of retaining a "winning" analyst.

Open-ended investment companies are retailed continually to investors. By law solicitation can be made only with a formal, SEC-approved statement called a *prospectus*. However, investors are attracted to mutual funds through newspaper advertising, direct mail campaigns, and other media forms. When sold by securities brokers, the mutual fund receives the amount invested less a sales charge—sometimes called a *load*—usually ranging from 7.50 to 8.75 percent of offering price for purchases of less than $10,000 to about 1.00 percent for purchases of $500,000 or more. When sold through brokers and dealers, the load is often split between the underwriter, who receives one-fourth for wholesaling the securities, and the retailer, who keeps three-fourths of the load for selling to investors. A second major distribution method is direct selling. The underwriting organization carries on, in addition to the wholesale function, the retailing function through an in-house staff of sales representatives. Alternatively, "no-load" mutual funds buy and sell their shares themselves at net asset value, employing neither an underwriter nor a local sales organization.

Asset Growth   Investment companies grew at an extraordinary rate from the end of World War II until the stock market doldrums of the late 1960s. Purchase of shares during the two decades after World War II were far greater than share redemptions, as investors turned from personal to investment company investing. Amounts are shown in Tables 14-1 and 14-2. In the 1960s *go-go funds*, which invested in highly risky securities, captured the imagination of speculative investors and added billions to the investment company industry. The extravagance of stock market speculation fell victim to the bear market of 1969–1970. The go-go funds fell in value, as the speculative stocks gave ground and price to the conservative, blue-chip stocks. Assets of investment companies declined sharply, and by the end of the two-year 1969–1970 period, mutual funds had lost $6.3 billion and closed-ended companies were down $1.1 billion. Since 1980 assets have expanded to new highs. Although the long-term average annual growth rate has been about 12 percent, the recent experience has been volatile, like the stock market.

Performance   The performance of mutual funds depends on the price and dividends of shares selected for the portfolio. Mathematically, we know that mutual fund prices are a function of external changes—market price and cash dividends. However, from a management perspective performance is a function of portfolio selection. Are mutual fund managers *selecting superior* securities and *controlling* costs? Mutual funds that advertise "professional" investment selection are purporting to offer investors something they cannot do on their own. The proof of security selection and portfolio management is in the results which the fund produces over time.

The major study by Michael Jensen (1968) compares investment company performance with stock market performance in general. Jensen evaluated performance in two dimensions: (1) increased returns on the portfolio through successful predictions of future security prices, and (2) reduced risk to shareholders obtained through diversification. Data for Jensen's study were taken from the standard source, Wiesenberger's *Investment Companies* (1955 and 1965). Jensen's conclusion startled many in the investment community:

> The evidence on mutual fund performance discussed above indicated not only that these 115 mutual funds were *on average* not able to predict security prices well enough to outperform a buy-the-market-and-hold policy, but also that there is very little evidence that any *individual* fund was able to do significantly better than that which we expected from mere random chance.[5]

No one has successfully challenged Jensen's conclusion.

---

[5] Jensen (1968), p. 415.

TABLE 14-1
MUTUAL FUNDS' STATEMENTS OF FINANCIAL ASSETS AND LIABILITIES, 1972–1984 (BILLIONS OF DOLLARS)

	1972	1973	1974	1975	1976	1977	1978	1979	1980	1981	1982	1983	1984
			Open-end investment companies (mutual funds)										
Total financial assets	58.9	46.6	35.2	43.0	46.5	45.4	45.8	51.2	63.5	63.8	89.5	129.4	161.9
Demand deposits and currency	0.9	0.7	0.5	0.6	0.7	0.7	0.7	0.7	0.8	0.8	1.2	1.7	2.1
Corporate equities	51.7	38.3	26.3	33.7	37.3	31.7	31.4	34.8	42.2	37.2	48.9	75.1	80.0
Credit market instruments	6.3	7.6	8.3	8.7	8.5	12.9	13.7	15.6	20.5	25.7	39.4	52.6	80.0
U.S. government securities	0.7	0.7	1.1	1.1	1.1	1.8	1.6	1.5	1.9	2.8	5.1	5.7	13.1
State & local obligations	—	—	—	—	0.5	2.2	2.7	4.0	6.4	9.3	21.1	30.1	44.8
Corporate & foreign bonds	4.2	4.3	4.9	5.6	6.0	7.0	6.4	7.2	8.5	10.1	10.2	13.0	15.2
Open-market paper	1.4	2.6	2.3	2.0	0.9	2.0	3.1	2.9	3.8	3.6	3.0	3.8	7.0
Total shares outstanding	58.9	46.6	35.2	43.0	46.5	45.4	45.8	51.2	63.5	63.8	89.5	129.4	161.9
			Money market mutual funds										
Total assets	—	—	2.4	3.7	3.7	3.9	10.8	45.2	74.4	181.9	206.6	162.6	209.7
Demand deposits and currency	—	—	*	*	*	*	0.1	0.1	0.2	-0.5	0.3	-0.3	-1.2
Time deposits	—	—	1.6	2.1	1.5	1.8	4.5	12.0	21.0	43.9	40.8	24.0	23.7
Security RPs	—	—	0.1	0.1	0.1	0.3	0.3	2.4	5.6	14.5	16.2	13.0	22.7
Foreign deposits	—	—	—	—	*	*	0.5	5.1	6.8	18.8	23.8	21.9	21.2
Credit market instruments	—	—	0.8	1.5	2.1	1.9	5.1	24.9	39.8	102.3	123.7	102.4	140.9
U.S. government securities	—	—	0.1	0.9	1.1	0.9	1.5	5.6	8.2	31.9	54.6	36.2	42.3
Open-market paper	—	—	0.6	0.5	0.9	1.1	3.7	19.3	31.6	70.4	69.1	66.2	98.7
Miscellaneous	—	—	-0.1	-0.1	-0.1	-0.2	0.3	0.7	1.1	2.9	1.8	1.5	2.4
Total shares outstanding	—	—	2.4	3.7	3.7	3.9	10.8	45.2	74.4	181.9	206.6	162.6	209.7

TABLE 14-2
MUTUAL FUNDS' FLOW OF FUNDS, 1972–1984 (BILLIONS OF DOLLARS)

	1972	1973	1974	1975	1976	1977	1978	1979	1980	1981	1982	1983	1984
Open-ended investment companies													
Current surplus	-1.6	-0.8	-0.9	-0.1	-0.1	-0.7	-0.8	-0.9	-2.0	-2.2	-2.1	-5.3	-6.3
Net acq. of financial assets	-1.4	-1.1	0.1	-0.4	-2.5	0.2	-0.9	-0.8	3.1	4.7	16.5	27.3	31.8
Demand deposits & currency	0.1	-0.2	-0.2	0.1	0.1	*	*	0.1	0.1	*	0.3	0.6	0.4
Corporate equities	-1.8	-2.2	-0.4	-0.9	-2.4	-3.7	-1.6	-2.8	-1.8	-0.6	3.5	13.6	5.6
Credit market instruments	0.3	1.3	0.7	0.5	-0.2	3.9	0.8	1.9	4.8	5.3	12.7	13.1	25.8
U.S. government securities	0.1	*	0.4	*	*	0.2	-0.2	*	0.3	0.9	2.3	0.6	7.4
State & local oblig.					0.5	1.6	0.5	1.4	2.0	2.9	10.9	8.9	13.4
Corporate bonds	0.5	0.1	0.6	0.7	0.3	1.1	-0.7	0.8	1.3	1.6	0.2	2.8	2.3
Open-market paper	-0.3	1.2	-0.4	-0.2	-1.1	1.1	1.1	-0.2	1.2	-0.1	-0.6	0.8	2.7
Net phase issues	*	-0.2	0.9	-0.3	-2.4	0.9	-0.1	0.1	5.2	6.8	18.6	32.6	38.1
Money market funds													
Net acq. of financial assets	*	—	2.4	1.3	*	0.2	6.9	34.4	29.2	107.5	24.7	-44.1	47.2
Demand dep. & curency	—	—	*	*	*	*	*	*	0.1	-0.7	0.8	-0.6	-1.0
Time deposits	—	—	1.6	0.5	-0.7	0.3	2.7	7.5	9.0	22.8	-3.1	-16.8	-0.3
Security RPs	—	—	0.1	0.1	*	0.1	0.1	2.1	3.2	8.9	1.7	-3.2	-9.6
Foreign deposits	—	—	—	—	—	*	0.5	4.6	1.7	-12.1	4.9	-1.8	-0.7
Credit market instruments	—	—	0.8	0.7	0.6	-0.1	3.2	19.8	14.9	62.5	21.4	-21.4	38.6
U.S. government securities	—	—	0.1	0.8	0.2	-0.3	0.6	4.2	2.6	23.7	22.7	-18.4	6.1
Open-market paper	—	—	0.6	-0.1	0.4	0.1	2.6	15.6	12.3	38.8	-1.3	-3.0	32.5
Misc.	—	—	-0.1	*	*	-0.1	0.5	0.4	0.4	1.9	-1.1	-0.4	1.0
Net phase issues	—	—	2.4	1.3	*	0.2	6.9	34.4	29.2	107.5	24.7	-44.1	47.2

Government Regulation

Investment companies are institutions subject to regulation by the Securities and Exchange Commission as a result of the Investment Company Act of 1940. Because of the investment rather than deposit nature of the securities offered, the agency does not provide temporary loans or insurance guarantees. Rather, it relies primarily on extensive regulation to maintain institutional integrity and public confidence. The affiliated distributors, called principal underwriters, of many mutual fund shares are excluded from government-sponsored insurance protection under the Securities Investor Protection Act, although bills have been introduced in Congress to extend this protection.

Investment companies are subject to extensive reporting and disclosure requirements. The information reported is generally publicly available and in addition is compiled and presented in periodic statistical publications by the SEC. Aggregate amounts of investment company shares sold and redeemed, which is included in such reports, has become a common barometer of the "popularity" of investment in these institutions.

REAL ESTATE INVESTMENT TRUSTS

It is appropriate to discuss REITs last, because these are relatively new financial intermediaries. Congress approved changes to the Internal Revenue Code in 1960 which established the framework within which all (IRS) qualified REITs operate. They invest in mortgages and property, offering their investors an opportunity to participate in real estate profits and tax benefits. Like investment companies REITs are taxed under the conduit theory; if at least 90 percent of their income is passed through to trust owners, they usually qualify for exemption from corporate income tax. Investors receive the benefits or losses of real estate investment, without the intermediary being taxed. Also, like investment companies the REITs are often established and operated by an adviser.

Trust Manager

Most trusts owe their existence to the management group that continues as the adviser and, in many instances, lends its name. Many trust advisers are mortgage banking companies or affiliates of financial institutions such as banks and life insurance companies. Other advisers are owned and operated by organizations with real estate backgrounds. Like investment companies, the board of trustees negotiates a contract with the adviser. The management contract provides for an advisory fee in return for services. The major functions of the adviser are to:

1 Conduct day-to-day operations of trust assets
2 Locate and evaluate new investment opportunities
3 Manage liabilities, including public offerings of debt and equity, bank borrowings, commercial paper sales, and direct placements of debt securities

Daily operation of real estate investments often entails a far greater number of personnel and facilities than is required for marketable stocks and bonds. Fund advisers must be knowledgeable specialists who can deal effectively in the building and housing industry. Furthermore, the adviser is relied upon to evaluate assets in a negotiated market where every property is unique and only approximately comparable to another property. We may conclude that many REIT managers assume responsibilities on a level comparable to bank, savings and loan, insurance company, and other managers who grant credit and negotiate investments directly.

Sources and Uses of Funds

Now we look at the balance sheet to put concrete form to our concept. The major assets and liabilities are shown in Table 14-3.

The first mortgage loans reflect the four stages of real estate development[6]:

1 Land is employed in a nonhousing use such as farming or foresting.
2 Land is purchased on speculation that it will be improved in the future.
3 Land is developed through:
   a Planning.
   b Off-site development.
   c On-site development.
   d Wholesale lots.
4 Land is improved with buildings. Factors in improvement include:
   a Building design and engineering.
   b Physical construction.
   c Retailing completed structures.

Land loans provide money for purchasing land which is ready for development, and then development loans finance the cost of planning (zoning, geology, transportation), off-site development (utility lines, major roads, golf courses, and so forth), and on-site development (streets, utilities, and grading). Next, construction loans are granted to pay for designing and building the physical structures (houses, motels, and office buildings). Upon completion an intermediate- or long-term loan may be granted, or a permanent lender (insurance company, pension fund, or other mortgage lender) will pay off construction loans and finance the occupied property. When the REIT buys a property (which it may finance during construction), it is called *property owned*. Some REITs specialize in mortgages, and others concentrate in property ownership, depending upon investor demand.

On the liability side we see that the major source of debt funding is bank loans. Commercial banks are major sources of short-term money which is relent to finance real estate development and construction, but they are reducing their lending to REITs (see Table 14-4). Because of very substantial losses

---

[6] These are defined by Ricks (1968).

TABLE 14-3
REAL ESTATE INVESTMENT TRUSTS' STATEMENTS OF FINANCIAL ASSETS AND LIABILITIES, 1972–1984

	1972	1973	1974	1975	1976	1977	1978	1979	1980	1981	1982	1983	1984
Physical assets	2.5	3.2	4.3	7.3	8.9	8.6	7.6	7.1	6.3	5.5	4.2	4.4	4.7
Multifamily structures	0.8	1.1	1.4	2.4	3.0	2.8	2.5	2.3	2.1	1.8	1.4	1.5	1.5
Nonresidential structures	1.7	2.2	2.9	4.9	6.0	5.7	5.1	4.7	4.2	3.7	2.8	3.0	3.1
Total financial assets	11.4	17.0	17.5	14.0	9.8	7.2	6.8	6.7	5.8	5.9	7.7	7.9	8.1
Home mortgages	1.2	1.9	1.7	1.4	1.1	0.9	0.7	0.5	0.4	0.3	0.1	0.1	0.2
Commercial mortgages	5.0	7.5	7.7	7.0	5.2	3.8	3.3	2.8	2.4	1.8	1.5	1.4	1.7
Multifamily mortgages	4.2	6.6	6.8	4.8	3.1	2.2	1.8	1.6	1.3	1.0	0.8	0.6	0.7
Miscellaneous assets	1.0	1.0	1.4	0.8	0.5	0.3	0.9	1.8	1.6	2.8	5.3	5.8	5.6
Total liabilities	8.8	14.4	16.6	17.8	16.0	13.0	11.5	10.2	8.1	8.3	8.4	8.4	8.7
Credit-market instruments	8.8	14.4	15.8	115.7	13.8	11.3	9.7	8.4	6.2	6.4	6.4	6.5	6.7
Mortgages	1.2	1.5	1.6	2.0	2.4	2.4	2.5	2.6	2.4	1.9	2.0	2.2	2.1
Multifamily residential	0.4	0.5	0.5	0.7	0.8	0.8	0.8	0.8	0.8	0.6	0.7	0.7	0.7
Commercial	0.8	1.0	1.1	1.4	1.6	1.6	1.7	1.7	1.6	1.3	1.4	1.4	1.4
Corporate bonds	1.4	1.9	2.1	2.1	1.9	1.8	1.6	1.6	1.4	0.7	0.7	0.7	0.7
Bank loans n.e.c.	3.0	7.0	11.4	10.8	8.9	6.5	4.9	3.5	1.8	3.2	3.3	3.4	3.6
Open-market paper	3.2	4.0	0.7	0.8	0.6	0.5	0.6	0.8	0.5	0.6	0.4	0.3	0.3
Miscellaneous liabilities	—	—	0.8	2.1	2.3	1.8	1.8	1.8	1.9	2.0	2.0	2.0	2.0

TABLE 14-4

REAL ESTATE INVESTMENT TRUSTS' FLOWS OF FUNDS, 1972–1984 (BILLIONS OF DOLLARS)

	1972	1973	1974	1975	1976	1977	1978	1979	1980	1981	1982	1983	1984
Physical investment	1.1	0.7	1.1	3.0	1.6	0.2	—	—	—	—	0.3	0.3	0.3
Net acq. of financial assets	5.0	5.5	0.5	-3.6	-4.1	-3.2	-1.4	-0.6	-1.7	-0.7	0.2	0.2	0.2
Mortgages	4.2	5.5	0.2	-4.8	-3.8	-2.4	-1.1	-1.0	-0.7	-1.1	-0.7	-0.3	0.4
Misc. assets	0.8	*	0.4	1.2	-0.3	-0.8	-0.3	0.3	-1.0	0.4	0.9	0.4	-0.2
Net increase in liabilities	6.3	6.5	1.4	*	-2.0	-2.4	-1.0	-0.3	-1.5	-0.5	0.7	0.7	0.7
Corporate equity issues	1.6	1.0	-0.9	-1.1	-0.3	0.6	0.6	0.9	0.6	-0.7	0.7	0.6	0.6
Credit-market inst.	4.6	5.5	1.5	-0.1	-1.9	-2.5	-1.4	-1.3	-2.2	0.2	0.1	0.1	0.1
Mortgages	0.5	0.4	0.2	0.4	0.4	*	0.1	*	-0.1	-0.5	0.1	0.1	*
Corporate bonds	0.3	0.5	0.2	—	-0.2	-0.1	-0.2	*	-0.2	-0.7	*	*	*
Bank loans n.e.c.	1.3	3.9	4.4	-0.6	-1.9	-2.4	-1.4	-1.4	-1.7	1.5	0.1	0.1	0.1
Open-market paper	2.5	0.7	-3.3	0.1	-0.3	*	0.1	0.1	-0.2	*	-0.1	-0.1	-0.1
Misc. liabilities	—	—	0.8	1.3	0.2	-0.5	-0.1	*	0.1	*	—	—	—

on loans to REITs, banks are reducing their exposure in this market. The mortgage loan liability represents loans on property owned by REITs which primarily own and operate rather than build real estate. Stockholders' equity represents the ownership by the investors who hold the REIT common stock. Note that REITs have debt as well as equity in their financial structure, unlike investment companies which typically are financed with only equity shares.

SUMMARY

Investment companies are financial intermediaries that attract large amounts of money from many individual investors, money which is pooled and invested in a diversified portfolio of securities. Real estate investment trusts offer the same service with pooled resources invested in mortgages, construction financing, and real estate.

Investment companies seek varying objectives in their investments as reflected by their varying investment techniques. Those seeking capital growth invest primarily in common stocks. Companies wishing to maximize current income generally concentrate their investments in interest-bearing bonds. Municipal bond funds invest in tax-exempt bonds, and money-market funds invest in short-term, prime-grade, highly liquid securities.

Investment companies are either open-ended or closed-ended. Open-ended companies, called mutual funds, continuously issue capital stock, which is redeemable at any time at its net asset value. Closed-ended companies are distributed in syndicated offerings and traded in secondary markets in the same manner as other corporate securities.

All investment companies have the option of being taxed under special provisions of the Internal Revenue Code, called Subchapter M. These provisions permit the investment company to escape taxation because income is taxed to the shareholders directly under the conduit theory.

Investment companies are sponsored by an entity called the investment manager. The manager provides, subject to a contract, investment advice and services in exchange for a fee which is based upon the value of the assets of the investment company. Open-ended investment company shares are sold either directly or through brokers at an offering price including a charge called a sales-load, or by the investment companies themselves, as is usually the case for no-load funds. Following two decades of impressive growth, investment company assets have fluctuated since the late 1960s. This is in part because of the volatility of the securities markets generally as well as the disappointing performance of investment companies.

Real estate investment trusts are similar to investment companies in several ways. Under a conduit theory of taxation, they usually avoid income taxes. They are sponsored and managed by a trust manager, who provides investment and management services to the trust in exchange for a fee subject to a contract. Assets of REITs generally reflect four stages of real estate development: land in nonhousing use, land held for speculation, land in development stages, and land improved with buildings. Unlike investment companies, REITs may finance some of their activities through borrowing.

TERMS

Investment Companies

common stock funds	conduit theory
balanced funds	Subchapter M
bond funds	investment manager
municipal bond funds	prospectus
money-market funds	sales load
open-ended investment company	no-load
net asset value	go-go funds
closed-ended investment company	mutual funds

Real Estate Investment Trusts

four stages of real estate development	off-site development
REITs	on-site development

QUESTIONS

1 Explain the difference between open-ended and closed-ended investment companies.
2 Name five common types of investment companies and explain how their investment strategy accomplishes their investment objectives.
3 How is net asset value computed?
4 What three types of distribution methods are used to sell shares of open-ended investment companies?
  What statement must accompany the sales solicitation?
5 Identify the services provided by the investment manager to the investment company. How is the investment manager compensated for these services?
6 What is a sales load? At what rate is it usually charged? Who receives the sales load? How are no-load funds usually sold?
7 What kind of investment strategy is pursued by go-go funds?
8 Why are REITs a "new" financial intermediary?
9 Why is the conduit theory of taxation a crucial factor in the existence of mutual funds and REITs?
10 What are the three major management functions of a REIT adviser?
11 List REIT assets which are used to finance real estate development for each of the four stages of property development.
12 What are the two major sources of funds to REITs?

SELECTED REFERENCES

Investment Companies

Friend, Irwin, F. E. Brown, Edward S. Herman, and Douglas Vickers: *A Study of Mutual Funds,* Securities Research Unit, Wharton School of Finance and Commerce, University of Pennsylvania, Philadelphia, 1962.

Friend, Irwin, Marshall Blume, and Jean Crockett: *Mutual Funds and Other Institutional Investors: A New Perspective*, McGraw-Hill, New York, 1970.

Good, W. R., R. Ferguson, and J. Treynor: "An Investor's Guide to the Index Fund Controversy," *Financial Analysts Journal*, November/December 1976, pp. 27–36.

Hakansson, N. H.: "The Purchasing Power Fund: A New Kind of Financial Intermediary," *Financial Analysts Journal*, November/December 1976, pp. 49–59.

Harless, Doris E.: *Nonbank Financial Institutions*, Federal Reserve Bank of Richmond, Richmond, Va., October 1975, chap. 6.

Ingersoll, J. E.: "A Theoretical and Empirical Investigation of the Dual Purpose Funds," *Journal of Financial Economics*, January/March 1976, pp. 83–123.

Investment Company Institute Annual Report, Investment Company Institute, Washington, D.C., annual publication.

Jensen, Michael C.: "The Performance of Mutual Funds in the Period 1945–1964," *Journal of Finance*, May 1968, pp. 389–419.

Mutual Funds Fact Book, Investment Company Institute, Washington, D.C., annual publication.

Litzenberger, R. H., and H. B. Sosin: "The Structure and Management of Dual Purpose Funds," *Journal of Financial Economics*, March 1977, pp. 203–230.

McDonald, John G.: "Objectives and Performance of Mutual Funds 1960–1969," *Journal of Financial and Quantitative Analysis*, June 1974, pp. 311–333.

Modigliani, F., and G. A. Pogue: "Alternative Investment Performance Fee Arrangements and Implications for SEC Regulatory Policy," *Bell Journal of Economics*, Spring 1975, pp. 127–160.

Scott, D. F., Jr., and R. C. Klemkosky: "Mutual Fund Performance and Unrealized Expectations," *Journal of Business Research*, January 1975, pp. 25–32.

Sharpe, William F.: "Mutual Fund Performance," *Journal of Business,* January 1966, pp. 119–138.

Wisenberger Services, Inc.: *Investment Companies*, Arthur Wisenberger and Company, New York, 1965.

Real Estate Investment Trusts

Levesque, J. R.: "Merchant Banks, REITs and MICs: Emerging Institutions in the Financial Sector," *Canadian Business Review*, Autumn 1974, pp. 18–21.

REIT Fact Book, National Association of REITs, Washington, D.C., annual publication.

Ricks, R. Bruce: "Real Estate Development Financing," *California Management Review,* Spring 1968, pp. 81–89.

Rosenberg, C., Jr., and P. Sack: "The High Risks of Open-End Real Estate Funds," *Journal of Portfolio Management,* Fall 1975, pp. 55–57.

Schulkin, Peter A.: "Real Estate Investment Trusts," *Financial Analysts Journal,* May/ June 1971, pp. 33–78.

Smith, K. V., and D. Shulman: "The Performance of Equity Real Estate Investment Trusts," *Financial Analysts Journal,* September/October 1976, pp. 61–66.

Wurtzebach, C. H.: "An Institutional Explanation for Poor REIT Performance," *Appraisal Journal,* January 1977, pp. 103–109.

CHAPTER 15

INTERNATIONAL MONEY MARKETS

The setting for institutions operating in the international sector is radically different from the domestic sector, as depicted in the following quotation:

> International finance is a game with two sets of players—the politicians and bureaucrats in national governments, and the presidents and treasurers of giant, large, medium, and small firms. The government officials want to win elections and secure a niche in the history of their countries. The corporate presidents and treasurers want to profit—or at least avoid losses—from the inevitable changes in exchange rates that government officials say will never occur—and yet always do. Since every major Western industrial country has changed the foreign exchange value of its currency in the last six years, the profit opportunities have been extensive.[1]

UNIQUENESS OF INTERNATIONAL TRANSACTIONS

The common denominator of international transactions is that one of the parties *must* deal in a foreign currency. An American buying a Toyota may pay in dollars or yen. If the buyer pays in dollars, then Toyota must convert dollars to yen. If the American wishes to pay in yen, then the dollars must be converted to yen before the purchase. The exchange of currencies is an inevitable consequence of foreign transactions, although the exchange may be delayed for a period of time. The financial mechanism for aiding such transactions is known as international intermediation.

The existence of different currencies presents a fundamental problem in international finance. Operationally, the problem is solved with a foreign ex-

[1] Robert Z. Aliber (1973), p. 3.

change market where businessmen and others can exchange one currency for another. However, the effects of foreign exchange on businessmen and financial institutions are substantial and foreign exchange dealings and decisions are complex. We first review the "three Cs" of international finance: currency, credit, and country. Then we study the *major* international financial institution—commercial banking—as it intermediates across national boundaries. In the final sections of this chapter, we survey programs of national governments designed to promote international trade and improve the economic conditions of developing countries with direct loans and loan guarantees.

INTERNATIONAL EXCHANGE RISKS

Currency Risk

Foreign exchange markets are places where currencies of various countries are bought and sold. For example, the market clears the exchange of dollars for francs at $0.20 per franc, when all potential suppliers and demanders of francs are satisfied. Thus, the link between currencies is independent of individual transactions, such as one American selling to one French person, and dependent on the total market. The currency market is cleared at the conversion price or *exchange rate*. Exchange rates, like other prices, are prone to fluctuation under supply and demand pressures. Currencies of two different countries are exchanged in an open market based on the buying and selling power of those currencies in the two countries. If the buying power of those currencies changes, then the exchange rate is likely to change, as well. The price is said to *float* when set solely by supply and demand forces. Alternatively, the price may be *pegged* by a national government so that the exchange rate varies only a small amount around a reference point.

With a *floating exchange rate,* price simply responds to the market's supply and demand forces. The concept is easily understood and its implementation presents few demands on government exchequers, but few countries allow their currencies to float freely. Those countries which do adopt a floating rate frequently participate in the market in order to dampen daily and weekly fluctuations. Sometimes floating rates are used by developed countries temporarily to "find" an acceptable range at which to peg their currency, but otherwise developed countries seldom allow their currencies to float. Many European countries floated their currencies briefly after World War I; and disagreement over exchange rates led most Western European countries and Japan to abandon pegs briefly in 1971 at the behest of the United States and induced Britain to release control of the pound prior to membership in the Common Market (January 1973).

Countries that *peg* their currencies commit themselves to maintaining a fixed parity between their currency and that of other countries. However, a government may also change the peg once in a while, once a year, or whenever they deem it desirable. For example, Britain changed the U.S. dollar-sterling parity from 2.80 to 2.40 in November 1967, and then up to 2.60 in December 1971. Countries change their exchange rate when the market value of their currency rises above or falls below the parity level.

Although most foreign countries peg their currencies to the U.S. dollar, some use gold as a reference point. The U.S. dollar has been a popular peg for other currencies because it was pegged to gold for a long time. The U.S. dollar was exchanged for gold at $20.67 per fine ounce for over a hundred years, before the official price was changed in 1933 and again in 1971 to bring the official parity to $42.50 per fine ounce. Now the United States no longer exchanges gold for dollars at parity, but the U.S. dollar remains an important international currency.

Since the transition to floating rates in 1973, potential fluctuations in exchange rates have concerned economic policy makers. Intervention in the foreign exchange market is a means of controlling foreign exchange rates. Intervention usually takes the form of purchases or sales of foreign currency with the domestic country's currency. In the United States such actions are usually conducted at the New York Federal Reserve Bank. Prior to February 1981, intervention transactions were executed regularly with the objective of moderating daily and weekly movements in currency values, but since February 1981, United States intervention in foreign exchange has been negligible. Studies of intervention suggest that intervention generally does not halt prolonged declines unless effective measures of dealing with the underlying causes are taken simultaneously. Further, U.S. dollar exchange rates with major trading partners increased only slightly after intervention was reduced in February 1981.[2]

Rates versus Reserves

When pegging exchange rates, countries let their reserves of gold and foreign currencies, rather than the price of their currency, fluctuate. A country running a payments surplus is selling its currency and purchasing gold or foreign currencies, while a country incurring payments deficits is buying its own currency by selling foreign currency and gold. (Incurring payments deficits means that the country is buying [paying for] more foreign goods from foreign consumers than it is selling [being paid for].) Hence pegging stabilizes the price of the currency but destabilizes the quantity of a government's stock of gold and foreign currency. A substantially overpriced currency causes an outflow of reserves because domestic buyers are able to buy foreign goods more cheaply than domestic goods. Eventually, a government is forced to alter its internal monetary and fiscal policies or devalue its currency. Devaluation may be accomplished by an official change in the exchange rate or de facto through import limits, tariffs, export subsidies, and foreign spending restrictions. Peg-

---

[2] For a very knowledgeable review of studies on intervention, see Henderson and Sampson (1983).

TABLE 15-1
DEVALUATION FREQUENCY IN
109 CURRENCIES (END OF 1948
TO END OF 1967)

Appreciation	1
No devaluation	12
One devaluation	27
Two devaluations	24
Three devaluations	24
Frequent devaluations	21
Total	109

Source: Lietaer (1971), p. 3, table 1.1.

ging exchange rates cannot isolate a country's economy from other countries over the long run; changes in exchange rates are the result of changes in the relative economic positions of trading countries.

Between 1948 and 1967 parity adjustments were made for most currencies and were commonplace for many. Table 15-1 shows that only 12 of 109 currencies remained constant during the 20-year period. Countries devaluing more than once included the United Kingdom, Austria, India, Greece, China, Ceylon (Sri Lanka), Ireland, New Zealand, Denmark, United Arab Republic, and France. Devaluation was in even greater evidence among the less-developed countries such as Bolivia, China, Paraguay, Uruguay, Colombia, Chile, Argentina, Brazil, and Yugoslavia. Rates of inflation are typically higher in less-developed countries, causing their currencies to be overvalued with respect to currencies of more stable economies.

The effects of devaluation (or revaluations) and price changes of floating currencies are the same from the viewpoint of foreign investors. When a firm has financial assets exceeding liabilities in a foreign currency, it is said to be in a *long* position. Firms owing more than they hold in financial claims is defined as being *short* in that currency. Those firms which are long tend to benefit from revaluations of foreign currencies, while those holding short positions tend to gain from currency devaluations.

Effect of Rate Fluctuations

Changes in exchange rates may alter the actual return earned on foreign investments; therefore, foreign investments are subject to *currency risk*. We can compare domestic and foreign investment returns by showing the effect of exchange rate changes. Exchange rates are quoted daily in *The Wall Street Journal,* and we shall use those shown in Tables 15-2 and 15-3 in our examples. *Spot* exchange rates are the current prices for currencies. *Future* exchange rates are prices which traders commit to now on future delivery or receipt of currencies. For example, the current price of francs may be $0.20. The present

TABLE 15-2
FOREIGN CURRENCY EXCHANGE QUOTATIONS, IN DOLLARS, NOVEMBER 25, 19X1

Country	Friday	Wednesday	Year ago
Argentina (Peso)	0.00182	0.001845	0.0042
Australia (Dollar)	1.1335	1.1325	1.2375
Austria (Schilling)	0.0633	0.0629	0.0586
Belgium (Franc)			
Commercial rate	0.028620	0.028495	0.027300
Financial rate	0.028630	0.028500	0.027325
Brazil (Cruzeiro)	0.0648	0.0648	0.085
Britain (Pound)	1.8200	1.8180	1.6475
30-Day Futures	1.8203	1.8203	1.6309
90-Day Futures	1.8198	1.8222	1.6017
180-Day Futures	1.8165	1.8223	1.5670
Canada (Dollar)	0.9016	0.9008	1.0057
30-Day Futures	0.9007	0.8996	*
90-Day Futures	0.9002	0.8992	*
180-Day Futures	0.8998	0.8984	*
China-Taiwan (Dollar)	0.0265	0.0265	0.0265
Colombia (Peso)	0.032	0.032	0.029
Denmark (Krone)	0.1631	0.1636	0.1700
Ecuador (Sucre)	0.0385	0.0385	0.04
Finland (Markka)	0.2385	0.2378	0.2618
France (Franc)	0.2064	0.2065	0.2005
30-Day Futures	0.2055	0.2056	*
90-Day Futures	0.2035	0.2036	*
180-Day Futures	0.2009	0.2011	*
Greece (Drachma)	0.0284	0.0284	0.028
Hong Kong (Dollar)	0.2147	0.2146	0.2108
India (Rupee)	0.1185	0.1185	0.1150
Indonesia (Rupiah)	0.002590	0.002590	*
Iran (Rial)	0.01415	0.01415	0.0143
Iraq (Dinar)	3.44	3.44	3.41
Israel (Pound)	0.0660	0.0660	0.1200
Italy (Lira)	0.001141	0.001141	0.001157

price for francs to be delivered in 90 days (90-day futures price) may be $0.22.
Investments and loans may be compared as follows:

   Domestic return = Foreign return

$$r_{US} = \left(\frac{LC_1 + LC_1 \, r_{LC}/M}{LC_0} \right)^M - 1 \qquad (15\text{-}1)$$

where

   LC_0 = free market spot rate of local currency at time 0 (purchase date)
   LC_1 = free market rate of local currency at time 1 (sale date)
   I_0 = investment (or loan)
   r_{LC} = interest rate of local currency

TABLE 15-2 (continued)

Country	Friday	Wednesday	Year ago
Japan (Yen)	0.004172	0.004170	0.003386
30-Day Futures	0.004195	0.004188	0.003386
90-Day Futures	0.004235	0.004214	0.003390
180-Day Futures	0.004267	0.004259	0.003395
Lebanon (Pound)	0.3260	0.3267	0.3846
Malaysia (Dollar)	0.4223	0.4218	*
Mexico (Peso)	0.0443	0.0443	0.0466
Netherlands (Guilder)	0.4172	0.4156	0.3986
New Zealand (Dollar)	1.0025	1.0040	0.9750
Norway (Krone)	0.1850	0.1844	0.1915
Pakistan (Rupee)	0.1025	0.0125	0.1030
Peru (Sol)	0.0087	0.0087	0.01523
Philippines (Peso)	0.1360	0.1360	0.1345
Portugal (Escudo)	0.0247	0.02475	0.0319
Saudi Arabia (Riyal)	0.2850	0.2850	0.2950
Singapore (Dollar)	0.4234	0.4227	0.4075
South Africa (Rand)	1.1522	1.1522	1.1535
South Korea (Won)	0.0021	0.0021	*
Spain (Peseta)	0.01215	0.01210	0.01465
Sweden (Krona)	0.2086	0.2088	0.2385
Switzerland (Franc)	0.4636	0.4575	0.4093
30-Day Futures	0.4657	0.4591	*
90-Day Futures	0.4689	0.4604	*
180-Day Futures	0.4747	0.4676	*
Thailand (Baht)	0.05	0.05	0.05
Uruguay (New Peso)	0.1870	0.1870	0.2780
Venezuela (Bolivar)	0.2331	0.2331	0.2340
West Germany (Mark)	0.4511	0.4483	0.4160
30-Day Futures	0.4522	0.4493	0.4161
90-Day Futures	0.4544	0.4515	0.4165
180-Day Futures	0.4582	0.4553	0.4176
Supplied by Bankers Trust Co., New York.			

* Information unavailable.
Source: The Wall Street Journal, November 28, 1977.

r_{US} = interest rate of domestic currency
M = 365 divided by number of days between purchase and sale dates

Example of Exchange Gain

Consider the case of a U.S. bank lending to a West German subsidiary of Consolidated Electronics, Inc. The loan is *denominated* in marks, the local currency of the subsidiary, according to the loan terms; the loan is granted for 91 days (November 25, 19X1, to February 28, 19X2). The loan is an open position *not hedged;* therefore, we compute *ex post* returns with spot market

TABLE 15-3
FOREIGN EXCHANGE QUOTATIONS IN DOLLARS, FEBRUARY 28, 19X2 (91 DAYS AFTER DATE IN TABLE 15-1)

Country	Tuesday	Monday	Year ago
Argentina (Peso)	0.001480	0.001480	0.00340
Australia (Dollar)	1.1385	1.1395	1.0974
Austria (Schilling)	0.0685	0.0680	0.0589
Belgium (Franc)			
Commercial rate	0.031855	0.031350	0.027280
Financial rate	0.031875	0.031390	0.027250
Brazil (Cruzeiro)	0.0618	0.0618	0.0800
Britain (Pound)	1.9420	1.9390	1.7100
30-Day Futures	1.9419	1.9388	1.6990
90-Day Futures	1.9412	1.9375	1.6772
180-Day Futures	1.9373	1.9345	1.6490
Canada (Dollar)	0.8970	0.8960	0.0528
30-Day Futures	0.8965	0.8957	*
90-Day Futures	0.8965	0.8955	*
180-Day Futures	0.8968	0.8952	*
China-Taiwan (Dollar)	0.0265	0.0265	0.0265
Colombia (Peso)	0.0290	0.0290	0.02760
Denmark (Krone)	0.1800	0.1787	0.1701
Ecuador (Sucre)	0.0382	0.0382	0.0365
Finland (Markka)	0.2405	0.2397	0.2623
France (Franc)	0.2103	0.2094	0.2008
30-Day Futures	0.2093	0.2085	*
90-Day Futures	0.2073	0.2064	*
180-Day Futures	0.2054	0.2039	*
Greece (Drachma)	0.0290	0.0290	0.0285
Hong Kong (Dollar)	0.2170	0.2172	0.2155
India (Rupee)	0.1252	0.1253	0.1150
Indonesia (Rupiah)	0.002590	0.002590	*
Iran (Rial)	0.0142	0.0142	0.0143
Iraq (Dinar)	3.44	3.44	3.41
Israel (Pound)	0.0656	0.0656	0.1150
Italy (Lira)	0.001174	0.001173	0.001135

prices at both the inception and maturity of the loan. If the loan carries a 10 percent interest rate, then the rate of return in U.S. dollars is computed using Eq. (15-1) and data from Tables 15-2 and 15-3.

$$r_{US} = \left(\frac{0.4970 + 0.4970(0.10/4.01)}{0.4511}\right)^{4.01} - 1$$

$$= 62.81\%$$

in which M is calculated as:

$$M = 365/91$$
$$= 4.01$$

TABLE 15-3 *(continued)*

Country	Tuesday	Monday	Year ago
Japan (Yen)	0.004203	0.004185	0.003548
30-Day Futures	0.004222	0.004203	0.003547
90-Day Futures	0.004254	0.004236	0.003538
180-Day Futures	0.004298	0.004279	0.003530
Lebanon (Pound)	0.3402	0.3402	0.3270
Malaysia (Dollar)	0.4246	0.4245	*
Mexico (Peso)	0.0441	0.0441	0.0450
Netherlands (Guilder)	0.4630	0.4565	0.4007
New Zealand (Dollar)	1.0280	1.0290	0.9600
Norway (Krone)	0.1895	0.1878	0.1900
Pakistan (Rupee)	0.1025	0.1025	0.1025
Peru (Sol)	0.0077	0.0077	0.01382
Philippines (Peso)	0.1360	0.1360	0.1345
Portugal (Escudo)	0.0249	0.0249	0.0305
Saudia Arabia (Riyal)	0.2895	0.2895	0.2850
Singapore (Dollar)	0.4321	0.4320	0.4070
South Africa (Rand)	1.1522	1.1522	1.1530
South Korea (Won)	0.0021	0.0021	*
Spain (Peseta)	0.01246	0.01245	0.01455
Sweden (Krona)	0.2185	0.2168	0.2368
Switzerland (Franc)	0.5495	0.5333	0.3926
30-Day Futures	0.5529	0.5368	*
90-Day Futures	0.5595	0.5432	*
180-Day Futures	0.5694	0.5532	*
Thailand (Baht)	0.05	0.05	0.05
Uruguay (New Peso)	0.1845	0.1845	0.2500
Venezuela (Bolivar)	0.2332	0.2332	0.2332
West Germany (Mark)	0.4970	0.4888	0.4177
30-Day Futures	0.4987	0.4905	0.4180
90-Day Futures	0.5024	0.4940	0.4184
180-Day Futures	0.5084	0.5005	0.4196
Supplied by Bankers Trust Co., New York.			

* Information unavailable.
Source: The Wall Street Journal, March 1, 1978.

Note that the reconversion (time 1) price of the currency is in the numerator and the current (time 0) price of the currency is in the denominator. Think of this equation as saying "the numerator is my return when each unit of foreign currency ($0.4970) plus interest [($0.4970 (0.1014.01)] is exchanged for dollars, divided by my investment of one unit of foreign currency at today's price ($0.4511)."

Example of Exchange Loss

Consider now an identical loan to the Brazilian subsidiary of Consolidated Electronics, Inc. The actual return is now:

$$r_{US} = \left(\frac{0.0618 + 0.0618(0.10)/4.01}{0.0648} \right)^{4.01} - 1$$

$$= -8.73\%$$

A modest decline in the Brazilian cruzeiro reduced the bank's actual return from 10.0 to −8.73 percent. Note that we are using *real data* in these examples to illustrate the significant impact of exchange rate changes on international investments. Because the position is open, spot prices are used when the loan is made and repaid; returns are *ex post* observations. *Currency risk* has been and will be a major consideration in international finance. We will consider some solutions later in this chapter.

Credit Risk

Loans and other credits extended to commercial and banking firms across international borders present special problems to domestic lenders. Greater geographical dispersion and differences in accounting practices and disclosure increase the difficulty of gathering information on prospective borrowers. When credit information is reported, it can be interpreted only by analysts who are familiar with that country's form of reporting and general economic conditions. A strong economy will tend to support business growth and reduce the credit risk of individual business. The problem of collecting losses is compounded by weak economies, as well as by foreign laws, courts,and customs.

Country Risk

Countries are sovereign powers and, therefore, may declare debts of foreigners void or otherwise restrict the movement of profits, interest, and capital. International trade and investment is a governmental policy tool which is exercised to the benefit of the domestic economy. Weak countries will continue to repay outstanding loans so as to be eligible for additional credits. As the debt service outflows increase and then exceed inflows from new loans, the financial benefit of defaulting increases. By declaring existing loans null and void, a country reduces its fixed obligations and may support new advances from eager importers (exporting countries) with its unencumbered export earnings. Countries may, in effect, default on their loans and other international commitments, but creditors may not "confiscate" pledged collateral.

Country risk depends upon political, economic, and cultural beliefs of the people and the government. Strong countries are characterized by the following:

1 Increasing per capita real income
2 Stable prices and costs of production
3 Governmental fiscal and monetary policy which balances taxes and expenditures, except under unusual domestic economic conditions

4 Labor union strength and goals in balance with management strength and labor productivity

5 Private and government domestic consumption expenditures in proportion to productive capacity[3]

6 Balanced or surplus balance of payments

7 Large foreign exchange and gold reserves

8 Large foreign direct investment in loans and real assets

Considerations such as these are used by bank management to rate the risk of individual countries. For more detail and a practical approach, see Korth (1979).

In recent years underdeveloped countries have maintained rates of growth in external borrowing that exceeded the growth of their economies or exports over a long period of time, incurring unsustainable debt-service burdens. Borrowing countries found international banks, both individually and as consortiums, willing to lend funds due to the attractive rate and growth opportunities available. Unfortunately, borrowers did not always tailor their borrowing programs to realistic assumptions about their prospects for general economic growth or their ability to earn foreign exchange. In some cases, borrowings appear to have been utilized not to finance additional investment, but at the margin to postpone needed downward adjustments in domestic consumption. The excessive borrowing was further confounded in several Latin American countries by rising interest rates that increased debt service requirements beyond the country's capacity to generate cash flows.[4]

CURRENCY RISK MANAGEMENT

Covering

American firms are increasing export sales at a quickening pace, while United States consumers are purchasing greater quantities of imports. Figure 15-1 shows the huge increase in exports since 1960. The financial transactions needed to accommodate exports are also substantial and are drawing U.S. bankers into the international money market.

Consider the position of Consolidated Electronics, Inc., when selling to France. To sell its electronics, Consolidated sells on open account with payment to be made within 90 days.[5] Assume here that the importer is of good

---

[3] The United States has made large increases in welfare expenditures since 1966, in addition to having incurred huge outlays for military operations. These expenditures have been increasing consumption in the short run while not improving production of goods and services and thus have been inflationary.

[4] See Teeters and Terrell (1983) for further discussion and statistics.

[5] Consolidated may also sell using commercial letters of credit. The letter is an instrument issued by the buyer's bank which agrees to pay drafts for contracted imports. In this manner, credit risk is shifted from the importer to the importer's bank and credit risk is usually eliminated.

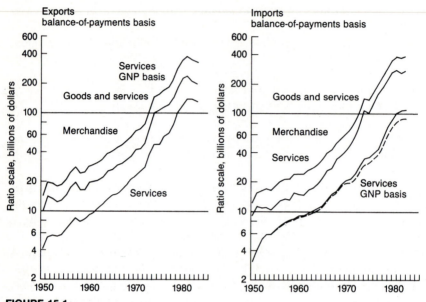

FIGURE 15-1
United States imports and exports of goods and services. (*Source*: Board of Governors of the Federal Reserve System.)

credit quality, so the major concern is currency risk. We wish to avoid possible exchange loss, preferring only to earn a profit through the manufacture and sale of goods.

Consolidated's treasurer can protect that company from currency risk by *covering* the sale with a forward contract to sell French francs 90 days hence. A *forward contract* is an agreement to exchange one currency for another at a future date and a stated price. Forward contracts are negotiated through banks and independent dealers that deal in the *forward market*. The market is made by traders who quote contract prices via telephone and teletypewriter to businesses and one another. These quotations, along with the spot (present) prices, are published daily in *The Wall Street Journal* (see Table 15-1). The forward contract *locks in* Consolidated's exchange profit or loss, as it no longer has a position in the local currency. We can compute the cost or profit from the currency exchange *now*. The future price of francs (LC) is fixed at the time of the sale (November 25). Using Eq. (15-1) and price information from Table 15-2, we have:

$$r_{US} = \left(\frac{0.2035 + 0.2035(0)/4.06}{0.2064}\right)^{4.06} - 1$$
$$= -5.58\%$$

Summary of Covering

Transaction	Position
Sell electronics to France	LONG in pounds sterling
	Nov. 25 Feb. 28
Futures contract to French francs	SHORT in pounds sterling
	Nov. 25 Feb. 28

(Note that $r_{LC} = 0$ because interest is not customarily charged on accounts receivable.) The certain exchange loss of 5.58 percent is preferred to the distribution of uncovered returns, which includes possibly substantially greater losses, such as 10, 20, or 30 percent.

Actually, the franc strengthened with respect to the U.S. dollar, and Consolidated would have earned a 7.89 percent (annual) return with a long position. Strengthening means that the currency increases in price. For example, francs increased in price from $0.2064 to $0.2103 from November 19X1 to February 19X2. We point out this example of the general rule that *covering eliminates the possibility for profit for the same reasons it reduces currency risk.* The commitment to deliver in the future at an agreed-upon exchange rate transfers the profit opportunity to the other party and leaves us with a relatively known, riskless position. As with most riskless positions, the possibility of large profits is eliminated with the chance of large losses.

Covering transactions may be impaired by market imperfections, such as transactions availability, costs, and defaults. Imperfect conditions prevent businesses from achieving the ideal results presented in these examples, and consequently, practitioners are advised to recognize that covering and hedging do not eliminate but merely substantially reduce risk.

Hedging

Financial assets of foreign subsidiaries denominated in foreign currencies may suffer exchange losses which substantially alter the earnings of the U.S. parent company. *Hedging* is a procedure for offsetting exchange losses on foreign financial assets through purchase or sale of futures contracts. *Long position* refers to ownership or right to own foreign currency; *short position* refers to an obligation to deliver foreign currency. A long position may be established in many ways, including purchases of currency in the spot market, contracting to purchase currency in the forward market, and selling goods on account in foreign currencies. Similarly, a short position is created in many ways, including borrowing in foreign currencies, importing goods on account in foreign currencies, and agreeing to deliver foreign currencies at a future date and at a fixed price (forward contract to deliver). We consider here a simple hedging strategy commonly used, although more complex models have been proposed.[6] The hedging strategy is devised in two stages:

1 Identification and quantification of exchange exposure
2 Selection of futures contracts which balance risk reduction and contract cost

Identification involves segregating balance sheet assets and liabilities according to those which would be affected by devaluation or revaluation. That is, financial assets denominated in foreign currencies are separated from other assets and liabilities. The accounting profession prefers the *net current asset* method of identification: short-term assets minus short-term liabilities. A more comprehensive approach is the *net financial asset method,* which subtracts short- and long-term debt from current assets. The financial asset method more properly recognizes the effect of exchange rate fluctuations on all liabilities—regardless of maturity—and has been adopted by many corporations.

Consolidated's German subsidiary may appear as in Table 15-4. The net exposed position is 200,000 marks (short). Fearing a revaluation of the mark and a devaluation of the dollar, Consolidated hedges its exposed position. A forward contract to purchase marks with dollars is negotiated, to take effect February 28 (again, see Table 15-3). Of course, the German subsidiary does not plan to liquidate its investment in 90 days and will not generate dollars to fulfill the contract. Instead, on February 28 it will purchase marks for dollars under the forward contract. The marks will be sold in the spot market for dollars.

Summary of Currency Hedging

Transaction	Position
Time of transaction: Nov. 25	
Balance sheet exposure (net financial assets)	SHORT in marks Nov. 25 Feb. 28
Futures contract to purchase marks	LONG in marks Nov. 25 Feb. 28
Time of transaction: Feb. 28	

Pay in dollars and receive marks under the futures contract signed Nov. 25.
Sell marks for dollars in the spot market

---

[6] A quadratic programming solution which incorporates portfolio concepts in a practical model is presented by Lietaer (1971).

TABLE 15-4
Consolidated Electronics, A.G.
Balance Sheet
November 25, 1977

(Marks)

Assets

Cash	200,000
Accounts receivable	1,000,000
Inventory	800,000
Fixed assets	800,000
Total assets	2,800,000

Liabilities

Current liabilities	1,000,000
Long-term debt	1,200,000
Net worth	600,000
Total liabilities and net worth	2,800,000

The exposure, computed with the net financial asset method, is:

Current assets	2,000,000 marks
Less: Current liabilites and long-term debt	2,200,000
Exposure	−200,000 marks

The annualized cost of hedging is computed with Eq. (15-1) just like the cost of covering.

$$r_{US} = \left(\frac{0.4544 + 0.4544(0)/4.06}{0.4511} \right)^{4.06} - 1$$

$$= 3.00\%$$

That is, we are contracting to purchase marks for more than the spot price. The hedge cost is incurred so that gains or losses on balance sheet items due to exchange rate changes are offset by losses and gains on the forward contract. If marks are revalued upward to $0.4970 per mark on February 28, then Consolidated earns a profit on its forward contract.

Gain from forward contract	
Receipt from sale of 200,000 marks at $0.4970 in spot market	99,400
Less: Purchase of 200,000 marks at $0.4544 per forward contract	90,880
Gain on forward contract	$8,520

Loss from balance sheet position	
Dollar value of exposed short position on November 22—200,000 marks @ $0.4511	90,220
Dollar value of exposed short position on February—200,000 marks @ 0.4970	99,400
Loss resulting from revaluation of mark	9,180

Consolidated incurs a $9180 loss when it purchases marks to repay the subsidiary's loan. However, the gain on the forward contract offsets that loss, except for the spread between the spot and forward price. The contract commits Consolidated to a cost equal to the spread, but protects it from a severe currency loss. The gain on the forward contract offsets most (all but $660 of the cost [2680.90]) of the mark revaluation on Consolidated's short position in marks (also referred to as an *exposed position*).

Swapping

Importers, foreign investors, and bankers making loans abroad also transact foreign exchange swaps to eliminate exchange risk. Under a *swap* agreement, an amount of one currency is exchanged for another today and the transaction reversed for an equivalent amount at a fixed future date. For example, 1000 U.S. dollars are traded for 4838 French francs today with the provision that 4,838 francs will be exchanged for 1000 dollars in 90 days. Swap transactions usually take place between soft and hard currencies.[7] Banks in a soft-currency country find this a cheap means of obtaining hard currency, while a swap creditor receives protection against devaluation of the soft currency.

The hard-currency lender pays interest on the soft currency swapped, although not receiving interest on its deposit. The soft-currency lender suffers the exchange rate change during the swap period and receives the interest paid on the soft currency. Thus, a U.S. bank may swap for Mexican pesos at 10 percent and lend to Consolidated's Mexican subsidiary at 20 percent. The profit would then be:

Gross yield on peso loan	20%
Cost of pesos swapped	10%
net yield on peso loan	10%

BANKING AND THE INTERNATIONAL MONEY MARKET

International Commercial Banks

Banks are the predominant financial institution in the international money market. International transactions are facilitated by bank traders who act as

[7] Soft currencies are those subject to frequent devaluation while hard currencies are stable and readily accepted as an international medium of exchange.

agents for others and take positions for their banks. The network of bank offices and correspondent relationships serve to transmit information about borrowers and money market conditions around the world. Although only the financial aspects of international banking are discussed here, we hasten to point out that banks also act as consultants on a wide variety of subjects including market, merger, and legal topics.

United States banks enjoy three competitive advantages in the international money market:

1 *Size*: Large banks can make the huge loans needed by multinational giants; also, substantial assets impart an image of confidence and safety. The three of the five largest banks in the world are U.S. banks. Citibank, N.A., of New York is larger than the entire Belgian banking system.

2 *Efficiency*: The very large number of U.S. banks (14,000) and their geographic dispersion has forced U.S. bankers to develop efficient transfer mechanisms and long-distance sales capabilities. United States banks have learned how to make loans efficiently and attract deposits in other major cities and states, and they are now transferring that knowledge to money centers around the world. Efficiency may be measured as the spread (difference) between the rate paid for deposits and that earned on loans. National barriers and the costs of international barriers and the costs of international transactions isolate money markets in different countries, so that not all banks need to be equally efficient to coexist.

3 *Preferred currency*: The U.S.dollar, America's domestic currency, is also the preferred international currency. A large number of foreign governments peg their exchange rates to the U.S. dollar, and foreign loans are frequently denominated in dollars. United States banks benefit from this fortuitous position, as their deposits are also denominated in dollars and tend to attract those who prefer dollars to yen, Swiss francs, or other currencies.

Eurodollar Banking

The development of the Eurodollar has been one of the most spectacular events in the money and capital markets during the last two decades. Not only is the Eurodollar market new, it is also enormous, complex, flexible, excitingly dangerous, and readily adaptable to vast international opportunities.

Eurodollars themselves are simply demand deposits of U.S. banks which are owned by foreign individuals, banks, or corporations. The dollar deposits are *always in the United States* and never leave, although the ownership may change from one foreigner to another. However, an important characteristic is that the Eurodollar lender does not expect to be paid by the U.S. bank but by a foreign branch of a U.S. bank.

Eurodollar transactions may be illustrated using the following example. Begin with the demand deposit account owned by an American corporation, Consolidated Electronics, Inc., in a New York bank.

New York Bank

	DD due Consolidated: $1

Suppose that Consolidated finds itself with excess cash balances which can be invested for 30 days. Consolidated asks a couple of U.S. banks what they are willing to pay and is quoted rates ranging from 7¼ to 7½ percent. However, a British bank quotes an 8½ percent rate, to which Consolidated agrees. The British bank now takes ownership of the United States balances, now termed Eurodollars.

Consolidated transfers its New York Bank account to the British bank:

New York Bank

	DD due Consolidated: 0
	DD due British bank: $1

British Bank

DD of N.Y. bank: $1	Time deposit due Consolidated: $1

The Eurodollars may then pass through several hands before returning to United States ownership. The British bank purchased the funds with the expectation of relending the funds to another bank, an individual, or a corporation. The British bank may lend the funds to a German bank, which in turn grants a loan to a German importer.

The British bank transfers funds to the German bank:

New York Bank

	DD due British bank: $0
	DD due German bank: $1

British Bank

DD of N.Y. bank: $0	Time deposit due Consolidated: $1
Time deposit of German bank: $1	

German Bank

DD of N.Y. bank: $1	Time deposit due British bank: $1

The German bank lends funds to an importer:

New York Bank

	DD due German bank: $1

British Bank

Time deposit of German bank: $1	Time deposit due Consolidated: $1

German Bank

DD of N.Y. bank: $1 Loan to German importer: $1	Time deposit due British bank: $1 Dollar denominated demand deposit due German importer: $1

The German importer may use the funds to purchase computers from a U.S. firm, which deposits the funds in a U.S. bank. The cycle is now complete; although the demand deposits may have been transferred from one U.S. bank to another, they never left the United States. The Eurodollar loans remaining on the British and German bank books will be retired according to their terms, but dollars are no longer owned by foreign parties.

The German importer pays for United States imports:

New York Bank

	DD due German bank: 0

British Bank

Time deposit due German bank: $1	Time deposit due investor: $1

German Bank

DD of N.Y. bank: 0 Loan to German importer: $1	Time deposit due British bank: $1 Dollar denominated demand deposit due German importer: 0

Eurodollars have the unique advantage of being available to users without any direct contact with a U.S. bank. Foreigners and foreign subsidiaries of domestic corporations desiring dollar credits may, therefore, deal directly with local bankers, who know them far better than officers of U.S. banks traveling abroad. Furthermore, special tax and other laws of the United States may apply to U.S. bankers dealing abroad but not to foreign banks, even though both may be selling demand deposits of the same U.S. bank.

The Eurodollar developed because foreign banks, accustomed to dealing in foreign currencies, were willing to make liability commitments denominated in dollars; and the practice blossomed because the worldwide loan demand for dollar-denominated notes and bonds has been expanding with the boom in international trade and investment. Now, only 15 years after the creation of the Eurodollar, virtually all foreign banks participate in the Eurodollar market and are developing Euroguilder, Euromark, and Eurofranc markets.

Risk of Eurodollar Dealing

Spreads and profits in the Eurodollar market have been declining, while the risks—real and potential—are increasing with the greater speed, size, and complexity of the transactions. Here are some of the risks:

1 Exchange traders are largely responsible for market operations but are effectively subject to only minimal surveillance by management. Commitments are usually made by telephone and rarely secured with collateral. Unlike commercial loans, credits to other banks are not carefully scrutinized with respect to credit quality by the traders, who are oriented toward the money market rather than toward individual institutions. The autonomy which permits traders to reap quick profits also permits them to make unauthorized commitments and take speculative positions.

2 Term structure misalignment is increasing as short-term borrowings are being used to finance long-term capital projects. Short-term funds are not always available at any price if the borrower is not of sufficient credit quality, and default becomes inevitable.

3 Unimpeachable bank credit quality is absolutely necessary but increasingly difficult to judge. Bank solvency is difficult to judge when the balance sheet consolidates Eurocurrency deposits or omits contingent commitments.

4 Eurodollars are "hot" money. A bank which is heavily dependent upon Eurodollars may suffer heavy outflows should rates in other countries rise sharply. Transactions are typically substantial and depositors are, by and large, very interest-rate sensitive.

5 A long chain of banks is interposed between the original lender and final borrower, exposing all the lenders to numerous credit, exchange, and political risks in addition to the risk of the final borrower. The original lender and banks in the chain depend upon the last bank in the chain to make prudent loans, but some Eurodollar transactions are made to business "raiders" and others for speculative purposes.

GOVERNMENT PROGRAMS

United States Agencies

The United States *Export-Import Bank* (Eximbank) provides financial assistance to stimulate the export of United States goods and services. Authorized $13.5 billion of credit, Eximbank grants direct loans and guarantees loans which facilitate exports. Direct loans are granted when private lenders are unwilling to assume the political or commercial risks of the transaction, but where the project financed has a reasonable chance of generating loan payments. Loan guarantees are made to private lenders and assist primarily small firms. Domestic and foreign lending institutions are eligible and qualifying loans are guaranteed up to 100 percent of the principal and interest.

The Agency for International Development (AID), an agency of the Department of State, provides nonmilitary assistance to friendly foreign countries.

Loans up to 40 years term are granted to foreign governments and private borrowers for procurement of the United States—manufactured portion of economic development projects. Also, AID grants local currency loans from local currencies received in payment for surplus agricultural produce; the loans provide for direct investment by local private enterprises. In addition to direct loans, AID guarantees new capital investment against losses due to expropriation, revolution, insurrection, and inconvertibility of local currency to dollars.

International Agencies

Commonly called the *World Bank,* the International Bank for Reconstruction and Development finances the foreign exchange portion of large projects in less-developed countries. The World Bank was established in 1944 as the development companion to the International Monetary Fund, which deals with currency exchange problems. Nearly one-third of loans granted have been to develop electric power production and distribution, one-third of its funds have paid for new transportation facilities, and one-third have been invested in water supplies and education. That is, the World Bank lends mainly to governments to improve the economic infrastructure of the country. The projects are usually massive and must be carefully planned and executed to qualify. Loan terms are rather liberal; maturities range from 10 to 30 years with a grace period before payments begin, and rates are close to high-quality money market rates. No losses have ever been suffered, largely because of the considerable effort expended to plan and select qualified developments.

The *International Finance Corporation* (IFC) accepts higher risk loans unqualified for the World Bank. Compared with the World Bank's paid-in capital of $2.5 billion, the $0.5 billion IFC is small. However, the IFC capitalizes only up to 50 percent of a project's cost so that the actions of the IFC have a multiplicative impact. Also, the IFC lends to and purchases equity interest from individuals, corporations, and other development banks. IFC funds support the development of such productive facilities as fertilizer, synthetic fiber, and petrochemical plants.

International Development Association (IDA) loans provide capital for infrastructure development of countries or projects not qualifying for World Bank credit but essential for the well-being of a people. IDA funds power, transportation, housing, education, and other social-purpose projects in less-developed nations. Loan terms are generous—interest is nominal and maturities range to 50 years with extended grace periods.

Regional development banks have also developed to serve nations with common geographical and economic problems. The major regional development banks are:

Inter-American Development Bank (IDB)—the Western hemisphere counterpart to the World Bank.

Asian Development Bank (ADB)—an Asian version of the IDA and one-third funded by developed nations.

European Investment Bank (EIB)—a European Common Market bank that integrates the Western European community through loans to finance inter-country projects, exploit comparative advantages, and develop depressed areas.

African Development Bank (AFDB)—a strictly regionally financed bank to promote the development of African nations.

SUMMARY

International financial institutions exploit the opportunity to intermediate among countries and are subject to the substantial uncertainty of changing currency values, massive credit losses, and expropriation. All international transactions involve the exchange of one currency for another; consequently, currency risk cannot be avoided. Furthermore, international lenders are confronted with added commercial credit risk and the unique country risk. Forward exchange contracts are one important means for reducing currency risk, but at a cost and only for short-term agreements. To support long-term loan arrangements, private lenders have relied upon Eurodollar- and Eurocurrency-denominated agreements.

Burgeoning international trade has clearly been supported, if not enlarged, by a vigorous private and governmental effort to develop financial institutions which can overcome international barriers to the free flow of money and capital. The U.S. government has encouraged exports with several agencies, principally the Eximbank and IDA. Additionally, numerous regional and worldwide agencies have been established during the past 40 years to provide long-term capital to developing countries and the European Common Market.

TERMS

exchange rate	hedging
float	Eurodollar
pegged	parity
long position	devaluation
short position	revaluation
currency risk	covering
credit risk	letter of credit
country risk	soft currency
futures contract	hard currency
futures market	swap agreement

LIST OF EQUATIONS

$$r_{US} = \left(\frac{LC_1 + LC_1\, r_{LC}/M}{LC_0}\right)^M - 1$$

QUESTIONS

1 What is the annual rate of return on a 180-day (pound) sterling loan to a British bank on November 25, 19X1, if the annual interest rate is 8 percent and the loan is fully hedged with futures contracts? Describe the differences in risk taken in this loan compared with a loan to a U.S. bank. Assume that the lender is owned and domiciled in the United States. (Use rates from Table 15-1.)

2 What financial risks are present in international transactions that are not usually found in domestic finance?

3 How can international finance reduce risk for a domestic company that exports products to foreign countries?

4 What is the difference between covering and hedging?

5 What is the exposed exchange position (net financial asset method) for ABC Corporation? What is the proper hedge to eliminate exchange risk?

ABC Corp.
Balance Sheet
December 31, 197X

(Yen)

Assets

Cash	3,000,000
Accounts receivable	12,000,000
Inventory	6,000,000
Fixed asset—net	5,000,000
Total assets	26,000,000

Liabilities

Current liabilities	5,000,000
Longer-term debt	10,000,000
Common stock	11,000,000
Total liabilities & net worth	26,000,000

6 What advantages do U.S. banks have over foreign banks in the international money market?

7 Trace the ownership of a $100,000 demand deposit from a wealthy Texas investor to a Russian importing agency through a British and a West German bank.

8 Evaluate the following investment alternatives by calculating their yields in U.S. dollars:

a French franc loan for 90 days bearing an annual interest rate of 12 percent.

b Swiss franc loan for 90 days bearing an annual interest rate of 6 percent.

Assume that the loan would be hedged, and assume that the full amount would be borrowed immediately.

Additional information: Foreign exchange rates are as follows:

Currency	Rate
France, spot	$0.2103
-30-day fut	0.2093
-90-day fut	0.2073
-180-day fut	0.2054
Switzerland, spot	0.5494
-30-day fut	0.5529
-90-day fut	0.5595
-180-day fut	0.5694

SELECTED REFERENCES

Aliber, Robert Z.: *The International Money Game,* Basic Books, New York, 1973.

Aliber, R.: "Monetary Independence under Floating Exchange Rates," *Journal of Finance,* May 1975, pp. 365–376.

"The Battle for Supremacy in the Euromarket," *Institutional Investor,* March 1976, pp. 81–85.

Brackenridge, A. B.: "Evaluating Country Credits," *Institutional Investor, International Edition,* June 1977, p. 13.

Brittain, B.: "Tests of Theories of Exchange Rate Determination," *Journal of Finance,* May 1977, p. 519.

Burt, J., F. R. Kaen, and G. G. Booth: "Foreign Exchange Market Efficiency under Flexible Exchange Rates," *Journal of Finance,* September 1977, pp. 1325–1330.

Cass, R. H.: "A Global Approach to Portfolio Management," *Journal of Portfolio Management,* Winter 1975, pp. 40–48.

Cornell, Bradford: "Inflation, Relative Price Changes, and Exchange Risk," *Financial Management,* Autumn 1980, pp. 30–34.

Dornberg, J.: "Government Financing: Financing the Communist Countries," *Institutional Investor, International Edition,* July 1976, pp. 42–48.

Frye, R.: "Foreign Banks in the U.S.–Chicago: How a New Law Opened the Door," *Institutional Investor,* September 1976, pp. 87–88.

Gardner, S. S.: "Statement to Congress," *Federal Reserve Bulletin,* July 1977, pp. 651–654.

Garrone, F., and B. Solnick: "A Global Approach to Portfolio Management," *Journal of Portfolio Management,* Summer 1976, pp. 5–14.

Giddy, I. H.: "An Integrated Theory of Exchange Rate Equilibrium," *Journal of Financial and Quantitative Analysis,* December 1976, pp. 883–892.

Graver, F. L. A.: "Sharing Rules and Equilibrium in an International Capital Market under Certainty," *Journal of Financial Economics,* June 1976, pp. 233–256.

Hausafus, K. F.: "Financial Institutions and International Capital Movements," *Journal of Money, Credit and Banking,* August 1976, pp. 359–371.

Henderson, Dale, and Stephanie Sampson: "Intervention in Foreign Exchange Markets," *Federal Reserve Bulletin,* November 1983, pp. 830–838.

Hewson, J., and E. Sakaibara: "A Qualitative Analysis of Euro-Currency Controls," *Journal of Finance,* May 1975, pp. 377–401.

————"The Effect of U.S. Controls on U.S. Commercial Bank Borrowing in the Eurodollar Market," *Journal of Finance,* September 1975, pp. 1101–1110.

Hewson, J., and E. Sakakibara: "A General Equilibrium Approach to the Eurodollar Market," *Journal of Money, Credit and Banking,* August 1976, pp. 297–323.

Korth, Christopher M.: "Developing a Country-Risk Analysis System," *Journal of Commercial Bank Lending,* December 1979, pp. 53–68.

Lessard, Donald: "International Portfolio Diversification: A Multivariate Analysis for a Group of Latin American Countries," *Journal of Finance,* June 1973, pp. 619–634.

Levy, Haim, and Marshall Sarnat: "International Diversification of Investment Portfolios," *American Economic Review,* September 1970, pp. 668–675.

Lietaer, Bernard A.: *Financial Management of Foreign Exchange: An Operational Technique to Reduce Risk,* MIT Press, Cambridge, Mass., 1971.

Mitchell, G. W.: "Statements to Congress," *Federal Reserve Bulletin,* February 1976, pp. 103–110.

Oldfield, G. S., and R. S. Messina: "Forward Exchange Price Determination in Continuous Time," *Journal of Financial and Quantitative Analysis,* September 1977, pp. 473–479.

Reich, C.: "The Flap Over Finland's AAA," *Institutional Investor, International Edition,* March 1977, pp. 48–49.

Reich, C.: "America's New Generation of International Bankers," *Institutional Investor, International Edition,* June 1977, pp. 37–44.

Shapiro, H. D.: "LDC Financing—the Search for Solutions to the LDCs' Problems," *Institutional Investor, International Edition,* October 1976, p. 38.

Shapiro, H. D.: "Forecasting Exchange Rates: The Battle of the New Services," *Institutional Investor, International Edition,* January 1977, pp. 64–71.

Solnik, B. H.: "Testing International Asset Pricing: Some Pessimistic Views," *Journal of Finance,* May 1977, p. 503.

Vernon, Raymond: *Manager in the International Economy,* 2d ed., Prentice-Hall, Englewood Cliffs, N.J., 1972.

Weston, J. Fred, and Bart W. Sorge: *International Business Finance,* Irwin, Homewood, Ill., 1972.

Zenoff, David B., and Jack Zwick, *International Financial Management,* Prentice-Hall, Englewood Cliffs, N.J., 1969.

PART FOUR

MANAGERIAL POLICY ISSUES

ORIENTATION

Managers of financial institutions develop policies for routine operations by analyzing risks, returns, expenses, laws, and regulations. Some of the policy issues require different solutions or take on greater meaning for financial institutions than for nonfinancial firms. Policy issues of particular concern or distinction for financial institutions managers are:

1 Credit policy (Chapter 16)
2 Operating economies of scale (Chapter 17)
3 Liquidity policy (Chapter 18)
4 Capital policy (Chapter 19)

Although these financial issues are not unique, they are particularly important because financial institutions specialize in performing financial functions, as listed in Chapter 1:

1 Payments mechanism
2 Security trading
3 Transmutation
4 Risk diversification
5 Portfolio management

In managing a portfolio of loans, for example, management develops a credit policy. With an efficient payments mechanism, management considers economies of scale in computer operations. Therefore, the commitment to perform financial functions leads to a common set of management issues.

Further, financial institution managers coordinate credit, liquidity, operating, capital, and other policies into plans for the coming years. The planning process begins with goal setting and market conditions analysis and proceeds through strategy/policy formulation to an action plan. The concept of financial planning is the same for all businesses, financial and nonfinancial alike. The implementation of financial planning, however, is different for financial intermediaries. Whereas *sales revenue* drives financial planning in nonfinancial firms, *assets and liabilities* drive financial planning in financial intermediaries. Therefore, special attention is paid to financial intermediary planning models in Chapter 20.

CHAPTER 16

CREDIT POLICY

Credit policy defines the institution's procedures for obtaining credit applicants, analyzing applications, deciding whether or not to grant credit, and collecting payments. Institutions carry out credit policy with personnel who market credit services, investigate applicants, make credit decisions, and collect payments. Coordinating credit activities so as to meet the institution's goals is the purpose of credit policy.

Granting credit is intrinsically risky. Some people are going to "skip" and others involuntarily fall into bankruptcy, causing the institution to sustain credit losses. The possibility of borrowers failing to repay loan principal and interest is called *default risk*. Default losses are undesirable, of course, but are a normal expense of the credit process. The relationship between default risk and other credit costs, methods of appraising loan applicants, and procedures for collecting delinquent accounts are discussed in this chapter.

CREDIT PROCESS

The credit process is diagrammed in Figure 16-1 to show the roles of risk analysis, profitability analysis, and collection effort in the selection of a portfolio of loans. *Risk analysis* is the process of estimating a potential or actual creditor's probability distribution of repayment of credit with given terms.

Profitability Analysis

Profitability analysis is the estimation of revenues and costs associated with the granting of a loan. Combining risk and profitability analysis, we find the

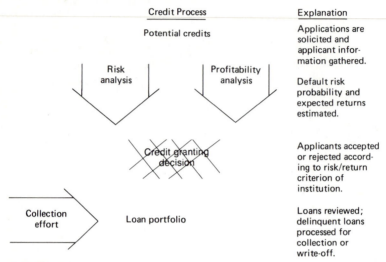

FIGURE 16-1
Components of the credit function.

expected value of granting credit. Then, the control procedure screens credits on the basis of risk criteria and overall firm objectives. Portfolio control then continues with periodic reviews to ensure that loans remain consistent with the institution's current policies.

Loan Loss Experience

It is the rare institution which does not experience loan losses as a regular part of its business. However, frequency and size of loan losses vary considerably from one institution to another. Finance companies typically suffer more losses than commercial banks, which, in turn, write off a greater proportion of bad loans than savings and loans. Before we consider the relationship between loan losses and net profit, we are going to review actual loss experience of a few major institutions. Disclosure of loss experience is neither uniform nor universal, because many executives and regulators believe that confidence in our financial institutions would be lessened if the general public knew of the billions of dollars worth of bad debts which are charged off every year. However, the current trend is toward full disclosure of loss experience and an attitude of accepting losses as an ordinary cost of lending money.

Home mortgages are generally considered to be very safe, and reported default rates are relatively low. Von Furstenberg (1969) conducted an extensive study of FHA-insured home mortgages of different maturities and borrower characteristics. Default data from Von Furstenberg's study are reproduced in Table 16-1. The mortgages which are only a few years old are more likely to default than those which have "aged." As the mortgage ages, the borrower reduces the amount of the loan and the value of the property increases. Toward

TABLE 16-1

ANNUAL DEFAULT RATES ESTIMATED OVER THE
TERM OF FHA-INSURED MORTGAGES

Default rate in yr. of age (t)*	Term		
	20	25	30
"New" home insurance			
1	0.0528%	0.0216%	0.1712%
2	0.0781	0.1016	0.4958
3	0.0858	0.1936	0.7201
4	0.0827	0.2722	0.8061
5	0.0727	0.3220	0.7631
6	0.0591	0.3367	0.6334
7	0.0446	0.3192	0.4691
8	0.0332	0.2782	0.3128
9	0.0209	0.2247	0.1896
10	0.0130	0.1694	0.1046
11	0.0076	0.1196	0.0527
12	0.0041	0.0793	0.0243
13	0.0021	0.0495	0.0103
14	0.0010	0.0291	0.0040
15	0.0005	0.0161	0.0014
16	0.0002	0.0085	0.0005
17	0.0001	0.0042	0.0001
18	–	0.0020	–
19	–	0.0009	–
20	–	0.0004	–
21-23		0.0002	
Total	0.5585%	2.5490%	4.7591%
"Existing" home mortgages			
1	0.1271%	0.3231%	0.3580%
2	0.3295	0.5347	0.6140
3	0.4420	0.6213	0.6734
4	0.4556	0.6250	0.6013
5	0.3929	0.5700	0.4607
6	0.2930	0.4794	0.3089
7	0.1920	0.3752	0.1831
8	0.1117	0.2746	0.0966
9	0.0579	0.1885	0.0454
10	0.0269	0.1215	0.0191
11	0.0112	0.0738	0.0072
12	0.0042	0.0422	0.0024
13	0.0014	0.0228	0.0007
14	0.0004	0.0116	0.0002
15	0.0001	0.0056	0.0001
16	–	0.0025	–
17	–	0.0011	–
18	–	0.0004	–
19	–	0.0002	–
20		0.0001	
Total	2.4459%	4.2736%	3.3711%

* Annual default rates are approximated by the ordinate at the midpoint of each interval. In the first year, for instance, t equals 0.5.

Source: Von Furstenberg (1969), p. 468.

the maturity data of a mortgage the default rate declines to nearly zero. Note that the default rate on mortgages of all maturities and ages are very low and does not exceed 0.81 percent annually. Most mortgagors make their payments on time, as shown by Rake's (1973) study of three St. Louis savings and loan associations. Rakes reports that conventional (uninsured) mortgage payments were received within 12 days of the due date from 85 percent of the borrowers.

CREDIT-GRANTING POLICY

The credit-granting decision, shown in Figure 16-1, involves both risk analysis and profitability analysis. The main purpose of a credit-granting policy is to define routine "accept" and "reject" rules for applicants and to provide guidelines by which exceptional credit applications can be evaluated. Most "accept" or "reject" decisions are made with one of three methods of analysis:

1 Credit analysts
2 Numerical credit scoring
3 Open season or no analysis

The three risk-analysis methods are described in the following sections.[1] Later sections deal with loan profitability analysis for consumer and commercial loans. Then risk and profitability are evaluated jointly to select the approach that maximizes stockholder wealth.

Practical lending policies, procedures, and decisions differ substantially with respect to structure, detail, formality, analysis, and objectives. Further, actual lending activities often vary from the desired approach due to practical considerations and legal limitations. Therefore, practical credit decision making is more complex than the process described here.

Credit Analysis

The traditional approach to credit analysis has been to hire and train credit analysts to investigate applicants, suggest improved agreements, and decide to accept or reject requests. Analysts analyze information about the applicant and the loan, advise applicants about financing options, and recommend that the institution accept or reject the request. The analyst's decisions are judgmental, based on credit experience and training. Important types of information and their relationship to credit decisions are reviewed next.

The credit investigation is primarily a credit-information gathering operations and ranges from a one-page application for credit cards to massive files and reports in the case of commercial credits. In either case, the basic tenet is the same: *Credit information is important if, when known, it would influence the credit decision.* It is annoying to the applicant and costly for the lender to

---

[1]Alternative explanations are presented in Mehta (1968), Edmister and Schlarbaum (1974), and Long (1976).

collect information. Management, therefore, first defines what information is requested and compiled. The information may be factual or in the form of opinion, with facts being preferred to opinions. which may reflect the contributor's prejudice and imagination rather than the character of the applicant. The credit information is historical, of course, but it is compiled to make a prediction of future behavior. Implicitly, credit analysts subscribe to the belief that history is a clue to the future.

Credit Information   For consumer credit based largely upon the merits of individual applicants, the following information is generally gathered:

1 *Payment record*. Past payment habits are regarded by many investigators as the most important fact in judging credit quality. A thorough investigation includes questions about the types and amounts of credit, current balances due and past due, the terms of repayment, and the date that credit was first extended.

2 *Income*. A household's greatest asset is its promise of future income, because consumer debts are usually repaid from the working member's wage and salary income. The name of the employer, type of position, amount of wages and salaries, and type of business are requested from the applicant and verified with the employer. Investigation of self-employed persons extends to their sources of income and parallels commercial credit applications. Also, commitments against income are estimated from existing loan repayment schedules and household expenditure habits. The analyst assembles this information to forecast the size and variability of income and fixed obligations to estimate the probability that the household will be *able* to repay its debts.

3 *Residence*. An address check is a routine part of the identification verification. Also, the size and type of residence are indicative of the applicant's housing expense, social responsibilities, and wealth. Signals which call for deeper investigation include: residence with a friend, in a hotel, furnished apartment, or rooming house; residence in an area frequently inhabited by criminals and perpetrators of credit frauds; persons living in luxurious residences and refusing to give verifiable references and sources of income.

4 *Marital status*. Information about single, married, widowed, divorced, or separated marital status is sometimes sought of all applicants and considered important by consumer credit analysts.[2] Not only are income and obligations affected by a marital relationship, but the person's happiness and attitude toward others are believed to be related as well. Loan defaults and collection problems repeatedly arise from marital maladjustment, because the person using the automobile, washer, or house is often not the one responsible for making the associated loan payments.

5 *Age*. Some analysts reject most applications of individuals under 25 and over 65 years of age. Young applicants are usually not established financially

[2] Federal legislation now prohibits credit discrimination by sex, age, or marital status, for certain types of consumer loans.

and are often considered transient and uncommitted. Older persons are recipients of limited incomes and prone to illness, leading analysts to refuse them credit. When considered on the basis of their individual ability and character, young and old persons may prove to be good risks, however, and the indiscriminate use of age as a predictor may erroneously eliminate a potentially good market.

6 *References and reputation.* Analysts check references to appraise the *willingness* of the applicant to repay. That is, character is reflected in the opinion of previous creditors, friends, and business associates. Persons who have treated others fairly and loyally are likely to give the same consideration to a new credit relationship.

7 *Reserve assets and collateral.* Assets and income that may be liquidated provide a backup means of payment when the income stream stops. Securities and real estate without heavy debt payments are good reserve assets, but items such as luxury boats and homes with large debt payments must be regarded as negative factors for credit purposes. Equity in the consumer good purchased is highly desirable, as the purchaser realizes that he or she stands to lose a great deal in the event of default, and the creditor's loss is reduced when the collateral is liquidated.

Commercial Credit Information   *Commercial credit* investigations frequently contain the same kinds of information as those for consumer applications, plus the following:

1 *Financial statements.* Financial statements, usually balance sheets and income statements, show with great clarity the position, trend, and flow of the applicant's business. The accounting precision and the certification of the statements by independent auditors or the firm's management provide a high degree of validity upon which to measure the ability of the business to meet its obligations. Laws in most states make it a crime to submit false financial statements for the purpose of obtaining credit.

2 *Customer and creditor listings.* Customers and creditor listings provide the means and authorization to make inquiries with those doing business with the applicant. Customers are asked about product satisfaction, expected future dealings, and accounts receivable reported on the applicant's balance sheet and supporting schedule. Creditors are contacted to verify accounts payable and other obligations and to relate their credit history with the applicant.

The foregoing information is often obtained from the following sources:

1 *Credit application.* Application forms are used by most lenders to assist the interviewer or applicant in recording basic information in an orderly fashion. The forms may be simple or extensive but usually contain spaces for name, residence address, former address, employer, bank, property claimed, references, remarks, and signature attesting to the authenticity of information supplied.

2 *Interview.* The credit manager or assistant credit manager usually interviews the applicant. The interviewer should be a person who knows the applicant, if possible, and should never make the interview an interrogation. As most applicants are accepted for credit, the interview also provides an opportunity to explain the terms of credit extended and to impress upon the applicant that the institution stands ready to help should the borrower's financial condition change. Collection problems are considerably easier (for all parties) when a good rapport is established at the initial meeting.

3 *Credit bureaus.* Retail credit bureaus are organized by lending institutions to exchange account information among members. The movement toward large cities, where individuals are usually unknown to lenders and the abuse of credit facilities by "skips" who borrow from everyone before leaving town, has encouraged the development of central information clearinghouses. Each member agrees to provide complete and factual information regarding all accounts and, in turn, may draw freely from the bureau's information bank.

Estimation of Credit Risk: Analyst Method   Having compiled a basic file of information and investigated avenues suggested by inconsistencies, derogatory comments, and favorable opinions, the analyst assesses the *willingness* and *ability* of the applicant to repay. The traditional standard has been the "four C's" of credit: character, capacity, capital, and conditions. Each of these describes an area of the person's or firm's credit worthiness.

1 *Character.* The quality of *desiring to repay debts when due* is ranked above all other considerations. Of course, honesty is a necessity, but character implies integrity and empathy for the lender's position as well. An established credit record (substantial borrowings and voluntary repayment) is one of the best evidences of a business's or individual's willingness to repay. Also, character is implied by the applicant's positions of trust accepted and fulfilled in business and social organizations. The character of business organizations follows that of the top management, its facilities for keeping records, the routinization of office functions, and relations with employees.

2 *Capacity.* Capacity is *the ability to repay* debts as scheduled. For households, the employment of the working members provides most of the income which is spent for consumer expendables, durables, and debt repayment. Consumer capacity is a reflection of the safety margin between income and committed outflows and the stability of each. The analyst must consider the effects of unusual events such as prolonged illness or unemployment on the economic capacity of the household. Business capacity, likewise, depends upon sales income, expenditure patterns, and debt commitments. However, the complexities of business operations are substantially greater than that of a household, requiring analysts highly trained in corporate finance and knowledge about the accounting, marketing, and financial peculiarities of the firm and its industry.

3 *Capital.* This is net worth or equity (assets minus liabilities); it provides a cushion to absorb operating and asset losses that might otherwise impair debt repayment. Accounting values are often adjusted for market values, encumbrances, and contingencies before computing capital for credit purposes.

4 *Conditions*. Borrowers may be subject to unfavorable economic conditions beyond their control. Repayment depends not only upon character, capacity, and collateral, but those factors over which the borrower exercises little or no control. The *long-run and short-run business cycle* affects nearly all persons and individuals, but certain industries are especially prone to oscillate between prosperity and depression. Credit analysts monitor industrial patterns, looking for early signs of weakness that would lead to unemployment, sales declines, and/or operating losses. Under the extreme adverse pressures of falling sales and loss of income, even strong, honest characters may subvert the loan relationship in order to preserve their economic position.

The analyst mentally takes account of the four C's, weighing each according to the particular circumstances. However, a general statement as to the usual importance of these factors can be made. Risk is dependent upon the *quality* found in each factor and the *combination* of the four C's. Assuming the same conditions prevail, these guidelines are suggested, beginning with the best possible combination:

Applicant characteristics	Credit risk
Character and capacity and capital	Very low
Character and capacity without capital	Low to moderate
Character and capital but insufficient capacity	Low to moderate
Capacity and capital but impaired character	Moderate
Capacity and capital without character	High
Character and capital without capacity	High
Character without capacity without capital	Very high
Capital without character without capacity	Very high
Capacity without character without capital	Fraudulent

Numerical Credit Scoring

Numerical credit scoring is an alternative that utilizes statistical techniques to summarize the credit experience of a particular group and then applies that summary to new applicants. Each application receives a score based on factual information, and the score is evaluated as good or bad according to preset policy levels. Credit scoring can be used by inexperienced personnel to make many of the decisions previously made by management and is more commonly implemented in high-volume consumer finance operations. The advantage of credit scoring over credit analysts is its low personnel cost. Training analysts to make accurate credit decisions requires a great deal of time and effort. Furthermore, most analysts are "burned" a few times before learning how to spot bad loan applicants. The institution suffers the loan losses resulting from inexperienced personnel. On the other hand, a clerical employee (or computer) can rapidly analyze thousands of applicants with a numerical credit formula.

The statistical problem is one of classifying an applicant as a member of one of two groups, success or failure, based upon a number of factual bits of information. Multiple discriminant analysis is the most common statistical procedure used and may be interpreted geometrically. The bivariate plot for groups I (loan failures) and II (loan successes) is shown in Figure 16-2. We may think of the variables X and Y as household characteristics, such as income and previous credit record. Old credit records are then examined with regard to these characteristics and the results plotted. The elliptical shapes represent the locus of points found in our credit files. A straight line is defined by the two points where the contours intersect. If a second line Z is constructed perpendicular to line A, and if the points in the X-Y space are projected onto Z, the overlap between the two distributions will be the smallest line. The characteristics of income and payment record are transformed by the discriminant function into a single discriminant score $\bar{z}$ located on Z. A value of z such as $0.50b$ divides the one-dimensional space into two regions, each having a probability of membership in I or II. (See Figure 16-3.)

The Z-score cutoff should be selected so as to equate the probability of type I and type II errors with the ratio of the explicit cost of accepting a failure to the opportunity cost of rejecting a success. This may be represented by the following equality:

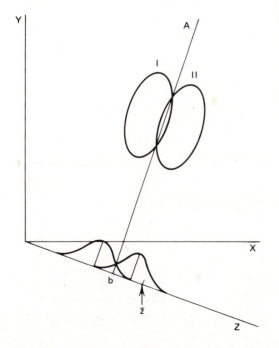

FIGURE 16-2
Bivariate plot of loan failures (I) and successes (II). (*Source*: Edmister, 1972, p. 1483.)

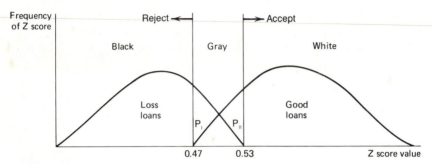

FIGURE 16-3
Credit score distributions and decision points. (*Source*: Edmister, 1971, p. 20.)

$$\frac{P_{II}}{P_I} = \frac{MC_I}{MC_{II}} \tag{16-1}$$

where

P_I is the probability of rejecting a loan to a successful firm (type I error),
P_{II} is the probability of accepting a loan to a failing firm (type II error),
MC_I is the marginal opportunity cost of rejecting a loan to a successful borrower, and
MC_{II} is the marginal actual cost of accepting a loan to a failing borrower.

This analysis provides the logical solutions for the Z- score cutoff for lenders who know their marginal costs. For example, if MC_I is $100 and MC_{II} is $500, then the cutoff is set so that the ratio of P_I to P_{II} is 0.20. Figure 16-3 is drawn to represent this relationship.

Open Season

The *open-season* approach accepts applicants without analysis and, consequently, individual qualifications are ignored. For example, the season may be defined as all applications received on Tuesday, every twentieth applicant, or applications with randomly selected identification numbers. Although such a policy may seem surprising on the surface, it has important advantages for *consumer lending*.

One important reason for accepting applicants without analysis is to establish a benchmark for evaluating numerical scoring functions. Applicant quality is estimated by declaring an open season and tracking the resulting loans to learn how many applicants are qualified and to relate applicant characteristics to repayment performance.

Occasionally, the net present value of an open-season approach is greater than that which would be earned with analysis. That is, the operating cost and the credit errors caused by analysis exceed the loan loss elimination benefits. (The factors and conditions necessary for finding that open season is better than other methods are discussed later in this chapter.) Of course, lenders do not publicize this approach but maintain a facade of credit analysis, because unqualified applicants would be attracted to an opportunity for unrestricted credit.

Profit Evaluation of the Credit-Granting Process

The credit policy problem is one of selecting the credit analysis method that maximizes the NPV. We begin by dividing loans into two categories:

1 *Good* loans
2 *Loss* loans

A *good loan* is defined as one that is repaid as agreed, while a *loss loan* is defined as one that is not repaid as agreed. Note also that applicants can be defined as good and loss, as well: *good applicants* would repay as agreed if granted a loan and *loss applicants* would default if granted a loan. When the borrower defaults, the lender does not receive full repayment of principal and interest and incurs unusually large collection expenses. (Collection procedures are discussed in a later section of this chapter.) The assumption of only two types of loans, good and loss, is convenient for analysis and reasonably realistic for most consumer and certain commercial loans.

Information needed to compute net present value for a credit selection method is summarized in the following list:

Net present values for good and loss loans
Number of good and loss loans
Cost of attracting applicants
Cost of analyzing applicants

In the next section, net present values for good and loss loans are estimated. Then, the number of good and loss loans selected from a given set of applicants is estimated.[3] Combined with the cost of attracting and analyzing applicants, the overall net present values of several methods is computed and compared to find the one that maximizes shareholder wealth.

NPV Computation

Net present values (NPV) for good and loss loans depend on cash inflows from principal and interest, cash outflows for expenses and income taxes, and the cost of funds. By definition, principal and interest are received in full with normal collection and accounting expenses. On the other hand, partial principal and interest are received and unusually large collection expenses are incurred

---

[3] Rejected applicants can be ignored without loss of analytical power, because this analysis implicitly solves a profit maximization function that is the dual of a minimization function using rejection rates. See Edmister and Schlarbaum (1974).

for loss loans. Thus, different cash flows are expected for good and for loss loans.

By discounting expected cash flows (funds dispersed to the borrower, loan repayments, and expenses), net present values for good loans (NPV$_g$) and loss loans (NPV$_1$) are computed. The discount rate is the cost of funds invested in the loan portfolio. This rate may be the same or, more likely, different from the intermediary's overall cost of capital. Of course, the after-tax rate is used because cash flows are net of taxes.

Example NPV Calculation

Consumer Loan Example For example, based on previous experience with similar consumer loans, we collect the critical information shown in Table 16-2. Note that all three payments are expected for the good loan, whereas only two payments are anticipated for a loss loan.

Based on the expected characteristics of loans to be granted, net present values for good loans and loss loans are computed in Table 16-2 in the following manner.

Loan disbursement ($10,000) and repayments in equal amounts ($10,000 times 0.4307 = $4307) are cash transactions.

Interest income is computed as the loan balance from the previous period times the interest rate (e.g., $1400 = 0.14 \times $10,000).

Principal payment is the difference between payments and interest income (e.g., $2907 = $4307 − $1400). Loan balance is reduced by the amount of principal payments (e.g., $7093 = $10,000 − $2907).

Collection expense is estimated for each loan payment (e.g., $25).

Income taxes reduce cash flow by the tax rate times the difference between interest income and collection expense. ($633 = 0.46 ($1400 − $25))

Net cash flow is calculated as the payment less cash expenses of collection and taxes (e.g., .$3650 = $4307 − $25 − $633).

Discount factor is the "present value of a future amount" for the after-tax cost of funds interest rate (e.g., 0.9488 = 1/(1 + (1 − 0.46) 0.10)).

Present value is the product of net cash flow and the discount factor, and *net present value* is the sum of present values for all items (e.g., $376 = −$10,000 +$3463 + $3454 + $3459).

Rounding occasionally causes small errors in the totals shown, because the totals were computed without rounding intermediate values to integers. When computing these values with a calculator, carry at least four significant digits through the problem to produce a reasonably accurate dollar result.

The NPV$_g$ of $376 is the net present value of attracting and granting a loan to one applicant who repays as agreed. Similarly, the NPV$_b$ of −$1368 represents the net present loss of disbursing funds to an applicant who defaults on the loan.

TABLE 16-2
CONSUMER LOAN CHARACTERISTICS

Loan Amount	$10,000
Maturity, years	3
Loan interest rate	14.00%
Pre-tax cost of funds	10.00%
Normal loan collection expense	$25
Loss loan collection expense	$500
Loss loan recovery amount	$1,000
Income tax rate	46.00%
Payment factor (PAY from Appendix B)	0.4307

Good loan

t	Transaction	Cash amount	Interest income	Principal payment	Loan balance	Collect expense	Income taxes
0	Loan disbursement	($10,000)			$10,000		
1	First payment	$4,307	$1,400	$2,907	$7,093	$25	$633
2	Second payment	$4,307	$993	$3,314	$3,778	$25	$445
3	Third payment	$4,307	$529	$3,778	$0	$25	$232

t	Transaction	Net cash flow	Discount factor	Present value
0	Loan disbursement	($10,000)	1.0000	($10,000)
1	First payment	$3,650	0.9488	$3,463
2	Second payment	$3,837	0.9002	$3,454
3	Third payment	$4,050	0.8540	$3,459
	Net Present Value (NPV)			$376

Loss loan

t	Transaction	Cash amount	Interest income	Principal payment	Loan balance	Collect expense	Income taxes
0	Loan disbursement	($10,000)			$10,000		
1	First payment	$4,307	$1,400	$2,907	$7,093	$25	$633
2	Second payment	$4,307	$993	$3,314	$3,778	$25	$445
3	Recovery	$1,000	$529	$471	$3,307	$500	($1,508)

t	Transaction	Net cash flow	Discount factor	Present value
0	Loan disbursement	($10,000)	1.0000	($10,000)
1	First payment	$3,650	0.9488	$3,463
2	Second payment	$3,837	0.9002	$3,454
3	Recovery	$2,008	0.8540	$1,715
	Net Present Value (NPV)			($1,368)

Commercial Loan Example Although the detail and form of commercial loan profitability analyses differ widely, the following example illustrates the general type of analysis employed by bankers. Assume that a commercial customer requests a $500,000 loan for three years at 12 percent interest. Assume that funds for commercial lending are acquired at the pretax rate of 10 percent. What are the net present values (NPVs) for good and loss loans?

To find net present values for good and loss commercial loans, set up cash flow statements like those presented for consumer loans. The amount of the loan, $500,000, is disbursed at time zero. (See line 0, Table 16-3.) At the end of the year, the bank receives principal and interest, and pays for processing costs and taxes. (See line 1, Table 16-3.) For a loss (default) loan, only $90,000 is collected in period 3.

Net cash flow is computed by summing cash inflows and subtracting cash outflows for each line. Future cash flows are converted to present values by multiplying each cash flow times its discount factor, as shown for the consumer loan example. Summing the present values, we find the net present values for good (NPV_g) and loss (NPV_1) loans are $9528 and $-$48,430, respectively. Thus, the larger individual loan amounts for commercial as opposed to consumer banking increases the potential for gain and loss resulting from each decision. As will be seen later, these differences are important in selecting the best credit policy.

Total Net Present Value

Generally, the total NPV expected for a given credit analysis method depends on four key items:

1 NPV of good loans (positive): the number of good loans accepted times the NPV for each good loan
2 NPV of loss loans (negative): the number of loss applicants accepted times the NPV for each loss loan
3 Cost of analysis (negative): expense incurred in making the credit accept/reject decision for all applicants
4 Cost of attracting applicants (negative): expenses incurred in motivating persons, businesses, and governments to request credit from this lending institution

Thus, these items account for revenues and expenses of good loans, partial revenues and expenses of loss loans, cost of capital, cost of analyzing applicants, and the cost of attracting applicants. Next we estimate the number of good and loss loans that are expected for each selection method.

Number of Good and Bad Loans

Money lent to applicants is analogous to bets placed on horses—winning depends on the amount of the bet and the ability to pick winners. The smart

TABLE 16-3
COMMERCIAL LOAN CHARACTERISTICS

Loan Amount	$500,000
Maturity, years	3
Loan interest rate (fraction)	12.00%
Pre-tax cost of funds (fraction)	10.00%
Normal loan collection expense	$500
Loss loan collection expense	$8,000
Loss loan recovery amount	$90,000
Income tax rate	46.00%
Payment factor (PAY from Appendix B)	0.4163

Good loan

t	Transaction	Cash amount	Interest income	Principal payment	Loan balance	Collect expense	Income taxes
0	Grant loan	($500,000)			$500,000		
1	First payment	$208,174	$60,000	$148,174	$351,826	$500	$27,370
2	Second payment	$208,174	$42,219	$165,955	$185,870	$500	$19,191
3	Third payment	$208,174	$22,304	$185,870	$0	$500	$10,030

t		Net cash flow	Discount factor	Present value
0	Grant loan	($500,000)	1.0000	($500,000)
1	First payment	$180,304	0.9488	$171,067
2	Second payment	$188,484	0.9002	$169,665
3	Third payment	$197,644	0.8540	$168,796
	Net Present Value (NPV)			$9,528

Loss loan

t	Transaction	Cash amount	Interest income	Principal payment	Loan balance	Collect expense	Income taxes
0	Grant loan	($500,000)			$500,000		
1	First payment	$208,174	$60,000	$148,174	$351,826	$500	$27,370
2	Second payment	$208,174	$42,219	$165,955	$185,870	$500	$19,191
3	Recovery	$90,000	$22,304	$67,696	$118,174	$8,000	($47,780)

t		Net cash flow	Discount factor	Present value
0	Grant loan	($500,000)	1.0000	($500,000)
1	First payment	$180,304	0.9488	$171,067
2	Second payment	$188,484	0.9002	$169,665
3	Recovery	$129,780	0.8540	$110,838
	Net Present Value (NPV)			($48,430)

gambler looks for a tout who will tilt the odds in his or her favor. Similarly in lending, the smart banker looks for credit information and analysis methods that accurately accept and reject applicants, while controlling costs. Consider the following three situations:

1 Open season
2 Credit analysts
3 Numerical credit scoring

Consumer Loan Example

Open Season or No Analysis   Let us begin our evaluation by assuming that historical loan statistics are unavailable. For example, the institution may be entering an unknown market or evaluating an existing system as if it were an unknown market. Financial institutions face unknown consumer loan markets when they expand to a new geographical territory, introduce a new type of loan, or direct sales campaigns toward new markets. Usually past experience suggests what may be expected and management has an opinion or a subjective estimate of the quality of applicants in the prospective market. Such an opinion is termed a *prior belief*. For example, management may estimate, based on experience with 3-year auto loans, that 80 out of every 100 applicants will repay as agreed.

As will become evident in later analysis, the accuracy of prior beliefs regarding applicant quality is important in evaluating alternative credit analysis methodologies. One means of obtaining applicant information is to accept every twentieth applicant until 100 applicants are accepted. Suppose we grant credit with such an open season to the 100 applicants represented as the entire circle in Figure 16-4. Some time later the actual credit histories are examined, and eighty borrowers are observed to be good credits and twenty are found to be loss credits. Thus, the pie chart is divided into two pieces, one of eighty and

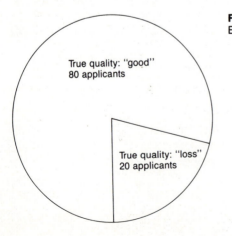

FIGURE 16-4
Example of 100 applicants divided by true quality.

True quality: "good"
80 applicants

True quality: "loss"
20 applicants

the other of twenty applicants, based on known historical experience. Next, we will compute the profit/loss for the case where open season is selected as a decision approach.

NPV for Open Season   By granting credit to all applicants, eighty good and twenty loss credits would be granted. The total NPV from good credits would be $30,080 (80 at $376) and NPV from loss credits would be −$27,3609 (20 at −$1,368); acceptance numbers and NPV values are shown in panel A of Table 16-4. The cost of analysis is zero, because no analysis is performed and the cost of attracting applicants is $14,000 by assumption. In summing the three row totals, we find total net present value of −$11,280. Thus, the open-season credit method is expected to *decrease* the wealth of the financial institution by $11,280 Therefore, credit would not be granted with this method, except occasionally to obtain information about applicants.

TABLE 16-4
CONSUMER CREDIT EXAMPLE: CREDIT POLICY EVALUATION FOR CONSUMER LOAN

Number of applicants	100
Acceptance rate	75.00%
Applicant quality	80.00%
Applicant cost	$14,000
Credit-analyst cost	$10,000
Credit-analyst loss rate	4%
Credit-scoring cost	$3,000
Credit-scoring accurancy—good loans	80.00%
Credit-scoring accuracy—loss loans	80.00%
NPV of good loan	$376
NPV of loss loan	($1,368)

Panel A
Open season grouping of applicants

	True quality		
Decision	Good	Loss	Total
Accept	80	20	100
Reject			
Total	80	20	100

Open-season net present value summary

	Number of loans	NPV of each loan	Row total
NPV, good loans	80	$376	$30,080
NPV, loss loans	20	($1,368)	($27,360)
Cost of applicants			($14,000)
Total net present value (NPV)			($11,280)

TABLE 16-4 *(continued)*

Panel B
Credit analyst's grouping of applicants

Decision	True quality		Total
	Good	Loss	
Accept	72	3	75
Reject			—
Total			100

Credit analyst's net present value summary

	Number of loans	NPV of each loan	Row total
NPV, good loans	72	$376	$27,072
NPVl, loss loans	3	($1,368)	($4,114)
Cost of applicants			($14,000)
Cost of credit analyst			($10,000)
Total net present value (NPV)			($1,032)

Panel C
Credit scoring grouping of applicants

Decision	True quality		Total
	Good	Loss	
Accept	64	4	
Reject		16	
Total	80	20	100

Credit scoring net present value summary

	Number of loans	NPV of each loan	Row total
NPVg, good loans	64	$376	$24,064
NPVl, loss loans	4	($1,368)	($5,472)
Cost of applicants			($14,000)
Cost of credit scoring			($3000)
Total net present value (NPV)			$1,592

Panel D
Summary of alternative credit selection policies

	Open season	Credit analyst	Credit scoring
Total net present value	($11,280)	($1,032)	$1,592

Historical Statistics for Credit Analysts   Virtually all institutions first use credit analysts before considering other credit methods.[4] By maintaining records on the number of applicants, the number of loans granted, and the numbers of good and loss loans, *management develops a historical record of analyst performance*.

Consider the 100 loan applicants discussed in the previous section. After performing a credit analysis, such as that described earlier, the analyst decides to accept seventy-five of the 100 applicants. (Accepted applicants are represented by the large section of the top circle in Figure 16-5.) The proportion of applicants accepted is termed the *acceptance rate*. In this example, the acceptance rate is 75 percent (75/100). Only rarely do financial institutions collect

[4] Most of the financial institutions listed in Chapter 1 employ credit analysts. Important exceptions are the securities brokers and dealers, who typically employ investment analysts.

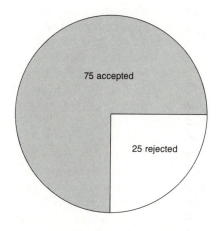

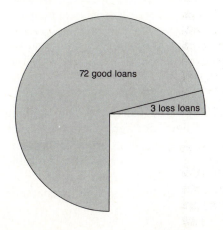

FIGURE 16-5
Example of 100 applicants divided according to analyst's decisions.

statistics on rejected loans, and consequently the "reject" group is ignored hereafter.

Of those applicants accepted, most repay their loans as agreed (good loans) while some default on their loans (loss loans). Actual loan results are used to subdivide applicants into good and loss loan categories, as reported in panel B of Table 16-4 and shown in Figure 16-5. The proportion of accepted applicants who default is termed the *loss rate* and is used to compute the number of applicants who are (1) accepted and loss credits and (2) accepted and good credits. Of the seventy-five accepted applicants, three fail to repay. Thus, the loss rate is 4 percent ($\frac{3}{75}$); alternatively, management may be told that the loss rate is 4 percent and compute that three of seventy-five credits would be losses. (Losses are represented in the bottom section of Figure 16-5 as a slice of the accepted section.)

Net Present Value (NPV) for Credit Analyst   As shown in Table 16-4, panel B, the number of good and loss loans accepted and the NPV of each are multiplied to find NPVs of good and loss loans. In adding the cost of analysis and applicants to net loan returns, the total NPV of $-\$1032$ is computed. Thus, the expected *decrease* in wealth when loans are granted with credit analysts is $1032. By comparing the total NPVs of the open-season and credit-analyst methods, we conclude that credit analysts are clearly better but not acceptably good. The *negative* total NPV for credit analysts means that granting credit is unprofitable under this method. Before quitting we should consider one more method of credit analysis—numerical credit scoring.

Statistics for Numerical Credit Scoring   Numerical credit scoring is often considered as an alternative to credit analysts, in which case statistics generated in the process of developing the scoring model are used to compare it with other methods. What statistics are available for credit scoring models? Review Figure 16-3 and note that the "accept" area under the curve covers a portion of the loss and good credits, indicating that only some of the good credits are correctly accepted and that some of loss credits are incorrectly accepted by the function. Again, the rejected applicants are ignored for reasons stated earlier. Thus, *the important statistics are the proportion of good credits accepted by the credit scoring analysis and the proportion of loss credits accepted by the credit scoring analysis.* These ratios are computed from test samples of previous applicants.

For example, consider a sample of 100 applicants, of which eighty repay (good) and twenty do not repay (loss) according to the loan terms. The grouping is reported in panel C of Table 16-4 ("Total" line) and represented in Figure 16-6 (left-hand circle). Of the eighty good credits, sixty-four are accepted; and of the twenty loss credits, four are accepted. See the "Accept" line in Table 16-4 and the "Accept" piece of pie in Figure 16-6. Also, note that the good-credit acceptance rate is 80 percent ($\frac{64}{80}$) and that the loss-credit acceptance rate is 20 percent ($\frac{4}{20}$).

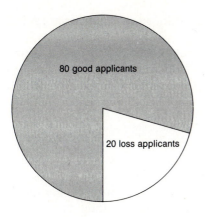

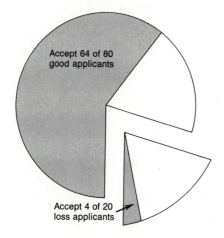

FIGURE 16-6
Example of 100 applicants divided first by true
quality and then by analyst's decision.

Using the acceptance and applicant quality rates, the number of good and loss loans that would be accepted is computed. In this example 80 percent of the applicants would be good credits. Assuming that 100 applications are received, then eighty would be "Good" and twenty would be "Loss" credits. (See panel C, Table 16-4, "Total" line.) Further, if the acceptance rates are 80 percent for good applicants and 20 percent for loss applicants, then sixty-four good applicants (80 percent times 80 applicants) and four loss applicants (20 percent times 20 applicants) are accepted. (See "Accept" line in Table 16-4.) In review, the computation sequence for the number of good and loss loans granted by the analyst is as follows:

1 The *quality ratio* divides applicants into total good (eighty) and loss (twenty) groups.

2 The *accuracy ratios* estimates number of good loans accepted (sixty-four) and loss loans rejected (sixteen).

3 The difference between *total* loss applicants (twenty) and *rejected* loss applicants (sixteen) is the number of accepted loss loans (four).

NPV for Numerical Credit Scoring   Similarly, NPV is computed for credit scoring by combining the number of accepted good and loss loans with NPVs for good and loss loans. The computations are summarized in panel C of Table 16-4. Total NPV for numerical credit scoring is $1592, an amount greater than the open season NPV ($-$11,280) and the credit analyst's NPV ($-$1032). Thus, we conclude that the function is superior to both the open-season and analyst methods. Further, the only method that produces a profit under these conditions is credit scoring: clearly the wealth maximizing method under these conditions is credit scoring.

Commercial Loan Example

Next, consider selecting a credit selection method for the commercial loan described earlier. (See Table 16-3). The credit policy may differ for commercial and consumer loans, because the policy variables are vastly different. Compared with consumer loans, commercial loan NPVs are larger, analytical costs are higher, applicant quality is more variable, and applicant marketing costs are greater. For example, see the scenario outlined in Table 16-5. Attracting 100 applicants is expected to cost $15,000 before analysis is conducted. If credit analysts are employed, an additional $300,000 will be spent; if a credit scoring method is adopted, the analysis cost will be $100,000. Analysts are expected to have an acceptance rate of 60 percent and a loss rate of 3 percent. The credit scoring method is 75 percent accurate on both good and loss applicants. The applicant quality is believed to be 65 percent, a relatively low quality resulting from an aggressive marketing effort aimed at new businesses. What is the optimal credit analysis method?

Open Season   Of the 100 applicants, sixty-five would be good (65 percent of applicants are believed to be good by assumption) and thirty-five would be losses. (See panel A, Table 16-5.) After combining the good and loss loan numbers with revenues and costs in the open-season net present value summary, we find this policy would generate a net present value of $-$1,090,730. This approach is like jumping naked into a snake pit.

Credit Analysis   The credit analysts are expected to accept sixty applicants of which an average 1.8 (3 percent times 60 percent) will be losses and the remainder (58.2) will be good loans. (See panel B, Table 16-5.) The loan numbers and costs, combined in the credit analysts' net present value summary, produce an expected total net present value of $152,356. The use of credit analysts is a feasible method. Before concluding that it is the optimal method, we consider credit scoring.

TABLE 16-5
CREDIT POLICY EVALUATION FOR COMMERCIAL LOANS

Number of applicants	100
Acceptance rate	60.00%
Applicant quality	65.00%
Applicant cost	$15,000
Credit-analyst cost	$300,000
Credit-analyst loss rate	3%
Credit-scoring cost	$100,000
Credit-scoring accuracy—good loans	75.00%
Credit-scoring accuracy—loss loans	75.00%
NPV of good loan	$9,528
NPV of loss loan	($48,430)

Panel A
Open season grouping of applicants

	True quality		
Decision	**Good**	**Loss**	**Total**
Accept	65	35	100
Reject			
Total	65	35	100

Open-season net present value summary

	Number of loans	**NPV of each loan**	**Row total**
NPVg, good loans	65	$9,528	$619,320
NPVl, loss loans	35	($48,430)	($1,695,050)
Cost of applicants			($15,000)
Total net present value (NPV)			($1,090,730)

Panel B
Credit analyst's grouping of applicants

	True quality		
Decision	**Good**	**Loss**	**Total**
Accept	58.2	1.8	60
Reject			
Total			100

Credit analyst's net present value summary

	Number of loans	**NPV of each loan**	**Row total**
NPVg, good loans	58.2	$9,528	$554,530
NPVl, loss loans	1.8	($48,430)	($87,174)
Cost of applicants			($15,000)
Cost of credit analyst			($300,000)
Total net present value (NPV)			$152,356

TABLE 16-5 *(continued)*

<table>
<tr><th colspan="4">Panel C
Credit scoring grouping of applicants</th></tr>
<tr><th></th><th colspan="2">True quality</th><th></th></tr>
<tr><th>Decision</th><th>Good</th><th>Loss</th><th>Total</th></tr>
<tr><td>Accept</td><td>48.75</td><td>8.75</td><td></td></tr>
<tr><td>Reject</td><td></td><td>26.25</td><td></td></tr>
<tr><td>Total</td><td>65</td><td>35</td><td>100</td></tr>
</table>

<table>
<tr><th colspan="4">Credit scoring net present value summary</th></tr>
<tr><th></th><th>Number
of loans</th><th>NPV of
each loan</th><th>Row
total</th></tr>
<tr><td>NPVg, good loans</td><td>48.75</td><td>$9,528</td><td>$464,490</td></tr>
<tr><td>NPVl, loss loans</td><td>8.75</td><td>($48,430)</td><td>($423,763)</td></tr>
<tr><td>Cost of applicants</td><td></td><td></td><td>($15,000)</td></tr>
<tr><td>Cost of credit scoring</td><td></td><td></td><td>($100,000)</td></tr>
<tr><td>Total net present value (NPV)</td><td></td><td></td><td>($74,273)</td></tr>
</table>

<table>
<tr><th colspan="4">Panel D
Summary of alternative credit selection policies</th></tr>
<tr><th></th><th>Open
season</th><th>Credit
analyst</th><th>Credit
scoring</th></tr>
<tr><td>Total net present value</td><td>($1,090,730)</td><td>$152,356</td><td>($74,273)</td></tr>
</table>

Credit Scoring   The credit-scoring method accepts 48.75 percent (75 percent of 65 percent) of the good and rejects 26.25 (75 percent of 35) of the loss applicants; it accepts 8.75 (35 − 24.5) loss loans. Combining accepted loan numbers and net present values in the credit-scoring net present value summary, we compute total net present values for this policy to be −$74,273. Thus, the credit-scoring method is infeasible. We conclude that the optimal method for commercial lending under these conditions is to hire credit analysts.

COLLECTION OF DELINQUENT AND DEFAULTED LOANS

Collections are the inevitable result of granting credit in an uncertain world; they ensue from insufficient credit analysis, faulty reasoning, and future circumstances unknown at the outset. Once we adjust our credit-analysis and granting policy, the institution must accept problem and loss loans as part of the overall credit function. The price paid for erroneous credit-granting decisions may be reduced, however, by alert and consistent management of the collection process. Good collection policies are carried out as a prompt, regular, and systematic effort.

The collection process begins when the borrower is sinking or sailing away, so that the first response should be made quickly. Collection efforts for poor credit should begin within 5 to 15 days after the payment is delinquent, while collection efforts for good customers may be delayed 30 to 60 days. Once the effort is started, regular inquiries are continued to remind the delinquent account of the money due and to impress upon him or her the intent to pursue the claim without fail. Delinquent accounts are gradually pressured until payment is received or the account is written off. The effect of each step is reinforced by the next step, as we move from friendly reminders to the formality of civil and criminal complaints in a court of law. The most common actions taken are listed as follows in the order of increasing severity:

1 Duplicate statements of account
2 Notices and reminders of past due account
3 Collection letters
4 Telephone calls
5 Dunning telegraph wire and registered letters
6 Personal visits by lender
7 Legal suit

The Fair Debt Collection Practices Act (1978) protects consumers by prohibiting abusive practices by debt collectors. The act covers collection of any debt incurred for personal, family, or household purposes; however, it does not apply to banks, other lenders, or businesses that collect their own accounts, using their own names. Under the act the collector may make reasonable efforts to communicate with a debtor but may not contact a debtor at an inconvenient or unusual time, an inconvenient place, at the debtor's place of employment if the employer prohibits such contact, or directly if represented by an attorney. Further, the law prohibits harassing, oppressing, or abusive conduct in connection with debt collection.

SUMMARY

The approach taken to credit policy selection and analysis presented in this chapter is analogous to a capital budgeting decision. The net present values computed for credit decisions require the investment of funds in loans, expenditures for servicing costs, and payment of taxes. Total net present value for various credit policies consist of the positive net present values contributed by good loans and negative net present values caused by loss loans, cost of analysis, and cost of applicants. Taken together in present value terms, these factors provide estimates of net changes in (stockholder) wealth which would result from various credit-analysis methods applied to the financial institution's loan market.

The three methods of credit solution are:

• Open season
• Credit analyst
• Credit scoring

Experience with each method provides critical information for credit policy evaluation. Open season provides an excellent estimate of applicant quality. Credit analysts generate observable acceptance rates and loan loss rates. Credit-scoring development provides credit function accuracy probabilities for good and loss loan applicants. Past experiences with two or three selection methods with expected future applicant volume and quality are combined to estimate the number of good and loss loans that will be granted. Good loans have positive and loss loans have negative net present values. By multiplying the number and net present values of good and loss loans together and subtracting applicant and analysis costs, the total net present value of each method is estimated. The method with the highest estimated net present value is preferred, in general, because it maximizes shareholders wealth.

The practice of credit analysis and the management of the credit function is complicated by changing market conditions, imperfect information, and personnel and organizational management problems. Obviously this chapter could not thoroughly treat all of the ramifications of credit policy, but has concentrated on basic principles. Interested students are encouraged to pursue this important facet of financial institutions management through further reading (see Selected References) and practice.

TERMS

credit policy	acceptance rate
default risk	numerical credit scoring
credit process	open season
credit analyst	net present value (NPV)
risk analysis	loan disbursement
profitability analysis	interest income
character capacity	principal payments
capital	net cash flow
conditions	discount factor

QUESTIONS

1 Why is it expensive to train credit analysts in the traditional methods?
2 Why is character given more emphasis than capital, capacity, and conditions by credit analysts?
3 Who pays for delinquent and defaulted loans? What would be the effect on loan interest rates of requiring financial institutions to lend to high-risk groups?
4 Assuming that credit analysts make errors in assessing the credit worthiness of applicants, how would you evaluate the ability of an analyst to grant loans? What would be the problems with comparing the performances of analysts located in different markets?
5 National Savings and Loan would like to know the net present value of making auto loans. It expects the average loan of $12,000 to yield a 14 percent interest over a period of 3 years. The savings and loan is in the 40 percent income tax bracket; it pays

10 percent (before taxes) for its funds and spends $15 to collect each payment. Loans usually fail after 1 year, and then National usually spends $1000 in unusual collection expenses and recovers $2000 of principal. (Assume that the loan is repaid in three equal installment payments at the end of the year.)

6 What is the net present value for a credit-scoring function approach for the following situtation?

  a 5000 loan applicants.

  b 90 percent of all applicants would repay their debt on time.

  c Net present value of good loans is $64 and net present value for loss loans is $289.

  d The credit-scoring function correctly classifies good loans 87 percent of the time and loss loans 86 percent of the time.

  e The credit-scoring method costs $50,000 and the other expenses total $30,000.

7 The Consumer Loan Department at Gotham Bank now spends $1000 to attract 100 applicants for automobile loans. The records show that analysts accept 75 percent of the applicants they review. Also, the bank estimates that the after-tax cost of this analysis approach is $2000. The bank's loss record is 4 percent of loans granted. The applicants are regarded as high quality, and open-season research indicates that 80 percent of everyone applying would repay if granted credit. Generally, those who repay generate a net present value of $376 whereas those who do not repay in full cause a net loss of $1368 in present value terms.

8 You are evaluating a proposal to change the credit-granting process to a credit-scoring system. The system would cost about $1000. The best estimate of its accuracy shows that it would correctly identify good loan applicants in 80 percent of the cases and bad (loss loan) applicants in 80 percent of the cases.

Calculate and compare the expected total net present values of all possible approaches.

9 (Comprehensive problem). Evaluate with three methods of credit analysis, given the following information:

Expected loan characteristics

Loan amount	$10,000
Maturity, years	3
Loan interest rate (fraction)	12.00%
Pretax cost of funds (fraction)	10.00%
Normal loan collection expense	$10
Loss loan collection expense (year 3)	$1,000
Loss loan recovery amount (year 3)	$1,000
Income tax rate	46.00%
Number of applicants	1000
Acceptance rate	70.00%
Applicant quality	80.00%
Applicant cost	$15,000
Credit analyst cost	$50,000
Credit analyst loss rate	5%
Credit scoring cost	$40,000
Credit scoring accuracy—good loans	85.00%
Credit scoring accuracy—loss loans	85.00%

SELECTED REFERENCES

Altman, Edward I.: "Financial Ratios, Discriminant Analysis and the Prediction of Corporate Bankruptcy," *Journal of Finance*, September 1968, pp. 589–609.

Carleton, Willard T., and Eugene M. Lerner: "Statistical Credit Scoring of Municipal Bond," *Journal of Money, Credit and Banking*, November 1969, pp. 750–764.

Cole, Robert H.: *Consumer and Commercial Credit Management*, 4th ed., Richard D. Irwin, Homewood, Ill., 1972.

Cooley, P. L.: "Bayesian and Cost Considerations for Optimal Classification with Discriminant Analysis," *Journal of Risk and Insurance*, June 1975, pp. 277–287.

Deshmukh, Sudhakar D., Stuart I. Greenbaum, and George Kanatas; "Lending Policies of Financial Intermediaries Facing Credit and Funding Risk," *Journal of Finance*, June 1983, pp. 873–886.

Edelstein, R. H.: "Improving the Selection of Credit Risks: An Analysis of a Commercial Bank Minority Lending Program," *Journal of Finance*, March 1975, pp. 37–56.

Edmister, Robert O.: Financial Ratios and Credit Scoring for Small Business Loans," *Journal of Commercial Bank Lending*, September 1971, pp. 10–23.

Edmister, Robert O.: "An Empirical Test of Financial Ratio Analysis for Small Business Failure Prediction," *Journal of Financial and Quantitative Analysis*, March 1972, pp. 1477–1493.

Edmister, Robert O., and Gary G. Schlarbaum: "Credit Policy in Lending Institutions," *Journal of Financial and Quantitative Analysis*, June 1974, pp. 335–356.

Hoeven, James A., "Predicting Default of Small Business Loans," *Journal of Commercial Bank Lending*, April 1979, pp. 47–60.

Long, Michael S.: "Effect of Lending Rate Ceilings and Money Costs on Extensions of Consumer Credit," *Journal of Bank Research*, Autumn 1976, pp. 206–212.

Mehta, Dileep: "The Formulation of Credit Policy Models," *Management Science*, October 1968, pp. 30–50.

Miller, Donald E., and Donald B. Relkin: *Improving Credit Practice*, American Management Association, New York, 1971.

Morton, T. G.: "A Comparative Analysis of Moody's and Standard and Poor's Municipal Bond Ratings," *Review of Business and Economics Research*, Winter 1975–1976, pp. 74–81.

Prochnow, Herbert V.: *Bank Credit*, Harper & Row, New York, 1981.

Rakes, G. K.: "A Numerical Credit Evaluation Model for Residential Mortgages," *Quarterly Review of Economics and Business*, Autumn 1973, pp. 73–84.

Sandor, R. L., and H. B. Sosin: "The Determinants of Mortgage Risk Premiums: A Case Study of the Portfolio of a Savings and Loan Association," *Journal of Business*, January 1975, pp. 27–38.

Smith, J. F.: "The Equal Credit Opportunity Act of 1974: A Cost Benefit Analysis," *Journal of Finance*, May 1977, p. 609.

Von Furstenberg, George M.: "Default Risk on FHA-Insured Home Mortgages as a Function of the Terms of Financing: A Quantitative Analysis," *Journal of Finance*, June 1969, pp. 459–477.

Webb, Bruce G.: "Borrower Risk under Alternative Mortgage Instruments," *Journal of Finance*, March 1982, pp. 169–183.

Winters, A. J.: "Banker Perceptions of Unaudited Financial Statements," *CPA*, August 1975, pp. 29–33.

CHAPTER 17

OPERATING ECONOMIES OF SCALE

Producing financial services requires substantial operating costs for personnel, facilities, and equipment. An important issue for both managers and regulators is the relationship between the scale of operations and the cost of operations. *Operating economies of scale* occur when the cost of operations increases proportionately less than the scale of operations. This chapter discusses the definition and application of operating economies of scale to financial institutions management.

OPERATING COST FUNCTION

The operating cost function relates the cost of producing financial services to the quantity of output, quality of output, price differences, and other factors. The following variables are typically specified in cost functions:

1 Total cost per month, quarter, or year, C
2 Output quantity per period, Q
3 Output quality, such as branch offices, special services, etc., H
4 Prices of factors, organizational structure, and management, P
5 Other factors, U

The general cost function is formulated as a Cobb-Douglas relationship to provide unbiased estimates of scale economies (for firms attempting to minimize costs at a given level of output). The common form of a cost function is:

$$C = b_0 Q^{b_1} H^{b_2} P^{b_3} U^{b_4} \tag{17-1}$$

where b_0, b_1, b_2, b_3, and b_4 are constant parameters. That is, cost is the product of volume, output quality, factor prices, and unspecified factors.[1]

Cost Function Example

A simple cost function is presented as an example here. We assume that operating costs (C) vary directly with the deposit quantity (Q), but that increases in deposit level cause a less than proportionate increase in operating costs, (Note: operating costs are the total dollar costs, unlike average operating costs, which are rates.) Assuming that all other factors are constant, we obtain the following:

$$C = b_0 Q^{b_1} \qquad (17\text{-}2)$$

That is, operating cost is equal to a constant times deposits raised to the b_1 power. The parameter b_1 indicates the degree of scale economies. When b_1 is less than 1, then scale economies exist.

The operating cost function depends upon the value of the parameters b_0 and b_1; for example, b_0 may be 0.0451 and b_1 may be 0.88. For any given level of deposits, the operating cost can be computed. Consider the cost at the $20 million level:

$$C = 0.0451(20)^{0.88}$$
$$= \$0.630 \text{ million}$$

Operating cost at the $20 million level of deposits is found to be $0.630 million or $630,000. (The computation is performed with a calculator having the function x^y.)

Furthermore, we know that economies of scale exist, because the coefficient b_1 is less than 1. Increases in deposits will cause less than proportional increases in operating costs. To prove this point, we compute C for a larger deposit level, such as $40 million:

$$C = 0.0451(40)^{0.88}$$
$$= \$1.159 \text{ million}$$

Operating costs at the $40 million level of deposits are computed to be $1.159 million. The operating costs at the $20 and $40 million levels are compared by computing the average operating cost (AC_0) at each level. Average operating costs are computed as follows:

---

[1] The Cobb-Douglas form restricts modeling to smooth, montonic functions. For a discussion of cost functions for financial institutions, see Benston (1972); Benston, Hanweck, and Humphrey (1982); and Murray and White (1983). The more recent papers suggest that translog cost functions represent the complex nature of institutional operations more precisely than a simple Cobb-Douglas model.

$20 Million Deposit Level $40 Million Deposit Level
$$AC_0 = C/Q \qquad\qquad AC_0 = C/Q$$
$$= 0.630/20 \qquad\qquad = 1.159/40$$
$$= 0.0315 \text{ or } 3.15\% \qquad = 0.0290 \text{ or } 2.90\%$$

We find that average operating cost declines from 3.15 to 2.90 percent, as deposits increase from $20 and $40 million (computed with the function $C = 0.0301\, Q^{0.88}$). This example of scale economies is typical of institutions such as commercial banks, savings and loans, and credit unions. Of course, the scale economies achieved by any particular institution depend upon its unique financial market, labor supply, and technology level.

COST FUNCTION ILLUSTRATIONS

A: Imperfect Deposit and Perfect Loan Markets

The operation of a depository intermediary that sells (supplies) savings deposits in a local market and buys (demands) loans in the national money market is illustrated here. At this point in the analysis, the objective to determine the optimal deposit level, given the deposit market, loan market, and operating cost function for this intermediary.

Operating Scale Economies By assumption, this intermediary achieves 12 percent economies of scale through personnel efficiencies and lower average equipment costs. Declining operating costs are illustrated in frame b, Figure 17-1.

Imperfect Deposit Market In its local market, time deposits are differentiated by the size, reputation, and location of the intermediary. Although important, the deposit interest rate is only one of many factors considered by depositors when selecting an intermediary; other factors are promotion, information, place, and contract terms. Other things remaining equal, the intermediary must pay a higher rate of interest to increase the quantity of deposits; the relationship between deposits and interest rates is positive, as shown in frame a, Figures 17-1.

Perfect Loan Market In the national loan market, this intermediary is one of many bidding for obviously high-quality loans. Bids are accepted by the borrowers when they are at or below the prevailing market interest rates; otherwise they are rejected. Thus, the intermediary finds that the loan interest rate is the same, regardless of the amount to be lent. The loan demand curve is drawn as a horizontal line in frame a, Figure 17-1; marginal revenue (MR) equals average revenue (AR), for all quantities.

Optimal Quantity What is the optimal deposit level for this intermediary? In general, the intermediary achieves maximum profits at the quantity Q^*

Frame a. Supply curve and deposit demand curve for Treasury bills

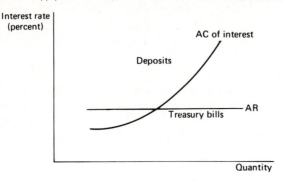

Frame b. Cost function for deposits

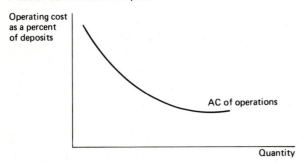

Frame c. Combined cost and revenue curves

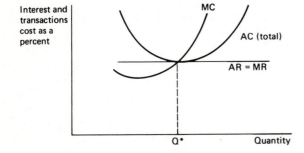

FIGURE 17-1
Average cost (AC), marginal
cost (MC), average revenue
(AR), and marginal revenue
(MR) for financial intermediary.

where marginal revenue (*MR*) is greater than or equal to marginal cost (*MC*).
(See frame c, Figure 17-1.) That is, management of the intermediary spends
money on personnel, facilities, and promotion up to the point where incremental expenditures are less than or equal to the marginal spread between loans and
deposits.

The graphic example presented earlier is more explicitly described with a
numerical example in this section. The Treasury bill investment opportunities
are represented with a constant revenue of 10 percent, regardless of the amount

TABLE 17-1
COST FUNCTION ILLUSTRATION A: IMPERFECT DEPOSIT AND PERFECT LOAN MARKETS
(AMOUNTS IN MILLIONS)

Account		Deposit level				
Item	Symbol	$10	$20	$30	$ 40	$50
Average revenue	AR	10.00%	10.00%	10.00%	10.00%	10.00%
Average interest cost	AC_i	5.95%	6.77%	7.00%	7.34%	7.62%
Average operating cost	AC_o	2.28%	2.10%	2.00%	1.93%	1.88%
Total average cost	TAC	8.23%	8.88%	9.00%	9.27%	9.50%
Average profit	AP	1.77%	1.12%	1.00%	0.63%	0.50%
Profit	P	$0.18	$0.22	$0.30	$0.25	$0.25

invested (see Table 17-1). The average deposit interest cost varies directly with the quantity of funds acquired, reflecting the imperfect deposit market within which the intermediary operates. To raise more funds from the sale of deposits, the intermediary must offer potential depositors a higher interest rate. Operating costs exhibit economies of scale, causing the average operating cost to decline as deposit volume increases. The average operating cost is inversely related to deposit volume and partially offsets the average interest cost, which is directly related to deposit volume.

To find the maximum profit level, average and total profits are computed from the revenue and cost information summarized in Table 17-1. The average profit (AP) is equal to the average revenue (AR) minus total average cost (TAC), as shown below:

$$AP = AR - TAC \qquad (17\text{-}3)$$

where total average cost is the sum of average interest cost (AC_i) and average operating cost (AC_0),

$$TAC = AC_i + AC_0 \qquad (17\text{-}4)$$

Average profit is the average rate of return (before taxes) earned on the deposit to Treasury bill intermediation function. We convert the average profit rate into profit amount (P) by multiplying average profit times the deposit level (D); this relationship is expressed as

$$P = AP(D) \qquad (17\text{-}5)$$

Profit (before taxes) is the dollar return earned by the intermediary in our example. Profit, average profit, and total average cost are presented in Table 17-1 for the financial intermediary example.

Profits from intermediations are maximized at the $30 million level of deposits, in this example. If the risk and regulatory constraints are assumed null or constant, the intermediary will choose to operate at the $30 million level, and maximize profits.

B: Imperfect Deposit and Imperfect Loan Markets

Now we evaluate a second example which illustrates an institution that both buys and sells securities in imperfect markets. (Our previous example dealt with a perfect asset and imperfect deposit market.) This would be an intermediary, such as a commercial bank, savings and loan, or credit union, which obtains funds by selling deposits and invests funds by making loans in its local market. The local loan market is assumed to be imperfect—the loan rate is a function of the loan level. As the intermediary attempts to attract more borrowers and make more loans, it finds that it must lower the loan rate. Thus, the relationship between loan level and interest rates is inverse.

Average revenue for this example is presented in Table 17-2 and is shown to decline from 12.28 percent at $10 million to 10.45 percent at $50 million of loans. Average operating cost is increased in this example from the previous example to reflect the greater cost of marketing and analyzing small local than large national loans. Average and dollar profit are calculated for our second example in the same manner as for the first example.

Note that the maximum profit level in this example is reached at the $20 million rather than the $30 million level of loans and deposits. The analysis of revenue, interest costs, and operating costs indicates that the size of this intermediary should be smaller than the size of the previous intermediary. This result illustrates an important point: the size of an intermediary depends on the characteristics of the financial market which the intermediary serves. Financial institutions management decisions are based on the joint analysis of the financial institution and the financial markets.

C: Perfect Deposit and Imperfect Loan Markets

In recent years the depositing public has become increasingly sensitive to interest rates as a result of the widely fluctuating rates. (Historical interest rates

TABLE 17-2
COST FUNCTION ILLUSTRATION B: IMPERFECT DEPOSIT AND IMPERFECT LOAN MARKETS (AMOUNTS IN MILLIONS)

Account		Deposit level				
Item	Symbol	$10	$20	$30	$40	$50
Average revenue	AR	12.28%	11.46%	11.00%	10.69%	10.45%
Average interest cost	AI	5.95%	6.77%	7.00%	7.34%	7.62%
Average operating cost	AOC	3.42%	3.15%	3.00%	2.90%	2.82%
Total average cost	TAC	9.37%	9.92%	10.00%	10.24%	10.44%
Average profit	AP	2.91%	1.54%	1.00%	.45%	.01%
Profit	P	$.29	$.31	$.30	$.18	$.01

were discussed in Chapter 3.) Spurred by the opportunity to earn greater returns without greater risk, the public invested heavily in money-market mutual funds, and drawing funds out of banks, savings and loans, and credit unions. In turn, banks, savings and loans, and credit unions created, based on authority provided in the 1980 and 1982 Banking Acts, a wide variety of interest-bearing checking and savings investments for households. The combination of greater interest sensitivity and investment alternatives means that households tend to move their funds more quickly in response to changes in risk and return opportunities than was the case historically.

Research indicates that banks drawing funds from large urban areas face a very interest-elastic deposit market. That is, small changes in deposit interest rate quotes cause large changes in deposit volume. Consequently, the bank ordinarily must pay interest rates similar to market interest rates to obtain funds. Can a depository intermediary exist under these conditions? What is the best size to maximize profit?

These questions can be answered by revising the revenue and cost values in the microeconomic model of a financial intermediary shown in Figure 17-1. Suppose that competition from money-market mutual funds and money-market securities forces the average interest cost to 7.00 percent, a deposit rate at the upper end of the optimum level for the imperfect market (Table 17-3). Obviously, the intermediary would prefer to pay the 6.77 percent interest rate associated with smaller size and greater dollar profit, but a 6.77 percent interest rate would attract zero deposits in the interest-sensitive market assumed in this example. On the other hand, the intermediary can issue any quantity of deposits it desires at the 7.00 percent interest rate, because the deposit market is perfectly interest elastic.

With this information we draw the deposit demand function as a horizontal, straight line at 7.00 percent. (See line AI in Table 17-3.) By using the same interest revenue and operating expense values assumed previously, average profit rates and dollar profits are computed for each deposit size level.

The greatest profit is now earned at the $40 million size where the average profit rate is 79 basic points. Compared with previous examples, this suggests a

TABLE 17-3
COST FUNCTION ILLUSTRATION C: PERFECT DEPOSIT AND IMPERFECT LOAN MARKETS (AMOUNTS IN MILLIONS)

Account		Deposit level				
Item	Symbol	10	20	30	40	50
Average revenue	AR	12.28%	11.46%	11.00%	10.69%	10.45%
Average interest cost	AI	7.00%	7.00%	7.00%	7.00%	7.00%
Average operating cost	AOC	3.42%	3.15%	3.00%	2.90%	2.82%
Total average cost	TAC	10.42%	10.15%	10.00%	9.90%	9.82%
Average profit	AP	1.86%	1.31%	1.00%	0.79%	0.63%
Dollar Profit	P	$0.19	$0.26	$0.30	$0.32	$0.31

larger institution operating size with a smaller profit percentage. This example is consistent with the events of the past few years—banks, insurance companies, securities brokers, and savings and loans have merged into large institutions that operate on a massive scale but often with reduced profit to asset percentages.

EMPIRICAL STUDIES OF SCALE ECONOMIES

Empirical studies of scale economies have been conducted for commercial banks and savings and loans. Results of these studies indicate the extent to which operating scale economies exist for many financial services.

Bank Economies of Scale

Bankers recognize the importance of knowing not only aggregate costs of operations but also functional area costs. Earlier in this chapter, the costs of the demand deposit and savings deposit functions were incorporated into the analysis of the total costs of deposit alternatives. Bank cost accounting information is utilized in a wide variety of bank management and regulatory decisions, and numerous methods are employed to gather and analyze cost data. One major system of cost accounting is the Functional Cost Analysis (FCA) Program sponsored by the Bank Relations Division of the district Federal Reserve Banks.

Banks voluntarily participate in the FCA program by gathering cost accounting information for each function. Salaries, wages, supplies, and other direct costs are assigned to these functions:

1 Demand deposits
2 Time deposits
3 Installment loans
4 Real estate loans
5 Business loans
6 Securities
7 Safe deposit
8 Trust

In large banks most direct costs are accounted for according to divisional lines corresponding to functions, and few costs are jointly determined. Small banks must allocate many costs because the same personnel perform several functions. Indirect costs, such as administration, business development, occupancy, and data processing, are reported separately by bank accountants. Each participating bank receives from the Federal Reserve an analysis of its operations and a comparison with similar banks. Thus, direct and indirect cost data for many functions are available to bankers who want a standard for comparison and to researchers studying bank operating costs.

The results of cost function studies are typified by the graph presented in Figure 17-2. The direct cost of demand deposit accounts is related to the num-

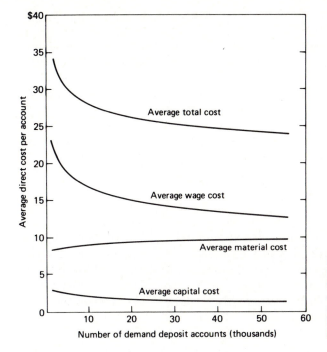

FIGURE 17-2
Relation between average wage, capital, and material cost, with the number of demand deposit accounts, annual basis, 1965. (*Source*: Bell and Murphy, 1968, p. 158.)

ber of accounts processed by a bank and disaggregated into capital, material, and wage factors.[2] Curves like those shown in Figure 17-2 are estimated for many functions.

Economies of scale are evident in most banking functions and for banks overall. Generally, a 10.0 percent increase in output at the average bank requires only a 9.3 percent increase in operating costs. Various cost studies provide estimates of economies of scale for particular functions, some of which are summarized as follows:

1 Demand deposits show economies of scale when computers are used, but not otherwise.

2 Time deposits exhibit economies of scale but to a smaller extent than banks overall.

3 Installment loans show large economies of scale.

4 Business loans are subject to economies of scale, except when on-premises computers are utilized.

---

[2] The Cobb-Douglas production function form ($C = b_0 Q^{b_1} H^{b_2} P^{b_3} U^{b_4}$) is transformed to a linear form for estimation. By taking the common logarithm of the equation and specifying the model with FCA accounts, Benston (1965) and Bell and Murphy (1968) obtained an equation that could be estimated with multiple regression. Data for Benston's (1965) classic study are for eighty to eighty-three Boston Federal Reserve District banks participating for the years 1959, 1960, and 1961. Bell and Murphy's (1968) study analyzes FCA statements of 210 to 283 banks in Boston, New York, and Philadelphia Federal Reserve Districts for the years 1963, 1964, and 1965.

5 Real estate loans are consistently subject to substantial economies of scale.

6 Scale economies are significant primarily for small banks and not significant for very large banks.

Furthermore, substantial scale economies are reaped as the average account size increases. Demand deposit costs increase only 3 to 4 percent when average balances increase 10 percent. Large-scale effects exist for all functions with respect to the size of the portfolio managed.

Savings and Loan Economies of Scale

Benston's (1972) study of the savings and loan industry covers 3159 of the 4332 insured associations. The savings and loan industry accounts for and reports total costs but does not account for costs by functional area. Consequently economies can be investigated only with respect to input factors, and costs cannot be separated between savings and lending functions. Output is measured as the number of loans serviced per year. The alternative specification of output, the number of savings accounts, was tested by Benston (1972), and similar results found.

Significant economies of scale are consistently evident in the savings and loan industry. Scale economies exist for salary and wage, occupancy, and other expenses. The overall elasticity of 0.92 for savings and loans implies that expenses rise 9.2 percent with each 10.0 percent increase in output. Saving and loan elasticities are very similar to bank elasticities. It appears that both banks and S & Ls are subject to the same economies of scale, particularly with respect to savings deposits and real estate loans. By any measure the cost functions of banks and savings and loan associations are strikingly similar. Like banks, savings and loans have a low elasticity of cost with respect to average size of loans (.46) and deposits (.73). Greater cost benefits occur for associations which increase the *dollar amount* of each savings account and loan rather than those that increase the *number* of accounts and loans.

SUMMARY

Operating economies of scale relate changes in the cost of operations relative to changes in the size of the intermediary, given output quality, factor prices, organizational structure, and management. When the costs of production change less than proportionately to the change in the level of production, then scale economies exist. The cost function specifies scale economies with an exponent of Q that is less than one.

Cost functions combined with deposit and loan market conditions determine optimal deposit and loan quantities for financial intermediaries. The optimal quantity sets marginal cost equal to marginal revenue, where marginal cost includes both interest and operating costs. As a result of differences in markets and production costs among intermediaries, the optimal quantity also differs among intermediaries. To determine the optimal size of its intermediary, management analyzes production and interest costs relative to loan opportunities. A more detailed description of the process of evaluating operating and market opportunities is presented in Chapter 20 in financial planning.

Empirical studies show that scale economies are small for deposit activities but often substantial for loan functions. Further, they show that scale economies are significant for the small- and medium-size banks but not necessarily important for large and very large banks. These findings must be regarded as tentative, however, due to measurement errors in allocating fixed costs to banking functions and to measuring financial service types of output. Thus, we tentatively conclude that large banks achieve operating economies in certain loan markets relative to similar banks but hasten to add that very large banks do not obtain smaller advantages over large banks. Therefore, we would expect that large and very large banks can compete on an equal cost basis in both deposit and loan markets and that all banks can compete on an equal basis in the deposit market.

TERMS

economies of scale
operating cost function
Cobb-Douglas cost function
functional cost analysis program

LIST OF EQUATIONS

$$C = f(Q, H, P, U)$$
$$C = b_0 Q^{b_1} H^{b_2} P^{b_3} U^{b_4}$$
$$C = b_0 Q^{b_1}$$

QUESTIONS

(Note: A calculator with an x^Y function is required.)

1 What is the optimal deposit level for XYZ Bank, if it believes that its cost and revenue structure is as follows?

Account	Deposit level (millions)				
	$300	$350	$400	$450	$500
Average revenue	9.0%	8.9%	8.8%	8.7%	8.6%
Average interest cost	4.5%	5.0%	5.5%	6.0%	7.0%
Average operating cost	5.0%	3.5%	2.8%	2.0%	1.5%

Average revenue declines as less desirable mortgages are accepted, while interest cost increases to attract more deposits.

2 What would be the operating costs for a financial institution with deposit quantity of $500, $1000, and $1500 million, if its operating cost function parameters are the following: $b_0 = 0.0727$ and $b_1 = 0.0902$

3 (Continuation of Question 2.) What would be the average operating costs for the financial institution in question? Describe the economies of scale, if any, shown in this problem.

4 A financial intermediary is analyzing its revenue and cost functions to determine its optimal size; for computational purposes, it is considering a size of $10, $20, $30, $40, or $50 million. From deposits and money-market sources, it can acquire funds in any quantity at the rate of 10 percent. These funds will be lent to businesses and individuals after a careful, confidential credit investigation. The cost of operating the institution, including credit investigations, is 2 percent of deposits at the $10 million level. Scale economies of 14 percent are expected each time the intermediary doubles in size. (*Hint:* Operating costs can be estimated with a standard Cobb-Douglas function in which the constant factor is 0.02 and an economy of scale the deposit exponent value is 0.86.) Because of the limited market area and reputation of the intermediary, increasing loan volume requires bidding lower loan rates. It is management's opinion that the following volume/rate schedule exists:

Volume	Rate
$10 million	13.31%
20	12.59
30	12.19
40	11.91
50	11.70

What is the profit rate on deposits and profit amount for each level of operations? What is the optimal level of operations with respect to maximum profits? To maximum rate of profits?

SELECTED REFERENCES

Auerbach, R.: "The Measurement of Economies of Scale: A Comment," *Journal of Business*, January 1976, pp. 60–61.

Bell, R. W., and N. B. Murphy: *Costs in Commercial Banking: A Quantitative Analysis of Bank Behavior and Its Relation to Bank Regulations*, Research Report No. 41, Federal Reserve Bank of Boston, 1968.

Benston, George J.: "Economies of Scale and Marginal Costs in Banking Operations," *National Banking Review*, June 1965, pp. 507–549.

Benston, George J.: "Economies of Scale and Financial Institutions," *Journal of Money, Credit and Banking*, May 1972, pp. 312–341.

Benston, George J., Gerald A. Hanweck, and David B. Humphrey: "Scale Economies in Banking," *Journal of Money, Credit and Banking*, November 1982, pp. 435–456.

"Cost of Operations and Economies of Scale in Savings and Loan Associations," *Study of the Savings and Loan Industry*, Federal Home Loan Bank Board, 1970, pp. 677–761.

Daniel, Donnie L., William A. Longbrake, and Neil B. Murphy: "The Effects of Technology on Bank Economies of Scale for Demand Deposits," *Journal of Finance*, March 1973, pp. 131–146.

Longbrake, William A.: "Computers and the Cost of Producing Banking Services: Planning and Control Considerations," *Journal of Bank Research*, Autumn 1973, pp. 194–202.

Murray, John D., and Robert W. White: "Economies of Scale and Economies of Scope in Multiproduct Financial Institutions: A Study of British Columbia Credit Unions," *Journal of Finance*, June 1983, pp. 887–902.

Smith, Paul F.: *Money and Financial Intermediation*, Prentice-Hall, Englewood Cliffs, N.J., 1978.

CHAPTER 18

LIQUIDITY POLICY

Liquidity policy is the plan for meeting the funding needs of the financial institution. Funds may be needed tomorrow, next week, or next year to meet promises to depositors, insured persons, borrowers, and other customers. When the promises come due, the financial institution must make payment in cash or equivalent funds; a default on its commitment nearly always causes a punishing response. Unlike a grocery store, which may have a "stock-out" of peanuts or frozen orange juice, a financial institution cannot run out of money needed to meet its customers' claims.

The default may be relatively minor, such as failing to lend to a business after having made verbal assurances that "the money will be there when you need it." The businessperson is angered and the intermediary's reputation for dependability is tarnished, but the intermediary survives. On the other hand, the default is serious if the institution cannot meet a legal commitment. The penalty for serious default is bankruptcy or an equivalent reorganization. Frequently, defaults lead to institutional liquidation or merger, management dismissal, board of director resignations, and stock value depression.

Thus, severe penalties provide strong motivation for management to plan adequately for future funding needs. Over the past two centuries, many concepts and ideas about liquidity planning have been developed. Today's liquidity planning is a hybrid of such concepts, subject to limitations imposed by law and changing with the advance of information technology.

FOUR CONCEPTS OF LIQUIDITY

As commercial banking is the oldest financial institution, predating savings and loans, insurance companies, and pension funds, the historical approaches were developed primarily for banking. However, the concepts underlying these approaches apply equally well to all financial institutions. Four important concepts are:

Commercial loan theory
Shiftability theory
Anticipated-income theory
Liabilities management

The first three theories are asset-based approaches and the last is a liability-based approach. The theories are summarized in Table 18-1 and discussed in the following sections.

Commercial Loan Theory

The accepted theory for nearly two centuries (until 1920) was the commercial loan theory. Under the commercial loan theory, the ideal assets are short-term, self-liquidating loans granted for working capital purposes. Short-term loans are considered the only type of asset appropriate for banks because banks raise

TABLE 18-1
SUMMARY OF BANK LIQUIDITY THEORIES THROUGH HISTORY

Commercial loan 18th–19th centuries (until 1920)	Under the traditional commercial loan theory, the ideal assets are short-term, self-liquidating loans granted for working capital purposes. These assets are considered the only type appropriate for banks because of their large proportion of demand and near-demand liabilities. In the event that deposits decrease, the maturing loans are not renewed and the funds are applied to depositors' withdrawals.
Shiftability theory 1920s	Broadened security markets in the 1920s and the desire of banks to make long-term loans fostered this theory. By holding secondary reserves composed of relatively short-term, high-grade, readily marketable securities, the bank satisfies its liquidity needs. Secondary reserves can be sold (shifted) without loss to meet deposit outflows. Given good quality and marketable securities, the bank can make such other loans as desired without respect to liquidity or maturity.
Anticipated-income theory 1940s	A growing proportion of amortized loans and the development of realistic repayment schedules for woking capital loans provided the basis for forecasting flows of funds. The massive flow of funds could be committed to reserve deficiencies or new loan demand, as circumstances dictated.
Liabilities-management theory 1960s	Rapidly developed and accepted by medium- and large-size banks, this theory holds that liquidity can be obtained through the issuance of liabilities rather than the sale of assets. Banks in need of funds can borrow Federal funds, issue negotiable certificates of deposit, sell consumer-type certificates of deposits, borrow from the Federal Reserve, issue capital notes and common stock, and raise funds in the Eurodollar market.

their capital with demand or near-demand commitments. If deposits decrease, maturing loans can be used to meet deposit withdrawals.

The commercial loan theory, however, suffered from a number of serious drawbacks. From the viewpoint of the economy as a whole, the practice of the commercial loan theory tended to accentuate economic collapse by breaking the cash-flow cycle of commerce and industry. Consider, for example, the case of a wheat farmer in the Midwest. In the spring he would borrow money to buy seeds, till the soil, and plant his crops. He anticipated repaying the loan by selling the crop at the end of the summer. He would harvest his crop and take it to a local mill. The miller would buy his crop with the intention of reselling it to the granary, which would ship the grain to Chicago. To finance his operation, the granary operator would borrow from the bank for 90 to 180 days. Under normal economic conditions the bank would plan to loan the money to the granary operator who in turn would buy the wheat from the farmer. In turn, the farmer would then repay the bank loan and deposit whatever profit he might have in the bank as well. The bank would use the farmer's loan repayment to finance the granary until the wheat was eventually sold later that year.

However, under adverse economic conditions, when the bank felt that it needed funds to meet depositor withdrawals, the bank would not advance funds to the granary. Of course, then the granary could not pay the farmers for their wheat crop, and the farmers could not repay their loans to the bank. The bank would be forced to foreclose on farm mortgages and liquidate the farm properties. The farmers were displaced from their means of livelihood, production of wheat was reduced, and the banks suffered loan losses. The commercial loan theory was an illusion. From the viewpoint of the community, the loan was outstanding throughout the period beginning with the purchase of the seed in the spring through the time when the grain was ultimately sold to distant converters. The bank was making not only short-term loans to individuals but also a long-term loan to the community. Economic collapse, bank robberies, and other events were accentuated by this myopic view of bank liquidity management.

Shiftability Theory

The commercial loan theory persisted for nearly two centuries, and only the advent of a well-organized secondary securities market in the 1920s permitted banks to consider an alternative means of meeting liquidity requirements. Bank managers saw that they could maintain liquidity reserves by holding a portfolio of relatively short-term, high-grade, readily marketable securities. The management strategy was clear; with a buffer of very liquid investments, the bank could enter into a more profitable long-term loan market. Given good-quality liquid reserves, the bank could make such other loans as desired without respect to liquidity or maturity consideration. If needed, the reserves could be sold (shifted) without loss to meet cash demand. Elements of the shiftability theory are evident in today's approaches to bank liquidity management, but shiftability theory had a lifespan of less than a decade. Because of the collapse of the securities market in the depression of the 1930s, the unprecedented outflow of deposits, and the restructuring of long-term loans, the shiftability theory was put aside. Bankers returned to a conservative loan posture and abandoned the aggressive financial structuring that had been the trend in the 1920s.

Anticipated-Income Theory

Following the economic collapse of the 1930s, bank management attempted to state realistic maturity terms for all loans they made. Loans made for working capital purposes were considered in light of the ability of the borrower to repay through reduction in inventory or accounts receivables. If the inventory or accounts receivables were constant over time, then the banks granted a long-term loan which would be repaid from profits, not from working capital. Similarly, real estate loans and equipment loans were put on amortization repayment schedules. Each month the borrower repaid a small portion of the loan so that at the end of 5 or 7 years the entire loan would be repaid. The development of realistic repayment schedules for working capital loans and for long-term loans provided the basis for the theory (developed in the 1940s) known as the anticipated-income theory. The concept of the *anticipated-income theory* is that the massive flow of funds can be committed to meet reserve deficiencies or new loan demand in the future. Every month mortgages are repaid in part, providing a regular and predictable flow of funds, which can be channeled either to provide for deposit outflows or to make new loans and commitments. The anticipated-income theory is a refreshing change from the commercial loan theory and the shiftability theory because it recognizes the dynamic nature of the banking business.

Liabilities-Management Theory

During the 1960s economic conditions changed dramatically and banking needs were altered. Banks had liquidated all their liquid assets that would qualify as shiftable in an effort to expand loan portfolios. In an expansionary phase, all the funds that were being generated by loan amortization and working-capital loan repayment were needed just to maintain a constant size. Banks needed more funds to grow and could not obtain these funds from asset sources that they had historically depended upon. The commercial loan theory, the shiftability theory, and the anticipated-income theory were all founded upon the notion that banks needed funds to meet *deposit withdrawals*. However, in the 1960s the problem was not one of contracting assets but of expanding liabilities. Banks turned their attention from managing assets to managing liabilities, hence the term *liabilities management*. Liabilities management means that banks in need of funds can obtain them in the form of:

1 Demand deposits
2 Federal funds

3 Negotiable certificates of deposit
4 Consumer-type certificates of deposit
5 Borrowings from the Federal Reserve
6 Capital notes
7 Capital stock
8 Borrowings from branches located abroad (Eurodollar market)

Heretofore liabilities were considered to be determined by forces outside the banking industry. Liabilities management introduced the concept that a banker may control the level (quantity) of liabilities. Compared with the commercial loan, shiftability, and anticipated-income theories, which assumed a given level of assets and liabilities, the liability-management concept allowed institutions to vary the total size by increasing or decreasing liabilities. Managers found that they were free to change the total hold of assets to meet demand and achieve optimal profitability.

Mixing Asset and Liability Liquidity Sources

The blend of asset and liability sources of liquidity depends largely on the ability of the institution to manage liquidity and the acceptance by the market of the institution's own securities. Greater management planning and economic expertise are required with liability management than with asset management, because the institution must always place itself in a position to tap the market. For example, Citicorp and its banking subsidiary, Citibank, have access to many sources of funds by borrowing from internationally diversified markets. Citicorp maintains its position as a preferred borrower so that it can tap sources of liquidity at the most favorable rates available. Likewise, finance companies maintain expert staffs to deal with commercial banks, corporate cash managers, and commercial paper dealers to provide immediate and continuing access to numerous sources of funds. With a strong liabilities liquidity position, the need for asset liquidity is reduced and a greater proportion of assets can be invested in higher yielding direct loans. On the other hand, a relatively unknown bank without an active money-market manager has few opportunities to borrow for liquidity purposes and is disfavored under tight money market conditions. The smaller banks cannot issue sufficient volumes of negotiable certificates of deposits to remain continuously active, and they rarely have foreign branches in the Eurodollar market. Thus, the smaller and unknown institutions must rely primarily on asset sources of liquidity.

LIQUIDITY RESERVE ESTIMATION

Desired Reserve Consideration

Liquidity reserves can be estimated by comparing *desired reserves* with *actual asset and liability reserves*. Desired reserves are estimated by analyzing assets and liabilities in terms of three considerations:

1 Variability
2 Velocity of turnover
3 Legal commitments

Typically, assets and liabilities are grouped separately and then subdivided into groups with similar variability and velocity. An alternative method is to classify by market, such as aggregating consumer loans and deposits. For some marketing decisions, categorization by market is more meaningful than grouping by the legal constituency of the security.

Tabular Presentation   In a tabular presentation, one table (Table 18-2) uses desired liquidity ratios to compute desired reserves and Table 18-3 compares the reserve position with desired reserves to determine if reserves are excessive or deficit. Reserves may be either primary or secondary; primary describes legal reserves as defined by the Federal Reserve for checking deposit balances, whereas secondary reserves are liquid assets and unused short-term borrowing capacity. The table may include both primary and secondary reserves, as shown in the following example.

Example of Table for Desired Reserves   Consider a depository intermediary with $8 million of demand deposits, $15,600,000 of time deposits, and $13,400,000 of loans. After studying liability accounts over time, they are divided into the categories of *volatile, vulnerable, and residual.* (See Table 18-2.) The volatile amounts are frequently withdrawn without notice and cannot be predicted accurately. To protect itself fully against unexpected with-

TABLE 18-2
PRIMARY AND SECONDARY RESERVE ALLOCATIONS (AMOUNTS IN THOUSANDS)

Account	Amount	Reserve ratios		Reserve allocations	
		Primary	Secondary	Primary	Secondary
Liabilities:					
Demand deposits					
Volatile	$ 1,000	12%	88%	$ 120	$ 880
Vulnerable	$ 2,000	12%	25%	$ 240	$ 500
Residual	$ 5,000	12%	0%	$ 600	$ 0
Time deposits					
Volatile	$ 600	3%	97%	$ 18	$ 582
Vulnerable	$ 3,000	3%	20%	$ 90	$ 600
Residual	$12,000	3%	0%	$ 360	$ 0
Assets:					
Volatile loan volume	$ 3,000		75%		$2,475
Seasonal loan volume	$ 1,100		20%		$ 220
Secular loan volume	$ 9,000		0%		$ 0
Total desired reserves				$1,428	$5,257

TABLE 18-3
SECONDARY RESERVE POSITION
(AMOUNTS IN THOUSANDS)

Secondary reserve assets	
Bankers' acceptances	$ 525
Commercial paper	$ 220
Loan participations bought	$1,300
Treasury bills	$ 600
Federal funds sold	$ 900
Total secondary reserve assets	$3,545
Liability liquidity	
Potential money-market borrowing	$8,300
Present money-market borrowings	$6,500
Unused liability liquidity	$1,800
Secondary reserve position	
Actual secondary reserves	$5,345
Desired secondary reserves	$5,257
Excess (or deficit) reserves	$ 88

drawals, the financial institution must invest all of these funds in either primary or secondary reserves. *Vulnerable* amounts are viewed as having only a moderate chance of being withdrawn unexpectably but, on infrequent occasions, all volatile and some vulnerable portions of demand deposits must be repaid by the financial institution with little warning.

Setting the secondary reserve ratio for vulnerable deposits requires comparing the risk of failing to meet an unexpected deposit withdrawal with the risk of underinvesting the institution's funds in high yielding loans. Extensive analysis of vulnerable deposit fluctuations aids in judging secondary reserve requirements but the final decision is a judgment call based on risk acceptance and managerial agility in a liquidity crisis.[1] In this example we decide to cover 25 percent of vulnerable demand deposits with secondary reserves. We believe that a 25 percent reserve would adequately cover declining deposits while we aggressively reduce the loan portfolio by rejecting loan applications, selling participations in existing loans, and arranging alternative financing sources for existing borrowers. *Residual* deposits are a solid core that is unlikely to be withdrawn unexpectedly, and consequently we maintain only the required primary reserves and no secondary reserves.

A similar analysis is performed on the time deposits to allocate additional primary and secondary reserves. Then total primary and second reserves ($1,428,000 and $5,257,000) are computed by adding the reserve allocation columns. Primary reserves are maintained by law as defined in Federal Reserve regulations. (Primary reserves are discussed in Chapter 22 in connection with

---

[1] See Baltensperger and Milde (1976), Boland (1975), Keown (1978), and Lifeson and Blackmarr (1973) for estimation of deposit variability.

monetary policy.) Secondary reserves are provided by asset and liability liquidity, the next topic considered.

Secondary Reserve Position

The secondary reserve position is computed in three parts (see Table 18-3):

1 Secondary reserve asset analysis
2 Unused liability liquidity analysis
3 Reserve excess or deficiency estimate

Secondary reserve assets are defined as those that may be sold nearly anytime during the day without loss of principal. The degree of certainty and speed at which securities may be sold at a price approaching their full value determines their liquidity.[2] That is, liquidity is defined as the ratio of the price obtainable from a "quick" sale to the price expected from an orderly, timely sale. When assets are sold quickly, the market does not have an opportunity to assess their values fully. Fewer potential buyers are available, of which only a portion can be contacted in a short time period.

Securities normally meeting the liquidity definition, as listed in Table 18-3, are:

Bankers' acceptances
Commercial paper
Loan participations bought
Treasury bills
Federal funds sold

These securities are actively traded in large denominations by a number of banks, bond dealers, and other financial institutions.

In addition to an asset being a liquid type of security, it must not be encumbered by liens or other legal restrictions for it to qualify as a secondary reserve asset. A commonly disqualified asset is a Treasury bill (TB) owned by a commercial bank and pledged as collateral for state or local government deposits. The bank cannot sell the TB without repaying the depositor, because the bank has agreed to collateralize all deposits with TBs. Therefore, the proceeds from the sale of such TBs would not be available to meet other funding needs.

In our example we have considered both the type of security and the legal restrictions for our assets. Secondary reserve assets and amounts are reported in Table 18-3; they total $3,545,000.

Liability liquidity is the difference between the maximum potential money market borrowings and actual money market borrowings. The financial institution can "control the level (quantity) of liabilities," as discussed earlier in the

---

[2] Hicks (1962) credits J. M. Keynes with first defining liquidity in terms of both realizable value and certainty. In the *Treatise of Money*, one thing is recognized as more liquid than another if it is "more certainly reliable at short notice without loss."

chapter, but the concept is limited by the market's acceptance of the institution's liabilities. Investors will not accept an infinite amount of money market debt but will accept a reasonable amount of debt from each financial institution. When the financial institution borrows less than the amount considered reasonable, then the opportunity to raise funds by increasing liabilities exists.

For the example we examined past money-market borrowings by our and similar financial institutions and consulted with money-market investors. Based on available evidence and opinion, we concluded that our institution could borrow quickly up to $8,300,000 with money-market liabilities. At the present time, money-market borrowings total $6,500,000. Therefore, the unused liability liquidity is $1,800,000 ($8,300,000 − $6,500,000).

The net position is the difference between total secondary reserves and desired secondary reserves. In our example, total secondary reserves are $5,345,000 ($3,545,000 + $1,800,000); desired secondary reserves of $5,257,000 are reported in Table 18-2. The net position of $88,000 is relatively close to zero, indicating that we hold neither excessive nor deficit secondary reserves but have a balanced liquidity position. We are the envy of the industry!

IMPORTANCE OF INVESTOR CONFIDENCE IN LIQUIDITY MANAGEMENT

Before leaving the subject of liquidity policy, the importance of investor confidence must be considered. Although an institution develops an excellent "plan for meeting the funding needs of the financial institution," it cannot maintain adequate liquidity if it loses investor confidence. As stated in the beginning of Chapter 1, "securities and deposits are supported *not by physical resources but by the confidence and desire of investors*. Consequently, financial institutions are supported by intangible assets and are subject to decline or collapse when trust and confidence wane."

The loss of investor confidence in massive funds outflows, creating funding needs beyond reasonable expectations and capabilities of even the most prudent management. For example, Continental Illinois National Bank lost billions of dollars per day when large certificate-of-deposit holders feared that its loan portfolio included substantial amounts of nonperforming and loss loans. This liquidity crisis was stemmed by lending billions of dollars immediately and only after the Federal Deposit Insurance Corporation, Comptroller of the Currency, and Federal Reserve reestablished a support package guaranteeing the repayment of all depositors.

SUMMARY

Because defaulting on their financial commitments often causes serious problems for financial institutions, they develop a liquidity policy. The policy is a plan for funding expected and unexpected funding needs. Over several centuries four means of providing liquidity have been developed: commercial loan theory, shiftability theory, anticipated-income theory, and liabilities management. Today liquidity policy embodies all of these theories in a comprehensive plan. A simple tabular approach to liquidity planning can be prepared by allocating reserves to liability and asset commitments and then comparing desired reserves with actual reserves. Such planning approaches can be incorporated in financial planning models such as that presented in the following chapter. Regardless of the planning policy adopted, managers of financial institutions recognize that continued liquidity depends foremost on the continued confidence of investors.

TERMS

liquidity policy	shiftability theory
commercial loan theory	liabilities management
anticipated-income theory	asset allocation

QUESTIONS

1 Explain the commercial loan theory of liquidity management using the liquid reserve reservoir concept.
2 How is the development of an orderly securities market related to the development of the shiftability theory?
3 The anticipated-income theory is an asset-management theory of liquidity management. Why is it so categorized?
4 What economic conditions of the 1960s precipitated the development of liability-management theory? What are the liability sources of funds?
5 List at least four types of securities meeting the definition of a liquid asset.
6 Why do some liquid assets not qualify as secondary reserve assets?
7 The Jasper Bank is attempting to determine if it maintains excess or deficit secondary reserves. It wants you to compute its secondary reserve position. Management has analyzed accounts and reserve needs and believes that the following information represents its views:
a Liabilities and assets are categorized by volatility:

Demand deposits	
Volatile	$3,000
Vulnerable	$5,000
Residual	$4,000
Time deposits	
Volatile	$6,000
Vulnerable	$3,000
Residual	$15,000
Money-market borrowings	$5,000
Loans	
Volatile	$5,000
Seasonal	$8,000
Secular	$12,000

Securities (unencumbered)	
Banker's acceptances	$2,000
Commercial paper	$1,000
Loan participations bought	$1,300
Treasury bills	$ 600
Federal funds sold	$3,000

b Management believes that volatile deposits must be fully reserved with either primary or secondary reserves. Vulnerable deposits should have secondary reserves equal to 30 percent of the amount of deposits. Volatile loan demand requires a 60 percent secondary reserve; seasonal loan demand needs a 20 percent secondary reserve; and secular demand requires no secondary reserve. Primary reserves are 12 percent for demand and 3 percent for time deposits, regardless of volatility.

c Knowledgeable money-market investors indicate that Jasper Bank could borrow up to $10,000 quickly and easily by issuing large certificates of deposit.

SELECTED REFERENCES

Baltensperger, E., and H. Milde: "Predictability of Reserve Demand, Information Costs, and Portfolio Behavior of Commercial Banks," *Journal of Finance,* June 1976, pp. 835–843.

Boland, Loraine (ed.): *An Introduction to Liquidity Management, Its Principles and Techniques,* The Institute of Financial Education, Chicago, 1975.

Cohen, Kalman J., and Frederick S. Hammer: "Linear Programming and Optimal Bank Asset Management Decisions," *Journal of Finance,* May 1967, pp. 147–165.

Cohen, Kalman J., and Sten Thore: "Programming Bank Portfolios Under Uncertainty," *Journal of Bank Research,* Spring 1970, pp. 42–61.

DeLong, Fred G.: "Liquidity Requirements and Employment of Funds," in Kalman J. Cohen and Frederick S. Hammer, *Analytical Methods in Banking,* Richard D. Irwin, Homewood, Ill., 1966, pp. 38–53.

Hicks, J. R.: "Liquidity," *Economic Journal,* December 1962; reprinted in part in Loraine, Boland (ed.), *An Introduction to Liquidity Management, Its Principles and Techniques,* Institute of Financial Education, Chicago, 1975, pp. 1–6.

Kane, Edward J., and Burton G. Malkiel: "Bank Portfolio Allocation, Deposit Variability, and the Availability Doctrine," *Quarterly Journal of Economics,* February 1965, pp. 113–134.

Keown, A. J.: "A Change-Constrained Goal Programming Model for Bank Liquidity Management," *Decision Sciences,* January 1978, pp. 93–106.

Keynes, John M.: *A Treatise on Money,* Harcourt, Brace & World, New York, 1930.

Lauch, Louis H., and Neil B. Murphy: "A Test of the Impact of Branching on Deposit Variability," *Journal of Financial and Quantitative Analysis,* September 1970, pp. 323–327.

Lifeson, K. A., and Brian R. Blackmarr: "Simulation and Optimization Models for Asset Deployment and Funds Sources Balancing Profit, Liquidity and Growth," *Journal of Bank Research,* Autumn 1973, pp. 239–255.

Lindow, W.: "In Defense of Bank Liability Management," *Journal of Portfolio Management,* Summer 1975, pp. 23–27.

McKinney, George W., Jr., and William J. Brown: *Management of Commercial Bank Funds,* American Institute of Banking, Washington, D.C., 1974.

Pulliam, Kenneth P.: "A Liquidity Portfolio Management Strategy Approach," *Journal of Bank Research,* Spring 1977, pp. 50–58.

Rangarajan, C.: "Deposit Variability in Individual Banks," *National Banking Review,* September 1966, pp. 61–71.

Woodworth, G. Walter: "Bank Liquidity Management: Theories and Techniques," *Bankers Magazine,* June 1967.

CHAPTER 19

CAPITAL POLICY

All financial institutions maintain a capital foundation, although the account titles and ownership of capital vary from one type of institution to another. In stock-chartered institutions, capital consists of capital stock, capital surplus, and retained earnings. In mutual associations, capital is called a *reserve* and accounts for the net worth (paid-in surplus and undivided profit).[1] Mutual life insurance associations retain "surpluses" as a general protection for policy obligations. Such surpluses, termed either *special surplus funds* or *unassigned surplus,* should be regarded as equivalent to capital because they serve the same functions as capital accounts in stock organizations. Given the large number and names for capital, we see that capital accounts are recognized by their position and function on the balance sheet rather than by a standard caption. Whatever the name, capital is the residual account on the liabilities side of the balance sheet and accumulates net profits and losses.

By giving liability holders a buffer against loss due to asset depreciation, employee defalcation, and mismanagement, capital improves public confidence in our financial institutions and economic system. Financial institutions can survive some loan defaults, stock price slumps, and falling bond values, if they have enough capital to absorb the losses. Those who provide capital realize that their capital is "at risk." Managers should know what risks are borne by capital, the amount of capital that is regarded as adequate by investors and

---

[1] Contrast this definition of reserves with that given in the liquidity discussion. In the banking world reserves are assets held against demand and time deposits. Also, policy reserves of U.S. life insurance companies are funds set aside to meet future obligations to policyholders and their beneficiaries. Policy reserves are, in effect, a liability of insurance companies owned by policyholders.

regulators, and the cost of capital. This chapter explains the meaning and concept of capital, the issues in capital adequacy determination, ratio measures of capital levels, and cost computations for debt and equity capital.

LEGAL FORMS OF ORGANIZATION

The legal form of organization defines the terms used to account for capital and the ownership interests in the residual worth of the institution. The initial organization of most financial institutions is legally recognized by a *charter* granted by the state or federal government. Most financial institutions are not permitted to operate without a charter and must cease operations if the charter is revoked. For example, if an organization accepts public time deposits and invests in long-term bonds, mortgage loans, and other investments, then it probably meets the legal definition of a savings bank. Because it operates as an established financial institution, it must be chartered by a national or state supervisory agency as a mutual savings bank. Among other things, the charter states the source of capital and the ownership of the institution.

Like other private business firms, some financial institutions are organized as corporations. Banks are chartered only as corporations, and savings and loans may choose whether or not to be incorporated. Pension funds are often established as trusts administered by a professional trustee. Many financial institutions are not incorporated but are chartered as mutual associations. The members of the association deposit money, buy life insurance policies, and borrow funds from their clublike organizations. Mutual savings banks, all federal and some state savings and loans associations, and many insurance companies are chartered by state and federal governments as mutual associations. Managers and investors decide which form of organization—corporate, mutual association, or trust—is legally possible and most profitable when the institution is established. Changes in legal form may occur later, but the original charter must be voided and a new charter accepted by the regulatory agency.

Example of Capital Accounts

The balance sheet of National Bank is shown in Table 19-1. The capital account section is more detailed than that shown in previous chapters. Which of the securities are capital items and which are part of the intermediary's portfolio? On the asset side, cash, investment securities, and loans are all part of the portfolio. We would expect that the real and other assets are owned to facilitate the operation of the securities portfolio. On the right side of the balance sheet, deposits are part of the liability portfolio. Deposits are not capital because they would be repaid before other accounts in the event of liquidation and they constitute the major business of the financial institution. Other liabilities are classified as part of the portfolio, because their short-term nature eliminates them from the "permanent" part of the capital definition.

TABLE 19-1
Reserve, Capital, and Classified Loan Information
National Bank (Example)
December 31, 19X1
(In Thousands of Dollars)

Assets		Liabilities and Capital	
Cash	82,400	Demand deposits	181,300
Securities	134,600	Time and savings deposits	227,300
Net loans	279,000	Federal funds and borrowings	68,700
Real and other assets	52,000	Accrued expenses and other	
Total assets²	548,000	liabilities	27,600
		Capital notes	4,000
		Common stock ($10 par value)	10,000
		Capital surplus	11,000
		Undivided profits	18,100
		Total liabilities and capital	548,000

Notes:
1 Reserve accounts changed as shown below during the year 19X1:

Beginning balance, reserve accounts	$1,000,000
Provision for losses	+100,000
Loan losses	−200,000
Loss loan recoveries	+50,000
Ending balance, reserve accounts	950,000

Loan amounts are reported after deducting reserves but include loans totaling $1,200,000 classified as substandard, doubtful, or loss.

2 Total assets as of January 1, 19X1 (beginning of the year) equaled $508,000,000.

Capital consists of *common stock, capital surplus,* and *undivided profits.* The *capital notes,* subordinated to claims of depositors and other creditors, serve the function of protecting senior claim holders (including depositors); however, capital notes require fixed payments for interest and principal, and consequently, do not qualify as capital in the full meaning of the word. "Common stock" is sold with a par value of $10 per share in this case; 1 million shares are outstanding (10,000 thousand at $10/share). "Capital surplus" of $11 million is obtained when shares are issued at a price greater than par. Through retention of profits, the "undivided profits" account has grown to $18 million. In all the intermediary has raised $43.1 million in capital since its inception.

Relationship of Capital to the Securities Portfolio

Now that we know how to account for capital, we can define its function in a financial institution. To describe the dual role played by capital, we divide the institution into two parts: capital and real assets are in one part, while the securities portfolio and its financing are in the other part. We separate capital (and operations) from the portfolio to highlight the function and cost of capital in a financial institution. The term "portfolio" is defined here to mean assets (loans and securities) and liabilities (deposits, insurance policies, and savings accounts) bought and sold by the institution in the normal course of business. Fluctuations in the values of assets and liabilities are referred to as asset portfolio risk or liability portfolio risk, respectively. The distinction between capital and portfolio securities is subtle, but it is important to understand the differences before analyzing the relationship. The relationship of capital to the portfolio may take one of two forms:

1 Capital is provided for management and operations only; the portfolio is legally separated from the capital account.

2 Capital is invested in a single entity combining the portfolio and operating balance sheets.

FIGURE 19-1
Relationship between capital and portfolio in investment companies (mutual funds) and financial intermediaries.

Panel a.   Investment Company or Trust:
            Portfolio is Separate from Capital

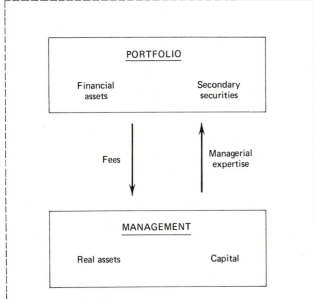

Panel b. Financial Intermediary:
            Portfolio and Capital are Combined in Same Legal Entity

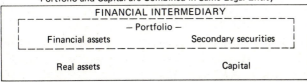

These organizational forms are illustrated in Figure 19-1 and discussed in this section. In the case of most investment companies (mutual funds), an independent management company receives fees for managing a portfolio owned by shareholders of the investment company (or trust). The investment company relationship to the management company is illustrated in panel A of Figure 19-1. Capital is invested for the purchase of real assets and provision of managerial services but does not bear portfolio risk. Fees are paid to the management company, and profits are earned when the fees exceed operating costs. The profits and losses of the securities portfolio accrue directly to the mutual find stockholders, financial risks are borne solely by the portfolio owners (mutual fund investors), and operating risks are assumed entirely by management owners.

Capital plays a much different role when the portfolio is legally combined with the management entity, as shown in panel B of Figure 19-1. When the portfolio and the management businesses are joined into a single organization, we create a financial intermediary and support the success of the securities portfolio with capital. Capital continues to bear the risk of operating losses, but if capital is insufficient, then portfolio owners assume the portfolio risks. For example, a bank owns loans and issues deposit liabilities. If the loans default on interest payments, then the loss is taken first by capital owners and second by depositors. Of course, returns from the loan portfolio in excess of interest costs paid to depositors belong to the capital suppliers. Profits due to controlling the cost of operations and to successful investment policies accrue to the common stockholders or, in the case of mutual organizations, to the capital reserve account.

CAPITAL RISKS

Although managers of financial institutions direct their efforts toward reducing risks, the financial markets are strewn with the relics of institutions and schemes that failed when the unusual or unexpected did occur. As in the 1977 blackout of New York City, the chance of lightning striking several times in critical places is small, but the effect is disastrous. In the 1970s the real estate investment trusts (REITs) were hit simultaneously by large credit losses in the building industry and unfavorable short-term interest rates. Then in the late 1970s, the savings and loans were squeezed between long-term low-rate mortgage revenues and short-term high-rate deposit interest expenses. Shortly thereafter many commercial banks were suffering severe losses from energy-related domestic loans and holding their breath over massive international credits. These examples illustrate the unfortunate but inevitable tenet: financial institutions are subject to unpredictable and substantial losses.

What are the most common risks that cause financial institutions to fail? Ranked roughly in order of severity, they are operating risk, credit risk, and term-structure risk. These are the most common problem areas but beware—other risks stalk the financial institution, as well.

Operating Risk

Operating risk refers to mismanagement, defalcation, fraud, and foreign currency trading losses. Mismanagement is a very broad reference encompassing erroneous decisions, inadequate internal controls, improper personnel practices, poor planning and budgeting, and generally failure to conduct a well-run business.

With regard to losses due to fraud and defalcation, minor losses are relatively frequent in large institutions and absorbed as a business expense; major losses are usually, but not always, covered by insurance. Uninsured fraudulent acts sometimes cause substantial losses and institutional failure. Just as most banks take painstaking precautions against fraud, they carefully control foreign exchange trading exposure. Foreign exchange risks, discussed in Chapter 15, exist as a normal part of maintaining inventories of foreign currencies and currency futures. Control over the level of exposure is effected by setting limits on employees' trading of currencies. However, currency losses sometimes are seen because traders ignore the limits or unusually large losses occur in many currencies over a short period of time.

Credit Risk

Credit risk, discussed with regard to individual borrowers in Chapter 16, is the variation in loan losses for the entire institution. Credit losses as a percent of outstanding loans fluctuate as a result of cycle conditions in the economy, chance, fraud, and credit mismanagement. Unusually large credit losses cause banks and other institutions to fail.[2] Sometimes the risks are not obvious when the loan is granted, or subsequent events cause financial deterioration. For example, a multimillion dollar loan to a large grocery chain operator was granted after the chain reported profits for many years. Subsequently, modestly higher operating expenses combined with a 0.2 percent decrease in gross operating margins combined to cause net operating losses. The grocery chain entered into bankruptcy, and creditors began the lengthy process for recovery. Like many problem credits, this one caused three types of losses:

1 Loss of principal
2 Loss of interest earnings
3 Abnormally high collection expenses

Some credit losses are a normal aspect of granting credit, as discussed in the last chapter, but unusually large losses cannot be absorbed by profits on good loans. As discussed in the following section, reserves and capital are required to meet large, unexpected losses.

---

[2] See Sinkey (1979) for research on causes of bank failures.

Term-Structure Risk

Term-structure risk, also referred to as interest-rate risk and discussed in Chapter 7, arises when asset and liability rates of return change differently for the same change in market interest rates. Although partially controllable, (1) the demands of the financial market, (2) limitations on communication of information, and (3) costs of transacting securities force institutions to accept some term-structure risk. Market demand, imperfect communications, and costly transactions are inherent in financial markets, and consequently, the resulting term-structure risk is a natural part of doing business as a financial intermediary. Those who invest the capital in financial intermediaries, therefore, accept the term-structure, as well as operating and credit risks.

Mismanagement of Credit and Term-Structure Risks

Avoidable credit and term-structure risks must be attributed to management rather than market imperfections. For example, one large bank intentionally purchased long-term assets with short-term deposit sources, on the speculation that short-term interest rates would soon decline. Unfortunately, short-term interest rates rose, and the bank's profit plummetted. Was this bank's decision a normal business risk or an unnecessary speculation? The action was speculative and unnecessary in this author's opinion, because short-term interest-rate changes fluctuate unpredictably and the bank could have earned normal profits without exposing itself to extreme term-structure risks. Therefore, the loss resulted from mismanagement, rather than bad luck thrown in the face of careful managers. (Subsequently, federal regulatory agencies effected substantial changes in the executive suite, injected additional capital funds, and forced the bank to eliminate unnecessary term-structure risks.)

A gray area between mismanagement and credit risk exist for losses attributable to borrower fraud. For example, mortgage frauds exposed in Florida bilked thousands of investors out of between $350 million and $1 billion. The Florida Attorney General said that the scope of fraud "has gone beyond our worst nightmares." The fraudulent scheme involved the use of fifty-six corporations that purchased land with first mortgage loans. After the land was improved, the tracts were sold and financed with another first mortgage. Thus, two mortgage investors believed that they held a first claim against the same property. When the loans were not repaid, the second group of investors were dismayed to find that they suffered losses as general creditors. Was the loss due to management's failure to analyze and monitor loans properly? Or was management acting in a reasonable manner in view of the costs of perfecting the credit-granting and -monitoring processes? These are questions of judgment, not problems with universal answers. The usual decision is to develop a reasonably good credit administration but recognize that unpredictable losses may occur. Next we consider means of protecting financial institutions and investors against unpredictable losses.

RESERVES, EARNINGS, CAPITAL, AND DEPOSIT INSURANCE

Losses from operations, credit, and term structure are absorbed by reserve accounts, current earnings, and capital accounts, and for depository intermediaries, by deposit insurance. Of course, losses are never welcomed, but they are expected and, consequently, provisions and procedures are established so that they can be sustained without destroying the institution or financial system. This section briefly describes those provisions.

Reserve Accounts

Reserve accounts are normally maintained for credit losses. Reserves are increased by the expense item "provision for losses" in the income statement; that is, losses are recognized as an expense during each period, although specific losses have not occurred. When losses do occur, they are charged to the reserve account. If funds are recovered from loans that were charged off, then the recovery is added back to the reserve account. All of these transactions can be illustrated with the information in the notes to Table 19-1.

The beginning balance of $1000 is increased by the provision for losses ($100) and recoveries from loans charged off ($50); it is reduced by $200 due to uncollectable loans and securities. The ending balance in the reserve account of $950 will be the beginning balance next year.

The reserve account performs two importance purposes. First, it adjusts the loan account for potential losses, and, therefore, the balance sheet fairly presents the value of the loan portfolio. Second, it buffers the income statement from fluctuations in actual loan losses. The provision for loan losses is generally smooth and controlled, while the actual loan losses are variable and random.

Earnings

What happens when the reserve account balances drop to zero or when provisions were not made for losses? Then earnings from other operations must absorb the losses. An uninsured defalcation, for example, becomes an expense that reduces earnings. An interest-rate loss would appear either as a decrease in revenue or as an increase in interest expense. Although such items are not explicitly charged against earnings, they all have the effect of decreasing earnings. Consequently, earnings are considered the second line of defense against losses.

Capital

What happens when current year earnings are insufficient to offset losses? Then the institution draws upon past years' retained earnings and initial capital contributions—the capital accounts. Capital should be great enough to absorb reasonable losses, but because rational individuals may and do disagree about what is reasonable, the acceptable level of capital is hotly disputed. For example, the bank regulatory agencies have not agreed on a common definition of capital and actively enforce different rules.

The FDIC's net capital ratio (NCR) illustrates the general concept of capital adequacy analysis. (Unlike the FDIC, the Federal Reserve and Comptroller of Currency include some long-term debt in their analysis.) The NCR is defined as follows: NCR = (Capital + Reserves − Classified assets)/Average assets (1). Classified assets are those listed as "substandard," "doubtful," or loss by bank examiners. Average assets are equal to beginning and ending total assets divided by two.

Research in banking indicates that a ratio of less than 2.74 percent very often means a "problem bank" classification will be assigned by the FDIC, while an NCR above 2.74 percent usually avoids such a classification.[3] Banks with negative capital are always classified as problems by the FDIC, as one would expect!

Example of NCR

For example, using information from Table 19-1, the NCR for National Bank is computed as follows:

$$NCR = (Capital + Reserves - Classified\ assets)/Average\ assets\ (1)$$
$$NCR = (29,100 + 950 - 1,200)/(508,000 + 548,000)/2$$
$$NCR = 5.46\%$$

Compared with the preferred standard of the FDIC, 6 percent, National Bank's NCR rates slightly low, but it is well above the level at which banks are classified as supervisory problems.

Deposit Insurance

Once a bank's own capital is depleted by losses, the depositor's position is threatened. In the days before deposit insurance, depositors in failed institutions actually lost their funds. The fear of loss was real and caused depositors to withdraw their deposits at the first hint of a problem. "Bank runs" threatened to bring the entire financial structure down during the depression of the 1930s. Therefore, depositor protection was deemed a socially desirable program and led to the establishment of the FDIC and the FSLIC. Also, a few states permit thrift institutions to operate with private insurance, such as that provided by the Maryland State Savings Insurance Corporation. Insurance premiums are paid by the insured institution and claims are paid to depositors

[3] Sinkey (1979).

of failed institutions by the insurance company, just as in the case of fire, theft, and health insurance programs. In recent years the Ohio and Maryland private insurance funds have failed to prevent bank runs, indicating that deposit loss fears are as important now as they were in the 1930s.

The nature of deposit insurance has led to special problems and controversies. First, unlike a broken leg, a failed bank or savings and loan is not clearly defined. Technically insolvent institutions (negative capital) can continue to receive and pay depositors from liquid reserves for a long period of time. There is almost always hope that poor-quality assets will improve, that operating problems will be solved, or that the unknown embezzler will be found. When should an institution be declared bankrupt? Although formal legal procedures are proscribed for a bankruptcy finding before closing any deposit institution, the problem of definition remains.

Second, all financial institutions pay about the same deposit premium but they are not all equally risky. Because of differences in managements and markets, the potential for failure differs widely. For example, some institutions concentrate in risky industries while others are diversified in low-risk loans. Yet all pay the same monthly premium.

Third, these problems are partially solved in two ways. First, deposit insurance applies only to a portion of total deposits, leaving some depositors uninsured. The uninsured depositors, primarily large corporations and investors, cautiously evaluate the deposit institution on a regular basis and stand ready to withdraw funds. That is, the threat of a "bank run" by part of the depositors is permitted by current regulation. This solution is referred to as *market discipline,* because the financial market takes actions against institutions with insufficient capital. Second, deposit insurers, both public and private, regularly analyze and investigate insured institutions. If the insurer perceives capital to be inadequate, it admonishes the institution either to reduce its risk exposure or to increase capital. This solution is referred to as *active supervision,* because the insurer aggressively pursues and forces institutions to conform to a set of standards.

A potential solution to deposit insurance problems is to vary the insurance premium according to the risk exposure. If the premium varied with risk, then insurance standards and active supervision could be relaxed. Relaxation of standards would permit a wider range of opportunities for financial institutions, which would, in turn, provide more types of credit services to the public. Further, explicit deposit premiums are believed to be less costly than the implicit premium imposed through active supervision. But while applauded for its conceptual merits, variable deposit premiums have not been applied because of the implementation obstacle of defining risk numerically.

Trend in Capital-to-Asset Ratios

The capital of financial institutions is far less now than in the past, according to common standards. Capital as a percent of bank assets was 5.7 percent in 1978 compared with 11.7 percent in 1961.[4] Likewise the capital of life insurance companies is down to 7.1 percent of total assets from 8.1 percent 15 years ago.[5] The net worth of savings and loans is declining in proportion to total assets. In 1960 savings and loan capital was 6.5 percent of assets and in 1975 it was 5.5 percent of assets. Similarly, net-worth-to-savings-balance ratios are decreasing nearly every year.[6]

However, decreased capital ratios do not necessarily indicate an inadequate level of capital. Currently, both managers and regulators recognize that an adequate capital level is determined by more than the ratios of capital to assets. Perhaps capital was unnecessarily large in 1960, and the financial system may have matured to a point where less risk exists and less capital is needed to absorb losses. Some economists consider recessions to be less frequent and severe than in past periods of history. Management of financial institutions is better now than 15 or more years ago, as managers are now better educated and informed than their predecessors. Managers are diversifying their portfolios geographically and across industries to reduce the risk of large loan concentrations. The development of short-term funding sources provides greater access to the money and capital markets, improving the ability of institutions to meet commitments. Federal insurance from the Federal Deposit Insurance Corporation (FDIC), Federal Savings and Loan Insurance Corporation (FSLIC), and National Credit Union Administration (NCUA) and temporary loans from the Federal Reserve are serving to prevent bank runs and stabilize institutional portfolio positions.

On the other hand, some economists point to the greater risks being taken by banks and other financial institutions now than in the past decades. Lending competition is intensifying, and lending in all forms of risky assets is increasing. Several banks sustained severe losses resulting from REIT loans and New York City bonds. Large loan commitments to underdeveloped countries and domestic municipalities are increasing the vulnerability of banks to domestic and foreign recessions. Ohio and Maryland savings and loan deposit runs in the 1980s suggest that the public is still very sensitive to such risks and quick to act on relatively little negative information. Furthermore, the greater dependence of large banks on liabilities management may increase interest-rate risk. Interest-rate fluctuations subject savings and loans, credit unions, and savings banks to the constant threat of disintermediation, short-term operating losses, and a growing reliance on short-term debt financing. Uncertain long-term bond rates and inflation rates create great uncertainties for pension plans with defined benefit plans. Finally, the increasing use of debt capital imposes required interest and principal payments not required of common-stock capital. In summary, clearly defined capital requirements do not exist because there are strong arguments for many levels of capital. Each manager considers his capital

---

[4] Increased nominal interest rates contributed substantially to decreasing capital to asset ratios during the late 1970s and early 1980s.

[5] *Life Insurance Fact Book, 1976,* p. 64.

[6] *Savings and Loan Fact Book 1976.*

requirements in light of the reasons for capital in general and the needs of his institution in particular.

COST OF CAPITAL

Recognizing that some capital is required to operate a financial institution, the profit-conscious manager must consider the cost of capital. The cost of capital influences not only the tenacity with which the manager will argue for lower capital requirements but also numerous internal decisions. To answer the fundamental question of "Can we operate in this area of the financial market with sufficient profit to justify raising capital?" or the more common question, "Is the rate of return expected on new investments greater than the cost of capital?," the manager needs a good estimate of capital cost. To manage the institution in the best interest of its stockholders (if a stock corporation), the manager must determine the rate of return expected by investors in the financial institution. Most reasonable investment alternatives return a positive rate of return, but is the return sufficient to justify investing new capital? For example, is the return expected from investing $500,000 in a new branch office greater than the cost of capital?

Computation of Cost of Capital

Although there are a number of acceptable approaches to computing cost of capital, the approach used here is based largely on the exquisite work by Lewellen (1969).[7]

Through a series of derivations, the cost of capital for a levered firm is defined in terms of the following equation:

$$K_e = \alpha + (\alpha - r)(1 - t_c)\left(\frac{D}{V_s}\right) \tag{19-1}$$

where

α = the cost of capital, that is, the discount rate applied by investors and indicating their expected rate of return

K_e = the earnings yield or ratio of earnings per share to price per share, which is also the current return on equity investment

r = the effective rate of interest currently paid on debt

D = the current dollar value of debt outstanding

t_c = the applicable corporate tax rate on earnings

V_s = the value of the outstanding stock of the financial institution (number of shares times share price)

---

[7] Readers who find this abridged presentation too abbreviated are encouraged to refer to the original Lewellen work for a detailed presentation and derivation of the equations presented here. Also, the theory of corporate finance may not be directly applicable to financial intermediary decision making due to the liquidity committments of intermediaries and the incomplete market for their capital. See Sealey (1983) for a discussion of capital structure theory applied to depository intermediaries.

The rate of return to the stockholder, on the left-hand side, is functionally related to the return on capital (α) and leverage (D/V_s).

Investors select a discount rate, K_e, depending on the perceived risk of future dividends and associated risks. Thus, the present value of dividends for N periods, and hence the price to be paid for the stock, is stated formally as

$$P = \sum_{t=1}^{N} \left(\frac{\bar{d_t}}{1 + K_e^t} \right) \tag{19-2}$$

where $\bar{d_t}$ is the dividend to be paid at the end of period t and K_e is the equity investors' discount rate. For a firm with dividends growing at the annual rate g, the present value of dividends into *perpetuity* may be expressesd as

$$P = \frac{\bar{d_1}}{K_e - g} \tag{19-3}$$

where $d_1 = d(1 + g)$ and d is the most current dividend. Solving for K_e, we use the equation

$$K_e = \frac{\bar{d_1}}{P} + g \tag{19-4}$$

where $\bar{d_1}$ is the dividend expected at the end of the present year. The *expectations* of investors are of crucial importance, although *actual* growth of the firm may not meet expectations. Investors are willing to pay the price P, because they believe the firm's growth rate is g.

Now the perfect markets cost of capital (α) can be computed. A suggested set of steps for computing α is as follows:

1 Estimate the expected growth rate of dividends and the expected dividend at the end of the current year.

2 Compute K_e by substituting values of $\bar{d}$, P, and g in Eq. (19-4).

3 Compute or estimate the market value of debt by using the bond's price or its equivalent.

4 Compute the market value of stock as the number of shares outstanding times the market price per share.

5 Substitute values of K_e, r, t_c, D, and V_s into (Eq. (19-1) and solve for α.

Example of Computation of Cost of Capital

This example, Security Financial, is a close reproduction of an actual financial institution and serves to illustrate the plausibility of applying standard corporate finance approaches to financial institutions management. Using the steps for finding α, the first step is estimating the investors' expectation of future growth. Data taken from Security Financial's annual report needed to compute α are as follows:

Security Financial

	19×0	19×1	19×2	19×3	19×4	19×5	Five-year compound growth rate
Assets*	$542	$563	$653	$742	$803	$875	10.1%
Stockholders' equity*	38	42	47	52	58	64	11.0%
Earnings/share†	1.49	1.87	1.91	2.06	2.46	2.61	11.9%
Cash dividends/share	0.71	0.79	0.87	0.94	0.97	1.19	10.9%

* Amounts in millions.
† There were 4.1 million shares outstanding during this period.

Although there is some disparity between the earnings growth rate and dividend payout growth rate, investor reports show that Security Financial is expected to have "continued good growth" and 11.9 percent is accepted as a good estimate of g. Substituting the current market price of the stock, $16 per share, and the current expected dividend $\bar{d}$ of $1.33 (the prior year's dividend of $1.19 per share plus the expected growth next year of 11.9 percent) into Eq. (19-4), we find the cost of equity capital.

$$K_e = \frac{1.33}{16.00} + 0.119$$
$$= 0.202 \text{ or } 20.2\%$$

Also, the market value of 4.1 million shares at $16 per share is $65.6 million.

Other pertinent information includes the following: Security Financial's capital rates as originally issued had a value of $7 million, but a market-wide shift in interest rates has caused the value of the bonds to decline to 58 as the yield increased to 9¼ percent. The bonds are now valued at $4.1 million. Also, the applicable corporate income tax rate is 48 percent or 0.48.

By substituting the above information into Eq. (19-1), we find α.

$$K_e = \alpha + (\alpha - r)(1 - t_c)(D/V_s)$$
$$0.202 = \alpha + (\alpha - 0.0925)(1 - 0.48)(4.1M/65.6M)$$
$$1.0325\,\alpha = 0.205$$
$$\alpha = 0.199 \text{ or } 19.9\%$$

Note that α varies very little from K_e due to the low leverage factor. This is not always the case, and α is sometimes substantially less than K_e.

Cost of Sources of Capital

In the previous discussion and example, the perfect market rate of return on capital that investors demand is computed. However, the actual cost of capital to a financial institution is not the same for all sources due to tax and transactions costs. The flow of funds between the investor and the institution is subject to levies by residents of Pennsylvania Avenue and Wall Street. Tax and transactions adjustments to α are required to find the real-world costs of added debt, retained earnings, and equity.

Debt If capital is raised with a debt issue, the after-tax costs, R_D, is α less the tax consequences $\alpha(t_c)$ resulting from expensing interest payments. The expression is, therefore,

$$R_D = \alpha(1 - t_c) \tag{19-5}$$

That is, the after-tax cost of debt is equal to α times 1 minus the income tax rate.

Retained Earnings Taxes impact more heavily on cash dividend than on capital gain income. Consider investors in institutions A and B, which are identical in all respects except for dividend payouts. A pays out all its earnings as dividends, while B retains all its earnings; A obtains additional capital by selling new stock, while B finances growth from retained earnings. We assume that investors will be indifferent between A and B if the after-tax returns are equal.

With some rearrangement of terms, the cost of retained earnings may be stated:

$$R_R = \alpha(1 - t_p)(1 - t_g) \tag{19-6}$$

where

t_p = the personal income tax rate
t_g = the personal capital gains tax rate
R_R = the before-tax rate of return for retained earnings

That is, the cost of retained earnings is equal to α times an investor tax adjustment ratio.

New Equity Institutional managers are concerned daily with the effort and risk required to sell many types of securities to investors, but only occasionally suffer the underwriting and legal expenses concomitant with *selling their own stock*. Bond issues are relatively inexpensive, but new stock issues incur large flotation expenses and a discounted sales price. Shares are discounted below the current market price in order to sell the large new issue quickly; net proceeds are likely to be from 5 to 15 percent below the prevailing market price. Consequently, the cost of new equity, R_E, is adjusted for transaction costs.

$$R_E = \alpha/(1 - b) \tag{19-7}$$

where b is the total flotation and price discount rate. The transaction cost of selling new equity issues increases the cost of equity capital beyond the perfect market rate α.

Example of Cost of Sources of Capital

What are full costs of debt, retained earnings, and new stock issues for Security Financial? The cost of debt capital is computed by substituting values from previous examples:

$$\begin{aligned} R_D &= \alpha(1 - t_c) \\ &= 0.199\,(1 - 0.48) \\ &= 0.103 \text{ or } 10.3\% \end{aligned}$$

Retained earnings costs depends upon the *stockholders'* marginal tax brackets for ordinary and capital gains income. The tax rates vary with the clientele owning shares, but an ordinary income tax rate (t_p) of 40 percent and a capital gains tax rate (t_g) of 25 percent serve here as good illustrations.

$$\begin{aligned} R_R &= \alpha(1 - t_p)/(1 - t_g) \\ &= 0.199\,(1 - 0.40)/(1 - 0.25) \\ &= 0.159 \text{ or } 15.9\% \end{aligned}$$

New issues of common shares may be sold through an investment banker for 7 percent at a discount of \$0.50 below market. Flotation costs (b) are, therefore, the sum of investment banking commissions and price discounts:

$$b = 0.50/16 + 0.07 = 0.101 \text{ or } 10.1\%$$

The cost of new equity capital is computed with Eq. (19-7) and the values of α and b.

$$\begin{aligned} R_E &= \alpha/(1 - b) \\ &= 0.199/(1 - 0.101) \\ &= 0.221 \text{ or } 22.1\% \end{aligned}$$

Weighted Average Cost of Capital

Capital obtained from the three sources is commingled and passed on for investment. *The average cost of capital depends upon the proportions of each type of capital.* Denoting the proportions of debt, retained earnings, and new equity as X_D, X_R, and X_E, the weighted average cost of capital, R_A, is given by:

$$R_A = (X_D)\,R_D + (X_R)R_R + (X_E)R_E \tag{19-8}$$

The proportions (weights) add to 1,

$$X_D + X_R + X_E = 1 \tag{19-9}$$

and R_D, R_R, R_E are the costs of three sources of capital computed previously.

Capital Structure Weights

After determining the cost of capital for each source, management is in a position to plan for future capital needs. Essentially management can continue to raise capital from the same sources and in the same proportions as it has done in the past. Alternatively management can alter the sources tapped and proportions used to optimize its cost of capital. The optimal structure satisfies these conditions:

    1 Requirements of the government regulatory agency are met.
    2 Investments with an expected return greater than the cost of capital are funded.
    3 A cost of capital lower than that of any other alternative capital structure is presented.

Historically, managers and regulators have been concerned almost exclusively with item 1. Capital adequacy was viewed as an absolute amount or ratio that would suffice during all but the most dire economic circumstances. Now, new investments, such as electronic funds transfer systems and data processing centers, are using capital. Financial institutions are increasingly faced with the classic question of real investment desirability; hence item 2 above. As the need for expansion, equipment, and facilities continues, additional capital will be raised and item 3 will become an issue.

Example of Weighted Average Cost of Capital

If the sources of capital are debt, retained earnings, and new equity and the target proportions, then the weighted average cost of capital is:

$$
\begin{aligned}
R_A &= (X_D)\, R_D + (X_R)R_R = (X_E)R_E \\
&= (0.50)0.103 + (0.30)0.159 + (0.20)0.221 \\
&= 1.43 \text{ or } 14.3\%
\end{aligned}
$$

The heavy weight give to low-cost debt is clearly beneficial in giving Security Financial a low-cost capital. Note that the advantage of debt is predicated on the assumptions of (1) differential tax structure favoring debt, and (2) investors pricing debt at the riskless rate. If these assumptions do not hold, then debt may not be advantageous.

Contemporary Issues in Capital Management

In the face of conflicting arguments for and against the current level and composition of capital held by financial institutions, setting capital standards remains an unresolved issue. Although it is generally (but not universally) believed that capital is necessary, the amount of capital needed for different types and individual institutions is hotly debated. Institutions and their supervisory agencies are contestants on nearly every issue of the role of regulation in the capital decision, including the following:

1 How is the responsibility for setting capital standards divided between management and regulators?

2 Are capital market pressures for capital sufficient to ensure adequate capital levels ("market test")?

3 Is long-term subordinated debt a legitimate form of capital?

4 Should regulators set standards not only for bank capital but for bank-holding company capital, too?

It is unlikely that managers and their regulatory counterparts will agree to unambiguous capital standards in the near future. Regualtors are using ratios to set minimum capital standards, and the manager may allow his or her institution to fall below the standards only if there is a willingness to incur significant regulatory pressure. The manager must compromise the desire for the optimal level of capital to win the blessing of the regulator who is attempting to create a stable financial system. In return, the institutions receive public accreditation and stature, as a safe depository. Recognized by the public as a secure haven for its money, the financial institution can sell its securities and raise funds at a low cost.

SUMMARY

Although the accounting definitions of capital depend on the legal form of the organization (corporation, trust, or mutual association), the purposes of capital remain the same for all types of institutions: provide an equity base to absorb potential losses from operating, term-structure, and credit risks. To determine whether capital is adequate to support these risks, various measures are used. The most widely used measure of capital adequacy is ratio analysis, as exemplified by the net capital ratio. In recent years there has been a general decline in capital levels among intermediaries, which has been at least partially offset by better institutions management and a generally healthier economic environment.

Of equal importance is the need for intermediary's management to determine whether the return on capital covers the cost of capital, thus justifying continuation of the use of capital as well as any expansion. Lewellen's method of computing cost of capital is presented. Since capital is obtained from borrowing, sales of equity securities, and retention of earnings, cost of capital from each source must be determined. Based on the cost and proportion of each capital source, the weighted average cost of capital is determined. Management uses this cost of capital information to plan for future capital needs consistent with obtaining an optimal capital structure.

TERMS

capital adequacy	loan loss capital
mutual association reserves	capital-to-loss exposure ratios
insurance policy reserves	variability of earnings ratios
special surplus funds	analysis of bank capital
unassigned surplus	risk assets
interest-rate risk	cost of capital
capital reorganization	financial leverage
operating risk	weighted average cost of capital
credit risk (default risk)	optimal capital structure

LIST OF EQUATIONS

$$K_e = \alpha + (\alpha - r)(1 - t_c)\left(\frac{D}{V_s}\right)$$

$$P = \sum_{t=1}^{N}\left(\frac{\overline{d_t}}{1 + K_e^t}\right)$$

$$P = \frac{\overline{d_1}}{K - g}$$

$$K = \frac{\overline{d_1}}{P} + g$$

$$R_D = \alpha(1 - t_c)$$
$$R_R = \alpha(1 - t_p)/(1 - t_g)$$
$$R_E = \alpha_t/(1 - b)$$
$$R_A = (X_D)R_D + (X_R)R_R + (X_E)R_E$$
$$X_D + X_R + X_E = 1$$

QUESTIONS

1 What are the functions of capital of a financial intermediary?

2 What account titles are used to designate capital in (1) an incorporated bank, (2) a mutual association, and (3) an insurance company?

3 What risk is suggested by losses resulting from an expansion of facilities beyond the level which can be covered by the revenues generated by the volume of business conducted?

4 If National Bank operates in a one-industry town and all its deposit and loan customers work in the industry, describe specific means by which the bank can mitigate the credit risk associated with a downturn in the town's industry.

5 Using the accompanying statement of financial position for Security Financial for December 31, 19X1, compute the following:
a Depositits-to-capital ratio
b Capital-to-loan ratio
c Capital-to-total asset ratio
d Capital-to-risk asset ratio
Comment on the adequacy of Security's capital ratios compared with that of banks in general in 19X1.

Security Financial
Statement of Financial Position
As of December 31, 19X1
(In Millions of Dollars)

Assets			Liabilities		
Cash		$71	Deposits:		
Investments:			Demand	$215	
Treasury bills	$41		Time	579	$794
FNMA notes	67				
Municipal bonds	26		Other liabilities		23
Corporate bonds	79				
Corporate stocks	56	269			
			Capital notes (4.85%)		7
Loans:					
Mortgages:					
FHA guaranteed	37		**Stockholders' Equity**		
VA guaranteed	45				
Conventional	232		Common stock		
			(par value $5/share)		20
Other:					
Gov't guaranteed	13				
Other	184	511	Capital surplus		14
Real and other assets		37	Retained earnings		30
			Total liabilities & stockholders'		
Total assets		$888	equity		$888

6 If Security has net income of $7 million in 19X1 and total assets were $835 million at December 31, 19X0, what was the rate of return on stockholders' equity and return on earnings assets for 19X1?
7 The Slocum National Bank has the following capital structure:

	Book value	Market value
Long-term bonds	$2,000,000	$1,500,000
Capital stock ($10 par)	1,000,000	
Capital surplus	3,000,000	7,600,000
Retained earnings	2,450,000	
Total	$8,450,000	$9,100,000

The long-term bonds pay a 6-percent coupon and yield 8 percent to maturity. The annual earnings per share is now $5.60 and expected to grow to $17.50 over the next 10 years. The dividend payment for the next period is expected to be $3.00. Taxes on income are 48 percent for corporate, 35 percent for personal ordinary, and 17.5 percent for personal capital gains income. The total transaction costs for new common stock are 15 percent of the funds raised.

a What is the expected annual compound growth *rate* in earnings per share?

b Estimate the rate of return which common-stock investors expect.

c What is the pure cost of capital (α) for this bank?

d Estimate the forecasted cost of additional capital raised during the next 10 years by issuing debt, 50 percent, retaining earnings, 30 percent, and issuing new stock, 20 percent.

SELECTED REFERENCES

Barnett, Robert E.: "Anatomy of Bank Failure," *Magazine of Bank Administration,* April 1972.

Booth, J. K.: "Government Supervision and Examination of Life Companies," *Conference of Actuaries in Public Practice, Proceedings,* 1974–1975, pp. 123–130.

Brown, W. J.: "Bank Capital in an Era of Liability Management," *Eastern Finance Association, Proceedings,* April 1975, pp. 45–46.

Buser, Stephen A., Andrew H. Chen, and Edward J. Kane: "Federal Deposit Insurance, Regulatory Policy, and Optimal Bank Capital," *Journal of Finance,* March 1981, pp. 51–60.

Collins, Robert A.: "An Empirical Comparison of Bankruptcy Prediction Models," *Financial Management,* Summer 1980, pp. 52–57.

Gibson, W. E.: "Alternatives to Explicit Regulation of Bank Capital Positions," *Financial Management,* Winter 1976, pp. 71–73.

Heggestad, A. A., and J. M. Mingo: "Capital Management by Holding Company Banks," *Journal of Business,* October 1975, pp. 500–505.

"An Introduction to a Symposium on the Capital Structure of Banks," *Financial Management,* Winter 1976, p. 53.

Jessup, P. F., and M. Bochnak: "Why Not Deregulate Bank Debt Capital?," *Financial Management,* Winter 1976, pp. 65–67.

Lewellen, Wilbur G.: *The Cost of Capital,* Wadsworth, Belmont, Calif., 1969.

Mingo, J. J.: "Capital Management and the Profitability of Prospective Holding Company Banks," *Journal of Financial and Quantitative Analysis,* September 1975, pp. 191–203.

Oldfield, G. S.: "The Free Market Regulation of Bank Capital," *Financial Management,* Winter 1976, pp. 56–58.

Orgler, Y. E.: "Capital Adequacy and Recoveries from Failed Banks," *Journal of Finance,* December 1975, pp. 1366–1375.

Pawelko, R. L.: "Solidity Regulation, Government Supervision and Examination of Life Companies," *Conference of Actuaries in Public Practice, Proceedings,* 1974–1975, pp. 99–122.

Pringle, John J.: "The Capital Decision in Commercial Banks," *Journal of Finance,* June 1974, pp. 779–795.

Santomero, A. M.: "Bank Capital: A Regulation Perspective," *Financial Management,* Winter 1976, pp. 59–64.

Santomero, A. M., and R. D. Watson: "Determining Optimal Capital Standard for the Banking Industry," *Journal of Finance,* September 1977, pp. 1267–1282.

Sealey, C. S.: "Valuation, Capital Structure, and Shareholder Unanimity for Depository Financial Intermediaries," *Journal of Finance,* June 1983, pp. 857–871.

Sinkey, Joseph F., Jr.: *Problem and Failed Institutions in the Commercial Banking Industry,* Greenwich, Conn., JAI Press, 1979.

Talley, S. H.: "Regulating Bank Holding Company Capital," *Financial Management,* Winter 1976, pp. 68–70.

Throop, A. W.: "Capital Investment and Entry in Commercial Banking," *Journal of Money, Credit and Banking,* May 1975, pp. 193–214.

Watson, R. D.: "Capital Evaluation Tools," *Financial Management,* Winter 1976, pp. 54–55.

CHAPTER 20

STRATEGIC PLANNING IN FINANCIAL INSTITUTIONS

Strategic planning deals with the problem of directing and coordinating the entire financial institution. The problem arises because many financial institutions are large, and employ thousands of people who make thousands of commitments on behalf of the institution. Because of the advantages of specialization, employees learn about a particular activity such as making loans, accounting for deposits, selling insurance policy, or underwriting stock issues. Specialization improves the efficiency and capability of the institution, but it also creates an information and management vacuum. When everyone is focusing on an individual task, then the entire institution may run into trouble. Those managers who look out for the institution's total financial welfare are senior management and the financial planning staff. The role, organization, and techniques of strategic planning are discussed in this chapter.

PURPOSE OF FINANCIAL PLANNING

Because of the central role of financial statements in financial planning, the planning function is synonomously referred to as *asset and liability management* or *balance sheet management*. Plans for the future are drawn to make better decisions today, and financial plans and statements are prepared to put the institution in a better position for forthcoming money and capital market conditions. We are consciously choosing among investment and financial alternatives with the objective of coordinating decisions in various parts of the institution and directing efforts toward financial goals, for example, a goal of increasing net income by 10 percent.

Financial planning usually takes place annually on an institution-wide scale and more frequently within departments. Peter Drucker describes planning as a continuous process:

> [Planning is] the continuous process of making present entrepreneurial decisions systematically and with the best possible knowledge of their futurity, organizing systematically the efforts needed to carry out these decisions, and measuring the results of these decisions against the expectations through an organized systematic feedback.[1]

As we change our opinion about future conditions and encounter organizational roadblocks, we need to evaluate and revise the financial plans. Past results are compared with the financial plan monthly or quarterly, providing feedback to managers and staff involved in developing and executing financial plans. When present and expected conditions indicate that the financial plan is no longer relevant, a revised plan is drawn and actions are based on the new plan. For plans to be useful, they must reflect our current expectations about the future of the money markets and our ability to deal profitability in future conditions.

Policy Coordination

The process of moving from financial goals to a written financial plan requires the accomplishment of several intermediate steps and the coordination of plans throughout the institution, as shown in Figure 20-1. Goals are set, supply and

[1] Drucker (1959), p. 239.

FIGURE 20-1
Financial planning in financial institutions.

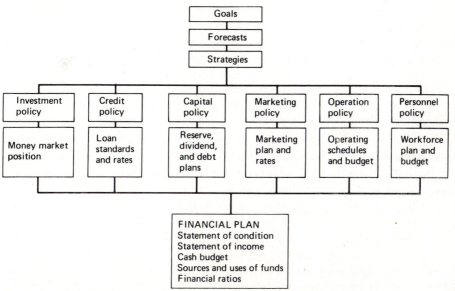

demand forecasted, strategies conceived, policies adopted, and *pro forma* financial statements prepared in the process of developing a financial map for the coming months and years.

The financial goals are defined in terms of profits, dividend payments, financial condition, and financial services to a community. Goals may be established after extensive discussion and written policy statements or through informal discussions by key executives, owners, and regulatory authorities. However determined, goals of the organization are important because they give rise to successful strategies. We have seen that different institutions succeed in the money and capital markets with different strategies. Life insurance companies use one strategy, and banks employ an entirely different strategy. Within the overall strategy of the institution, policies are set by management. The major policy areas of financial institutions are:

- Investment policy
- Credit policy
- Capital policy
- Marketing policy
- Operations policy
- Personnel policy

Policies determine what actions are taken. The results of these actions are measured quantitatively in the financial results. We measure financial results primarily with the following types of financial reports:

- Statement of condition
- Statement of income
- Financial ratios

Statements of Condition and Income

The basic financial statements of financial institutions are the statement of condition and the statement of income. The statement of condition is the financial institution's balance sheet, which presents an itemized statement of assets, liabilities, and capital. The income statement reports revenues, expenses, and profits of the financial institution for a period of time. The condition and income statements are the basic reports for beginning analysis of past operations and for starting to plan for the future. We have used statements of condition and income to describe the institutions composing the money and capital markets in previous chapters. Now we will use financial statements as a management tool for decision making.

The financial statements of the hypothetical National Bank are shown in Tables 20-1 and 20-2.[2] The balance sheet reports ownership of the major asset categories: cash, securities, loans, real assets, and other assets. Commitments

---

[2] National Bank is used as an example in the text and is the basis of some of the problems at the end of the chapter.

TABLE 20-1
National Bank Statement of Condition
December 31, 19X1
(Thousands of Dollars)

Assets

Cash	82,400
Securities	134,600
Loans	279,000
Real and other assets	52,000
Total assets	548,000

Liabilities and Capital

Demand deposits	181,300
Time and savings deposits	227,300
Federal funds and borrowings	68,700
Accrued expenses and other liabilities	27,600
Capital notes	4,000
Stockholders' equity	39,100
Total liabilities and capital	548,000

TABLE 20-2
National Bank Statement of Income
Year Ending December 31, 19X1
(Thousands of Dollars)

Security revenue	9,335
Loan revenue	29,260
Total interest revenue	38,595
Interest expense	19,829
Net interest revenue	18,766
Other revenue	3,742
Net revenue	22,508
Operating expense	16,160
Net income from operations	6,348
Interest on capital notes	320
Net income before taxes and security gains (losses)	6,028
Income taxes	1,972
Net income before security gains (losses)	4,056
Security gains and (losses) net of income taxes	300
Net income	4,356

of the bank are listed as the liabilities: demand deposits, time and savings deposits, other liabilities, and capital notes. Demand deposits are payable immediately and are listed before time and savings deposits, which are subject to payment delays of 30 days or more. The bank's first obligation is to the depositors, then to other creditors. Depositors and others lending money to National Bank would receive first priority to assets in the event of liquidation. Federal funds and borrowings are advances and funds borrowed from the Federal Reserve Bank. The account "accrued expenses and other liabilities" includes loans from other banks and accrued liabilities for purchases and wages, and miscellaneous other credits. Capital notes are bonds issued by the bank to investors who are willing to subordinate their claim on assets to other creditors. Hence, capital notes are a residual type of liability and different from deposits and other liabilities. Stockholders' equity accounts for ownership by National Bank shareholders, and it consists of common stock, capital surplus, and retained earnings. Net income retained since the bank was started is accumulated in retained earnings. In general, stockholders' equity is the residual portion of the condition statement and changes with the success or failure of the bank.

Income Statement Determinants

The statement of income reflects the income and expense results of investment, financing, and operating decisions of the financial institution. The basic factors influencing net income are:

- Interest revenue and expense
- Operating revenue and expense
- Income distribution

Interest Income   Interest income is produced by security and loan investments. For example, National Bank received $38,595 thousand in revenue from security and loan investments totaling $413,600 thousand. Interest revenue is a function of the interest rate and the amount invested, as shown below (amounts in thousands):

	Average interest rate	Amount invested	Interest revenue
Securities	6.94%	$134,600	$ 9,335
Loans	10.49%	279,000	29,260
		$413,600	$38,595

Also, interest is paid for deposits and other sources of money invested in securities and loans. Interest expense of $19,829 thousand represents the cost of money to the bank. Money is the commodity bought by the bank, and interest is the rent paid for money. National Bank pays for the use of money as follows (amounts in thousands):

	Average interest rate	Amount borrowed	Interest expense
Time and savings deposits	6.34%	$227,300	$14,406
Other liabilities	7.89%	68,700	5,423
Total		$296,000	$19,829

Net interest revenue is the difference between interest income and interest expense. Bankers and other money managers sometimes call the difference between interest revenue and expense the *interest spread*. Financial institutions pay for their operations and earn profits on the spread between the rate paid for money and the rate received from investments. Therefore, we need to compute the amount of *net interest revenue*. The amount of net interest revenue is a function of the amount invested, the rate of return on investments, and the interest cost of borrowed funds. The amount invested is largely dependent on the size of the institution and grows with the expansion of the institution's portfolio. Interest income is determined by decisions on what types of investments are selected for the portfolio, prices charged for loans, rates paid depositors and other customers, and the amount of funds borrowed from the money market. Each of these areas is explored in depth in following chapters, as the balance sheet and the investment, loan, and liquidity policies are analyzed.

Other Income and Net Revenue   Other income consists of fees for loans and financial services, charges for checking account overdrafts, discounts on credit card sales, sale of credit life insurance, and similar revenues. Although incidental to the usual business of brokering money, other income is not an interest type of charge. The amount is not usually computed on the basis of the amount borrowed, lent, or on deposit. Fees are paid for bookkeeping, trust services, information, and security transactions services. When other income is added to net interest revenue, the result is termed *net revenue*.

Operating Expense   Outlays for personnel, advertising and promotion, loan loss provisions, and other noninterest costs are shown as operating expense. The $16,160 of operating expense for National Bank consists of the following (amounts in thousands):

Personnel	$ 5,740
Advertising and promotion	425
Provision for loan losses	1,545
Other	8,450
Total operating expenses	$16,160

Personnel costs are typically a large part of the total operating expenses of financial institutions, because institutions are service-oriented businesses that deal directly with the public. Personal selling is the mainstay of the marketing mix, and advertising and promotion are usually small. The provision for loan losses is shown separately to emphasize the importance of losses as an expense item. Large loan losses, such as those experienced by banks in 1975–1976, can increase expenses and reduce profits substantially. Other expenses include the costs of buildings, equipment, and supplies. Growing use of electronic data processing equipment and the boom in electronic funds transfer (EFT) is causing a rapid increase in the other expense category. Institution managers hope that the increase in EFT expenses will be more than offset by a decrease in personnel costs as money mechanization replaces clerical financial services.

Net Income   After deducting operating expenses from net revenue, we have net income from operations (operating income). The claims of customers lending money to the institution and operating expenses have been paid, but the income taxes and residual owners are not yet paid. At this point we begin dividing the current profits among the government and the residual owners. The first claim on income is given to the capital-note holders. The interest paid on capital notes is a tax-deductible expense and is subtracted from operating income before taxes. After deducting interest on capital notes from net income from operations, we obtain net income before taxes and security gains (losses). State and federal income taxes are then subtracted to arrive at net income before security gains (losses). Stockholders and managers view net income before security gains (losses), as important, because it reflects the "regular" profits earned from operations. It is a measure of how well net interest revenue and operating expenses are managed, and it is independent of security gains and losses. Price fluctuations in marketable securities cause security gains and losses, which are real changes in the wealth of stockholders but less subject to managerial control than operating income. After taking security gains or losses, the bottom-line figure is net income. As in any business, net income is profit earned by stockholders. Net income is the final measure of current operations from the viewpoint of stockholders.

For institutions organized as mutual trusts, net income represents the amount retained as a reserve against future losses and is owned communally by members of the institution. In a savings and loan association, for example, net income is transferred to a capital reserve account. If the association takes unusually large losses during a future year, then the loss is borne by the capital reserve account rather than by savings depositors. Thus, current net income provides safety and assurance to future depositors of a mutual savings and loan association. In summary, net income is used to pay dividends, finance additional growth, and absorb losses.

Techniques for Financial Planning

The last section reviewed basic accounting for commercial banks. Accounting for transactions is historical in nature—it looks at the past. But managerial decisions impact on the future of the institution—today's decisions are reported in future accounting statements. Therefore, accounting systems using historical data are inadequate for judging decisions that affect the future. Rather, financial institution managers use planning models that begin with the present financial condition and commitments and then project *pro forma* financial conditions and operations. A *planning model* is a procedure for combining the many proposed decisions with preexisting conditions in an orderly manner. Despite differences in complexity and use, planning models generally have the following features:

1 Managerial input

2 Report output

3 Computational support

These features can be illustrated with a simple example. This example reduces financial institutional accounting to the most basic level to create a situtation that can be solved with a four-function calculator.

Example Financial Plan

Consider an institution with the assets, liabilities, and capital shown in Table 20-3, panel A. What will the balance sheet look like at 19X2? What profit will the institution earn during 19X2? Obviously, these questions can not be answered without additional information—management's input about plans and expectations for 19X2. That is, management is responsible for thinking ahead about the year 19X2, projecting financial market conditions, and committing to financial, personnel, and capital resources. Conditions and commitments resulting from management decisions are the inputs needed to complete our financial plan. Financial statement outputs based on management decisions may then be compared with institutional goals to judge the merit of the proposed plan.

The market conditions and management commitments include projections of interest rates, demand for and supply of funds, operating expenses, and other aspects of the financial institution. In our example the conditions and commitments are summarized in Table 20-3, panel B. Forecasted interest rates are our assessment of the price for funds bought and sold by our institution for various financial contracts. The operating expenses are estimates for personnel and other resources required to service the flow of funds through the intermediary.

The beginning condition and management inputs are combined to form the projected condition and operation for 19X2. The results are shown in Table 20-3, panel C, and the computations are detailed below:

1 Liabilities are recorded from panel B.

2 Assets depend on both the change in the sources of funds (liabilities) and in capital. The equation to find assets for this type of problem is as follows[3]:

$$\text{Assets}_2 = (\text{Liabilities}_2 \, (1 - \text{Liability rate}_2 + \text{Capital}_1 \\ - \text{Operating expense})/(1 - \text{Asset rate}_2) \qquad (20\text{-}1)$$

This equation says "*pro forma* assets equal projected liabilities adjusted for

---

[3] This equation is a reduction of the following equations:

$$\text{Assets}_2 = \text{Liabilities}_2 + \text{Capital}_1 + \text{Income}_2$$
$$\text{Income}_2 = \text{Asset rate}_2 \times \text{Assets}_2 - \text{Liability rate}_2 \times \text{Liabilities}_2 - \text{Operating expense}$$

The first equation is the balance sheet identity, and the second is the definition of income. The equations are solved simultaneously for the unknown assets2, using common alegebraic rules.

TABLE 20-3
EXAMPLE FINANCIAL INSTITUTION—FINANCIAL PLANNING
STATEMENTS

Panel A Historical financial performance, 19X1	
Assets	$1,000,000
Liabilities	$900,000
Equity capital	$100,000
Net income	$14,000

Panel B Projections by management, 19X2	
Projected liability balances	$1,050,000
Predicted interest rate—assets	12.00%
Predicted interest rate—liabilities	10.00%
Planned operating expenses	$19,000

Panel C Computation of ending assets, 19X2	
Projected liabilities	$1,050,000
Times (1 − liability interest rate)	0.90
Equals liabilities after interest expense	$945,000
Subtract operating expenses	($19,000)
Add beginning equity capital	$100,000
Divide by (1 − asset interest rate)	0.88
Equals ending assets for *pro forma* balance sheet	$1,165,909

Panel D *Pro forma* balance sheet, 19X2	
Assets	$1,165,909
Liabilities	$1,050,000
Equity capital	$115,909

Panel E *Pro forma* income statement, 19X2	
Interest revenue	$139,909
Interest expense	$105,000
Net interest margin	$34,909
Operating expenses	$19,000
Net income	$15,909

Panel F Ratio analysis, 19X2	
Return on assets	1.36%
Return on equity	13.73%
Capital to assets	9.94%
Asset growth rate	16.59%
Net income growth rate	13.64%

interest plus beginning capital less operating expenses, all divided by 1 minus the asset interest rate." It solves for assets whenever the balance sheet and income statement have the form presented in Table 20-3.

3 Interest expense is equal to the amount of liabilities times the projected interest rate.

4 Interest revenue is the product of the predicted interest rate and assets for 19X2.

5 Interest expense is the product of the predicted rate and liabilities for 19X2.

6 Net interest margin equals interest revenue less interest expense.

7 Operating expense is assumed equal to planned operating expenses.

8 Income equals net interest expense less operating expense.

Application of *Pro Forma* Statement Model

Now consider how the *pro forma* planning model can be put to work analyzing two familiar management problems of financial institutions:

1 Fluctuating interest rates
2 Changing interest sensitivity of savers

Note as we work through these problems that the impact of proposed changes is not necessarily obvious, even for the elementary situations analyzed here. In reality the number of changes proposed create some very complex problems. (*Hint:* Test yourself by writing the *pro forma* income amount before looking at the results in Table 20-4.)

Fluctuating interest rates are likely to affect the interest rates received on assets and paid on deposits, if the term structure differs for assets and liabilities. (See Chapter 7 for discussion of term-structure management.) For example, rising short-term market rates would cause the liability interest rate to increase more than the asset interest rate if the maturity of liabilities is shorter than the maturity of assets. In our example management predicts that the rising market interest rates might cause the asset rate to be 12.50 percent and the liability rate to be 11.00 percent in 19X2. What will be the impact on 19X2 net interest income? By following the computations described earlier, the statements in panel A, Table 20-4, are prepared. As shown, the impact of rising market interest rates would be a decline in projected 19X2 income from $15,909 to $10,286. Thus, management would recognize that the unbalanced term structure is a substantial risk with respect to income and could consider actions now that would reduce this risk.

Changing interest sensitivity of savers affects the amount of liabilities, liability interest rates, and operating expenses simultaneously. Suppose that management believes that savers are increasingly sensitive about interest rates and, by comparison, decreasingly concerned about the institution's services.

TABLE 20-4
EXAMPLE FINANCIAL INSTITUTION—ALTERNATIVE CONDITIONS
AND COMMITMENTS

Panel A Fluctuating market rates—example	
Projected liability balances	$1,100,000
Predicted interest rate—assets	12.50%
Predicted interest rate—liabilities	11.00%
Planned operating expenses	$20,000

Pro forma income statement, 19X2	
Interest revenue	$151,286
Interest expense	$121,000
Net interest margin	$30,286
Operating expense	$20,000
Income	$10,286

Pro forma balance sheet, 19X2	
Assets	$1,210,286
Liabilities	$1,100,000
Capital	110,286

Panel B Changing interest-rate sensitivity of savers	
Management inputs for 19X2	
Projected liability balances	$1,115,000
Predicted interest rate—assets	12.00%
Predicted interest rate—liabilities	10.50%
Planned operating expenses	$15,000

Pro forma income statement, 19X2	
Interest revenue	$151,943
Interest expense	$120,750
Net interest margin	$31,193
Operating expense	$15,000
Income	$16,193

Pro forma balance sheet, 19X2	
Assets	$1,266,193
Liabilities	$1,150,000
Capital	$116,193

Then management might consider increasing the rate paid on liabilities from 10.00 to 10.25 percent. Further, management plans to reduce branch office operations, thereby saving $5000 in 19X2. The marketing manager projects that these changes would result in total 19X2 liabilities of $1,150,000. What would be the impact on income?

Results of our computations are shown in panel B, Table 20-4. Thus, this strategy increases income from $15,909 to $16,193, a modest but positive improvement. Now management can weigh the nonfinancial considerations, knowing that the financial impact would be favorable.

Alternative Financial Planning Models

Although the basic example presented previously illustrates the process of developing *pro forma* statements, it lacks the detail needed to represent actual financial institutions. Consideration must be given to income taxes, specific asset and liability securities and contracts, line item budgets for operations, historical financial commitments, existing capital assets, legal restrictions, and other aspects of current operations. Such considerations expand the number of accounts and add restrictions that increase the complexity of planning beyond the reach of manual accounting methods. Accounts are highly interrelated; therefore, each time an account or restriction is added, the total plan expands geometrically. In practice, the accounting statements often specify hundreds of accounts and restrictions. Thus, practical planning models are frequently large systems solved with computers.

Two different types of large-scale planning models can be classified according to the form of management inputs. The first type is a *pro forma statement model,* similar to but larger than the previous example, in which all conditions and commitments are specified directly by management. (For example, the Table 20-3, panel B, projections of assets and liabilities are controlled by management.) The results of a *pro forma* statement model are analyzed separately with respect to management's goals. The second type of planning model is the *optimization programming model,* in which management specifies part of the conditions and commitments and sets a goal to be maximized. The program model solves mathematically for that set of management commitments that best achieves management goals. Thus, planning models may take one of two forms:

1 *Pro forma* statement model
2 Optimization programming model

The form depends on the manner in which management inputs are incorporated into the model. In the next section, optimization programming models are examined more closely.

OPTIMIZATION PROGRAMMING MODELS

Following the classic article on bank optimization programming by Chambers and Charnes (1961), financial intermediaries began developing and applying mathematical optimization models. The optimization models determine an optimal financial structure over several time periods, while satisfying liquidity, capital, and other conditions. Compared with manual *pro forma* statement approaches, programming models are extremely efficient for solving large, complex financial structure problems. Many banks, savings and loan associations, and other intermediaries develop short- and intermediate-term plans with programming models. The models' speed, accuracy, and multiperiod capability are well worth the personnel and computer expenses. Furthermore, programming models easily accommodate simultaneous asset and liabilities management decisions, whereas tabular and algebraic approaches can evaluate only prespecified changes in liabilities.

Linear Programming

Linear programming models consist of an objective function and a series of constraints that are linear or may be transformed to a linear form. Constraints represent policy, legal, and market restrictions, while the objective function specifies rates of return and costs. The policy constraints include liquidity and capital minimums, risky investment maximums, and volatile liability source maximums. Legal constraints restrict the financial structure in conformance with contractual obligations and regulatory authority rules. Marketing constraints place upper limits on sales or purchases of securities at given rates. For interperiod models adjustment (from period to period) constraints and tying constraints are necessary.

Model Specification

Consider formulating the financial statements of National Bank as a linear programming model. (Terms are defined in Table 20-5.) If the objective is to maximize profits for a given amount of capital, then the following profit function may be used[4]:

$$\text{Max } [(i_c)\, \text{CASH} + (i_I)\, \text{INVEST} + (i_L)\, \text{LOANS} - (i_D)\, \text{DEP}]$$

Policy constraints are specified as four ratios in this example. The ratios are

---

[4] Other objectives may be specified, although profit is used here for simplicity. For example, Cohen and Hammer (1967) suggest and discuss these alternatives: maximum stockholder equity at the end of the planning period, maximum present value of net income plus capital gains, and maximum present value of net income plus capital gains plus ending stockholders' equity. Note that profit implies profitability, because capital is held constant here.

TABLE 20-5
DEFINITION OF TERMS

Statement of condition			
	Notation		
	Amount	Rate	Example
Cash	CASH	i_C	0
Investment securities	INVEST	i_I	8.2%
Loans	LOANS	i_L	8.5%
Total assets	TA		
Deposits	DEP	i_D	6.8%
Capital	CAPITAL	–	–

Policy ratios			
	Notation	Policy	Example
Ratio of deposits to capital	DEP/CAPITAL	a	11.00
Ratio of cash to deposits	CASH/DEP	b	0.20
Ratio of investments to deposits	INVEST/DEP	c	0.29
Ratio of loans to deposits	LOANS/DEP	d	0.65

transformed to a linear equation in which the left side is less than or equal to a constraint on the right side[5].

As initially stated	Transformed to LP model
DEP/CAPITAL $\leq$ a	DEP – a CAPITAL $\leq$ 0
CASH/DEP $\geq$ b	b DEP – CASH $\leq$ 0
INVEST/DEP $\geq$ c	c DEP – INVEST $\leq$ 0
LOANS/DEP $\leq$ d	d DEP + LOANS $\leq$ 0

Of course, the balance sheet must have equal assets and liabilities plus capital; the balance sheet equality may be stated as follows:

$$CASH + INVEST + LOANS = DEP + CAPITAL$$

---

[5] When multiplying both sides of an inequality by a negative number, the inequality is reversed. That is, "greater than" becomes "less than." Using this rule and other rules of algebra, ratio constraints are transformed to linear constraints. For example:

Step 1: CASH/DEP	$\geq$ b	Initial form
Step 2: CASH	$\geq$ b DEP	Multiply by DEP
Step 3: CASH – b DEP	$\geq$ 0	Subtract b DEP
Step 4: b DEP – CASH	$\leq$ 0	Multiply by –1

or

CASH + INVEST + LOANS − DEP − CAPITAL = 0 (transformed to LP model)

Also, accounts cannot be less than zero; therefore, we include a nonnegativity constraint:

CASH, INVEST, LOANS, DEP, CAPITAL ≥ 0

which is transformed in the LP model to:

−CASH, −INVEST, −LOANS, −DEP, −CAPITAL ≤ 0

The complete model is shown in Table 20-6.

Numerical Example

Consider the situation where the business cycle is experiencing an expansion stage, when loan demand is strong at high interest rates and deposit growth is

TABLE 20-6
SUMMARY OF LINEAR PROGRAMMING MODEL

Maximize $[(0)$ CASH $+ (i_I)$ INVEST $+ (i_L)$ LOANS $- (i_D)$ DEP$]$

Subject to:

	CASH	INVEST	LOANS	DEP	CAPITAL	
Asset allocation constraints				DEP	− a CAPITAL	≤ 0
	− CASH			+ b DEP		≤ 0
		− INVEST		+ c DEP		≤ 0
			− LOANS	+ d DEP		≤ 0
Balance sheet constraint	CASH	+ INVEST	+ LOANS	− DEP	− CAPITAL	= 0
Nonnegativity constraints	− CASH					≤ 0
		− INVEST				≤ 0
			− LOANS			≤ 0
				− DEP		≤ 0
					− CAPITAL	≤ 0
Market constraint				DEP		≤ DEP*
Liquidity constraint		INVEST				− INVEST*
Capital constraint					CAPITAL	= CAPITAL*

moderate. To provide additional funds, deposits can be sold at a total cost (interest and transaction costs) of 6.8 percent. Loans would yield 8.5 percent and investments would yield 8.2 percent. A deposits-to-capital ratio of 11, cash-to-deposits ratio of 0.20, investments-to-deposits ratio of 0.29, and a loans-to-deposit ratio of 0.65 are maintained. Deposits are constrained to the $10 million believed available in the local market. What is the maximum profit which can be earned? Projected earnings are found by substituting our example values into the linear programming model shown in Table 20-6. The final version of the problem in matrix form is shown in Table 20-7. The matrix version of the problem may be solved using linear programming computer algorithms or the Doolittle method.[6] The optimal solution to the example yields earnings of $78,000 and the following statement of condition (thousands of dollars):

Assets		Liabilities and capital	
CASH	2,000	DEP	10,000
INVEST	2,500	CAPITAL	1,000
LOANS	6,500		11,000
TA	11,000		

We find that the highest yielding asset, LOANS, is constrained by the policy ratio of LOANS/DEPOSITS (0.65). Because the return on INVEST is greater than the cost of DEP, funds are allocated to INVEST until we reach the total amount of deposits and capital available. Earnings are computed by multiplying

---

[6] See Hempel and Yawitz (1977) for a discussion of the Doolittle solution technique. Linear programming solutions are described by Hempel and Yawitz (1977).

TABLE 20-7
PARAMETERS FOR NUMERICAL EXAMPLE OF LINEAR PROGRAMMING MODEL

	Cash	Invest	Loans	Dep	Capital		Constant
Maximize:	0	.082	.085	.068			
Subject to:				1	−11	≤	0
	−1			.20		≤	0
		−1		.29		≤	0
			−1	.65		≤	0
	1	1	1	−1	−1	≤	0
	−1					≤	0
		−1				≤	0
			−1			≤	0
				−1		≤	0
					−1	≤	0
				1		≤	10,000,000
					1	=	1,000,000

the interest rate times the amount of each source and use of funds and then summing positive revenues and negative costs.

PROGRAMMING MODELS UNDER UNCERTAINTY

The linear programming model previously described assumes certainty exists and that perfect forecasts can be made. The assumption of certainty is weak and often criticized by both model antagonists and protagonists. One alternative is a model using two-stage linear programming with discrete distribution functions.[7] The first stage of the program allows the intermediary to set balance sheet values, such as CASH, INVEST, LOANS, DEP, etc. In the second stage stochastic changes in DEP and other uncertain accounts occur and the model makes optimal adjustments to the financial structure in response to the changes. By trying a number of first-state decisions, management can evaluate the effects of various policy proposals under conditions of uncertainty.

SUMMARY

Strategic planning in financial institutions coordinates the funds acquisition and investment activities with the operating policy decisions. It focuses financial and human resources on financial markets that have the greatest potential for profitable employment of the stockholder's capital.

To predict the results of alternative investment, credit, capital, marketing, operations, and personnel policies, management inputs projections into a financial planning model. The inputs consist of financial market predictions, policy projections, and institutional responses. The planning model then generates either *pro forma* or optimal balance sheets and income statements, depending on the form of management input. *Pro forma* statements use management input in the form of accounting-like entries, whereas optimization procedures require management inputs in the form of maximization and constraint function(s). After processing planning inputs, financial results are evaluated by management in light of the institution's goals and economic environment. Once a plan is found to be acceptable on both financial and policy levels, it is implemented as the strategic plan coordinating actions throughout the institution.

TERMS

asset and liability management
balance sheet management
pro forma statements
interest-rate margin
comparative statistics

optimization programming models
linear programming models
constraints
objective function

---

[7] For example, the Cohen and Thore (1970) model is a two-stage type.

QUESTIONS

1 How is financial planning related to current decision making?
2 What are the major policy areas a financial institution's manager must consider in formulating a financial plan?
3 Prepare a *pro forma* income statement and balance sheet like that shown in Table 20-3 for 19X2, given the following information:

Balance sheet 19X1	
Assets	$1,000,000
Liabilities	900,000
Capital	100,000

Management inputs for 19X2	
Projected liability balances	$1,200,000
Predicted interest rate—assets	12.00%
Predicted interest rate—liabilities	10.00%
Planned operating expenses	$25,000

4 Given the following information:

Historical financial performance 19X1	
Assets	$2,000,000
Liabilities	$1,900,000
Equity capital	$100,000
Net income	$16,000

Projections by management 19X2	
Projected liability balances	$2,100,000
Predicted interest rate—assets	11.20%
Predicted interest rate—liabilities	8.80%
Planned operating expenses	$45,000

compute these ratios:

Return on assets
Return on equity
Capital to assets
Asset growth rate
Net income growth rate

5 Suppose that interest rates increase beyond those assumed in Question 3. If all other assumptions remain the same, except that the interest rate on assets and liabilities rise to 12.50 and 11.00 percent, respectively, project income for the year 19X2.
6 Compare and contrast *pro forma* statement planning models with optimization planning models, with respect to (a) ease or difficulty in specifying management inputs, (b) computational requirements, (c) information provided by the analysis, and (d) acceptance of results by management.

SELECTED REFERENCES

Aghili, P., R. H. Cramer, and H. E. Thompson: "Small Bank Balance Sheet Management: Apply Two-Stage Programming Models," *Journal of Bank Research*, Winter 1975, pp. 246–256.

Black, Fischer: "Bank Funds Management in an Efficient Market," *Journal of Financial Economics*, December 1975, pp. 323–339.

Boland, Loraine (ed.): *An Introduction to Liquidity Management, Its Principles and Techniques*, Institute of Financial Education, Chicago, 1975.

Carleton, Willard T.: "An Analytical Model for Long-Range Financial Planning." *Journal of Finance*, May 1970, pp. 291–315.

Carleton, Willard T., Charles L. Dick, Jr., and David H. Downes: "Financial Policy Models: Theory and Practice," *Journal of Financial and Quantitative Analysis*, December 1973, pp. 691–709.

Chambers, D., and A. Charnes: "Inter-Temporal Analysis and Optimization of Bank Portfolios," *Management Science*, July 1961, pp. 393–410.

Cohen, Kalman J., and Frederick S. Hammer: "Linear Programming and Optimal Bank Asset Management Decisions," *Journal of Finance*, May 1967, pp. 147–165.

Cohen, Kalman J., Steven Maier, and James H. Vander Weide: "Recent Developments in Management Science in Banking," *Management Science*:, October 1981, pp. 1097–1119.

Drucker, Peter F.: "Long-Range Planning: Challenge to Management Science," *Management Science*, April 1959.

Fortson, James C., and Robert R. Dince: "An Application of Goal Programming to Management of a Country Bank," *Journal of Bank Research*, Winter 1977, pp. 311–319.

Goldstein, Alice B., and Barbara G. Markowitz: "SOFASIM: A Dynamic Insurance Model with Investment Structure, Policy Benefits and Taxes," *Journal of Finance*, May 1982, pp. 595–607.

Haslem, John A.: "Concepts of Bank Funds Management," *Bankers Magazine*, May/June 1982, pp. 92–97.

Hayes, Douglas A.: *Bank Funds Management:* Ann Arbor, University of Michigan, 1980.

Hempel, George H.: *Bank Funds Management under Deregulation*, American Bankers Association, Washington, D.C., 1981.

Hempel, George H., and Jess B. Yawitz: *Financial Management of Financial Institutions*, Prentice-Hall, Englewood Cliffs, N.J., 1977.

Holmberg, S. R.: "Commercial Bank Strategic Planning: The Role of the Business Economist," *University of Michigan Business Review*, March 1978, pp. 25–29.

Hopelain, D. G., and D. W. Jones: "Managing Change in Modern Investment Institutions," *Financial Analysts Journal*, September/October 1976, pp. 27–34.

Kahane, Y., and D. Nye: "A Portfolio Approach to the Property-Liability Insurance Industry," *Journal of Risk and Insurance*, December 1975, pp. 579–598.

Kingsland, Louis: "Projecting the Financial Condition of a Pension Plan Using Simulation Analysis," *Journal of Finance*, May 1982, pp. 577–584.

Lifson, K. A., and Brian R. Blackmarr: "Simulation and Optimization Models for Asset Deployment and Funds Sources Balancing Profit, Liquidity and Growth," *Journal of Bank Research*, Autumn 1973, pp. 239–255.

McKinney, G. W., Jr.: "A Perspective on the Use of Models in the Management of Bank Funds," *Journal of Bank Research*, Summer 1977, pp. 122–127.

MacMillan, Ian C., and Mary Lynn McCaffery: "Strategy for Financial Services: Cashing in on Competitive Inertia," *Journal of Business Strategy*, Winter 1984, pp. 58–65.

Minsky, H. P.: "Banking and a Fragile Financial Environment," *Journal of Portfolio Management*, Summer 1977, pp. 16–22.

Nicholson, E. A. and R. L. Litschert: "Long-Range Planning in Banking: Ten Cases in the U.S. and Britain," *Journal of Bank Research*, Spring 1973, p. 31.

Royer, M. H.: "Simulation at Banque de Bruxelles," *Journal of Bank Research*, Winter 1975, pp. 237–245.

Shank, John K.: "Long Range Planning Systems: Achieving both 'Realism' and 'Reach'" *Journal of Bank Research*, Autumn 1973, pp. 185–193.

Steans, Harrison I.: "The Business of Banking," *Journal of Commercial Bank Lending*, April 1977, pp. 57–63.

Taylor, Bernard W., and Laurence J. Moore: "A Simulation Approach to Planning Bank Projects," *Journal of Bank Research*, Autumn 1976, pp. 225–228.

Winklevoss, Howard E., "Plasm: Pension Liability and Asset Management Simulation," *Journal of Finance*, May 1982, pp. 585–594.

Yalif, Anat: "Strategic Planning Techniques," *Magazine of Bank Administration*, April 1982, pp. 22–26.

Yeo, Edwin H., III: "A Management View of Financial Planning, or the Best Laid Schemes," *Journal of Bank Research*, Autumn 1973, pp. 207–211.

Zoltners, Andris A.: "A Manpower Sizing and Resource Allocation Model for Commercial Lending," *Journal of Bank Research*, Summer 1983, pp. 134–143.

PART FIVE

PUBLIC POLICY TOWARD FINANCIAL INSTITUTIONS

ORIENTATION

Trust and confidence in the financial system is not only a prerequisite for the existence of financial institutions, but a condition demanded by the public. Governmental response to the public demand for a safe, sound, and supportive financial system has been a great deal of state and federal legislation that codifies acceptable behavior and maintains regulatory bodies that monitor financial institutions and securities activities. This part deals with two aspects of public policy toward financial institutions:

Purpose and structure of regulation (Chapter 21)
Money and banking public policy (Chapter 22)

The chapter on the purpose and structure of regulation presents the basic tenets of governmental oversight of private financial institutions. Then it considers reform history and prospects that are intended to adjust governmental policy legislation and regulation in tune with the rapidly evolving financial sources industry.

The chapter on money and banking public policy reviews the Federal Reserve's monetary policy function. So as to promote economic stability and growth, the Federal Reserve alters the size and business of the financial institutions system. The means applied by the Federal Reserve and the controversial results obtained are important to both managers and observers of financial institutions.

CHAPTER 21

PURPOSES AND STRUCTURE OF REGULATION

Changes in the forms and delivery modes of financial services offered by commercial banks and other financial institutions have occurred at an unprecedented pace in the past decade. Pressure from innovative nonbank institutions such as the money-market mutual funds already spurred Congress to pass significant deregulation of banking in 1980 and 1982. Yet the regulatory oversight of financial institutions remains largely unchanged from the structure cast by legislation enacted during the Great Depression. Far more sweeping reforms in regulatory oversight will be required to deal with the market-oriented, high-technology institutions of the next decade.

PURPOSE OF REGULATION

For more than a century, American consumers and businesspersons have called for public policies that make financial institutions competitive and sound.[1] In response to the public demand, the state and federal governments have legislated standards of conduct and created regulatory agencies. The avowed purpose of this legislation was usually to improve the welfare of the general public. The Investment Company Act of 1940 was enacted "to eliminate the (certain) conditions . . . which adversely affect the national public interest and the interest of investors."[2] As financial market and social conditions changed, new legislation was enacted to change the authority of regulatory agencies. The Securities Exchange Act of 1934 was amended in 1975

---

[1] *Report of the President's Commission on Financial Structure and Regulation* (1971), p. 1.
[2] Investment Company Act of 1940, H.R. 10065, Public Law No. 768, 76th Congress, p. 2.

"to remove barriers to competition, to foster the development of a national securities market system and a national clearance and settlement system. . . ."[3] Through the prohibition of undesirable acts and the promotion of competition and common objectives, regulation is intended to improve the effectiveness and efficiency of financial institutions and markets.

Proposed changes in the structure of regulation are based on a set of general objectives. The view of the Board of Governors of the Federal Reserve System is that regulation be designed to accomplish the following[4]:

1 Increase competition
2 Improve the flexibility of financial institutions to respond to changing needs of individuals and businesses
3 Maintain a base for effective monetary policy
4 Preserve a sound and resilient financial system

These objectives are intended to promote a stable and growing standard of living. Also, regulation is designed to increase confidence and stability. Confidence in the financial system promotes the flow of savings to investment.

The financial markets are fragile structures, not having physical form and subject to the failure of human resolve under stress and temptation.[5] To the extent that government regulation supports confidence and promotes strength in the financial system, the flow of capital into investment is enhanced. Therefore, confidence may be as important an objective as efficiency when evaluating regulatory structure.

Effect of Regulation on Institutions Management

Regulation changes the alternative actions available to financial institutions managment and, consequently, becomes a factor in management decision making.[6] As depicted in Figure 21-1, government regulations cause changes in the investment portfolios, security issues, and operations of financial institutions. In turn, the derivative actions of the financial institutions are intended to achieve the public policy objectives of financial stability, high economic growth, stable prices, full employment levels of output, and a balance of international trade.

Many management decisions are influenced in some way by regulation.[7] For

---

[3] Securities Acts Amendments of 1975, Public Law 94-29, 94th Congress, S. 249, June 4, 1975, p. 1.

[4] Holland (February 1976), p. 96.

[5] Wojnilower (1976), p. 13.

[6] In responding to pressures of competition, technological advance, and customer demand for different and expanded services, Holland states that "the most effective role here for the Congress and the regluatory agencies is one of channeling and containing these developments within prudent limits" (Holland, February 1976, p. 96).

[7] While not generally considered in the same vein as regulated public utilities in the power, communications, or transportation industries, depository institutions—commerical banks, savings and loan associations, and mutual savings banks—are among the most highly regulated of all firms. See Tuccillo (1977), p. 577.

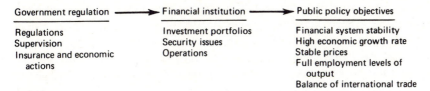

FIGURE 21-1
Government regulation causes changes in financial institutions to achieve public-
policy objectives.

example, the Securities Acts Amendment of 1975, which abolished fixed commission charges for trading securities, prevented the New York Stock Exchange management from setting standard prices for trading securities listed on
the New York and other organized stock exchanges. Under competitive pressures, commission charges fell drastically for large, institutional trades. Some
brokerage firms responded to lower commission revenues by shifting their
marketing efforts from the institutional sector to retail sector and to portfolio
management.[8] Other brokerage firms recognized the market opportunity afforded by the abolition of fixed commission rates quickly offered securities
exchange services without research services but at commission rates substantially below prevailing rates, and they successfully captured that segment of the
market that desired only the execution of securities transactions. Thus, new
regulation eliminates alternatives for some and opens the door for other financial institutions.

Cost of Regulation

Regulation not only provides benefits but also imposes costs on financial
institutions and markets. In general, consumers are best served by financial
institutions that desire and are able to provide services freely. A freely competitive financial structure prevails where institutions are "wealth maximizing
competitors that are neither subsidized, penalized or regulated by the government and where entry into and exit from the market is not constrained."[9]
Therefore, the imposition of regulation usually entails a movement away from
free competition and toward greater costs or suboptimal portfolios. For example, deposit institutions must submit to regular examinations by government
auditors, which they pay for explicitly in the form of fees and implicitly in the
form of business disruption. Mutual savings banks are restricted by law to
mortgage loan investments, although the supply of mortgages of the risk class
that they wish to accept may be limited. When the supply of desirable mort-

---

[8] Williams (1978) discusses the movement into and out of the institutional brokerage market
following May day when commissions became negotiable for all transactions.
   [9] Benston (1973), p. 220.

gages is less than the quantity of funds available, the mutual savings bank must make marginal mortgages or invest funds elsewhere.[10]

The cost of regulation is a form of tax assessed explicitly and implicitly.[11] Differences in regulation cause the implicit tax to vary from one type of institution to another. For example, required reserves on depostis at depository institutions are an implicit tax. The amount of the tax equals the lost earnings on the nonearning reserve asset; the U.S. Treasury receives the tax as a transfer payment from the Federal Reserve's interest revenues earned on U.S. government bills, notes, and bonds purchased with required reserve balances. Another example of an implicit tax is active supervision. Financial institutions are required by law to provide extensive financial and other reports of operations, to open their offices frequently for examination, and to comply with a variety of special rules and regulations. Complying with active supervisory requests requires personnel and other resources, which increase operating expenses and reduce profits. Supervisory fees charged to institutions by the regulatory agencies are explicit operating expenses; they are accounted for as operating expenses and separately from explicit taxes assessed by local, state, and federal governments. In general, the agencies that regulate financial institutions are supported not by general tax revenues but from assessments paid by financial institutions. These assessments are relatively small compared with the amount of assets and revenues of the institutions.

FINANCIAL SYSTEM EFFICIENCY AND STABILITY

Financial system stability means establishing and maintaining a structure of financial institutions and markets having a reasonable level of risk; efficiency means that the demand for financial services is anticipated and services provided to the public at the least cost for a given level of quality.[12] The explicit and implicit costs of regulation imply that regulations imposed to promote system stability are likely to reduce system efficiency. The two objectives are often inconsistent, and compromises are frequently necessary to develop reasonable regulations.

Proposals for Change

The difficulties of developing a regulatory system balancing the sometimes conflicting objectives of efficiency and stability are many. Sometimes regulations designed to promote stability hold back desirable changes and interfere

---

[10] Benston (1972), p. 136. Benston argues that "greater diversity rather than specializatin would help the MSBs manage their funds more efficiently." These and other implicit taxes and subsidies are described by Kane (1973), also.

[11] This discussion is based on Tuccillo's (1977) research, which applies regulated industry concepts to depository institutions and estimates differential taxation effects.

[12] The definition of efficiency is based on the optimal banking structure concept of Benston (1973). This definition is a practical interpretation of market perfection discussed in Chapter 3.

with the ability of the sytem to adapt efficiently to a new environment. For example, branch banking laws and court decisions have retarded the development of electronic funds transfer systems, when capital investment needs are shifting with changes in technology and international business. Unfortunately, new laws to accommodate interest rate, money flow, and capital investment changes are written only after significant events in the financial market.

The difficulties of anticipating tomorrow's public policy requirements adds to the problems of designing today's laws. Concern for future public policy is reflected in the Hunt commission, which quotes a 1970 report of the Council of Economic Advisers:

> Financial services required by tomorrow's economy will differ in as yet undefinable ways from those appropriate today. The demands on our flow of national savings . . . will be heavy in the years ahead, and our financial structure must have the flexibility that will permit a sensitive response to changing demands.[13]

In response to changing conditions and needs, agency officials, economists, and financial institutions executives undertake studies and recommend regulatory changes in great numbers and with nearly a daily frequency. The House Committee on Banking, Currency, and Housing and the Senate Committee on Banking, Housing, and Urban Affairs meet regularly to listen to testimony from industry spokespersons and agency representatives. State legislators hear and consider legislative proposals affecting financial institutions in their states in nearly every session. The volume of proposed (or even enacted) legislation is substantial, and summarizing all of it would be beyond the scope of this book. On the other hand, a few major study commissions have undertaken reviews covering major segments of the U.S. financial system. The study commissions, composed of economists, lawyers, and legislators, provide a capsulized and thoughtful view of regulation of the depository institutions, the organized securities markets, consumer finance institutions, and the electronic funds transfer network. These important areas of the financial system are addressed in the following major studies:

Official Title	*Reference Title*
1 The President's Commission on Financial Structure and Regulation	Hunt commission
2 Securities and Exchange Commission *Institutional Investor Study*	*Institutional Investor Study*
3 National Commission on Consumer Finance	*Consumer Credit in the United States*
4 National Commission on Electronic Fund Transfers	*EFT in the United States: Policy Recommendations and the Public Interest*

---

[13] Report of the Council of Economic Advisers, February 1970, p. 104, quoted in *Report of the President's Commission on Financial Structure* (1971), pp. 1–2.

Also, related reports and studies provide insight into the direction of regulatory evolution. For example, *Financial Institutions and the Nation's Economy* (FINE) presented "discussion principles" for developing legislation. The major studies stimulate a great deal of discussion and writing among legislators, regulators, executives, and economists, because they bring controversial issues to light in a systematic and thorough manner.

Hunt Commission

Scope of Study   The so-alled Hunt commission report (named for the chairman, Reed O. Hunt) was the most recent and important study of the U.S. financial system. Officially termed The President's Commission on Financial Strucutre and Regulation, this group issued a study that proposed sweeping legislative changes in the regulation of financial institutions. The scope was defined at its earliest meeting, where the commission experts decided to concentrate on commercial banks, credit unions, reserve life insurance companies, and private pension funds. Key problems and areas addressed were the following:

1 Deposit rate regulations
2 Chartering and branching
3 Deposit insurance
4 Reserves and taxation
5 Effects of regulation on social priority investments
6 Competition among institutions
7 Organization of the regulatory agencies

Obviously, this study was very extensive and designed to set the legislative tone for a decade.

Reasoning that a package of balanced recommendations was more rational than a series of independent suggestions, the commission proposed a set of legislative guides. The report recommended seven points, four of which were substantially incorporated into the 1980 and 1982 Banking Acts. A later study, *Financial Institutions and the Nation's Economy* (FINE), supported these recommendation as well as advocated universal reserve requirements. The 1980 Deregulation and Monetary Control Act (DIDMCA) was an omnibus bill containing several titles. The major features, as summarized by Cargill and Garcia (1980), are described here.

Financial System Reform

Interest-rate Ceilings   Interest-rate ceilings were to be entirely eliminated over time, and under the following provisions:

1 There was to be an "orderly phaseout and the ultimate elimination of the

limitations on the maximum rate of interest and dividends'' on deposit accounts by 1986 (Title II, Section 202).

2 Authority to set interest-rate ceilings (Federal Reserve Regulation Q) was transferred from various federal agencies to the newly created Depository Institutions Deregulation Committee (DIDC).

3 DIDC is required to give due regard for the ''safety and soundness of depository institutions . . . '' (Title II, Section 204).

4 State laws limiting interest rates on mortgage loans were superseded; limits were placed on maximum interest rates for business and agricultural loans, credit union loans, and other loans.

Funding   Funding sources were greatly expanded by authorizing depository institutions to permit depositors to make withdrawals by ''transferable instruments for the purpose of making transfers to third parties'' (Title III, Section 303). This provision expanded NOW accounts to all depository institutions, but left intact the commercial bank monopoly over demand deposits.

Lending powers were expanded for all depository institutions, particularly the savings and loans. Important changes for the savings and loan associations were:

1 Portfolio composition restrictions were removed for account loans, single-family loans, multifamily loans, U.S. government securities, home improvement and manufactured home loans, and loans to other financial institutions.

2 They were authorized to lend up to 90 percent of appraised value on single- and multifamily loans.

3 They were authorized to make commercial real estate and consumer loans within certain limits.

4 They were authorized to issue credit cards and engage in related operations.

That is, savings and loans were given many lending powers previously limited to commercial banks.

Federal Reserve Powers   Federal Reserve control over the monetary aggregates was improved in response to declining membership (member banks were relinquishing national charters in favor of state charters) and to expanding nonbank depository intermediaries. The act solved the problem simply by requiring that ''each depository institution shall maintain reserve against its transaction accounts . . . ,'' ''Each depository institution shall maintain reserves against its non-personal time deposits . . . ,'' and ''Foreign branches, subsidiaries, and international banking facilities of nonmember depository institutions shall maintain reserves to the same extent required by the Board of foreign branches, subsidiaries, and international banking facilities of member banks'' (Title I, Section 103). Further, the Federal Reserve was required to expand discount and borrowing privileges and other services to all depository institutions. Thus, depository institutions were placed on a level playing field with respect to maintaining reserves and receiving services at the Federal Reserve.

Recommendations versus Actions   Many of the recommendations and much of the philosophy of the Hunt report and the FINE study were enacted in the 1980 Deregulation and Monetary Control Act. However, the 1980 act differed from study recommendations on several significant points, noted by Cargill and Garcia (1982). First, previous studies recommended that all depository institutions be authorized to issue demand deposit accounts. The 1980 act authorized NOW accounts for nonbank depository institutions but did not expand demand deposit authority for corporate demand deposit accounts; that is, corporations are not permitted interest-bearing checking accounts. Second, the 1980 act did not abolish the prohibition of interest payments on demand deposit accounts, as recommended by the FINE study. However, liberalization of checking-type accounts with interest payments was effected in both the 1980 and 1982 acts. Third, entry and charter restrictions were largely unchanged by the 1980 and 1982 Banking Acts, thereby maintaining barriers to entry and change by new or existing financial institutions. Fourth, income tax inequalities among depository institutions were criticized in the previous studies, but the acts avoided this politically sensitive issue. Thus, the 1980 and 1982 Banking Acts did not adopt all of the recommendations of the earlier commissions. Further, they did not deal with the need for a restructured regulatory regime. The unfinished agenda of institutional reform and developing problems of regulating a reformed industry no doubt, will, be the subject of subsequent commissions.

Regulatory Reform Task Group

This 1983 task group focused on only the question of simplifying the regulatory bureaucracy. It recommended that the structure of regulation should be functional, delegating all antitrust matters to the Justice Department (currently the joint responsibility of many banking agencies) and securities regulation to the SEC, regardless of the type of institution providing the service. Further it recommended that deposit insurance premiums vary with institutional risk and that large, uninsured deposits not be honored in the case of failed institutions.

Institutional Investor Study

The *Institutional Investor Study*, completed in 1971, fulfilled a congressional mandate to study the effect of institutional purchases, sales, and holding of securities "upon the maintenance of fair and orderly securities markets . . . the stability of such markets . . . the interests of the issuers . . . and upon the interests of the public. . . ."[14] The resolution to study institutional effects on the securities markets was prompted by the growing importance of

[14] Public Law No. 90-438, July 29, 1968. This federal law authorized the *Institutional Study.*

pension, profit-sharing, and mutual funds in the equity securities markets. (In Part Two of this book, the rapid growth of institutions that hold and trade equity securities was shown.) At the same time that institutional ownership of stocks was growing, the household ownership of stocks was declining.[15] The *Institutional Investor Study* undertook to analyze the structure and efficiency of the securities markets under changing institutional conditions. Results of the study were summarized under three headings[16]:

1 Institutional trading patterns and price impacts
2 Performance of the market-making function
3 Impacts of the fixed minimum commission rate system upon institutional trading

Institutional Trading Patterns   In response to the allegation that institutions systematically trade the same stocks at the same time and way (buying or selling), the study analyzed subgroups of investors. Parallel trading could be caused by either performance-oriented managers who follow trading actions by fund leaders or analysts simultaneously reaching trade decisions on the basis of new information. The study concludes that "the incidences of apparent parellelism are no more frequent than would be expected from chance given independent trading decisions."[17] Institutions did not appear to "gang up" on the same side of the market but rather produced passive patterns that did not affect prices. The finding that institutional trading habits neither strain the market nor systematically impact on prices (with some minor exceptions) served to squelch a movement toward greater restrictions over the size and trading activities of institutional portfolios.

Performance of the Market-Making Function   Market makers, exchange specialists, and third-market dealers supply liquidity to the securities markets by changing their own inventories. The study analyzed the inventory positions of active market makers in ninety-three New York Stock Exchange listed stocks over a 15-month period. Specialist and dealer inventories changed in an inverse relationship to price changes, indicating that market makers tend to stabilize the markets in which they deal. Furthermore, institutional trading was found to produce less uncertainty, not more, as is commonly believed.

Institutions were executing block trades off the exchange floors through dealers. Block trades were advantageous to institutions because they were unreported, not subject to New York transfer taxes, traded later in the day (on the west coast), avoided undesired participation by the specialist and public, and were executed at substantially lower fees in some cases. However, block trades were found to reduce market efficiency, because the quality of report-

---

[15] The study reported changes in the distribution of holdings in vol. 1, chap. 3.
[16] This summary is based on Jones (1972). For a brief description of the methodology, readers are referred to Jones (1972) or the study report cited at the end of the chapter.
[17] Jones (1972), p. 309.

ing, and, therefore, investor information, was reduced. The study affirmed the need for greater disclosure of block trades.

Impact of the Fixed Minimum Commission Rate System upon Institutional Trading Commissions were fixed for most trades at the time of the study. Many problems of the secondary equity market were attributed to the market structure itself rather than to institutional trading effects. Under the fixed commission rate schedule, commissions charged on institutional accounts exceeded costs. Investment managers were able to obtain reciprocal services from brokers who recognized the excessive profitability of institutional accounts. By trading frequently (rapid portfolio turnover), some institutions obtained reciprocal services from brokers. Thus, the structure of brokerage commissions was found to cause undesired trading. That is, institutional trading patterns that were undesirable from a public policy viewpoint were the result of an inefficient market structure. Ironically, the commission structure was supported by federal law. Subsequent legislation abolished fixed minimum commission rate structures, and market competition forced brokerage commissions to fall substantially for institutional investors.[18]

National Commission on Consumer Finance

The National Commission on Consumer Finance (NCCF) was established as part of the Consumer Credit Protection Act of 1968 and reported its findings on December 31, 1972.[19] The study appraised the functioning and structuring of the consumer finance industry and consumer credit transactions. Issues investigated included consumer credit rates, unfair practices, and industry structure. Government regulation and chartering were evaluated, particularly the possibility of federal chartering. Not only did the study deal with specific topical issues, but it also compiled historical, descriptive information on the consumer credit industry. The breadth of the study was far too wide for us to cover its conclusions adequately in a short space. A significant contribution of the study, however, was the revelation that government overregulation reduced market efficiency without achieving significant social goals.

The commission's primary assessment is "that the essentials of how much credit, to whom, and at what price should be left to the free choice of consumers in the marketplace—provided that the marketplace is competitive."[20] Just as the commission could not say if the price of hamburgers or shoes was fair, it could not say that the price of credit was fair. The allocation of credit among consumers, like the allocation of hamburgers and shoes, should be made by the industry itself. Determination of what part of a family's income can safely be devoted to monthly payments on credit obligations is an activity the industry is

---

[18] The effects of "unfixing" commission rates are shown in Edmister (1978).

[19] Except where noted, this section is based on the *Report of the National Commission on Consumer Finance* (1972).

[20] *Report of the National Commission on Consumer Finance* (1972), p. 3.

constantly attempting to improve through personnel training and statistical analysis. (See Chapter 16, for a discussion of credit analysis.) It is the responsibility of management motivated by the opportunity for profit, to make as much credit available as possible at fair prices and to all credit-worthy individuals. Through competition, lenders attempting to charge excessive rates or withholding credit unfairly are displaced by competitors who grant loans at the lowest possible rates to persons able to repay.

A significant finding by this government-sponsored study is that "state legislation especially has tended to restrain competition and unnecessarily segment the consumer credit market."[21] Existing laws and regulation tend to inhibit competition, rather than promote free access to businesses willing to provide consumer credit. Principal impediments to consumer credit granting are:

1 State laws containing unrealisticly low (outdated) rate structures

2 Convenience and advantage statutes and licensing laws

3 Laws preventing retailers from making cash loans and other laws segmenting the industry

4 Statutes prohibiting savings and loan associations, mutual savings banks, and life insurance companies from making certain types of consumer loans

5 Laws preventing banks from charging market loan rates

6 Restrictions on inter- and intrastate branch banking

An unrealistic rate structure is imposed by some states in an attempt to reduce the cost of credit to consumers, but the effect of such legislation is not necessarily in the consumer's interest. Laws and institutional provisions establishing maximum legal interest rates are called *usury laws* and exist in all states except New York, Massachusetts, and New Hampshire.[22]

The effects of usury laws are subtle, because price is only one facet of the credit offer function.[23] The credit offer function consists of the following:

1 Interest rate

2 Maturity

3 Down payment

4 Security and collateral

5 Availability of irregular payment plans

6 Willingness of credit granters to assume risk of default

7 Convenience of location

8 Status of credit grantor in view of consumer

9 Collection methods

[21] *Report of the National Commission on Consumer Finance* (1972), p. 3.

[22] Curiously, Massachusetts led the American colonies in passing the first usury statute in 1641. Other colonies adopted similar statutes but failed to repeal them when Massachusetts rescinded its usury laws in 1867. Today, Massachusetts and New Hampshire limit finance charges only on specific forms of consumer credit.

[23] *Report of the National Commission on Consumer Finance* (1972), chap. 3.

10 Prepayment penalty

11 Delinquency and deferral charges

If a low ceiling is imposed effectively on credit contracts, two consequences are likely: (1) credit availability is reduced, and (2) credit is subsidized by cash buyers. Forced reduction in interest rates reduces the revenue necessary to pay for loan defaults; therefore, lenders are less willing to grant credit to high-risk borrowers (credit offer function number 6). At the margin credit availability is reduced, and the group first affected is low-income families. Restrictive rates in the District of Columbia caused credit to become partially unavailable there. Reductions in the maximum rate in Arkansas, Minnesota, Wisconsin, and Washington led to a decrease in the availability of credit and an effort by lenders to make up for the loss in income. Lenders who also sell the goods financed may transfer a portion of the finance charge to the price of goods sold. Although retailing is a highly competitive business, some retailers can emphasize sales financing, raise the price of goods, and thereby increase the effective rate of return from consumer credit. Cash buyers patronizing such retailers also pay the higher price, which includes finance charges, and inadvertently subsidize consumer credit purchases by others. The commission studied numerous other aspects of consumer lending in terms of their overall effect on the public. Generally, legislation (such as usury laws) that seeks one improvement produces undesirable side effects, such as reduced credit availability or service. Pushing on one facet of the credit function causes a bulge in another place.

In addition to advocating the repeal of restrictive state legislation, the commission recommended improving consumer knowledge and industry competition. The consumer has a "right to know" and the government has a responsibility to ensure that the industry follows the truth-in-lending legislation in practice and spirit. The industry should be restricted from mergers and other actions which tend to reduce the interinstitution and interfirm competition. On the other hand, the government's approach should be consistent. Laws and regulation to ensure free access, open competition, and elimination of harmful and socially undesirable practices should be accompanied by elimination of inhibiting rate ceilings.

National Commmission on Electronic Fund Transfers

The National Commission on Electronic Fund Transfers (EFT commission), which presented its findings in 1977, followed a congressional charge to complete a comprehensive view of EFT and to provide explicit recommendations for public policy in the United States.[24] The purposes of the EFT commission were (1) to recognize the need to preserve competition among financial institutions and other businesses using EFT systems, (2) to promote competition and minimize government regulation in EFT systems, (3) to prevent unfair and

---

[24] Except where noted, this summary is based on the study report, *EFT in the United States* (1977).

discriminatory practices in EFT systems, and (4) to stimulate maximum user convenience and privacy in EFT systems. The EFT commission's report dealt with the effects of EFT on consumers, the development of EFT systems, the technology of EFT, the role of the federal government, and international developments.

Consumer Interests   Consumers have accepted EFT reluctantly, according to the study, for reasons of privacy and lack of experience. The commission concluded that the privacy of financial information was not adequately safeguarded by present laws. Privacy could be violated in four areas identified by the study:

1 New types of financial transactions records
2 Expanded transactions records
3 Improved ease of access to records
4 Increased number of institutions that can access individual transactions records

For example, a centralized EFT system would permit system users the privilege of surveilling a person's physical and financial activities, such as eating at a restaurant (paid by EFT) or buying securities (purchased through EFT). The commission recommended that EFT systems not provide government surveillance information except within strict procedures, not release data to third parties without consumer approval, and not collect unnecessary information. To combat the potential lack of information about EFT account activity, the commission recommended that institutions mail statements to consumers, carefully describe credit terms, and provide credit file information for consumer verification. These and other consumer interests dictated the development of more extensive legislation on the acquisition and dissemination of financial information about consumers.

Development of EFT Systems   Developmental issues led to recommendations for separate legislation covering terminals offering EFT services, the rules for deploying and offering services through terminals, approaches to shared EFT systems, competitive impacts of EFT, credit availability with EFT options, and the economics of EFT systems. The study concluded that terminals should not be considered brick-and-mortar branches of financial institutions and not be subject to branching restrictions. The commission concluded that freedom of entry would promote geographical development of funds-transfer services. After considering the argument that an unrestricted approach to terminal dissemination might lead to domination of financial markets by a few depository institutions, the commission found that potential harmful effects could be prevented by current regulations. This recommendation implied that banks and other financial institutions could open unattended terminals in new locations without government approval. Unrestricted entry for terminals, a radical concept not accepted by the courts and many regulatory agencies, would give bank managers accessibility to markets previously barred by branch application approval delays and contestations.[25]

Large EFT systems are expensive to build and operate but can serve a large number of users. Sharing EFT systems is an economical approach to overcoming the fixed costs of deployment and operation, and the EFT commission supported *procompetitive* sharing. On the other hand, the power to control access to an EFT network could be used to preclude competitive institutions from EFT services, and thereby reduce competition. The EFT commission recognized that the conflicting arguments of cost and competition could not be resolved by specific legislation. It recommended, therefore, that the "appropriate State and Federal regulatory agencies continue to monitor the proliferation of EFT systems and take appropriate action consistent with the agencies charter." The recommendation is weak but consistent with the finding that the commission "found no evidence for immediate concern." Again, the commission decided in favor of a freely competitive EFT structure for this infant industry where future costs are uncertain.

The commission's study of point-of-scale (POS) EFT systems found that scale economies are realized as system size increases. Potential scale economies could substantially affect changes in market shares and the structure of the retail financial service industry. Large-scale institutions and institutions associated with large-scale POS EFT systems could obtain increased market shares. However, the lack of useful cost data precluded estimating the limits of scale economies, and rapidly decreasing prices for EFT system components prevented predicting the future cost structure. Therefore, the resulting optimal institutional structure could not be constructed. To allow the industry to adjust to future cost structures, the commission recommended that rules and regulations not be imposed now, but that the market be monitored for market share impacts.

MAJOR REGULATORY ISSUES

New regulatory policy issues will arise in the 1980s and 1990s because of continuing advances in information technology, additional but partial deregulation, and unpredictable fluctuations in interest rates and economic activity. Among the many important issues that may develop, four stand out as well-recognized, crucial areas of concern. These are:

- Deposit insurance coverage and cost
- Bankruptcy proceedings for large depository institutions

---

[25] Currently, depository institutions must receive approval to open or close branch offices. The application may be dissapproved by the regulating body after due process, which includes public hearings. Protestants, which may include competing banks, may claim that the additional branch in their market area would be seriously harmful to their institution or that it would not significantly improve the financial services available to the public; or they may offer other causes for denying approval of the application.

- Product and line-of-business restrictions
- Geographical restrictions on depository institutions

These issues span the entire financial institutions sector and regulatory structure.

Deposit Insurance Coverage and Cost

Deposit insurance occupies a pivotal role in the regulatory regime because most depository institutions are insured by government agencies. The Banking Act of 1933 established the Federal Deposit Insurance Corporation (FDIC) to insure deposit accounts of commercial banks. One year later the Federal Savings and Loan Insurance Corporation (FSLIC) was chartered to insure accounts at savings and loan associations. Also, private and state deposit insurance companies insure deposits in state-chartered banks and savings and loans. Virtually all depository intermediaries insure their deposits, a requirement for all new state and federal depositories.

Bank failures have declined since the enactment of deposit insurance. One purpose of deposit insurance was to eliminate the financial panics and bank runs that plagued U.S. banking during the nineteenth and early twentieth centuries. In spite of the establishment of a national currency, requirement of reserves, and formation of the Federal Reserve System, thousands of banks failed in 1933. Since that date the number of bank failures, as reflected in FDIC liquidations, has averaged about twelve annually. There is strong evidence that deposit insurance was a necessary element in the solution to the historic bank-run problem.

Far from being a regulatory shackle, deposit insurance is a competitive advantage for intermediaries. The rapid growth is attributable to the advantage of reducing deposit risk for a small insurance premium. Deposit insurance converts investors' rights from a claim on a portfolio of risky assets to a claim on private, state, or federal resources. With either FDIC or FSLIC insurance, there is an implicit guarantee that the full taxing power of the federal government stands behind insured deposits. In state programs the financial strength is less, but still greater than that of any single private institution. On the other hand, deposit insurance premiums are small, about one-twelfth of 1 percent, relative to default premiums commonly observed in the private money and capital market. The net effect of risk reduction through government-supported insurance permits individual intermediaries to offer deposit accounts with superior risk characteristics for a given rate of return and maturity.

If deposit insurance proved useful in stabilizing the financial system, won acceptance from intermediaries, and induced investors to save billions of dollars, then why is the deposit insurance system an issue? The answer is that the cure for bank runs produced a regulatory regime that nurtures excessive risk taking by individual intermediaries. Depository intermediaires shift part of their risk to the deposit insurance system, which, by virtue of its federal agency status, shifts part of the risk onto the public. Certainly, the public accepted some risk sharing with the passage of enabling legislation in 1933 and 1934. However, such legislation was not intended to be a license to insure risk assets around the world or for any venture. Further, the permanent subsidy to investors was limited by the maximum insured account size.

The issue is one of controlling the use of deposit insurance so as to provide a stable financial foundation under the economic system, on the one hand, and to retaining the credibility of the deposit system, on the other hand. A broad, expansive insurance coverage tends to support a large, diverse financial system. But the demands of an expansive insurance program tax the credibility of the insurance companies—the FDIC, FSLIC, and state-chartered deposit insurers. For reasons of both insurance company ability and taxpayer equity, deposit insurance may be more limited in the future.

In summary, deposit insurance, developed as a wonder drug in the 1930s to quell bank runs, has safeguarded the private sector from deposit risks for 50 years. However, serious, long-term side effects of depositor and bank management indulgence are surfacing. Bank depositors are relying heavily on government insurance and examination, rather than their own analysis, when selecting a bank account. In turn, management is relieved of the responsibility for building depositor confidence, and government regulatory agencies have grown from being a backstop for troubled banks to acting as an involved participant in bank management. The extended role of the federal government raises questions concerning its role in competitive private businesses, the ability of government examiners to monitor and control massive private banking companies, and the equity of committing taxpayers to insure private investors against private banking losses.

Bankruptcy for Large Banks

Deposit insurance nominally protects only small (under $100,000) depositors, but the bankruptcy procedures applied by the FDIC and FSLIC effectively insure large depositors and large banks as well. Currently, many large depositors do not perceive themselves to be completely at risk with a large bank, because history supports the thesis that the FDIC nearly always arranges full payment for all depositors following a bank failure. The FDIC usually assists failed banks to merge, sometimes by infusing cash, guarantees, and options into the failed bank to convince a sound bank to acquire the failed institution. The surviving bank honors all deposits, including those of the failed bank. Since the FDIC was established, no depositor in an insured bank with more than $1 billion in total deposits has suffered a loss. Thus, consistently arranging mergers has established a *de facto* policy of insuring large depositors.

The FDIC justification for merging rather than liquidating failed banks goes beyond considerations of financial system stability to bankruptcy costs. Losses of the failed institution are frequently less when mergers are arranged than for formal bankruptcy proceedings. Legal proceedings restrict the use of billions of dollars of assets and deposits, cost large sums for attorneys and related professionals, and absorb management and regulator effort for years. When bankruptcy occurs, borrowers and depositors are disrupted by the uncertain future of the relationship and the inflexible commitment to prebankruptcy contracts. Economic pressures provide strong rationale for continuing to merge weak banks rather than process them as bankruptcy organizations.

Under the current bankruptcy system, depositors perceive themselves to be partially at risk despite *de facto* insurance. Foreign investors seem more skeptical than domestic depositors about the reliability of the FDIC's exclusive use of the merger solution. Also, the dramatic increase in the number and size of bank failures may exceed the capacity of the FDIC to bail out failed banks through merger and subsidization. Evidence indicating partial risk bearing is seen in the Continental Bank problem. In the weeks prior to a firm commitment by the FDIC and FED officially to support Continental, the large CD interest rate for Continental carried a 40-basis-point premium over that of other large banks. Apparently investors were demanding a substantial risk premium for investing in a large bank they perceived as more risky than other banks. Advocates of greater market discipline would expand market pressures by actually withdrawing FDIC and FED support for uninsured deposits, while advocates of strong governmental intervention point to the success of the existing deposit insurance program promoting economic stability.

Product and Line-of-Business Restrictions

Financial institutions have traditionally been subject to federal and state laws restricting their business activities. Insurance, investment banking, commercial banking, and savings banking were separated by the Glass-Steagall Act (Banking Act of 1933) into independent firms. One important section (20) of Glass-Steagall states:

> No member bank shall be affiliated in any manner—with any corporation, association, business trust, or other similar organization engaged principally in the issue, flotation, underwriting, public sale, or distribution at wholesale or retail or through syndicate participation of stocks, bonds, debentures, notes, or other securities.

This and other sections defined the separation of deposit-taking and securities-underwriting institutions. These definitions prevent banking and securities firms from engaging in each other's activities. Should a loophole exist in this law (such as use of the word "principally"), then banks would gain additional entry rights to the securities industry. Traditional structures have been upset by recent horizontal mergers across lines of business and technical developments, however. The conglomerate financial institutions, financial supermarkets, offer wide lines of financial services needed by individuals and businesses. Product-line expansion brings into question the safety, soundness, and efficiency of a financial system that includes mega-institutions. Will the establishment of broad-based financial firms promote concentration, instability, and undesired trade practices?

Proponents argue that product-line expansion promotes economic efficiency by reducing production and marketing costs. Fixed costs are spread over a larger number of activities, and technical processes developed in one activity are transferred to another activity. Marketing costs are reduced by providing the same customer with multiple services, rather than selling many customers a limited number of services. Further, consumers and businesses benefit from the greater convenience of a single rather than many relationships with the financial system. For example, consumers generally prefer shopping at supermarkets rather than specialty food shops because they can buy everything with one stop.

There is widespread belief among managers that synergies exist in the financial services industry, although empirical benefit and cost information provides little support for any opinion on the issue. It is too early to judge the synergies for the several large firms that recently integrated insurance, real estate, securities underwriting and securities brokering into one organization. Studies of operating synergies outside of the financial services industry report mixed results, depending on the industry and the study methodology. Therefore, the only indication that synergies exist is the recent commitment by some institutions to expand rapidly and substantially to a broad array of integrated services.

On a more limited scale, commercial banks would like to broaden their lines of business to include general securities underwriting (banks have limited underwriting authority now), insurance underwriting and sales, real estate development, and management consulting. Many banks currently operate related businesses, such as some municipal security underwriting, credit life insurance sales, real estate lending, and financial consulting. Thus, the broadened powers build upon the existing expertise and customer base. For example, it is a relatively small step from real estate lending to equity financing or from credit life to whole life insurance sales. Consequently, proponents argue that synergies are likely to be substantial while new product expenses and problems are minimal.

Opponents of line-of-business expansion, on either a broad or limited scale, raise the specter of undue risk taking, unacceptable concentrations of power, conflicts of interest, and unfair competitive practices. Excessive risk taking is controlled now by the active supervision of regulatory agencies. However, monitoring and judging risks of equity investments may be too complex and subjective for supervisory techniques. Without safeguards against intermediaries taking excessive risks, depositors and deposit insurance agencies unknowingly, and perhaps unjustifiably, permit excessive risks.

The excessive risk argument is especially persuasive when line-of-business regulation is not coupled with deposit insurance deregulation, Deposit insurance regulations tend to shift the cost of asset risk from shareholders to the government, as explained earlier in the deposit insurance section. As the asset risk level rises, the risk premium earned by the intermediary increases. However, neither the cost of insurance nor deposit interest expense increases. Consequently, the intermediary retains the entire risk premium return earned on risky assets rather than compensating the insurer for greater risks. That is, the unassessed deposit insurance premium is earned by those banks with high-risk-asset portfolios.

The powerful incentive offered by the current deposit insurance structure, therefore, would encourage institutions to underwrite the greater risks possible in deregulated lines-of-business environment. In view of the difficulty of controlling asset risk under current regulations, restricting asset risk under a fully decontrolled structure might prove infeasible.

Relaxing Geographical Restrictions

Geographical restrictions limit depository intermediaries from branching outside legal jurisdictions but usually ignore nondepository institutions. Depository intermediaries have accepted, if not promoted, geographical limitations because of the advantages of creating local monopolies and oligopolies. However, the geographical market barriers are being circumvented by nondepository institutions that introduce close substitutes. By producing the substitute services with large-scale operations, the nondepository institutions can operate at a low cost and set a low price. Money-market services by securities underwriting and brokerage firms are motivating banks to cast aside the previously coveted geographical market limitation in favor of the opportunity to expand volume. Larger volume, according to advocates, promotes efficiency and reduces consumer prices. On the other hand, opponents fear increased concentration by large banks, development of unfair trade practices, and increased instability.

The geographical boundary most debated is the state line, although intrastate restrictions and international ownership issues continue to arise. Commercial banks, savings banks, and savings and loans are prohibited in all states from establishing branches across state lines. However, some states permit holding companies to own banks in more than one state. The historical rationale for such restrictions apparently was the control of capital outflows from rural to the money centers in New York City and Chicago. The fear of money-center power continues to be a common argument, despite the fact that local banks now routinely invest funds anywhere in the United States, including the major money centers. Improvements in bank communications and transfer capabilities have completely eroded the concept of recycling funds within a geographically defined community.

Part of the interstate banking controversy stems from the interstate legal restrictions, which are a set of federal and state laws and regulations governing different types of depository institutions. At the federal level, banks are controlled by the McFadden Act and the Bank Holding Company Act of 1956. The

Federal Home Loan Bank Board limits interstate branching, except in cases of failing institutions. State-chartered savings and loans are subject to laws limiting their operations in other states. Amid the tangle of laws and regulations on geographical branching, three important exceptions are permitting *de facto* deregulation, which, in turn, will lead to repeal of geographical restrictions. The three important exceptions are:

1 Definition of the word "bank" by the Bank Holding Company Act of 1956
2 States' rights to permit interstate banking
3 Last-resort mergers of failing institutions

The exceptions are more important than the restrictions, because the exceptions provide the channels to avoid prohibition against interstate expansion. Taken together with technological innovations, these exceptions have permitted widespread *de facto* interstate banking.

A bank, defined in the Bank Holding Company (as amended in 1970), is an institution that *both* accepts demand deposits and makes commercial loans. Performing either function alone excludes the institution from definition as a bank, and, of course, from the consequent limitations under the act. Banks that accept deposits or make commercial loans but do not perform both functions are termed "nonbank banks." (The terminology reveals the inconsistent state of banking practice and regulation.) Further, such an institution may be owned by a bank holding company. The net result is that a bank holding company may own a bank operating in one state and a nonbank bank operating in other states. A number of nonbank banks operate currently and applications are pending for several hundred more.

The Garn-St. Germain Depository Institutions Act of 1982 empowered bank regulatory authorities to permit acquisition of failing institutions across state lines. Several savings and loans have been acquired by out-of-state commercial banks and savings and loans. Although the number of regulator-authorized exceptions is likely to remain small, they break the precedent of exclusive intrastate banking.

In addition to changes in the regulatory regime, advances in communications and information systems technology are improving the capacity of large institutions to operate and manage distant branches. The reduced cost and improved speed of voice and data transfer methods are significantly different from the technology existing in the 1930s–1960s—the period during which laws limiting interstate banking were written. With improved communications devices, state boundaries are no longer an effective barrier to out-of-state financial institutions that conduct business directly with a state's consumers.

Deregulation Heightens Disclosure Issue

Deregulation of deposit insurance, interstate banking, and product lines will increase the government's responsibility for the disclosure of information to investors. Disclosure will develop into a central issue of deregulation for two important reasons. First, the power and responsibility for disciplining financial institutions are shifted from a few government agencies that are empowered with substantial legal rights and audit resources to many private investors who have limited access to a financial institution's information. The right of investors to have access to information about current and potential information is an accepted prerequisite for an efficient market and a privilege of property ownership. However, increased disclosure will be contested for reasons of cost, competitive secrecy, and management flexibility. Second, deregulation allows financial institutions greater latitude to assume risk. As differences in risk increase among institutions, better information is needed to evaluate the risk of an individual institutions accurately and economically.

SUMMARY

Institutions are regulated both with respect to the liabilities and securities they may offer to the public and to the assets in which public funds may be invested. The regulations are intended to encourage prudent economic growth, to maintain institutional identities, to maintain the effectiveness of monetary policy, and to discourage abuses of public confidences.

Four national studies conducted in the past decade have echoed similar recommendations for regulation, after exhaustive studies of major segments of the financial markets. Legislatures were urged to avoid intricate social judgments over the design, development, and deployment of financial markets, institutions, and communications. The Hunt commission recommended the elimination of restricted interest rates and types of loans for depository institutions. The National Commission on Consumer Finance urged the repeal of state and federal statutes on loan and demand deposit interest rates. The *Institutional Investor Study* recommended the abolition of fixed commission rates and the prohibition of demand deposit interest repayments. Likewise, the National Committee on EFT suggested only minimal legislation for the burgeoning electronics fund transfer industry.

Rather than propose detailed regulation to achieve public policy objectives, the major national commissions of recent years have affirmed the principle of free competition with full disclosure. Generally, financial institutions are left with the task of developing and providing financial services, while the government promotes entry of new firms, protects against monopolization of existing markets, and safeguards consumer rights through education and selective prohibitions of unfair practices. The commissions have felt that the welfare of the general public is best served by managers who can direct their institutions toward saving and credit needs without legal restriction rather than by the "public utility" type of financial institutions operated by managers under tight bureaucratic controls.

Managers of financial institutions may wish to have the burden of state and federal laws lifted but should realize that reduced regulation almost certainly will lead to increased competition. As financial institutions that are now distinguished by law receive the freedom to offer services and securities of other institutions, the number of competitors will increase. When savings and loans are permitted to make any type of consumer loan, finance companies will face a new group of competitors—with thousands of offices and well-trained personnel. Although the savings and loans will receive the privilege of granting loans banks have offered, they will compete without protection when banks are permitted to pay the same interest rate on time deposits as savings and loans pay. Thus institutional distinctions, as known today, will tend to diminish; and managers will need to develop new positions based on their expertise to remain competitive in the money and capital markets.

Crucial public policy issues to be resolved are (1) deposit insurance coverage and cost, (2) bankruptcy proceedings for large depository institutions, (3) product and line-of-business restrictions, and (4) geographical restrictions on depository institutions. The highly successful deposit insurance system is inadvertently rewarding institutional risk taking and investor apathy in an increasingly market-oriented financial system. The problem of large institution bankruptcy confounds the insurance issue, because large institutions receive additional government safeguards owing to their strategic importance in the money market. Further, the insurance and bankruptcy issues are complicated by expanding product lines and geographic ranges by all institutions. To say the least, legislation enacted in an era of relatively simple, local banking and securities firms is not appropriate for multiproduct and multimarket international financial supermarkets.

TERMS

implicit tax	NCCF
financial system stability	EFT
financial system efficiency	ACH
entry and exit of institutions	POS
Hunt commission	Bank Holding Company Act (1956)
Institutional Investor Study	Glass-Steagall Act (1933)
Consumer Credit in the United States	McFadden Act (1927)

QUESTIONS

1 Describe the desirable aspects of government regulations of financial institutions.
2 What are the explicit and implicit costs of regulating financial institutions?
3 Why are security market efficiency and stability opposing objectives? Provide an example of a law that favors efficiency to the detriment of stability. Then provide an example of a law that supports stability at the cost of efficiency.
4 What were the major recommendations of the Hunt commission?
5 What prompted the *Institutional Investor Study?* What were the major contributions of this study?
6 Why is it illogical to regulate interest charges on consumer credit in order to subsidize low-income families?

7 What are the potential impacts of EFT on consumers? On financial institutions?

8 Why did the EFT commission recommend that the federal government not become heavily involved in the development and operations of EFT systems?

9 What are the common concepts advocated by the four studies presented in this chapter? What is the likely impact of future regulation of financial institutions on the structure of U.S. financial markets?

10 Describe the changes in banking that are attributable to the Deposit Institutions Deregulation and Monetary Control Acts of 1980 and 1982.

11 Why is the successful federal deposit insurance program an important public issue? What is the relationship between deposit insurance and large bank failure?

12 What federal legislation separates banking and securities activities into different financial institutions? In what year was it passed?

13 Why would deregulation of banking product lines increase the need for bank financial disclosure?

SELECTED REFERENCES

Aharony, Joseph, and Itzhak Swary: "Effects of the 1970 Bank Holding Company Act: Evidence from Capital Markets," *Journal of Finance*, September 1981, pp. 841–853.

Benston, George J.: "Savings Banking and the Public Interest," *Journal of Money, Credit and Banking*, February 1972, pp. 133–226.

Benston, George J.: "The Optimal Banking Structure: Theory and Evidence," *Journal of Bank Research*, Winter 1973, pp. 220–237.

Boorman, John T., and Manfred Peterson: "The Hunt Commission and the Mortgage Market: An Appraisal," *Journal of Bank Research*, Autumn 1972, pp. 155–165.

Cargill, Thomas F., and Gillian G. Garcia: *Financial Deregulation and Monetary Control: Historical Perspective and Impact of the 1980 Act*, Hoover Institution Press, Stanford University, Stanford, Calif., 1982.

Carron, Andrew S.: "Banking on Change: The Reorganization of Financial Regulation," *Brookings Review*, Vol. 2, Spring 1984, pp. 12–21.

Daskin, Alan J., and Jeffrey C. Marquadt: "The Separation of Banking from Commerce and the Securities Business in the United Kingdom, West Germany, and Japan." *Issues in Bank Regulation*, Summer 1983, pp. 16–24.

Edmister, Robert O.: "A New Kind of Supermarket," *Maryland*, February 1976, p. 23.

Edmister, Robert O.: "Commission Cost Structure: Shifts and Scale Economies," *Journal of Finance*, May 1978, pp. 477–486.

EFT in the United States: Policy Recommendations and the Public Interest, National Commission on Electronics Funds Transfer, Washington, D.C., October 28, 1977.

"Financial Market Deregulation," Chapter 6 in *Economic Report of the President*, February 1984, pp. 145–174.

Gart, Alan: *The Insider's Guide to the Financial Services Revolution*, McGraw-Hill, 1984.

Holland, R. C.: "Statement to Congress," *Federal Reserve Bulletin*, January 1976, pp. 33–37.

Holland, R. C.: "Statements to Congress," *Federal Reserve Bulletin*, February 1976, pp. 96–100.

Institutional Investor Study Report of the Securities and Exchange Commission, 92d Congress, 1st Session, House Doc. #92-64, GPO, Washington, D.C., 1971.

Issac, William M.: "The Role of Deposit Insurance in the Emerging Financial Services Industry," *Yale Journal of Regulation*, Vol. 1, 1984, pp. 195–215.

Jacobs, Donald P., and Almarin Phillips: "The Commission on Financial Structure and Regulation: Its Organization and Recommendations," *Journal of Finance*, May 1972, pp. 319–328.

James, Christopher, and Mark Flannery: "An Analysis of the Impact of Deposit Rate Changes on Common Stock Returns," *Journal of Finance*, December 1982, pp. 1259–1276.

Jones, Lawrence D.: Some Contributions of the Institutional Investor Study," *Journal of Finance*, May 1972, pp. 305–317.

Kane, Edward J: "Taxation of S&L's and Commercial Banks," *Federal Home Loan Bank Board Journal*, July 1973, pp. 10–17.

Lindsay, Robert, discussion of "The Commission on Financial Structure and Regulation: Its Organization and Recommendations," *Journal of Finance*, May 1972, pp. 333–339.

Longbrake, William A., and John A. Haslem: "Commercial Banking Structure in the United States: Its Development and Future," *Baylor Business Studies*, May, June, July 1975, pp. 7–35.

Report of the National Commission on Consumer Finance, GPO, Washington, D.C., December 1972.

Report of the President's Commission on Financial Structure and Regulation, GPO, Washington, D.C., 1971.

Sprinkle, Case M.: "A Theoretical Framework for Evaluating the Impact of Universal Reserve Requirements," *Journal of Finance*, September 1981, pp. 825–840.

"Survey of Investor Protection and the Regulation of Financial Intermediaries," U.S. General Accounting Office, Washington, D.C., July 13, 1983.

Tuccillo, John: "Taxation by Regulation: The Case of Financial Intermediaries," *Bell Journal of Economics*, Autumn 1977, pp. 577–587.

Williams, Dave H.: "The Changing Shape of Investment Research," *Financial Analysts Journal*, January/February 1978, pp. 18–21.

Wojnilower, Albert M.: "Financial Crises and Social Values," *Journal of Portfolio Management*, Fall 1976, pp. 11–13.

CHAPTER 22

MONEY AND BANKING PUBLIC POLICY

Bank monetary policy is the topic of a separate chapter because it is different and important. Banks (defined broadly to include all depository institutions) are unique in that they issue checkable deposits, and checkable deposits are one form of money. That is, private banks create money, a great deal of money, and they keep track of money for many of us. Banks are special because they handle our money supply, and they are important because the money supply affects the economy. By controlling the money supply, the federal government controls the *supply of credit* and influences *short-term interest rates* in the United States.[1] This chapter describes how money is created by banks and controlled by the federal government. We see how the Federal Reserve uses its power to influence the economy. It is important to recognize that in the process of controlling the money supply, the Federal Reserve significantly affects the amount of credit flowing through the financial markets. Managers of nonbank as well as bank financial institutions watch the Federal Reserve because it is a major contributor to the flow of funds which, in turn, partially determines short- and long-term interest rates.

MONEY DEFINED

Before showing how banks create money, a more precise definition of money is required. What is money? *Money* is any asset people readily accept as a

---

[1] Virtually all economists recognize the need for government regulation of the money supply, but for an interesting discussion of regulation versus free competition of the money supply, see Klein (1974). The genesis of U.S. bank regulation is developed by Hall (1974).

payment. The acid test of whether or not something is accepted as money is the question, "Can I buy my lunch with it?" An essential characteristic of money is that it is *acceptable*. Behind an asset's acceptability are supporting characteristics, such as its status under the law, the issuer's integrity, and pledges of gold. In the U.S. economy, a growing number of assets are accepted as money. The Federal Reserve now defines the "narrow" money stock, M_1, to include:

- Currency outside the Treasury, Federal Reserve Banks, and vaults of commercial banks
  - Traveler's checks of nonbank issuers
  - Demand deposits at commercial banks and mutual savings banks
  - Negotiable order of withdrawal (NOW) accounts
  - Automatic transfer service (ATS) accounts
  - Credit union share draft (CUSD) accounts

A broader definition of money includes investments easily convertible to a payment account. The Federal Reserve defines the broader measure M_2 to be M_1 plus the following:

- Money market deposit accounts (MMDAs)
- Savings and small-denomination time deposits
- Overnight repurchase agreements at commercial banks
- Overnight Eurodollars held by U.S. residents
- Money-market mutual funds of the general-purpose and broker/dealer type

The even broader measure of money, M_3, consists of M_2 plus the following:

- Large-denomination time deposits
- Term repurchase agreements
- Money-market mutual funds of the institution-only type

The M_3 definition recognizes that large corporation and financial institutions fund payments on a daily basis by liquidity money-market investments. For example, a $1 million bank certificate of deposit usually sells within hours if negotiated at market prices through a bond dealer. Because of the very large size and commercial nature of such a transaction, only large investors and money managers access this market regularly. Therefore, institutional money-market securities are classified separately in M_3.

DEPOSIT AND CREDIT CREATION

In this section we see how banks create demand deposits by extending credit. ("Credit" means making loans.) Banks have been doing this for over 800 years—the process is not a secret.[2] However, only in the last 100 years has the U.S. government sought to control banking powers to accomplish public goals.

---

[2] The classic paper on deposit expansion, upon which this and most modern explanations are based, is by Crick (1927).

After an illustration in this section of how banks create money, the control of banks by public agencies is discussed in the next section.

National Bank Example

At the beginning of the explanation, one hypothetical bank is used to demonstrate banking principles. (Later, other banks are added to form a *banking system*). The bank is called National Bank and is imbued with high standards of integrity and public esteem. Initially, consumers are attracted to the bank and deposit $1000 of their money. The books of the bank record the deposit in double-entry form. Assets and liabilities are shown on the left and right, respectively, in T-account form.

National Bank

Assets	Liabilities
Cash $1000	Consumer deposit $1000

With the public's confidence and $1000 of its money, we are prepared to expand our banking business. At this time only one bank exists in the economy, an assumption which is relaxed later.

Credit Creation

When we take a check in payment for books, clothes, or rent, we accept the check as money. The check may be written by a depositor or by the bank itself. Banks can give us money by "crediting our account" at their institution. A credit is an increase in our checking account balance. In return for increasing our deposit balance, we (the consumer) sign a note for borrowed money. The bank lends us money by using its power to increase our checking account. Money (demand deposits) and credit (loans) are created by the bank in the process of lending to its customers.

Example of Credit Creation

For example, National Bank makes a business loan of $2000. When the business signs the note (IOU), the bank credits the business accounts for $2000. National Bank's T account shows the loan asset (debit on left side) and deposit liability (credit on right side):

National Bank

Assets	Liabilities
Cash $1000	Consumer deposit $1000
Loan $2000	Business deposit $2000

The net result is an increase in the supply of money and credit by $2000. Cash remains the same, because the business is paid through the creation of a new demand deposit (money). The money supply is increased in this manner and will continue to increase until either National Bank demand deposits are no longer accepted as money or a governmental authority limits further expansion.

Limits on Credit Creation

If banks could increase deposits without limit, the money supply would be uncontrollable and massive. Money is most valuable when it is scarce, and bank deposits would cease to function as money if credit were extended infinitely. The public-policy issue here is how to control the money supply without limiting the freedom of banks to accept deposits and grant loans. The solution developed in the U.S. monetary system is called the *reserve banking system*. Banks are required to maintain primary reserves equal to or greater than a specific percentage of their deposits. (See Table 22-1.) Primary reserves are defined as vault cash and deposits with the Federal Reserve Bank. The amount of primary bank reserves created by the Federal Reserve Bank, a public-policy arm of the government, and the ratio of primary reserves to demand deposits determines the maximum amount of demand deposits in the banking system. Thus by controlling the total amount of bank reserves, the total amount of deposits created by banks is limited.

The amount of reserves (R) needed for demand deposits is computed by multiplying demand deposits (DD) times the required reserve rate (rr). The relationship among the amount of reserves, the reserve rate, and the amount of deposits is as follows:

$$R = rr \cdot DD \tag{22-1}$$

Example of Reserve Requirement

Suppose National Bank is required to maintain primary reserves of at least 12 percent of deposits. What amount must be held as a reserve? Is it meeting its reserve requirements?

National Bank has $3000 ($1000 reserves + $2000 loans) in deposits and is required to maintain a reserve ratio of 12 percent. Substituting these values for DD and rr in Eq. (22-1), we find:

$$\begin{aligned} R &= rr \cdot DD \\ &= (0.12)(3000) \\ &= 360 \end{aligned}$$

Primary reserves of $360 are required, and National Bank easily meets this requirement by holding $1000 in cash. In fact, excess reserves of $640 ($1000 minus $360) are being held. Why not invest these funds in an interest-bearing security?

TABLE 22-1

RESERVE REQUIREMENTS

Type of deposit, and deposit interval[1]	Percent
Net transaction accounts[2,3]	
$0–$26.3 million	3
Over $26.3 million	12
Nonpersonal time deposits[4]	
By original maturity	
Less than 1½ years	3
1½ years or more	0
Eurocurrency liabilities	
All types	3

[1] The Garn-St Germain Depository Institutions Act of 1982 (Public Law 97–320) provides that $2 million of reservable liabilities (transaction accounts, nonpersonal time deposits, and Eurocurrency liabilities) of each depository institution be subject to a zero percent reserve requirement. The Board is to adjust the amount of reservable liabilities subject to this zero percent reserve requirement each year for the next succeeding calendar year by 80 percent of the percentage increase in the total reservable liabilities of all depository institutions, measured on an annual basis as of June 30. No corresponding adjustment is to be made in the event of a decrease. Effective Dec. 9, 1982, the amount of the exemption was established at $2.1 million. In determining the reserve requirements of a depository institution, the exemption shall apply in the following order: (1) nonpersonal money market deposit accounts (MMDAs) authorized under 12 CFR section 1204.122; (2) net NOW accounts less allowable deductions); (3) net other transaction accounts; and (4) nonpersonal time deposits or Eurocurrency liabilities starting with those with the highest reserve ratio. With respect to NOW accounts and other transaction accounts, the exemption applies only to such accounts that would be subject to a 3 percent reserve requirement.

[2] Transaction accounts include all deposits on which the account holder is permitted to make withdrawals by negotiable or transferable instruments, payment orders of withdrawal and telephone and preauthorized transfers (in excess of three per month) for the purpose of making payments to third persons or others. However, MMDAs and similar accounts offered by institutions not subject to the rules of the Depository Institutions Deregulation Committee (DIDC) that permit no more than six preauthorized, automatic, or other transfers per month of which no more than three can be checks—are not transaction accounts (such accounts are savings deposits subject to time deposit reserve requirements.)

[3] The Monetary Control Act of 1980 requires that the amount of transaction accounts against which the 3 percent reserve requirement applies be modified annually by 80 percent of the percentage increase in transaction accounts held by all depository institutions determined as of June 30 each year. Effective Dec. 31, 1981, the amount was increased accordingly from $25 million to $26 million; and effective Dec. 30, 1982, to $26.3 million.

[4] In general, nonpersonal time deposits are time deposits, including savings deposits, that are not transaction accounts and in which a beneficial interest is held by a depositor that is not a natural person. Also included are certain transferable time deposits held by natural persons, and certain obligations issued to depository institution offices located outside the United States. For details, see section 204.2 of Regulation D.

Note: Required reserves must be held in the form of deposits with Federal Reserve Banks or vault cash. After implementation of the Monetary Control Act, nonmembers may maintain reserves on a pass-through basis with certain approved institutions.

Source: Federal Reserve Bulletin, November 1983, A7.

Maximum Credit Creation

Being motivated to earn the greatest profit possible for given risk levels, the bank manager recognizes that cash is a poor investment choice. Investing excess reserves in Treasury bills is a far more profitable decision than holding currency and Federal Reserve deposits (cash), because the bank earns some interest without any added risk.

The wise banker finds it profitable to reduce primary reserves to the minimum level and invest the maximum amount available in securities and loans. From the viewpoint of the banking system, assets and deposits are expanded to the point where required reserves just equal available reserves. (We see later how the government controls the amount of reserves available.) We find the amount of demand deposits (DD) that are created given a quantity of primary reserves (R) and a required reserve rate (rr):

$$DD = \frac{R}{rr} \qquad (22\text{-}2)$$

Because rr is less than 1, deposits expand as a multiple of reserves. The fractional reserve system is so named because the reserve requirement (rr) is a percentage of deposits. Another way of stating Eq. (22-2) is:

$$DD = \frac{1}{rr} \cdot R \qquad (22\text{-}3)$$

The term $1/rr$ is the *money multiplier,* and is a number greater than 1. Multiplying the amount of reserves by the money multiplier gives the amount of deposits that can be supported by the given amount of reserves. Hence, bank deposits are referred to as *derivative* deposits; they are derived from the reserve base. We hasten to point out that in actuality derivative deposits are less than the theoretical maximum due to imperfections in the system. (Major "leakages" are considered in a later section.)

In spite of some very sophisticated communications equipment and legal arrangements, bankers are not always able to invest all their excess reserves. They may not know exactly how much is available to invest or they may postpone their investment decision until too late in the date to buy securities. However, bank money managers are careful to avoid carrying excess funds overnight (and senior bank management is quick to chastise the money manager who fails to keep the bank fully invested), so that only very small quantities of excess reserves exist in the banking system.

Example of Deposit Creation Maximum

National Bank realizes that it has excess reserves and plans to invest them. It creates deposits by extending credit. The maximum amount of deposits is computed using Eq. (22-2), as shown on the following page:

$$DD = \frac{R}{rr}$$
$$= \frac{1000}{0.12}$$
$$= 8333$$

The maximum amount of loans is equal to the maximum deposits minus initial reserves. After deposits increase to their maximum $8333, the T account appears as shown below:

National Bank

Assets	Liabilities
Cash $1000	Deposits (consumer
Loans $7333	and business) $8333

Individual Banks versus Banking System

To this point we assumed that only one bank existed in the economy, and that bank (National Bank in the examples) held primary reserves, created deposits, and made loans. If National were the only bank in the system, then the deposits it created would continue to exist as long as customers preferred deposits to cash. The loan made to Farmer Fran in the form of a deposit credit would remain a deposit even when Farmer Fran pays Feedstore Fred, because Fran's account is reduced and Fred's account is increased by the transaction, and total deposits remain unchanged.

Now, *relax the assumption of a one-bank system and allow many banks to exist*. If Fran's check is deposited by Fred at a competing bank, then the competing bank will demand payment in cash (the request is called a *cash letter*) from Fran's bank. Cash and deposits are transferred from one bank to another by order of the deposit owner. Although the federal government regulates the total amount of deposits created, the customers divide the deposits among individual banks.

Transfers of reserves and deposits among banks by customers neither increases nor decreases total available reserves or deposits. The quantity of money derived from a given reserve base is the same regardless of the number of banks. Deposits created in the process of granting loans may be transferred to someone else without changing the total value of deposits.

However, the individual bank loses deposits and reserves when a customer orders funds transferred to a customer of another bank. Bank managers realize that the deposits created by granting loans are not going to remain in their bank very long. (Why would one borrow money unless he or she desired to purchase goods and services?) With 14,000 competing banks in the United States, banks expect to lose a large percentage of new loan deposits to other banks. Therefore, a bank does not lend more than its excess reserves. If the bank lent more than its excess reserves, then it would have to draw down its reserves as the borrower made payments that were deposited at other banks.

The deposit-expansion process works just as powerfully in reverse as it does in forward, and the lending bank suffers a severe contraction. In a competitive banking system, it is sound practice for an individual bank to restrict loan expansion only to the amount of its excess reserves. Then, if some deposits return to the individual bank, the bank can expand loans further. Otherwise the excess reserves will become a second bank's deposits. The second bank will, in turn, expand loans.[3]

Example of Overexpansion by Individual Bank

Consider the plight of National Bank, once the only bank in the system, when a competitor opens. During the first week of the grand opening promotion by Super Bank, customers withdraw $500 from National Bank and deposit it in Super Bank. Then the T accounts become:

National Bank				Super Bank		
Assets		**Liabilities**		**Assets**		**Liabilities**
Cash	$ 500	Deposits $7833		Cash $500		Deposits $500

Because the reserve requirement is 12 percent, National Bank should hold cash of $940 against deposit liabilities of $7833, and Super Bank should maintain cash of $60 against deposits of $500. National Bank has a reserve deficiency of $440, while Super Bank has excess reserves of $440. One bank is violating the legal reserve requirements, while the other is wasting funds by holding non-interest-bearing cash. How do the banks attain an equilibrium position? National Bank sells some of its loans for cash. Who buys the loans? Super Bank buys the loans with its $440 excess reserves (cash). (Alternatively, National Bank could refuse to grant new loans as existing loans matured and were repaid. Borrowers would then go to Super Bank for loans.) Then both banks return to equilibrium positions:

National Bank				Super Bank		
Assets		**Liabilities**		**Assets**		**Liabilities**
Cash	$ 940	Deposits $7833		Cash	$ 60	Deposits $500
Loans	$6893			Loans	$440	

In response to a loss in deposits and cash, National Bank liquidates a portion of the loan portfolio to restore lost reserves. The increases in deposits and

---

[3] Bank deposit expansion and contraction for a single bank in a multibank system are demonstrated in *Modern Money Mechanics* (1975), pp. 6–10.

reserves experienced by Super Bank initiates an expansion of the loan portfolio. In practice, bank managers constantly monitor the deposit inflows and outflows to detect changes in deposits and makes corresponding changes in the investment policy of the bank.

Money Multiplier with Currency and Time Deposits

To expand the money multiplier to account for more real-world conditions, currency (C) and time deposits (TD) are added as leakages from the expansion of the money supply, which was previously based on demand deposits alone. As currency and time deposit leakages increase, demand deposits decrease with a multiple effect. Each dollar of currency outside the banking system is a loss of a dollar in potential reserves. Each dollar shifted to time deposits decreases the amount of demand deposits the system can create. The reserve requirement for time deposits is lower than the reserve requirement for demand deposits. Therefore, the decrease in M_1 caused by shifting from demand to time deposits is not as great as shifting from demand deposits to currency holdings.

The equation for the money supply, which includes the effects of currency and time deposit holdings in the determination of M_1, is given below:

$$M_1 = \frac{1 + c}{rr_d + rr_{td}t} R \tag{22-4}$$

where the money multiplier (m) is:

$$m = \frac{1 + c}{rr_d + rr_{td}t} \tag{22-5}$$

Explanation of the terms useful in solving for M_1, with time deposits and currency in the money multiplier model, are listed below:

C = currency (amount)
c = proportion of currency holdings to demand deposits
DD = demand deposits (amount)
M_1 = money supply
MB = monetary base

R = reserves (amount)
R_d = reserves supporting demand deposits
R_{td} = reserves supporting time deposits
rr_d = reserve requirement on demand deposits
rr_{td} = reserve requirement on time deposits
t = propensity of the public to hold time deposits
TD = time deposits (amount)

Using the terms defined above, a list of important equations follows. The propensity of the public to hold currency (c) is the ratio of currency (C) to demand deposits (DD).[4]

$$c = \frac{C}{DD} \tag{22-6}$$

The amount of demand deposits (DD) in the system is determined by dividing the amount of reserves supporting demand deposits (R_d)(by the reserve requirement on demand deposits (rr_d):

$$DD = \frac{R_d}{rr_d} \tag{22-7}$$

The equation for the narrow money supply (M_1) is currency (C) plus demand deposits (DD):

$$M_1 = C + DD \tag{22-8}$$

The monetary base (MB) is the amount of reserves —R) and currency (C) upon which the money supply is based:

$$MB = R + C \tag{22-9}$$

The total amount of reserves (R) is the sum of the reserves on demand deposits (R_d) and reserves supporting time deposits (R_{td}):

$$R = R_d + R_{td} \tag{22-10}$$

The propensity of the public to hold time deposits (t) is the ratio of the amount of time deposits (TD) to the amount of demand deposits (DD):[5]

$$t = \frac{TD}{DD} \tag{22-11}$$

The amount of time deposits (TD) is the proportion of reserves on time deposits (R_{td}) to the reserve requirement for time deposits (rr_{td}):

$$TD = \frac{R_{td}}{rr_{td}} \tag{22-12}$$

---

[4] The ratio of currency to demand deposits (c) actually varies over time. An interesting analysis of variation in c related to the business cycle is presented by Hess (1971).

[5] The ratio of time deposit to demand deposit changes over time with variations in the demand for money balances. Although the demand for money depends in part on its need for transactions, other factors influence the public's desired holdings of money. For a review of current (conflicting) explanations of desired money balances, see Meyer and Neri (1975).

Examples of Money Multiplier with Currency and Time Deposits

Solving for M_1 with T Accounts   Initially, the (illustrative) banking system has $1000 in reserves (cash), $7333 in loans, and $8333 in demand deposits. The T account for the entire system is shown below:

Banking System

Assets	Liabilities
Reserves $1000	Demand deposits $8333
Loans $7333	

Here M_1 is equal to demand deposits of $8333.

What is the effect of a depositor withdrawing $280 in currency and holding it?[6] The bank must contract credit (loans) and thus demand deposits and the money supply. The reason this contraction of the system must take place is that the amount of reserves ($720 = 1000 − 280$) no longer meets the legal requirements to support $8333 in demand deposits ($1000). The smaller reserve base cannot support as many loans and demand deposits as before the currency withdrawal. Loans are collected or sold until the amount of reserves is sufficient legally to support the remaining demand deposits. The new T account, with the effect of currency holdings of $280, appears as follows:

Banking System

Assets		Liabilities	
Reserves	$ 720	Demand deposits	$6000
Loans	5280		
	$6000		$6000

M_1 $(C + DD)$ decreases to $6280 ($280 + 6000). A $2053 decrease in the money supply has taken place due to an increase in currency holdings of $2053 by the public.

Now consider the effect of using $123 of the bank's reserves to support time deposits. The reserve requirement on time deposits is 0.03. The total amount of time deposits is equal to the reserves for time deposits ($123) divided by the reserve requirement on time deposits (0.03). Using Eq. (22-12), time deposits are computed to be $4100.

$$TD = \frac{R_{td}}{rr_{td}}$$

---

[6] The figure of $280 is used because the actual currency in circulation is approximately 28 percent of M_1 (*Federal Reserve Bulletin*, December 1984, p. 13).

$$TD = \frac{123}{0.03} = 4100$$

Likewise, maximum demand deposits are determined by dividing reserves available for demand deposits ($220) by the reserve requirement on demand deposits (0.12). Total demand deposits in the banking system with currency and time deposit leakages are $1833. Using Eq. (22-7), demand deposits are computed:

$$DD = \frac{R_d}{rr_d}$$

$$DD = \frac{220}{0.12} = 1833$$

The T account after currency and time deposit leakages appears below:

Banking System

Assets		Liabilities	
Reserves on demand deposits	$ 220	Demand deposits	$1833
Reserves on time deposits	$ 123	Time deposits	$4100
Loans	$5590		
	$5933		$5933

The money supply (M_1) is equal to currency ($657) plus demand deposits ($1833) (Eq. 22-8):

$$M_1 = C + DD$$
$$M_1 = 657 + 1833 = 2490$$

Solution Using Equations Using Eq. (22-4), the same results can be achieved simultaneously in a single equation with the information provided: currency is $657, reserves are $343 ($220 on demand deposits and $123 on time deposits), and the reserve requirements on time and demand deposits are 0.03 and 0.12 respectively. Using Eqs. (22-7) and (22-10), demand deposits are computed as $1833 and time deposits are found to be $4100. Now the calculations of c and t are needed in order to solve for the money supply. The propensity of the public to hold currency (c) is equal to currency outstanding (vault cash excluded) divided by demand deposits.

$$c = \frac{C}{DD}$$

$$c = \frac{657}{1833} = 0.36$$

The proportion of time deposits the public decided to hold (t) is simply time deposits divided by demand deposits.

$$t = \frac{TD}{DD}$$

$$t = \frac{4100}{1833} = 2.24$$

The money supply, M_1, can now be found with Eq. (22-4):

$$M_1 = \frac{1 + c}{rr_d + rr_{td}t} R$$

$$= \frac{1 + .36}{0.12 + 0.03\,(2.24)}\ 343$$

$$= (7.26)\ 343$$

$$= 2490$$

In this equation, 7.26 is the money multiplier with currency and time deposit leakages. The addition of currency and time deposits to the money multiplier reduces the multiplier from 8.33, shown in the previous example, to 7.26. The money multiplier is always reduced by the recognition of currency and time deposit leakages.

Application of Money Multiplier

Federal Reserve policies to change the money supply depend on the money multiplier. When the Federal Reserve changes the amount of reserves, the variations in the money supply depends upon the variables (c, t, rr_d, and rr_{td}) in the money multiplier. The reserve requirements on demand and time deposits are controlled by the Federal Reserve. Changes in reserve requirements have such a powerful effect on the money supply that altering them could be destabilizing to the economy. Because of this, reserve requirements are seldom changed and, consequently, the Federal Reserve does not directly modify the money multiplier. On the other hand, the public's allocation of currency, time deposits, and demand deposits is a principal determinant of the size of the money multiplier. It is the public's behavior that determines the values of c and t, and thus the size of the money multiplier.

Once the Federal Reserve has approximated the money multiplier, its ability to control the amount of reserves in the banking system allows it to change the money supply. The amount by which the money supply varies is equal to the change in reserves times the money multiplier. If the amount of reserves is increased, the money supply will increase. Alternatively, if reserves are decreased, the money supply will decrease. Federal Reserve monetary policy that affects the amount of reserves is discussed in greater detail later in this chapter.

FEDERAL RESERVE FUNCTIONS AND POLICIES

The Federal Reserve[7] is the central bank for the United States. The U.S. Treasury and commercial bankers use the Federal Reserve as we use our personal bank to deposit and withdraw money. The Federal Reserve does not deal with individuals but with bankers and brokers to carry out its primary function: to control the economy's supply of money and credit by restricting the amount of legal reserves and setting the reserve requirement ratio. The Federal Reserve tries to control the money supply in order to promote the economic stability and growth. Restrictive monetary policy involves decreasing the money supply or its rate of growth, whereas expansive monetary policy requires increasing the money supply. If inflation threatens the economy, the Fed tightens the availability of money and credit to hold back spending.[8] If unemployment increases in a sluggish economy, the Fed loosens the reins on money to stimulate spending, investment, and job vacancies. In a growing economy with stable prices, the Fed seeks to provide a corresponding increase in money. During each year the Fed increases and decreases money to meet seasonal needs, such as farm harvests, Christmas spending, and summer vacations. The Fed is the caretaker of our money supply and uses its power to keep the economy green and healthy. The Federal Reserve operates within guidelines specified in the Federal Reserve Act and subsequent government legislation.[9]

Five Links between Reserves and Economic Activity

How can our central bank, the Federal Reserve, expand or constrain economic activity? The critical elements in the process are reserves—deposits at the Federal Reserve and vault cash.[10] We know, from previous discussion, that banks must hold a stated percentage of their deposits in reserves. The Federal Reserve controls reserves, and consequently the money supply. The amount of money and credit influences investment by business, income of individuals, and total spending.

The five links between reserves and economic policy objectives are as follows:

1 The Federal Reserve specifies the percentage of demand and deposits that must be held in reserves.

---

[7] Officially termed Federal Reserve System but referred to as the Federal Reserve or simply the Fed.

[8] Anti-inflation postures are often difficult to take, and (former) chairman of the Federal Reserve Arthur Burns has argued that the independence of the Federal Reserve from the federal government is required for a meaningful anti-inflation policy. See Burns (1977).

[9] The Federal Reserve Act was passed in 1913 and the Federal Reserve Banks were established in 1914. This is the latest establishment of a central bank among the major economic powers of the world. For further history and development of the Federal Reserve System, see Hall (1974).

[10] Two officers of the New York Federal Reserve Bank succinctly present the strategy for monetary control in general and for 1975 in Holmes and Sternlight (1976).

2 Money supply expands and contracts with changes in demand deposits and currency holdings.

3 Loan supply changes with the deposit component of the money supply.

4 Real investment is altered by changes in the availability and cost of loans.

5 Income and spending rise and fall with real investment expenditures.

Reserves and Loanable Funds

Reserves are increased or decreased to expand or contract, respectively, the availability of credit to member banks. As described earlier in this chapter, changes in the reserves available to banks allow banks to change the levels of deposits and loans.[11] Thus a change in the money supply changes the availability of credit to individuals, businesses, and governments. An increase in reserves would cause an increase in loans and a decrease in interest rates, if everything else is constant.[12]

When the Federal Reserve contracts the money supply, then credit becomes less available. As deposits decline (or do not increase as fast as they need to meet rising demand), banks find themselves without enough money to meet borrower's demands. The profitable action for banks to take is to make loans to the borrowers willing to pay the highest rate (commensurate with the borrower's risk). Interest rates are bid higher as borrowers compete in a scarce credit market. Some potential borrowers are unwilling to pay the higher interest rate and cancel or postpone their loan requests. In tight credit periods, we see a decline in state and local government bond issues, new mortgage loans, and long-term bonds from corporations. Borrowers sensitive to increases in interest rates drop out of the money and capital market. The desired effect occurs: total borrowing is reduced and available credit is rationed among those who can best use it.

Link between Loan Expansion and Real Investment

Changes in credit availability causes changes in real investment. This step occurs outside of the banking and financial markets. First, consider the case of an increase in credit and loans. Money obtained from mortgage loans, inventory loans, state and local bond issues, and equipment loans is spent for real things. Consumers, businesses, and governments spend money for houses, cars, plants and equipment, roads, and schools. If interest rates are low and lenders are aggressively searching for loans, then borrowers are more likely to

---

[11] The term "loans" is used here to encompass all securities purchased by banks. For an analysis of the effect of monetary policy actions on bank investment portfolios, see the study by Barth, Kraft, and Wiest (1977). They find that the effectiveness of monetary policy hinges on how great an adjustment banks make in their investment portfolios.

[12] Of course, conditions do not remain constant because of or in spite of changes in reserves. The substantially more complex but realistic relationships between reserves, interest rates, and deposits have been studied extensively. For a synthesis, see Hendershott and DeLeeuw (1970).

decide to build a new plant, enlarge the inventory of merchandise, or build a new house. For example, the interest rate and availability of credit are important when you consider building a new house. As the interest rate on a 30-year mortgage loan declines from 8¼ percent to 7¼ percent, the monthly payment decreases by $27.63 for a $40,000 mortgage. The lower payment may be small enough to fit your budget, and you can build now. You make the decision to build a house, thereby translating the Federal Reserve's credit policy into real (physical) investment.

Effect of Credit Restraint on Investment Tightening credit acts to restrain real private and public investment. Now loans are more expensive, as interest rates are bid higher by eager (desperate!) borrowers. What investment should be financed? New investments are carefully analyzed to determine whether or not they return a rate above the cost of money. Although some projects would have been accepted under the previous lower rates, they are rejected now. The rising interest rate is too great a hurdle for investment opportunities returning less than the currently higher rate. Consequently, we decide not to build a new plant, buy a new car, or increase our inventory. Higher interest rates are causing us to hold back on real investment. This is the desired effect of a reduction in reserves made available by the Federal Reserve.

Investment Multiplier Income and spending are changed as real investment rises and falls. The increase in real investment decisions propelled by the larger money supply is seen by producers as an increase in demand. How does business meet the greater demand in sales? Output is increased by hiring more employees and building new plant capacity, and prices are increased if the demand outstrips the ability of the industry to produce. Spending increases with output: more is spent for salaries and wages, and more is spent for plant and equipment. The increased spending in turn promotes sales of consumer and industrial products. The new employee spends his or her paycheck for housing, food, a car, and other goods. The second round of spending stimulates sales and investment, just as the initial decision spurred new investment. Thus, the total effect of new investment on spending is greater than the initial amount spent for plant and equipment. As the original investment money is spent, respent, and spent again, income is increased by a multiple of the initial change in investment. This process of expanding a dollar of investment into money dollars of income is called the multiplier effect.

Recapitulation

In summary, the Federal Reserve uses small changes in reserves to effect large changes in interest rates, investment, spending, and income through the private banking system. The process is sketched in Figure 22-1. The reserves are called *high-powered* money because one dollar of reserves expands to many dollars of bank deposits. Banks invest their new-found money in securities and loans, and

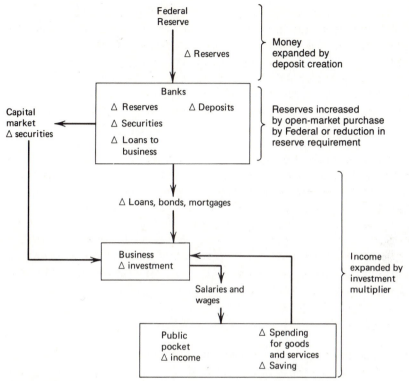

FIGURE 22-1
Federal Reserve use of reserve changes to influence income and spending.

money ultimately pours into business for new investment. Investment spending flows to the public pocket as wages and salaries. Investment spending is multiplied as the public spends a large part of its new income. The initial stimulus from the Federal Reserve is expanded by deposit expansion and the investment multiplier. By increasing reserves, the Federal Reserve can greatly stimulate income and consumer spending. Conversely, consumer spending can be checked by reducing reserves and thereby draining funds from the business investment pool.[13]

Deposit Expansion Variability

The deposit expansion and contraction relationships presented earlier in this chapter assume a fixed reserve-to-deposit multiplier. The constant multiplier assumption is an oversimplification of the actual condition, especially in the

[13] The relationships among monetary actions, wealth, expenditures, and interest rates have been modeled extensively. A simple macroeconomic framework illustrated with equations and graphs is shown by Meyer (1974).

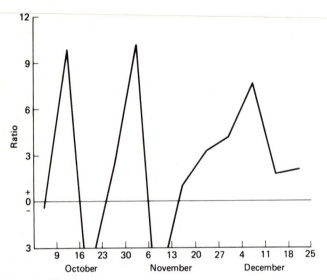

Frame a. Weekly

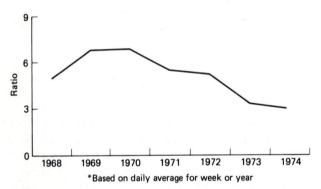

*Based on daily average for week or year

Frame b. Annual

FIGURE 22-2
Ratio of demand deposits to bank reserve, fourth quarter 1974
(frame A) and 1968 through 1974 (frame B). (*Source:* "Modern
Money Mechanics," Federal Reserve Bank of Chicago, p. 30.)

short run. A principal cause for variations in the multiplier are changes in
utilization of reserves. Although we mentioned earlier that the profit incentive
strongly motivates banks to invest all available reserves, the level of excess
reserves in the banking system does vary. Some excess reserves always exist in
the banking system, due to frictions and lags in the flow of funds through the
14,600 commercial banks. Furthermore, reserve requirement rate differences
among member and nonmember banks, a topic discussed later in this chapter,
cause unpredictable variations in the multiplier. For example, see Figure 22-2,
frame a, which shows short-run variations in the multiplier. Although the

multiplier is relatively stable over the long run (see Figure 22-2, frame b), monetary actions to control deposits in the short run do not have exactly the desired effect due to unpredictable changes in the multiplier from week to week.[14]

MONETARY POLICY IN ACTION

Now that we have a concept of why a central bank would want to control the money supply, we are ready to study the tools that make the concept a reality. The Federal Reserve is an effective economic entity because it has several means by which it can control the money supply. What are the main instruments of Federal Reserve policy? Here we survey two instruments of the Federal Reserve:

1 Open-market operations
2 Discount window policy

Open-market operations involve buying and selling U.S. government securities and thereby increasing or decreasing, respectively, bank reserves. Reserve ratios are set by the Federal Reserve, and occasionally the required ratio is changed. The discount window policy may be strict or lenient, although still conforming to the general policy discussed earlier in this chapter. Now look at the three instruments in more detail.

Federal Reserve Balance Sheet Control

Control of selected assets and liabilities is the principal means by which the Federal Reserve influences the money market and the money supply. The key relationship to understand is that between the assets and liabilities of the Federal Reserve itself. Look at the major assets and liabilities of the Federal Reserve as shown in the balance sheet (Table 22-2). The first asset is the central bank's cash—gold certificates (representing real gold stored by the U.S. Treasury), and foreign currency. United States government securities are interest-bearing bills, notes, and bonds issued by the U.S. Treasury and federal agencies. Cash items in process of collection are checks deposited by commercial banks. Checks are recorded as an asset while awaiting payment from another bank; this account represents the Federal Reserve *float* in the bank clearing system. Now move to the liabilities section of the balance sheet. "Currency outside banks" is the paper bills in our wallets. (Look at the inscription on your money. Does it say "Federal Reserve note"?) Deposits are accepted primarily from the U.S. Treasury and commercial banks. Other liabilities and capital are trivial amounts and are unimportant monetary policy instruments.

---

[14] Four a discussion of alternative reserve measures, deposit expansion relationships, and forecasting accuracy, see Laufenberg (1976). Also, lagged accounting rules affect the current period responsiveness of banks to changes in reserve levels. See Pierce (1976).

TABLE 22-2
MONETARY AUTHORITY STATEMENT OF FINANCIAL ASSETS AND LIABILITIES, 1972–1984 (BILLIONS OF DOLLARS)

	1972	1973	1974	1975	1976	1977	1978	1979	1980	1981	1982	1983	1984
Total financial assets	97.6	106.9	113.4	124.6	134.5	143.0	156.2	166.7	173.8	182.0	193.2	201.9	218.4
Gold and foreign exchange	10.5	11.5	11.6	11.7	11.7	11.7	13.2	13.6	16.2	16.2	16.9	14.8	14.6
Treasury curr. & SDR. ctfs.	8.7	9.1	9.7	10.6	12.0	12.6	13.1	14.9	16.4	17.8	18.4	18.4	16.4
Federal Reserve float	4.0	3.1	2.0	3.7	2.6	3.8	6.5	6.8	4.5	1.8	2.7	1.6	0.9
F.R. loans to domestic banks	2.0	1.3	0.3	0.2	*	0.3	1.2	1.5	1.8	1.6	0.7	0.9	3.5
Credit market instruments	71.3	80.6	86.7	95.3	105.1	112.2	119.2	126.9	131.4	140.5	150.3	161.2	169.6
U.S. government securities	71.2	80.5	85.7	94.1	104.1	111.3	118.6	126.2	130.6	140.3	148.8	160.8	169.6
Treasury issues	69.9	78.5	80.5	87.9	97.0	102.8	110.6	117.5	121.3	131.0	139.3	151.9	160.9
Agency issues	1.3	2.0	5.2	6.2	7.1	8.5	8.0	8.7	9.3	9.4	9.5	8.9	8.8
Acceptances	0.1	0.1	1.0	1.1	1.0	1.0	0.6	0.7	0.8	0.2	1.5	0.4	—
Bank loans n.e.c.	—	—	—	—	—	—	—	—	—	—	—	—	—
Miscellaneous assets	1.1	1.4	3.2	3.2	3.0	2.4	3.0	3.1	3.6	4.1	4.1	5.1	8.8
Total liabilities	97.6	106.9	113.4	124.6	134.5	143.0	156.2	166.7	173.8	182.0	193.2	201.9	218.4
Member bank reserves	25.6	27.1	25.8	26.1	25.2	26.9	31.2	29.8	27.5	25.2	26.5	21.4	21.8
Vault cash of coml. banks	8.6	10.7	11.6	12.3	12.1	13.9	15.5	18.5	19.8	18.6	19.5	20.7	18.7
Demand deposits and currency	60.4	65.0	71.9	82.5	93.1	98.0	104.3	112.5	121.5	132.4	141.3	153.9	171.4
Due to U.S. government	2.2	2.9	3.3	7.8	10.9	7.5	4.4	4.6	3.5	4.7	5.5	4.1	5.8
Due to foreign	0.4	0.3	0.5	0.5	0.6	0.6	0.7	0.8	0.5	0.7	0.4	0.5	0.4
Currency outside banks	57.9	61.8	68.1	74.3	81.6	89.9	99.2	107.1	117.4	126.9	135.4	149.3	165.1
Miscellaneous liabilities	2.9	4.2	4.0	3.8	4.1	4.2	5.2	6.0	5.1	5.8	5.9	5.9	6.6

* SDR refers to *Special Drawing Rights*.
Note: "—" denotes data not available, and "*" indicates negligible values.
Source: Board of Governors of the Federal Reserve System.

Open-Market Operations

Buying and selling U.S. government securities are *open-market operations* of the Federal Reserve. Bonds are bought and sold every day through bond dealers. The dealers trade securities for many buyers and sellers, allowing the Federal Reserve to acquire securities from the private sector. The Federal Reserve pays for its purchases with a check drawn on itself. The steps for clearing bond dealer checks and increasing reserves are:

1 Fed pays by check to bond dealer who sells bonds.
2 Bond dealer deposits check in a commercial bank.
3 Commercial bank deposits Fed check in its account at the Federal Reserve Bank.
4 Federal Reserve increases deposit balance of commercial bank. Because Fed deposit balances are reserves, the commercial bank now has more reserves.

Of course, the Fed could buy or sell using Federal Reserve notes, but cash is hard to handle in multimillion-dollar amounts! The check is worth as much as cash, because banks can exchange the check for Federal Reserve notes anytime. (The Fed is able to print notes when the public demands currency.)

Control over open-market operations is vested in the Federal Open Market Committee (FOMC). Twelve economic experts sit on the FOMC and decide open-market policy. Decisions by the FOMC provide directions to the operating staff of the Federal Reserve. For example, the FOMC may instruct the staff to hold the growth in the money supply (M_1) "within ranges of 4½ to 6½ percent."

How is money supply growth held within a range of 4½ to 6½ percent? The answer lies in making commercial bank reserves increase by about 4½ to 6½ percent. Banks use the increased reserves for loans and the money supply expands. This is exactly the process described in Figure 22-1. Reserves are increased by buying U.S. government securities with Federal Reserve checks.

A 5 percent increase in the $40 billion deposit basis means the Federal Reserve must purchase $2 billion of securities. As the Federal Reserve purchases $2 billion in securities during the year from bond dealers, member bank deposits (reserves to the commercial banks) rise. If the expansion factor is 5 times reserves, then the money supply grows by 5 times $2 billion, or $10 billion. The Federal Reserve receives daily reports on deposits and checks actual money supply growth against the policy target. If it is shooting too high, then reserves are decreased by *selling* securities. The multiplier works in reverse, too, and a $1 billion decline in bonds and Federal Reserve deposits reduces commercial bank reserves by about $5 billion. Open-market operations are a quick, direct means for executing FOMC policy decisions.

Changes in the assets and liabilities of the Federal Reserve over time are shown in Tables 22-2 and 22-3.[15] End-of-year amounts outstanding are shown

---

[15] These tables show annual amounts and changes; weekly transactions by the Fed are released and reported weekly in the financial press and by electronic news services.

TABLE 22-3
MONETARY AUTHORITY FLOW OF FUNDS, 1974–1984 (BILLIONS OF DOLLARS)

	1974	1975	1976	1977	1978	1979	1980	1981	1982	1983	1984
Current surplus	0.1	0.2	*	0.2	0.7	0.2	0.2	0.4	0.1	0.5	1.1
Net acq. of financial assets	6.5	11.3	9.7	8.5	13.3	10.9	7.1	8.2	12.4	9.4	14.6
Gold and foreign exchange	0.1	0.1	0.1	*	1.6	0.7	2.6	*	0.6	-2.1	-0.1
Treasury currency	0.5	1.0	0.6	0.5	0.5	1.3	0.7	0.7	0.6	0.7	0.7
SDR certificates	—	0.1	0.7	0.1	0.1	0.5	0.7	0.8	1.3	—	-10.7
Federal Reserve float	-1.1	1.7	-1.1	1.2	2.7	0.3	-2.3	-2.7	1.0	-1.2	0.7
F.R. loans to domestic banks	-1.0	-0.1	-0.2	0.2	0.9	0.3	0.4	-0.2	-0.9	0.2	2.7
Credit market instruments	6.2	8.5	9.8	7.1	7.0	7.7	4.5	9.2	9.8	10.9	8.4
U.S. government securities	5.2	8.4	10.0	7.2	7.3	7.6	4.4	9.8	8.5	12.0	8.8
Treasury securities	2.0	7.4	9.1	5.8	7.7	6.9	3.9	9.6	8.4	12.6	8.9
Agency issues	3.2	1.0	0.9	1.4	-0.4	0.7	0.6	0.1	0.1	-0.7	-0.1
Acceptances	0.9	0.1	-0.1	*	-0.4	0.1	0.1	-0.6	1.3	-1.1	-0.4
Bank loans n.e.c.	—	—	—	—	—	—	—	—	—	—	—
Miscellaneous assets	1.8	*	-0.2	-0.6	0.5	0.2	0.5	0.5	*	1.0	3.7
Net increase in liabilities	6.4	11.1	9.7	8.3	12.6	10.7	6.9	7.8	12.2	8.9	13.4
Member bank reserves	-1.2	0.2	-0.9	1.7	4.4	-1.4	-2.3	-2.2	1.3	-5.0	0.4
Vault cash of coml. banks	1.0	0.6	-0.1	1.8	1.5	3.0	1.3	-1.2	0.9	1.5	-2.3
Demand deposits and currency	6.9	10.7	10.6	4.8	6.3	8.2	9.0	10.9	10.2	13.0	15.8
Due to U.S. government	0.4	4.5	3.1	-3.3	-3.1	0.1	-1.1	1.2	0.7	-1.3	1.7
Due to foreign	0.2	*	0.2	*	0.1	0.1	-0.2	0.1	-0.2	*	*
Currency outside banks	6.3	6.3	7.4	8.2	9.3	8.0	10.3	9.5	9.7	14.3	14.2
Miscellaneous liabilities	-0.3	-0.4	0.1	*	0.4	0.9	-1.1	0.3	-0.1	-0.5	-0.5

Note: "—" denotes data not available, and "*" indicates negligible values.
Source: Board of Governors of the Federal Reserve System.

in Table 22-2 for the years 1965 through 1976. Changes in year-end amounts are reported as flows in Table 22-3. Legal reserves of member banks are the lines labeled "member bank reserves" and "vault cash of commercial banks." Thus, the Federal Reserve reports bank reserves separately from other liabilities and makes the figures available on a regular and timely basis.[16]

Discount Window

The Federal Reserve discount window makes loans to all insured banks.[17] The loans are called *advances* and are reported in Tables 22-2 and 22-3 as "F.R. loans to domestic banks." Like U.S. government securities, the loans (1) are an interest-bearing asset of the Federal Reserve and (2) are purchased with increases in Federal Reserve deposits. Increases and decreases in discounts (loans from the Fed) cause about the same changes in the money supply as open market operations. (Unlike open-market operations, member bank loans are sold to only one clientele: member banks.) By lowering the discount rate, loans are made more attractive and borrowing increases. To restrict credit and the money supply, the Federal Reserve raises the discount rate to reduce the desirability of its loans.[18]

Federal Reserve Policy Example

Tools for controlling the money supply are very much available to and used daily by the U.S. central bank. The best summary of FOMC thinking is stated by the FOMC itself in the following directive issued on May 17, 1977:

> The information reviewed at this meeting suggests that real output of goods and services is growing at a rapid rate in the current quarter. In April industrial output and employment continued to expand at a substantial pace, and the unemployment rate declined from 7.3 to 7.0 percent. Total retail sales remained at the advanced level reached in March. The wholesale price index for all commodities rose substantially in April for the third consecutive month; increases again were particularly sharp among farm products and foods, and they remained sizable for industrial commodities.
>
> The average value of the dollar against leading foreign currencies has changed little on balance over the past month. The U.S. foreign trade deficit widened further in March; for the first quarter as a whole the deficit was twice as large as for the preceding quarter.
>
> The increase in M-1, which had been moderate in the first quarter, was exceptionally large in April. Inflows of the time and savings deposits included in the

[16] More disaggregated data are available for study, as well. For example, similar data are published for each of the twelve Federal Reserve Districts to provide information of regional conditions.

[17] Actually, the discount "window" is simply an office of the Federal Reserve.

[18] Borrowing rules and administration of the discount window are different among the Federal Reserve regions. The Federal Reserve Act of 1913 established twelve regions with independent authority to provide for geographical differences, and differences in the discount facility are evident today. See Berman (1976) for an empirical study of distinct discount window facilities.

broader aggregates were slower than earlier in the year, but because of the rapid expansion in M-1, growth in M-2 and M-3 accelerated. Business short-term borrowing expanded sharply while corporate financing in the capital markets was reduced. Market interest rates have risen in recent weeks.

In light of the foregoing developments, it is the policy of the Federal Open Market Committee to foster bank reserve and other financial conditions that will encourage continued economic expansion and help resist inflationary pressures, while contributing to a sustainable pattern of international transactions.

At its [last] meeting . . . , the Committee agreed that growth of M-1, J-2, and M-3 within ranges of 4½ to 6½ percent, 7 to 9½ percent, and 8½ to 11 percent, respectively, from the first quarter of 1978 appears to be consistent with these objectives. These ranges are subject to reconsideration at any time as conditions warrant.

The Committee seeks to encourage near-term rates of growth in M-1 and M-2 on a path believed to be reasonably consistent with the longer-run ranges for monetary aggregates cited in the preceding paragraph. Specifically, at present it expects the annual growth rates over the May–June period to be within the ranges of 0 to 4 percent for M-1 and 3½ to 7½ percent for M-2. In the judgement of the Committee such growth rates are likely to be associated with a weekly average Federal funds rate of about 5⅜ percent. If, giving approximately equal weight to M-1 and M-2, it appears that growth rates over the 2-month period will deviate significantly from the midpoints of the indicated ranges, the operational objective for the Federal funds rate shall be modified in an orderly fashion within a range of 5¼ to 5¾ percent.

If it appears during the period before the next meeting that the operating constraints specified above are proving to be significantly inconsistent, the Manager is promptly to notify the Chairman who will then decide whether the situation calls for supplementary instructions from the Committee.

Inflation Counter-Effect

The loanable funds effects depend upon many other economic conditions remaining constant. Two conditions that may not be constant are the price inflation rate and the net borrowings from the rest of the world. The most important economic condition that does not remain constant is the price inflation rate. As the discussion on the relationship between inflation rates and interest rates in Chapter 3 shows, short-term nominal interest rates will rise as expected inflation rates increase. A possible side effect of an increase in the money supply is higher inflation expectations, which, in turn, tend to cause interest rates to rise. Consequently, the downward effects of increased availability may be partially or wholly offset by the upward effects of higher inflation expectations. Also, borrowings from the rest of the world certainly depend upon interest rates in the United States compared with other countries. If interest rates rise (fall) domestically, then funds will flow into (out of) domestic financial markets in a way that tends to maintain interest rates at constant levels. Combining inflation and international worst-case effects leads to the conclusion that increases in the money supply lead to an increase in prices, an outflow of capital, and no change in real interest rates and productivity. Because of the possibility of significant adverse side effects, one must interpret the loanable funds effects on real interest rates and activity with great caution. The short- and long-term effects of Federal Reserve adjustments on the U.S. economy remain somewhat mysterious.

SUMMARY

Banks, broadly defined to include all depository institutions, are unique among financial institutions in that they alone can create money. Money in this context means cash and demand deposits. As banks' customers deposit cash in the bank, the cash becomes primary reserves, which form the basis for non-cash-deposit expansion. The bank is then able to make loans to other customers by crediting the customers' deposit account. The Federal Reserve regulates deposit and credit expansion by requiring that a minimum percentage of deposits be held by banks as primary reserves. The relationship between the amount of reserves required to be held (R), the required reserve rate (rr), and the amount of deposits (DD) is expressed algebraically as:

$$R = rr \cdot DD$$

Reserve requirements limit deposit expansion to a determinable multiple. The expansion multiple is the inverse of the reserve rate. Because there are many banks in the banking system that are continually interacting in deposit, loan, and transfer activities, bank managers must continually monitor deposit and reserve levels in order to ensure that required reserves are maintained and that idle reserves are quickly invested.

The Federal Reserve Bank is the central bank of the United States. Like any bank, the Federal Reserve receives deposits, makes loans, and performs transfer functions for private commercial banks. Its primary function is to conduct monetary policy so as to balance inflation, economic activity, unemployment, and international financial goals. This is executed primarily through the process of controlling available reserves, which in turn influences economic activity. As reserves are contracted or expanded, interest rates are raised or lowered. In turn, interest rates influence the attractiveness of borrowing and investment. Investment and borrowing impact on real investment as money is spent for homes, equipment, schools, and other capital investment.

The two main instruments which the Federal Reserve uses to control reserves are:

1 Open-market operations
2 Discount window policy

Open-market operations consist of transactions by the Federal Reserve in U.S. government securities that increase or decrease deposits held as reserves by commercial banks. The Federal Open Market Committee (FOMC) establishes the policy to be followed with respect to open-market transactions. The discount rate is the rate of interest charged by the Federal Reserve on loans to insured banks. As the rate is decreased, loans are more attractive and borrowing increases. On the other hand, as the rate increases, borrowing becomes less attractive and bank loans decline.

TERMS

money	reserve rate
narrow money stock	required reserves
money supply	real investment
M_1	loanable funds
deposit creation	loan expansion
credit creation	high-powered money
derivative deposits	monetary policy
investment multiplier	discount rate
monetary base	open-market operations
money multiplier	Federal Open Market Committee (FOMC)

LIST OF EQUATIONS

$$R = rr \cdot DD$$

$$DD = \frac{R}{rr}$$

$$DD = \frac{1}{rr} \cdot R$$

$$c = \frac{C}{DD}$$

$$DD = \frac{R_d}{rr_d}$$

$$M_1 = C + DD$$

$$MB = R + C$$

$$R = R_d + R_{td}$$

$$t = \frac{TD}{DD}$$

$$TD = \frac{R_{td}}{rr_{td}}$$

$$M_1 = \frac{1 + c}{rr_d + rr_{td}t} R$$

$$m = \frac{1 + c}{rr_d + rr_{td}t}$$

QUESTIONS AND PROBLEMS

1 What is the narrow money stock? What is the essential characteristic of money? What are the principal assets used as money?

2 Complete the following T accounts to show the maximum amount that loans and deposits can be expanded, assuming a 12 percent reserve requirement against deposits and that cash is fixed at $500 by the monetary authority.

Banking System

Cash	$ 500	Deposits	$2000
Loans	1500		
Total	$2000	Total	$2000

3 How do banks create money? What power does the central bank have to create money that commercial banks do not have?

4 National Bank has deposits of $30,000 and cash of $30,000. If the current reserve rate is 12 percent, how much excess reserves does the bank have?

5 Fourth National Bank opens for business with capitalization of $4 million, of which $1 million is used to establish operations and $3 million is held as cash reserves. Assuming that a reserve rate of 12 percent is in effect, compute the amount deposits can be expanded. Use T accounts to show the effect the expansion has on the bank's balance sheet.

6 What profit incentive does the bank manager have for maintaining reserves at the minimum possible level?

7 What are derivative deposits?

8 Briefly explain how Federal Reserve monetary actions change short-term interest rates.

9 Explain the five steps through which Federal Reserve monetary policy implements government economic policies.

10 Explain why high interest rates allocate credit among borrowers on the basis of economic need.

11 Why are spending increases a multiple of real investment increases?

12 What are the two principal instruments of Federal Reserve monetary policy?

13 How do open-market operations by the Federal Reserve influence commercial bank reserves? Who determines open-market policy?

14 Compare open-market operations and discount rate policy as instruments of monetary policy.

15 How does the Federal Reserve increase the supply of lendable funds?

16 Why are member bank deposits at the Federal Reserve called high-powered money?

17 Try this teaser problem that many banks face. Assume that a bank is started with $3 million in capital and cash reserves. When it makes a loan, 50 percent of the loan is maintained as a deposit and 50 percent is withdrawn from reserves. The required primary reserve rate is 12 percent of deposits. What is the maximum amount of deposit and credit expansion possible? (*Hint:* Use the balance sheet identity as a format and solve algebraically for deposits, given the relationships described in the problem.)

SELECTED REFERENCES

Barth, J. A. Draft, and P. Wiest: "A Utility Maximization Approach to Individual Bank Asset Selection," *Journal of Money, Credit and Banking,* May 1977, pp. 316–327.

Berman, P. I.: "Differential Discount Facility Administration: Some Empirical Evidence," *Journal of Bank Research,* Summer 1976, pp. 158–165.

Boorman, John T., and Thomas M. Havrilesky: *Money Supply, Money Demand, and Macroeconomic Models,* AHM Publishing Corp., Arlington Heights, Ill., 1972.

Burns, Arthur F.: "The Importance of an Independent Central Bank," *Federal Reserve Bulletin,* September 1977, pp. 777–781.

Cox, William: "The Money Stock," *Monthly Review.* (Federal Reserve Bank of Atlanta), November 1973, pp. 178–181.

Crick, W. F.: "The Genesis of Bank Deposits," *Economica,* 1927.

Gurley, John G., and E. S. Shaw: *Money in a Theory of Finance,* The Brookings Institution, Washington, D.C., 1960.

Hall, William: "How the American System of Bank Regulation Developed," *The Banker,* September 1974, pp. 1101–1107.

Havrilesky, Thomas M., and John T. Boorman: *Current Perspectives in Banking,* AHM Publishing Corp., Arlington Heights, Ill., 1976.

Hendershott, Patric H., and Frank De Leeuw: "Free Reserves, Interest Rates, and Deposits, A Synthesis," *Journal of Finance,* June 1970, pp. 599–613.

Hess, Alan C.: "An Explanation of Short-Run Fluctuations in the Ratio of Currency to Demand Deposits," *Journal of Money, Credit and Banking,* August 1971, pp. 666–679.

Holmes, Alan R., and Peter D. Sternlight: "The Strategy of Monetary Control," *Federal Reserve Bulletin,* May 1976, pp. 411–421.

Kaminow, Ira: "Why Not Pay Interest on Member Bank Reserves?" *Business Review* (Federal Reserve Bank of Philadelphia), January 1975, pp. 3–9.

Klein, Benjamin: "The Competitive Supply of Money," *Journal of Money, Credit and Banking,* November 1974, pp. 423–453.

Laufenberg, Daniel E.: "Reserve Measures as Operating Variables of Monetary Policy: An Empirical Analysis," *Journal of Finance,* June 1976, pp. 853–864.

Logue, Dennis E., and Lemma W. Senbet: "External Currency Market Equilibrium and Its Implications for Regulation of the Eurocurrency Market," *Journal of Finance,* May 1983, pp. 435–447.

Mayer, T.: "Should Large Banks Be Allowed to Fail?," *Journal of Financial and Quantitative Analysis,* November 1975, pp. 603–610.

Meyer, Laurence H.: "Wealth Effects and the Effectiveness of Monetary and Fiscal Policies," *Journal of Money, Credit and Banking,* November 1974, pp. 481–502.

Meyer, Paul A., and John A. Neri: "A Keynes-Friedman Money Demand Function," *American Economic Review,* September 1975, pp. 610–623.

Modern Money Mechanics, Federal Reserve Bank of Chicago, 1975.

Pierce, David A.: "Money Supply Control: Reserves as the Instrument under Lagged Accounting," *Journal of Finance,* June 1976, pp. 845–852.

Polakoff, Murray E., et al.: *Financial Institutions and Markets,* Houghton Mifflin, Boston, 1981.

Rea, John D.: "Monetary Policy and the Cyclical Behavior of the Money Supply," *Journal of Money, Credit and Banking,* August 1976, pp. 347–358.

Santomero, Anthony M., and Jeremy J. Siegel: "A General Equilibrium Money and Banking Paradigm, *Journal of Finance,* May 1982, pp. 357–369.

Wood, John H.: "Two Notes on the Uniqueness of Commercial Banks," *Journal of Finance,* March 1970, pp. 99–108.

Wrightsman, Dwayne: *An Introduction to Monetary Theory and Policy,* 3d ed., Free Press, New York, 1983.

PART SIX

APPENDIXES

COMPOUND-INTEREST EQUIVALENTS

$$R = (1 + i/M)^M - 1$$
(percent)

Compounding frequency				
Annual *i*	Semiannual *R*	Quarterly *R*	Monthly *R*	Daily *R*
4.00	4.04	4.06	4.07	4.08
4.25	4.30	4.32	4.33	4.34
4.50	4.55	4.58	4.59	4.60
4.75	4.81	4.84	4.85	4.86
5.00	5.06	5.09	5.12	5.13
5.25	5.32	5.35	5.38	5.39
5.50	5.58	5.61	5.64	5.65
5.75	5.83	5.88	5.90	5.92
6.00	6.09	6.14	6.17	6.18
6.25	6.35	6.40	6.43	6.45
6.50	6.61	6.66	6.70	6.72
6.75	6.86	6.92	6.96	6.98
7.00	7.12	7.19	7.23	7.25
7.25	7.38	7.45	7.50	7.52
7.50	7.64	7.71	7.76	7.79
7.75	7.90	7.98	8.03	8.06
8.00	8.16	8.24	8.30	8.33
8.25	8.42	8.51	8.57	8.60
8.50	8.68	8.77	8.84	8.87
8.75	8.94	9.04	9.11	9.14
9.00	9.20	9.31	9.38	9.42
9.25	9.46	9.58	9.65	9.69

$$R = (1 + i/M)^M - 1$$
(percent)

Compounding frequency				
Annual i	Semiannual R	Quarterly R	Monthly R	Daily R
9.50	9.73	9.84	9.92	9.96
9.75	9.99	10.11	10.20	10.24
10.00	10.25	10.38	10.47	10.52
10.25	10.51	10.65	10.75	10.79
10.50	10.78	10.92	11.02	11.07
10.75	11.04	11.19	11.30	11.35
11.00	11.30	11.46	11.57	11.63
11.25	11.57	11.73	11.85	11.91
11.50	11.83	12.01	12.13	12.19
11.75	12.10	12.28	12.40	12.47
12.00	12.36	12.55	12.68	12.75
13.00	13.42	13.65	13.80	13.88
14.00	14.49	14.75	14.93	15.02
15.00	15.56	15.87	16.08	16.18
16.00	16.64	16.99	17.23	17.35
17.00	17.72	18.11	18.39	18.53
18.00	18.81	19.25	19.56	19.72

INTEREST RATE TABLES

PRESENT VALUE GLOSSARY AND EQUATIONS

Values contained in this table may be computed with calculators and computers programmed with the following equations:

Future Value (or a present amount)

$$FV = (1 + R)^n$$

Present Value (of a future amount)

$$PV = \frac{1 - (1 + R)^{-n}}{R}$$

Annuity Future Value

$$AFV = \frac{(1 + R)^n - 1}{R}$$

Annuity Present Value

$$APV = \sum_{t=1}^{n} \frac{1}{(1 + R)^t}$$

Payment

$$PAY = \frac{R}{1 - (1 + R)^{-n}}$$

Interest Rate of ⅓ Percent

n	Compound amount — Future value of a present amount FV	Present value — Present value of a future amount PV	Annuity compound amount — Future value of an annuity AFV	Annuity present value — Present value of an annuity APV	Payment — Annuity repaying a present amount PAY	n
1	1.0033	.9967	1.0000	.9967	1.0033	1
2	1.0067	.9934	2.0033	1.9900	.5025	2
3	1.0100	.9901	3.0100	2.9801	.3356	3
4	1.0134	.9868	4.0200	3.9669	.2521	4
5	1.0168	.9835	5.0334	4.9504	.2020	5
6	1.0202	.9802	6.0502	5.9306	.1686	6
7	1.0236	.9770	7.0704	6.9076	.1448	7
8	1.0270	.9737	8.0940	7.8813	.1269	8
9	1.0304	.9705	9.1209	8.8518	.1130	9
10	1.0338	.9673	10.1513	9.8191	.1018	10
11	1.0373	.9641	11.1852	10.7831	.0927	11
12	1.0407	.9609	12.2225	11.7440	.0851	12

n	Compound amount — Future value of a present amount FV	Present value — Present value of a future amount PV	Annuity compound amount — Future value of an annuity AFV	Annuity present value — Present value of an annuity APV	Payment — Annuity repaying a present amount PAY	n
48	1.1732	.8524	51.9596	44.2888	.0226	48
60	1.2210	.8190	66.2990	54.2991	.0184	60
72	1.2707	.7869	81.2226	63.9174	.0156	72
84	1.3225	.7561	96.7541	73.1593	.0137	84
96	1.3764	.7265	112.9185	82.0393	.0122	96
108	1.4325	.6981	129.7414	90.5718	.0110	108
120	1.4908	.6708	147.2498	98.7702	.0101	120
132	1.5516	.6445	165.4714	106.6477	.0094	132
144	1.6148	.6193	184.4354	114.2168	.0088	144
156	1.6806	.5950	204.1721	121.4896	.0082	156
168	1.7490	.5717	224.7128	128.4777	.0078	168
180	1.8203	.5494	246.0904	135.1922	.0074	180

n					
13	1.0442	.9577	13.2632	12.7017	.0787
14	1.0477	.9545	14.3074	13.6561	.0732
15	1.0512	.9513	15.3551	14.6074	.0685
16	1.0547	.9481	16.4063	15.5556	.0643
17	1.0582	.9450	17.4610	16.5006	.0606
18	1.0617	.9419	18.5192	17.4424	.0573
19	1.0653	.9387	19.5809	18.3812	.0544
20	1.0688	.9356	20.6462	19.3168	.0518
21	1.0724	.9325	21.7150	20.2493	.0494
22	1.0760	.9294	22.7874	21.1787	.0472
23	1.0795	.9263	23.8633	22.1050	.0452
24	1.0831	.9232	24.9429	23.0283	.0434
25	1.0868	.9202	26.0260	23.9484	.0418
26	1.0904	.9171	27.1128	24.8655	.0402
27	1.0940	.9141	28.2032	25.7796	.0388
28	1.0977	.9110	29.2972	26.6906	.0375
29	1.1013	.9080	30.3948	27.5986	.0362
30	1.1050	.9050	31.4961	28.5036	.0351
31	1.1087	.9020	32.6011	29.4056	.0340
32	1.1124	.8990	33.7098	30.3046	.0330
33	1.1161	.8960	34.8222	31.2006	.0321
34	1.1198	.8930	35.9382	32.0936	.0312
35	1.1235	.8901	37.0580	32.9837	.0303
36	1.1273	.8871	38.1816	33.8708	.0295

n						months
13	1.8945	.5279	268.3390	141.6439	.0071	192
14	1.9716	.5072	291.4940	147.8430	.0068	204
15	2.0520	.4873	315.5923	153.7994	.0065	216
16	2.1356	.4683	340.6725	159.5227	.0063	228
17	2.2226	.4499	366.7745	165.0219	.0061	240
18	2.3131	.4323	393.9399	170.3059	.0059	252
19	2.4074	.4154	422.2120	175.3830	.0057	264
20	2.5055	.3991	451.6360	180.2613	.0055	276
21	2.6075	.3835	482.2588	184.9487	.0054	288
22	2.7138	.3685	514.1293	189.4526	.0053	300
23	2.8243	.3541	547.2981	193.7801	.0052	312
24	2.9394	.3402	581.8183	197.9383	.0051	324
25	3.0591	.3269	617.7449	201.9337	.0050	336
26	3.1838	.3141	655.1353	205.7726	.0049	348
27	3.3135	.3018	694.0489	209.4613	.0048	360
28						
29						
30						
∞				300.0000	.0033	∞

Source: Schall, Lawrence D. and Charles W. Haley: *Introduction to Financial Management*, McGraw-Hill Book Co., New York, 1983, p. 807.

Interest Rate of ½ Percent

n	Compound amount Future value of a present amount FV	Present value Present value of a future amount PV	Annuity compound amount Future value of an annuity AFV	Annuity present value Present value of an annuity APV	Payment Annuity repaying a present amount PAY	n
1	1.0050	.9950	1.0000	.9950	1.0050	1
2	1.0100	.9901	2.0050	1.9851	.5038	2
3	1.0151	.9851	3.0150	2.9702	.3367	3
4	1.0202	.9802	4.0301	3.9505	.2531	4
5	1.0253	.9754	5.0503	4.9529	.2030	5
6	1.0304	.9705	6.0755	5.8964	.1696	6
7	1.0355	.9657	7.1059	6.8621	.1457	7
8	1.0407	.9609	8.1414	7.8230	.1278	8
9	1.0459	.9561	9.1821	8.7791	.1139	9
10	1.0511	.9513	10.2280	9.7304	.1028	10
11	1.0564	.9466	11.2792	10.6770	.0937	11
12	1.0617	.9419	12.3356	11.6189	.0861	12

n	Compound amount Future value of a present amount FV	Present value Present value of a future amount PV	Annuity compound amount Future value of an annuity AFV	Annuity present value Present value of an annuity APV	Payment Annuity repaying a present amount PAY	n
48	1.2705	.7871	54.0978	42.5803	.0235	48
60	1.3489	.7414	69.7700	51.7256	.0193	60
72	1.4320	.6983	86.4089	60.3395	.0166	72
84	1.5204	.6577	104.0739	68.4530	.0146	84
96	1.6141	.6195	122.8285	76.0952	.0131	96
108	1.7137	.5835	142.7399	83.2934	.0120	108
120	1.8194	.5496	163.8793	90.0735	.0111	120
132	1.9316	.5177	186.3226	96.4596	.0104	132
144	2.0508	.4876	210.1502	102.4747	.0098	144
156	2.1772	.4593	235.4473	108.1404	.0092	156
168	2.3115	.4326	262.3048	113.4770	.0088	168
180	2.4541	.4075	290.8187	118.5035	.0084	180

13	1.0670	.9372	13.3972	12.5562	.0796	13	192	2.6055	.3838	321.0913	123.2380	.0081	192
14	1.0723	.9326	14.4642	13.4887	.0741	14	204	2.7662	.3615	353.2311	127.6975	.0078	204
15	1.0777	.9279	15.5365	14.4166	.0694	15	216	2.9368	.3405	387.3532	131.8979	.0076	216
16	1.0831	.9233	16.6142	15.3399	.0652	16	228	3.1179	.3207	423.5799	135.8542	.0074	228
17	1.0885	.9187	17.6973	16.2586	.0615	17	240	3.3102	.3021	462.0409	139.5808	.0072	240
18	1.0939	.9141	18.7858	17.1728	.0582	18	252	3.5144	.2845	502.8741	143.0908	.0070	252
19	1.0994	.9096	19.8797	18.0824	.0553	19	264	3.7311	.2680	546.2259	146.3969	.0068	264
20	1.1049	.9051	20.9791	18.9874	.0527	20	276	3.9613	.2524	592.2514	149.5110	.0067	276
21	1.1104	.9006	22.0840	19.8880	.0503	21	288	4.2056	.2378	641.1158	152.4441	.0066	288
22	1.1160	.8961	23.1944	20.7841	.0481	22	300	4.4650	.2240	692.9940	155.2069	.0064	300
23	1.1216	.8916	24.3104	21.6757	.0461	23	312	4.7404	.2110	748.0719	157.8091	.0063	312
24	1.1272	.8872	25.4320	22.5629	.0443	24	324	5.0327	.1987	806.5469	160.2602	.0062	324
25	1.1328	.8828	26.5591	23.4456	.0427	25	336	5.3431	.1872	868.6285	162.5688	.0062	336
26	1.1385	.8784	27.6919	24.3240	.0411	26	348	5.6727	.1763	934.5392	164.7434	.0061	348
27	1.1442	.8740	28.8304	25.1980	.0397	27	360	6.0226	.1660	1004.5150	166.7916	.0060	360
28	1.1499	.8697	29.9745	26.0677	.0384	28	∞						
29	1.1556	.8653	31.1244	26.9330	.0371	29					200.0000	.0050	∞
30	1.1614	.8610	32.2800	27.7941	.0360	30							
31	1.1672	.8567	33.4414	28.6508	.0349	31							
32	1.1730	.8525	34.6086	29.5033	.0339	32							
33	1.1789	.8482	35.7817	30.3515	.0329	33							
34	1.1848	.8440	36.9606	31.1955	.0321	34							
35	1.1907	.8398	38.1454	32.0354	.0312	35							
36	1.1967	.8356	39.3361	32.8710	.0304	36							

Interest Rate of ⅔ Percent

n	Compound amount — Future value of a present amount — FV	Present value — Present value of a future amount — PV	Annuity compound amount — Future value of an annuity — AFV	Annuity present value — Present value of an annuity — APV	Payment — Annuity repaying a present amount — PAY	n
1	1.0067	.9934	1.0000	.9934	1.0067	1
2	1.0134	.9868	2.0067	1.9802	.5050	2
3	1.0201	.9803	3.0200	2.9604	.3378	3
4	1.0269	.9738	4.0402	3.9342	.2542	4
5	1.0338	.9673	5.0671	4.9015	.2040	5
6	1.0407	.9609	6.1009	5.8625	.1706	6
7	1.0476	.9546	7.1416	6.8170	.1467	7
8	1.0546	.9482	8.1892	7.7652	.1288	8
9	1.0616	.9420	9.2438	8.7072	.1148	9
10	1.0687	.9357	10.3054	9.6429	.1037	10
11	1.0758	.9295	11.3741	10.5724	.0946	11
12	1.0830	.9234	12.4499	11.4958	.0870	12

n	Compound amount — Future value of a present amount — FV	Present value — Present value of a future amount — PV	Annuity compound amount — Future value of an annuity — AFV	Annuity present value — Present value of an annuity — APV	Payment — Annuity repaying a present amount — PAY	n
48	1.3757	.7269	56.3499	40.9619	.0244	48
60	1.4898	.6712	73.4769	49.3184	.0203	60
72	1.6135	.6198	92.0253	57.0345	.0175	72
84	1.7474	.5723	112.1133	64.1593	.0156	84
96	1.8925	.5284	133.8686	70.7380	.0141	96
108	2.0495	.4879	157.4295	76.8125	.0130	108
120	2.2196	.4505	182.9460	82.4215	.0121	120
132	2.4039	.4160	210.5804	87.6006	.0114	132
144	2.6034	.3841	240.5084	92.3828	.0108	144
156	2.8195	.3547	272.9204	96.7985	.0103	156
168	3.0535	.3275	308.0226	100.8758	.0099	168
180	3.3069	.3024	346.0382	104.6406	.0096	180

Table for periods 13–36:

n						n
13	1.0902	13.5329	12.4130	.0806	.9172	13
14	1.0975	14.6231	13.3242	.0751	.9112	14
15	1.1048	15.7206	14.2293	.0703	.9051	15
16	1.1122	16.8254	15.1285	.0661	.8991	16
17	1.1196	17.9376	16.0217	.0624	.8932	17
18	1.1270	19.0572	16.9089	.0591	.8873	18
19	1.1346	20.1842	17.7903	.0562	.8814	19
20	1.1421	21.3188	18.6659	.0536	.8756	20
21	1.1497	22.4609	19.5357	.0512	.8698	21
22	1.1574	23.6107	20.3997	.0490	.8640	22
23	1.1651	24.7681	21.2579	.0470	.8583	23
24	1.1729	25.9332	22.1105	.0452	.8526	24
25	1.1807	27.1061	22.9575	.0436	.8470	25
26	1.1886	28.2868	23.7988	.0420	.8413	26
27	1.1965	29.4754	24.6346	.0406	.8358	27
28	1.2045	30.6719	25.4648	.0393	.8302	28
29	1.2125	31.8763	26.2896	.0380	.8247	29
30	1.2206	33.0889	27.1088	.0369	.8193	30
31	1.2287	34.3094	27.9227	.0358	.8138	31
32	1.2369	35.5382	28.7312	.0348	.8085	32
33	1.2452	36.7751	29.5343	.0339	.8031	33
34	1.2535	38.0203	30.3320	.0330	.7978	34
35	1.2618	39.2737	31.1246	.0321	.7925	35
36	1.2702	40.5356	31.9118	.0313	.7873	36

Table for periods 192–360 and ∞:

n						n
192	3.5814	.2792	387.2092	108.1169	.0092	192
204	3.8786	.2578	431.7973	111.3267	.0090	204
216	4.2006	.2381	480.0861	114.2906	.0087	216
228	4.5492	.2198	532.3830	117.0273	.0085	228
240	4.9268	.2030	589.0204	119.5543	.0084	240
252	5.3357	.1874	650.3588	121.8876	.0082	252
264	5.7786	.1731	716.7882	124.0421	.0081	264
276	6.2582	.1598	788.7312	126.0315	.0079	276
288	6.7776	.1475	866.6454	127.8684	.0078	288
300	7.3402	.1362	951.0265	129.5645	.0077	300
312	7.9494	.1258	1042.4111	131.1307	.0076	312
324	8.6092	.1162	1141.3807	132.5768	.0075	324
336	9.3238	.1073	1248.5646	133.9121	.0075	336
348	10.0976	.0990	1364.6448	135.1450	.0074	348
360	10.9357	.0914	1490.3596	136.2835	.0073	360
∞				150.0000	.0067	∞

Interest Rate of ¾ Percent

n	Compound amount Future value of a present amount FV	Present value Present value of a future amount PV	Annuity compound amount Future value of an annuity AFV	Annuity present value Present value of an annuity APV	Payment Annuity repaying a present amount PAY	n
1	1.0075	.9926	1.0000	.9926	1.0075	1
2	1.0151	.9852	2.0075	1.9777	.5056	2
3	1.0227	.9778	3.0226	2.9556	.3383	3
4	1.0303	.9706	4.0452	3.9261	.2547	4
5	1.0381	.9633	5.0756	4.8894	.2045	5
6	1.0459	.9562	6.1136	5.8456	.1711	6
7	1.0537	.9490	7.1595	6.7946	.1472	7
8	1.0616	.9420	8.2132	7.7366	.1293	8
9	1.0696	.9350	9.2748	8.6716	.1153	9
10	1.0776	.9280	10.3443	9.5996	.1042	10
11	1.0857	.9211	11.4219	10.5207	.0951	11
12	1.0938	.9142	12.5076	11.4349	.0875	12

n	Compound amount Future value of a present amount FV	Present value Present value of a future amount PV	Annuity compound amount Future value of an annuity AFV	Annuity present value Present value of an annuity APV	Payment Annuity repaying a present amount PAY	n
48	1.4314	.6986	57.5207	40.1848	.0249	48
60	1.5657	.6387	75.4241	48.1734	.0208	60
72	1.7126	.5839	95.0070	55.4768	.0180	72
84	1.8732	.5338	116.4269	62.1540	.0161	84
96	2.0489	.4881	139.8562	68.2584	.0147	96
108	2.2411	.4462	165.4832	73.8394	.0135	108
120	2.4514	.4079	193.5143	78.9417	.0127	120
132	2.6813	.3730	224.1748	83.6064	.0120	132
144	2.9328	.3410	257.7116	87.8711	.0114	144
156	3.2080	.3117	294.3943	91.7700	.0109	156
168	3.5089	.2850	334.5181	95.3346	.0105	168
180	3.8380	.2605	378.4058	98.5934	.0101	180

n													n
13	1.1020	.9074	13.6014	12.3423	.0810	13	192	4.1981	.2382	426.4104	101.5728	.0098	192
14	1.1103	.9007	14.7034	13.2430	.0755	14	204	4.5919	.2178	478.9183	104.2966	.0096	204
15	1.1186	.8940	15.8137	14.1370	.0707	15	216	5.0226	.1991	536.3517	106.7869	.0094	216
16	1.1270	.8873	16.9323	15.0243	.0666	16	228	5.4938	.1820	599.1727	109.0635	.0092	228
17	1.1354	.8807	18.0593	15.9050	.0629	17	240	6.0092	.1664	667.8869	111.1450	.0090	240
18	1.1440	.8742	19.1947	16.7792	.0596	18	252	6.5729	.1521	743.0469	113.0479	.0088	252
19	1.1525	.8676	20.3387	17.6468	.0567	19	264	7.1894	.1391	825.2574	114.7876	.0087	264
20	1.1612	.8612	21.4912	18.5080	.0540	20	276	7.8638	.1272	915.1798	116.3781	.0086	276
21	1.1699	.8548	22.6524	19.3628	.0516	21	288	8.6015	.1163	1013.5375	117.8322	.0085	288
22	1.1787	.8484	23.8223	20.2112	.0495	22	300	9.4084	.1063	1121.1219	119.1616	.0084	300
23	1.1875	.8421	25.0010	21.0533	.0475	23	312	10.2910	.0972	1238.7985	120.3770	.0083	312
24	1.1964	.8358	26.1885	21.8891	.0457	24	324	11.2564	.0888	1367.5139	121.4882	.0082	324
25	1.2054	.8296	27.3849	22.7188	.0440	25	336	12.3123	.0812	1508.3037	122.5040	.0082	336
26	1.2144	.8234	28.5903	23.5422	.0425	26	348	13.4673	.0743	1662.3006	123.4328	.0081	348
27	1.2235	.8173	29.8047	24.3595	.0411	27	360	14.7306	.0679	1830.7435	124.2819	.0080	360
28	1.2327	.8112	31.0282	25.1707	.0397	28	8						8
29	1.2420	.8052	32.2609	25.9759	.0385	29					133.3333	.0075	
30	1.2513	.7992	33.5029	26.7751	.0373	30							
31	1.2607	.7932	34.7542	27.5683	.0363								
32	1.2701	.7873	36.0148	28.3557	.0353								
33	1.2796	.7815	37.2849	29.1371	.0343								
34	1.2892	.7757	38.5646	29.9128	.0334								
35	1.2989	.7699	39.8538	30.6827	.0326								
36	1.3086	.7641	41.1527	31.4468	.0318								

Interest Rate of 1.00 Percent

n	Compound amount — Future value of a present amount — FV	Present value — Present value of a future amount — PV	Annuity compound amount — Future value of an annuity — AFV	Annuity present value — Present value of an annuity — APV	Payment — Annuity repaying a present amount — PAY	n
1	1.0100	.9901	1.0000	.9901	1.0100	1
2	1.0201	.9803	2.0100	1.9704	.5075	2
3	1.0303	.9706	3.0301	2.9410	.3400	3
4	1.0406	.9610	4.0604	3.9020	.2563	4
5	1.0510	.9515	5.1010	4.8534	.2060	5
6	1.0615	.9420	6.1520	5.7955	.1725	6
7	1.0721	.9327	7.2135	6.7282	.1486	7
8	1.0829	.9235	8.2857	7.6517	.1307	8
9	1.0937	.9143	9.3685	8.5660	.1167	9
10	1.1046	.9053	10.4622	9.4713	.1056	10
11	1.1157	.8963	11.5668	10.3676	.0965	11
12	1.1268	.8874	12.6825	11.2551	.0888	12

n	Compound amount — Future value of a present amount — FV	Present value — Present value of a future amount — PV	Annuity compound amount — Future value of an annuity — AFV	Annuity present value — Present value of an annuity — APV	Payment — Annuity repaying a present amount — PAY	n
48	1.6122	.6203	61.2226	37.9740	.0263	48
60	1.8167	.5504	81.6697	44.9550	.0222	60
72	2.0471	.4885	104.7099	51.1504	.0196	72
84	2.3067	.4335	130.6723	56.6485	.0177	84
96	2.5993	.3847	159.9273	61.5277	.0163	96
108	2.9289	.3414	192.8926	65.8578	.0152	108
120	3.3004	.3030	230.0387	69.7005	.0143	120
132	3.7190	.2689	271.8959	73.1108	.0137	132
144	4.1906	.2386	319.0616	76.1372	.0131	144
156	4.7221	.2118	372.2091	78.8229	.0127	156
168	5.3210	.1879	432.0970	81.2064	.0123	168
180	5.9958	.1668	499.5802	83.3217	.0120	180

n						n
13	1.1381	.8787	13.8093	12.1337	.0824	13
14	1.1495	.8700	14.9474	13.0037	.0769	14
15	1.1610	.8613	16.0969	13.8651	.0721	15
16	1.1726	.8528	17.2579	14.7179	.0679	16
17	1.1843	.8444	18.4304	15.5623	.0643	17
18	1.1961	.8360	19.6147	16.3983	.0610	18
19	1.2081	.8277	20.8109	17.2260	.0581	19
20	1.2202	.8195	22.0190	18.0456	.0554	20
21	1.2324	.8114	23.2392	18.8570	.0530	21
22	1.2447	.8034	24.4716	19.6604	.0509	22
23	1.2572	.7954	25.7163	20.4558	.0489	23
24	1.2697	.7876	26.9735	21.2434	.0471	24
25	1.2824	.7798	28.2432	22.0232	.0454	25
26	1.2953	.7720	29.5256	22.7952	.0439	26
27	1.3082	.7644	30.8209	23.5596	.0424	27
28	1.3213	.7568	32.1291	24.3164	.0411	28
29	1.3345	.7493	33.4504	25.0658	.0399	29
30	1.3478	.7419	34.7849	25.8077	.0387	30
31	1.3613	.7346	36.1327	26.5423	.0377	31
32	1.3749	.7273	37.4941	27.2696	.0367	32
33	1.3887	.7201	38.8690	27.9897	.0357	33
34	1.4026	.7130	40.2577	28.7027	.0348	34
35	1.4166	.7059	41.6603	29.4086	.0340	35
36	1.4308	.6989	43.0769	30.1075	.0332	36

n						n
192	6.7562	.1480	575.6220	85.1988	.0117	192
204	7.6131	.1314	661.3078	86.8647	.0115	204
216	8.5786	.1166	757.8606	88.3431	.0113	216
228	9.6666	.1034	866.6588	89.6551	.0112	228
240	10.8926	.0918	989.2554	90.8194	.0110	240
252	12.2740	.0815	1127.4002	91.8527	.0109	252
264	13.8307	.0723	1283.0653	92.7697	.0108	264
276	15.5847	.0642	1458.4726	93.5835	.0107	276
288	17.5613	.0569	1656.1259	94.3056	.0106	288
300	19.7885	.0505	1878.8466	94.9466	.0105	300
312	22.2981	.0448	2129.8139	95.5153	.0105	312
324	25.1261	.0398	2412.6101	96.0201	.0104	324
336	28.3127	.0353	2731.2720	96.4680	.0104	336
348	31.9035	.0313	3090.3481	96.8655	.0103	348
360	35.9496	.0278	3494.9641	97.2183	.0103	360
∞				100.0000	.0100	∞

Interest Rate of 1.25 Percent

n	Compound amount — Future value of a present amount — FV	Present value — Present value of a future amount — PV	Annuity compound amount — Future value of an annuity — AFV	Annuity present value — Present value of an annuity — APV	Payment — Annuity repaying a present amount — PAY	n	Compound amount — Future value of a present amount — FV	Present value — Present value of a future amount — PV	Annuity compound amount — Future value of an annuity — AFV	Annuity present value — Present value of an annuity — APV	Payment — Annuity repaying a present amount — PAY	n
1	1.0125	.9877	1.0000	.9877	1.0125	1	1.8154	.5509	65.2284	35.9315	.0278	48
2	1.0252	.9755	2.0125	1.9631	.5094	2	2.1072	.4746	88.5745	42.0346	.0238	60
3	1.0380	.9634	3.0377	2.9265	.3417	3	2.4459	.4088	115.6736	47.2925	.0211	72
4	1.0509	.9515	4.0756	3.8781	.2579	4	2.8391	.3522	147.1290	51.8222	.0193	84
5	1.0641	.9398	5.1266	4.9178	.2076	5	3.2955	.3034	183.6411	55.7246	.0179	96
6	1.0774	.9282	6.1907	5.7460	.1740	6	3.8253	.2614	226.0226	59.0865	.0169	108
7	1.0909	.9167	7.2680	6.6627	.1501	7	4.4402	.2252	275.2171	61.9828	.0161	120
8	1.1045	.9054	8.3589	7.5681	.1321	8	5.1540	.1940	332.3198	64.4781	.0155	132
9	1.1183	.8942	9.4634	8.4623	.1182	9	5.9825	.1672	398.6021	66.6277	.0150	144
10	1.1323	.8832	10.5817	9.3455	.1070	10	6.9442	.1440	475.5395	68.4797	.0146	156
11	1.1464	.8723	11.7139	10.2178	.0979	11	8.0606	.1241	564.8450	70.0751	.0143	168
12	1.1608	.8615	12.8604	11.0793	.0903	12	9.3563	.1069	668.5068	71.4496	.0140	180

13	1.1753	.8509	14.0211	11.9302	.0838	13	192	10.8604	.0921	788.8326	72.6338	.0138	192
14	1.1900	.8404	15.1964	12.7706	.0783	14	204	12.6063	.0793	928.5014	73.6540	.0136	204
15	1.2048	.8300	16.3863	13.6005	.0735	15	216	14.6328	.0683	1090.6225	74.5328	.0134	216
16	1.2199	.8197	17.5912	14.4203	.0693	16	228	16.9851	.0589	1278.8054	75.2900	.0133	228
17	1.2351	.8096	18.8111	15.2299	.0657	17	240	19.7155	.0507	1497.2395	75.9423	.0132	240
18	1.2506	.7996	20.0462	16.0295	.0624	18	252	22.8848	.0437	1750.7879	76.5042	.0131	252
19	1.2662	.7898	21.2968	16.8193	.0595	19	264	26.5637	.0376	2045.0953	76.9884	.0130	264
20	1.2820	.7800	22.5630	17.5993	.0568	20	276	30.8339	.0324	2386.7139	77.4055	.0129	276
21	1.2981	.7704	23.8450	18.3697	.0544	21	288	35.7906	.0279	2783.2493	77.7648	.0129	288
22	1.3143	.7609	25.1431	19.1306	.0523	22	300	41.5441	.0241	3243.5296	78.0743	.0128	300
23	1.3307	.7515	26.4574	19.8820	.0503	23	312	48.2225	.0207	3777.8020	78.3410	.0128	312
24	1.3474	.7422	27.7881	20.6242	.0485	24	324	55.9745	.0179	4397.9611	78.5708	.0127	324
25	1.3642	.7330	29.1354	21.3573	.0468	25	336	64.9727	.0154	5117.8136	78.7687	.0127	336
26	1.3812	.7240	30.4996	22.0813	.0453	26	348	75.4173	.0133	5953.3856	78.9392	.0127	348
27	1.3985	.7150	31.8809	22.7963	.0439	27	360	87.5410	.0114	6923.2796	79.0861	.0126	360
28	1.4160	.7062	33.2794	23.5025	.0425	28	∞						
29	1.4337	.6975	34.6954	24.2000	.0413	29					80.0000	.0125	∞
30	1.4516	.6889	36.1291	24.8889	.0402	30							
31	1.4698	.6804	37.5807	25.5693	.0391	31							
32	1.4881	.6720	39.0504	26.2413	.0381	32							
33	1.5067	.6637	40.5386	26.9050	.0372	33							
34	1.5256	.6555	42.0453	27.5605	.0363	34							
35	1.5446	.6474	43.5709	28.2079	.0355	35							
36	1.5639	.6394	45.1155	28.8473	.0347	36							

Interest Rate of 1.50 Percent

n	Compound amount — Future value of a present amount FV	Present value — Present value of a future amount PV	Annuity compound amount — Future value of an annuity AFV	Annuity present value — Present value of an annuity APV	Payment — Annuity repaying a present amount PAY	n
1	1.0150	.9852	1.0000	.9852	1.0150	1
2	1.0302	.9707	2.0150	1.9559	.5113	2
3	1.0457	.9563	3.0452	2.9122	.3434	3
4	1.0614	.9422	4.0909	3.8544	.2594	4
5	1.0773	.9283	5.1523	4.7826	.2091	5
6	1.0934	.9145	6.2296	5.6972	.1755	6
7	1.1098	.9010	7.3230	6.5982	.1516	7
8	1.1265	.8877	8.4328	7.4859	.1336	8
9	1.1434	.8746	9.5593	8.3605	.1196	9
10	1.1605	.8617	10.7027	9.2222	.1084	10
11	1.1779	.8489	11.8633	10.0711	.0993	11
12	1.1956	.8364	13.0412	10.9075	.0917	12

n	Compound amount — Future value of a present amount FV	Present value — Present value of a future amount PV	Annuity compound amount — Future value of an annuity AFV	Annuity present value — Present value of an annuity APV	Payment — Annuity repaying a present amount PAY	n
40	1.8140	.5513	54.2679	29.9158	.0334	40
44	1.9253	.5194	61.6889	32.0406	.0312	44
48	2.0435	.4894	69.5652	34.0426	.0294	48
52	2.1689	.4611	77.9249	35.9287	.0278	52
56	2.3020	.4344	86.7975	37.7059	.0265	56
60	2.4432	.4039	96.2147	39.3803	.0254	60
64	2.5931	.3856	106.2096	40.9579	.0244	64
68	2.7523	.3633	116.8179	42.4442	.0236	68
72	2.9212	.3423	128.0772	43.8447	.0228	72
76	3.1004	.3225	140.0274	45.1641	.0221	76
80	3.2907	.3039	152.7109	46.4073	.0215	80
84	3.4926	.2863	166.1726	47.5786	.0210	84

n						n
13	1.2136	.8240	14.2368	11.7315	.0852	13
14	1.2318	.8118	15.4504	12.5434	.0797	14
15	1.2502	.7999	16.6821	13.3432	.0749	15
16	1.2690	.7880	17.9324	14.1313	.0708	16
17	1.2880	.7764	19.2014	14.9076	.0671	17
18	1.3073	.7649	20.4894	15.6726	.0638	18
19	1.3270	.7536	21.7967	16.4262	.0609	19
20	1.3469	.7425	23.1237	17.1686	.0582	20
21	1.3671	.7315	24.4705	17.9001	.0559	21
22	1.3876	.7207	25.8376	18.6208	.0537	22
23	1.4084	.7100	27.2251	19.3309	.0517	23
24	1.4295	.6995	28.6335	20.0304	.0499	24
25	1.4509	.6892	30.0630	20.7196	.0483	25
26	1.4727	.6790	31.5140	21.3986	.0467	26
27	1.4948	.6690	32.9867	22.0676	.0453	27
28	1.5172	.6591	34.4815	22.7267	.0440	28
29	1.5400	.6494	35.9987	23.3761	.0428	29
30	1.5631	.6398	37.5387	24.0158	.0416	30
31	1.5865	.6303	39.1018	24.6461	.0406	31
32	1.6103	.6210	40.6883	25.2671	.0396	32
33	1.6345	.6118	42.2986	25.8790	.0386	33
34	1.6590	.6028	43.9331	26.4817	.0378	34
35	1.6839	.5939	45.5921	27.0756	.0369	35
36	1.7091	.5851	47.2760	27.6607	.0362	36

n						n
88	.0205	48.6822	180.4605	.2698	3.7069	88
92	.0201	49.7220	195.6251	.2542	3.9344	92
96	.0197	50.7017	211.7202	.2395	4.1758	96
100	.0194	51.6247	228.8030	.2256	4.4320	100
104	.0190	52.4944	246.9341	.2126	4.7040	104
108	.0188	53.3137	266.1778	.2003	4.9927	108
112	.0185	54.0858	286.6023	.1887	5.2990	112
116	.0182	54.8131	308.2801	.1778	5.6242	116
120	.0180	55.4985	331.2882	.1675	5.9693	120
∞	.0150	66.6667				∞

Interest Rate of 2.00 Percent

n	Compound amount Future value of a present amount FV	Present value Present value of a future amount PV	Annuity compound amount Future value of an annuity AFV	Annuity present value Present value of an annuity APV	Payment Annuity repaying a present amount PAY	n	Compound amount Future value of a present amount FV	Present value Present value of a future amount PV	Annuity compound amount Future value of an annuity AFV	Annuity present value Present value of an annuity APV	Payment Annuity repaying a present amount PAY	n
1	1.0200	.9804	1.0000	.9804	1.0200	1	2.2080	.4529	60.4020	27.3555	.0366	40
2	1.0404	.9612	2.0200	1.9416	.5150	2	2.3901	.4184	69.5027	29.0800	.0344	44
3	1.0612	.9423	3.0604	2.8839	.3468	3	2.5871	.3865	79.3535	30.6731	.0326	48
4	1.0824	.9238	4.1216	3.8077	.2626	4	2.8003	.3571	90.0164	32.1449	.0311	52
5	1.1041	.9057	5.2040	4.7135	.2122	5	3.0312	.3299	101.5583	33.5047	.0298	56
6	1.1262	.8880	6.3081	5.6014	.1785	6	3.2810	.3048	114.0515	34.7609	.0288	60
7	1.1487	.8706	7.4343	6.4720	.1545	7	3.5515	.2816	127.5747	35.9214	.0278	64
8	1.1717	.8535	8.5830	7.3255	.1365	8	3.8443	.2601	142.2125	36.9936	.0270	68
9	1.1951	.8368	9.7546	8.1622	.1225	9	4.1611	.2403	158.0570	37.9841	.0263	72
10	1.2190	.8203	10.9497	8.9826	.1113	10	4.5042	.2220	175.2076	38.8991	.0257	76
11	1.2434	.8043	12.1687	9.7868	.1022	11	4.8754	.2051	193.7720	39.7445	.0252	80
12	1.2682	.7885	13.4121	10.5753	.0946	12	5.2773	.1895	213.8666	40.5255	.0247	84

n						n
13	1.2936	.7730	14.6803	11.3484	.0881	13
14	1.3195	.7579	15.9739	12.1062	.0826	14
15	1.3459	.7430	17.2934	12.8493	.0778	15
16	1.3728	.7284	18.6393	13.5777	.0737	16
17	1.4002	.7142	20.0121	14.2919	.0700	17
18	1.4282	.7002	21.4123	14.9920	.0667	18
19	1.4568	.6864	22.8406	15.6785	.0638	19
20	1.4859	.6730	24.2974	16.3514	.0612	20
21	1.5157	.6598	25.7833	17.0112	.0588	21
22	1.5460	.6468	27.2990	17.6580	.0566	22
23	1.5769	.6342	28.8450	18.2922	.0547	23
24	1.6084	.6217	30.4219	18.9139	.0529	24
25	1.6406	.6095	32.0303	19.5235	.0512	25
26	1.6734	.5976	33.6709	20.1210	.0497	26
27	1.7069	.5859	35.3443	20.7069	.0483	27
28	1.7410	.5744	37.0512	21.2813	.0470	28
29	1.7758	.5631	38.7922	21.8444	.0458	29
30	1.8114	.5521	40.5681	22.3965	.0446	30
31	1.8476	.5412	42.3794	22.9377	.0436	31
32	1.8845	.5306	44.2270	23.4683	.0426	32
33	1.9222	.5202	46.1116	23.9886	.0417	33
34	1.9607	.5100	48.0338	24.4986	.0408	34
35	1.9999	.5000	49.9945	24.9986	.0400	35
36	2.0399	.4902	51.9944	25.4888	.0392	36

n						n
88	5.7124	.1751	235.6177	41.2470	.0242	88
92	6.1832	.1617	259.1618	41.9136	.0239	92
96	6.6929	.1494	284.6467	42.5294	.0235	96
100	7.2446	.1380	312.2323	43.0984	.0232	100
104	7.8418	.1275	342.0919	43.6239	.0229	104
108	8.4883	.1178	374.4129	44.1095	.0227	108
112	9.1880	.1088	409.3981	44.5581	.0224	112
116	9.9453	.1005	447.2673	44.9725	.0222	116
120	10.7652	.0929	488.2582	45.3554	.0220	120
∞				50.0000	.0200	∞

Interest Rate of 3.00 Percent

n	Compound amount — Future value of a present amount — FV	Present value — Present value of a future amount — PV	Annuity compound amount — Future value of an annuity — AFV	Annuity present value — Present value of an annuity — APV	Payment — Annuity repaying a present amount — PAY	n
1	1.0300	.9709	1.0000	.9709	1.0300	1
2	1.0609	.9426	2.0300	1.9135	.5226	2
3	1.0927	.9151	3.0909	2.8286	.3535	3
4	1.1255	.8885	4.1836	3.7171	.2690	4
5	1.1593	.8626	5.3091	4.5797	.2184	5
6	1.1941	.8375	6.4684	5.4172	.1846	6
7	1.2299	.8131	7.6625	6.2303	.1605	7
8	1.2668	.7894	8.8923	7.0197	.1425	8
9	1.3048	.7664	10.1591	7.7861	.1284	9
10	1.3439	.7441	11.4639	8.5302	.1172	10
11	1.3842	.7224	12.8078	9.2526	.1081	11
12	1.4258	.7014	14.1920	9.9540	.1005	12

n	Compound amount — Future value of a present amount — FV	Present value — Present value of a future amount — PV	Annuity compound amount — Future value of an annuity — AFV	Annuity present value — Present value of an annuity — APV	Payment — Annuity repaying a present amount — PAY	n
40	3.2620	.3066	75.4013	23.1148	.0433	40
44	3.6715	.2724	89.0484	24.2543	.0412	44
48	4.1323	.2420	104.4084	25.2667	.0396	48
52	4.6509	.2150	121.6962	26.1662	.0382	52
56	5.2346	.1910	141.1538	26.9655	.0371	56
60	5.8916	.1697	163.0534	27.6756	.0361	60
64	6.6311	.1508	187.7017	28.3065	.0353	64
68	7.4633	.1340	215.4436	28.8670	.0346	68
72	8.4000	.1190	246.6672	29.3651	.0341	72
76	9.4543	.1058	281.8098	29.8076	.0335	76
80	10.6409	.0940	321.3630	30.2008	.0331	80
84	11.9764	.0835	365.8805	30.5501	.0327	84

n					
13	1.4685	.6810	15.6178	10.6350	.0940
14	1.5126	.6611	17.0863	11.2961	.0885
15	1.5580	.6419	18.5989	11.9379	.0838
16	1.6047	.6232	20.1569	12.5611	.0796
17	1.6528	.6050	21.7616	13.1661	.0760
18	1.7024	.5874	23.4144	13.7535	.0727
19	1.7535	.5703	25.1169	14.3238	.0698
20	1.8061	.5537	26.8704	14.8775	.0672
21	1.8603	.5375	28.6765	15.4150	.0649
22	1.9161	.5219	30.5368	15.9369	.0627
23	1.9736	.5067	32.4529	16.4436	.0608
24	2.0328	.4919	34.4265	16.9355	.0590
25	2.0938	.4776	36.4593	17.4131	.0574
26	2.1566	.4637	38.5530	17.8768	.0559
27	2.2213	.4502	40.7096	18.3270	.0546
28	2.2879	.4371	42.9309	18.7641	.0533
29	2.3566	.4243	45.2189	19.1885	.0521
30	2.4273	.4120	47.5754	19.6004	.0510
31	2.5001	.4000	50.0027	20.0004	.0500
32	2.5751	.3883	52.5028	20.3888	.0490
33	2.6523	.3770	55.0778	20.7658	.0482
34	2.7319	.3660	57.7302	21.1318	.0473
35	2.8139	.3554	60.4621	21.4872	.0465
36	2.8983	.3450	63.2759	21.8323	.0463

n					
88	13.4796	.0742	415.9854	30.8605	.0324
92	15.1714	.0659	472.3789	31.1362	.0321
96	17.0755	.0586	535.8502	31.3812	.0319
100	19.2186	.0520	607.2877	31.5989	.0316
104	21.6307	.0462	687.6913	31.7923	.0315
108	24.3456	.0411	778.1863	31.9642	.0313
112	27.4012	.0365	880.0391	32.1168	.0311
116	30.8403	.0324	994.6754	32.2525	.0310
120	34.7110	.0288	1123.6996	32.3730	.0309
∞				33.3333	.0300

Interest Rate of 4.00 Percent

n	Compound amount — Future value of a present amount — FV	Present value — Present value of a future amount — PV	Annuity compound amount — Future value of an annuity — AFV	Annuity present value — Present value of an annuity — APV	Payment — Annuity repaying a present amount — PAY	n
1	1.0400	.9615	1.0000	.9615	1.0400	1
2	1.0816	.9246	2.0400	1.8861	.5302	2
3	1.1249	.8890	3.1216	2.7751	.3603	3
4	1.1699	.8548	4.2465	3.6299	.2755	4
5	1.2167	.8219	5.4163	4.4518	.2246	5
6	1.2653	.7903	6.6330	5.2421	.1908	6
7	1.3159	.7599	7.8983	6.0021	.1666	7
8	1.3686	.7307	9.2142	6.7327	.1485	8
9	1.4233	.7026	10.5828	7.4353	.1345	9
10	1.4802	.6756	12.0061	8.1109	.1233	10
11	1.5395	.6496	13.4864	8.7605	.1141	11
12	1.6010	.6246	15.0258	9.3851	.1066	12

n	Compound amount — Future value of a present amount — FV	Present value — Present value of a future amount — PV	Annuity compound amount — Future value of an annuity — AFV	Annuity present value — Present value of an annuity — APV	Payment — Annuity repaying a present amount — PAY	n
40	4.8010	.2083	95.0255	19.7928	.0505	40
44	5.6165	.1780	115.4129	20.5488	.0487	44
48	6.5705	.1522	139.2632	21.1951	.0472	48
52	7.6866	.1301	167.1647	21.7476	.0460	52
56	8.9922	.1112	199.8055	22.2198	.0450	56
60	10.5196	.0951	237.9907	22.6235	.0442	60
64	12.3065	.0813	282.6619	22.9685	.0435	64
68	14.3968	.0695	334.9209	23.2635	.0430	68
72	16.8423	.0594	396.0566	23.5156	.0425	72
76	19.7031	.0508	467.5766	23.7312	.0421	76
80	23.0498	.0434	551.2450	23.9154	.0418	80
84	26.9650	.0371	649.1251	24.0729	.0415	84

n					
13	1.6651	.6006	16.6268	9.9856	.1001
14	1.7317	.5775	18.2919	10.5631	.0947
15	1.8009	.5553	20.0236	11.1184	.0899
16	1.8730	.5339	21.8245	11.6523	.0858
17	1.9479	.5134	23.6975	12.1657	.0822
18	2.0258	.4936	25.6454	12.6593	.0790
19	2.1068	.4746	27.6712	13.1339	.0761
20	2.1911	.4564	29.7781	13.5903	.0736
21	2.2788	.4388	31.9692	14.0292	.0713
22	2.3699	.4220	34.2480	14.4511	.0692
23	2.4647	.4057	36.6179	14.8568	.0673
24	2.5633	.3901	39.0826	15.2470	.0656
25	2.6658	.3751	41.6459	15.6221	.0640
26	2.7725	.3607	44.3117	15.9828	.0626
27	2.8834	.3468	47.0842	16.3296	.0612
28	2.9987	.3335	49.9676	16.6631	.0600
29	3.1187	.3207	52.9663	16.9837	.0589
30	3.2434	.3083	56.0849	17.2920	.0578
31	3.3731	.2965	59.3283	17.5885	.0569
32	3.5081	.2851	62.7015	17.8736	.0559
33	3.6484	.2741	66.2095	18.1476	.0551
34	3.7943	.2636	69.8579	18.4112	.0543
35	3.9461	.2534	73.6522	18.6646	.0536
36	4.1039	.2437	77.5983	18.9083	.0529

n					
88	31.5452	.0317	763.6310	24.2075	.0413
92	36.9035	.0271	897.5868	24.3226	.0411
96	43.1718	.0232	1054.2960	24.4209	.0409
100	50.5049	.0198	1237.6237	24.5050	.0408
104	59.0836	.0169	1452.0911	24.5769	.0407
108	69.1195	.0145	1702.9877	24.6383	.0406
112	80.8600	.0124	1996.5012	24.6908	.0405
116	94.5948	.0106	2339.8705	24.7357	.0404
120	110.6626	.0090	2741.5640	24.7741	.0404
∞				25.0000	.0400

Interest Rate of 5.00 Percent

n	Compound amount — Future value of a present amount — FV	Present value — Present value of a future amount — PV	Annuity compound amount — Future value of an annuity — AFV	Annuity present value — Present value of an annuity — APV	Payment — Annuity repaying a present amount — PAY	n
1	1.0500	.9524	1.0000	.9524	1.0500	1
2	1.1025	.9070	2.0500	1.8594	.5378	2
3	1.1576	.8638	3.1525	2.7232	.3672	3
4	1.2155	.8227	4.3101	3.5460	.2820	4
5	1.2763	.7835	5.5256	4.3295	.2310	5
6	1.3401	.7462	6.8019	5.0757	.1970	6
7	1.4071	.7107	8.1420	5.7864	.1728	7
8	1.4775	.6768	9.5491	6.4632	.1547	8
9	1.5513	.6446	11.0266	7.1078	.1407	9
10	1.6289	.6139	12.5779	7.7217	.1295	10
11	1.7103	.5847	14.2068	8.3064	.1204	11
12	1.7959	.5568	15.9171	8.8633	.1128	12
40	7.0400	.1420	120.7998	17.1591	.0583	40
44	8.5572	.1169	151.1430	17.6628	.0566	44
48	10.4013	.0961	188.0254	18.0772	.0553	48
52	12.6428	.0791	232.8562	18.4181	.0543	52
56	15.3674	.0651	287.3482	18.6985	.0535	56
60	18.6792	.0535	353.5837	18.9293	.0528	60
64	22.7047	.0440	434.0933	19.1191	.0523	64
68	27.5977	.0362	531.9533	19.2753	.0519	68
72	33.5451	.0298	650.9027	19.4038	.0515	72
76	40.7743	.0245	795.4864	19.5095	.0513	76
80	49.5614	.0202	971.2288	19.5965	.0510	80
84	60.2422	.0166	1184.8448	19.6680	.0508	84

n						n						n
13	1.8856	.5303	17.7130	9.3936	.1065	13	88	73.2248	.0137	1444.4964	19.7269	.0507	88
14	1.9799	.5051	19.5986	9.8986	.1010	14	92	89.0052	.0112	1760.1045	19.7753	.0506	92
15	2.0789	.4810	21.5786	10.3797	.0963	15	96	108.1864	.0092	2143.7282	19.8151	.0505	96
16	2.1829	.4581	23.6575	10.8378	.0923	16	100	131.5013	.0076	2610.0252	19.8479	.0504	100
17	2.2920	.4363	25.8404	11.2741	.0887	17	104	159.8406	.0063	3176.8120	19.8749	.0503	104
18	2.4066	.4155	28.1324	11.6896	.0855	18	108	194.2872	.0051	3865.7450	19.8971	.0503	108
19	2.5270	.3957	30.5390	12.0853	.0827	19	112	236.1574	.0042	4703.1473	19.9153	.0502	112
20	2.6533	.3769	33.0660	12.4622	.0802	20	116	287.0508	.0035	5721.0151	19.9303	.0502	116
21	2.7860	.3589	35.7193	12.8212	.0780	21	120	348.9120	.0029	6958.2397	19.9427	.0501	120
22	2.9253	.3418	38.5052	13.1630	.0760	22	∞						
23	3.0715	.3256	41.4305	13.4886	.0741	23					20.0000	.0500	∞
24	3.2251	.3101	44.5020	13.7986	.0725	24							
25	3.3864	.2953	47.7271	14.0939	.0710	25							
26	3.5557	.2812	51.1135	14.3752	.0696	26							
27	3.7335	.2678	54.6691	14.6430	.0683	27							
28	3.9201	.2551	58.4026	14.8981	.0671	28							
29	4.1161	.2429	62.3227	15.1411	.0660	29							
30	4.3219	.2314	66.4388	15.3725	.0651	30							
31	4.5380	.2204	70.7608	15.5928	.0641	31							
32	4.7649	.2099	75.2988	15.8027	.0633	32							
33	5.0032	.1999	80.0638	16.0025	.0625	33							
34	5.2533	.1904	85.0670	16.1929	.0618	34							
35	5.5160	.1813	90.3203	16.3742	.0611	35							
36	5.7918	.1727	95.8363	16.5469	.0604	36							

Interest Rate of 6.00 Percent

n	Compound amount — Future value of a present amount — FV	Present value — Present value of a future amount — PV	Annuity compound amount — Future value of an annuity — AFV	Annuity present value — Present value of an annuity — APV	Payment — Annuity repaying a present amount — PAY	n
1	1.0600	.9434	1.0000	.9434	1.0600	1
2	1.1236	.8900	2.0600	1.8334	.5454	2
3	1.1910	.8396	3.1836	2.6730	.3741	3
4	1.2625	.7921	4.3746	3.4651	.2886	4
5	1.3382	.7473	5.6371	4.2124	.2374	5
6	1.4185	.7050	6.9753	4.9173	.2034	6
7	1.5036	.6651	8.3938	5.5824	.1791	7
8	1.5938	.6274	9.8975	6.2098	.1610	8
9	1.6895	.5919	11.4913	6.8017	.1470	9
10	1.7908	.5584	13.1808	7.3601	.1359	10
11	1.8983	.5268	14.9716	7.8869	.1268	11
12	2.0122	.4970	16.8699	8.3838	.1193	12
40	10.2857	.0972	154.7620	15.0463	.0665	40
44	12.9855	.0770	199.7580	15.3832	.0650	44
48	16.3939	.0610	256.5645	15.6500	.0639	48
52	20.6969	.0483	328.2814	15.8614	.0630	52
56	26.1293	.0383	418.8223	16.0288	.0624	56
60	32.9877	.0303	533.1282	16.1614	.0619	60
64	41.6462	.0240	677.4367	16.2665	.0615	64
68	52.5774	.0190	859.6228	16.3497	.0612	68
72	66.3777	.0151	1089.6286	16.4156	.0609	72
76	83.8003	.0119	1380.0056	16.4678	.0607	76
80	105.7960	.0095	1746.5999	16.5091	.0606	80
84	133.5650	.0075	2209.4167	16.5419	.0605	84

n						n
13	2.1329	.4688	18.8821	8.8527	.1130	13
14	2.2609	.4423	21.0151	9.2950	.1076	14
15	2.3966	.4173	23.2760	9.7122	.1030	15
16	2.5404	.3936	25.6725	10.1059	.0990	16
17	2.6928	.3714	28.2129	10.4773	.0954	17
18	2.8543	.3503	30.9057	10.8276	.0924	18
19	3.0256	.3305	33.7600	11.1581	.0896	19
20	3.2071	.3118	36.7856	11.4699	.0872	20
21	3.3996	.2942	39.9927	11.7641	.0850	21
22	3.6035	.2775	43.3923	12.0416	.0830	22
23	3.8197	.2618	46.9958	12.3034	.0813	23
24	4.0489	.2470	50.8156	12.5504	.0797	24
25	4.2919	.2330	54.8645	12.7834	.0782	25
26	4.5494	.2198	59.1564	13.0032	.0769	26
27	4.8223	.2074	63.7058	13.2105	.0757	27
28	5.1117	.1956	68.5281	13.4062	.0746	28
29	5.4184	.1846	73.6398	13.5907	.0736	29
30	5.7435	.1741	79.0582	13.7648	.0726	30
31	6.0881	.1643	84.8017	13.9291	.0718	31
32	6.4534	.1550	90.8898	14.0840	.0710	32
33	6.8406	.1462	97.3432	14.2302	.0703	33
34	7.2510	.1379	104.1838	14.3681	.0696	34
35	7.6861	.1301	111.4348	14.4982	.0690	35
36	8.1473	.1227	119.1209	14.6210	.0684	36

n						n
88	168.6227	.0059	2793.7123	16.5678	.0604	88
92	212.8823	.0047	3531.3721	16.5884	.0603	92
96	268.7590	.0037	4462.6505	16.6047	.0602	96
100	339.3021	.0029	5638.3681	16.6175	.0602	100
104	428.3611	.0023	7122.6844	16.6278	.0601	104
108	540.7960	.0018	8996.5995	16.6358	.0601	108
112	682.7425	.0015	11362.3743	16.6423	.0601	112
116	861.9466	.0012	14349.1103	16.6473	.0601	116
120	1088.1877	.0009	18119.7958	16.6514	.0601	120
∞				16.6667	.0600	∞

Interest Rate of 7.00 Percent

n	Compound amount — Future value of a present amount — FV	Present value — Present value of a future amount — PV	Annuity compound amount — Future value of an annuity — AFV	Annuity present value — Present value of an annuity — APV	Payment — Annuity repaying a present amount — PAY	n
1	1.0700	.9346	1.0000	.9346	1.0700	1
2	1.1449	.8734	2.0700	1.8080	.5531	2
3	1.2250	.8163	3.2149	2.6243	.3811	3
4	1.3108	.7629	4.4399	3.3872	.2952	4
5	1.4026	.7130	5.7507	4.1002	.2439	5
6	1.5007	.6663	7.1533	4.7665	.2098	6
7	1.6058	.6227	8.6540	5.3893	.1856	7
8	1.7182	.5820	10.2598	5.9713	.1675	8
9	1.8385	.5439	11.9780	6.5152	.1535	9
10	1.9672	.5083	13.8164	7.0236	.1424	10
11	2.1049	.4751	15.7836	7.4987	.1334	11
12	2.2522	.4440	17.8885	7.9427	.1259	12

Interest Rate of 8.00 Percent

n	Compound amount — Future value of a present amount — FV	Present value — Present value of a future amount — PV	Annuity compound amount — Future value of an annuity — AFV	Annuity present value — Present value of an annuity — APV	Payment — Annuity repaying a present amount — PAY	n
1	1.0800	.9259	1.0000	.9259	1.0800	1
2	1.1664	.8573	2.0800	1.7833	.5608	2
3	1.2597	.7938	3.2464	2.5771	.3880	3
4	1.3605	.7350	4.5061	3.3121	.3019	4
5	1.4693	.6806	5.8666	3.9927	.2505	5
6	1.5869	.6302	7.3359	4.6229	.2163	6
7	1.7138	.5835	8.9228	5.2064	.1921	7
8	1.8509	.5403	10.6366	5.7468	.1740	8
9	1.9990	.5002	12.4876	6.2469	.1601	9
10	2.1589	.4632	14.4866	6.7101	.1490	10
11	2.3316	.4289	16.6455	7.1390	.1401	11
12	2.5182	.3971	18.9771	7.5361	.1327	12

n						n						n
13	2.4098	.4150	20.1406	8.3577	.1197	13	2.7196	.3677	21.4953	7.9038	.1265	13
14	2.5785	.3878	22.5505	8.7455	.1143	14	2.9372	.3405	24.2149	8.2442	.1213	14
15	2.7590	.3624	25.1290	9.1079	.1098	15	3.1722	.3152	27.1521	8.5595	.1168	15
16	2.9522	.3387	27.8881	9.4466	.1059	16	3.4259	.2919	30.3243	8.8514	.1130	16
17	3.1588	.3166	30.8402	9.7632	.1024	17	3.7000	.2703	33.7502	9.1216	.1096	17
18	3.3799	.2959	33.9990	10.0591	.0994	18	3.9960	.2502	37.4502	9.3719	.1067	18
19	3.6165	.2765	37.3790	10.3356	.0968	19	4.3157	.2317	41.4463	9.6036	.1041	19
20	3.8697	.2584	40.9955	10.5940	.0944	20	4.6610	.2145	45.7620	9.8181	.1019	20
21	4.1406	.2415	44.8652	10.8355	.0923	21	5.0338	.1987	50.4229	10.0168	.0998	21
22	4.4304	.2257	49.0057	11.0612	.0904	22	5.4365	.1839	55.4568	10.2007	.0980	22
23	4.7405	.2109	53.4361	11.2722	.0887	23	5.8715	.1703	60.8933	10.3711	.0964	23
24	5.0724	.1971	58.1767	11.4693	.0872	24	6.3412	.1577	66.7648	10.5288	.0950	24
25	5.4274	.1842	63.2490	11.6536	.0858	25	6.8485	.1460	73.1059	10.6748	.0937	25
26	5.8074	.1722	68.6765	11.8258	.0846	26	7.3964	.1352	79.9544	10.8100	.0925	26
27	6.2139	.1609	74.4838	11.9867	.0834	27	7.9881	.1252	87.3508	10.9352	.0914	27
28	6.6488	.1504	80.6977	12.1371	.0824	28	8.6271	.1159	95.3388	11.0511	.0905	28
29	7.1143	.1406	87.3465	12.2777	.0814	29	9.3173	.1073	103.9659	11.1584	.0896	29
30	7.6123	.1314	94.4608	12.4090	.0806	30	10.0627	.0994	113.2832	11.2578	.0888	30
35	10.6766	.0937	138.2369	12.9477	.0772	35	14.7853	.0676	172.3168	11.6546	.0858	35
40	14.9745	.0668	199.6351	13.3317	.0750	40	21.7245	.0460	259.0565	11.9246	.0839	40
45	21.0025	.0476	285.7493	13.6055	.0735	45	31.9204	.0313	386.5056	12.1084	.0826	45
50	29.4570	.0339	406.5289	13.8007	.0725	50	46.9016	.0213	573.7702	12.2335	.0817	50
55	41.3150	.0242	575.9286	13.9399	.0717	55	68.9139	.0145	848.9232	12.3186	.0812	55
60	57.9464	.0173	813.5204	14.0392	.0712	60	101.2571	.0099	1253.2133	12.3766	.0808	60
∞				14.2857	.0700	∞				12.5000	.0800	∞

Interest Rate of 9.00 Percent

n	Compound amount Future value of a present amount FV	Present value Present value of a future amount PV	Annuity compound amount Future value of an annuity AFV	Annuity present value Present value of an annuity APV	Payment Annuity repaying a present amount PAY	n
1	1.0900	.9174	1.0000	.9174	1.0900	1
2	1.1881	.8417	2.0900	1.7591	.5685	2
3	1.2950	.7722	3.2781	2.5313	.3951	3
4	1.4116	.7084	4.5731	3.2397	.3087	4
5	1.5386	.6499	5.9847	3.8897	.2571	5
6	1.6771	.5963	7.5233	4.4859	.2229	6
7	1.8280	.5470	9.2004	5.0330	.1987	7
8	1.9926	.5019	11.0285	5.5348	.1807	8
9	2.1719	.4604	13.0210	5.9952	.1668	9
10	2.3674	.4224	15.1929	6.4177	.1558	10
11	2.5804	.3875	17.5603	6.8052	.1469	11
12	2.8127	.3555	20.1407	7.1607	.1397	12

Interest Rate of 10.00 Percent

n	Compound amount Future value of a present amount FV	Present value Present value of a future amount PV	Annuity compound amount Future value of an annuity AFV	Annuity present value Present value of an annuity APV	Payment Annuity repaying a present amount PAY	n
1	1.1000	.9091	1.0000	.9091	1.1000	1
2	1.2100	.8264	2.1000	1.7355	.5762	2
3	1.3310	.7513	3.3100	2.4869	.4021	3
4	1.4641	.6830	4.6410	3.1669	.3155	4
5	1.6105	.6209	6.1051	3.7908	.2638	5
6	1.7716	.5645	7.7156	4.3553	.2296	6
7	1.9487	.5132	9.4872	4.8684	.2054	7
8	2.1436	.4665	11.4359	5.3349	.1874	8
9	2.3579	.4241	13.5795	5.7590	.1736	9
10	2.5937	.3855	15.9374	6.1446	.1627	10
11	2.8531	.3505	18.5312	6.4951	.1540	11
12	3.1384	.3186	21.3843	6.8137	.1468	12

Left-hand interest table:

n					
13	3.0658	.3262	22.9534	.1336	7.4869
14	3.3417	.2992	26.0192	.1284	7.7862
15	3.6425	.2745	29.3609	.1241	8.0607
16	3.9703	.2519	33.0034	.1203	8.3126
17	4.3276	.2311	36.9737	.1170	8.5436
18	4.7171	.2120	41.3013	.1142	8.7556
19	5.1417	.1945	46.0185	.1117	8.9501
20	5.6044	.1784	51.1601	.1095	9.1285
21	6.1088	.1637	56.7645	.1076	9.2922
22	6.6586	.1502	62.8733	.1059	9.4424
23	7.2579	.1378	69.5319	.1044	9.5802
24	7.9111	.1264	76.7898	.1030	9.7066
25	8.6231	.1160	84.7009	.1018	9.8226
26	9.3992	.1064	93.3240	.1007	9.9290
27	10.2451	.0976	102.7231	.0997	10.0266
28	11.1671	.0895	112.9682	.0989	10.1161
29	12.1722	.0822	124.1354	.0981	10.1983
30	13.2677	.0754	136.3075	.0973	10.2737
35	20.4140	.0490	215.7108	.0946	10.5668
40	31.4094	.0318	337.8824	.0930	10.7574
45	48.3273	.0207	525.8587	.0919	10.8812
50	74.3575	.0134	815.0836	.0912	10.9617
55	114.4083	.0087	1260.0918	.0908	11.0140
60	176.0313	.0057	1944.7921	.0905	11.0480
∞				.0900	11.1111

Right-hand interest table:

n					
13	3.4523	.2897	24.5227	.1408	7.1034
14	3.7975	.2633	27.9750	.1357	7.3667
15	4.1772	.2394	31.7725	.1315	7.6061
16	4.5950	.2176	35.9497	.1278	7.8237
17	5.0545	.1978	40.5447	.1247	8.0216
18	5.5599	.1799	45.5992	.1219	8.2014
19	6.1159	.1635	51.1591	.1195	8.3649
20	6.7275	.1486	57.2750	.1175	8.5136
21	7.4002	.1351	64.0025	.1156	8.6487
22	8.1403	.1228	71.4027	.1140	8.7715
23	8.9543	.1117	79.5430	.1126	8.8832
24	9.8497	.1015	88.4973	.1113	8.9847
25	10.8347	.0923	98.3471	.1102	9.0770
26	11.9182	.0839	109.1818	.1092	9.1609
27	13.1100	.0763	121.0999	.1083	9.2372
28	14.4210	.0693	134.2099	.1075	9.3066
29	15.8631	.0630	148.6309	.1067	9.3696
30	17.4494	.0573	164.4940	.1061	9.4269
35	28.1024	.0356	271.0244	.1037	9.6442
40	45.2593	.0221	442.5926	.1023	9.7791
45	72.8905	.0137	718.9048	.1014	9.8628
50	117.3909	.0085	1163.9085	.1009	9.9148
55	189.0591	.0053	1880.5914	.1005	9.9471
60	304.4816	.0033	3034.8164	.1003	9.9672
∞				.1000	10.0000

Interest Rate of 11.00 Percent

n	Compound amount — Future value of a present amount — FV	Present value — Present value of a future amount — PV	Annuity compound amount — Future value of an annuity — AFV	Annuity present value — Present value of an annuity — APV	Payment — Annuity repaying a present amount — PAY	n
1	1.1100	.9009	1.0000	.9009	1.1100	1
2	1.2321	.8116	2.1100	1.7125	.5839	2
3	1.3676	.7312	3.3421	2.4437	.4092	3
4	1.5181	.6587	4.7097	3.1024	.3223	4
5	1.6851	.5935	6.2278	3.6959	.2706	5
6	1.8704	.5346	7.9129	4.2305	.2364	6
7	2.0762	.4817	9.7833	4.7122	.2122	7
8	2.3045	.4339	11.8594	5.1461	.1943	8
9	2.5580	.3909	14.1640	5.5370	.1806	9
10	2.8394	.3522	16.7220	5.8892	.1698	10
11	3.1518	.3173	19.5614	6.2065	.1611	11
12	3.4985	.2858	22.7132	6.4924	.1540	12

Interest Rate of 12.00 Percent

n	Compound amount — Future value of a present amount — FV	Present value — Present value of a future amount — PV	Annuity compound amount — Future value of an annuity — AFV	Annuity present value — Present value of an annuity — APV	Payment — Annuity repaying a present amount — PAY	n
1	1.1200	.8929	1.0000	.8929	1.1200	1
2	1.2544	.7972	2.1200	1.6901	.5917	2
3	1.4049	.7118	3.3744	2.4018	.4163	3
4	1.5735	.6355	4.7793	3.0373	.3292	4
5	1.7623	.5674	6.3528	3.6048	.2774	5
6	1.9738	.5066	8.1152	4.1114	.2432	6
7	2.2107	.4523	10.0890	4.5638	.2191	7
8	2.4760	.4039	12.2997	4.9676	.2013	8
9	2.7731	.3606	14.7757	5.3282	.1877	9
10	3.1058	.3220	17.5487	5.6502	.1770	10
11	3.4785	.2875	20.6546	5.9377	.1684	11
12	3.8960	.2567	24.1331	6.1944	.1614	12

n					n
13	3.8833	.2575	26.2116	6.7499	.1482
14	4.3104	.2320	30.0949	6.9819	.1432
15	4.7846	.2090	34.4054	7.1909	.1391
16	5.3109	.1883	39.1899	7.3792	.1355
17	5.8951	.1696	44.5008	7.5488	.1325
18	6.5436	.1528	50.3959	7.7016	.1298
19	7.2633	.1377	56.9395	7.8393	.1276
20	8.0623	.1240	64.2028	7.9633	.1256
21	8.9492	.1117	72.2651	8.0751	.1238
22	9.9336	.1007	81.2143	8.1757	.1223
23	11.0263	.0907	91.1479	8.2664	.1210
24	12.2392	.0817	102.1742	8.3481	.1198
25	13.5855	.0736	114.4133	8.4217	.1187
26	15.0799	.0663	127.9988	8.4881	.1178
27	16.7386	.0597	143.0786	8.5478	.1170
28	18.5799	.0538	159.8173	8.6016	.1163
29	20.6237	.0485	178.3972	8.6501	.1156
30	22.8923	.0437	199.0209	8.6938	.1150
35	38.5749	.0259	341.5896	8.8552	.1129
40	65.0009	.0154	581.8261	8.9511	.1117
45	109.5302	.0091	986.6386	9.0079	.1110
50	184.5648	.0054	1668.7712	9.0417	.1106
55	311.0025	.0032	2818.2042	9.0617	.1104
60	524.0572	.0019	4755.0658	9.0736	.1102
8				9.0909	.1100

n					n
13	4.3635	.2292	28.0291	6.4235	.1557
14	4.8871	.2046	32.3926	6.6282	.1509
15	5.4736	.1827	37.2797	6.8109	.1468
16	6.1304	.1631	42.7533	6.9740	.1434
17	6.8660	.1456	48.8837	7.1196	.1405
18	7.6900	.1300	55.7497	7.2497	.1379
19	8.6128	.1161	63.4397	7.3658	.1358
20	9.6463	.1037	72.0524	7.4694	.1339
21	10.8038	.0926	81.6987	7.5620	.1322
22	12.1003	.0826	92.5026	7.6446	.1308
23	13.5523	.0738	104.6029	7.7184	.1296
24	15.1786	.0659	118.1552	7.7843	.1285
25	17.0001	.0588	133.3339	7.8431	.1275
26	19.0401	.0525	150.3339	7.8957	.1267
27	21.3249	.0469	169.3740	7.9426	.1259
28	23.8839	.0419	190.6989	7.9844	.1252
29	26.7499	.0374	214.5828	8.0218	.1247
30	29.9599	.0334	241.3327	8.0552	.1241
35	52.7996	.0189	431.6635	8.1755	.1223
40	93.0510	.0107	767.0914	8.2438	.1213
45	163.9876	.0061	1358.2300	8.2825	.1207
50	289.0022	.0035	2400.0182	8.3045	.1204
55	509.3206	.0020	4236.0050	8.3170	.1202
60	897.5969	.0011	7471.6411	8.3240	.1201
8				8.3333	.1200

Interest Rate of 13.00 Percent

n	Compound amount — Future value of a present amount — FV	Present value — Present value of a future amount — PV	Annuity compound amount — Future value of an annuity — AFV	Annuity present value — Present value of an annuity — APV	Payment — Annuity repaying a present amount — PAY	n
1	1.1300	.8850	1.0000	.8850	1.1300	1
2	1.2769	.7831	2.1300	1.6681	.5995	2
3	1.4429	.6931	3.4069	2.3612	.4235	3
4	1.6305	.6133	4.8498	2.9745	.3362	4
5	1.8424	.5428	6.4803	3.5172	.2843	5
6	2.0820	.4803	8.3227	3.9975	.2502	6
7	2.3526	.4251	10.4047	4.4226	.2261	7
8	2.6584	.3762	12.7573	4.7988	.2084	8
9	3.0040	.3329	15.4157	5.1317	.1949	9
10	3.3946	.2946	18.4197	5.4262	.1843	10
11	3.8359	.2607	21.8143	5.6869	.1758	11
12	4.3345	.2307	25.6502	5.9176	.1690	12

Interest Rate of 14.00 Percent

n	Compound amount — Future value of a present amount — FV	Present value — Present value of a future amount — PV	Annuity compound amount — Future value of an annuity — AFV	Annuity present value — Present value of an annuity — APV	Payment — Annuity repaying a present amount — PAY	n
1	1.1400	.8772	1.0000	.8772	1.1400	1
2	1.2996	.7695	2.1400	1.6467	.6073	2
3	1.4815	.6750	3.4396	2.3216	.4307	3
4	1.6890	.5921	4.9211	2.9137	.3432	4
5	1.9254	.5194	6.6101	3.4331	.2913	5
6	2.1950	.4556	8.5355	3.8887	.2572	6
7	2.5023	.3996	10.7305	4.2883	.2332	7
8	2.8526	.3506	13.2328	4.6389	.2156	8
9	3.2519	.3075	16.0853	4.9464	.2022	9
10	3.7072	.2697	19.3373	5.2161	.1917	10
11	4.2262	.2366	23.0445	5.4527	.1834	11
12	4.8179	.2076	27.2707	5.6603	.1767	12

n						n
13	4.8980	.2042	29.9847	6.1218	.1634	13
14	5.5348	.1807	34.8827	6.3025	.1587	14
15	6.2543	.1599	40.4175	6.4624	.1547	15
16	7.0673	.1415	46.6717	6.6039	.1514	16
17	7.9861	.1252	53.7391	6.7291	.1486	17
18	9.0243	.1108	61.7251	6.8399	.1462	18
19	10.1974	.0981	70.7494	6.9380	.1441	19
20	11.5231	.0868	80.9468	7.0248	.1424	20
21	13.0211	.0768	92.4699	7.1016	.1408	21
22	14.7138	.0680	105.4910	7.1695	.1395	22
23	16.6266	.0601	120.2048	7.2297	.1383	23
24	18.7881	.0532	136.8315	7.2829	.1373	24
25	21.2305	.0471	155.6196	7.3300	.1364	25
26	23.9905	.0417	176.8501	7.3717	.1357	26
27	27.1093	.0369	200.8406	7.4086	.1350	27
28	30.6335	.0326	227.9499	7.4412	.1344	28
29	34.6158	.0289	258.5834	7.4701	.1339	29
30	39.1159	.0256	293.1992	7.4957	.1334	30
35	72.0685	.0139	546.6808	7.5856	.1318	35
40	132.7816	.0075	1013.7042	7.6344	.1310	40
45	244.6414	.0041	1874.1646	7.6609	.1305	45
50	450.7359	.0022	3459.5071	7.6752	.1303	50
55	830.4517	.0012	6380.3979	7.6830	.1302	55
60	1530.0535	.0007	11761.9498	7.6873	.1301	60
∞				7.6923	.1300	∞

n						n
13	5.4924	.1821	32.0887	5.8424	.1712	13
14	6.2613	.1597	37.5811	6.0021	.1666	14
15	7.1379	.1401	43.8424	6.1422	.1628	15
16	8.1372	.1229	50.9804	6.2651	.1596	16
17	9.2765	.1078	59.1176	6.3729	.1569	17
18	10.5752	.0946	68.3941	6.4674	.1546	18
19	12.0557	.0829	78.9692	6.5504	.1527	19
20	13.7435	.0728	91.0249	6.6231	.1510	20
21	15.6676	.0638	104.7684	6.6870	.1495	21
22	17.8610	.0560	120.4360	6.7429	.1483	22
23	20.3616	.0491	138.2970	6.7921	.1472	23
24	23.2122	.0431	158.6586	6.8351	.1463	24
25	26.4619	.0378	181.8708	6.8729	.1455	25
26	30.1666	.0331	208.3327	6.9061	.1448	26
27	34.3899	.0291	238.4993	6.9352	.1442	27
28	39.2045	.0255	272.8892	6.9607	.1437	28
29	44.6931	.0224	312.0937	6.9830	.1432	29
30	50.9502	.0196	356.7868	7.0027	.1428	30
35	98.1002	.0102	693.5727	7.0700	.1414	35
40	188.8835	.0053	1342.0251	7.1050	.1407	40
45	363.6791	.0027	2590.5648	7.1232	.1404	45
50	700.2330	.0014	4994.5213	7.1327	.1402	50
55	1348.2388	.0007	9623.1343	7.1376	.1401	55
60	2595.9187	.0004	18535.1333	7.1401	.1401	60
∞				7.1429	.1400	∞

Interest Rate of 15.00 Percent

n	Compound amount — Future value of a present amount — FV	Present value — Present value of a future amount — PV	Annuity compound amount — Future value of an annuity — AFV	Annuity present value — Present value of an annuity — APV	Payment — Annuity repaying a present amount — PAY	n
1	1.1500	.8696	1.0000	.8696	1.1500	1
2	1.3225	.7561	2.1500	1.6257	.6151	2
3	1.5209	.6575	3.4725	2.2832	.4380	3
4	1.7490	.5718	4.9934	2.8550	.3503	4
5	2.0114	.4972	6.7424	3.3522	.2983	5
6	2.3131	.4323	8.7537	3.7845	.2642	6
7	2.6600	.3759	11.0668	4.1604	.2404	7
8	3.0590	.3269	13.7268	4.4873	.2229	8
9	3.5179	.2843	16.7858	4.7716	.2096	9
10	4.0456	.2472	20.3037	5.0188	.1993	10
11	4.6524	.2149	24.3493	5.2337	.1911	11
12	5.3503	.1869	29.0017	5.4206	.1845	12

Interest Rate of 16.00 Percent

n	Compound amount — Future value of a present amount — FV	Present value — Present value of a future amount — PV	Annuity compound amount — Future value of an annuity — AFV	Annuity present value — Present value of an annuity — APV	Payment — Annuity repaying a present amount — PAY	n
1	1.1600	.8621	1.0000	.8621	1.1600	1
2	1.3456	.7432	2.1600	1.6052	.6230	2
3	1.5609	.6407	3.5056	2.2459	.4453	3
4	1.8106	.5523	5.0665	2.7982	.3574	4
5	2.1003	.4761	6.8771	3.2743	.3054	5
6	2.4364	.4104	8.9775	3.6847	.2714	6
7	2.8262	.3538	11.4139	4.0386	.2476	7
8	3.2784	.3050	14.2401	4.3436	.2302	8
9	3.8030	.2630	17.5185	4.6065	.2171	9
10	4.4114	.2267	21.3215	4.8332	.2069	10
11	5.1173	.1954	25.7329	5.0286	.1989	11
12	5.9360	.1685	30.8502	5.1971	.1924	12

n						n
13	6.1528	.1625	34.3519	5.5831	.1791	13
14	7.0757	.1413	40.5047	5.7245	.1747	14
15	8.1371	.1229	47.5804	5.8474	.1710	15
16	9.3576	.1069	55.7175	5.9542	.1679	16
17	10.7613	.0929	65.0751	6.0472	.1654	17
18	12.3755	.0808	75.8364	6.1280	.1632	18
19	14.2318	.0703	88.2118	6.1982	.1613	19
20	16.3665	.0611	102.4436	6.2593	.1598	20
21	18.8215	.0531	118.8101	6.3125	.1584	21
22	21.6447	.0462	137.6316	6.3587	.1573	22
23	24.8915	.0402	159.2764	6.3988	.1563	23
24	28.6252	.0349	184.1678	6.4338	.1554	24
25	32.9190	.0304	212.7930	6.4641	.1547	25
26	37.8568	.0264	245.7120	6.4906	.1541	26
27	43.5353	.0230	283.5688	6.5135	.1535	27
28	50.0656	.0200	327.1041	6.5335	.1531	28
29	57.5755	.0174	377.1697	6.5509	.1527	29
30	66.2118	.0151	434.7451	6.5660	.1523	30
35	133.1755	.0075	881.1702	6.6166	.1511	35
40	267.8635	.0037	1779.0903	6.6418	.1506	40
45	538.7693	.0019	3585.1285	6.6543	.1503	45
50	1083.6574	.0009	7217.7163	6.6605	.1501	50
55	2179.6222	.0005	14524.1479	6.6636	.1501	55
60	4383.9987	.0002	29219.9916	6.6651	.1500	60
∞				6.6667	.1500	∞

n						n
13	6.8858	.1452	36.7862	5.3423	.1872	13
14	7.9875	.1252	43.6720	5.4675	.1829	14
15	9.2655	.1079	51.6595	5.5755	.1794	15
16	10.7480	.0930	60.9250	5.6685	.1764	16
17	12.4677	.0802	71.6730	5.7487	.1740	17
18	14.4625	.0691	84.1407	5.8178	.1719	18
19	16.7765	.0596	98.6032	5.8775	.1701	19
20	19.4608	.0514	115.3797	5.9288	.1687	20
21	22.5745	.0443	134.8405	5.9731	.1674	21
22	26.1864	.0382	157.4150	6.0113	.1664	22
23	30.3762	.0329	183.6014	6.0442	.1654	23
24	35.2364	.0284	213.9776	6.0726	.1647	24
25	40.8742	.0245	249.2140	6.0971	.1640	25
26	47.4141	.0211	290.0883	6.1182	.1634	26
27	55.0004	.0182	337.5024	6.1364	.1630	27
28	63.8004	.0157	392.5028	6.1520	.1625	28
29	74.0085	.0135	456.3032	6.1656	.1622	29
30	85.8499	.0116	530.3117	6.1772	.1619	30
35	180.3141	.0055	1120.7130	6.2153	.1609	35
40	378.7212	.0026	2360.7572	6.2335	.1604	40
45	795.4438	.0013	4965.2739	6.2421	.1602	45
50	1670.7038	.0006	10435.6488	6.2463	.1601	50
55	3509.0488	.0003	21925.3050	6.2482	.1600	55
60	7370.2014	.0001	46057.5085	6.2492	.1600	60
∞				6.2500	.1600	∞

Interest Rate of 18.00 Percent

n	Compound amount — Future value of a present amount — FV	Present value — Present value of a future amount — PV	Annuity compound amount — Future value of an annuity — AFV	Annuity present value — Present value of an annuity — APV	Payment — Annuity repaying a present amount — PAY	n
1	1.1800	.8475	1.0000	.8475	1.1800	1
2	1.3924	.7182	2.1800	1.5656	.6387	2
3	1.6430	.6086	3.5724	2.1743	.4599	3
4	1.9388	.5158	5.2154	2.6901	.3717	4
5	2.2878	.4371	7.1542	3.1272	.3198	5
6	2.6996	.3704	9.4420	3.4976	.2859	6
7	3.1855	.3139	12.1415	3.8115	.2624	7
8	3.7589	.2660	15.3270	4.0776	.2452	8
9	4.4355	.2255	19.0859	4.3030	.2324	9
10	5.2338	.1911	23.5213	4.4941	.2225	10
11	6.1759	.1619	28.7551	4.6560	.2148	11
12	7.2876	.1372	34.9311	4.7932	.2086	12

Interest Rate of 20.00 Percent

n	Compound amount — Future value of a present amount — FV	Present value — Present value of a future amount — PV	Annuity compound amount — Future value of an annuity — AFV	Annuity present value — Present value of an annuity — APV	Payment — Annuity repaying a present amount — PAY	n
1	1.2000	.8333	1.0000	.8333	1.2000	1
2	1.4400	.6944	2.2000	1.5278	.6545	2
3	1.7280	.5787	3.6400	2.1065	.4747	3
4	2.0736	.4823	5.3680	2.5887	.3863	4
5	2.4883	.4019	7.4416	2.9906	.3344	5
6	2.9860	.3349	9.9299	3.3255	.3007	6
7	3.5832	.2791	12.9159	3.6046	.2774	7
8	4.2998	.2326	16.4991	3.8372	.2606	8
9	5.1598	.1938	20.7989	4.0310	.2481	9
10	6.1917	.1615	25.9587	4.1925	.2385	10
11	7.4301	.1346	32.1504	4.3271	.2311	11
12	8.9161	.1122	39.5805	4.4392	.2253	12

n						n	n						n
13	8.5994	.1163	42.2187	4.9095	.2037	13	13	10.6993	.0935	48.4966	4.5327	.2206	13
14	10.1472	.0985	50.8180	5.0081	.1997	14	14	12.8392	.0779	59.1959	4.6106	.2169	14
15	11.9737	.0835	60.9653	5.0916	.1964	15	15	15.4070	.0649	72.0351	4.6755	.2139	15
16	14.1290	.0708	72.9390	5.1624	.1937	16	16	18.4884	.0541	87.4421	4.7296	.2114	16
17	16.6722	.0600	87.0680	5.2223	.1915	17	17	22.1861	.0451	105.9306	4.7746	.2094	17
18	19.6733	.0508	103.7403	5.2732	.1896	18	18	26.6233	.0376	128.1167	4.8122	.2078	18
19	23.2144	.0431	123.4135	5.3162	.1881	19	19	31.9480	.0313	154.7400	4.8435	.2065	19
20	27.3930	.0365	146.6280	5.3527	.1868	20	20	38.3376	.0261	186.6880	4.8696	.2054	20
21	32.3238	.0309	174.0210	5.3837	.1857	21	21	46.0051	.0217	225.0256	4.8913	.2044	21
22	38.1421	.0262	206.3448	5.4099	.1848	22	22	55.2061	.0181	271.0307	4.9094	.2037	22
23	45.0076	.0222	244.4868	5.4321	.1841	23	23	66.2474	.0151	326.2369	4.9245	.2031	23
24	53.1090	.0188	289.4945	5.4509	.1835	24	24	79.4968	.0126	392.4842	4.9371	.2025	24
25	62.6686	.0160	342.6035	5.4669	.1829	25	25	95.3962	.0105	471.9811	4.9476	.2021	25
26	73.9490	.0135	405.2721	5.4804	.1825	26	26	114.4755	.0087	567.3773	4.9563	.2018	26
27	87.2598	.0115	479.2211	5.4919	.1821	27	27	137.3706	.0073	681.8528	4.9636	.2015	27
28	102.9666	.0097	566.4809	5.5016	.1818	28	28	164.8447	.0061	819.2233	4.9697	.2012	28
29	121.5005	.0082	669.4475	5.5098	.1815	29	29	197.8136	.0051	984.0680	4.9747	.2010	29
30	143.3706	.0070	790.9480	5.5168	.1813	30	30	237.3763	.0042	1181.8816	4.9789	.2008	30
∞				5.5556	.1800	∞	∞				5.0000	.2000	∞

Interest Rate of 25.00 Percent

n	Compound amount — Future value of a present amount — FV	Present value — Present value of a future amount — PV	Annuity compound amount — Future value of an annuity — AFV	Annuity present value — Present value of an annuity — APV	Payment — Annuity repaying a present amount — PAY	n
1	1.2500	.8000	1.0000	.8000	1.2500	1
2	1.5625	.6400	2.2500	1.4400	.6944	2
3	1.9531	.5120	3.8125	1.9520	.5123	3
4	2.4414	.4096	5.7656	2.3616	.4234	4
5	3.0518	.3277	8.2070	2.6893	.3718	5
6	3.8147	.2621	11.2588	2.9514	.3388	6
7	4.7684	.2097	15.0735	3.1611	.3163	7
8	5.9605	.1678	19.8419	3.3289	.3004	8
9	7.4506	.1342	25.8023	3.4631	.2888	9
10	9.3132	.1074	33.2529	3.5705	.2801	10
11	11.6415	.0859	42.5661	3.6564	.2735	11
12	14.5519	.0687	54.2077	3.7251	.2684	12

Interest Rate of 30.00 Percent

n	Compound amount — Future value of a present amount — FV	Present value — Present value of a future amount — PV	Annuity compound amount — Future value of an annuity — AFV	Annuity present value — Present value of an annuity — APV	Payment — Annuity repaying a present amount — PAY	n
1	1.3000	.7692	1.0000	.7692	1.3000	1
2	1.6900	.5917	2.3000	1.3609	.7348	2
3	2.1970	.4552	3.9900	1.8161	.5506	3
4	2.8561	.3501	6.1870	2.1662	.4616	4
5	3.7129	.2693	9.0431	2.4356	.4106	5
6	4.8268	.2072	12.7560	2.6427	.3784	6
7	6.2749	.1594	17.5828	2.8021	.3569	7
8	8.1573	.1226	23.8577	2.9247	.3419	8
9	10.6045	.0943	32.0150	3.0190	.3312	9
10	13.7858	.0725	42.6195	3.0915	.3235	10
11	17.9216	.0558	56.4053	3.1473	.3177	11
12	23.2981	.0429	74.3270	3.1903	.3135	12

n						n	n						n
13	.3102	3.2233	97.6250	.0330	30.2875	13	13	.2645	3.7801	68.7596	.0550	18.1899	13
14	.3078	3.2487	127.9125	.0254	39.3738	14	14	.2615	3.8241	86.9495	.0440	22.7374	14
15	.3060	3.2682	167.2863	.0195	51.1859	15	15	.2591	3.8593	109.6868	.0352	28.4217	15
16	.3046	3.2832	218.4722	.0150	66.5417	16	16	.2572	3.8874	138.1085	.0281	35.5271	16
17	.3035	3.2948	285.0139	.0116	86.5042	17	17	.2558	3.9099	173.6357	.0225	44.4089	17
18	.3027	3.3037	371.5180	.0089	112.4554	18	18	.2546	3.9279	218.0446	.0180	55.5112	18
19	.3021	3.3105	483.9734	.0068	146.1920	19	19	.2537	3.9424	273.5558	.0144	69.3889	19
20	.3016	3.3158	630.1655	.0053	190.0496	20	20	.2529	3.9539	342.9447	.0115	86.7362	20
21	.3012	3.3198	820.2151	.0040	247.0645	21	21	.2523	3.9631	429.6809	.0092	108.4202	21
22	.3009	3.3230	1067.2796	.0031	321.1839	22	22	.2519	3.9705	538.1011	.0074	135.5253	22
23	.3007	3.3254	1388.4635	.0024	417.5391	23	23	.2515	3.9764	673.6264	.0059	169.4066	23
24	.3006	3.3272	1806.0026	.0018	542.8008	24	24	.2512	3.9811	843.0329	.0047	211.7582	24
25	.3004	3.3286	2348.8033	.0014	705.6410	25	25	.2509	3.9849	1054.7912	.0038	264.6978	25
26	.3003	3.3297	3054.4443	.0011	917.3333	26	26	.2508	3.9879	1319.4890	.0030	330.8722	26
27	.3003	3.3305	3971.7776	.0008	1192.5333	27	27	.2506	3.9903	1650.3612	.0024	413.5903	27
28	.3002	3.3312	5164.3109	.0006	1550.2933	28	28	.2505	3.9923	2063.9515	.0019	516.9879	28
29	.3001	3.3317	6714.6042	.0005	2015.3813	29	29	.2504	3.9938	2580.9394	.0015	646.2349	29
30	.3001	3.3321	8729.9855	.0004	2619.9956	30	30	.2503	3.9950	3227.1743	.0012	807.7936	30
8	.3000	3.3333				8		.2500	4.0000				8

Interest Rate of 40.00 Percent

n	Compound amount — Future value of a present amount — FV	Present value — Present value of a future amount — PV	Annuity compound amount — Future value of an annuity — AFV	Annuity present value — Present value of an annuity — APV	Payment — Annuity repaying a present amount — PAY	n
1	1.4000	.7143	1.0000	.7143	1.4000	1
2	1.9600	.5102	2.4000	1.2245	.8167	2
3	2.7440	.3644	4.3600	1.5889	.6294	3
4	3.8416	.2603	7.1040	1.8492	.5408	4
5	5.3782	.1859	10.9456	2.0352	.4914	5
6	7.5295	.1328	16.3238	2.1680	.4613	6
7	10.5414	.0949	23.8534	2.2628	.4419	7
8	14.7579	.0678	34.3947	2.3306	.4291	8
9	20.6610	.0484	49.1526	2.3790	.4203	9
10	28.9255	.0346	69.8137	2.4136	.4143	10
11	40.4957	.0247	98.7391	2.4383	.4101	11
12	56.6939	.0176	139.2348	2.4559	.4072	12

Interest Rate of 50.00 Percent

n	Compound amount — Future value of a present amount — FV	Present value — Present value of a future amount — PV	Annuity compound amount — Future value of an annuity — AFV	Annuity present value — Present value of an annuity — APV	Payment — Annuity repaying a present amount — PAY	n
1	1.5000	.6667	1.0000	.6667	1.5000	1
2	2.2500	.4444	2.5000	1.1111	.9000	2
3	3.3750	.2963	4.7500	1.4074	.7105	3
4	5.0625	.1975	8.1250	1.6049	.6231	4
5	7.5938	.1317	13.1875	1.7366	.5758	5
6	11.3906	.0878	20.7813	1.8244	.5481	6
7	17.0859	.0585	32.1719	1.8829	.5311	7
8	25.6289	.0390	49.2578	1.9220	.5203	8
9	38.4434	.0260	74.8867	1.9480	.5134	9
10	57.6650	.0173	113.3301	1.9653	.5088	10
11	86.4976	.0116	170.9951	1.9769	.5058	11
12	129.7463	.0077	257.4927	1.9846	.5039	12

n					n		n						n
13	79.3715	.0126	195.9287	2.4685	13	.4051	13	194.6195	.0051	387.2390	1.9897	.5026	13
14	111.1201	.0090	275.3002	2.4775	14	.4036	14	291.9293	.0034	581.8585	1.9931	.5017	14
15	155.5681	.0064	386.4202	2.4839	15	.4026	15	437.8939	.0023	873.7878	1.9954	.5011	15
16	217.7953	.0046	541.9883	2.4885	16	.4018	16	656.8408	.0015	1311.6817	1.9970	.5008	16
17	304.9135	.0033	759.7837	2.4918	17	.4013	17	985.2613	.0010	1968.5225	1.9980	.5005	17
18	426.8789	.0023	1064.6971	2.4941	18	.4009	18	1477.8919	.0007	2953.7838	1.9986	.5003	18
19	597.6304	.0017	1491.5760	2.4958	19	.4007	19	2216.8378	.0005	4431.6756	1.9991	.5002	19
20	836.6826	.0012	2089.2064	2.4970	20	.4005	20	3325.2567	.0003	6648.5135	1.9994	.5002	20
21	1171.3556	.0009	2925.8889	2.4979	21	.4003	21	4987.8851	.0002	9973.7702	1.9996	.5001	21
22	1639.8978	.0006	4097.2445	2.4985	22	.4002	22	7481.8276	.0001	14961.6553	1.9997	.5001	22
23	2295.8569	.0004	5737.1423	2.4989	23	.4002	23	11222.7415	.0001	22443.4829	1.9998	.5000	23
24	3214.1997	.0003	8032.9993	2.4992	24	.4001	24	16834.1122	.0001	33666.2244	1.9999	.5000	24
25	4499.8796	.0002	11247.1990	2.4994	25	.4001	25	25251.1683	.0000	50500.3366	1.9999	.5000	25
∞				2.5000	∞	.4000	∞				2.0000	.5000	∞

INDEX